**Religion in Latin American
Life and Literature**

Religion in Latin American Life and Literature

Edited by

Lyle C. Brown
Department of Political Science
Baylor University

and

William F. Cooper
Department of Philosophy
Baylor University

MARKHAM PRESS FUND
Waco, Texas

To J. Lloyd Mecham

Copyright © 1980 by Markham Press Fund of
Baylor University Press, First edition 1980

All rights reserved. No portion of this book may
be reproduced in any form or by any means without
written permission of the publisher.

Library of Congress Catalog Card Number: 80-83665
International Standard Book Number: 0-918954-23-1

Printed in the United States of America
Baylor University Press, Waco, Texas 76798

This book was set in Melior, was printed by
Baylor University Press, and was bound by
Universal Bookbindery, Inc.

CONTENTS

Preface ....

Part I. GENERAL 1
  1. Some Perspectives on the Church as an Agent
     of Modernization in Latin America 2
      James D. Cochrane, Tulane University
  2. The Changing Church in Latin America 19
     Father *Teodoro de la Torre*,
     formerly Dominican College, Houston
  3. Recent Themes in Catholic Social Thought
     in Latin America 29
      Walter B. Redmond, Universidad Autónoma
      del Estado de Puebla
  4. The Perils of Success: Post-World War II
     Latin American Protestantism 52
      Richard L. Millett, University of
      Southern Illinois at Edwardsville

Part II. MEXICO 67
  A. History 69
  5. The Inquisition in Colonial Mexico: Heretical
     Thoughts on the Spiritual Conquest 70
      Richard E. Greenleaf, Tulane University
  6. The Catholic Church in the Mexican Period
     of New Mexican History: Interpretation
     and Archival Source Material 83
      Gerald Theisen, Eastern New Mexico University
  7. The Cristero Rebellion, 1926-1929: A Violent
     Chapter in the History of Church-State
     Relations in Mexico 90
      Roberto Cortés, Instituto Irlandés
  8. Tomás Garrido Canabal and the Repression
     of Religion in Tabasco 106
      Alan M. Kirshner, Ohlone College
  9. Church and State in Mexico, 1931-1936:
     An Overview 119
      Harriet Denise Joseph,
      Texas Southmost College

10. Mexican Catholics and Socialist Education
    of the 1930s 135
    Sister *Maria Ann Kelly*, C.S.J.,
    College of Saint Rose

B. Social Science 149
   11. Evangelical Expansion in Mexico: A Study
       of the Number, Distribution, and Growth
       of the Protestant Population, 1857-1970 150
       Julian C. Bridges, Hardin-Simmons University
   12. La Religión como Trasfondo en la Vida Familiar
       del Mexicano: Respuesta a Oscar Lewis 169
       Manuel Mendoza, Stephen F. Austin
       State University
   13. The "Politics" of Iván Illich and Small Group
       Political Behavior at CIDOC—Cuernavaca, 1972 177
       William R. Garner, Southern Illinois
       University at Carbondale

C. Literature 189
   14. The Virgin of Guadalupe in Mexican Culture 190
       Harvey L. Johnson, University of Houston
   15. Calderón de la Barca in Nahuatl 204
       Norris MacKinnon, Eastern Kentucky University
   16. The General and the Lady: Two Examples
       of Religious Persecution in the Mexican Novel 212
       Vivian M. Gruber, Stephen F. Austin
       State University
   17. "Así en la Tierra como en el Cielo":
       Religión, Mito, Superstición y Magia en las
       "Novelas de la Tierra" de Agustín Yáñez 220
       Roberto Bravo-Villarroel, Texas Tech
       University
   18. El Tema Religioso en *Al Filo del Agua*
       de Agustín Yáñez
       Lino García, Pan American University
   19. Octavio Paz: Mexico, the United States,
       and the World 241
       John H. Haddox, University of
       Texas at El Paso

Part III. SPANISH SOUTH AMERICA AND THE CARIBBEAN 249
   A. History 250

20. Sixteenth Century Colonial Education
    and Indoctrination of the Andean Indians 251
       Brother Robert D. Wood, S.M.,
       Saint Mary's University
21. The Jesuit Settlement Frontier
    in Southern Brazil 262
       C. Gary Lobb, California State University,
       Northridge
22. The Inquisition and the Enlightenment Library
    of Antonio Nariño 278
       Jerrold S. Buttrey, St. Stephen's
       Episcopal School
23. Spain and the Spiritual Reconquest
    of Santo Domingo, 1861-1865 289
       Jess H. Stone, College of William and Mary

B. Social Science 295
   24. The Influence of González Prada on the
       Attitudes toward Religion of Mariátegui
       and Haya de la Torre 296
          Judith Walker, University of Houston
   25. The Catholic Church and Political Development
       in Colombia 304
          Steven J. Brzezinski, University of Wyoming
          at Laramie
   26. Catholic Radicalism and Political Change
       in Argentina 316
          Michael Dodson, Texas Christian University

C. Literature...331
   27. Time and Eternity in Victor Massuh's
       Philosophy of Religion 332
          Niels C. Nielsen, Jr., Rice University
   28. Religion in Colombia as Seen in the Works
       of García Márquez 339
          Bertie Acker, University of Texas
          at Arlington
   29. The Limits of Exorcism and the Poetry of
       Humberto Díaz Casanueva 351
          S. Alan Schweitzer, Lorain Community College

Part IV. BRAZIL 361
   30. The Roots of Brazilian Regalism 362
          Tarcisio Beal, Incarnate Word College

31. Brazilian Positivism and the Military Republic 377
    Don Whitmore, Texas Woman's University
32. Sources of Brazilian Protestantism:
    Historical or Contemporary? 385
    John L. Robinson, Abilene Christian University
33. The Catholic Right in Contemporary Brazil:
    The Case of the "Society for the Defense
    of Tradition, Family, and Property" (TFP) 394
    Thomas Niehaus, Tulane University
    Brady Tyson, American University

Editors and Contributors 411

Index 415

PREFACE

History, social science, and literature all contribute to our understanding of religion and how it has influenced the lives of individuals, the course of national development, and the conduct of international relations. This volume features thirty-three studies that relate to religion in Latin America. Although these essays are not intended to provide systematic and encyclopedic coverage of nearly five hundred years of Latin American religious experience, they do touch many of the great religious issues and developments from the heroic era of European exploration and conquest to the troubled decade of the 1970s.

In dealing with controversial topics, there is merit in diversity of authorship. Contributors represent a variety of academic disciplines, educational backgrounds, and theological orientations. Also, their approaches represent a wide range of personal religious commitment. Some authors have written from the perspective of detached but interested spectators, while others have taken hold of their topic in a more personal and passionate manner. In all cases, however, the authors have been directly involved with their subjects through observation, participation, or archival and bibliographic research.

This volume should serve as a source of useful information for scholars and general readers; and perhaps it will provide inspiration for further research and writing on religious topics and themes. The four essays in Part I clarify many of the issues related to changing perspectives on religious life in twentieth-century Latin America. These studies delineate major phases of contemporary institutional and theological situations, and they describe important aspects of problems and events stemming from pressures for rapid social change. The three remaining parts cover a wide variety of religious involvement in distinct geographic areas: Mexico, Spanish South America and the Caribbean (including South Brazil during its Spanish missionary era), and Brazil.

Although the task of publishing this volume has exceeded original estimates of time and resources, for the editors it has been a labor of love for the subject and of pride in associating with cooperative contributors. Expressions of appreciation are at best inadequate, but they are genuinely extended to the Southwestern Council of Latin American Studies (SCOLAS) for providing a forum for the original presentation and discussion of these studies, to Baylor University for hosting the forum and for underwriting much of its expense, to donors who established the Markham Press Fund that has financed this publication, and to personnel of Baylor University Press for their craftsmanship in producing this book. Although limitations of space prevent acknowledging the efforts of many individuals, mention must be made of the contributions of two eminent authorities on religion in Latin America: Richard E. Greenleaf (Professor of History, Tulane University) and J. Lloyd Mecham (Professor Emeritus of Government, University of Texas at Austin). Professor Greenleaf presented two provocative lectures (one of which is published herein) at the SCOLAS meeting devoted to religion in Latin American life and literature; and Professor Mecham, to whom this volume is dedicated and whose *Church and State in Latin America* has guided two generations of scholars, honored that meeting with his presence as its distinguished guest.

Editing chores were made lighter as a result of assistance and advice rendered by two Baylor colleagues: Professor Robert T. Miller, Chairman of the Department of Political Science, and Professor James Leo Garrett, Jr., Director of Church-State Studies. Last but not least in importance were the professional typing services rendered by Mrs. Dorothy Hitt, and innumerable research and editing chores performed by two graduate assistants: Mr. William Higgins and Sr. Juan David Grima.

Lyle C. Brown
William F. Cooper

This volume is the tenth volume published by the Markham Press Fund of Baylor University Press, established in memory of Dr. L. N. and Princess Finch Markham of Longview, Texas, by their daughters, Mrs. R. Matt Dawson of Waco, Texas, and Mrs. B. Reid Clanton of Longview, Texas.

Kent Keeth
Chairman, Markham Press Fund
of Baylor University Press

**Religion in Latin American
Life and Literature**

PART I

GENERAL

Throughout three centuries of Spanish and Portuguese colonial rule, Roman Catholicism was the established religion in Latin America. Even after independence was achieved by twenty Latin American countries, the Catholic Church continued to exercise a virtual monopoly over organized religion; however, political independence paved the way for disestablishment and for the entry of Protestantism. Today the status of the Catholic Church varies from country to country; but throughout Latin America, Catholicism is confronted by the external challenge of secular materialism and by an internal struggle between traditionalists and reformers of different callings. Growth of Protestantism has been slow in some countries; but in others, Protestants (or Evangelicals, as they prefer to be called) have increased rapidly in number and in influence—especially since World War II. At any event, one can no longer equate Latin American Christianity with Roman Catholicism; neither can one assume that Latin American bishops and priests are in agreement concerning the role of the Catholic Church in a troubled world.

1. Some Perspectives on the Catholic Church in Latin America as an Agent of Modernization

JAMES D. COCHRANE

Professor Cochrane discusses the diversity that characterizes the Catholic Church's approach to modernization in Latin America. He describes the limited number of techniques that modernizing elements have at their command and points to a variety of obstacles that confront those Catholic elites who are committed to modernization. In conclusion, Professor Cochrane offers four generalizations concerning his topic.

There is no dearth of literature on the Church—the Roman Catholic Church—in Latin America; but there is considerable ambiguity and contradiction in the literature. The ambiguity and contradiction are particularly great concerning the stance of the Church toward modernization (i.e., economic development, political development, and social change), the role that it is playing in promoting modernization, and the skills and resources that it has to promote modernization. Bruneau very aptly describes the state of the literature on the Church:

> A review of the popular and even scholarly literature dealing with the Catholic Church in Latin America during the last decade will leave the reader confused. The books, articles, and media coverage in comparison with each other are ambiguous and at times contradictory. If on the one hand the Church is described as the fastest changing institution on the continent, there is on the other hand ample proof put forth that the institution is stagnant and in many cases apparently bankrupt. While some students point to the emergence of militant clergy groups such as the Golconda movement in Colombia or Priests of the Third World in Argentina, others as easily argue that these movements are beyond the institution and without significance in the larger society. And for every time the Church is shown siding with the poor and oppressed, two instances are held up in which words are not followed by action. It must

be emphasized that these apparent contradictions apply not only to popular reporting but to more scholarly works as well.[1]

There are varying reasons for the ambiguity and contradiction that are found in the literature.

Incomplete analysis is one reason for the ambiguity. Seeing only what one wants to see and ignoring or glossing over what one does not want to see is another reason. The Church itself is still another reason. On more than one occasion it has changed its position. An example is the Argentine Church during Perón's first tenure in the *Casa Rosada*. Regarding the Argentine Church and Perón, Snow reports: "While Perón had the almost total support of the Church in 1946, by about 1951 its position had changed to one of hesitant neutrality, and by 1955 to virtually complete opposition."[2] (One could argue that the Argentine Church really did not change its position at all, that it consistently held to a position of protecting and promoting its interests, that it merely used different techniques at different times to do so. Nonetheless, it is easy to see how differing, contradictory—but equally accurate—statements could be made about the Argentine Church's attitude toward dictatorial government.)

Yet another reason for the ambiguity and contradiction is that individual Catholics—laymen and clerics—often express very divergent opinions on any number of subjects. The writings of two Chilean laymen illustrate sufficiently that point. Jorge Iván Hübner Gallo, a man with decidedly conservative views, asserts: "Only an authoritarian, honest, impersonal, and efficient regime, which does not represent the majority but rather the best, can instill in the masses a sense of obedience and implant in the social life the principles of order, hierarchy, and discipline, which are indispensable for attaining the common good and national progress."[3] Eduardo Frei Montalva, a Christian Democrat and former President of Chile, expresses a point of view diametrically opposed to that of Hübner. Frei writes:

> Associated with democracy we can now discover unjust economic systems, horror, misery, hatred, selfishness, and overweaning ambition. The reason for this is that human society requires Christianity to a degree that it does not now possess. But simply because democracy now abounds in imperfections are we going to renounce it and abandon all

---

[1]Thomas C. Bruneau, "Obstacles to Change in the Church: Lessons from Four Brazilian Dioceses," *Journal of Inter-American Studies and World Affairs* 15 (November 1973): 395.

[2]Peter G. Snow, *Political Forces in Argentina* (Boston: Allyn and Bacon, 1971), p. 83.

[3]Jorge Iván Hübner Gallo, "Catholic Social Justice, Authoritarianism, and Class Stratification," in *The Conflict between Church and State in Latin America*, ed. Frederick B. Pike (New York: Knopf, 1964), p. 207. To Hübner, Franco's Spain represents the ideal sociopolitical order.

hope? To place ourselves under the authority of a master would be to abandon hope.[4]

Frei continues, declaring:

> Our task is to realize the possibilities of democracy, to enrich it in order to defend it. We will serve it insofar as we make it dynamic and perfect the means for the representation of all the people. We will defend it by using the goods of the nation for the advantage of all Chileans. Then, the man trembling in the night will be replaced by a citizen who can feel a sense of participation in the community and who can understand that he is part of a great family.[5]

Pointing out that ambiguity and contradiction exist in the literature is very much in order; and it is a useful endeavor—provided that it serves to stimulate the drawing of a less confused picture of the Church and modernization.

This essay is concerned with the Church as an agent of modernization. Three general questions are taken up: What is the stance of the Church in Latin America toward modernization? What techniques does the Church have to promote modernization? What obstacles confront the Church in promoting modernization? Hopefully, in directing attention to these questions, not only will a measure of insight be achieved regarding the Church as an agent of modernization but also some of the ambiguity and contradiction in the literature will be explained.

The Church: Agent of Modernization?

The first and most basic question to be asked about the Church and modernization is simple but all-important: Is the Church an agent of modernization? Does it champion and promote modernization of society? Or, does it seek either to maintain the status quo or, at least, to slow the pace of modernization?

The literature does not provide a single answer to those questions. Rather, at least two general lines of thought are apparent. One portrays the Latin American Church—sometimes in very strong terms—as being on the side of modernization and a promoter of it. John J. Kennedy, comparing the Church of 1930 with that of 1960, declares:

> There is little doubt that the situation of the Church today is radically different. Contrasts between 1930 and 1960 establish the difference. At the earlier date, rightly or wrongly, the Church was widely regarded as exerting what pressure it could on behalf of the *status quo* in opposition to incipient social change. Now, when pressing social demands portend

---

[4]Eduardo Frei Montalva, "Catholic Social Justice, Democracy, and Pluralism," in *The Conflict between Church and State in Latin America*, ed. Pike, pp. 212-13.
[5]Ibid., p. 213.

yet deeper and more far-reaching transformation, the Church appears to have given vigorous endorsement to these demands. Most of the alliances with reaction have long since disappeared. Conservative and Catholic are no longer interchangeable symbols in the language of party politics.[6]

Robert J. Alexander expresses a very similar view of the Church. Concerning the Church in the Colonial Period and the 19th century, he writes:

> The role of the Catholic Church in Latin American social and political life has been changing in recent years. In the latter part of the colonial period and during the long Church-State struggle of the nineteenth century and the early years of the present one, the Church generally stood on the side of the status quo. Its hierarchy was usually aligned with the landlords and the mercantile ruling classes. It found no difficulty in living on friendly terms with dictatorial regimes of all kinds, so long as those regimes did not interfere with the Church's own privileges. Seldom was a Church voice raised against the injustices and cruelties of the long list of tyrants who plagued the Latin American countries during their first century of independence.... During this long period the Church in the Latin American countries seemed to be more concerned with maintaining its temporal status than in answering the needs of its flock.[7]

The 20th century, according to Alexander, has seen a profound change in the stance of the Church: "The Church has tended to shift its emphasis from defense of the economic, social, and political status quo and of its own privileges, to a more critical attitude toward the Latin American society in which it is ministering. This new attitude is reflected in the development, particularly since World War II, of both Catholic trade-union movements and Christian Democratic parties."[8]

Russell H. Fitzgibbon is yet another who sees the Church as an agent of modernization:

> The third of the classic institutions, the Catholic church, has also undergone great change over a century. Traditionally, it was regarded as almost wholly conservative, or even reactionary, an all but automatic supporter of the established lay authority and an unquestioning ally of the hereditary landed aristocracy. Although ostensibly keyed to divine rather than mundane authority, the Church in Latin America ... did not hesitate to use its great weight for political ends.... But the Church, perhaps partly because of its very institutionalization, probably partially due to its sophistication, and certainly in part because of its inheritance of centuries of experience, was better fitted than the other two classic institutions [the armed forces and landed aristocracy] to bend to the

---

[6]John J. Kennedy, "Dichotomies in the Church," *The Annals*, 334 (March 1961): 57.

[7]Robert J. Alexander, *Today's Latin America*, 2d ed., Anchor Books (Garden City, N.Y.: Doubleday, 1968), pp. 218-19.

[8]Ibid., p. 220.

wind of change. The first alternation seemed to come with Pope Leo's famous *Rerum Novarum* in 1891. Other evidences of adaptation followed in course, spurred by the catalyst of additional important encyclicals in 1931 and 1961. The Church became active here and there in organizing and directing Catholic-oriented labor unions; some of its hierarchy advocated distribution of its surplus lands among the landless; most significant of all, perhaps, Christian Democratic parties started to modernize the conservative image of the Church in politics.[9]

The foregoing statements represent one point of view concerning the Church in contemporary Latin America, and it is the characterization of the Church that one most frequently encounters. However, a second line of thought about the Church and modernization is discernible in the literature. It expresses a more restrained, questioning view of the Church's stance toward modernization and promotion of it, although it does not characterize the Church as a reactionary institution committed to maintaining the status quo. Robert F. Adie and Guy E. Poitras note that while the Church recognizes that socioeconomic change or modernization in society cannot be avoided, it looks at specific changes in terms of whether they will threaten the survival of the Church. If interpreted as threatening, the change or changes will be opposed. They write: "No matter what the specific changes—for better or worse—that emerge, almost all members of the Church can agree that institutional survival must be maintained. Threats to institutional survival will be opposed by nearly all members, but threats are subject to different interpretations."[10] The same authors note that on the part of at least one segment of the clergy, the conservatives, the attitude toward modernization and pressures in society for it is roughly as follows: "If the situation becomes grave and something must be done as a last resort, the conservatives emphasize the importance of braking rather than accelerating change through public policy."[11]

Martin C. Needler, although noting that the attitude of the Church is different now than it was in the Colonial Period and the 19th century, contends: "The identification of the Church with the forces of social conservatism, in general, continues to this day. . . ."[12] He does, however, report that the conservative identification of the Church has been or is being moderated somewhat by the papal encyclicals of a social nature and the tendency of 20th century dictators to attempt to gain influence, if not control, over all organizations, including the

---

[9]Russell H. Fitzgibbon, "Components of Political Change in Latin America," *Journal of Inter-American Studies and World Affairs* 12 (April 1970): 195.

[10]Robert F. Adie and Guy E. Poitras, *Latin America: The Politics of Immobility* (Englewood Cliffs, N.J.: Prentice-Hall, 1974), p. 167.

[11]Ibid., p. 174.

[12]Martin C. Needler, *Latin American Politics in Perspective*, rev. ed. (Princeton, N.J.: Van Nostrand, 1967), p. 14.

Church—a factor that has made the Church more cautious in the political alliances it forms and the sorts of governments it supports.[13] While the thrust of his case is not that the Church is in all respects a reactionary, status quo-oriented institution, the remarks of Emanuel de Kadt about the content of education in Catholic secondary schools in Brazil also raises a question about the extent to which the Church—at least as far as education in that country is concerned—is either an advocate or agent of modernization. He states, "Those who pass through the Church schools are exclusively exposed to the pietistic outlook, . . . with its limited and limiting stress on certain specific sins (particularly sexual ones) and its virtually total disregard for the social teachings of the Church. They learn to believe that 'all is well with the Church'—an attitude often referred to as triumphalism—and, incidentally, that all is well with society."[14] Clearly, then, there is no generally-agreed-on answer to the question of whether the Church in Latin America is an agent of modernization; and a good deal of supportive evidence can be marshalled to back conflicting answers to the question.

The Problem of Generalizing

Ambiguity and contradiction on whether the Church is or is not a proponent of modernization stems, in the main, from the tendency of many writers to generalize about the Church—to generalize about the Roman Catholic Church in all of Latin America or to generalize about the Church in a single country, often on the basis of limited, partial data which apply to a specific situation but not to the Church as a whole.

The point so frequently overlooked is that the Church differs in various ways—resources, strength, the extent and nature of Church-State relations, size, quality and outlook of clergy, and so on—from one country to another. Moreover, and this is even more frequently overlooked, in many instances the Church even within a particular country is not a unified, cohesive, monolithic entity. "At no level," in the words of a Rand Corporation study, "does the Roman Catholic Church, despite the unifying religious symbolism of the Papacy, exist in fact as a single, united entity."[15] And, as de Kadt puts it:

> In discussions of the social and political problems of Latin America one nowadays often hears the question asked: Where does the Church stand on this matter? It is not necessarily a very enlightening question.

[13]Ibid., pp. 14-15.

[14]Emanuel de Kadt, "Religion, the Church, and Social Change in Brazil," in *The Politics of Conformity in Latin America*, ed. Claudio Veliz (New York: Oxford University Press, 1967), p. 203.

[15]Luigi Einaudi, Richard Maullin, Alfred Stepan, and Michael Fleet, *Latin American Institutional Development: The Changing Catholic Church*, Memorandum RM-6136-DOS (Santa Monica., Calif.: The Rand Corporation, October, 1969), p. 9.

> Although in many countries of the continent "the Church" continues to be a near-monolithic entity, in others conflicting tendencies and groups have become more and more distinct from each other. To talk about "the Church" in countries such as Chile, Venezuela, and Brazil—and Churchmen themselves are particularly prone to do so—therefore merely befuddles the issues.[16]

Thomas G. Sanders, in discussing the change that is taking place in the Church throughout Latin America, notes:

> Like many cultural changes, however, this one has been neither as abrupt nor as total as casual observers have often reported. Just as the Church was never as monolithic or reactionary as its critics claimed, recent reform movements have not totally captured the Catholic community or followed a single, unified path. Rather, the Church is in a continuous transition which has greatly intensified in the last decade, building on a long tradition of division and dissent that dates as far back as the early sixteenth century....[17]

Because policies of the Catholic Church differ from one country to another and even within a country, failure to recognize these diversities accounts, in large part, for the conflicting views as to whether the Church is or is not an agent of modernization. The views that describe the Church as an agent of modernization are not inaccurate. They apply to the Church in some countries or, more correctly, to segments of the Church. But, they do not have universal validity for the Church throughout Latin America. The same applies to those statements that describe the Church as not being an agent of modernization or, at least, as not being a very enthusiastic one.

Catholic Elite[18]

The diversity within the Church concerning modernization, as well as other matters, is best revealed by looking at the elements within the Church who comprise what can be termed the Catholic elite. A member of the elite is, to quote Sanders,

> ... an individual who ... has internalized Catholic beliefs and values to a sufficient degree that he justifies his social and political outlook and actions chiefly by his Catholicism rather than by other norms, institu-

---

[16]de Kadt, "Religion, The Church, and Social Change in Brazil," p. 192. It may well be that de Kadt is actually somewhat overstating the situation when he says that in "many" countries of Latin America the Church remains nearly monolithic.

[17]Thomas G. Sanders, "The Church in Latin America," *Foreign Affairs* 47 (January 1970): 285.

[18]This section is based on Thomas G. Sanders, "Types of Catholic Elites in Latin America," in *Latin American Politics: Studies of the Contemporary Scene*, ed. Robert D. Tomasek, 2d ed., Anchor Books (Garden City, N.Y.: Doubleday, 1970), pp. 180-96; Adie and Poitras, *Latin America*, pp. 150-88; and, to a much lesser extent, Ivan Vallier, "Religious Elites: Differentiations and Developments in Roman Catholicism," in *Elites in Latin America*, ed. Seymour Martin Lipset and Aldo Solari (New York: Oxford University Press, 1967), pp. 190-232.

tions, or pressures. The most cursory observation of Latin American culture reveals that the overwhelming majority of those who call themselves Catholic, though often deeply religious, adhere to forms of culture religion that reflect only a slight, confused understanding of normative Catholic belief and no understanding of the social teaching of the Church which supposedly provides the framework for political action. We cannot then ascribe the political functioning of the masses to Catholic conviction, though in some instances they may be mobilized for actions, usually defensive, that certain Catholics rationalise as expressions of Church interests. . . . It is among the elites, then, those who have been trained in thought about their beliefs and who are trying to apply them to decisions, that a genuine relationship between Catholicism and politics appears. Elites are usually educated and have participated in Catholic institutions where they absorbed a perspective that modified the unreflective culture religion common to Latin America. Bishops, priests, or laymen compose elites. In general, though, bishops are more limited in their capacity to assume unusual political and social position than priests and laymen, because they symbolize the unity of the Church in their dioceses and have pastoral responsibilities for all the Catholics there.[19]

The Catholic elite in Latin America is fragmented. Four distinct elite types can be identified. Moving from the Right to the Left of the political spectrum, they are identified as follows: Reactionaries, Conservatives, Progressives, and Radicals.

Reactionaries. The Reactionaries are definitely not agents of change—unless it be that of turning the clock backward to an earlier century. In this category are clerics—including some of high level—and laymen. Although Reactionaries are to be found in all segments of society, most come from the upper class. Younger as well as older members of society are to be found in the ranks of the Reactionaries. According to Adie and Poitras, the Reactionaries "are highly disturbed by change of almost any scope or direction. For example, the Reactionaries find it difficult to discriminate between liberal reform and revolutionary upheaval. Particularly disturbed about the alleged threat of communism to Latin America, they launch indiscriminate attacks on those who seek or even approve of changes of any kind."[20] The Reactionaries equate change with communism or, what they see as equally evil, socialism. They champion an authoritarian, highly structured, stratified society. According to Sanders, "the absolute which they defend is private property. . . ."[21] If nothing else, the Reactionaries are consistent. Their attitudes toward the Church as a religious institution match their attitudes on political, economic, and social questions. They oppose, with vigor, the Church reforms of Vatican II and the social encyclicals.

[19]Sanders, "Types of Catholic Elites in Latin America," pp. 182-83.
[20]Adie and Poitras, *Latin America*, pp. 171-72.
[21]Sanders, "Types of Catholic Elites in Latin America," p. 185.

The Reactionaries are few in number and their influence varies from country to country. They are probably most numerous and influential in the least developed countries of Latin America. Throughout Latin America, their "greatest impact comes on isolated issues such as opposition to divorce and agrarian reform, where it can appeal to innate sympathies in a large section of the populace."[22]

Conservatives. Compared to the Reactionaries, the Conservatives may appear to be "flaming liberals." But liberals they are not. In fact, the Conservatives hold nearly all of the same positions and values as the Reactionaries do; however, they do not have the militancy that characterizes the Reactionaries. It is that lack of militancy that is the main distinction between these two elements of the Catholic elite. Like the Reactionaries, the Conservatives—who constitute the bulk of the Catholic clergy, dominate the Catholic hierarchy, and perhaps constitute the bulk of the practicing laity—are not agents of modernization. Indeed, it is the Conservatives, because of their majority position, who are responsible for the image of the Church in Latin America as a tradition-bound, status quo-oriented institution. According to Adie and Poitras, "Unconditionally loyal to an institution that is threatened by its failure to adapt to socioeconomic change, the conservatives are largely responsible for perpetuating a Church increasingly out of touch with the masses. Like the Reactionaries, the conservative clergy active in politics are more likely to do nothing to change Latin American society than they are to suggest concrete proposals for promoting change."[23]

Given their number, both in the clergy and among the laity, and the positions that they hold in the clergy, there is no question about the Conservatives' influence.

Progressives. The Progressives among the Catholic elite believe that the Church can and should play a role, an active role, in the modernization of Latin American society and that it has not done so. The Progressive, Sanders reports, "has absorbed the changes in the official thinking of the Church since 1960, believes that the Church is making significant adjustments and suggestions to the modern world, and wants to follow the Church's guidance. While he assumes that further innovations will come in the future, he thinks that the Vatican II documents and subsequent encyclicals, as well as major hierarchical statements, outline a sound position for the present. He tries to work carefully within the Church. His intellectual inspiration on social matters tends to be the reasonable, balanced neo-Thomism of Jacques Maritain. . . ."[24] The Progressives are both realists and idealists. They recognize that the Church is weak, lacking influence

---

[22]Ibid., p. 186.
[23]Adie and Poitras, *Latin America,* p. 174.
[24]Sanders, "Types of Catholic Elites in Latin America," p. 188.

over a majority of the Latin American population, but are convinced that with new methods and effort it can achieve a position of influence. It is the Progressives, along with the Radicals, who are responsible for the image of the Church as an agent of modernization.

The strength and influence of the Progressives are difficult to characterize. They are probably less strong numerically and less influential politically than may be suggested by the vast amount of attention they receive from scholars and journalists. Given the segments of society they represent and the public policies they advocate, the Progressives not infrequently "lack the [essential] contacts with important power groups in and out of government...."[25] What is clear is that the Progressives are stronger and more influential in some countries than in others.

Radicals. The Radicals are both similar to and different from the Progressives. Like the Progressives, the Radical members of the Catholic elite believe that the Church can and should play an active role in the modernization of Latin America, and that it has not done so in the past. However, the Radicals go farther, much farther, than the Progressives:

> The Radical considers himself as good a Catholic as the Progressive and quotes encyclicals where he can, but he stretches the obvious meaning of the Church's position. He considers the changes only a partial adjustment to what is necessary. In terms of certain vital social interests—relevance to development, political effectiveness, modernity—he regards the consensus as lagging. He sees himself on the frontier of new problems and knows that the Church must learn from the ideas and experiences of innovating Catholics like himself.[26]

While the Progressives tend to work mainly within the Church, the Radicals do not confine themselves to doing so. They are doubtful that their aims can be attained within the framework of the Church and tend to look to broad-based or mass movements—including alliances with Marxist groups—as a more promising means of achieving their ends. The Radicals tend toward socialism, although not necessarily Marxism, while the Progressives oppose Marxism and seek some middle ground between capitalism and socialism. The Radicals are essentially revolutionary while the Progressives are evolutionary.

As with the Progressives, it is difficult to characterize precisely the strength and influence of the Radicals; but Adie and Poitras provide some insight:

> Unlike the progressive clergy, the radicals are prone to form coalitions with Marxists and other extremists, the demands of which are more likely to provoke governmental hostility than governmental compliance.

[25]Adie and Poitras, *Latin America*, p. 176.
[26]Sanders, "Types of Catholic Elites in Latin America," p. 188.

> The radicals are not uninfluential in some ways; their small numbers underrepresent their impact. However, given militancy and fondness for utopian remedies, the radical clergy have tended to present polemical, rather than concrete, demands which the leaders of Latin American political systems generally cannot meet, even if they were inclined to do so.[27]

Moreover, according to the same authors, "because the radical clergy do not play the game of political influence like most groups that accept the current system, their activities have . . . sometimes counterproductive results."[28]

The foregoing is in no way a comprehensive description of the four types found within the Catholic elite of Latin America. But it is perhaps sufficient to show (1) the diversity that exists within the Church on the question of modernization, and (2) the impossibility of making any meaningful generalizations about whether the Church as a whole in this or that Latin American country is or is not an agent of modernization or of describing the sort of modernization advocated, let alone the possibility of characterizing the Latin American Church as a whole on the modernization question. The diversity that exists among members of the Catholic elite is not amazing. Large-scale organizations, whether religious or not, are rarely, if ever, monolithic entities. Sanders states:

> The outlooks represented by Reactionary, Conservative, Progressive, and Radical elites are common to large institutions that include people from diverse social, economic, and educational backgrounds, especially when the demand for change presents itself. They represent those who fight against change, those who ignore it, those who proceed prudently with it, and those who criticize radically and take advanced positions. The Latin American Church includes patterns of analysis that can be found in non-Catholic institutions. . . .[29]

In sum, observers have erred in looking for a single stance on the part of the Church on the question of modernization. They have erred even more by ascribing a single stance to it. Although it is not as neat or as easy to handle, the reality is that the Church—or its various elements—have several different attitudes regarding modernization.

Modernization: Techniques and Obstacles

Some segments within the Church are not agents of modernization; instead, they oppose or resist it. Other segments (the Progressives and Radicals), however, do advocate modernization and

---

[27]Adie and Poitras, *Latin America*, p. 182.
[28]Ibid., p. 183. For a sample of the thought of a Revolutionary, see Camilo Torres, "Crossroads of the Church in Latin America," in *The Roman Catholic Church in Modern Latin America*, ed. Karl M. Schmitt (New York: Knopf, 1972), pp. 139-46.
[29]Sanders, "Types of Catholic Elites in Latin America," p. 194.

are acting to promote it. What techniques do these elements who are committed to the modernization of society possess to promote it? What obstacles do these elements face in their efforts to promote that modernization?

Techniques

The techniques which the modernizing elements of the Church have at their command are not very numerous. Public pronouncements constitute one technique: statements directed to the faithful, the public at large, and political decision-makers—statements that identify problems, suggest remedies, call for corrective action, criticize existing policies and practices, and so on. Moral suasion, not entirely distinct from public pronouncements, is another technique—persuading the faithful, the general population, and political decision-makers on the basis of Catholic theology and social doctrine that various sorts of activities that would promote modernization are morally right and that they should be pursued for moral reasons. Sponsoring programs of a developmental nature is yet another technique that may be employed; examples are operating educational programs, organizing labor unions and peasant groups, providing credit and technical assistance, operating clinics, sponsoring co-operatives, and constructing low-cost housing. Occupying political decision-making positions is another technique; but given present patterns of political power distribution in most Latin American countries, that technique is one that is open to very, very few of the modernization-oriented Catholic elites. Not only are the techniques available to the modernization-oriented Catholic elites fairly few in number, but also their effectiveness is not as great as might appear at first glance.

Obstacles

A variety of obstacles confront those elites within the Church who are committed to promoting the modernization of society. The obstacles fall under several headings: extent of Church influence, characteristics of the clergy, scarcity of resources, nature of some development programs, failure of those committed to modernization to confront some major social problems, and vulnerability to attack by government.

Church influences. The population of Latin America is overwhelmingly Catholic. Probably 90 percent of the population is formally Catholic;[30] however, the Church's influence in Latin America is not commensurate with the size of its membership. For a variety of reasons, Church influence has waned since the Colonial Period and the 19th century. Probably no more than about 10 percent of Latin

---

[30]Alexander T. Edelmann, *Latin American Government and Politics*, rev. ed. (Homewood, Ill.: Dorsey Press, 1969), p. 142.

America's Catholics are practicing Catholics.[31] The low number of formal Catholics who are practicing Catholics limits, although it certainly does not wholly eliminate, the effectiveness or impact that public pronouncements and attempts at moral suasion are likely to have. Glenn A. Nichols shows the limits of the Church's political influence in Rio de Janeiro:

> The Church was notoriously unsuccessful in influencing the electoral outcomes of the city of Rio de Janeiro. One prominent Catholic layman told the author that to many candidates the Church's endorsement was welcomed like the "kiss of death." In 1950, . . . only five of the 25 UDN *vereador* candidates endorsed by LEC [the Catholic Electoral League] were elected to office. In 1954, only 9 of the 47 UDN *vereador* candidates supported by LEC won office. Despite the overwhelming Catholic population in the city of Rio, few Catholics appear to have followed LEC's advice. In 1962, with an attempt to pick probable winners, ALEF [Electoral Alliance for the Family] fared little better. In the deputy race 6 of 17 of ALEF's candidates were elected. Since 4 of the 6 had been elected prior to ALEF's existence and enjoyed the benefits of incumbency, ALEF's influence should probably be reduced to 2. In the state legislature race, ALEF had supported only 11 of the 55 elected candidates.[32]

There is no reason to think that the situation Nichols found in Rio de Janeiro is peculiar to that city, although the same situation may not characterize every Latin American electoral situation.

Characteristics of the clergy. Various characteristics of the clergy, too, are obstacles to effectiveness on the part of those clerics within the Catholic elite who are committed to modernization. Six of these obstacles can be summarized as follows:

1. The clergy does not enjoy the esteem of large numbers of Latin Americans. As one source puts it, "Not only does a priest receive very little status from the prestige class of modern times but even members of the working class refuse to defer to the clergy."[33] The situation that faced the clergy in pre-Castro Cuba was extreme but is suggestive of the general situation. According to Alexander T. Edelmann, "Any male who regarded himself as *macho* did not want to be seen speaking civilly to a priest or entering a church on Sunday. For if he violated the *macho* code, he might be charged with effeminacy and lack of virility."[34] To gain some measure of respect from fellow males in Cuba, more than one priest openly kept a mistress.

---

[31]François Houtart and Emile Pin, *The Church and the Latin American Revolution*, trans. Gilbert Barth (New York: Sheed and Ward, 1965), p. 152.

[32]Glenn Alvin Nichols, "Toward a Theory of Political Party Disunity: The Case of the National Democratic Union Party of Rio de Janeiro, Brazil" (Ph.D. dissertation, Tulane University, 1974).

[33]Charles F. Denton and Preston Lee Lawrence, *Latin American Politics: A Functional Approach* (San Francisco: Chandler, 1972), p. 147.

[34]Edelmann, *Latin American Government and Politics*, p. 141.

2. There is a dearth of clergy in Latin America. One estimate puts the figure at roughly 1 priest per 5,000 persons in the population.[35] According to Adie and Poitras, "The great lack of clergy detracts significantly from the ability of the Church as a renovated institution to reach the Latin American masses and thereby play a significant role in promoting socioeconomic change."[36] It means that the clergy is not close to the people, cannot be close, and that it cannot have the close rapport with the faithful that would aid it in influencing thought and behavior. Also, the shortage of clergy limits the number of priests who can be freed from parish and other essential religious duties to direct various development programs or, at a minimum, reduces the amount of time they can devote to such activities.

3. One-third of the clergy in Latin America is non-Latin American.[37] Whatever may be their orientation, foreign priests are probably not in a particularly good position to promote modernization in Latin America. They are aliens; and when they criticize existing conditions and suggest corrective action, they are likely to be regarded as meddling, intruding, perhaps creating resistance to change instead of impetus for it. Further, many foreign priests, particularly during their initial years in Latin America, probably have relatively little understanding of Latin America, a factor that further hinders their effectiveness as agents of modernization.

4. In most Latin American countries, these elements in the clergy who are committed to modernization lack "clout." They are, for the most part, in the lower reaches of the clergy rather than well-placed in the upper reaches of the hierarchy. That makes it difficult for them to influence Church policy and action, and makes them vulnerable to sanctions by superiors who do not share their values. Much the same applies to many modernization-oriented laymen.

5. Modernization-oriented Catholic elites, both clergy and laymen, in many Latin American countries lack political skills and influence with political decision-makers. They lack skills because they have little or no political experience. They lack political influence, in part, because the views they express are not held by most decision-makers. Another reason for lack of political influence stems from the limited influence the Church in general has in society. As Denton and Lawrence express it: "Once an extremely important political interest group in Latin America, the Roman Catholic church has gradually lost its ability to make demands for resources or to provide supports for particularly amenable authoritative decision makers."[38]

6. The members of the clergy come largely, although not wholly, from the upper reaches of the social structure. That has at least two

[35]Houtart and Pin, *The Church and the Latin American Revolution*, p. 146.
[36]Adie and Poitras, *Latin America*, p. 161.
[37]Einaudi et al., *Latin American Institutional Development*, p. 17.
[38]Denton and Lawrence, *Latin American Politics*, pp. 146-47.

adverse effects so far as modernization is concerned. It contributes to the negative attitude toward the Church held by a large part of the lower classes, and it hinders the efforts of the clergy to establish close rapport with members of the lower classes.

Resources. Modernization requires resources—human and material. In the main, the Church in most Latin American countries does not have an abundance of either sort of resource. The previously noted shortage of priests is one indication of the human resource inadequacy. Another indication is the sort of seminary education that most Latin American priests receive. Regarding this matter, Adie and Poitras have written:

> Seminarians are subjected to a traditionalistic education in which values of pre-modern theology rather than the values of contemporary social justice are stressed. The religious training of the seminary ill prepares the priest for the modern life to which many must adjust or face social ineffectiveness. For example, although claiming much concern for the family as an institution, the Church, through its seminaries, fails to provide the students with any practical knowledge about the family and its problems in today's world. Generally, then, the molding of the priest within the seminaries is inadequate for today's Latin America and is inadequate as a device to train Church personnel for effective roles in promoting changes in society. The seminarian's understanding of the complex process of change with which he may be required to grapple is at best faulty, because he has little practical involvement with them.[39]

Undoubtedly, large numbers of modernization-oriented laymen receive a similar education if their education is obtained in a Catholic school.

The Roman Catholic Church is often portrayed as a vastly wealthy organization. In fact, the Church in many Latin American countries is not very well endowed with material resources. In large measure, it must depend on the charity of the wealthy—who are not especially generous—for its finances. And, not infrequently, in those Latin American countries where the Church does possess wealth there is little or no willingness on the part of those in the hierarchy who control the Church's resources to expend those resources on modernization programs. (The Church in Chile is a notable exception. It has given quite generous support to modernization programs.)

Lack of understanding. There is basis for questioning whether sincere, well-intentioned, modernization-oriented elites within the Church have the kind of understanding of societal problems, alternative solutions to them, and probable clientele reaction that is necessary for a successful assault on the problems. Pike, commenting on the Church and modernization in Chile and Peru, writes:

---

[39] Adie and Poitras, *Latin America,* p. 164.

> There is some evidence, based largely on the statements of renowned Catholic intellectual leaders, including laymen, priests and bishops, to suggest that the Church in Peru and Chile is not meeting its obligation to be well informed on social and economic problems, except for compiling statistics to prove that such problems exist. It is in the realm of suggesting feasible solutions to the problems that responsibility and obligations are most commonly ignored.[40]

Often simplistic panaceas and utopian proposals are put forward. Ill-conceived assaults on basic problems are little better than no assault at all; and perhaps they are worse. An assault that fails may produce disillusionment on the part of all involved, whereas when a problem goes unattacked there may be a hope at least that *eventually* something may be done about it.

Failure to confront fundamental problems. The elites within the Church who are committed to modernization have ignored certain basic problems. Perhaps the most notable instance of ignoring a basic problem is the way the demographic problem has been handled or, more correctly, not handled. Thus, Pike states:

> Although churchmen could not be an effective force for family limitation, even if given the approval of Rome, unless many of them changed their whole approach to socioeconomic reform, at the present time they contribute nothing whatsoever to the resolution of the demographic problem, which is perhaps the most serious menace to social justice now confronting Latin America. Instead the clergy, in many instances, seem insistent upon making the problem worse. While it is true that Chile's enlightened Cardinal-Archbishop Raúl Silva Henríquez has not interfered with the operation of birth control clinics in his country, many churchmen have continued to thunder with undiminished passion and vigor that procreation is the sole end of matrimony.[41]

Vulnerability to government. Government suppression or repression is another obstacle, or potential obstacle, to the efforts of these Catholic elites who are promoting modernization of society. Not all governments look with favor on the activities of these Church elements, and governments have various techniques which they can use to hinder the activities of those within the Catholic elite who are seeking to promote modernization. Bruneau has detailed the suppression—if not outright persecution—of some modernization-oriented Catholic elites in Brazil by the post-1964 military government;[42] and the Brazilian experience is not unique. Similar suppressions have taken place elsewhere in Latin America. Further, it is not only conservative governments, military and civilian, that im-

---

[40]Frederick B. Pike, "The Catholic Church and Modernization in Peru and Chile," *Journal of International Affairs* 20 (1966): 278.
[41]Ibid., p. 285.
[42]Bruneau, "Obstacles to Change in the Church," pp. 395-414.

pede or may impede Catholic modernizers. There is, for example, some indication that Goulart intended to take control of the Catholic-sponsored peasant organizations in Brazil. He failed to do so only because of his ouster from the presidency.

Conclusion

Four generalizations can be offered by way of conclusion:

1. The Church in contemporary Latin America can neither be described as an unqualified agent of modernization nor as an unqualified opponent of it. Elements within the Church in each of the Latin American countries oppose modernization while other elements are working to promote it.[43]

2. Although the subject was not discussed here, the Church in some countries (e.g., Chile, at least until the 1973 coup) is more modernization-oriented as an institution than it is in other countries.

3. Throughout Latin America, except for Cuba where the Church is proscribed, elements of the Catholic elite are carrying out programs to modernize society. The extent and effectiveness of these programs not only differs from country to country but from one area of a country to another and from one sort of program in a country to another sort of program within the same country.

4. In promoting modernization, Catholic elites have a relatively small arsenal of techniques at their disposal and they confront a variety of obstacles.

---

[43]For an essay that contends that elements in the Church both can and do promote modernization, see Ivan Vallier, "Church 'Development' in Latin America: A Five-Country Comparison," in *The Roman Catholic Church in Modern Latin America*, ed. Schmitt, pp. 167-93. For a somewhat contrary view, see David E. Mutcher, "Adaptations of the Roman Catholic Church to Latin American Development: The Meaning of Internal Church Conflict," in *The Roman Catholic Church in Modern Latin America*, ed. Schmitt, pp. 194-216.

2. The Changing Church in Latin America

FATHER TEODORO DE LA TORRE

Noting that the traditional social and religious apparatus of the Catholic Church in Latin America began to crumble in the 1930s, the author asserts that the Church was unprepared for the transformation of society that has attended population explosion and rapid urbanization. He points out, however, that the Church has become aware of these significant socioeconomic changes, and he describes how the Church has attempted to reform Catholic pastoral activities in three directions: development (which emphasizes helping the poor to help themselves); revolution (which seeks to transform society, as in the case of Camilo Torres and the Golconda group); and liberation (which seeks to reformulate Christian theology in terms of other relevant social and political categories).

The situation prevailing in Latin America and the Catholic Church during the last three centuries can be outlined as follows:

1. In the arid highlands of the Andean countries, Central America, and Mexico, the inhabitants, mostly Indians, were the poorest people of the whole continent. Not having much to expect from their life on earth, they placed their hope in the life of heaven. The priests played the role of intermediaries between the landlords and the masses; they were greatly revered.

2. In the tropical lowlands, in which vegetation is either parched as in northeastern Brazil or luxuriant as in the Amazon region, the people, often black in whole or in part, were only slightly better off than in the highlands. Nevertheless, attuned to the exuberance of their environment, they tended to enjoy their earthly lives as much as possible. Their religious practices were often spirited and gay; the priests, always scarce in number, were looked upon mostly as performers of ritual ceremonies and were treated with kindness rather than with reverence.

3. In the fertile and more temperate lands (e.g., Argentina, Uruguay, Venezuela, Cuba, southern Brazil), there was a great amount

of European immigration and foreign investment. Periods of prosperity alternated with periods of depression. The priests, many foreign-born, did not exercise widespread influence, but had the support of a religiously cultivated minority. There were numerous church-related institutions, such as schools, youth centers, and benevolent homes.

4. Finally, everywhere throughout Latin America, there were enclaves of the native bourgeoisie, mostly white and highly educated. They protected the Catholic Church as part of the *status quo* that they tried to maintain.

This social and religious apparatus began to crumble in the 1930s. The economic depression, halting and actually reversing the outflow of foreign immigration and investment, paralyzed development of the more advanced regions; but improved health care caused an excess of population in the more destitute sections of Latin America. The result was massive emigration from the country to slums in and around all the largest cities.

The Catholic Church, unprepared for the unexpected and sudden transformation of society, delayed her adjustment to the new circumstances. Communism, on the other hand, found in the resulting turmoil abundant opportunities for its activism. Recently the Church has become fully aware of radical socioeconomic changes and has been greatly affected by this recognition.[1] Reference is made primarily to the Catholic Church, but the situation of the Protestant churches is very similar.[2]

The Church's attempt to reform her pastoral activities has taken three directions: development, revolution, and liberation.

Development

Recently, in the Houston Medical Center where he was hospitalized, this writer met Father José María Vélaz, a Chilean Jesuit

[1] The literature on this subject is abundant: François Houtart and Emile Pin, *The Church in the Latin American Revolution*, trans. Gilbert Barth (New York: Sheed and Ward, 1965); Marcos McGrath, "The Signs of the Times in Latin America Today," and Eduardo F. Pironio, "Christian Interpretation of the Signs of the Times in Latin America Today," in *The Church in the Present-Day Transformation of Latin America in the Light of the Council*, Position Papers of the Second General Conference of Latin American Bishops, Medellín, Colombia, 1968 (Bogotá: General Secretariat of CELAM, 1970), pp. 1, 79-106, and 107-128; Paul E. Sigmund, "Latin American Catholicism's Opening to the Left," *Review of Politics* 35 (January 1973): 61-76.

[2] As early as 1966, various Evangelical denominations met to consider the adjustment of their Churches to the changing Latin America society: Segunda Consulta Latinoamericana de Iglesia y Sociedad, *America hoy* (Montevideo: ISAL, 1966); on the same problem, see Christian Lalive d'Epinay, "La Iglesia evangélica y la revolución latinoamericana," in *CIDOC*, no. 78 (Cuernavaca, Mor.: Centro Intercultural de Documentación, 1968). For a critical appraisal of radicalism in the Evangelical Churches of Latin America, see Florencio Sáez, Jr., *Entre Cristo y Che Guevara* (San Juan de Puerto Rico: Palma Real, 1972).

priest. He is the founder and director of Faith and Joy (Fe y Alegría), a movement begun in 1955 to provide education for underprivileged children of the Caracas slums. The movement operates in seven nations: Venezuela, Ecuador, Peru, Bolivia, Panama, El Salvador, and Colombia. More than 100,000 students attend elementary and high schools established by Faith and Joy, as well as trade schools of commerce, agriculture, husbandry, mechanics, and even a very specialized school of tourism in Mérida, Venezuela. Although primarily educational in intent, the movement also offers such services as free clinics, cooperatives, sports activities, and leadership training. There are plans for it to enter the field of housing.

The program is directed by 15 Jesuits with the cooperation of 300 men and women of 50 religious communities, but it is carried on mostly by 3,000 salaried employees. Volunteers are used exclusively for promotional and fund-raising purposes.

An enterprise of this caliber requires a great amount of money, which is obtained from private donors and corporations and, in some countries, through public subsidies. These contributions tie the work of Father Vélaz with the rich and with the political authorities, but he considers this fact an inevitable evil. He has decided that compromise is necessary, unless one prefers to remain at the level of utopian thinking.

Let us take another example. Father Domingo Effio,[3] a Peruvian-born priest, decided to open a catechetical center in a shantytown of Bogotá. Received at first with suspicion by the three hundred families of the area, he gained their friendship when, changing his clerical habit for work clothes, he began to share in their endless operation of building shacks and keeping them from falling apart.

Once he became their leader, Father Effio undertook new projects: fixing a street; opening a drainage ditch; installing a public faucet of running water; building a chapel, a school, a clinic, and a community center; creating a voluntary service of night watchmen; and establishing an employment agency.

Although Father Effio relied mainly on the communal work of the slum-dwellers—and he saw in this work a redeeming value—he searched for and obtained outside help in the form of money and, especially, personal services. Many families of the affluent society of Bogotá (sometimes in teams of husband, wife, and children) came to participate in the work of the priest and his people. Finally the end arrived. Most of the construction was on private property. The owners demanded their legal right to the land; and, under police protection, bulldozers began to tear down the shaky houses. Expelled from the

---

[3]Domingo Effio, P.O., "The Sad, Hidden Side of a Modern City," *World Campus*, February 1967, p. 3; Graciela Giraldo Moscoso, "El trabajo, lazo de unión entre habitantes del Barrio Juan XXIII," *La República* (Bogotá, Colombia), January 17, 1967.

country, Father Effio came to Texas, where he works in a Mexican-American parish.

From the point of view of the legal establishment, this second case is less orthodox than the first because here we have a case of trespassing. Father Effio permitted trespassing and cooperated with the trespassers, because he knew the personal problems of those with whom he was working. When they were unable to pay rent, some families with six to eight children were evicted from the notorious slum area of South Bogotá. But Father Effio was not a revolutionary; he actually thought that the only way of preventing revolution was to undertake generous programs of social assistance.

In these two cases, as in the many others of their kind thoughout Latin America, the motivating force has been fundamentally religious; the work of these apostles of charity is a witness to the depth of their conscience. But they also have a sociological reason. They believe that there cannot be progress unless it is preceded by the acculturation of Latin America's marginal masses.

Revolution

Now let us examine an entirely different approach: the revolutionary attempts of some members of the clergy to transform the Latin American society.

Camilo Torres[4] was born into an upper-class Colombian family. Upon his return from the University of Louvain, where he studied sociology, he was appointed chaplain of the anti-clerical National University of Bogotá in 1959. Later, he became a professor of social sciences at that university. Increasingly disenchanted with all the programs designed to improve the conditions of the poor, Camilo began to voice his criticism of the political authorities. After being warned by Cardinal Concha of the provisions of the Colombian concordat with the Holy See, which forbids priests from entering politics, Father Torres asked for and obtained his laicization. Immediately, he began a tour of the country in an effort to unite workers, students, and other political groups in a political coalition against the ruling National Front. Subject to continuous harassment by the police, and having been the target of various assassination attempts, Camilo Torres joined the National Liberation Army. After four months of fighting as a guerrilla, he was killed in a skirmish with regular Colombian soldiers on February 15, 1966.

---

[4]Camilo Torres, *Revolutionary Writings* (New York: Herder and Herder, 1969); *Revolutionary Priest; The Complete Writings and Messages of Camilo Torres,* ed. John Gerassi (New York: Vintage Books, 1971). Works on Camilo Torres include Germán Guzmán Campos, *Camilo Torres,* trans. John D. Ring (New York: Sheed and Ward, 1969); Javier Darío Restrepo, "Priest-Guerrillas (Camilo Torres Started Something)," *Revista Familia,* Bogotá, reprinted in LADOC 1 (November 1970).

In July 1968, a group of Colombian priests, claiming to be the successors of Camilo, met at a farm known as "Golconda"[5] and issued a manifesto calling for overthrow of the capitalist system, abolition of all political and economic dependency on the United States, and organization of a socialist society. At least one of the Golconda priests, Father Domingo Laín, a Spaniard, joined the Colombian guerrillas; the others preferred to dedicate themselves to stirring the revolution among students, workers, and peasants.

After obtaining the support of Bishop Valencia Cano of Buenaventura, members of the Golconda group increased their radicalism against American imperialism and the native bourgeoisie. They asked for separation of Church and state, rejected all developmentalist attitudes (among which they included the efforts of the Christian Democrats), accused the Church of hypocrisy and phariseeism, demanded abolition of the national constitution, and asked for disbandment of the armed forces.

To reach the masses, still profoundly religious in Colombia, the Golconda activists have used liturgical and paraliturgical devotions. For example, in the Holy Week of 1969, they prepared special skits to give revolutionary meaning to the traditional exercise of the "Seven Words of Jesus Christ on the Cross": Jesus' exclamation "I thirst" became "I thirst for justice, for equality, for liberation from want, for education, etc." "Why hast Thou abandoned me?" was dramatized by a child crying "I'm hungry, I'm hungry."

Golconda priests do not hide their intention of turning religion upside down by transforming the classical categories of Christianity: *faith* is for them a factor of change directed toward a more just and humane society, not the assent to God's revelation; *hope* is the craving for liberation from socio-economic structures, not the expectation of another life or the trust in God's grace; *charity* is the solidarity of men and women struggling for a better future, not a love which can be more sentimental than beneficial; *incarnation* is the commitment of the oppressed to political action, not a mystery concerning Jesus alone; *revelation* is the awareness of man's needs in his present situation, not God's manifestation in history; *resurrection* is the birth of the

---

[5]"The Golconda Statement," trans. J. E. and M. Goff, Apartado 1024, Cuernavaca, Mor., México, November 10, 1969; Rick Edwards, "Religion in the Revolution? A Look at Golconda," *NACLA Newsletter* (North American Congress on Latin America), February 1970, reprinted in LADOC 1 (January 1971): 49b. Attached to Edwards's article is an excerpt from the write-up that resulted from an interview with Golconda strategist Germán Zabala by Héctor Borrat, published first as "Las rutas de Camilo" in *Marcha* (Montevideo), November 14, 1969, trans. NACLA staff under a new title, "How Golconda Organizes." See also, Joseph Novitski, "Radical Priests in Colombia, Heirs to Slain Guerrilla, Have Forged an Open Marxist-Catholic Alliance," *New York Times*, February 16, 1970. For a statement by one of the main spokesmen for the movement, see "Father René García Speaks to Colombian Students," a talk made at the National University in Bogotá, April 11, 1969, reprinted in *LADOC* 1 (November 1970): 39c.

new society, not an ancient miracle in Christ's life. They do not hesitate to sacrifice the Church itself for the sake of revolution. In the words of Father Noel Olaya, "In the last analysis we could say that the only way to save the Church is that it not be important to us."[6]

Golconda has obtained wide publicity by moving the people's feelings when the rebel priests have been tortured by the police or disciplined by their bishops. It is interesting to contrast the radical social ideas of the Golconda group with those of their hero Camilo Torres; the latter look moderate by comparison. Contrary to Golconda's anti-clericalism and demythologizing of Christian doctrine, Camilo was respectful of the hierarchy almost to the end of his life; and he remained loyal to the Catholic faith.

Liberation

In almost all the countries of Latin America, priests' groups have been organized to encourage involvement of the Church in the transformation of society. Included among these groups are "Priests of the Third World," originally from Argentina; the "Priestly Movement ONIS," of Peru; and "Priests for the People," of Mexico.[7] Generally, rather than engage directly in revolutionary activism, they prefer to lay the ideological foundation for the revolution or, in more moderate cases, for radical social action. One result is a theological battle that has occupied numerous Latin American theologians. *A Theology of Liberation*, by Peru's Gustavo Gutiérrez,[8] is an example of the literature of liberation thought.

According to Gutiérrez, traditional theology exalts the transcendent at the expense of the worldly and stresses the revelation contained in the Bible more than the permanent work of the Spirit in the Church, as expressed by the scientific, anthropological, and sociological knowledge of each generation. Therefore, he asks for a "theology of temporal realities," not of the kind that has been developed in the rich countires but one in consonance with the Latin American situation of dependence.

Gutiérrez prefers the word "liberation" to "development" or "revolution." To speak of a "theology of development," he insists, implies

---

[6] Quoted by Borrat, "Las rutas de Camilo."
[7] On these movements, see "Conclusiones del II Encuentro Nacional de ONIS," *Movimiento Sacerdotal ONIS, Declaraciones* (Lima: Centro de Estudios y Publicaciones, 1970); Fernando Boasso, "The Third World Movement: Recent Events and What to Do Now," excerpts from an article published in *Revista del CIAS* (Buenos Aires), (August-September, 1970), reprinted in *LADOC* 1 (December 1970): 42b; "Posición revolucionaria de Mons. Mendez Arceo y otros mexicanos," interview published by *Panorama* (Argentina) on the occasion of the First Latin American Encounter of Christians for Socialism, *NADOC* (Lima), June 21, 1972. In the same issue is the manifesto of the movement, "Priests for the People."
[8] Gustavo Gutiérrez, *A Theology of Liberation: History, Politics and Salvation*, trans. and ed. Sister Caridad Inda and John Eagleson (Maryknoll, N. Y.: Orbis Books, 1973).

that there is a possible remedy for the socioeconomic structures, which is not the case of Latin America.[9] On the other hand, his "theology of revolution" stresses use of violence, which might be a necessary means but is not the direct purpose of theology. Convinced that Marxism is the best scientific and dialectical approach to Latin American problems and their solution, Gutiérrez has attempted an interpretation of Christianity in the light of Marxism. He believes that he has as much right to do so as Saint Thomas had to use the pagan philosophy of Aristotle for his theological synthesis. Searching for Christian ideas that apply better to the circumstances in question, the Peruvian theologian reinterprets such concepts as creation, salvation, the covenant, the eschatological promises, the building of the kingdom, the liberating mission of Christ, and ideas such as hope, fraternal love, and poverty.

His solution to the apparent contradiction between the Christian precept of love for the enemy and the Marxist insistence on class-struggle can serve as a sample of Gutiérrez's reasoning. Class-struggle, he says, is a fact which has not been created by Marxism but by the ruling classes that discriminate against the poor. To be realistic, the Church cannot ignore the existence of this struggle; and, to be loyal to her mission, she must side with the oppressed against the oppressors. The Church exercises true Christian love only when she helps the poor ransom their freedom and opposes unjust domination by the rich (who, in the process, are also liberated from their sinful conduct). On the other hand, the Church does not display this love when she distributes the token contributions by which the oppressors placate their guilt-feelings and by which the human dignity of the recipients is destroyed and their awakening to the call of salvation is hampered. The symbiosis of Christianity and Marxism is especially difficult in the case of Gutiérrez, who does not demythologize the Christian dogmas. For him, God is a person; Christ is God made flesh; the resurrection of Christ is a historical fact; and the eternal life of the heavens is the last end of man.

Ideas and language of the theology of liberation were favorably received and used by the Second General Conference of Latin American

---

[9]For works on the theology of underdevelopment, see Jürgen Moltmann, *Theology of Hope*, trans. J. W. Leitch (New York: Harper and Row, 1967); Hugo Assmann, "Caraterização de uma Teologia de Revolução," *Ponte Homen*, September-October 1968; Richard A. McCormick, S. J., "The Theology of Revolution," *Theological Studies* 29 (December 1968): 685-97; Jürgen Moltmann, *Religion, Revolution and the Future*, trans. M. Douglas Meeks (New York: Charles Scribner's Sons, 1969); *In Search of a Theology of Development: A SODEPAX Report* (Lausanna: Consultation of Theology of Development, 1970); Gerhard Bauer, *Towards a Theology of Development: An Annotated Bibliography* (Geneva; Committee on Society, Development, and Peace, 1970); René Laurentin, *Liberation, Development and Salvation*, trans. Charles U. Quinn (Maryknoll, N. Y.: Orbis Books, 1972).

Bishops (CELAM), held in Medellín, Colombia, in August 1968.[10] Granted that the final text of the Medellín Declaration softens the Marxist tone and strengthens the Christian aspects of liberation doctrine, still the Bishops' expressions seem to legalize an existing tendency within the Church to polarize the classes and favor the revolutionary activism of some elements in behalf of the Latin American population. Rick Edwards believes that the Medellín documents were "prepared by theological and sociological experts rather than by the much more conservative bishops," and he is of the opinion that the Bishops approved them "seemingly unaware of their troublesome potential."[11] The author's personal conversations with some of the signatories indicate that this assumption, partially at least, corresponds to fact.

This review of the various revisionist positions within the Latin American Church concludes with a brief note concerning Dom Hélder Câmara.[12] Upon being made Archbishop of Recife, he was shocked by socioeconomic conditions in Brazil's Northeast, which inhabitants of the richer South try systematically to ignore.

Although many years have passed since Dom Hélder Câmara first called the attention of the world to the scandal of underdevelopment, his preaching has not changed much. It sounds moderate today because he opposes violence while supporting the liberating force of moral pressure, and he rejects both capitalist and communist systems of oppression. It is interesting to note that conclusions of the Department of Social Action of CELAM, announced at the Rio de Janeiro meeting in June 1972,[13] take a position which more closely resembles the moderate doctrine of Dom Hélder than that of the Medellín Conference.

In reply to the conclusions of the "First Encounter of Christians and Socialists," held in Santiago de Chile in April 1972, the CELAM Commission warned the faithful against the tendency of capitalist and socialist systems to use the Church for their own purposes: in the case

---

[10]The proceedings were published by the General Secretariat of CELAM (Bogotá, 1970). For other declarations of the Latin American Bishops, see *Between Honesty and Hope: Documents from and about the Church in Latin America,* issued by the Peruvian Bishops' Commission for Social Action, trans. John Drury (Maryknoll, N. Y.: Maryknoll Publications, 1970).

[11]Edwards, "Religion in the Revolution?" p. 1.

[12]Hélder Câmara, *Pronunciamientos de Dom Hélder,* Nordeste II, Secretariado Regional, CNBB, Recife, Brazil; idem, *Church and Colonialism: The Betrayal of the Third World,* trans. William McSweeney (Denville, N. J.: Dimension Books, 1969); idem, *Spirale de la violence* (Paris: Desclée, de Brouwer, 1970); idem, *Revolution Through Peace,* ed. Ruth N. Anshen, trans. Amparo McLean (New York: Harper and Row, 1971); "Bishop Calls for Action," *The Catholic Worker,* December, 1972, pp. 1, 3.

[13]"Instrumentalizición política de la Iglesia en América Latina," title under which the conclusions of the Rio de Janeiro meeting were published by *Catolicismo* (Bogotá), August 27, 1972, reprinted in *NADOC* (Lima), November 15, 1972.

of capitalism, to increase profits; under socialism, to concentrate political control. Both attitudes are detrimental to the Church, and both systems result in domination of the people. Catholics should be aware of these maneuvers, abstain from supporting them, and search in the depth of Christian doctrine for solutions that the Latin American nations so urgently need at the present.

Some social activists consider the new position of the Church as a betrayal of her commitment to the poor, which was made at Medellín. Conversely, for others, the new developments are a sign of maturity: The Church was shocked and paralyzed in her work when she discovered that many of her members were living in infrahuman conditions and that she had ignored the extent of this fact. Now, because the Church has accepted her responsibility for the massive injustice—and this happened at Medellín—she can and must renew her social action, in the new direction required by the circumstances.

Conclusions and Perspectives

Traditionally, Latin America's priests have not joined guerrillas or engaged in revolutionary activism; although during the Independence period, there were some who did follow these causes. In recent history, this kind of activity is a real innovation. But now as then, revolutionary priests constitute the exception rather than the rule.

Programs of social work are not news: They began in Latin America with the missionaries in colonial times. The only novelty is that, at present, they are turning from paternalistic assistance to cooperative programs.[14]

Other changes are rather symbolic: departure of nuncios and bishops from their palaces to live among the poor;[15] more emphasis on the social implications of the Gospel in preaching and catechetical instructions;[16] greater communication between priests and their superiors, and between priests and the laity.

What is entirely new is an acute awareness of the unjust structures of the society in which the Latin American Church exercises her ministry. Also new is the breach in the monolithic unity of the Catholic doctrine and its rigid discipline. This writer cannot foresee all the consequences of this sudden change, but there are two facts that appear to be most obvious: the Church's position as a rampart against socialism has been greatly weakened; and the number of nominal Catholics will drop, because not all can withstand the winds of change.

[14]Regional Latin American Justice and Peace Secretariats, "Cooperative Social Action Beyond Social Assistance," *Latin America Calls!*, October 1972, p. 4.

[15]"Vacant Palace," *Latin America Calls!*, August-September 1972, p. 7.

[16]Bernardino Pinera (Bishop of Temuco), "Chile Today and Catechesis," *World Parish*, February 1973.

Hopefully, the Christian community will gain in quality what it loses in quantity. Also, it is hoped that the influence of the Church—with its spiritual values that materialistic socialism cannot offer—will be an important factor in shaping the new society which is inevitably in the making.

3. Recent Themes in Catholic Social Thought in Latin America

WALTER B. REDMOND

Professor Redmond describes the course of Catholic social thought in Latin America since the middle of the twentieth century and summarizes the principal elements of liberation theology. Furthermore, he explains how this new school of theology has been used to support and give direction to political efforts, and even to military operations, designed to change or to overthrow those socioeconomic structures that are considered to be unjust.

In recent years, the social movement of the Catholic Church in Latin America has produced surprises.[1] Some priests, for example, tell us that the coming kingdom has more to do with this world than with worlds after and beyond, and they feel so strongly that they occasionally go off into the wilds as guerrilla fighters to help make it come sooner. These new attitudes are often referred to as a theology of liberation, and the object of this essay is to offer some observations on its history and content.

Liberation theology is in conflict with the older, "traditional" way of thinking and acting; indeed, division in the Church today is deeper and seemingly more irreconcilable than at any other time in the last 150 years. Differences between traditionalists and intellectuals of the liberation movement not only constitute distinct theologies but practically amount to separate views of reality. Conservatives usually hold for a scholastically inspired view of world, man, and Church. On the other hand, theologians of liberation approach a consensus[2] on re-

---

[1] Cf. Ivan Vallier, *Catholicism, Social Control, and Modernization in Latin America* (Englewood Cliffs, N.J.: Prentice-Hall, 1970), p. 3.

[2] This in fact creates a problem of documentation. In the first part of this study, the notes are usually not exhaustive. The following are bibliographies related to Latin American Catholic social thought: "Bibliografía de la teología de la liberación," *Boletín bibliográfico ibero americano* (Madrid: OCSHA, 1972); Jesús M. Díaz Baizán, Antonio Guillén Paredes, and Juan I. Gutiérrez Fuente, "Bibliografía," in *Fe cristiana y cambio social en América Latina: Encuentro de El Escorial, 1972* (Salamanca: Ediciones

vamping much of the old moral and dogmatic systems, although they work individually within philosophic frames that vary in content and sophistication. In general, their perspectives are not highly elaborated; and they admit this incompleteness, pleading more urgent concerns.[3]

In their criticism of the Church (and of Western culture, for that matter), liberation theologians often use an historical analysis of the theoretical support underlying attitudes and activities. Many reject Hellenic influence as "unrevealed" and even as untrue. This excision naturally leads them to search the Scriptures anew for fresh insight on which to base a theology committed to Latin American problems, but their reading of the Bible is hardly arbitrary. Without exception, they are respectful of biblical scholarship and, usually, are conversant with it; but they are also aware of Hellenistic influence on the Bible. Liberation theologians are familiar with North Atlantic theology and make free use of modern philosophy and social science. However, if generally not original, they are aware of the dangers of uncritically accepting and applying foreign ideas; thus, they have sharply attacked not only progressive theology and exegesis but also, at times, Western thinking in general. The historical sensitivity of liberation theology compels its thinkers to monitor the course of their movement and constantly to question the validity of its reflection and the effectiveness of its praxis. Indeed, this self-consciousness enters into the definition of theology itself, which is seen as critical reflection on the Church's activity.

Some might see this theologizing as a rationalization process whereby these Latin American theologians would be offering a complex justification for radical positions held mainly for other reasons (for example, because these positions are widespread in Latin American intellectual circles). But psychological considerations aside, these thinkers present their view of Christianity and their appraisal of the world political scene as probable and based on fact. They have been somewhat successful in persuading others with their view and have also aroused lively resistance.[4] Of course, they have no intention of "proving" socialism from the Bible or the history of Church thought, but they insist that socialism is compatible with Christian

Sígueme, 1973), pp. 391-414; Richardo Ortiz, "Fuentes bibliográficas para una teología de la secularización en América Latina," in *Fe y secularización en América Latina,* ed. Joseph Comblin et al., Colección IPLA, no. 12 (Bogotá: CELAM, 1972) pp. 69-79; R. Valenzuela M., "De la dependencia a la teología de la liberación: Notas bibliográficas," Doc. 1/1. CIDOC, pp. 73/386ff; F. P. Vanderhoff, *Bibliography: Latin American Theology of Liberation* (Ottawa, 1972) (mimeographed); Roger Vekemans, *Desarrollo y revelación, Iglesia y libertad,* bibliografía (Barcelona: Herder, 1972).
[3]Hugo Assman, "Evaluación crítica de la teología de la liberación," *Pasos,* May 28, 1973.
[4]Cf. Alexander Wilde, review of *The Church as a Political Factor in Latin America: With Particular Reference to Colombia and Chile,* by David E. Mutchler, in *Contemporary Sociology: A Journal of Reviews* 2 (August 1973): 543.

teaching. They wish to be able to use Marx in their analysis of society and to work toward socialist solutions—and to carry out this commitment within the Church as loyal Christians.

Rise of the Liberation Movement

In the middle of our century, the Latin American Church experienced changes, implications of which are now being strongly felt; and the outcome is still very much in doubt. These changes are naturally linked to the social, economic, political, and cultural transformation of the region.[5] The shift on the theoretical and ideological level has affected a relatively small but intellectually important group in the Latin American Church, and some observers have viewed it as the Latin American counterpart of a crucial turning point in the general history of Christianity. For example, Enrique Dussel believes the Catholic Church has entered upon the third stage of its history since the 1960s. He sees the Church seeking expression in all human culture, after previously being restricted to Jewish and later, under Christendom, to Hellenistic world views.[6]

We may trace the history of the Latin American Church through the following periods: encounter with America, Christendom, Neo-Christendom, and the present day. Segundo Galilea notices a theologically significant parallel between the first and last stages, a development which he explains in terms of tension. For the Church to be free to play its critical role, he says, it must be adapted to society but must stand off from society. Tension was high during the conquest when men like Bartolomé de Las Casas challenged crown policy; then it dropped during the Christendom period; but recently it has become strong again.[7] Dussel calls Las Casas a theologian of liberation and points to a similarity between Spain's quest for gold and foreign economic domination of Latin America today.[8]

Latin American Christendom began with consolidation of the Church in the colonial period and continued into the republican period, lasting until well into the 20th century; but a process of decline set in during the first half of the 19th century.[9] Under Spanish domination the church was given over to the exigencies of the royal

---

[5]Rubem Alves, "Religion, Oppression and Freedom" (New York, 1971), p. 10. (Mimeographed.)

[6]Enrique Dussel, *The History of the Church in Latin America—An Interpretation,* trans. Walter Redmond (San Antonio, Tex.: Mexican-American Cultural Center, 1974), p. 10.

[7]Segundo Galilea, "La teología de la liberación como crítica de la actividad de la Iglesia en América Latina," in *Fe y secularización,* pp. 53-55.

[8]Enrique Dussel, "Historia de la fe cristinana y cambio social en América Latina," in *Fe cristiana y cambio social,* p. 68 and note 39, p. 78.

[9]Dussel, *The History of the Church,* pp. 21-22 and 27-29; Galilea, "La teología de la liberación," p. 54.

patronage system; later, it became divided over the question of independence from Spain. During the 19th century and much of the 20th century, the Church tended to ally itself with conservative political parties in an effort to guard privileges against liberal and, more recently, Marxist opposition. In Europe, the First Vatican Council (1869-70) and the encyclicals of Pope Leo XIII[10] sought to insulate the Church from naturalism and liberalism by promoting Thomistic philosophy and putting forward a "social doctrine of the Church." Especially after the Latin American Plenary Council in Rome (1899), efforts to implement ultramontane objectives in Latin America were not notably successful. During the Christendom period, Christianity was presented as a mass religion. At best, salvation outside the Church was problematic. Ritual was stressed in the ministry, and the priests' function was seen as spiritual. The profane or "temporal" sphere was not considered as autonomous but as practically subject to the Church.[11]

Theologians of liberation who have written on the history of the Church tend to see an intermediate period that began around 1930 and extended to a great turning point in the 1960s. The thought dominating at least the first phase of this period was influenced by Jacques Maritain and is frequently referred to as New Christendom. Unlike the Old Christendom (which it did not displace), Neo-Christendom was not a social state of affairs but an ideal aiming at remaking secular society along lines favorable to properly Christian activity.[12] Catholic Action began to flourish in the 1930s, which was a time for the laity, for Catholic minorities.[13] It was also a time when social justice became an important concern for Catholics—after publication of a second social encyclical in 1931[14] and an increase in Marxist influence. A lull in the Church's direct political activity occurred when it diminished reliance on and support of the traditional conservative parties and began to concentrate on promoting social ethics.[15] There was also a theoretical reason for this lull. In reaction to the Christendom view of the temporal, and following a biblical distinction between creation and redemption and Maritain's interpreta-

---

[10] *Aeterni Patris*, 1879; *Rerum Novarum*, 1891.

[11] Gustavo Gutiérrez, *A Theology of Liberation: History, Politics, and Salvation*, trans. and ed. Sister Caridad Inda and John Eagleson (Maryknoll, N.Y.: Orbis Books, 1973), pp. 53-54; Segundo Galilea, "Politics and the Church," trans. Walter Redmond, pp. 2-5 (Manuscript); Joseph Comblin, "The Three Catholicisms of Latin America," trans. Walter Redmond, pp. 1-4 (Manuscript); Dussel, *The History of the Church in Latin America*, p. 30.

[12] Comblin, "The Three Catholicisms," pp. 4-5; Gutiérrez, *A Theology of Liberation*, p. 55 and note 8, p. 59. Jacques Maritain's *True Humanism* (New York: Charles Scribner's Sons, 1938) circulated in Spanish translation in the 1930s.

[13] Dussel, *The History of the Church in Latin America*, pp. 36-37.

[14] Pius XI, *Quadragesimo Anno*.

[15] Galilea, "Politics and the Church," p. 5.

tion of the Thomistic distinction of nature and grace, many Latin American churchmen accepted a theoretical and practical dualism of the profane and religious spheres, admitting the autonomy of the former. This dualism was applied to the individual Christian: he was considered to act precisely as a Christian when he went to Mass, for example; but when engaged in politics, he was merely acting according to Christian principles without compromising the official Church. A double role was often attributed to the Church: religious ("evangelization," aiming at salvation) and temporal ("humanization" or "pre-evangelization," aiming at social development).[16] The most visible feature of the New Christendom was the founding of institutions, only indirectly connected with the Church, through which Christians could carry out their social commitment. The Latin American Church sponsored cooperatives, labor unions, newspapers, and political parties, often with foreign financial backing. In the 1930s, Tristão de Athayde (Alceu Amoroso Lima) and Eduardo Frei were active in political organizations that later became Christian Democratic parties in Brazil and Chile. The ideology behind Christian Democracy was linked to the social doctrine of the Church, which was presented as a "third way" or middle course between capitalism and communism.

A newer apostolic approach soon became influential and marks a transition to the deeper changes of the 1960s.[17] Unlike Neo-Christendom, it saw Christianity in a pluralistic context, not necessarily as a majority religion, and criticized the institutional approach to the apostleship because it made the Church dependent on foreign sources for money to finance organizations and even for the personnel to run them. Advocates of this approach also objected to the top-heavy organization of Catholic Action and stressed the importance of grass-roots communities, which required little financing; this emphasis on small groups of lay people later became the main thrust of Christian social praxis in the base community. After the Second World War, Catholic Action became diversified. Organized according to the nature of the participating group (e.g., students, workers, businessmen), the new movement combined diversification with grass roots organization; and sometimes it employed the *révision de vie* of the European worker movement to structure the reflection and activity of Catholic Action units. At a meeting, cell members would analyze a "fact of life" or moral event witnessed by one of them and then would decide on relevant action. Many cells of the same movement could meet to discuss and act upon a structural problem

[16]Cf. Segundo Galilea, *Reflexiones sobre la evangelización*, Colleción IPLA, no. 10 (Quito: Don Bosco, 1970).

[17]Gutiérrez, *A Theology of Liberation*, pp. 56ff; Gustavo Gutiérrez, *Líneas pastorales de la Iglesia en América Latina: Análisis teológico* (Lima: CEP, 1970), pp. 27ff.

often noticed in the cell meetings, and even higher-level assemblies within one movement or of several movements were envisioned. Thus, in theory, a powerful, coordinated movement could be mounted to influence many sectors of society. Dualism was still strong however; parallel organizations were often set up to carry out the Church's direct and indirect missions. For example, there might be two organizations of university students: one for religious activity and another, perhaps a party or "front" within university politics, through which they could express social commitment. The mission of the priest in both the Neo-Christian and the *révision* approach was that of *asesor* (advisor, consultant).

The hour of truth came in the 1960s,[18] when the Second Vatican Council (1962-65) cast doubt on the very ultramontane aims of Vatican I. After opening the Church to "outside" thought, many deemed it pointless to go on defending the past or trying to restore a Christendom situation through a rigid scholasticism or a conservative social doctrine.[19] In Latin America, it came clear for many intellectuals that the "third way" of the social doctrine of the Church was but an updated version of the old first way and only looked different because it spoke an archaic language. Paradoxically, as Christian Democracy reached the height of its power in Chile, many churchmen looked upon its theoretical base as outdated.[20] The dualism of the intermediate period, which grounded basic notions of how the Church should operate in the world, was also shaken. For the newer generation, the temporal world is not "pro-fane" because before God nothing is "outside the temple." Creation and redemption coincide basically, because creation is God's first saving act and redemption means the creation of a new man.[21] Suppression of the distinction between matters profane and sacred has led the Church to rediscover history and relate itself in new ways to politics.[22]

Priests suddenly found themselves with a direct temporal mission, and they were not slow in becoming involved in politics. Camilo Torres, a Colombian priest who joined a guerrilla movement and was killed in a skirmish with government troops in 1966, has left a profound impression on the younger clergy. Priests in many countries formed themselves into groups to express their social commitment (e.g., Golconda in Colombia, Priests for the Third World in Argentina,

---

[18]Expression from Joseph Comblin, "Movimientos e ideologías en América Latina," in *Fe cristiana y cambio social*, p. 123.
[19]Comblin, "The Three Catholicisms," p. 6.
[20]Comblin, "Movimientos e ideologías," p. 123.
[21]Gutiérrez, *A Theology of Liberation*, pp. 66ff, 153ff, 190ff. Cf. José Porfirio Miranda, *Marx y la Biblia: Crítica a la filosofía de la opresión* (Salamanca: Ediciones Síguema, 1972), pp. 101-102; and idem, *El ser y el Mesías* (Salamanca: Ediciones Síguema, 1973), ch. 2.
[22]Dussel, *The History of the Church in Latin America*, pp. 38 and 40-41.

ONIS in Peru). In fact, leadership of the social movement within the Church has passed from the laity to the clergy.[23] Many priests no longer see the third way as viable. Their choice is between capitalism and socialism, and they have chosen the latter.

Earlier, the Church entered politics for its own ends and shared responsibility for injustice in society.[24] Today, many clergy and laity feel their participation in politics is different; they belong to the left, and their aim is not to guard the institutional Church but to serve the oppressed.[25] Catholic allegiance to the right wing remains strong, however. Most bishops are conservative and either support the political right or claim neutrality, supposing the Church to be above politics. Leftist Christians are quick to point out that behind this stated neutrality lurks a conservative ideology that supports the status quo.[26] Thus there is deep polarization in the Church which has become more acute in the last few years.

Politics has become a part of the pastoral mission that emphasizes the need for Christians to be committed to changing society.[27] Sometimes called prophetic because of its stress on involvement in history,[28] without necessarily politicizing Christian doctrine or practice, the new pastoral program downplays individualistic, alienating elements and aims at "conscienticizing" the people, helping them to think more realistically about the forces shaping their lives and giving them hope to assume a more active role in society.[29] The liturgy could be altered, some suggest, to gain a more historical bearing. Instead of omitting exorcisms from the christening service, as priests commonly do, says Segundo, we could name the devil who is being expelled: "Go out of this child, thou unclean spirit of capitalism, so that he may enter society as a living hope and not as another burden."[30] In present-day pastoral approaches, the base community is still fundamental, but dualistic lay apostolic movements have waned.[31]

[23]Comblin, "Movimientos e ideologías," p. 124.
[24]Galilea, "Politics and the Church," pp. 4-5.
[25]Ibid., pp. 6-7.
[26]See, for example, ibid., p. 10.
[27]Ibid., pp. 10-12.
[28]Gutiérrez, Líneas pastorales, pp. 29-31; Gustavo Gutiérrez, "Problemas teológicos latinoamericanos" (Mimeographed); Segundo Galilea, "Profetas en la pastoral" (September 1970), pp. 7-14; Segundo Galilea, Hacia una pastoral vernácula: (Artículos de pastoral latinoamericana) (Santiago de Chile: Dilapsa, 1966; Barcelona: Nova Terra, 1966); Dussel, The History of the Church in Latin America, pp. 48-50; cf. Comblin, "The Three Catholicisms," pp. 14-20.
[29]Segundo Galilea, "La fe como principio crítico de promoción de la religiosidad popular," in Fe cristiana y cambio social, p. 157. Paulo Freire has developed the concept of conscientização in his Pedagogy of the Oppressed, trans. Myra Bergman Ramos (New York: Seabury, 1971).
[30]Juan Luis Segundo, "Theology and Ideology," trans. Walter Redmond, p. 8. (Manuscript.)
[31]Gutiérrez, A Theology of Liberation, p. 64.

Theologians of liberation approach the Church's mission from new views of salvation. In the Old and New Christendoms, the Church's mission was thought to be the salvation of souls. Today, many Catholic theologians reject the idea that the Church is the exclusive vehicle of salvation. Furthermore, they do not understand salvation in a dualistic context of saving the spiritual part of man and relegating to some nonreligious category like humanization the task of assisting historical man. For them, salvation is continuous with creation and bears upon profane evils like poverty and ignorance that keep man from being more fully man. The Church's mission of salvation, according to this view, involves freeing man from what holds him back from self-realization; it is liberation in a wide sense.[32]

But the Church's liberating mission is not abstract; it must be embodied, "incarnate" in a particular historical situation through praxis. An important aspect of this Christian praxis is political action, especially in Latin America. Involvement in leftist politics is often linked to the Gospel through the following reasoning process. Effective obedience to Jesus' command of loving our neighbor demands intelligent analysis of the causes of his suffering. If we find that a significant number of these causes are inherent in the social and economic structures of society, clearly we must endeavor to replace such structures with ones promising more justice. This replacement, according to a usage common in Latin America, is called revolution, a word not necessarily implying violence. Left-wing Christians share a conviction that is widespread in Latin America today: that injustice in the capitalistic system is indeed the greatest obstacle to liberation of the poor. Since effort to change socio-economic structures is political action, Christians who accept this appraisal of structural injustice feel they must become politically active in order to carry out the Christian imperative. They also share a common belief that the most promising replacement of the old structures is a form of socialism.[33]

But how should the Christian become politically active? Exactly how does the Church become incarnate in history? There are two aspects to this practical question (evidence of a lingering dualism): we can ask what the official Church should do and what Christians should do. With regard to the second question, theologians of liberation do not advocate the formation of Christian parties but speak rather of changing the social structure in a meaningful and effective way and of associating with all men in this endeavor. Christian militants not only are willing to work with Marxists but also to make use of Marxist thought in analyzing political conditions and guiding their

[32]Ibid., ch. 9.
[33]Segundo, "Theology and Ideology," pp. 1-2; Galilea, "Politics and the Church," pp. 10-11; Jordan Bishop, "Marxism and Theology in Latin America," pp. 12-13 (Manuscript); Gutiérrez, *A Theology of Liberation*, p. 48.

praxis. Many Catholics and Protestants have been pleasantly surprised to find themselves together in their social concern; in this practical ecumenism, they show little interest in the classical debates that would force them apart. The scandal for many leftist Christians is not collaboration with Marxists but the fact that those calling themselves Christians, even bishops, contribute to the oppression of the poor.[34] The base comunity has become the main vehicle of the Christian social apostleship. Small cells of poor people with elected leaders meet to discuss and remedy their problems, sometimes maintaining only minimal contact with the institutional church. In face of the lack of vocations to the priesthood, networks of these groups provide an effective outreach which, under repressive regimes, are the only critical organization possible.

For militants, violence is a most difficult practical problem that is still an open question and is very much discussed in the liberation literature. It can be stated in the following terms (and the mere statement suffices to challenge simplistic "nonviolent" positions of both conservatives and liberals): Revolution is sometimes seen as a series of violent acts breaking the peace of a previous state of nonviolence. However, say revolutionary Christians, reality is more complex and demands a more careful analysis. The fundamental datum, the state ot affairs we start with, is a condition of constant violence against the poor caused largely by unjust social structures. The rich overlook this violence to the poor and see instead a situation of law and order. The point is to change unjust structures that cause violence against the poor. Ideally, this change should come in a lawful, peaceful way; but powerful, wealthy minorities block needed social change in order to guard their privileged position in society, thus forcing those who are concerned to take counterviolent measures. Hence, the question is whether the Christian can or should use counterviolence against those who (perhaps unwittingly) condone violence against the poor, if there is no other way to bring about social change.[35] The question is further complicated by the fact that wealthy minorities have at their disposal stupendous armed power, which they do not hesitate to use (even in the name of Christ) when their privilege is threatened. Hélder Câmara, a Brazilian bishop, disavows counterviolence partially on the grounds that it will be met by the repressive violence of the powerful.[36] Some

[34]Segundo, "Theology and Ideology," p. 6.
[35]See, for example, Gonzalo Castillo-Cárdenas, "Christians and the Struggle for a New Social Order in Latin America" (Paper presented at the World Conference on Church and Society, Geneva, July 12-26, 1966), p. 5. (Mimeographed.)
[36]Dom Hélder Câmara, "Violence in the Modern World," in *Between Honesty and Hope: Documents from and about the Church in Latin America*, trans. John Drury, Maryknoll Documentation Series (Maryknoll, N.Y.: Maryknoll Publications, 1970), p. 53; J. J. Rossi, *Iglesia y desarrollo*, 2d ed. (Buenos Aires: Ediciones Búsqueda, 1968), p. 33; Dussel, *The History of the Church in Latin America*, pp. 201-202; Segunda Conferencia General del Episcopado Latinoamericano, *La Iglesia en la actual transforma-*

Christian revolutionaries reluctantly conclude that counterviolence is unavoidable; and a few, like Camilo Torres, actually make use of it. Most, however, remain profoundly distrustful of all violence. They leave the theoretical question open and, in practice, opt for nonviolent but urgently necessary tasks leading to social transformation (for example, conscienticizing the people and promoting base communities). The fact that violence is already a reality, according to leftist Christians, is one reason neutrality is impossible; inaction when action is called for, even if considered nonideological or apolitical, condones existing violence against the poor.

The other question concerning what the official Church should do is equally delicate. The liberation movement was given a charter, on principle at least, in the Second General Bishops Conference held in Medellín (1968). There the bishops issued statements endorsing many of the above-mentioned ideas: seeing society, for example, not as law and order but as the established disorder of "institutionalized violence"; leaving the question of counterviolence open; and stressing the duty of the Christian to take part in social change.[37] Latin American theologians believed that the discussion in the Vatican Council had little to do with problems on their continent and saw the Medellín meeting as the Vatican II of Latin America. The Council and the Bishops Conference together constitute an official counterpart of the transformation of the Latin America Church.

The liberation movement was jubilant over the official support of Medellín, but the euphoria soon vanished.[38] Most bishops never seemed really comfortable with the new social thought; and, despite the Medellín documents, they often showed their mistrust in practice by failing to back or even by opposing liberation initiatives.[39] "To put it bluntly," writes Galilea, "many Latin American bishops have not yet committed themselves to history."[40] There is evidence to indicate Vatican involvement with an organized resistance to the liberation movement. Certain consultants were not permitted to address the Medellín conference, allegedly on orders from Rome.[41] By August

ción de América Latina a la luz del Concilio, vol. 2: Conclusiones (México, D.F.: 1970), p. 74.

[37]Segunda Conferencia General del Episcopado Latinoamericano, La Iglesia en la actual transformación, 2:72-74.

[38]Hugo Assmann, Teología desde la praxis de la liberación: Ensayo teológico desde la América dependiente, Agora (Salamanca: Ediciones Sígueme, 1973), p. 95.

[39]Segundo, "Theology and Ideology," p. 1; cf. "Sacerdocio y política (I)," and "Sacerdocio y política (II)," in Iglesia latinoamericana: Protesta o profecía? ed. Juan José Rossi (Avellaneda, Argentina: Ediciones Búsqueda, 1969), pp. 129-44.

[40]Galilea, "Politics and the Church," p. 9.

[41]François Houtart and André Rousseau, The Church and Revolution: From the French Revolution of 1789 to the Paris Riots of 1968; from Cuba to Southern Africa; from Vietnam to Latin America, trans. Violet Nevile (Maryknoll, N.Y.: Orbis Books, 1971), p. 223.

1972, "programming" was suspected behind attacks on the liberation movement by Pope Paul, Latin American bishops, and even the Chilean Christian Democratic Party.[42] Belgian Jesuit Roger Vekemans, advisor of Frei during his presidency and an enemy of liberation theology, is said to figure prominently in a campaign directed against this new political orientation in the Church.[43] It has been suggested (and denied) that the Vatican sponsored the two candidates elected in November 1973 to key offices in the Latin American Bishops Council (CELAM, founded in 1955), which formerly sheltered the growth of liberation ideas.[44] At any event, Bishop Alfonso López Trujillo, the new secretary general, who is claimed to have proposed holding another general conference to nullify Medellín positions, has already begun to revamp CELAM training programs in the name of evangelization.[45] Liberation criticism of the older theology on the relation of Church and state has not convinced most bishops. Many claim political neutrality but warn against Marxist ideology (even advising against voting for Marxist candidates), and official statements from the CELAM conference held in Lima (March 1974) are reminiscent of the third way.[46] However, a small but articulate minority in the hierarchy still supports liberation theology. In fact, the bishops are as polarized as their priests and laymen and the people of Latin America in general.

Liberation theologians, who consider themselves faithful sons of the Church, are naturally dismayed at this opposition and the distortion of their own views that it so often embodies. We can realize better their frustration when we recall that they are subject to persecution by right-wing governments all over Latin America. Members of the liberation movement have been exiled, tortured, and even killed. They do not often counterattack the hierarchy directly; to do so, some theologians claim, diverts attention from the real enemy, the oppressors of the poor, and saps energy in ecclesiastical infighting.[47] Others say that criticism of institutionalized religion and its politics is useless because this represents the "most superficial" aspect of Chris-

---

[42]Assmann, *Teología desde la praxis de la liberación*, pp. 234-35.

[43]Agostino Bono, "Five Years after Medellín: Social Action Fades in Latin America," *National Catholic Reporter*, November 9, 1973, p. 6; Genaro Alarcón, "Revelaciones sobre la campaña organizada contra la teología de la liberación," *Noticias Aliadas*, February 2, 1973, reprinted in *Teología desde la praxis de la liberación*, pp. 238-39.

[44]Bono, "Five Years after Medellín," pp. 6-7.

[45]Ibid.

[46]Cf., for example, " 'Necesito apoyo decidido de la Iglesia católica,' declaró Odúber," *Excelsior*, February 10, 1974, p. A16; "Capitalismo y comunismo, incompatibles con el cristianismo, afirma el CELAM," *Excelsior*, March 9, 1974, p. A1.

[47]Assmann, "Evaluación crítica"; Assmann, *Teología desde la praxis de la liberación*, p. 37; Gutiérrez, *A Theology of Liberation*, pp. 262 and 268. Harvey Cox has commented on this intramural preoccupation of Catholic theologians in "Harvey Cox, Trend-maker," *National Catholic Reporter*, November 16, 1973, p. 5.

tianity. They emphasize the need to evaluate the religion of the people, the true agent, of liberation.[48] Ironically, liberation theology criticizes Christians for not getting involved in politics in favor of the masses, while the conservative element, by act or supposed neutrality, has been and remains involved, but on the right. There is no consensus among liberation theologians themselves on whether the Church should officially support socialism, but the question is being asked.[50] Many are reluctant to relate any political system to the Gospel; but some suggest that the Church may have the "obligation to publicly rectify, with specific options of another character," its past justification of dominating power.[51]

Liberation Theology

Dussel sees three phases in recent theological activity in Latin America.[52] In the Neo-Christendom period, foreign theology was often imported from Europe and adapted or applied uncritically to Latin American situations.[53] Theologians were often out of contact with their own national intellectual life, felt unsure of their role in the Church, and had to subordinate their studies to the active ministry. During the second phase, many churchmen (especially in connection with the pastoral, catechetical, and liturgical programs set up under CELAM in the 1960s) began a more careful reflection on social problems proper to the region. The third period, beginning with the discovery that prophetism exists on the continent, has produced truly Latin American theology that is practically identified with the liberation movement.[54]

Liberation theologians themselves see many factors contributing

---

[48]Comblin et al., "Interpretación no religiosa del Nuevo Testamento y teología de la liberación," in Fe y secularización, p. 23.
[49]Hugo Assmann, "Presentación," and "¿Reflexión teológica a nivel estratégico-táctico?" in Pueblo oprimido: Señor de la historia, Biblioteca Iglesia y sociedad (Montevideo: Tierra Nueva, n.d.).
[50]Cf. Martín de la Rosa, "Revolutionary Christianity in Latin America," trans. Walter Redmond, p. 5 (Manuscript); Dussel, The History of the Church in Latin America, pp. 37-38; Assmann, "Evaluación crítica"; Gutiérrez, A Theology of Liberation, p. 138.
[51]Hugo Assmann, Seminar on "Conciencia cristiana y situaciones extremas en el cambio social," in Fe cristiana y cambio social, p. 343.
[52]Dussel, The History of the Church in Latin America, pp. 50-52.
[53]Joseph Comblin, "El porvenir de los estudios teológicos en Latinoamerica" (Typewritten); Enrique Dussel, Hipótesis para una historia de la Iglesia en América latina (Barcelona: Estela, 1967); Galilea, Hacia una pastoral vernácula; Lucio Gera, "En asemblea permanente con monseñor Parteli y Lucio Gera," Víspera, November-December 1969, pp. 3-12; Lucio Gera, "Iglesia y mundo," La Iglesia y el país (Buenos Aires: Ediciones Búsqueda, 1967), pp. 7-19; Lucio Gera, "Problemas teológicos latinoamericanos" (Mimeographed); Gutiérrez, Líneas pastorales; Gutiérrez, "Problemas teológicos"; Sergio Méndez Arceo, "Desacralización para el desarrollo," La Iglesia, el subdesarrollo y la revolución (México, D.F.: Nuestro Tiempo, 1968), pp. 239-47.
[54]Dussel, The History of the Church in Latin America, pp. 51-52.

to the rise of the movement. They point to intellectual influences, like the theologies of secularization (Bonhoeffer), hope (Moltmann), and politics (Metz), as well as to Marx, Marcuse, Levinas, and others.[55] Liberation theologians stress as particularly important a critical process within the Church that is related to the recent historical experience of Latin America.[56] This experience includes the increased misery and hopelessness of the poor, the failure of the "decade of development" to bring about improvement in social conditions, and an escalated repression against people working toward a socialist transformation of society.

Within this context, a turnabout in attitudes toward development has been of great significance for the rise of liberation theology.[57] Underdevelopment, development, and progress had been seen in terms of the capitalist consumer model. United States aid programs have been conceived from this perspective. In the 1960s, however, many Latin American thinkers began to see underdevelopment as resulting partially from capitalistic development, and they often refer pejoratively to any theoretical or practical use of the capitalistic model as "developmentalism" (*desarrollismo*).[58] They prefer to work with the concept of dependency, judging the main problem to be the dependence of developing nations upon international centers of wealth and power, and upon the national minorities representing them. Many Christians also reject developmentalism and speak instead of liberation, especially after the Medellín conference,[59] not only to allude to the need to free Latin America from unjust social structure but also to place this process in a wider humanistic and biblical context.

The liberation movement defines theology in terms of this historical experience and the Church's reaction to it. Theology was earlier defined under Hellenic influences as wisdom (in the Patristic period) and science (in the Middle Ages); however, in Latin America at the present moment, it is commonly seen as critical reflection on praxis.[60] Theology has two inputs: faith (from Scripture) with its historical mediations ("tradition") and the present reality (analyzed with the help of the sciences), plus Christian praxis operating on this reality.[61] In Latin America, not only the historical fact of suffering and in-

[55]Comblin, "Crítica de la teología de la secularización," in *Fe y secularización*, pp. 35-37; Gutiérrez, *A Theology of Liberation*, ch. 11.

[56]Assmann, *Teología desde la praxis de la liberación*, p. 33.

[57]Gutiérrez, *A Theology of Liberation*, chs. 2, 6; Walter Redmond, "Christian Thought in Latin America Today" (Master's thesis, Aquinas Institute of Theology, 1972), pp. 9-10.

[58]Christian Lalive d'Epinay, "Culture et dépendance en Amérique latine: Note sur la place et le programme d'une sociologie de la culture intégrée à une sociologie de la dépendance" (Geneva, 1970), pp. 1-2. (Mimeographed)

[59]Assmann, *Teología desde la praxis de la liberación*, pp. 29-30.

[60]Gutiérrez, *A Theology of Liberation*, ch. 1.

[61]Assmann, *Teología desde la praxis de la liberación*, p. 46.

justice, but also Christian attempts (through political and other means) to eliminate suffering and injustice are part of the spiritual experience which is a source of theology.[62] This concept of theology obviously esteems the efficiency of liberating action and rejects views of religion as mere orthodoxy, much as Marx criticized mere cognitive philosophy. Liberation theologians also criticize the classical distinction between dogma and moral, orthodoxy and orthopraxis, because of the close association between belief and behavior found in the Bible.[63]

Such a definition of theology not only localizes or differentiates theologizing according to situation and unites it when the situation is broad, but it also furnishes a basis for judging the relevancy of theology. Efficacy becomes a necessary (if not sufficient) criterion for evaluating ecclesial activity. Liberation theologians find their own thought as well as North Atlantic thought lacking when they apply the criterion. Their basic criticism of foreign theology is that it is historically unrealistic. It does not take sufficient account of the implication of the developed countries in the oppression of the Third World, is naive about the supposed neutrality of theological activity itself, and is accommodating toward bourgeois consumer capitalism. Even political theology is too abstract to touch the actual political world. It underrates the role of international politics in underdevelopment and does not question sufficiently the Church's social thought. Much North Atlantic theology, say liberation theologians, is still highly individualistic and even apologetic; and by paying more attention to living religiously with reality than to changing reality, it is fideistic.[64] They chide biblical scholars for not venturing out into contemporary history.[65] Even the "Dutch heresies" are irrelevant, because much more is at stake than intraecclestical reform.[66] Thus, Dussel asks: "Are European and North American Christians aware that their fellow Christians in the Third World are being persecuted as subversives for opposing a system of international oppression from which these same European and North American Christians, yes, even their progressive dogmatic and pastoral theologians, calmly benefit?"[67]

---

[62]Juan Carlos Scannone and Fernando Urbina, "Necesidad y posibilidades de una teología socio-culturalmente latinoamericana," in *Fe cristiana y cambio social*, p. 370.
[63]Miranda, *El ser y el Mesías*, pp. 78-80.
[64]These criticisms are taken from Assmann, "Conciencia cristiana," pp. 335ff; Assmann, "¿Reflexión teológica a nivel estragético-táctico?"; Assmann, *Teología desde la praxis*, pp. 42-46; Comblin, "Crítica de la teología," pp. 35-51; Comblin et al., "Interpretación no religiosa del Nuevo Testamento," pp. 20-21; Dussel, *The History of the Church in Latin America*, pp. 48-49.
[65]Hugo Assmann, "Nota previa: La dinámica de un encuentro de teología," in *Pueblo oprimido*, pt. 2.
[66]Assmann, "Evaluación crítica."
[67]Dussel, *The History of the Church in Latin America*, p. 44.

When Paul of Tarsus, in one of the memorable unsuccessful speeches in history, mentioned the resurrection of the dead, his Athenian audience scoffed or promised to come back later; afterwards, in his letters, he was hardly complementary of Greek wisdom. Christians today feel uncomfortable with the idea of resurrection, because our usual category of survival after death, like that of Paul's hearers, is the immortality of the soul, the spiritual component of man distinguished from his material body.[68] Latin American theologians often analyze critically the intellectual framework within which past theology (and philosophy and science) has moved.[69] They object basically to implications of an ontological and anthropological dualism. Reality for the Greeks falls into two realms: truth, the eternal, necessary world of essence; and our contingent world of matter changing in time, which participates in the stability of the world of truth. Man consists of a soul, through which he attains the truth of essence, and a material body. The Greeks sometimes took the soul's ascent to the world of truth as an ethical goal, because essence and the soul that knows essence are good, and because matter and the body that holds soul captive are bad. Now, if the contingent world shares in the same essences, nothing radically new happens; history becomes repeated sameness. For the Greeks, the world of essence is the highest being and is the object of our noblest mental powers; the world of matter in itself, considered without participation in essence, is meaningless, unknowable. Even in Thomas Aquinas, an Aristotelian, man's understanding of the contingent material thing is indirect, and the very basis of material individuality is difficult to explain. Although the Greeks did not ignore man's duty to the state, many thought it to be more important for man to contemplate truth than to be overly worried about the world of changing matter. In the Bible, the value of abstract knowledge is not stressed and man's contingent history is of decisive importance. Moreover, Greek dualism provides man with a heaven into which he can flee (or better, should flee) contingent instability, both now (psychically) and after death (physically). When biblical salvation enters this Greek world, what is saved is primarily the soul; and, especially in a Catholic version, it is saved from history. The content of salvation is contemplative: man can and should contemplate God in this life, and he is called to the beatific vision in the next. Hence, the Church has conceived its saving mission to be supernatural, spiritual, and religious—and as touching upon contingent, temporal history only in a secondary sense. Hence also the

[68]Miranda, *Marx y la Biblia*, pp. 322-23; cf. Acts 17:31-32; 1 Cor. 1:22 and 2:1-5; Col. 2:8.
[69]Dussel, *The History of the Church in Latin America*, pp. 13-15, 17-19; Miranda, *Marx y la Biblia*, pp. 15-20; Assman, *Teología desde la praxis de la liberación*, pp. 42-44.

dualisms which have influenced the Church's behavior in the world: the religious and temporal spheres, the direct and indirect missions, evangelization and humanization.[70]

For Christians, God causes and transcends the world, and it is important for them to know this fact. The ancient Hebrews also believed that the world originates in God, and other peoples in the ancient Near East shared this belief.[71] But God appears in the Bible more as savior than creator: he is conceived as immanent, dynamic, breaking into history to free oppressed Jews.[72] Exodus is a paradigmatic theme in the Bible. A key passage in the Yahwistic tradition manifests its basic meaning; God speaks to Moses in the burning bush:

> I have seen the affliction of my people in Egypt and have heard their cry ... and have known their suffering. And I have come down to free them from the hand of the Egyptians and lead them out of that land into a good and spacious land, a land flowing with milk and honey.... (Exod. 3:7-14)

Expressions like "I am Yahweh, your God who brought you out of Egypt" precede the decalogue (Exod. 20 and Deut. 5) and appear frequently in the later law.[73] The law aimed at safeguarding human rights and keeping out of Israel the evils suffered by the Hebrews in Egypt.[74] Theologians of liberation see the exodus as a "political action" indicating how God acts and is, as well as indicating how his people should act and be.[75]

The name of God given in Exod. 3:14, *ehyeh ašer ehyeh* or simply

---

[70]Cf. Miranda, *Marx y la Biblia*, pp. 15-20, 64-66, 85-86, 91-93, 163, 273-82, 295ff.; Miranda, *El ser y el Mesías*, chs. 1-2, 4, 9; Assmann, *Teología desde la praxis de la liberación*, pp. 62ff.; Assmann, *¿Reflexión crítica?*; Dussel, *The History of the Church in Latin America*, pp. 4-5, 7-8, 11-15, 17-19; Segundo Galilea, *Contemplación y apostolado*, Colección IPLA, no. 17 (Bogotá: CELAM, 1972), p. 40; Galilea, "Politics and the Church," pp. 5, 9; Comblin et al., "Interpretación no religiosa del Nuevo Testamento," pp. 11-12, 16-17; Comblin, "Crítica de la teología," pp. 46-47; Gutiérrez, *A Theology of Liberation*, pp. 165-67, 193-94, 10ff., 66-72, 151ff., 169ff.; Lucio Gera, "Reflexión teológica," in *Sacerdotes para el tercer mundo: Crónica-documentos-reflexión* (Buenos Aires: Movimiento de Sacerdotes para el Tercer Mundo, 1970), pp. 123-58; Rubem Alves, report on a speech given in CICOP, *The Tablet*, February 8, 1968; Joseph Comblin, "Cristo en la Iglesia de hoy y de mañana," in *Cristología y pastoral en América Latina*, pp. 11-48; Enrique Dussel, *Cultura latinoamericana e historia de la Iglesia* (Mendoza, 1968), chs. 2-3; Noel Olaya, "Anteproyecto del plan pastoral" (Bogotá, 1966) (Mimeographed); Juan Luis Segundo, transcription of talks given in 1964 to foreign missionaries to Latin America, 5th lecture (Typewritten).

[71]Miranda, *El ser y el mesías*, ch. 2.

[72]Gutiérrez, *A Theology of Liberation*, p. 165; Miranda, *Marx y la Biblia*, pp. 101-102; Miranda, *El ser y el Mesías*, ch. 2. However, difficulties like the *herem* in the invasion of Canaan are not reconciled.

[73]Miranda, *Marx y la Biblia*, pp. 103ff.

[74]Ibid., p. 166; Miranda, *El ser y el Mesías*, ch. 2.

[75]Gutiérrez, *A Theology of Liberation*, p. 155; Dussel, *The History of the Church in Latin America*, p. 60; cf. Assmann, *Teología desde la praxis de la liberación*, p. 38.

ehyeh (*yhwh* in a third person form), has received in the past many translations, usually stating something about God's being: absolute ("I am who am"), transcendent ("I shall not reveal my name"), creative ("I am he who causes what is"). Some Latin American theologians prefer interpretations indicating God's intervention in human history, not his being "in himself." Gutiérrez gives this paraphrase: "I shall be ready to act, to rescue you, lead you to the land, . . ."[76] For Miranda, justifying his use of the future tense on linguistic grounds, God is "he who shall be," he who intervenes in history "to form a mankind in whom he can be at last."[77] With due respect to our ontological categories, says Miranda, Yahweh is not but shall be.[78]

God is future in the sense that he will "be" when man recognizes his moral imperative: "Then I shall be their God and they will be my people" (Jer. 31:33).[79] Yahweh is experienced as imperative, commanding, and as interpellation, calling to account; and the object of the imperative and interpellation is human justice.[80] This ethical characterization sets the biblical God apart from idols and, according to Miranda, constitutes the main revelation of the Scriptures.[81] The first two commandments of the decalogue show how Yahweh is to be held unique; there will be no strange gods and no images. Images of God are forbidden, not for fear of anthropomorphic theologizing but to emphasize that God is not to be seen but heard in his imperative.[82] The last eight commandments spell out the imperative in terms of human justice.

The experience of God as imperative accounts for the close relationship between knowing God and doing justice in the Bible. Yahweh is found not in mystical experience but in the "radicalism of a life of service."[83] God is not made an object of our knowledge; he remains "transcendent," other, in the cry of the poor.[84] When a man forgets justice, he worships an idol; God wants justice before liturgical reform: "You disregard God's commandments and cling to human

---

[76]Gutiérrez, *A Theology of Liberation*, p. 165.

[77]The LXX usually translates *ehyeh* as *esomai*; in *Grammaire de l'hébreu biblique* (Rome, 1947), Joüon says in note 113a that in stative verbs the imperfect has a future sense. Miranda, *Marx y la Biblia*, pp. 327-28; idem, *El ser y el Mesías*, p. 46.

[78]Miranda, *Marx y la Biblia*, p. 328.

[79]Miranda, *El ser y el Mesías*, pp. 34, 48.

[80]Miranda, *Marx y la Biblia*, p. 68; cf. p. 66 citing Rudolf Bultmann, *Glauben und Verstehen*, 4 vols. (Tubingen: Mohr, 1925), 1:26-37.

[81]Miranda, *Marx y la Biblia*, p. 78.

[82]Ibid., pp. 59ff, 97. Note that the second commandment is often excluded from later lists and the commandment against coveting (originally one commandment) is split to give ten.

[83]Comblin et al., "Interpretación no religiosa del Nuevo Testamento," p. 16; cf. Gutiérrez, *A Theology of Liberation*, p. 205.

[84]Miranda, *Marx y la Biblia*, pp. 91-93, quoting Emmanuel Levinas, *Totalité et infini*, 2d ed. (The Hague: Nijhoff, 1965), pp. 196, 46, 48, 61ff, 156.

tradition [ritual of washing hands]" (Mark 7:8).[85] Likewise, in the words of an Old Testament prophet, "it is mercy I desire, not sacrifice; knowledge of God rather than holocausts." (Hos. 6:6) The relation between knowing God and doing justice is not merely one of likeness or causation but "synonymy," "identity."[86] In Jeremiah (22:12), dispensing justice to the weak and poor is equated with true knowledge of God. In the famous Immanuel passage of Isaiah (11:1-9), the spirit of the knowledge of God which shall rest on the son of Jesse is related to justice for "he shall judge the poor with justice" (vv. 4-5), and knowledge reappears in the second part of the inclusion structure (v. 9). The theme is also found in the New Testament:

> Let us love one another
>   because love is of God;
> Everyone who loves is born of God
>   and has knowledge of God. (John 4:7)[87]

God can be loved only indirectly, through justice to neighbor, says Miranda; any attempt to contact him directly will fail.[88] God "is" (as far as man is concerned) inasmuch as he is "known" (in the sense of doing justice). The identity of love of God and neighbor is taken as a specifically biblical doctrine and is considered an important Christian contribution to the revolutionary movement in Latin America.[89]

The first picture of concrete man given in the Bible occurs in the account of Cain: fratricide; and the point is that evil depends upon human autonomy and that we are indeed our brother's keeper.[90] St. Paul sees mankind in the grip of *hamartia*: evil, injustice, a supraindividual, almost mythical entity concretely penetrating worldly wisdom, civilization and its law, social structures. *Hamartia* is a constant in man, but it is not part of human nature, and it is suppressible.[91] Justice in the Bible, on the other hand, in spite of frequent translations of ṣedaqah as "almsgiving" and the like, is commanded by law and is not a work of supererogation. The world is still divided between Cains and Abels, and the biblical God continues to take sides; God is a "moral dualist."[92] He opposes the "unjust" (reša 'im,

---

[85] Miranda, *Marx y la Biblia*, p. 82.
[86] Ibid., pp. 68-69.
[87] Ibid., pp. 67-77. Here Miranda discusses technically these and other texts.
[88] Miranda, *El ser y el Mesías*, pp. 48, 132; idem, *Marx y la Biblia*, p. 91.
[89] Comblin et al., "Interpretación no religiosa del Nuevo Testamento," p. 16; Assmann, *Teología desde la praxis de la liberación*, p. 137.
[90] "Adam" (not "haadam," "man") appears first in Gen. 4:25. Man is like God in the Yahwistic tradition for knowing good and evil and in the priestly code for having freedom of action (Gen. 1:26-4:16); Miranda, *Marx y la Biblia*, p. 118; idem, *El ser y el Mesías*, ch.. 2.
[91] Miranda, *Marx y la Biblia*, pp. 214ff. Idem, *El ser y el Mesías*, ch. 1; cf. Gutiérrez, *A Theology of Liberation*, p. 175.
[92] Miranda, *El ser y el Mesías*, ch. 5. See James Cone, *Black Theology of Liberation* (Philadelphia: Lippincott, 1970).

po·'alei-awen), oppressors, cheats, the merciless and violent; and he defends the "just" (saddiqim), associated with the poor and oppressed (dallim, 'anawim...).[93] For Assmann, God's people today are those who are kept away from decision-making in society, especially the "condensors" of social consciousness and conscience, the prophets.[94] However, for the Bible, justice will win out. The closing of the inclusion mentioned above is "The earth shall be filled with knowledge of God as water covers the sea," and the point is made in Psalm 37 (28-9):

> The posterity of the unjust will be cut off;
> The just shall possess the land and dwell in it forever.

The beatitudes and "woes" in Luke (6:20-6; cf. Matt. 5:3-12) repeat this moral dualism. The poor man is blessed and the rich threatened. Liberation theologians, like exegetes of all ages, inquire what "poor (in spirit)" means; and they tend to understand it as real economic poverty, which the Bible condemns as unjust and evil, plus another good quality such as mercy (but not mere detachment from one's wealth).[95] Miranda sees the beatitudes and woes as denouncing the difference between the right and poor; for Gutiérrez, "Christian poverty" today means a commitment of solidarity with the poor as protest against injustice.[96]

Jesus appears as Yahweh's word, the "compassion and kindness" interpellating man.[97] He does the work of Yahweh (John 14) and, as in the case of Yahweh, the point is to obey his word commanding love of others. Jesus, when questioned about a biblical text on the love of God and neighbor (Deut. 6:5 and Lev. 19:18b), tells the story of the Samaritan (Luke 10: 25-37). The unity of love of God and neighbor is shown again in the only New Testament account of the content of the last judgment (Matt. 25:31-46). The theme appears in the Old Testament where God appears as šofet, "savior" rather than "judge," or as warrior defending the poor and oppressed.[98] The phrase "last judgment" connotes that God at last frees the poor and defeats their enemies. Gutiérrez defends his interpretation of "least brothers" in "As often as you did it for one of my least brothers, you did it for me" (Matt. 25:40) as meaning "all the needy, not just Christians"; and he

---

[93]Miranda, Marx y la Biblia, pp. 125-31; Gutiérrez, A Theology of Liberation, p. 291.
[94]Assmann, Teología desde la praxis de la liberación, p. 98.
[95]Gutiérrez, A Theology of Liberation, pp. 291ff; Hector Borrat, "Las bienaventuranzas y el cambio social," in Fe cristiana y cambio social, pp. 213-29; Miranda, Marx y la Biblia, pp. 38-39.
[96]Miranda, Marx y la Biblia, pp. 38-39; Gutiérrez, A Theology of Liberation, pp. 299-302.
[97]John 1:14 ḥaris kai aléthpeia renders the Hebrew phrase ḥesed weemet and relates to justice; Miranda, El ser y el Mesías, ch. 7; idem, Marx y la Biblia, pp. 268-69.
[98]Miranda, Marx y la Biblia, pp. 137ff, quoting Ps. 82, Matt. 25, Zeo. 3:17. On p. 150, Miranda gives a list of texts where warrior god and oppressed appear together.

concludes that we meet God by committing ourselves to history, through a necessary human mediation, and that communion and brotherhood are the "ultimate meaning of human life."[99]

The judgment scene forms part of the eschatological motif in the Bible. If for the Greeks history is characterized by a certain sameness, in the Bible history goes somewhere, has an "at last," an esḥaton, a solution. Miranda is more forthright in his treatment of the esḥaton than other Latin American theologians who are cautious on this question, especially on the possibility of survival after death. First, he says, we cannot reduce the kingdom in Greek fashion to an inner or otherworldly experience; careful exegesis does not sanction removing from this world the elimination of injustice. The "reward in heaven" passage (Matt. 5:12) means that our acts accumulate like treasure before God, not that we will be rewarded for them in an afterlife.[100] For Jesus, Paul, John, and the Synoptics, the kingdom comes on earth.[101] The messianic kingdom, the esḥaton, is already here, in fact, since it was inaugurated by the death and resurrection of Jesus the Messiah. But the kingdom is also still to come in the sense that it will be brought to perfection, when man will no longer be unjust and the kind will rule the earth.[102] Faith takes its meaning from this eschatological context, for by faith we believe (and hope) that Jesus is the Messiah.[103] Miranda affirms that because of a connection between injustice and death, when the esḥaton is fully realized, death will be absent: if the gaining of justice is a miracle, so too is the defeat of death.[104] Assmann considers speculation on death a Christian contribution to revolutionary thought, because in this matter Marx was not satisfactory.[105]

Possible parallels between this world view and Marx are clear. Religion is not an escape from contingent history; on the contrary, praxis in the search for justice is the highest ethical value. Biblical ethics is not eudaimonistic in the Greek, Christian, or utilitarian sense; it is deontological. Miranda remarks that if God had no care for the needy, we ought to oppose him even in the face of eternal damnation.[106] Marx was an atheist because, if God "is" in the experience of

---

[99]Gutiérrez, A Theology of Liberation, pp. 194, 196, 198. He criticizes J. C. Ingelaere, "La 'parabole' de Jugement Dernier (Matthieu 25:31-46)," Revue d'Histoire et de Philosophie Religieuse 50:1 (1970): 23-60; and H. J. Holtzmann, Die Synoptiker, 3d ed. (Tubingen, 1901).

[100]Miranda, El ser y el Mesías, ch. 9: idem, Marx y la Biblia, p. 289. Miranda also treats other seemingly contrary passages (Luke 16:23 and 23:43; 2 Cor. 12:4; Phil. 1:23) in Marx y la Biblia, pp. 31-33, and El ser y el Mesías, p. 59.

[101]Miranda, Marx y la Biblia, p. 83.

[102]Ibid., pp. 272 ff; Miranda El ser y el Mesías, p. 59.

[103]Miranda, Marx y la Biblia, pp. 228ff.

[104]Ibid., pp. 319-20.

[105]Assmann, Teología desde la praxis de la liberación, p. 137.

[106]Miranda, El ser y el Mesías, chs. 2 and 9.

justice, there was, could be, no God for him to know.[107] On the other hand, some older Christian doctrines that have fallen into disuse suggest parallelisms between Christian and Marxist ethics: communitary value and socialism, usury and the critique of capitalism, even the "just war" applied to class-struggle.[108] However, the great similarity that Miranda notes between Marx and the Bible is hope in an esḥaton; Marx, too, believed justice will be attained in this world.[109] Both Marx and the Bible are utopian; they see the world's evil as man-made and suppressible: "The old order has passed away; now all is new" (2 Cor. 5:17). Echoing a sentiment of Teilhard de Chardin, Miranda sees humanity divided into two bands: those who believe the world has a solution here below and those who do not.[110] Marx and Paul belong to the first group.

Segundo has remarked that the Church's mission to the world has changed for many Christians, but the theology supporting the former mission has not been replaced. Now, new concepts of God, sin, sacrament, and even ecclesial unity are needed.[111] This is especially true if the philosophical content of the old supporting theology is thrown into question. Building of new theologies is a task concerning the whole Church, but Latin American theologians have put forward interesting suggestions, taking their lead from North Atlantic thinkers. It would be a mistake simply to label these attempts "naturalism." Miranda speaks about what might be termed a theology of the "outcry" (se ʽa-qah). The only thing we cannot objectivize or assimilate into ourselves is the "hard otherness" of the appeal of the needy, identified with God. Only the cry of the oppressed can overcome "idealism," break in upon our aloneness and yet remain other.[112] Dussel and Assmann discuss prophetism within the context of a constant dissatisfaction with the present, with the totalities we shape our world into, in the name of an expectation of otherness beyond.[113] Assmann judges a pragmatic view of truth to be more compatible with biblical knowing than the theory of eternal essence. Such a view considers truth efficient praxis, underlining its historical dimension against any attempt to "base the content of truth on a step previous to its verification (its 'coming true, being made true [hacerse verdad]')." The faith is his-

---

[107]Miranda, Marx y la Biblia, pp. 316, 329.
[108]Jordan Bishop, Cristianismo radical y marxismo (México, D.F.: Nuestro Tiempo, 1970), p. 39; Miranda, Marx y la Biblia, pp. 11-12.
[109]Miranda, Marx y la Biblia, pp. 228, 246, 288.
[110]Ibid., p. 258.
[111]Segundo, "Theology and Ideology," p. 3.
[112]Miranda, El ser y el Mesías, chs. 2-3, 7; cf. idem, Marx y la Biblia, p. 115.
[113]Dussel, "Historia de la fe cristiana y cambio social," pp. 69, 74, citing Levinas, Totalité et infini, and F. W. Schelling, Philosophie der Offenbarung (Werke, Vol. 4); Assmann, Teología desde la praxis, pp. 146-47. Cf. Gutiérrez on "Eschatology and Politics" in his A Theology of Liberation, pp. 213-50.

torically true when it is "made true [*se hace verdad*]," that is, "when it is historically efficatious for man's liberation."[114]

Miranda draws upon Kant, Sartre, and Heidegger in speaking of the God of the Bible. Kant was right, he says, in disassociating God from the being accessible to the understanding and relating him instead to the practical reason. Marx and the Bible also reject ontic gods in the name of ethics. God is linked with the ethical imperative, a condition for the possibility of human conscience.[115] God has to do with conscience, rooted in man's freedom, the sphere of being which depends upon man's decision, and not with the *en-soi*, for Sartre the area of "objective" being open to science. Miranda also ties eschatology to human freedom, through the concept of time, another condition for the possibility of conscience. Kierkegaard emphasized the temporal, individual aspect of our life against Hegel; for Heidegger, temporality is essential to the meaningfulness of our world and the future is the most important phase of temporality. Now, says Miranda, the future itself is made meaningful by the key event it contains, the *esḥaton*, which will come in real time and founds hope in a new creation.[116]

It should not be surprising, given the strong emphasis in liberation theology on action to benefit neighbor and the high Platonic content of traditional Christian mysticism, that one of the greatest crises in the Latin American Church concerns spirituality.[117] Galilea sees the problem as getting back an "authentic Christian mysticism" after clearing it of its monastic flavor, Greek dualism of body and soul, individualism, and evasive transcendentalism.[118] Experience is commonly seen as the basis of spirituality.[119] But the problem lies in defining this experience and relating it to love of neighbor, because it is axiomatic for liberation theologians that there is no union with God without union with man. Gutiérrez sees the conversion to the oppressed as essential to this spiritual experience; and Galilea points to a double encounter, found in the New Testament, with Jesus, the Other, and with our neighbors, the others.[120] Leaving self to find others entails suffering; when man approaches God through man he is

---

[114]Assmann, *Teología desde la praxis de la liberación*, pp. 65, 71.

[115]Miranda, *El ser y el Mesías*, pp. 34, 181.

[116]Ibid., chs. 1-3.

[117]Gutiérrez, *A Theology of Liberation*, pp. 203-208 and p. 212, note 48; Galilea, *Contemplación y apostolado*, especially ch. 4; Scannone and Urbina, "Necesidad y posibilidades," p. 372.

[118]Galilea, *Contemplación y apostolado*, p. 40; Scannone and Urbina, "Necesidad y posibilidades," p. 372; Gutiérrez, *A Theology of Liberation*, p. 7.

[119]Gutiérrez, *A Theology of Liberation*, p. 204; Scannone and Urbina, "Necesidad y posibilidades," p. 365; Galilea, *Contemplación y apostolado*, p. 40.

[120]Gutiérrez, *A Theology of Liberation*, pp. 205, 207; Galilea, *Contemplación y apostolado*, pp. 43-44.

stripped naked.[121] There is no solution yet; when it comes, says Gutiérrez, living witness, not theology, will find it.[122] In the liberation movement, what people do is much more important than what they say.[123] But St. John of the Cross must be reread; perhaps Ernesto Cardenal's psalms will some day also become a text to be glossed.

> Listen to my words, oh Lord
> Hear my protest.
> . . . .
> There is no truth in their speeches,
> No sincerity in their press releases.
> They discuss peace at their conferences
> But in secret ready for war.
> . . . .
> Thou shalt deliver me from their plans,
> They speak with the mouth of machine guns.
> . . . .
> Punish them, oh Lord, confound their policies.
> Thou shalt be my refuge
> > In the hour of the air raid;
> Be Thou with me
> > On the day of the bomb. . . .[124]

---

[121]Galilea, *Contemplación y apostolado*, p. 45; Gutiérrez, *A Theology of Liberation*, p. 206.

[122]Gutiérrez, *A Theology of Liberation*, p. 308.

[123]Francisco Bravo, "Religion as Problem in Latin America," trans. Walter Redmond, p. 32 (Manuscript); Bishop, *Marxism and Theology*, pp. 19-20.

[124]From Ernesto Cardenal, *Salmos* (Buenos Aires: Ediciones C. Lohlé, 1969), pp. 13-14; cf. Ernesto Cardenal, *Psalms of Struggle and Liberation*, trans. Emil G. McAnay (New York: Herder and Herder, 1971).

4. The Perils of Success: Post-World War II Latin American Protestantism

RICHARD L. MILLETT

Professor Millett describes recent increases in the size and influence of Protestantism in Latin America, comments on changes in relations between Latin American Protestant groups and the Catholic Church, and outlines new problems and responsibilities facing Latin American Protestants.

The past three decades have witnessed remarkable growth in both the size and influence of Latin America's Protestant community. Accompanied by major alterations within the Roman Catholic Church, these changes have served to shatter the area's image as a center of religious stagnation and traditionalism. Protestantism's new strength and influence represents a degree of success that was virtually unimagined before World War II. With this success, however, has come a host of new problems and responsibilities. Efforts to deal with these have been only partially successful, at best; often, they have produced even further fragmentation within the already badly divided evangelical community.

In 1916, Protestants claimed only 93,337 communicants in South America, 10,422 in Central America, and 22,282 in Mexico.[1] A high percentage were immigrants: notably Germans, Englishmen, and North Americans. From 1916 thru the 1930s, Protestantism experienced generally steady but unspectacular growth. A major development in this period was the appearance of indigenous Pentecostal churches and of independent "faith mission" churches, which in many areas began to equal or surpass the size of older denomina-

---

[1] William Read, Victor Moterroso, and Harmon Johnson, *Latin American Church Growth* (Grand Rapids, Mich.: Eerdmans, 1969), p. 41.

tions. By the late 1930s, the Protestant community numbered over two million, the majority of whom were Latins.[2]

Achieving even this limited growth had not been easy. Protestants often encountered determined and at times violent opposition from local Roman Catholics. Their churches were often tiny and isolated; their members were drawn heavily from the lower class; and, usually, their denominational organizations were foreign controlled and dependent upon external financial support for survival. Immigrant churches, notably Lutherans in Brazil and Argentina, often reacted to this situation by isolating themselves from the surrounding society. They continued to use their own national language, usually German, and made little if any effort to win converts from the surrounding Latin populations. Most of their pastors came directly from the United States or Europe.[3] However, indigenous churches and those founded by missionaries developed a highly defensive self-image. They viewed themselves a tiny, persecuted minority that contended bravely for the faith against the awesome powers of evil—powers which were often identified with Roman Catholicism. Most were militantly anti-Catholic, denouncing the Church as idolatrous and debased, accusing it of offering superstition in place of faith, exploiting the poor and supporting all the ills which beset Latin American society. Catholics responded in kind. They denounced Protestants as heretics and perverters of the social order; and they classified Protestantism with Communism, spiritualism, and materialism as a threat to the future of the hemisphere.[4] In the mid-1940s, an Argentine archbishop reportedly went so far as to declare, "Argentina is a Catholic Country. Those in the country who abandon Catholicism are traitors. And traitors are shot in the back."[5]

This constant struggle with Catholicism, a struggle upon which the survival of the evangelical community often seemed to depend, encouraged Protestants to focus what limited political influence they had upon questions of church-state relations. Issues often appeared deceptively simple. If an administration was pro-Catholic, restricting Protestant activities and/or making Catholic religious instruction compulsory in the schools, Protestants opposed it and often attacked such governments in their publications in the United States. Support was given to "liberal," anti-clerical regimes. Efforts were made to counter

[2]These figures are taken from a course outline on the History of Evangelical Christianity in Latin America prepared by Dr. Wilton Nelson of the Seminario Bíblico Latinoaméricano in Costa Rica.
[3]This information was furnished by the Rev. Fred Pankow, director of Latin American work for the Lutheran Church, Missouri Synod.
[4]This description of Latin American Protestantism is attributed by both Protestants and Catholics to Pope Pius XII.
[5]José Míguez-Bonino, "Roman Catholic-Protestant Relations in Latin America," The Religious Situation 1969, ed. Donald Cutler (Boston: Beacon Press, 1970).

Catholic attacks upon such governments, as exemplified during certain phases of the Mexican Revolution, and any opportunities offered by such regimes for increasing Protestant activities were usually warmly accepted.[6] This alliance with liberal parties, combined with the polemical nature of many Protestant critiques of a traditional social structure that was intimately identified with Roman Catholicism, gave evangelicals a progressive, anti-establishment image.[7] Protestant schools become noted centers for training liberal, even radical leadership.[8] The depth of any commitment to liberalism by the majority of the Protestants, however, is open to serious question. Beyond involvement in church-state issues, most Protestants usually avoided any political involvement—perhaps because their minority status and dependence upon foreign support made the risks of such involvement unacceptably high.

The relatively extensive social programs of many Protestant groups often contributed to their progressive image. Most of their pre-World War II medical and social welfare programs, however, were undertaken primarily to assist in the winning of converts. A similar motive was responsible for much of their educational work, although it also served the purpose of making available for the children of missionaries and converts an educational system free from the Roman Catholic religious instruction that was often compulsory in other schools.

Dependence upon foreign support, combined with militant rejection not only of Catholicism but of all cultural values associated with the Church, often produced a form of cultural alienation among members of evangelical churches. They produced their own subculture, often imitating Anglo-Saxon models.[9] In this regard, they conformed to one of the worst aspects of late 19th and early 20th century Latin American liberalism: a tendency to reject Latin America's own cultural and social heritage and to seek development along European or North American lines. This attitude shaped the churches' internal practices as well as their external attitudes. Services became virtual carbon copies of foreign, middle-class models; hymns were usually direct, often awkward, translations from English-language hymnals.[10]

[6]For examples, see Richard Millett, "The Protestant Role in Twentieth Century Latin American Church-State Relations," *Journal of Church and State* 15 (Autumn 1973): 369-73.

[7]Samuel Escobar, "El Reino de Dios, la escatología y la ética social y política en América Latina" (1973), p. 7. (Manuscript).

[8]James E. Helms, "Origins and Growth of Protestantism in Mexico to 1920" (Ph.D. dissertation, University of Texas, 1955), p. 553. APRA leader Raul Haya de la Torre is perhaps the best known example of this influence.

[9]Samuel Escobar, "The Social Responsibility of the Church in Latin America," *Evangelical Missions Quarterly* 6 (Spring 1970): 136.

[10]Orlando Costas, "La realidad de la Iglesia Evangélica Latinoamericana," unpublished ms., pp. 17-19.

Seminaries and bible schools followed curricula based on somewhat simplified models of those used in North American institutions. Exceptionally promising students often received advanced education in the United States or in Europe; and upon returning to Latin America, they usually found employment with foreign missions or service organizations. Such employment, however, was usually at a subordinate level; control of such organizations usually remained firmly in foreign missionary hands. It is therefore not surprising that as recently as twenty years ago Latin American Protestants had produced virtually no distinctive theology, social commentary or philosophy.[11]

In the past three decades, several important developments have forced a major re-examination of the traditional position and self-image of Latin American Protestants. The most obvious factor has been the rapid growth of the evangelical community. By 1967, Protestant churches in Latin American, excluding the Caribbean countries and the Guianas, had a total membership of 4,915,477.[12] Addition of members in Cuba, Haiti, the Dominican Republic, and Puerto Rico would put the total well over 5,500,000. Because most denominations in Latin America admit to membership only those with a conversion experience, this virtually eliminates all persons under age ten. Furthermore, because membership often requires adherence to rigid standards of faith and conduct, the actual size of the total Protestant community is much larger. Various formulas, most of which multiply membership figures between two and four times, have been used to determine the total population that should be identified as Protestant. This would place total Protestant strength in 1967 somewhere between eleven and twenty-two million. A figure somewhat under fifteen million would probably be a reasonable estimate. Accepting such a figure as well as indications that a relatively rapid growth rate of at least five percent per year has been maintained since 1967, one concludes that by the late 1970s the total Protestant community in Latin America probably numbered somewhere in excess of twenty-five million.

This great increase in size has been accompanied by a significant change in composition. Growth rates of most traditional denominations, such as Methodists and Presbyterians, have lagged well behind the rate for the region as a whole. Churches sponsored by non-denominational, faith missions have done somewhat better, perhaps due to the overwhelming numbers of missionary personnel that these groups have poured into the area.[13] By far the most spectacular in-

---

[11] It is interesting to note that a pioneering effort in this direction, Richard Shaull's *El Cristianismo y la Revolución Social* (Buenos Aires: La Aurora, 1954), was written by a North American missionary.

[12] Read, Monterroso, and Johnson, *Latin American Church Growth*, p. 48.

[13] Such groups reportedly provide 32.4 percent of all Protestant missionaries, but their

creases have been those recorded by Pentecostals and by Seventh Day Adventists. As recently as 1960 most studies of Latin American Protestantism made little if any reference to Pentecostals; at most, only passing mention of their existence was made.[14] Today, any study that does not devote extensive attention to these churches is of extremely limited usefulness; Pentecostals now make up approximately 60 percent of the entire evangelical community.[15] A large percentage of the Pentecostals belong to churches which are wholly indigenous, free of any ties with foreign churches. Their strength, along with that of the Adventists (a denomination which many of the more fundamentalist bodies refuse to recognize as truly "Christian") has led many of the more traditional denominations to a critical re-examination of their programs of outreach and worship.

Changes in influence and self-image produced by this remarkable growth are even greater than statistics indicate. Much of Latin American Catholicism is nominal. A Guatemalan bishop has commented that the majority of the Catholics in his diocese come to church only to be "hatched, matched, and dispatched."[16] Today in Chile, Haiti, and perhaps even Brazil, it is possible that on a given Sunday more Protestants than Catholics attend worship services. Given the low level of educational preparation required for the ministry by many Pentecostal groups and fundamentalist denominations, and because of the small size of many evangelical congregations, there has been a great increase in the number of Protestant ministers. With priestly vocations declining within the Roman Catholic community, this has produced a situation where even in Honduras, a country in which Protestants constitute less than 3 percent of the population, there are more Protestant ministers than Catholic priests.

Along with the increase in strength has come a distinct rise in social status and political influence. Thirty years ago, a Protestant professional or government official was something of a rarity in most areas. Today, there are Protestants occupying important positions in virtually every Latin American nation. The most conspicuous example is Brazil where the President, four of the twenty-one state gov-

---

churches contain only 1.5 percent of Protestant church members. *Escobar*, "El Reino de Dios," p. 12.

[14] This is thoroughly documented in Norbert E. Johnson's "The History, Dynamic and Problems of the Pentecostal Movement in Chile" (Th.M. thesis, Union Theological Seminary, Richmond, Va., 1970), pp. 92-95.

[15] This figure was derived largely from data contained in Read, Monterroso, and Johnson, *Latin American Church Growth*, and from *Haiti: Status of Christianity* (Monrovia, Calif.: Missions Advanced Research and Communication Center, 1971). The percentage of Pentecostals in the Latin American Protestant community is apparently still growing.

[16] This comment was made to me in 1972 by a bishop who may wish to remain anonymous.

ernors, and several members of the Congress were Protestants in 1972.[17]

While this rapid growth in size and influence has undermined the Protestants' self-image as a small persecuted minority, the ecumenical movement and the effects of Vatican II upon the Roman Catholic Church have created a serious challenge to traditional anti-Catholic attitudes. The mutual anathemas of the first half of this century have been replaced largely by a growing dialogue. Once bitterly condemned as *herejes*, Protestants are now classified as *hermanos separados*—often with more emphasis being placed upon the *hermano* than upon the *separado*. Participation of a Protestant leader in a major Catholic meeting or speaking in a Catholic seminary is no longer unusual. Catholics, in turn, are often participants in Protestant-sponsored gatherings.[18]

Not all Protestants have found these changes easy to accept. In fact, many have been slow to adapt their own position to this new reality, which is more likely to confront them with the problem of how to respond to an invitation to address a local gathering of priests than it is to confront them with the traditional problem of preventing forcible disruption of their services. Some conservatives have warned that Protestant-Catholic dialogue threatens internal unity among evangelicals and that it may also cause converts to question why they ever left the Catholic Church.[19] For others, the reality of the ecumenical movement has come as a distinct personal shock. One young North American missionary arrived in Central America a few years ago full of stories of the persecution of Protestants by fanatical priests and of determined Catholic efforts to prevent their congregations from reading the Bible. After several weeks of language school, he embarked upon his first venture in missionary service: distributing copies of the New Testament in a small village. He parked near the plaza and began to unload his books; suddenly, the black-robed local priest appeared and inquired as to his purpose in the area. Summoning up his courage he boldly declared, in broken Spanish, that he had come to distribute the word of God. "Wonderful," responded the priest. "I'll ring the church bell and summon some of my people to help you." When I encountered this individual a few days later, his world view was still in a state of considerable disarray.

One area in which many Latin American Catholics have sought

---

[17]Rick Edwards, "Protestant Ethic and Imperial Mission: The Latin American Case," *NACLA's Latin America and Empire Report* 4 (February, 1972): 10.

[18]For a fuller description of the changes involved, see Miguez-Bonino, "Roman Catholic-Protestant Relations in Latin America." For a description of the changes and problems produced in one small nation, see Richard Millett, "Protestant-Catholic Relations in Costa Rica," *Journal of Church and State* 12 (Winter 1970): 41-57.

[19]Emilio Antonio Nuñez, "Perilous Ecumenical Overtures," *Evangelical Missions Quarterly* 5 (Summer 1969): 193-94.

dialogue and even cooperation with Protestants has been in developing a response to the area's ever deepening socioeconomic crisis. Responses to this situation have deeply divided the Protestant community. Obviously, traditional social service programs of medical aid and education are totally inadequate in dealing with the area's massive problems; yet, efforts to define a new, more active program of social action have led to serious conflicts within the evangelical community. Growing pressure for radical change from the political left, coupled with increasingly violent repression from the right, has served to further aggravate this situation.

Problems have also arisen in Protestant church bodies as a result of the growing spirit of nationalism throughout Latin America. This has limited the effectiveness of North American missionaries, especially in pastoral ministries, and, increasingly, has freed Latin church leaders to question and criticize programs proposed by foreigners. This, in turn, is forcing a long overdue examination of the basically paternalistic relationships that have existed between many Latin American churches and denominational authorities or mission boards in the United States.

The aforementioned developments have created a critical need for *evangélicos* to re-define their position within society. The urgency of this task varies from nation to nation, being less critical in a relatively static society such as Paraguay than it is in the more modernized and urbanized environment of Argentina or Chile; nevertheless, the necessity is clearly present in every nation. Divisions along national and denominational lines, and especially along political-theological lines, however, have made it virtually impossible to achieve any consensus on the churches' role in contemporary society.

Many fundamentalist *evangélicos* continue to resist all pressures to alter their traditional positions. Often they echo North American conservative arguments that equate social activism with modernism in theology and communism in politics. Their churches tend to be highly suspicious of approaches to other denominations, viewing any deviation from their own doctrines as dangerously heretical. Due, in part, to their own self-imposed isolation, the influence of these churches upon the total evangelical community is rather limited.

While some Pentecostal groups fall within the above category, many find themselves in a more open position with regard to both ecumenical and social programs.[20] Unlike many of the older denominations that have been transformed into increasingly middle-class churches and have been alienated from the mass of the popula-

[20]For an example of the Pentecostal groups most opposed to any form of social, political or ecumenical action, see Cornelia Butler Flora, *Mobilizing the Masses: The Sacred and the Secular in Colombia* (Ithaca, N. Y.: Cornell University Press, 1970). For a more recent account, see idem, *Pentecostalism in Colombia* (Cranbury, N. J.: Associated University Presses, 1976).

tion, Pentecostals have managed to retain an intimate identification with the lower classes.[21] Their ministers are largely drawn from this segment of society, and they usually live in or near their churches that are generally located within lower class neighborhoods.[22] This continuing class identification means that their appreciation of the material as well as the spiritual needs of their congregations is experienced directly, not simply understood intellectually.

The actual role of Pentecostals in promoting meaningful social change has been the subject of considerable debate. Professor Emilio Willems of Vanderbilt University sees them as "protest movements against the existing class structure" and views their basic social impact as positive.[23] Walter Hollenweger, a German scholar, supports this view. He notes that among Brazilian Pentecostals "political and social engagement goes hand in hand with evangelization."[24] Cristian LaLive d'Epinay, a Swiss sociologist, argues, however, that the Pentecostals of Chile "reactivate the basic paternalistic power structure and become centripetal and exclusive societies with a Manichaen vision of their environment. In this sense the religious communities strengthen oppression and harden the oppressed consciousness of men."[25] Orlando Costas, a Puerto Rican theologian, takes a moderating position on this issue. He gives Pentecostals credit for producing an individual liberating effect, but he criticizes their inability to translate concern for individuals into meaningful, organized social involvement.[26]

Part of this disagreement over the social role of the Pentecostals may be due to the wide variety of leadership and social doctrine which exists within the movement. An interesting example of this diversity is provided by the Brazil para Cristo church headed by the charismatic Manuel de Melo. This church has encouraged political involvement; has opened orphanages, hospitals, and schools; and, to the astonishment of many, has joined the World Council of Churches.[27]

[21]Charles F. Denton, "Protestantism and the Latin American Middle Class," *Practical Anthropology* 9 (January-February 1971): 24-28; Charles Troutman, "Evangelicals and the Middle Class in Latin America," *Evangelical Missions Quarterly* 7 (Winter 1971): 80.

[22]C. Peter Wagner, *Look Out! The Pentecostals Are Coming* (Carol Stream, Ill.: Creation House, 1973), pp. 89-100; Key Yuasa, "A Study of the Pentecostal Movement in Brazil: Its Importance," *The Reformed and Presbyterian World* 29 (June 1966): 67.

[23]Emilio Willems, *Followers of the New Faith* (Nashville, Tenn.: Vanderbilt University Press, 1967), p. 218.

[24]Walter J. Hollenweger, *The Pentecostals*, trans. R. A. Wilson (Minneapolis, Minn.: Augsburg, 1972), pp. 80 and 107.

[25]Cristian LaLive d'Epinay, "La Iglesia Evangélica y la Revolución Latinoamericana," *Cristianismo y Sociedad* 6: Nos. 16 and 17 (1968): 29.

[26]Costas, "La realidad de la Iglesia Evangélica Latinoamericana," pp. 29-36.

[27]Howard J. Wiarda and Iêda Siqueira Wiarda, "The Churches and Rapid Social Change: Protestants and Catholics in Brazil," *Journal of Church and State* 12 (Winter 1970): 26-27.

De Melo has explained this last action by expressing a need to join with other Christians in order to attack social problems. He has been quoted as saying, "What good does it do to convert a million people if at the same time the Devil unconverts ten million through hunger, disease and military dictatorship. These sorts of things one can't overcome by holding wonderful religious services, but by organizing one's forces and joining with others who have similar interests."[28] If nothing else, this quotation serves to illustrate that a very real, if still largely unrealized, potential for social action does exist within the Pentecostal churches.

While Seventh Day Adventists make up one of the largest Protestant bodies in Latin America, it has been virtually impossible to include them within the scope of this study. Data are difficult to obtain and there are almost no independent studies of this major group. They have remained relatively isolated from other Protestants, a situation due not only to theological differences but also to other denominations' resentment over their aggressive, proselyting efforts.[29]

Problems produced by collapse of the traditional self-image and changes in the social status of Protestants are most clearly seen and probably most acute within the older, more traditional denominations. This would include immigrant churches (Lutherans, Mennonites, and Waldensians), mainline Protestants (notably Methodists, Presbyterians, Episcopalians, and Baptists), and some churches fostered by the older and larger interdenominational missions. These groups share several common situations. First, while many are still growing at a rate near to or even greater than the rate of national population growth, their relative strength within the Protestant community has declined steadily in recent decades due to the much more rapid growth of the Adventists and Pentecostals.

These churches also face the problem of an emerging second generation that was born into Protestantism, not converted from Catholicism, or, in the case of the immigrant churches, born into a Latin rather than a European environment. In both cases, ties of the second generation to traditional church patterns are weaker than those of their parents; at the same time, however, their concern for national problems is often stronger. Among immigrant groups there is growing pressure to hold services in Spanish or Portuguese and to integrate the church into the national community. In all these groups, there is a growing questioning of traditional patterns of social and political

---

[28]Walter J. Hollenweger, "Pentecostalism and the Third World," *Dialog* 9 (Spring, 1970): 125.

[29]William R. Read and Frank A. Ineson, *Brazil, 1980: The Protestant Handbook* (Monrovia, Calif.: Missions Advanced Research and Communication Center, 1973), pp. 98-100; Read, Monterroso, and Johnson, *Latin American Church Growth*, pp. 58-60. Harmon A. Johnson, *The Growing Church in Haiti* (Coral Gables, Fla.: West Indies Mission, 1970), pp. 46-48.

response. At the Latin American Conference on Evangelism in 1969, Professor Samuel Escobar of Peru quoted a Protestant youth as saying:

> In the past they told us not to worry about changing society because what we need is to change men. New men will change society. But when the new men begin to worry about changing society they are told not to worry, that the world has always been bad, that we await new heavens and a new earth and that this world is condemned to destruction. Why try to make it better? What's even worse is that those who teach this are the ones who enjoy all the advantages that this passing world offers and they passionately defend them whenever they are endangered.[30]

Another common factor for many of these churches is their increasing identification with the middle class. According to Orlando Costas, this means that most Latin American evangelicals who do recognize the need for social action and justice strive to achieve this within the framework of "an ideology of change which responds to the interests of the middle class."[31] This is combined with a traditional approach to social problems that is highly individualistic and moralistic, stressing drunkenness, sexual vices, and various forms of popular amusements as the great evils of society. Even when hunger, disease, and illiteracy are added to this list of social problems, there remains a clear tendency to concentrate on treating the symptoms while ignoring the structural basis of society which produces existing conditions.[32]

The weakness of most Protestant social action programs is aggravated by an acute shortage of capable, educated pastoral leadership. As the social and educational levels of many congregations have risen in recent years, the need for a better qualified clergy has increased; but neither the manpower nor the monetary resources needed to meet this need have been forthcoming.[33] Efforts to solve the shortage by expanding and upgrading traditional seminary facilities have been somewhat less than successful. Major union seminaries have been created in many areas, notably in Buenos Aires and Mexico City, but have suffered from a lack of students. Recently, the Buenos Aires seminary complex (I.S.E.D.E.T.) had only forty-six full-time theology students for a faculty of fourteen full-time and eleven part-time instructors.[34] Graduates of such seminaries often find that there

---

[30]Escobar, "The Social Responsibility of the Church in Latin America," p. 132.

[31]Orlando Costas, "La crisis de la Iglesia Evangélica en América Latina," rev. ms. of a paper read at the Latin American Conference of the Church of God, Alajuela, Costa Rica, August 3, 1973, p. 11.

[32]Ibid., p. 12.

[33]For a detailed analysis of this problem as it affected one denomination, see Werner Kaschel, "Baptist Ministry and Underdevelopment in Brazil," (Th.D. diss., Southern Baptist Theological Seminary, 1971).

[34]These statistics are taken from a pamphlet describing the I.S.E.D.E.T. program in 1972.

are few churches that can or will support ministers with their educational and social qualifications. In addition, the relatively liberal education which they receive tends to alienate them from the membership of their own denominations. As a result, many, if not most of the best graduates of these institutions go into administrative or teaching positions—or they leave church work altogether.[35]

Efforts to provide additional leadership have taken other forms. Some major urban churches, unable to obtain qualified national pastors, have turned to Cuban exiles, to local seminary professors, to Puerto Ricans, and even to former North American missionaries. In an effort to improve the education of pastors of rural churches and smaller urban churches, a massive effort at theological education by extension has been undertaken throughout Latin America.[36] Despite such efforts, the problem of recruiting and supporting capable pastoral leadership remains acute in most nations.

All but the most conservative and isolated groups have recognized that Latin Americans should assume responsibility for the Protestant work, but efforts in this direction have led to a multitude of problems. First, where Protestant work has been heavily dependent upon foreign contributions, usually from North America, moves toward relinquishing control have often been accompanied by major reductions in financial support. This is due to a variety of reasons. Recently, some major denominations have experienced financial problems; therefore, cutting support in the name of nationalism and local autonomy has seemed increasingly attractive. In other cases, major conflicts have arisen between the parent church body and Latin American churches over programs of social action. Interestingly enough, in several of these disputes, the Americans have advocated more aggressive social action and have diverted resources into the support of activist sociopolitical organizations and movements whose connections with the Latin American church is tenuous at best.[37]

---

[35]This problem has been experienced, though perhaps to a lesser degree, by the graduates of some relatively conservative seminaries, such as the Seminario Bíblico in Costa Rica, as well as by the graduates of such institutions as I.S.E.D.E.T. and the union seminary complex in Mexico City.

[36]A massive literature and a regular newsletter on this movement exist. For example, the latest book list of the Church Growth Book Club lists thirteen separate titles under the heading "Theological Education by Extension."

[37]Relations between the Presbyterian Church in the U.S.A. and the Presbytery of the South in Colombia, especially the conflict over the American Church's decision to appropriate funds for the work of the "ROSCA de Investigación y Acción Social," a group headed by individuals closely connected with ISAL in Colombia, provide an excellent example of this. As relevant documents, see the release of the Presbyterian Information Office, 1972 Series, No. 2, for the letter from Pbro. Javier Zarate Pérez, Stated Clerk of the Presbytery of the South Synod of the Presbyterian Church in the U.S.A., and the "Declaration of Position of the Presbytery of the South Synod of the Presbyterian Church in Colombia" approved at its Regular Meeting in Ibague, Tolima, January 5-7, 1972. Another example is provided by the angry reaction of Brazilian Lutherans to the

Finally, there is a marked reluctance on the part of many churches in the United States to transfer support from an American missionary, whom they often know, to a Latin American whom they may never have met. As one Ecuadorian Protestant leader somewhat bitterly expressed it: "Most North Americans seem only interested in sending their money to other North Americans who come back from time to time to entertain them with photographs of naked Indians."[38] Whatever the reason, this reduction of support often creates heavy burdens for an emerging national church, especially when it also inherits a large infrastructure of schools, hospitals, and other church-related institutions.

At times, church boards in the United States have approached nationalizing mission church leadership with considerable suspicion and fear. Programs for this purpose have often been characterized by a heavy-handed paternalism. The parent denomination or board, while paying lip service to the necessity for indigenous leadership and an end to dependency relations, demands, at the same time, that it have final judgment on the pace of transition, financial arrangements involved, and, in some cases, even the selection of "national leaders" who will assume control. Bitterness produced by such attitudes should not be underestimated.[39]

Pressures of responding to change both within and outside the Protestant community have produced serious divisions among Latin American evangelicals and have caused conflicts between missionaries and indigenous leaders. A small but active minority, including many of the best educated and most articulate Latin American churchmen, has called for the church to take radical action in favor of social justice and political change.[40] Although it has existed for many years, this group's emergence as a significant factor within the Protestant community can probably be dated from the Huampaní Conference on "The Responsibility of the Protestant Church in the Face of Rapid Social Changes," which was held in Peru during July 1961. The Latin American Board on Church and Society (ISAL) was formed at this conference, and it has served as an organizational center for studies and publications advocating increasingly activist and often radical roles for the churches of Latin America.[41] In 1963, ISAL began publishing a journal, *Cristianismo y Sociedad*, which provided a

decision of World Lutheran leaders to cancel a proposed World Confederation meeting in Brazil as a gesture of protest against the policies of Brazil's military government.

[38]The author heard this statement in Ecuador in September 1971. For obvious reasons, the source must remain anonymous.

[39]The author encountered this problem repeatedly in discussions with Latin American church leaders in recent years, most notably in Venezuela in 1971.

[40]Most estimates place support for this viewpoint at no more than 5 percent of the total Protestant community.

[41]Jorge Lara-Braud, *Social Justice and the Latin Churches* (Richmond, Va.: John Knox, 1969), pp. 9-13.

means for further dissemination of such arguments throughout Latin America. Additional calls for radical social action on the part of the churches characterized the Second Latin American Conference on Church and Society held in Chile in 1966.[42] At this same time, the hemisphere-wide Provisional Commission for Latin American Evangelical Unity (UNELAM) seemed to many to be coming increasingly under the influence and direction of ISAL supporters. These developments alarmed conservative church leaders, who responded by attacking proposals advanced through ISAL and by accusing its spokesmen of theological liberalism and of a political alliance with Marxism.[43] In the late 1960s, a bitter dispute broke out over selecting delegates and planning the program for the Third Latin American Evangelical Congress.[44] After repeated postponements, the Conference was finally held in Buenos Aires. Many conservative denominations boycotted the meeting, although others, including some Pentecostal bodies, sent delegates. Arguments in sessions on social action and ecumenical ties seemed to signal an almost complete split within Latin American Protestantism.[45]

Later, in 1969, conservative groups conducted their own Latin American Conference on Evangelism in Bogotá. To the surprise of many, several speakers openly criticized the churches for their lack of meaningful social involvement. These remarks received generally favorable responses from the 920 delegates.[46] The concluding *Declaración Evangélica de Bogotá* stated that "the hour has come for the evangelicals to become aware of our social responsibilities."[47] The extent to which ISAL activities influenced this belated recognition of social responsibilities is questionable; but whatever the cause, this discussion and self-criticism within the ranks of the more conservative or traditional churches have continued and have expanded with each passing year.

While the gap between conservative and liberal church factions has by no means been healed by events since 1969, the near total polarization which seemed to be developing has apparently been de-

---

[42]The previously cited work by Jorge Lara-Braud is largely a summary of this meeting.

[43]See C. Peter Wagner, *Latin American Theology, Radical or Evangelical?* (Grand Rapids, Mich.: Eerdmans, 1970). It should be noted that the Spanish version of this work appeared in 1969.

[44]For differing views of this conflict, see Peter Savage, "Protestantism in Latin America Today," *Christian Heritage*, November 1968, pp. 26-29, and J. Gordon Chamberlin, "Ecumenical Tangle," *Christian Century*, January 17, 1968, pp. 75-77.

[45]Dayton Roberts, "Latin American Protestants; Which Way Will They Go?" *Christianity Today*, October 10, 1969, p. 16.

[46]Costas, "La crisis de la Iglesia Evangélica en América Latina," p. 1. For the reactions of several Protestant leaders to the meeting, see the special issue of *En Marcha Internacional* (San José, Costa Rica), January-June 1970.

[47]"Declaración Evangélica de Bogotá," reprinted in *En Marcha Internacional*, January-June 1970, p. 3.

layed if not halted. A moderate faction, including such notable figures as José Míguez-Bonino of I.S.E.D.E.T. and Samuel Escobar, President of the conservative-dominated Fraternidad Teológica Latinoamericana, has begun to emerge, seeking a means of adequately expressing both traditional theological concerns and active social involvement. The strident attacks upon the ISAL theologians and others of the Protestant left, which C. Peter Wagner made in 1969, have since been criticized by conservative as well as liberal spokesmen.[48] Criticism of American policy or of the cultural dependency created by various missions has become a not uncommon topic at conferences sponsored by conservative as well as liberal Protestants.

Despite such developments, the basic differences within Latin American Protestantism have not been overcome and are not likely to be overcome in the foreseeable future. There are basic theological as well as methodological issues involved. For example, in 1971 there was a dispute that centered around a liberal-radical sponsored seminar on "Mission and Development" held in Bogotá. Other disputes have featured continuing arguments over Protestant responses to the developing "Theology of Liberation," a theology which began within Latin America's Roman Catholic Church, but which has exercised great influence upon contemporary Protestant thought.[49] Perhaps the emergence of moderates within both liberal and conservative ranks may be a sign of more splintering to come rather than an indication of any real movement towards reconciliation or consensus among competing ideologies. However, one thing is certain: the days of ideological and social stagnation within Latin America's Protestant community have come to an end.

Over the past few decades, the perils of success have become increasingly clear for Latin American Protestants. Simple formulas by which they could gauge responses to most social and political situations and could tell friend from foe largely on the basis of attitudes towards Catholicism are gone forever. Growth and respectability have brought conflict, fragmentation, and tension rather than peace and unity. But with these problems have come new opportunities and new resources. For the first time, Protestants have both the numbers and the indigenous leadership to make a major contribution to Latin America's future. There is a continuing struggle to develop a Protestant community which is authentically Latin, relating to rather than

---

[48]C. Rene Padilla, "A Steep Climb Ahead for Theology in Latin America," *Evangelical Missions Quarterly*, 7 (Winter 1971): 99-106.

[49]For an appraisal of the dispute over the Bogotá Conference, see the April 1971 press release by the Evangelical Confederation of Colombia entitled "The National Council of Churches of the United States Sponsors a Seminar on Mission and Development in Bogotá, Colombia," and the reply to this document issued by the Rev. William Wipfler on behalf of the Latin American Division of the National Council of Churches, April 20, 1971.

denying its cultural heritage and its own national problems, and which is also free, free of foreign control, free to adapt from other sources and ideologies; but, also free to develop its own distinctive approaches to the shaping of the hemisphere's future. Undoubtedly, the struggle will continue for many more years. Upon the outcome of this struggle with the perils of success will rest the future of Protestantism in Latin America.[50]

---

[50]The theme of struggling to create a church which is "evangélica, latina y libre" has been repeated to the author dozens of times by various church leaders in recent years.

Part II

MEXICO

From the sixteenth-century days of Zumárraga, Las Casas, and Vasco de Quiroga to the decade of the 1970s, religion has been a major factor in Mexico's society and politics. The passion with which Mexicans have embraced or rejected religion has resulted in conflicting attitudes and conduct (as may be illustrated by a vast literature of Christian apologetics and of criticism by agnostics and atheists), in dogmatic sermonizing and rabidly anticlerical violence, in the burning of heretics and the persecution of the faithful. Under the influence of religion, many Mexicans have been inspired to perform noble deeds in the service of both God and their fellow man; yet others have been motivated by religion to wage holy war, to conduct guerrilla campaigns, or to commit acts of terrorism and assassination—although all of this violence has brought death and destruction to both true believers and servants of Satan. Most of Mexico's religious history is the history of the Roman Catholic Church, which in that country has been strongly influenced by medieval and Counter-Reformation theology, on one hand, and by indigenous pre-Colombian paganism, on the other. This clash of European and Indian religions has produced a spiritual and cultural syncretism exemplified in the Mariolatry of the Virgin of Guadalupe. In addition to the dominant Catholic influence, modern Mexico has been affected by Protestantism. Transplanted to Mexican soil largely through the efforts of missionaries from the United States, Protestantism grew slowly at first; but today Mexican Protestants are increasing rapidly in number, and their influence is expanding.

HISTORY

Many Mexican church buildings constructed during the colonial era are still in use. Some are used for the religious purposes intended by their builders; others now house public schools, libraries, and government offices or serve even more mundane secular purposes. The former stand as monuments to the Spanish Catholic conquest, which was dogmatic, intolerant, monolithic, and pervasive—and which still influences Mexican life. The latter are symbols of independence, disestablishment, and social revolution that have been experienced over the past one and one-half centuries. Each of the following essays deals with a part of Mexico's religious history, ranging from the Inquisition of the colonial period to Catholic opposition to socialist education in more recent times.

5. The Inquisition in Colonial Mexico: Heretical Thoughts on the Spiritual Conquest

RICHARD E. GREENLEAF

With the experience of many years of archival research in Mexico and Spain, Professor Greenleaf discusses the objectives, procedures, and influence of the Holy Office of the Inquisition in colonial Mexico. Special attention is given to treatment of Indians, Jews, Protestants, and foreigners. The author comments on the historian's problems of research, methodology, and analysis in dealing with this controversial institution.*

Recently a professor who had done no archival research echoed what might be called a "liberal establishment interpretation" of the effects of the Holy Office of the Inquisition in colonial Mexico. He maintained that "the very existence of the Inquisition made possible a massive corruption of public morality" and that the thought control imposed by the Inquisition had such a "deleterious effect on all creative, intellectual, and scientific development in Mexico" that "when, in the nineteenth century, the Mexican Inquisition finally came to an end, [Cecil] Roth's conclusion regarding Spain could well be applied to Mexico: it was 'a country drained of its inspiration, of its genius, of its wealth....' "[1]

The whole history of Mexico belies this interpretation and suggests that reasonable men need to cast aside centuries-old clichés and find new, valid yardsticks for evaluation which are grounded in sound historical research. They may still disagree on historical and

---

*Portions of this study rely on the author's "The Mexican Inquisition and the Indians: Sources for the Ethnohistorian," paper read at the XLI International Congress of Americanists, México, D.F., September 5, 1974; a published version under the same title is printed in *The Americas: A Quarterly Review of Inter-American Cultural History* 34 (January 1978): 315-37.

[1] Norton B. Stern, Review of *The Mexican Inquisition of the Sixteenth Century* by Richard E. Greenleaf, *Journal of the West* 9 (January 1970): 138.

contemporary meanings of what they discover, but at least they will have the solid bedrock of data and interpretations necessary to support their conclusions. Only then can they accurately analyze the Mexican Inquisition as an instrument of Spiritual Conquest.

Here, use of the phrase "Spiritual Conquest" must be understood to mean not only the Christianization process wherein friars and priests reduced native populations to Spanish control—probably in at least 65 percent of the geographical area of modern Mexico—but also to encompass the ideological conquest of New Spain that accompanied the three centuries of colonization. In this sense, Robert Ricard's ideas of spiritual conquest and John L. Phelan's concept of "Many Conquests—demographic, spiritual, philosophical, bureaucratic, and social"—have been combined because there were many conquests and the Roman Catholic Church in Mexico participated in all of them.[2]

The Holy Office of the Inquisition in colonial Mexico had as its purpose the defense of Spanish religion and Spanish Catholic culture against individuals who held heretical views and against people who showed lack of respect for religious principles. As such, the institution tried to cast an aura of influence over the whole range of colonial life and society; but the extent to which the Holy Office was able to exert this influence is highly arguable. Inquisition archives and other sources suggest that only a negligible portion of Mexico's population was ever affected by the Holy Office's activities.

The Indians and the Inquisition

One special area of concern to the Mexican Inquisition was how to deal with the Indian populations. During the sixteenth century, a debate raged over whether the Indians of Mesoamerica as recent converts should be subject to the Inquisition's procedures. It was decided in 1571 that each archbishopric should establish a bureaucracy parallel to the Inquisition to deal with native transgressions against the faith because, as neophytes in the religion, Indians were as yet unable to comprehend it fully. This hiatus lasted for the rest of the colonial era, although the Holy Office gradually assumed more control over the Christianized Indian in successive centuries.[3]

[2]See Robert Ricard, *The Spiritual Conquest of Mexico* (Berkeley and Los Angeles: University of California Press, 1966); and John L. Phelan, "Many Conquests: Some Trends and Some Challenges in Mexican Historiography (1945-1969): The Sixteenth and Seventeenth Centuries," in *Investigaciones contemporáneas sobre historia de México: Memorias de la Tercera Reunión de Historiadores Mexicanos y Norteamericanos* (México, D.F.: Universidad Nacional Autónoma de México, 1971), pp. 125-48; and Richard E. Greenleaf, ed., *The Roman Catholic Church in Colonial Latin America* (New York: Knopf, 1971).

[3]See Richard E. Greenleaf, "The Inquisition and the Indians of New Spain: A Study in Jurisdictional Confusion," *The Americas: A Quarterly Review of Inter-American Cultural History* 22 (October 1965): 138-66.

By the end of the sixteenth century and throughout the seventeenth century, paganism, idolatry, sorcery, religious syncretism, and native resistance to absorption into Spanish Catholic culture accentuated among many groups of Mesoamerican Indians. In spite of protests of individual clergy, who had gained some appreciation of Mexican ethnohistory, the church and the viceregal government tolerated these practices. Their permissiveness allowed native religions to survive and to submerge themselves into a new "religious baroque" in Mexico, a religion that often was Catholic in form but pagan in substance and function. Missionary chroniclers, scholarly friars, and priests wrote about these developments and usually deplored them. Many of the writers were provincial commissioners of the Inquisition; hence, their letters and reports are filed in the Holy Office's archive. Perhaps unwittingly, these writers attest to the fact that the Roman Catholic Church in colonial Mexico did accommodate itself to a variegated populace with regional Indian beliefs and practices. On the one hand, the church followed its own ancient tradition of syncretism, which had begun in the Mediterranean world in the first century of the Christian era. On the other hand, the Indians of central Mexico, Oaxaca, and the Yucatán peninsula followed a pre-conquest tradition of syncretism and absorption of new gods and new religious ideas into their own pantheon. Although missionary clergy and secular priests of colonial Mexico believed that spiritual conquest first had to be destructive of the old religions before it could be instructive in Christianity, they began to realize at the turn of the seventeenth century that they had failed to destroy the old beliefs—hence, the pessimism that characterized much of their writing about the Indian church from the 1580s until 1650. This same pessimism, combined with fear of fostering nativistic florescence of pre-conquest practices, probably accounts for the decline of missionary scholarship in ethnohistory and linguistics after the time of Sahagún.

Throughout the colonial era, but especially in the sixteenth century, the Inquisition *procesos* reveal fascinating data on the use of idolatry, sorcery, and sacrifice within a political context of native resistance to Spanish power. In general, Indians attempted to manipulate inquisitional procedures by denouncing Spanish-appointed *caciques* of idolatry in order to deprive them of office. There were also denunciations for idolatry and human sacrifice by Indians who wanted to attack their own political enemies, hoping to replace them in the new political hierarchy. The *procesos* also illuminate subversive activities of Indian sorcerers, curers, witches, and seers who tried to perpetuate old beliefs. Of particular concern to the Mexican Inquisition were groups of native priests and sorcerers who openly defied the "spiritual conquest" by establishing schools or apprenticeships among the young. Indian teachers made a frontal attack on Catholicism and Spanish Catholic culture. They ridiculed the new religion and urged a return to native religious practices. Branded as "dogmatizers" by the inquisitors, these men were considered especially dangerous by the missionary clergy. Thus, the native priesthood preached a counter-culture and a counter-religion, and they took the lead in performing sorceries and sacrifices. They supported the ancient practices of concubinage and bigamy as symbols of resistance to the new religion—and the dogmatizers also ridiculed the Inquisition. Students of ritual humor among the Maya, notably Professor Victoria R. Bricker, in recent times have found survivals of plays and dances performed in jest of the Holy Office. It is obvious that this same set of attitudes impelled native doctors or curers to continue the use of preconquest medicine—and to transmit Aztec, Maya, and Mixtec medical lore to future generations of Indians and mestizos in colonial Mexico.

Obviously, trials of Indians initiated by the Inquisition are peripheral to other documentation about social discontent in sixteenth and seventeenth century Mexico, but they are reliable bench marks of what was taking place. Trials of all genre of *mestizos*, *pardos*, and others are indicative of developing syncretism, accommodation, and resistance to the culture of the conqueror. But most resistance to the Spanish social structure probably came in more passive ways—however much some writers would like to link forced acculturation with Indian rebellions in colonial Mexico. It is certain that native religion was important in Indian rebellions and that paganism became a catalyst in the upheavals, but documentary studies of causal factors still await scholarly investigation.

Irving A. Leonard's concept of the Baroque is a useful model for the study of colonial Mexican religion, both Spanish-Catholic and syncretic.[4] His delineation of Mexican "Baroque Society" can provide the ethnohistorian with a multiphasic framework for evaluation of beliefs, attitudes, and institutions. Certainly, his view of the hybrid population, underscored by Magnus Morner's discussion of the Societies of Castes,[5] deserves to be tested and documented by studies of religious syncretism and nativism, so that historians can perceive the degree of truth to his contention that the hybrid population was miserable, ignorant, and exploited, and that

> their neglect and superstition made them a ready prey to a swarm of sorcerers and quacks who practiced magic rites and the black arts inherited from African and Indian barbarism. Faith in witchcraft, illuminati, animism, omens, charms, astrology, and the occult flourished in all castes and classes, including the dominant whites. Baroque, in-

---

[4]Irving A. Leonard, *Baroque Times in Old Mexico: Seventeenth Century Persons, Places and Practices* (Ann Arbor: University of Michigan Press, 1967).
[5]Magnus Morner, *Race Mixture in the History of Latin America* (Boston: Little, Brown, 1967).

deed, does this profusion of ethnological detail, intricate hierarchy, and superstitious credulity of a New World society appear. . . .[6]

What seems clear from the Inquisition papers is that one must examine hundreds of actual trials before generalizations on nativism and syncretism in colonial Mexico can be valid. Anthropological and historical literature based on other sources viewed the clash of Mesoamerican and Spanish religions from different points of view. Bradley W. Case aptly characterizes the two major schools of thought:

> One school emphasized the compromise made by the diverse cultures of colonial Mexico to reach a common ground which could be shared by all and, at the same time, served as a mechanism of acculturation and social control for imperial Spain. The other school considered the acculturation of native American and African cultures to the Spanish world view to be minimal. The adherents to the latter view were convinced that the conquered peoples dwelling in Mexico merely worshipped their old gods using Spanish forms, because this was the easiest way for them to maintain cultural continuity with their past. For these writers, therefore, religious syncretism was a type of passive resistance rather than an accommodation.[7]

Case is certainly correct when he claims that different peoples responded in different ways to forced acculturation, depending upon the given circumstances. Indian Inquisition trials show this to be true.

Successively administered by monastic prelates, bishops, and professional judges in colonial Mexico, the Holy Office of the Inquisition played only a haphazard role in the process of forced acculturation as the native peoples were integrated into Spanish Catholic culture. The degree to which *Procesos de Indios* actually document "cultural repression" is arguable and depends on the many different criteria that might be used for evaluation. After examining masses of documentation on the Church and the Indians of the Valley of Mexico, Charles Gibson concluded:

> What, finally, did the Church accomplish? On the surface, it achieved a radical transition from pagan to Christian life. Beneath the surface, in the private lives and covert attitudes and inner convictions of Indians, it touched but did not remold native habits. Our fullest evidence for pre-conquest survivals derives from modern Indian practices rather than from colonial records, for the latter, however informative in individual incidents, are unsystematic for the whole. Modern Indian society, on the other hand, abundantly and consistently demonstrates a pervasive supernaturalism of pagan origin, often in syncretic compromise with Christian doctrine. Although it cannot really be demonstrated, it may be assumed that the pagan components of modern

---

[6]Leonard, *Baroque Times in Old Mexico*, p. 52.
[7]Bradley W. Case, "Working Paper on Social Discontent in Seventeenth Century Mexico" (Ithaca, N.Y.: Cornell University, 1974).

Indian religions have survived in an unbroken tradition to the present day.[8]

It is certain that the Mexican Holy Office of the Inquisition was no more successful than the larger structure of the Spanish Church in forcing the Indians to acculturate. The *Procesos de Indios* are important milestones in that imperfect process.

Jews, Protestants, and Foreigners

Europeans in the Mexican colony were the major concern of the Inquisition in the sixteenth century.[9] Colonial immigration policies forbade non-Spaniards and non-Catholics from entering the colony, for the most part; however, many foreigners considered by the Holy Office as heretics did find their way illegally into colonial Mexico, often under forged passports and assumed names. Although Lutheranism never constituted a threat to Mexican orthodoxy, fear that its doctrines would undermine the ideological status quo was foremost in the minds of the inquisitors. Lutherans began to be tried in the 1530s, and Calvinists and other Protestants were prosecuted throughout the sixteenth and seventeenth centuries. Many English, French, and Dutch corsairs were brought before the Mexican Inquisition after they were captured while raiding ships or attacking coastal towns. Some of the pirates were executed, while others were sentenced to the galleys or textile *obrajes*.

The *judaizante*, or Jewish pseudo-convert to Catholicism, was a particular problem for the Mexican Inquisition. *Judaizantes* and *conversos* (actual converts to Catholicism) often came to Mexico under aliases to engage in conquest and commercial enterprises, and more importantly to the Inquisition, to practice the Jewish faith in private. Such people had come with Cortés and were tried in the 1520s by the first friar-inquisitors. Their number rapidly increased all over the Mexican viceroyalty, especially in the central valley, Puebla, Nuevo León, and the far northwest. In the last decades of the sixteenth century, members of the famous Carvajal family of Nuevo León were tried for relapsing into Judaism; and several of them, including some women, were burned at the stake. The Holy Office wished to use the Carvajal burnings as a threat to the Jewish community in Mexico; but it failed to eradicate the *judaizantes*, who continued to practice the old religion in private and to proselytize. The size of the Jewish or crypto-Jewish community continued to increase in the seventeenth century despite church and state caveats.

[8]Charles Gibson, *The Aztecs Under Spanish Rule: A History of the Indians of the Valley of Mexico, 1519-1810* (Stanford, Calif.: Stanford University Press, 1964), p. 134.
[9]See Richard E. Greenleaf, *Zumárraga and the Mexican Inquisition, 1536-1543* (Washington, D.C.: Academy of American Franciscan History, 1962).

Many scholars who have written about the Mexican Inquisition over the past few decades have tended to overemphasize the Holy Office's persecution of *judaizantes*. This is not unnatural because the majority of the authors have approached their subject from the perspective of Jewish history rather than Mexican history. As a result, the student of colonial Mexico gets a number of misconceptions. One mistaken impression is that the Inquisition constantly was preoccupied with prosecuting crypto-Jews throughout the colonial period. On the contrary, the vast majority of its cases dealt with breaches of faith and morals of the colonists: blasphemy, bigamy, superstition, doctrinal error, clerical morality, and Indian transgressions.

In-depth investigations in the Inquisition archive lead this writer to believe that there were many more Protestants and Jews in colonial Mexico than is commonly supposed, and the documents hint that only a small number of these ever came before the Holy Office.[10] For the most part, the Inquisition left them alone. Both groups constituted a nebulous subculture in the colony, lending variety to the social scene and to the intellectual milieu. Except when they challenged the Church or Spanish authority in an open manner or when they particularly rankled the Mexican Spaniard as a business competitor or as a political rival, these "heretics" did not appear in the halls of the Inquisition. The Tribunal was so reduced in its concern about Jews and Protestants in the eighteenth century that it tried almost no cases. Instead, the Inquisitors used the Tribunal's bureaucracy as an agency to instruct those who sincerely wished to convert to Catholicism.[11]

Whether the attitude of tolerance, or inaction, or benign neglect vis-à-vis Jews and Protestants as well as towards Catholic transgressions against faith and morals led to the growth of irreligion and massive corruption is a controversial topic. Critics of the Holy Office often espouse this interpretation, but the burden of proof is on them to demonstrate that it was so. To date no professional historian has undertaken the wide-ranging research needed to test this untested generalization.

Scholarly Analysis of the Mexican Inquisition

Scholarly writing on the Holy Office of the Inquisition in Spain or in the colonies poses many problems of research, methodology, and analysis. It is difficult to rid one's self of political and philosophical preconceptions and cultural biases as one begins to interpret such a controversial institution. In this brief discussion, an attempt is made to report on eighteen years of research in Mexican Inquisition

---

[10]See Richard E. Greenleaf, *The Mexican Inquisition of the Sixteenth Century* (Albuquerque: University of New Mexico Press, 1969).

[11]Richard E. Greenleaf, "North American Protestants and The Mexican Inquisition, 1765-1820," *A Journal of Church and State* 8 (Spring 1966): 186-99.

archives and related primary documentation; and the author will grapple with some untested generalizations and interpretations about the Mexican Inquisition as an institution. There are more than 1600 *legajos* of manuscripts in the Mexican Inquisition archive and at least three hundred bundles of Mexican Holy Office materials in Spain. A survey of these documents was completed before the writing of the author's first two books on the Mexican Inquisition in the sixteenth century. This research will result in two final volumes on the Mexican Inquisition in the Baroque Age and the Mexican Inquisition during the Bourbon Century.

There is considerable disagreement among historians over the proper role of religion in colonial Mexican society. Interpretation of the Church is made difficult because of the disagreement. Evaluation of the Inquisition is even more polemical because those who interpret the documents wish to do so from an Enlightenment and twentieth-century standard of political and legal theory, and they insist upon making religious toleration the central focus of their evaluation. Later on this writer will suggest a wider sociological analysis of intolerance that seems more appropriate in understanding the problem.

As a twentieth-century man, the author deplores repressive religious and repressive political institutions; but, as an historian of religious institutions, one feels constrained to view them in a perspective of sixteenth- and seventeenth-century Mexico. Thus it seems fairer to judge the Mexican Inquisition from the vantage point of the prevailing judicial system and ideological structure of Spain and Spanish Catholicism than from the more equalitarian point of view. Some may call this a "White Legend" interpretation, but the writer prefers to see the Inquisition in the "historical present" in much the same way that the anthropologist would view the ethnographic present of the colonial period.

The balance between the safety of society, as defined in a particular historical era, and the dignity and rights of its individual members, as viewed today, was never easy to maintain. In colonial Mexico and in Spain, church, state, the ruling class, and large numbers of the common people felt that preservation of certain ideals was of paramount importance. Today, however, we believe that the interests of society are not necessarily bound up with an ideological status quo; and we contend that it is not enough for the guardian of social institutions to be a man of zeal. He must also be possessed of uncommon good sense and moderation because we feel that if he lacks these, no matter how righteous he knows his cause to be, the problems of liberty and license become a mere exercise in semantics.

But must not the research scholar also proceed with moderation? It appears to this writer (as a Protestant, often a dissenter, and yet still somewhat of an "establishment liberal") that one can believe that suppression of dissent is wrong and yet can examine the Mexican Holy Office of the Inquisition from a professional historian's vantage point with temperance and objectivity. Nevertheless, many scholars find it difficult or politically unacceptable to assume this stance.

Procedure of the Holy Office

In Spain and in Mexico the Holy Office of the Inquisition was an internal security organization charged with protecting a civilization and its culture—culture in its broadest sense: religious, political, and social. Even today the social scientist has great difficulty measuring the effects or the degree of repressiveness of internal security organizations and their procedures. Enlightenment and twentieth-century political philosophy and jurisprudence certainly call into question rules of evidence, procedures, and judicial torture of the Mexican Inquisition. Prior to the legal reformism of Beccaria and the Benthamites, however, the Holy Office operated within a framework of procedures prescribed by canon law; and these procedures were consistent with the rules of law of the era. Examination of thousands of Inquisition trial records has demonstrated to this writer that within the prescribed rules and regulations the Inquisitors acted with zeal but also with fairness and common sense in the vast majority of cases. Again, one must add, this does not mean that we approve of these procedures today.

Critics of the Mexican Inquisition, and of the Spanish government, contend that the mere fact that the Holy Office required denunciations and proceeded with investigations is a good index of repression. Perhaps this argument can be supported on philosophical grounds but it is more difficult to substantiate statistically. As social scientists using techniques of quantification study modern police records, they encounter many of the same problems of analysis facing the investigator in the Inquisition archive. It appears that 95 percent of the total population of colonial Mexico never had any contact with the Inquisition. Of 5 percent who did, 5/6 of them never came to trial because of insufficient evidence; and of that 1/6 who were tried by the Holy Office, perhaps 2 percent were convicted, 1/2 of one percent were subjected to judicial torture, and less than 1/10 of one percent were executed. These figures, while deplorable to the modern man, stand out in stark contrast to the accounts of the gothic writers on the Inquisition who give a very distorted picture of the institution's outreach into society.

Gothic writing on the Holy Office has of course emphasized that the Inquisition "surrounded its operations with extreme secrecy while recording them in meticulous detail," a procedure which some modern scholars feel led to the lurid myths about all phases of inquisitorial activities.[12] It is perhaps true that obsession with secrecy fostered lurid myths about the Holy Office; but because the greater part of viceregal operations took place in a climate of extreme confidentiality, it appears that this interpretation has been exaggerated. Certainly, Protestant and Jewish historiography of the era contributed much to the distortions and luridness.[13]

The view almost universally held that the Mexican Holy Office prosecuted heretics in order to line its pockets is open to question. Until competent scholars have analyzed many hundreds of volumes of detailed Mexican Inquisition account books and have proved the contrary, Clarence Haring's view that it would be difficult to sustain these charges must be allowed to stand as well as his judgment that "there is no clear evidence that the economic backwardness of the colonies can be ascribed to the Inquisition."[14] Most generalizations about Mexican Inquisition finance have resulted from published data on a financial scandal of the middle of the seventeenth century when a group of impoverished and greedy Inquisitors did indeed try to rob the Jews. However, this writer's preliminary investigations of the account books, and the study done of the scandal by Helen Phipps many decades ago, show that this was an atypical situation and that up until the middle of the seventeenth century the Mexican Holy Office was an impoverished institution.[15] Researches by the author show that wealth of the Tribunal increased after the latter quarter of the seventeenth century and throughout the eighteenth century—but that it did not increase appreciably from judicial fines or confiscation of property of heretics. The Holy Office received property and money in trust and in the wills of the faithful, and the rents and monies were invested by the Tribunal in the same manner that nunneries and other arms of the ecclesiastical establishment invested and increased their properties. As such, the Treasury of the Holy Office was an investment institution serving primarily the economic needs of the creole elite.

Influence of the Mexican Inquisition

In Mexico and in Spain, the phenomenon of intolerance—even

---

[12]See, for instance, Nancy M. Farriss, Review of *The Mexican Inquisition of the Sixteenth Century* by Richard E. Greenleaf, *Hispanic American Historical Review* 50 (August 1970): 588-89.

[13]Consult Philip W. Powell, *Tree of Hate* (New York: Basic Books, 1971), pp. 60-112, passim.

[14]Clarence Haring, *The Spanish Empire in America* (New York: Oxford University Press, 1952), p. 205; see also Greenleaf, *The Roman Catholic Church in Colonial Latin America*, pp. 12-13, passim.

[15]Helen Phipps, "Notes on Medina Rico's 'Visita de Hacienda' to the Inquisition of Mexico," *Todd Memorial Volumes*, 3 vols. (New York: Columbia University Press, 1930), 2: 79-89.

with the presence of the Inquisition—can be studied meaningfully only if intolerance is related to a wide complex of historical circumstances. Henry Kamen has investigated these factors in the Iberian peninsula, and he has concluded that the religious issue was not the most prominent or the most relevant factor.[16] The writer's research suggests that insularity, exclusivism, xenophobia, even racial attitudes, were more important factors than religion in developing the climate of intolerance that prevailed from the fifteenth century to the 1800s. In Mexico as in Spain, the Inquisition was not a tyrannical body imposed on the populace; nor was the Spanish Inquisition a logical outgrowth of Catholicism. Rather, it was a logical expression of prevalent social prejudices. The Tribunal of the Holy Office was neither a "despotic body in control of a hypocritical nation" nor was it by nature primarily anti-Protestant or anti-Jewish.[17]

During Hapsburg times, and until the middle of the eighteenth century in Mexico, the Inquisition found ready support from the ruling elite and from the humble masses. For the most part, the focus of inquisitorial activities was on Indians and foreigners; thus, the Mexican populace regarded the Holy Office as a relatively benign institution that protected society and religion from traitors and fomentors of social revolution. The only real opposition to the Tribunal came from *conversos*, the converted Jews. But even in the matter of the Jews, it should be remembered that anti-Semitism came first and then the Inquisition.

In colonial Mexico, the Tribunal and its agents were never able to effect thought control over either the colonial population or the Indian groups. Studies on colonial printing in Mexico, the book trade, literary production, scientific investigation, and colonial art show that a vital intellectual atmosphere prevailed and that the intellegentsia, both clergy and colonist, read, speculated, and wrote with a degree of freedom not found in Spain during the imperial era. In Mexico, as in Spain, those who wished to read about the new scientific ideas from abroad were allowed to do so, because none of those works ever appeared on the Index of prohibited reading.

Therefore, as an agency of social control the Mexican Inquisition worked as all such agencies do: to constrain but not to intimidate. Generalizations of the more popular writers to the contrary, actual evidence of intimidation is lacking in all but a very few isolated cases. There were debates, theological arguments, and ideological disputes within the clerical establishment, within the universities, and within the military and political bureaucracies—debates which might have led to security investigations in a more rigid intellectual milieu. But

---

[16]Henry Kamen, *The Spanish Inquisition* (New York: New American Library, 1965).
[17]Ibid., p. 293, passim.

in Mexico they did not, at least until the middle of the eighteenth century.

The political role of the Holy Office in eighteenth century Mexico needs serious study.[18] To conclude, as some writers have, that the Holy Office in Mexico declined in power and became decadent in the Bourbon Century (1700 to 1820) because it developed into a political instrument seems fallacious. The Holy Office was a political instrument from the time of its founding in New Spain. Only when Enlightenment publicists and French Revolutionary activists tried to split religion and politics did the distinction between political heresy and religious heresy become clear in Mexico. For the most part, the Mexican Inquisition rejected the idea that politics and religion could be separated. The Holy Office tried heretics as traitors, and traitors were tried as heretics. For the Mexican inquisitors, Enlightenment social and political philosophy was heresy. Actually, the political role of the Holy Office in eighteenth century Mexico tended to strengthen the mission of the Holy Office rather than to produce decadence. In the second half of that century, some of the Mexican clergy and many of the intelligentsia adopted philosophical eclecticism; this tendency revived the mission of the Inquisition to defend orthodoxy and the political system. This same movement in Spain—the attempt by many to use non-Spanish ideas to solve domestic political and economic problems—escalated the Holy Office's activities there and began to net the institution the only articulate and effective criticism it had received since its founding.

In various researches and writings on the Inquisition and the Church in Spain and Mexico, Henry Kamen and this writer have independently reached similar conclusions. Those of the writer are tentative ones; Kamen's are articulated. He views the Holy Office as "an organic function of a corporate whole, inseparable from the social and economic forces which affected the whole body of society."[19] Kamen claims that "the ruling class of Spain was the demiurge of an ideology, which for good or ill, has dominated Spanish society into modern times";[20] and he feels that "this class content in ideology cannot be too strongly emphasized as the main factor in the creation of the closed society of traditional Spain."[21] His research led him to conclude that "wherever it was established, the Inquisition drew its strength from the common people and the nobility over them, who

---

[18]Consult Richard E. Greenleaf, "The Mexican Inquisition and The Enlightenment: 1763-1805," *New Mexico Historical Review* 41 (July 1966): 181-96; and by the same author, "The Mexican Inquisition and the Masonic Movement: 1751-1820," *New Mexico Historical Review* 44 (April 1969): 92-117.

[19]Kamen, *The Spanish Inquisition*, p. 301.
[20]Ibid., p. 305.
[21]Ibid.

together became the steadfast pillars of the traditional order in Spain."[22]

Research in the Mexican Inquisition papers has revealed the relevance of some of Kamen's ideas in the New World. The interesting thing that happened in Mexico, however, was that the ruling class ideology of the creole elite and the common people changed at the turn of the nineteenth century; and with this development, the posture of orthodoxy changed. It became more flexible, more eclectic, and more amenable to attack on the Spanish monarchy from a political standpoint.

Conclusions

Revisionist studies must begin to view the Inquisition as a mirror of the Mexican society in which it ministered rather than as a causal force that brought degeneracy to a civilization. Causal forces are difficult to substantiate, and political and social repressions are difficult to measure. The real importance to the historian of Inquisition trials may not be their religious content but the social and intellectual data which they contain. These data may well provide the social scientist with new viewpoints and revised interpretations within the framework of liberal historiography.

In any event, modern historians—no matter what their political affiliations and religious views—should be willing to do the documentary depth probes, rather than to rely on tired clichés, when they interpret the coercive power of the colonial church. Whatever their findings, the purposes of history will have been served by professionals rather than by polemicists.

[22]Ibid.

6. The Catholic Church in the Mexican Period of New Mexican History: Interpretations and Archival Source Material

GERALD THEISEN, © 1974

Many writers have commented on the immorality of the clergy and the decadence of the Catholic Church in New Mexico from the time of Mexico's Independence until ecclesiastical control was relinquished by the Bishop of Durango in 1851. Professor Theisen discusses some of the factors that have prompted this criticism, and he describes major archival holdings that should be consulted by researchers desiring to conduct an objective study of the Catholic Church in the Mexican period of New Mexican history.

The period of Mexican sovereignty in New Mexico lasted only a generation. Hardly had Mexico achieved independence from Spain when much territory in the North was lost to Anglo expansionists. New Mexico was included in the area ceded by Mexico in the Treaty of Guadalupe-Hidalgo in 1848. Even though United States troops had been in New Mexico since 1846, ecclesiastical control was retained by Mexico's bishop of Durango for five additional years. Thus, the Mexican-controlled Church continued to exist in a period of United States political dominance. Because of this situation, many Anglos ventured opinions relative to the Mexican Catholic Church. One of the earliest such comments appeared in the Santa Fe *Republican*, the first English-language newspaper in New Mexico. An issue published in January 1848 carried an article in which the Mexican clergy were described as exerting the "most baneful domination over the minds of the people."[1]

W. W. H. Davis, who had served as United States Attorney in New Mexico, published in 1857 an unusually thoughtful book en-

[1]January 15, 1848, p. 1.

titled *El Gringo; or, New Mexico and Her People.* Perhaps less critical than others, he nevertheless commented strongly on the Catholic Church and the Mexican clergy. Davis wrote:

> Under the Spanish and Mexican governments no other religion was tolerated, and the rites of the Church were administered with a degree of bigotry and fanaticism almost incredible. The natural consequence of this undisputed sway for near three centuries was the growth of many and serious abuses, some of which have remained to this day, and call loudly for redress. . . . The priests of New Mexico were noted for their corruption, . . . and instead of being teachers of morality they were leaders in vice. Their lascivious pleasures were quite as public and notorious as their priestly duties, and there was hardly a priest in the country who did not rear a family of illegitimate children, in direct violation of his holy vows and the laws of religion and morality.[2]

A number of other nineteenth-century residents of New Mexico also expressed their opinions concerning the character of the Catholic Church during the generation of Mexican sovereignty. Almost without exception, these comments were likewise critical of the Church as it existed under the direction of Mexican clerics. Some of the more significant observations were from Joseph P. Machebeuf. This French priest came to Santa Fe in 1851 as Vicar-General to assist Bishop Jean Baptiste Lamy in his efforts to assume ecclesiastical control of New Mexico. Upon arrival, Machebeuf revealed his preconceived ideas concerning the Mexican Church in New Mexico:

> This is a country of ancient Catholicity, but, alas, how times have changed! Instead of piety and practical religion which marked the days of the Mission, we now have but the forms and the exterior of religion. . . . But, alas! the great obstacle to the good which the Bishop is disposed to do among them, does not come from the people but from the priests themselves, who do not want the Bishop, for they dread a reform in their morals, or a change in their selfish relations with their parishioners. One of the great neglects of the priests of New Mexico is that they seldom or never preach. But how could such priests preach?[3]

One of the most vocal denunciations of the Mexican clergy came from a native New Mexican. In 1856, Miguel A. Otero contested the reelection of José Manuel Gallegos as Delegate to Congress. Gallegos was a former Mexican priest who had been elected in spite of the active support that Bishop Lamy had given to the defeated Otero. In testimony taken by a congressional investigating committee, Otero characterized the Catholic Church at the time of Lamy's arrival as having "sunk into the most deplorable condition of immorality. The priests themselves were notoriously addicted to the grossest vices.

---

[2]W. W. H. Davis, *El Gringo; or, New Mexico and Her People* (New York: Harper and Bros., 1857), pp. 227, 229.

[3]Letter of 1851 as reprinted in W. J. Howlett, *Life of the Right Reverend Joseph P. Machebeuf, D. D.* (Pueblo, Colo.: Franklin Press Co., 1908), pp. 164-65.

They were, in many instances, the disgrace of every gambling house and drinking saloon, and open frequenters of the brothels. In a word, they personified vice in all its hideous and revolting aspects."[4]

It is just such comments as these which have been responsible for creating a Black Legend concerning the Catholic Church in New Mexico during the period of Mexican administration. Scarcely a secondary work dealing with Southwestern history in the period fails to mention the "decadent Church."[5] Certainly the observations of Josiah Gregg in his *Commerce of the Prairies* (1844) have had their input into this generalization.[6] However, it has not been historical works which have popularized this conception. Credit for this accomplishment must be given to Willa Cather. In her novel *Death Comes for the Archbishop*,[7] she succeeded in creating the picture of two totally pious French priests correcting the excesses of certain Mexican clergymen who had almost no redeeming qualities.

It is not my intent to suggest that these nineteenth-century observers were totally mistaken in their judgments of the Mexican Church and the Catholic clergy in New Mexico. One should remember, however, that all these authors were writing from a position that placed them in opposition to the Mexican clergy. Many of the native priests actively opposed the United States' occupation of New Mexico and resented the Anglos and their French bishop. As a result, these newly arrived residents and their Hispanic allies, such as Miguel A. Otero, sought to expose what they thought to be a corrupt institution. Moreover, their comments are based upon opinion and not upon a thorough examination of historical facts.

It is my purpose to outline major archival holdings that can serve as the basis for a reexamination of the role of the New Mexican Catholic Church and clergy during the Mexican period. Familiarity with these sources stems from my research for a biography of José Manuel Gallegos (1815-75), a Mexican cleric who, after the arrival of Lamy, left the priesthood and devoted himself to politics.

The archive that has preserved some of the day-to-day material necessary to construct a picture of the Church in Mexican New Mexico is that of the Archdiocese of Santa Fe.[8] Using documents in this

---

[4]*Congressional Globe*, July 23, 1856, p. 1734.
[5]Howard Roberts Lamar, *The Far Southwest, 1846-1912: A Territorial History* (New York: W. W. Norton, 1970), p. 29.
[6]"The padres themselves are foremost in most of the popular vices of the country: first at the fandango—first at the gaming table—first at the cock-pit—first at bacchanalian orgies—and by no means last in the contractions of those liaisons which are so emphatically prohibited by their vows." Josiah Gregg, *Commerce of the Prairies: The Journal of a Santa Fe Trader* (1844; reprint ed., Dallas, Tex: Southwest Press, 1933), p. 173.
[7]Willa Cather, *Death Comes for the Archbishop* (New York: Alfred A. Knopf, 1927).
[8]Fray Angélico Chávez, *Archives of the Archdiocese of Santa Fe* (Washington, D. C.: Academy of Franciscan History, 1957).

archive as a basis, it is possible to demonstrate that isolation experienced in the Mexican period was not as complete as it had been at the turn of the nineteenth century. At that time the New Mexican representative stressed "the neglect and isolation of the province" in his 1812 *Exposición* to the Spanish Cortes.[9] After independence, both the Franciscan superior and later the diocesan vicar often sought to make their people aware of the political struggles within central Mexico. On one occasion, Juan Rafael Rascón gave public thanksgiving upon the capture of Vicente Guerrero. Two years later, in 1833, Juan Felipe Ortiz issued a circular concerning the San Felipe law by which the Mexican government ended the legal obligation to render tithes to the Church. Disregarding the question of clerical involvement in politics, this shows that the ranking clerics in New Mexico sought to give leadership necessary to end the isolation by involving New Mexicans in the national life of Mexico.[10]

There is other archival material which supports the supposition that New Mexico was less isolated in the Mexican period than it had been during the years of Spanish sovereignty. In 1760 Bishop Pedro Tamarón y Romeral undertook an official *visita* to New Mexico in an effort to exert his ecclesiastical jurisdiction over the area. Over the more than sixty years that remained before Mexican independence, extant documents do not record the visit of another bishop.[11] In the Mexican period, however, Bishop José Antonio Laureano de Zubiría y Escalante made three *visitas* to New Mexico during the twenty years that the area was under his jurisdiction. Certainly, this can be taken as an indication that Bishop Zubiría sought to bring New Mexico out of the isolation experienced in the colonial period. It should be noted, nevertheless, that the bishop's efforts to strengthen New Mexican Catholicism were not always successful. At times his attempts to exert authority met with an unresponsive laity. For example, after his *visita* of 1845, Zubiría expressed disappointment that abuses noted during his previous *visita* had yet to be corrected.[12]

It was Bishop Zubiría who personally supervised much of the training undergone by New Mexican students at the diocesan seminary in Durango. This is illustrated by the example of José

[9]Pedro Bautista Pino, "Exposición sucinta y sencilla de la Provincia del Nuevo-México: Hecha por su diputado en Cortés," in *Three New Mexico Chronicles*, trans. H. Bailey Carrol and J. Villasana Haggard (Albuquerque, N.M.: The Quivira Society, 1942), p. 35.

[10]See Gerald Theisen (ed.), "Opinions on the Newly Independent Mexican Nation: Documents from the Archives of the Archdiocese of Santa Fe, New Mexico, 1820-43," *Revista de Historia de América*, 72 (July-November 1971), 484-96.

[11]In his Exposición, Pino argued for the creation of a bishopric in New Mexico. Although the Cortés issued such a decree in 1813, it did not become a fact until 1853. See *Three New Mexico Chronicles*, pp. 50-53, 188-89n; and Archives of the Archdiocese of Santa Fe (AASF), Loose Documents, 1853, no. 12.

[12]AASF, Books of Patents, 1845.

Manuel Gallegos. Through an examination of his ordination file, it is clear that Gallegos was in close contact with his bishop during his three years of study.[13] Such personal attention apparently served to give Bishop Zubiría a great deal of rapport with his priests. This was certainly true regarding Gallegos. Even after he had been dismissed from his duties by Bishop Lamy, Gallegos continued a warm correspondence with Bishop Zubiría. In 1854, while he was serving as Delegate to Congress in Washington, D. C., Gallegos wrote to Durango giving his former bishop personal impressions of the eastern United States and of American Catholicism.[14]

Other priests in New Mexico also maintained direct contact with their bishop. This is certainly true of Juan Felipe Ortiz, whose term as vicar coincided almost exactly with Bishop Zubiría's period of jurisdiction over New Mexico. In this position, as the bishop's representative within New Mexico, Vicar Ortiz made *visitas* in order to oversee properly the state of religion in the area.[15] On occasion various parish priests also communicated directly with Bishop Zubiría. For example, from his church in Taos, Antonio José Martínez wrote to the bishop and commented upon the arrival of Lamy as well as upon the poor situation caused by locusts and drought.[16] Thus, the clergy of New Mexico was not isolated from the influence of Bishop Zubiría. Even priests such as Antonio José Martínez, who had studied in Durango before the bishop assumed control, had an obvious rapport with their ecclesiastical superior in Durango.

In the last decade of the Mexican period, many inhabitants of New Mexico were becoming less patriotic toward their native Mexico. This can be partially explained by such realities as the economic pull resulting from the Santa Fe trade. Throughout this period, however, the clergy as a group remained active supporters of the Mexican Republic. In fact, such priests as José Manuel Gallegos were called upon to loan money to the government in Santa Fe so that it could meet various operating expenses.[17] Perhaps their years of study at the seminary in Durango gave these priests this deep loyalty to the national government. Certainly, their patriotism presents another focus for a reevaluation of the role of the clergy in the Mexican period.

It would seem clear that the archive at the Archdiocese of Durango contains much material relevant to a study of the Catholic Church in New Mexico.[18] Not only are there files on each priest who

[13] Archives of the Archdiocese of Durango, Mexico (AAD), Ordenes: Gallegos, 1839.
[14] AASF, Loose Documents, 1854, no. 7.
[15] For example, see AASF, Books of Patents, 1845.
[16] AASF, Loose Documents, 1851, no. 13.
[17] State Records Center and Archives (SRCA), Mexican Archives of New Mexico (MANM), Governor's Papers, July 12, 1840; and Alvarez Papers, SRCA, 1839-48 Ledger, February 13, 1845.
[18] The library of the University of Texas at El Paso has microfilm copies of these documents.

studied at the seminary, but there also exists a great amount of correspondence pertaining to New Mexico. Proportionately, a large percentage of the documents dates from the Mexican period, with decreasing amounts of material dating from earlier periods. This is as might be expected, because prior to the nineteenth century, there were few priests from Durango in New Mexico. In 1820, for example, twenty-three of twenty-eight priests were Fransciscan friars.[19]

After the independence of Mexico, many European-born Spaniards were expelled from the Republic. Most of the Franciscans serving in New Mexico were affected, and gradually their number dwindled. This loss drastically altered the structure of the Church within the territory, because there were not enough secular priests for replacements. Those friars who did manage to remain were treated with distrust and their effectiveness was limited. In 1826, Agustín Fernández San Vicente, Vicar from the Cathedral of Durango, made an official *visita* to New Mexico. He was under specific instructions from President Guadalupe Victoria to investigate both moral and political actions of the Franciscans and to determine the number of Europeans still among them.[20] By the end of the Mexican period, no friars remained in the territory.

On his *visita* in 1833, Bishop Zubiría lamented the fact that the priests were forced to endure difficult conditions due to the lack of clergy.[21] Unfortunately, he was able to do little. Zubiría had only recently taken over the vacant See of Durango; and since the period of Mexican independence, education and ordination of secular priests had been disrupted. Thus, there were too few priests available in other parts of the diocese to allow a significant number of transfers to New Mexico. Also, the loss of the Franciscans came so suddenly that there had not been enough time to recruit and train an adequate number of native clergy. The pastor in Taos, Antonio José Martínez, had established a school; and throughout much of the Mexican period he prepared young men to enter the seminary in Durango. When Bishop Lamy arrived in 1851, however, there were only fifteen priests to minister to a Catholic population estimated by Vicar-General Machebeuf to total 70,000.[22] Any criticism of the Mexican clergy must consider the impossible task that confronted these men. They were without the resources of Bishop Lamy and thus unable to accomplish dramatic progress. The abrupt decrease in the number of priests in New Mexico and the corresponding detrimental effect upon the

[19]AASF, Books of Accounts, Book LXII.
[20]AASF, Loose Documents, 1826, no. 16.
[21]AASF, Books of Marriages, M-35. The previous year Antonio Barreiro in his *Ojeada sobre Nuevo-México* had mentioned the hardships this shortage forced the people to endure; also he had suggested the establishment of the bishopric. See *Three New Mexico Chronicles*, pp. 53-55.
[22]Letter of 1851 as reprinted in Howlett, *Life of Machebeuf*, p. 164.

Church were matters beyond the control of these few clerics and their bishop in Durango. This consideration would seem to form part of a basis for a reinterpretation of the Black Legend of New Mexican Catholicism during this period.

In addition to various administrative documents contained in the archdiocesan archives in both Durango and Santa Fe, there is a large body of other source material pertinent to a study of the Church in this period of New Mexican history. For example, the Biblioteca Nacional de México in Mexico City houses a sizeable collection of Franciscan documents concerning New Mexico during these years of the nineteenth century. Also notable are the various surviving official papers for the period of Mexican administration. These are housed at the State Records Center and Archives of New Mexico and in government depositories in Mexico, especially the Archivo General de la Nación. While some significant collections remain under individual ownership, other such private papers have been deposited at various centers. These include the Henry E. Huntington Library and Art Gallery, the Bancroft Library, the University of New Mexico's Zimmerman Library, and the State Records Center and Archives in Santa Fe.

It is hoped that this brief presentation suggests the wealth of archival material available for a scholarly study of the Church in the Mexican period of New Mexican history. A topic as significant as this deserves an evaluation that is objective, rather than one based upon contemporary opinions of those all too involved in the events of the times.

CHAPTER 7

The Cristero Rebellion, 1926-1929: A Violent Chapter in the History of Church-State Relations in Mexico

Roberto Cortés

This essay is based on the author's more extensive work, "The Role of the Catholic Church in Mexico's Cristero Rebellion, 1926-1929" (M.A. thesis, Baylor University, 1969). Professor Cortés describes the role of the Catholic episcopacy in the religious insurrection, comments on the scope of military operations during three years of guerrilla warfare, gives special attention to military and diplomatic events involved in the last stages of the armed revolt, and analyzes the results of the *modus vivendi* negotiated by leaders of church and state.

Mexico's Catholic clergy opposed the Revolution that began in 1910; and the anti-clerical provisions of the Constitution of 1917 (especially Articles 3, 5, 27, and 130) provoked similar opposition. Not until the administration of President Plutarco Elías Calles (1924-1928), however, did the federal government begin to enforce the Constitution's religious restrictions and to encourage development of the schismatic Orthodox Catholic Apostolic Mexican Church. On March 14, 1925, militant Catholic laymen responded to Calles' policies by organizing the National Religious Defense League (later known as the National League of Religious Liberty) for the purpose of "detaining the enemy and reconquering religious liberty and other liberties that are derived from it."[1]

Ten months later, on January 27, 1926, Mexico City's *El Universal* published an article announcing that the Catholic Church would

---
[1] For the text of the League's program, see Miguel Palomar y Vizcarra, *El caso ejemplar mexicano*, 2d ed. (México, D.F.: Editorial Jus, 1966), pp. 144-47.

begin a campaign against laws that it considered to be unjust. Archbishop Mora y del Río confirmed this information in an interview that was published in the same newspaper on February 4. Subsequently, his attorney denied that the archbishop had been correctly quoted; but on February 8 the Mexican episcopacy (including Mora y del Río) issued a collective protest against the Constitution's religious provisions. In the months that followed, actions by national and state governments resulted in deportation of foreign-born clergy, closure of convents and parochial schools, limitations on the number of clergy allowed to function, and requirements that ministers of all religious organizations register with civil authorities. In response, the National Religious Defense League called for a national boycott of commercial activity; and with the approval of the Pope, the Mexican episcopacy announced that religious services would be suspended throughout the country, beginning on August 1. Thus, by the end of the summer of 1926, Mexico was on the brink of a civil war.[2]

Role of the Catholic Episcopacy

Apparently convinced that negotiations with the Calles government would have little or no chance of success, and influenced by the League's increasing agitation for use of force, the Mexican episcopacy sent a committee of bishops to Rome for the purpose of securing papal approval for a resort to arms. Composed of Monsignors José María González y Valencia, Emeterio Valverde y Téllez, and Jenaro Méndez del Río, the committee left Mexico on September 19, 1926, and arrived in Rome on October 27. When the Pope received the Mexican prelates, he informed them that an encyclical was to be written on religious persecution in their country. As for the attitude of the Vatican with regard to armed conflict, the Pope was clear: "We cannot remain impartial, we must always be on the side of justice." Nevertheless, when Secretary of State Gasparri was asked if Church funds could be used to support an insurrection, he advised the committee that only money not designated for the performance of masses and other rites should be utilized. But Gasparri added that if he were a Mexican bishop, he would sell his jewelry to help the cause.[3]

The encyclical promised by the Pope was made public on November 18. Entitled "Concerning the Calamitous Conditions of the Catholic Religion in Mexico" and referred to as *Iniquis afflictisque*, the papal pronouncement condemned "the Mexican government's implacable hatred against religion" as manifested in its evil and op-

---

[2]See J. Lloyd Mecham, *Church and State in Latin America: A History of Politico-Ecclesiastical Relations* (Chapel Hill: University of North Carolina Press, 1934), pp. 476-93.

[3]Antonio Rius Facius, *México cristero: Historia de la ACJM, 1925 a 1931* (México, D.F: Editorial Patria, 1960), pp. 160-62.

pressive restrictions. Referring to the refusal of the Calles regime to heed the protests and petitions of the Church, the Pope concluded:

> Nothing more remains, venerable brothers, but that we ask and implore of Our Lady and Celestial Patroness of the Mexican Nation, Santa María de Guadalupe, that pardoning the injuries committed against her, she may deign to grant to her people the return of peace and harmony; but if as a result of the mysterious design of God that greatly desired day is far off, that She shall wish to comfort the hearts of the faithful Mexicans and to strengthen them so that they may continue struggling on behalf of their freedom to profess the [Catholic] Religion.[4]

Although the Pope did not exhort Mexican Catholics to rebel against the government, it is significant that he took pains to praise those Catholic lay organizations that were most militant in their opposition to the government. The Pontiff asserted:

> With most singular praise we pay tribute to the Catholic associations that in the present conflict maintain themselves as an auxiliary militia on the flank of the Clergy.... And this is true of all, but we wish to say something about the principal associations so that each one of them may know that it is vehemently approved and praised by the Vicar of Jesus Christ.... We refer also to the National Defense League of Religious Liberty, which was finally instituted when it appeared clearer than the sun that an immense accumulation of evils menaced Catholic life. Having extended itself throughout the Republic, its members work harmoniously and assiduously with the end of directing and instructing all Catholics to oppose their adversaries with a most solid and united front.

And concerning the work of the Union of Catholic Women and the Catholic Action of Mexican Youth (*Acción Católica de la Juventud Mexicana*, ACJM), the Pope commented: "In effect, both to these associations second and support, and make others second and support, in all parts the initiative taken by the cited National Defense League of Religious Liberty."[5]

Only eight days after publication of *Iniquis afflictisque*, a memorable meeting took place on the afternoon of November 26 when sixteen members of the episcopacy conferred in Mexico City with League representatives Lic. Rafael Ceniceros y Villarreal, Miguel Palomar y Vizcarra, and Luis G. Bustos. On this occasion the episcopacy was presented with the League's "Memorial" requesting positive support that would consist of episcopal action designed to influence public opinion to accept armed rebellion as "lawful, laudable, meritorious, and legitimate." Also, the "Memorial" asked for appointment of

---

[4]For this portion of the encyclical, see Joaquín Blanco Gil [Andres Barquín y Ruiz], *El clamor de la sangre* (México, D.F.: Editorial "Rex-Mex," 1947), p. 421.

[5]This part of the encyclical is quoted in Palomar y Vizcarra, *El caso ejemplar mexicano*, pp. 149-59.

military chaplains to serve with rebel forces according to canon law; and it requested that the prelates should encourage rich Catholics to make financial contributions to the Cristero cause.[6]

After studying the "Memorial," on November 30 Archbishop Ruiz y Flores and Bishop Díaz y Barreto presented the episcopacy's reply to representatives of the Directing Committee of the League. While recognizing the legitimacy of the revolt, the episcopacy was not prepared to undertake the task of soliciting financial support for the struggle from the wealthy. With regard to the matter of military chaplains, the League representatives were informed that individual priests desiring to minister to the Cristero forces in the field could seek permission from their bishops.[7]

By the end of November 1926, at a time when some Cristero groups were already in the field, the League had been praised publicly by the Pope and had been assured by the Mexican Episcopacy that resort to arms would be considered legitimate. Therefore, the League took final steps to mobilize all Catholic lay organizations for the impending armed struggle against the Calles regime. Reliable statistics concerning the size of the League's membership are not available. One Catholic writer has stated that by August 1, 1926, the League had extended its organization into all parts of Mexico and that more than 300,000 members were enrolled in Mexico City alone.[8] Regardless of what the membership was, certainly only a small percentage took part in the actual fighting, because, in all probability, there were never more than 20,000 Cristeros in the field at any time between 1926 and 1929.[9] During this particular era, Mexico's total population amounted to roughly 16,000,000.[10] The League did not restrict its activities to Mexico. For the purpose of obtaining support for the Cristero cause in Europe, the International Union of Honorary Members of the League was organized. Another European group was founded by Antonio

---

[6]The "Memorial" is printed in Alicia Olivera Sedano, *Aspectos del conflicto religioso de 1926 a 1929: Sus antecedentes y consecuencias* (México, D.F: Instituto Nacional de Antropología e Historia, 1966), p. 133.

[7]For accounts of this meeting, see ibid., pp. 134-37; Alberto María Carreño, *El arzobispo de México, exmo, Sr. Dr. Don Pascual Díaz, y el conflicto religioso*, 2d ed. (México, D.F.: Ediciones Victoria, 1943), pp. 92-106; Rius Facius, *México cristero*, pp. 153-55; and James and Edna Wilkie, *México visto en el siglo xx: Entrevistas de historia oral* (México, D.F.: Instituto Mexicano de Investigaciones Económicas, 1969), pp. 442-43.

[8]Aquiles P. Moctezuma [Eduardo Iglesias], *El conflicto religioso de 1926: Sus orígenes, su desarrollo, su solución*, 2d ed., 2 vols. (México, D.F: Editorial Jus, 1960), 2: 379.

[9]See James W. Wilkie, "The Meaning of the Cristero Religious War Against the Mexican Revolution," *A Journal of Church and State* 7 (Spring 1966): 230.

[10]Charles C. Cumberland, *Mexico, The Struggle for Modernity* (New York: Oxford University Press, 1968), p. 367. This rough estimate is derived from census totals of 14,334,000 for 1921 and 16,553,000 for 1930.

López Ortega and titled International Union of Friends of the League, commonly referred to as VITA.[11]

The importance of the League in preparing the way for rebellion, in disseminating propaganda (handbills, pamphlets, stickers, and even balloons carrying anti-government statements), and in supplying and equipping guerrilla bands, cannot be underemphasized. Most important of all, however, was the role that the League played as an intermediate link between the Vatican and the Mexican episcopacy, on one hand, and the Cristero troops in the field, on the other hand. Without assuming responsibility for directing the rebellion against the Mexican government, the Catholic hierarchy was able to exercise a controlling influence over Catholic laymen, both combatants and non-combatants, who were directly involved.

Guerrilla Warfare

Although small skirmishes between rebelling Catholics and government forces took place in Zacatecas during August 1926, the origin of the Cristero Rebellion is commonly traced to the taking of the town of Pénjamo in the state of Guanajuato. Luis Navarro Origel led the attack and has come to be known as the "First Cristero." Educated in the Conciliar Seminary of Morelia, Navarro was greatly impressed by the writings of the Spanish mystics, Santa Teresa de Jesús and San Juan de la Cruz. In his correspondence he mentioned frequently the possibility of being shot and dying for Christ.[12]

After entering public life at an early age, he was elected as mayor of Pénjamo while only twenty-four years old. However, he soon abandoned that office at about the same time that he participated in founding a unit of the ACJM in that city. Accompanied by three brothers (Jesús, Manuel, and Ignacio) and a few friends, Navarro took Pénjamo in a surprise attack on September 29, 1926; however, this victory was short-lived because federal forces expelled the rebels on the following day. Subsequently, Navarro retreated into Michoacán where he allied himself with two notorious bandits, Serapio Cifuentes and "El Perro" Ibáñez. For a period of two years, until killed in battle on August 10, 1928, the former mayor of Pénjamo succeeded in inflicting heavy casualties on Mexican army forces in the Michoacán-Guanajuato area. Most of his troops were peasants, who could be depended upon for service for several months each year, but who often slipped away to their fields during the rainy season to plant crops.[13]

Until the last days of the rebellion, the most secure stronghold of

---

[11]Blanco Gil, *El clamor de la sangre*, p. 16. See also, "Organización mundial filial de la Liga N.D. de la L. Religiosa," *David* 1 (August 1952): 6.

[12]See Martín Chowell [Alfonso Trueba], *Luis Navarro Origel: El primer cristero* (México, D.F.: Editorial Jus, 1959), pp. 12-26, 92-109.

[13]See ibid., pp. 86-91, 115-49.

the Cristeros was the Colima volcano area that includes not only the state of Colima but also portions of western Michoacán and Jalisco. Led by Dionisio Eduardo Ochoa, Rafaél G. Sánchez, and Antonio C. Vargas, guerrilla bands engaged federal forces in over two hundred skirmishes from January 1926 to July 1929. Familiar with the mountainous terrain, the Cristeros of the volcano region consistently succeeded in harrassing larger bodies of government troops and in raiding agrarian settlements where the people were loyal to the Calles regime. In dealing with this subject, Catholic writers have tended to glorify the Cristeros and to exaggerate the losses of government forces; likewise, pro-government authors have gone to the opposite extreme.[14]

Contrary to the picture that is presented by some writers, Cristero soldiers were not always idealists or fanatics motivated by a religious zeal. Many were unsophisticated country boys who were skillfully recruited by parish priests or by laymen representing the League, the ACJM, or some other Catholic group. Others were discontented peasants who had not shared in the benefits of the government's land reform program. Although few men of wealth were to be found in the Cristero ranks, some owners of large rural estates took up arms to defend their properties from plunder by Mexican army units. On occasion, unscrupulous army officers charged both merchants and landowners with Cristero activity merely to provide an excuse for

[14]Concerning all aspects of the Cristero Rebellion, the most objective treatment is David C. Bailey, ¡Viva Cristo Rey! The Cristero Rebellion and the Church-State Conflict in Mexico (Austin: University of Texas Press, 1974). For the most extensive coverage of the subject, see Jean A. Meyer, La Cristiada (originally presented as a doctoral dissertation at the University of Paris-Nanterre), trans. Aurelio Garzón del Camino, 3 vols: I, La guerra de los Cristeros; II, El conflicto entre la Iglesia y el Estado en México; III, Los Cristeros: Sociedad e ideología (México, D.F.: Siglo Veintiuno Editores, 1973-1974). For one-volume versions of this work, see Meyer's La Christiade: L'Eglise, l'Etat et le Peuple dans la Révolution Mexicaine (Paris: Payot, 1975) and his corresponding version in English, The Cristero Rebellion: The Mexican People Between Church and State, trans. Richard Southern (Cambridge: Cambridge University Press, 1976). A related work, consisting of documents and commentary, is Meyer's Apocalypse et Révolution au Méxique: La guerre des Cristeros (Paris: Gallimard, 1974). For a Marxist interpretation, see Nicolas [Nicolaĭ Sergeevich] Larin, La rebelión de los Cristeros, translation of the original Russian edition, 1965 (México, D.F.: Ediciones Era, 1968). Donald J. Mabry analyzes differing views in "Mexican Anticlerics, Bishops, Cristeros, and the Devout during the 1920s: A Scholarly Debate," Journal of Church and State 20 (Winter 1978): 75-82; and Alicia Olivera de Bonfil describes her research, including oral history interviews, in "La Iglesia en México, 1926-1970," in Contemporary Mexico: Papers of the IV International Congress of Mexican History, ed. James W. Wilkie, Michael C. Meyer, and Edna Monzón de Wilkie (Berkeley: University of California Press, 1976), pp. 295-316. Luis González y González has provided a detailed account of how a village in Michoacán was affected by the Cristero Rebellion: Pueblo en vilo: Microhistoria de San José de Gracia, 2d ed. (México, D.F.: El Colegio de México, 1972), ch. 5; for the English version, see idem, San José de Gracia: Mexican Village in Transition, trans. John Upton (Austin: University of Texas Press, 1974), ch. 5.

seizing merchandise and grain or livestock, or for extorting payments of money as the price for escaping death before a firing squad. At the same time, former bandit elements who were recruited to serve the Cristero cause often continued to practice the crimes to which they had been accustomed. Frequently chosen as targets for Cristero raids were villages to which the Calles regime had donated land taken from large landholders.[15] During the latter months of the conflict, a pro-government force of 15,000 armed peasants commanded by General Saturnino Cedillo was employed successfully in waging counter-guerrilla warfare against the Cristeros.[16]

Last Stages of the Armed Revolt

Throughout 1927 a high level of military activity was maintained by various Cristero bands operating in Central and Southwestern Mexico. By the end of the year, however, the rebel movement showed the weakening effects of loss of many of its more important leaders, lack of unified direction, shortages of supplies, and increased pressure from government forces. Despite these adverse conditions, there were no indications that the rebels were contemplating surrender or that federal forces could suppress the insurrection in a short period of time. According to reports found in the archives of the League, at the end of 1927 major concentrations of Cristero troops were distributed as follows: Pacific coast region of Michoacán, 7,000; Central Michoacán, 1,000; Colima, Jalisco, Nayarit, and southern Zacatecas, 10,000; northern Zacatecas, 500; Aguascalientes, 500; Guanajuato, 800; and State of Mexico, 1,500. Smaller contingents were to be found in Durango, Tlaxcala, Oaxaca, San Luis Potosí, Puebla, Morelos, Sinaloa, Hidalgo, and Guerrero.[17] Neither the sparsely populated desert regions of the North nor the Isthmus of Tehuantepec and other areas of the South were affected by Cristero operations.

With members of the Directing Committee of the League meeting clandestinely in Mexico City, communications with commanders in the field presented serious problems. Capistrán Garza, the Supreme Chief of the Cristero movement, had been occupied in the United States until his dismissal; and throughout 1927 and for most of 1928 there was no military leader empowered to exercise command over all rebel forces. Finally, in October 1928, General Enrique Gorostieta y Velarde, commander of Cristero troops in Jalisco, was named by the League as "Military Chief of the Liberating Movement." Thirty-nine years of age at the time he was placed in command of all Cristero

[15] See Olivera Sedano, *Aspectos del conflicto religioso*, pp. 211-12; and John W. F. Dulles, *Yesterday in Mexico: A Chronicle of the Revolution, 1919-1936* (Austin, Tex.: University of Texas Press, 1961), pp. 310-11.
[16] Wilkie and Wilkie, *Mexico visto en el siglo xx*, p. 505.
[17] Olivera Sedano, *Aspectos del conflicto religioso*, pp. 184-85.

forces, Gorostieta had been educated in Mexico's Military College and had served as an officer under the Huerta government. His successes in directing Cristero operations in Jalisco had resulted in selection as commander-in-chief.[18]

Assuming his new command on October 28, General Gorostieta issued on that date a "Manifesto to the Nation" explaining that the League had seen fit to appoint a "visible chief." The bases of the Cristero program were summarized in fourteen points. Included were provisions for reestablishing the Constitution of 1857 without the Reform Laws, conferring the name "National Guard" upon Cristero military forces, and creating the office of Civil Chief of the Liberating Movement to be filled by appointment of the Directing Committee of the League with the consent of the Military Chief. In conclusion, Gorostieta declared that "victory is near" and he exhorted his followers to strive so that "on all sides and at all hours, only our war cry will be heard: Long live Christ the King! Long live the Virgin of Guadalupe! Death to the bad Government!"[19]

As a result of the assassination of President-elect Alvaro Obregón, it was the constitutional responsibility of the Mexican Congress to name a provisional president who would hold office until another national election could be conducted. Thus, on September 25, 1928, the Senate and Chamber of Deputies chose Emilio Portes Gil, former Secretary of *Gobernación*, to become the nation's chief executive. Also on that day the Congress fixed November 20, 1929, as the date for holding a national election to choose a president to fill out the remainder of Obregón's term.[20]

Although most Mexicans assumed that the election would be conducted in such a way as to guarantee victory for a candidate picked by Calles, on November 10, 1928, Lic. José Vasconcelos announced his candidacy. Speaking at the border town of Nogales, Sonora, Vasconcelos voiced his opposition to the Calles regime and called for an end to the religious strife, "which for years has been tearing out the intestines of the fatherland. . . ." He added, "To feel hatreds for questions of supernatural creeds, or to impose laws that provoke rebellions for reasons of worship, is something so unusual, so sterile and antisocial, that now in none of the civilized nations of the earth—or in the uncivilized—are questions that transcend human reason itself carried to the extreme of bloodshed. . . ."[21] On that same day he commented

---

[18]Ibid., pp. 193-96; and Miguel Palomar y Vizcarra, "Gorostieta," *David* 2 (October 1955): 233-35.

[19]The text of the manifesto is printed in Manuel González Ramírez, ed., *Planes políticos y otros documentos*, vol. 1 of *Fuentes para la Revolución Mexicana* (México, D.F.: Fondo de Cultura Económica, 1954), pp. 280-87.

[20]Dulles, *Yesterday in Mexico*, p. 393.

[21]Portions of this speech are printed in Gustavo Casasola, *Historia gráfica de la Revolución Mexicana, 1900-1960*, 4 vols. (México, D.F.: Editorial F. Trillas, 1962), 3: 1916-17.

that "fanaticism is combatted with books, not with machine guns."[22]

In the course of his campaign, Vasconcelos arrived at Guadalajara on January 27, 1929. He reports that shortly thereafter he was sought out by two men carrying credentials issued by General Gorostieta and bearing an offer of asylum with Cristero forces in the region of Los Altos. According to Vasconcelos, he told the Cristero representatives that he expected to take to the battlefield against the Calles regime but that he would wait until after the election when he could claim to be President-elect. Despite the conviction that the government would not allow him to gain the presidency by peaceful means, Vasconcelos felt certain that the nation would come to his support once he raised the standard of revolt. Thus, he wrote that he told Gorostieta's men, "Tell the general that after the election I shall escape toward his camp."[23] (Before the election was held, however, Gorostieta was killed and the Cristero revolt ended.)

On March 1, 1929, supporters of former President Calles gathered at Querétaro to organize a new political party and to nominate a presidential candidate. Consequently, the Mexican Revolutionary Party came into existence; and on March 3, Pascual Ortiz Rubio was nominated. That same day news reached Querétaro that General Jesús M. Aguirre had rebelled in Veracruz; also, it became known that a group of generals (all of whom had been close associates of Obregón) had signed the Plan of Hermosillo proclaiming themselves in revolt and recognizing General José Gonzalo Escobar as Supreme Chief of the movement. With almost 30,000 men—or about a quarter of the troops in the army, including most of those forces in the northern part of the country—these elements, if allied with the Cristeros, would have posed a most serious threat to Portes Gil's government.[24] In fact, some two weeks before the Plan of Hermosillo was issued, persons connected with the League's Directing Committee met with General Escobar and drew up a pact which later was approved by General Gorostieta.[25] The Plan of Hermosillo denounced Calles as "the Jew of

[22] Alfonso Taracena, *Mi vida en el vértigo de la Revolución Mexicana* (México, D.F.: Ediciones Botas, 1936), p. 607.

[23] José Vasconcelos, *El proconsulado*, 3d ed. (México, D.F.: Ediciones Botas, 1946), p. 116. In another of his autobiographical works, Vasconcelos wrote: "The most distinguished of all the rebel chiefs, Gen. Gorostieta, . . . had promised his support. . . ." See *La Flama: Los de arriba en la Revolución: Historia y tragedia* (México, D.F.: Compañía Editorial Continental, 1959), p. 196.

[24] Dulles, *Yesterday in Mexico*, pp. 427-32, 442.

[25] Rius Facius, *Mexico cristero*, p. 413. Another account of the Escobar revolt indicates that direct negotiations between Escobar and Gorostieta took place in Mexico City. Ricardo Topete, brother of General Fausto Topete who was also a signer of the Plan of Hermosillo, made the following statement to José C. Valadés, publisher of *La Prensa* of San Antonio, Texas: "The thing improved when Fausto, my brother, won over General Enrique Gorostieta. The Cristeros were very suspicious, but since Fausto is a strong Catholic, it seems that they believed him; consequently, Gorostieta went to Mexico City to talk with General José Gonzalo Escobar, who named him Chief of the Army Corps of

the Revolution" and charged him with planning to impose his puppet in the presidency. Also, for the purpose of appealing to Cristero elements for support, the Plan condemned "the massacre of fellow countrymen in the states of Jalisco, Colima, and Michoacán for the simple reason that they claim the sacred right on which liberty of conscience is based."[26]

Shortly after the Plan of Hermosillo was proclaimed, Gorostieta issued Circular Order No. 5 explaining to his forces the reasons why he had accepted the pact with Escobar. First, he pointed out that the agreement guaranteed full freedom of religion and of education; and, second, it recognized the National Guard as a military entity.[27] To strengthen his appeal to the Cristeros, on March 12 General Escobar issued a decree abolishing both the Article 130 Regulating Law and the Calles Law.[28] That this decree had an immediate effect is indicated by a March 13 message from General Francisco R. Manzo to Escobar, which stated: "Numerous groups previously taking up arms against the Calles regime, and for reasons of circumstances, unfurling the religious flag, have adhered to the revolution, accepting the fact that the revolutionary movement is essentially secular and will restore with all its purity the basic principles of liberalism which are freedom of conscience, freedom of worship, and the secular state—principles violated by the reactionary Calles regime which, in fact, has converted itself into a religious government by intervening directly in the internal affairs of religious sects."[29]

Because both Vasconcelos and the rebels who proclaimed the Plan of Hermosillo had been associated closely with Obregón, it appears that Gorostieta and the League must have dealt with them out of sheer desperation. Due to its armed strength, the Escobar movement held forth the promise of badly needed military assistance; however, under the personal direction of Calles, who was named by Portes Gil as Secretary of Defense at the outbreak of the revolt, columns of loyal troops under the command of General Lázaro Cárdenas and General Juan Andreu Almazán soon smashed the rebel forces. By the begin-

---

Central Mexico." Published in *La Prensa*, August 11, 1929, this account is printed in Froylán C. Manjarrez, *La jornada institucional*, pt. 2: *La crisis de la violencia* (México, D.F.: Talleres Gráficos Editorial, 1939), p. lix.

[26]For the text of the Plan of Sonora, see González Ramírez, *Planes políticos*, pp. 295-300.

[27]A portion of the text of Circular Order No. 5 is printed in Rius Facius, *Mexico cristero*, pp. 413-14.

[28]See Escobar's press release of March 12, 1929, printed in Manjarrez, *La jornada institucional*, pt. 2, pp. xliii-xliv.

[29]This telegram is printed in ibid, p. xxxvi. Another of Escobar's generals did not find the Cristeros to be reliable allies. For an account of General Juan Gualberto Amaya's dealings with Colonel Aurelio R. Acevedo during the period of March 11-13, 1929, see Amaya's *Los gobiernos de Obregón, Calles y regímenes "peleles" derivados del callismo* (México, D.F: n.p., 1947), pp. 256-58, 262-64.

ning of May the revolt had been crushed.[30] At the same time that Escobar's units were being routed, early in April a force of 15,000 irregular armed peasants was sent to Jalisco under the command of General Saturnino Cedillo. Using counter-guerrilla tactics, Cedillo's men scored several successes over Gorostieta's hard-pressed Cristeros in the region of Los Altos.[31] The most important blow was struck on June 2 when a detachment of Cedillo's troops engaged a small group of rebels at El Valle ranch about eighteen miles from Atotonilco. As a result of this skirmish, General Gorostieta was killed.[32]

With the death of Gorostieta, on June 4 the Directing Committee of the League appointed General Jesús Degollado Guízar as Supreme Chief of the National Guard.[33] Three days later the new Cristero commander issued his "Manifesto to the Nation" in which he declared: "I pick up the flag of Christ the King and I swear, before the corpse of General Gorostieta, to continue the struggle until I see our essential liberties won or until I perish in it."[34]

General Degollado's struggle was destined to end within less than three weeks. He did not win and he did not perish. Although hard-pressed by government forces, his guerrilla bands still operated in many states; however, the Vatican and the Mexican episcopacy had decided that there was no chance of victory on the battlefield. Hopes that had been aroused by the Escobar revolt had faded fast as loyal forces crushed the rebelling federal troops. Gorostieta's death was the final blow.

Results of the 'Modus Vivendi'

After coming to terms with Portes Gil,[35] Archbishop Ruiz was faced with the necessity of explaining the need for this action to the

---

[30] See Dulles, *Yesterday in Mexico*, pp. 444-58; and Manjarrez, *La jornada institucional*, pt. 2, passim.

[31] For an account of the Cristero defeat at Tepatitlán on April 19, see portions of Cedillo's report to Secretary of War Calles printed in Manjarrez, *La jornada institucional*, pt. 2, pp. 137-39. Among the Cristeros killed in this encounter was the famous fighting priest, J. Reyes Vega.

[32] Rius Facius, *México cristero*, pp. 425-29. For a firsthand account by a member of Gorostieta's staff who later became a Jesuit priest, see Heriberto Navarete, S.J., *"Por Dios y por la Patria": Memorias de mi participación en la defensa de la libertad de conciencia y culto durante la persecución religiosa en México de 1926 a 1929* (México, D.F.: Editorial Jus, 1961), pp. 242-54.

[33] The text of the communication naming Degollado Guízar to this post is printed in Jesús Degollado Guízar, *Memorias de Jesús Degollado Guízar, último general en jefe del ejercito cristero* (México, D.F.: Editorial Jus, 1957), pp. 265-66.

[34] The manifesto is printed in ibid., pp. 266-67.

[35] Concerning negotiations that led to the modus vivendi, two books are of special importance: Harold Nicolson, *Dwight Morrow* (New York: Harcourt, Brace and Co., 1935); and Elizabeth Ann Rice, *The Diplomatic Relations Between the United States and Mexico, 1925-1929* (Washington, D.C.: Catholic University of America Press, 1959). The best articles on this subject are Edward J. Berbusse, "The Unofficial Intervention of the United States in Mexico's Religious Crisis, 1926-1930," *The Americas* 23 (July 1966): 28-63;

clergy and to all Mexican Catholics, especially those who had risked life and property in support of unsuccessful political and military actions designed to resist, and if possible, to overthrow, the government. On June 25, only four days after concluding negotiations with Portes Gil, the Apostolic Delegate issued a pastoral letter in which he emphasized that the Pope had approved the *modus vivendi*; thus Ruiz stated: "We prelates and priests, by conviction and discipline, agree completely with the High Pontiff; therefore it is just that every sincere Catholic should accept wholeheartedly that which has been agreed upon." Further, he declared, "This arrangement is not in contradiction with that which has been said and taught by the Pope and the Mexican Episcopacy in matters of dogma; . . ." The Papal Delegate reported that the President had been advised that a definitive settlement of the religious question through action by Congress would have been preferred—action based on "a friendly separation between the Church and the State. . . ." This, he explained, would have involved approval of Catholic petitions; and as a result, "with the Church recovering its judicial personality, with her rights and freedoms of association, of worship, of education, of sacraments, and of property necessary for her social functioning—the evils which we deplore would be remedied effectively, and the fatherland would enjoy the blessings of sincere harmony between the Catholic people and the Government." However, Ruiz noted, "This solution not having been possible before resuming public worship, . . . we believed the case foreseen in the instructions of the High Pontiff had arrived, that of seeking an arrangement which, permitting the faithful of the Church to profess their religious belief and to practice legally our Catholic worship, will remedy the evils that the suspension of worship has caused and the even greater evils that would be caused to customs and public morals." While expressing the firm conviction that a definitive solution to the religious question would be reached in time, Ruiz emphasized that "it is not the desire of the Church to impose or to depose governments, nor to declare itself in favor of any political candidate, but rather to strengthen the principle of authority and to accept unquestionably the freedom that it needs from the hands of any government." In conclusion, the Archbishop of Morelia and principal representative of the Vatican in Mexico asserted:

Miguel Cruchaga Tocornal, "El conflicto religioso mexicano," *Revista chilena de historia y geografía* 113 (January-June 1949): 216-55; Ethan Ellis, "Dwight Morrow and the Church-State Controversy in Mexico," *Hispanic American Historical Review* 38 (November 1958): 482-505; Walter Lippmann, "Church and State in Mexico: The American Mediation," *Foreign Affairs* 8 (January 1930): 186-207; Stanley R. Ross, "Dwight Morrow, Ambassador in Mexico," *The Americas* 14 (January 1958): 273-89; and idem, "Dwight Morrow and the Mexican Revolution," *Hispanic American Historical Review* 38 (November 1958): 506-28.

We have offered to cooperate with the Government in all just and moral efforts leading to the welfare and betterment of the people; in order to prove this in practice, the priests and the faithful will take care to heed with docility and self-denial the instructions that the Episcopacy may dictate for the purpose of achieving such an end.

We give thanks to God with all our heart for this step in the pacification of spirits; let us ask Him that he may continue and finish His work, and we shall all cooperate with prayer, with a good example and Christian charity that excludes nobody from the sphere of his love, in order to hasten the day of solid and true peace within the Mexican family, with Most Holy Mary of Guadalupe as its Mother and Lady and with Christ as its Sovereign and its King. All of that we shall obtain from the Holy Spirit, to whom we, the Mexican Prelates, have consecrated our dioceses with all confidence that He will unite us with the sweet ties of Charity.[36]

On June 22, at the same time that Mexico's press was publishing the statements made by Ruiz and Portes Gil on the previous day, the following announcement appeared in *Excelsior,* one of the national capital's leading newspapers: "The Directing Committee of the National Defense League of Religious Liberty declares its unconditional, sincere, and filial submission to the resolutions of His Holiness, Pope Pius XI, with respect to the Mexican religious question, and takes this opportunity to make public its sentiment of respect for and adherence to the Apostolic Delegate and the Mexican Episcopacy."[37] In the days that followed, however, there was much discussion and dissention within League ranks concerning the policy that the organization would pursue.[38] Finally, although it did not end the controversy, on July 12 a broadside entitled *Manifiesto a la Nación* was issued by the organization's Directing Committee. Emphasizing that "neither the Venerable Episcopacy, nor much less, the Holy See, had any responsibility for this armed struggle," the manifesto declared that League and National Guard chiefs must heed the decisions of the Pope regarding the liberties that they should struggle for. It pointed out that because of the recent arrangements made by Portes Gil and the Apostolic Delegate, public worship had been restored; however, note was made of the fact that freedom of "teaching, association, social action, etc." had not been obtained. Nevertheless, the Directing Committee explained, "Because as Catholics we have full confidence in the high and delicate prudence of the Sovereign Pontiff and in his firmness, the League is of the opinion that the decisive moment has arrived for ending the armed struggle, in order to dedicate itself to another class of activities that will always be conducive to the welfare of the Fatherland and to our faith." According to the manifesto, in the

[36] For the full text of the pastoral letter, see Moctezuma, *El conflicto religioso,* 2: 541-44.
[37] Quoted in ibid., p. 548.
[38] See Carreño, *El arzobispo de México,* passim.

future the League would involve itself in a program of "Catholic Action"; in this respect, it was proposed that the League should give special attention to arranging a national referendum for the purpose of petitioning Mexican authorities for changes in the nation's Constitution and laws.[39]

Even before the League's manifesto of July 12, some members of the National Guard, including a few high-ranking officers, surrendered to commanders of Mexican army units. Hearing of the arrangement for resumption of public worship and noting that the morale of his forces was unfavorably affected, General Degollado Guízar made his way to Mexico City for the purpose of conferring with the League's Directing Committee. Here he was informed that he must arrange for the disbanding of the Cristero troops.[40] Represented by Luis Beltrán y Mendoza, who was assisted by Archbishop Ruiz, the general obtained from President Portes Gil acceptance of the following terms: guarantees for the lives of National Guard personnel so that they might return to their homes; similar guarantees for civilians who had aided the movement; release of persons imprisoned for religious reasons, both civilian and military; repatriation of persons exiled for religious reasons; payment of twenty-five pesos for each rifle surrendered by National Guard soldiers; authorization for officers to keep their pistols and to receive such financial assistance as might be judged proper by Mexican Army chiefs; and disbanding of troops of the National Guard in the presence of Mexican Army chiefs.[41]

Shortly before his death, and at a time when much publicity was being given to the possibility of settling the church-state conflict, General Gorostieta had issued a strongly-worded statement in opposition to any negotiations between Church representatives and the Mexican government.[42] But the statement had not prevented negotiations that produced the *modus vivendi*; and within a month after this arrangement had been made, Gorostieta's successor had been forced to take steps to dissolve the National Guard. Then in August, General Degollado Guízar issued a final order directing those Cristeros still in the field to lay down their arms. This order explained that "His Holiness, the Pope, by means of His Excellency, the Apostolic Delegate, for reasons which we do not know but which we accept as Catholics, has disposed that, without abolishing the laws, worship services be

---

[39] A copy of the broadside was made available to the writer by Professor James W. Wilkie, Department of History, University of California, Los Angeles. Portions of this document are quoted in Moctezuma, *El conflicto religioso*, 2: 549-50.
[40] See Degollado Guízar, *Memorias*, pp. 270-73.
[41] For the text of General Degollado Guízar's letter of instruction to Luis Beltrán y Mendoza, together with the appended terms presented to, and accepted by, Portes Gil, see ibid., pp. 268-70.
[42] For the text of this statement dated May 16, 1929, see *David* 5 (January 22, 1961): 174-77.

resumed and the priest . . . begin to exercise his public ministry." Such a development, the last Cristero General-in-Chief explained, had produced a special problem for the priest: "If he condemned our activities, he would perhaps condemn the best of his flock. . . . If, to the contrary, he shall declare himself in our favor, by this single act, in addition to placing himself in grave danger of perishing as a victim of our enemies, there will remain the impossibility of exercising his ministry among the noncombatant population." Such a situation, it was predicted, would lead to divisions among noncombatant supporters of the Cristero troops, with the result that the National Guard would loose its "most abundant and secure source of supply." Pointing out that the *modus vivendi* "has changed our situation," General Degollado Guízar declared that the time had come to cease combat. He emphasized that the "National Guard has assumed all responsibility for the conflict, but this responsibility will not be imputed to it for the period since the 21st of June. . . ." With another note of bitterness, the rebel commander asserted, "the National Guard disappears, not defeated by its enemies, but, in reality, abandoned by those who were the first to receive the most valuable fruit of its sacrifices and self-denials." His final words were those of a man who considered himself a martyr:

> Christ, help those of us who for Thee go to humiliation, to exile, and perhaps to an inglorious death, victims of our enemies; with all submissiveness, with the most fervent love, we hail Thee; and, once more, we acclaim Thee as King of our Fatherland!
> Long live Christ the King! Long live Holy Mary of Guadalupe![43]

According to Portes Gil, more than 14,000 Cristeros surrendered.[44] Some, like General DeGollado Guízar, merely went into hiding;[45] others found their way home without the formality of laying down arms; and former bandits no doubt remained in the field where they had been operating when they took up the Cristero cause.[46] Thousands of rebels who bore arms in the name of Christ the King were killed in combat or died of disease. Concerning these losses, Professor James W. Wilkie has written:

> No precise statistics concerning the number of Cristeros killed are available, but according to Portes Gil, the Ministry of War reported deaths on both sides as running about 800 to 1,000 monthly, including participants and noncombatants. Since the major action of the guerrilla war took place in 1927 and 1928 and in the first six months of 1929,

---

[43] The text of this final order is printed in Degollado Guízar, *Memorias*, pp. 270-73.
[44] Emilio Portes Gil, *Quince años de política mexicana*, 3d ed. (México, D.F.: Ediciones Botas, 1954), p. 330.
[45] Degollado Guízar, *Memorias*, p. 278.
[46] For a firsthand account of one Cristero's experiences at the end of the conflict, see Navarrete, "*Por Dios y por la Patria*," pp. 260-70.

total deaths may have reached 24,000 to 30,000. Assuming that the Cristeros suffered at least half of these casualties, their losses would have reached 12,000 to 15,000. A figure of 12,000 dead for the Cristeros would be roughly in line with the surrender of 14,000 Cristeros in 1929, if we accept the League's own count of 25,000 followers in 1927. All of these figures seem high, however, for no major battles were fought in the guerrilla war.[47]

Because of bitterness caused by the conflict, an unknown number of Cristero veterans were killed after laying down arms and returning to their homes. In some cases, the government did not fulfill the terms of the amnesty that had been agreed upon; in other cases, former members of the National Guard were assassinated by private citizens. At any event, all bloodshed did not end with the disbanding of rebel forces.[48]

Conclusion

In conclusion, all evidence indicates that the Vatican and the Mexican episcopacy did not openly call for armed revolt; on the other hand, neither did the hierarchy discourage such a development. In fact, papal praise of militant lay organizations, which did so much to prepare many Catholics for rebellion against the government, was a significant factor in producing the revolt. Had the Pope and all members of the Mexican episcopacy fearlessly and publicly called for a holy war against the Calles regime, perhaps a larger number of the faithful would have taken up arms; however, there was no guarantee that such a course of action would have assured a victory. Total war against the government would have raised the possibility of total defeat, with resulting liquidation of clerical personnel and an end of Catholic organizational activity in the country. Many priests and laymen were willing to take this gamble, but the Pope and the prelates were not prepared for such an extreme measure. As it turned out, halfway measures were unsuccessful; but defeat did not prove to be disastrous. Today, half a century after the conclusion of the Cristero Rebellion, the Mexican Catholic Church enjoys more prosperity and influence than at any time since the outbreak of the Revolution of 1910.

---

[47]Wilkie, "The Meaning of the Cristero Religious War Against the Mexican Revolution," pp. 230-31.
[48]One author states that within a year after the truce, five hundred Cristeros had been killed. See Joaquín Cardoso, *Los mártires mexicanos: El martirologio católico de nuestros días*, 2d ed. (México, D.F.: Buena Prensa, 1958), p. 453. For descriptions of various assassinations of Cristeros, see Blanco Gil, *El clamor de la sangre*, passim.

CHAPTER 8

Tomás Garrido Canabal and the Repression of Religion in Tabasco

ALAN M. KIRSHNER

Many readers first learn of Garrido Canabal's antireligious campaigns as a result of reading Graham Greene's famous novel, *The Power and the Glory*, or Greene's journal entitled *Another Mexico*. In this study, Professor Kirshner provides a concise survey of Garrido's career in state politics, his brief but stormy tenure as minister of agriculture in the Cárdenas administration, and the destruction of his repressive regime in Tabasco.

In the 1920s and early 1930s, Tomás Garrido Canabal was the political strong man of Mexico's southeastern state of Tabasco. During this era, he continually received presidential acclaim for what was considered to be dynamic fulfillment of the goals of the Revolution. Alvaro Obregón, President from 1920 until 1924, referred to Tabasco as the "Bulwark of the Revolution." Lázaro Cárdenas, while on a presidential campaign trip in 1934, spoke of Tabasco as the "Laboratory of the Revolution." Cárdenas even cast his own vote for Garrido in the presidential election of that year;[1] later, he appointed Garrido to the office of Secretary of Agriculture in his administration. Plutarco Elías Calles, President of Mexico between 1924 and 1928 and political boss

[1] A photograph of Cárdenas casting his vote for Garrido can be seen in the "Rotograbado" section of *El Nacional* (México, D.F.), December 20, 1934, p. 1. A facsimile of the ballot cast by Cárdenas can be seen in *Opiniones* (n.p., n.d.), p. 3. On January 14, 1969, in a taped interview with Emilio Portes Gil (President of Mexico, 1928-1929), the author was informed that it was quite usual for presidential candidates to cast their ballot for someone they considered worthy. Portes Gil said that Cárdenas voted for Garrido because he was a good revolutionary and a radical. Luis I. Rodríguez, private secretary to Cárdenas in 1935, indicated in an interview on January 24, 1969, that he did not know why Cárdenas voted for Garrido; but he added that people have the right to vote for whom they wish.

of the country until 1935, praised Garrido in such glowing terms that the press asked Calles if he intended Garrido to succeed Cárdenas as President of Mexico.[2]

Mexican Catholics viewed Tomás Garrido Canabal differently. Many considered him to be the anti-Christ. Rumors spread that if he were not the devil incarnate, then Lucifer was at his side. In part, this could be considered correct, because a nephew named Lucifer often accompanied Garrido during his travels. Tomás Garrido's reputation in Mexico was based on the fanatical campaign he waged to destroy the Catholic Church in his state. Fulfilling provisions of the Mexican Constitution of 1917, which allowed each state to regulate the number of clergymen officiating therein, he could boast that not one priest existed in Tabasco by the end of the 1920s. Reports did speak of a lone priest, Padre Macario Fernández Aguado, hiding in the forests and swamps of Tabasco, always one step ahead of the police and death. After a trip through Mexico (including Tabasco) in the late 1930s, Graham Greene wrote his classic novel, *The Power and the Glory*, based on these stories.[3]

Part of the Mexican political tradition after *La Reforma*, the liberal movement of the 1850s, had as its goal the separation of church and state; but the dynamic character of the Mexican Revolution brought an end to this liberalism. Nationalism became the new crusading spirit, and the revolutionary government found itself locked in mortal combat with the Catholic Church for the souls of the Mexican people.[4]

Elimination of the Catholic religion appeared to be the order of the day, at least in the rhetoric and limited actions of many revolutionaries—including Garrido's mentors, Alvaro Obregón and Plutarco Elías Calles. For Tomás Garrido Canabal, repression of religion became a passion. Born into a family of conservative Tabascan *hacienda* owners, Garrido became a left-wing revolutionary who hated religion in general and the Catholic Church in particular. Many theories have been propounded to account for his abhorrence of religion as well as an equally strong hatred of alcohol. Pointing to Garrido's fanatical campaigns against religion and alcohol, some of his opponents have explained that this conduct stemmed from an adolescent rebellion against his parents: a devout Catholic mother and an alcoholic father.[5]

[2]*El Hombre Libre* (México, D.F.), December 26, 1934, p. 1.
[3]An account of Greene's adventures can be found in his travelogue *Another Mexico* (New York: The Viking Press, 1939).
[4]Robert E. Quirk, *The Mexican Revolution and the Catholic Church, 1910-1929* (Bloomington: Indiana University Press, 1973), pp. 22-23.
[5]Garrido's father, Pío, is reported to have defied his son's edicts against drinking hard liquor. Trinidad Malpica H., propaganda minister during Garrido's reign in Tabasco, told the author that he often drank in Pío Garrido's house in Villahermosa during this

Garrido's Tabascan *hacienda* background probably explains his attitude. As the *cacique* of Tabasco, he became the *patrón* of an enlarged *hacienda*. An efficient *hacienda* demands productivity from the workers. Garrido's *hacienda* experiences convinced him that alcoholism and religion created unproductive peasants. He realized that *hacienda* owners, concerned with ego-power and not efficiency, gave liquor and God to their *peones* to enable them to forget the horrors of this world. A worker's ability to judge himself and his life was warped by these escape mechanisms, which reduced his efficiency but made him pliable for the *hacienda* owner. Thus, Garrido desired to eliminate the consumption of alcohol and the practice of religion in order to better the lives of his people and to develop a productive working force that would enrich his enlarged *hacienda*, the state of Tabasco.

Another factor in Tomás Garrido's actions against the Catholic Church can be analyzed through the very nature of absolute power itself. As with most dictators, Garrido's thirst for power meant the need to control or eliminate any institution that might oppose him. The Catholic Church was definitely a competing source of power, if not in Tabasco, then certainly in other parts of Mexico—and Garrido was an ambitious politician.

While other revolutionaries worked to destroy the political influence of the Catholic Church in Mexico, Garrido strove to eliminate religion. On one occasion, he stated: "In order to be free, it is necessary to eliminate the root [of oppression], the religious virus."[6] According to one writer, Garrido asked, "How can any sane person read history without coming to the fixed conclusion that religion and alcohol have ever been humanity's greatest curses?"[7] For Garrido there was "no other God but work, nor any other religion than truth and justice."[8] He intended to secure his "truth and justice" by destroying the Church.

One propaganda minister, who served in Garrido's regime, boasted: "Garrido was an extremist who burned the saints and destroyed the Church."[9] Because the Catholic Church had never been strong in Tabasco, Tomás Garrido's actions to eliminate religion came easier than similar attempts made by other state governments.[10] Catholic churches in Tabasco generally remained empty and people in the

epoch. (Interview taped in Villahermosa, Tabasco, February 4, 1969.) Although Garrido's enemies claim that he allowed his mother to practice Catholicism, the author could find no evidence to verify this assertion.

[6]*Redención* (Villahermosa, Tab.), June 24, 1931, p. 2.
[7]George Creel, "The Scourge of Tabasco: Mexico's Hottest Dictator," *Collier's*, February 23, 1935, p. 10.
[8]*Redención*, October 23, 1931, p. 1.
[9]Taped interview with Trinidad Malpica H., Villahermosa, Tab., February 4, 1969.
[10]Charles S. MacFarland, *Chaos in Mexico: The Conflict of Church and State* (New York: Harper and Brothers, 1935), p. 204.

rural countryside seldom saw a priest.[11] This indifference towards religion has been accounted for by the fact that the Franciscans, Augustinians, Dominicans, and Jesuits never established missions in Tabasco.[12] According to a memorandum to the Cortes of Cádiz dated July 24, 1811, the early clergy who did settle in the state were among the worst with regard to exploitation of the natives.[13] This is quite a charge in a country where the Catholic Church has had a reputation for exploitation.

General Francisco J. Múgica, interim governor of Tabasco in 1915, prepared the way for Garrido's repression of religion. Múgica, a rabid anticleric, later became the guiding force behind those articles in the Constitution of 1917 that place severe restrictions on clerical involvement in Mexican politics.[14] During his interim governorship, General Múgica abolished San Juan Bautista as the name of the state's capital city and restored its original name, Villahermosa.[15] Through appointment by General Múgica, Tómas Garrido obtained his first position in the government of Tabasco as head of the state's Legal Department.[16] Subsequently, Garrido rose rapidly. When he became interim governor in 1919, laws were enacted that greatly restricted religious activity in Tabasco. One of Garrido's laws divided the state into sectors and permitted only one priest in each sector.[17] Other legislation limited the number of churches to one for every 6,000 inhabitants and prohibited the building of churches in rural fields, ranches, or farm communities. Only masonry construction of churches was allowed, and foreign priests were prohibited from officiating in the state.[18]

Various individuals alternated with Garrido as interim governors of Tabasco between 1920 and 1923, but real political power remained in his hands.[19] In 1922, Garrido won a very questionable election after the federal government headed by Alvaro Obregón intervened to force the withdrawal of a strong opposition candidate.[20] Following this election, Tomás Garrido functioned as Governor for only a short

[11]Arcadio Zentella, *Tabasco* (Villahermosa, Tab.: Redención, 1929), p. 102; Quirk, *The Mexican Revolution and the Catholic Church*, p. 6.

[12]Charles Bennett, *Tinder in Tabasco: A Study of Church Growth in Tropical Mexico* (Grand Rapids, Mich.: William B. Eerdmans Publishing Co., 1969), p. 32.

[13]Zentella, *Tabasco*, p. 102.

[14]See Quirk, *The Mexican Revolution and the Catholic Church*, pp. 83-99.

[15]Mariano Tovar, *El dictador de Tabasco: Reivindicación y justica* (Villahermosa, Tab.: n.p., 1936), p. 14.

[16]Francisco J. Santamaría, *El periodismo en Tabasco: Un balance políticosocial de la Independencia al Garridismo* (México, D.F.: Ediciones Botas, 1936), pp. 193-94.

[17]Tomás Garrido Canabal, *Manifiesto a los obreros organizados de la República y al elemento revolucionario* (Villahermosa, Tab., May 14, 1925), pp. 10-11. Hereafter cited as *Manifiesto*.

[18]Partido Socialista Radical, *Tabasco actual* (Villahermosa, Tab., 1929), p. 29.

[19]Santamaría, *El periodismo en Tabasco*, p. 198.

[20]See articles by José Domingo Ramírez Garrido, "La cuestión electoral tabasqueña, 1923-1926," *Tabasco* (México, D.F.), March 1955-March 1956.

period of time before rebel forces supporting Adolfo de la Huerta occupied Villahermosa. Tabasco became one of the chief strongholds of the *delahuertista* movement, and Garrido was forced to flee to Guatemala. With the collapse of the De la Huerta Rebellion, Tomás Garrido returned to Tabasco. Because most of Garrido's opponents had joined De la Huerta, execution or exile of these individuals eliminated any effective resistance to his rule.

As an adroit politician, Tómas Garrido always mirrored the attitudes of Mexico's political bosses, moving to carry out their policies in a manner designed to win presidential favor. When President Alvaro Obregón considered it politic to avoid enforcing religious restrictions in the Constitution of 1917, Garrido avoided direct confrontation with the Church. But when Plutarco Elías Calles, an implacable enemy of the Catholic Church, succeeded Obregón and undertook to implement the religious restrictions of the Constitution, Tomás Garrido embarked on a program of total elimination of religion in Tabasco. Enforcement of legislation enacted in Tabasco in 1919 failed to destroy the Church in his state, so Garrido began a new series of repressive activities. First, with the assistance of Manuel González Punaro, a schismatic priest, Garrido attempted to form an independent Catholic Church.[21] This project failed, as did a national effort in 1925 to create a Mexican Catholic Church independent from Rome.[22] Garrido's second step proved more successful. On March 6, 1925, the state legislature passed a law establishing the following qualifications for priests officiating in Tabasco:

I. To be Tabascan or Mexican by birth, with five years residency in the state.
II. To be older than forty.
III. To have studied the primary and the preparatory courses in the official schools.
IV. To be of good moral antecedents.
V. To be married.
VI. Not to have been, nor be subject to any lawsuits.[23]

Inspiration for this legislation was far from original with Garrido. At the Mexican Constitutional Convention in 1917, delegates from Yucatán proposed that all clergy be Mexican-born, more than fifty years of age, and married.[24] Forty percent of the convention's delegates actually voted in favor of compelling priests to marry.[25] When a

[21]Ignacio Muñoz, *Verdad y mito de la Revolución Mexicana*, 4 vols (México, D.F.: Ediciones Populares, 1960-1965), 4:212.
[22]See Nathaniel and Sylvia Weyl, *The Reconquest of Mexico: The Years of Lázaro Cárdenas* (London: Oxford University Press, 1939), p. 147.
[23]*Manifiesto*, p. 12.
[24]Quirk, *The Mexican Revolution and the Catholic Church*, p. 96.
[25]Ibid., p. 97.

reporter from the United States asked Tomás Garrido why the Tabascan legislature had included the provision that all priests must marry, he replied that he wanted to legitimize their children.[26] Whatever the truth about priests and their illegitimate children in Tabasco, Garrido knew that such a provision would effectively eliminate the Catholic Church in Tabasco. All that remained was to destroy the vestiges of Catholicism remaining in the homes and the lives of the people.

Further decrees ordered eating of meat on Catholic holy days and removing all monuments from graves, allowing only plain earthen mounds without crosses.[27] Garrido also created an organization of "shock troops" who violated the sanctity of the home, confiscated religious symbols, and burned confiscated items every Sunday in large bonfires.[28] These gangs of youths razed many churches to the ground and turned the land into athletic fields or parks. They converted other churches into schools, centers of fine arts, or depositories used by producer and consumer cooperatives.[29]

The first group that served Garrido's bidding by destroying church property and private religious symbols took the name Volunteers of Tabasco. They formed an elite corps of the Leagues of Resistance, which basically were unions that were created after Garrido's return to the state in 1924 and were organized after the pattern of the Leagues in Yucatán.[30] Meeting halls used by the Tabascan Leagues of Resistance contained all types of antireligious propaganda. One observer noted: "Every inch of wall space was taken up by paintings that ... went to the edge of obscenity in lampooning religion and its priests."[31] A New York Times reporter provided more graphic de-

[26]Ernest Gruening, Mexico and Its Heritage (New York: The Century Co., 1928), pp. 270-71.
[27]New York Times, June 3, 1934, p. 28.
[28]Photographs of the burning of images, relics, and crosses can be found in Severo García, El Indio Gabriel: La Matanza de San Carlos (México, D.F.: Editorial Jus, 1957), pp. 58-59; and in Carlos María de Heredíz, Tabasco renace en Cristo (México, D.F.: J. Aguirre B., 1939), pp. 9-15. Garrido seemed to have spared the crosses on the highways in order that obscene slogans could be written on them, according to Andrés Iduarte, El mundo sonriente (México, D.F.: Fondo de Cultura Económica, 1968), p. 38.
[29]Código obrero (Villahermosa, Tab.: Redención, 1925), p. 41. According to George Creel, Garrido took pride in driving every priest from Tabasco and tearing down the churches. Creel reported: "A tennis court, surrounded by grassy lawns, was shown to me as the site of a church that had been demolished, and on another corner only some piles of stone remained to show the fate of the ancient cathedral. Still farther on, my hosts pointed out a gaping hole in the ground where un templo bell, they exclaimed delightedly, had been melted and made into a statue of General Obregón." Creel, "The Scourge of Tabasco," p. 10.
[30]Vespasiano Lasta et al., Texto de la segunda acusación presentada ante la Comisión Permanente del Congreso de la Unión contra el Gobernador de Tabasco Lic. Tomás Garrido Canabal (México, D.F.; Guerrero Hnos., 1925), p. 6.
[31]Creel, "The Scourge of Tabasco," p. 10.

tails when he described decorative pictures of nude priests adorning the walls of the local Federation of Workers hall in Villahermosa.[32]

The Revolutionary Vanguard superseded the Volunteers of Tabasco in 1928, but a more enduring movement replaced the Vanguard in 1929. The new organization, Bloc of Young Revolutionaries, was popularly known as the Red Shirts because of the uniforms they wore.[33] With the revival of the church-state conflict in Mexico in 1933, this Red Shirt organization spread throughout Mexico. The largest contingent developed in the capital city after Garrido became Secretary of Agriculture in the Cárdenas administration.[34] Tomás Garrido and his Red Shirts obtained minimal success in their nationwide antireligious campaigns, because all Mexico was not Tabasco. With the shooting of five Catholics attending mass in the Mexico City suburb of Coyoacán on December 30, 1934, the Red Shirts and their mentor lost the favor of Mexico's closed political establishment and were unable to fulfill their hope of eliminating the Church throughout Mexico as they had done in Tabasco.[35]

The Red Shirts and their predecessors held guerrilla-style theatres where they dressed in bizarre outfits to mock the Church. They published newspapers and magazines expounding their antireligious doctrines,[36] and they founded Atheist Clubs under names of famous Mexican figures like Benito Juárez.[37] One of their baseball teams even took the name "Atheists."[38] They observed "Anti-Clerical Wednesdays," when speakers clamored against the belief in God.[39] Concerning a meeting of this sort, a humorous story was told about one speaker's method of thundering against God. While addressing an assembly, Arnulfo Pérez H. reportedly proclaimed:

> I am the personal enemy of God. God does not exist. Do you want some proof? If God exists ... he will kill me this very moment! I give you,

---

[32]New York Times, May 19, 1937, p. 1.

[33]Redención, August 4, 1929, p. 1. Trindad Malpica H. (taped interview, February 3, 1969) informed the author that the Blocs were organized in 1929. Agapito Domínguez, once President of the Bloc of Young Revolutionaries of the Federal District, wrote the author that the Red Shirt movement began in 1928. (Memorandum for Alan M. Kirshner, México, D.F., January 13, 1969.) However, first mention of these Blocs appeared in issues of Redención published in 1929.

[34]Stories of the period that were published in Redención, the official party paper of Tabasco, told of the organization of new Blocs and of their activities.

[35]See Alan M. Kirshner, "A Setback for Tomás Garrido Canabal's Desire to Eliminate the Church in Mexico," Journal of Church and State 13 (Autumn 1971): 479-92.

[36]Santamaría, El periodismo en Tabasco, p. 1.

[37]Redención, March 27, 1931, p. 1. An "Atheist Club" in Yucatán took the name "Tomás Garrido Canabal." Redención, July 29, 1933, p. 4.

[38]Redención, June 29, 1933, p. 4.

[39]For a typical example of a schedule of events on an "Anti-Clerical Wednesday," see Redención, September 19, 1934, p. 4.

> God, three minutes to kill me. Three minutes that I will count on my watch . . . one . . . two . . . three! Did you see it? God does not exist![40]

Another tale about the same orator's defiance of God reads as follows:

> "God, You do not exist; I apostrophize You and challenge You that if You really exist You strike down this building on my head." After a pause in the roofless open-air theatre the speaker went on to address his audience saying: "You see, gentlemen, the building has not fallen and so God does not exist."[41]

While serving Garrido as Chief Clerk of the Ministry of Agriculture, Pérez proudly distributed calling cards which read: "Arnulfo Pérez H., Chief Clerk of the Ministry of Agriculture and Development. Deputy to the Federal Congress. Member of the Partido Nacional Revolucionario. Personal Enemy of God."[42]

Indoctrination in antireligious and atheistic doctrines became mandatory for all school children. One follower of Garrido proudly reported that on a visit to Tabasco he found school children repeating the following phrases: "The saints do not exist, they are made of straw, and they only serve to be burned"; "The Church is the enemy of the poor"; "The priest and the capitalist take the bread from our mouth."[43] Tomás Garrido termed this education "Rationalist," which in reality was a forerunner of the socialist education amended into Article III of the Constitution in 1934. Mexican Catholics interpreted such education as a plot to destroy religious values and substitute atheistic communism. Yet rationalist education or socialist education actually taught empirical scientific methodology. Perhaps the purpose and effects of the so-called socialist education can best be understood in Mariano Tovar's report of an interview with a Tabascan peasant. When asked if it were true that when mangoes fall they obey the will of God, the peasant replied: "Excuse me . . . when the mangoes fall they are obeying the laws of physics."[44]

The curriculum of Tabascan schools included sex education. This fed the paranoia of conspiracy adherents, convincing them that it was part of an international, anti-Christ, atheistic, communist plot. An anonymous author, who claimed he was present at an interview

---

[40]Roberto Blanco Moheno, *Crónica de la Revolución Mexicana*, 3 vols. (México, D.F.: Editorial Diana, 1967), 3: 339.

[41]John W. F. Dulles, *Yesterday in Mexico: A Chronicle of the Revolution, 1919-1936* (Austin: University of Texas Press, 1961), p. 622.

[42]Ibid.; Rodulfo Brito Foucher, "Recursos demagógicos del garridismo, ateísmo alcoholismo: II," *El Día*, February 15, 1936, pp. 3, 5; Jesús Guisa y Azevedo, "Luzbel Garrido Canabal y el enemigo personal de Dios," *Hoy*, September 1, 1956, p. 24.

[43]Roberto Hinojosa, *El Tabasco que yo he visto*, 2d ed. (Tacubaya, D.F.: Talleres Gráficos de la Oficina de Publicaciones y Propaganda de la Secretaría de Agricultura y Fomento, 1935), p. 38.

[44]Mariano Tovar, *Un pueblo, una causa, un hombre* (San José, Costa Rica: Editorial Borrase Hnos., 1939), p. 13.

between Tomás Garrido Canabal and United States Ambassador Josephus Daniels, told an interesting anecdote relating to Tabasco's sex education courses:

> The newspaperman and diplomat from South [sic] Carolina asked the lawyer Garrido: "Is it true that you impart sex education in the schools of Tabasco and reveal to the students the mysteries of animal reproduction?" Without wincing or adopting a sarcastic tone the Tabascan educator answered Daniels: "No, Mr. Ambassador, in Tabasco we are not accustomed to falsifying the mission entrusted to the North American cinema."[45]

Tabascan educators were organized into Leagues of Atheist Teachers.[46] The Leagues encouraged teachers from other states to visit Tabascan schools for the purpose of studying rationalist education, and they worked to develop a nationwide program of socialist education based on precepts of the amended Article III of the national Constitution.

Tomás Garrido, always proud of the success his atheist teachers had achieved and desirous of winning student support for his political ambitions, invited the First Congress of Socialist Students to meet in Tabasco. When the 230 delegates arrived, the Red Shirts urged them to participate in what was described as a true socialist exercise: the demolition of one of the few remaining churches in the state of Tabasco.[47] While the Red Shirts' band played "La Golondrina," delegates led by a Sonoran proceeded to demolish the church stone by stone.[48]

In the summer of 1934, Tomás Garrido opened a special agricultural fair designed to run concurrently with a session of the state legislature.[49] Generally such fairs were used to degrade religion. Along with the typical harangues against religion and the anti-church poems and songs, it was common to see Garrido exhibiting his own livestock. In one such fair in 1930, Garrido presented his prizewinning zebu bull named God, an ass labeled Christ, a cow called the Virgin, a pig tagged the Pope, and a horse titled Bishop Pascual Díaz.[50]

The real Bishop Pascual Díaz had been forced to leave Tabasco after Garrido's legislation of 1925. Thus, it is understandable why he became one of the most outspoken critics of the Mexican government's religious policy and gave indirect support to the Cristero rebels

---

[45]Pin [pseud.], "In memoriam: Tomás Garrido Canabal," *El Nacional*, April 8, 1951, p. 3.

[46]Alfonso Taracena, *La verdadera revolución mexicana*, 18 vols. (Mexico, D.F.: Editorial Jus, 1960-65), 18: 166.

[47]*Redención*, July 31, 1934, p. 1.

[48]Ibid.

[49]*El Nacional*, July 30, 1934, p. 7.

[50]*El Hombre Libre*, July 16, 1930, p. 1.

in 1926.[51] Later however, Díaz sought a peaceful resolution of the conflict,[52] for which the Pope named him Archbishop of Mexico.

The Cristero Rebellion had little impact in Tabasco. By 1926, any Tabascan clergyman or layman who could have led a rebellion had been eliminated. Opposition groups did appear in Mexico City, but the leaders of these groups never allied themselves with the Church. Whenever these opposition groups sent expeditions from the national capital to Tabasco in an attempt to liberate the state from Garrido's oppression (as was done in 1929, 1932, 1934, and 1935), they always encountered a number of simple, devout peasants who were ready to aid them.[53] One such individual was named Isabelino Alegría. Residing in Playas del Rosario, he coordinated clandestine religious activities in the hamlets and villages near Villahermosa after Garrido's return to the state in 1934.[54] For many years the people of Playas del Rosario and a nearby village called Parrilla hid a priest in their midst and protected their small church from the destructive forces of the *garridistas*.[55] The only uprising that can be compared with Cristero violence took place in 1929, when the villagers of San Carlos refused to replace their saint's day with a "Yucca Fair." This local rebellion was led by a lay priest, whose brother immortalized it in a book entitled *El Indio Gabriel*.[56] Tabascan authorities killed seventeen people, and the following year the Indian Gabriel was hunted down by the forces of Garrido and slain in the state of Chiapas.[57] Despite such

---

[51]Quirk, *The Mexican Revolution and the Catholic Church*, p. 197.

[52]Ibid, pp. 204-5.

[53]After the *modus vivendi* between church and state obtained by President Emilio Portes Gil in 1929, Tabascan exiles believed the federal government would withdraw its support of Garrido. Expeditions into Tabasco with the pretense of participating in election campaigns were launched. Portes Gil's successor, President Pascual Ortiz Rubio, received strong backing from Tabascan exiles. Perhaps this accounted for his cool attitude toward Garrido, who mistakenly worked for Aarón Sáenz (a relative of Calles), and his interference on behalf of the *anti-garridistas* when their expeditions failed. (See Archivo de Brito Foucher, letter from President Ortiz Rubio, México, D.F., to Tomás Garrido Canabal, Villahermosa, Tab., May 26, 1931.) In any case, though Mexican Presidents between 1929 and 1934 tried to maintain a national equilibrium in religious affairs, they permitted state governors like Tomás Garrido Canabal to continue their oppressive antireligious activities. Probably this reflected the true sentiments of Plutarco Elías Calles, Mexico's political boss during that era. See John B. Williman, "Adalberto Tejeda and the Third Phase of the Anticlerical Conflict in Twentieth Century Mexico," *Journal of Church and State* 15 (Autumn 1973): 443.

[54]Isabelino Alegría Jiménez, "Historia de los tiempos pasados," (Playas del Rosario, Tab., 1960), p. 1. (Manuscript.)

[55]Taped interview with Filemon León, Félix García, and Isabelino Alegría at Parrilla, Tab., February 6, 1969.

[56]See above, note 28.

[57]Efraín Huerta, "La huella de sangre," *Así* (México, D.F.), May 24, 1941, p. 15; Salvador Camelo Soler, *Tomás Garrido Canabal: El Sátrapa* (México, D.F.: n.p., 1933), p. 17; and Tovar, *Un pueblo, una causa, un hombre*, pp. 200-4.

sporadic uprisings, extensive organized opposition never existed inside of Tabasco.

Led by Rodulfo Brito Foucher, a former dean of the Law School of the National University in Mexico City, an opposition force did move successfully to liberate Tabasco from Garrido's control in July 1935. This development came after Garrido sided with Plutarco Elías Calles in the power struggle with President Cárdenas.

In June 1935, Brito Foucher learned that Garrido had joined with Calles,[58] but the Cárdenas government did not contemplate any action against Garrido after removal from his cabinet position.[59] In mid-June, Cárdenas reorganized his complete cabinet to assure loyalty to himself; and Tomás Garrido returned to Tabasco. Saturnino Cedillo, a procleric from San Luis Potosí, replaced Garrido as Secretary of Agriculture. This action by Cárdenas seemed to Catholics, as well as to the Tabascan exiles in the Federal District, to be a sign that religious repression would end in Mexico.[60] Yet Garrido's removal did not mark any radical change in the government's policy toward the Church.[61] It was strictly a political maneuver that strengthened Cárdenas' position. Cedillo, a popular hero, was a supporter of Cárdenas, but Garrido's loyalty was questionable.

Brito and his émigré friends soon learned that Garrido had realized his mistake in supporting Calles and was professing his loyalty in daily letters and telegrams sent to President Cárdenas.[62] They decided to act immediately because they feared that Garrido would soon be back in Cárdenas's good graces. Thus, Brito led an expedition to Tabasco in mid-July 1935. It was composed of twenty-one Tabascan exiles, most of whom were students at the National University. After Brito's men arrived in Villahermosa, violence erupted between them

---

[58]Rodulfo Brito Foucher, "Mi expedición a Tabasco: o un año de contacto con la política mexicana, " *Hoy,* July 9, 1938, p. 17.

[59]Ibid.; Marcelino Morales M., "El derrocamiento de Garrido y el Sr. Brito," in "¿Quién es quién en la Revolución?" *La Prensa* (México, D.F.), May 23, 1939, p. 11.

[60]Archbishop Díaz even led Mexican Catholics in a prayer for religious liberty, stating that now was the time for tranquility. *New York Times,* July 1, 1935, p. 7.

[61]A more conciliatory policy began in the early part of 1936, and an accommodation was basically achieved in 1937. See Lyle Clarence Brown, "General Lázaro Cárdenas and Mexican Presidential Politics, 1933-1940: A Study in the Acquisition and Manipulation of Political Power" (Ph.D. diss., University of Texas, 1964), pp. 139-46; Albert Louis Michaels, "Mexican Politics and Nationalism from Calles to Cárdenas" (Ph.D. diss., University of Pennsylvania, 1966), pp. 156-59; and Eduardo J. Correa, *El balance del cardenismo* (México, D.F.: Acción, 1941), pp. 261-311.

[62]During June 13-16, 1935, Redención printed telegrams from the Red Shirts and other *garridista* organizations declaring their support for Calles. After his return to Tabasco on June 16, Garrido's words left little doubt that he was a Calles man. But after June 20, the *garridistas* apparently realized which way the wind was blowing, because they began to profess their loyalty to President Cárdenas. See correspondence in Archivo del Presidente Lázaro Cárdenas, Archivo General de la Nación, as well as letters and telegrams printed in Redención after June 20, 1935.

and the Red Shirts; a number of combatants on both sides were killed. Subsequently, emotional protests against Tomás Garrido's "massacre" of innocent students were voiced all over Mexico. President Cárdenas, apparently pressured by these protests and annoyed by disturbances that were destroying national tranquility, forced the strong man of Tabasco to seek refuge in Costa Rica on August 12, 1935. It was announced that Garrido had been commissioned to study agriculture in Central America.[63]

Tomás Garrido's exile caused little basic change in the prevailing system in Tabasco for many years. Graham Greene, who visited the state in 1938, reported his conversation with a local dentist:

"Well," I said, "I suppose things are better than in Garrido's time."
"Not on your life," he said. "There was discipline in those days. . . . Garrido was all right, only his friends went too far." "Why," he said, "that woman there, my wife, she's his niece. I was Garrido's dentist in Villahermosa. He never went to anyone else."
"Did he pay you?"
"I never sent a bill," he said. "I wasn't that crazy. But I got protection. All that was wrong with Garrido was—he went against the Church. It never pays," he said. "He'd be here now if he hadn't gone against the Church."
"But he seems to have won," I said; "no priests, no churches. . . ."
"Oh," he said illogically, "they don't care about religion around here. It's too hot."[64]

A short while before Graham Greene visited Tabasco, the first break came in the vigorous enforcement of Garrido's statutes. In May 1937, the Mexican Supreme Court ruled unconstitutional a Chihuahua law permitting only one priest to function in the state. The incumbent *garridista* governor of Tabasco, Victor Fernández Manero, announced that the court's decision was not applicable to his state. He explained that Tabascan law permitting a priest to officiate only when married existed as part of the state constitution. Although Fernández Manero declared that all churches would remain closed, he did promise that Catholics would be allowed to worship in their own homes.[65]

A little over a year after Governor Fernández Manero's intransigent stand on church worship, several hundred Catholics marched on Villahermosa and held a pray-in at the ruins of the Church of Concepción. Salvador Abascal had recently come to the state to lead them. He acted as an organizer for the newly formed *Sinarquistas*, a proclerical movement.[66] This twenty-eight-year-old

---

[63]See Dulles, *Yesterday in Mexico*, pp. 650-58. The author has numerous taped interviews with participants in the events of July and August 1935.
[64]Greene, *Another Mexico*, pp. 127-28.
[65]*New York Times*, May 19, 1937, p. 1.
[66]Michaels, "Mexican Politics and Nationalism," p. 166; Hugh Gerald Campbell, "The

zealot, who has been described as "the most important leader the Sinarquista movement was to have,"[67] was successful in implementing his policy of Catholic militancy.[68] Yet his victory came in the traditional manner of change in Tabasco—state troops opened fire, killing several Catholics and causing a national uproar.[69] President Cárdenas reacted by ordering Governor Fernández Manero to repeal Garrido's antichurch laws.[70]

Tomás Garrido's attack on the Catholic Church in Tabasco reflected the Mexican Revolutionary leadership's desire to create a new society with a new mentality.[71] Tomás Garrido and the *garridistas* went to extemes in an effort to eliminate the Church. Success was dependent upon the prevailing ideology of Mexico's revolutionary ruling class, which hated the Church's economic and mental control of the Mexican people and its constant interference in the political life of the nation. When Mexico's politicians, especially President Lázaro Cárdenas, felt the need to become conciliatory toward the Church, religious repression came to an end in Tabasco, as in the rest of the nation.

Radical Right in Mexico, 1929-1949" (Ph.D. diss., University of California at Los Angeles, 1968), pp. 258-59.
[67]Campbell, "The Radical Right in Mexico," p. 255.
[68]Ibid., p. 259.
[69]Ibid.; Frank L. Kluckhohn, *The Mexican Challenge* (New York: Doubleday, Doran, and Co., 1939), p. 277; Betty Kirk, *Covering the Mexican Front: The Battle of Europe vs. America* (Norman: University of Oklahoma Press, 1942), p. 132; Evelyn Waugh, *Mexico: An Object Lesson* (Boston: Little, Brown and Co., 1939), pp. 296-97.
[70]Campbell, "The Radical Right in Mexico," p. 259; Kirk, *Covering the Mexican Front*, p. 132; Michaels, "Mexican Politics and Nationalism," p. 166.
[71]Quirk, *The Mexican Revolution and the Catholic Church*, pp. 22-23.

9. Church and State in Mexico, 1931-1936: An Overview

HARRIETT DENISE JOSEPH

This study surveys six years of intensive church-state struggle. Beginning in 1931 with state legislation limiting the number of priests and with church festivities commemorating the four hundredth anniversary of the appearance of the Virgin of Guadalupe, the period ends with President Cárdenas's order exiling the rabidly anticlerical Plutarco Elías Calles and with the Vatican's appointment of conciliatory Luis María Martínez to the post of archbishop of Mexico. Dr. Joseph's overview of the era that was bracketed by these events provides a detailed narrative of the government's program of socialist education and its policies restricting religious personnel and practices.

In 1916, Mexican revolutionaries met in Querétaro to draft a new constitution for their country. Participants at the constitutional convention wished to form a modern nation free from control by the large landowner, the foreign investor, and the conservative Roman Catholic Church.

To curb the traditional power and aspirations of the Roman Catholic clergy, convention delegates inserted into the Mexican Constitution of 1917 several articles designed to subject the Catholic Church to civil control. Various provisions deprived religious bodies of juridical personality, nationalized church property, required all clergymen to be native Mexicans, prohibited clerics from voting or holding public office, and required ministers in charge of religious buildings to register with the government.

Mexico's revolutionary politicians believed that the Catholic Church, through its predominant influence in Mexican education, instilled in the people acceptance of the status quo. To achieve their revolutionary goals, convention delegates concluded they must not only prevent the clergy from interfering in temporal matters but must also break the hold of the Church over the minds of Mexican youth. Article 3, intended to accomplish this latter purpose, stated that primary education—both public and private—must be secular. No religious corporation or clergyman would be allowed to establish or direct any primary school.[1]

While the Roman Catholic episcopate strongly objected to this and other anticlerical provisions of the Constitution of 1917, no immediate clash resulted between church and state. Governments in power from 1917 to 1924 were too preoccupied with other problems to devote much energy to enforcement of constitutional provisions objectionable to the Catholic Church. This situation changed in 1924 when a strong-minded Sonoran, Plutarco Elías Calles, became president of Mexico. The new chief executive initiated a vigorous campaign to enforce the religious articles of the Constitution. Calles's action led to a clerical strike in 1926 and the Cristero Rebellion. When both strike and rebellion ended in 1929, the federal government had proven its strength and ability to demand obedience to the national Constitution.[2]

The year 1929 marked the beginning of an uneasy truce that lasted only two years. In June 1931, the legislature of Vera Cruz exercised its constitutional prerogative by limiting the number of clergymen of each faith allowed to officiate within the state. The resultant law permitted only one Catholic cleric for each one hundred thousand state inhabitants. Two months later, the Director of Education in this same state dismissed all primary and secondary school teachers who professed Catholicism. Despite complaints from priests and petitions from outraged Catholics, President Pascual Ortiz Rubio insisted that the federal government would respect the rights of individual states. Consequently, he refused to intervene in Vera Cruz.[3]

Church-state relations became more hostile in December 1931, when the Catholic clergy organized a series of elaborate festivities to commemorate the four-hundredth anniversary of the appearance of Mexico's patron saint, the Virgin of Guadalupe. Because certain "prominent Mexicans," including powerful ex-President Calles, felt that the celebrations were a "heathenish feast" and a "vulgar farce," a new wave of anticlericalism swept the country. The national congress enacted a law restricting the number of priests for the Federal District

---

[1]Albert L. Michaels, "Mexican Politics and Nationalism from Calles to Cárdenas" (Ph.D. diss., University of Pennsylvania, 1966), p. 146; *Diario de los debates del congreso constituyente, 1916-1917*, 2 vols. (México, D.F.: Ediciones de la Comisión Nacional para la Celebración del Sesquicentario de la Proclamación de la Independencia Nacional y del Cincuentario de la Revolución Mexicana, 1960), 2: 1181-82.

[2]For recent scholarly works on the church-state conflict of the 1920s, see David C. Bailey, ¡*Viva Cristo Rey! The Cristero Rebellion and the Church-State Conflict in Mexico* (Austin: University of Texas Press, 1974); and Jean Meyer, *La cristiada*, trans. Aurelio Garzón del Camino, 2d ed., 3 vols. (México, D.F.: Siglo Veintiuno Editores, 1974).

[3]J. Lloyd Mecham, *Church and State in Latin America: A History of Politico-Ecclesiastical Relations* (Chapel Hill: University of North Carolina Press, 1934), p. 499; *Excelsior*, June 11, 1931; *New York Times*, August 11, 1931, p. 6; *Current History* 35 (October 1931): 114. (*New York Times* hereafter cited as *NYT*, and *Current History* hereafter cited as *CH*.)

and the territories of Baja California to one per fifty thousand inhabitants. Pascual Díaz y Barreto, Archbishop of Mexico, labeled this and similar laws, which already existed in other Mexican states, unconstitutional and unpatriotic; but the Mexican Supreme Court disagreed with the Archbishop and affirmed the constitutionality of the restrictive measures. Thereafter, those Mexican states that did not already have limiting laws began enacting measures that severely regulated the number of authorized clergymen.[4]

While this occurred, Mexico changed presidents. Calles, the true wielder of power in Mexican politics from 1925 to 1935, became dissatisfied with Ortiz Rubio and secured his resignation in September 1932. Congressional appointee Abelardo Rodríguez, a veteran politician acceptable to Calles, then assumed the presidency.[5]

In the month of this presidential turnover, Pope Pius XI expressed his views on "The New Persecutions of the Church by the Mexican Government." The Pope declared any restriction on the number of Catholic priests allowed to exercise their functions to be a "grave violation of Divine Rights." Concerning the Mexican government's hostility toward the Catholic Church, he complained that "not only is religious instruction forbidden in the primary schools, but not infrequently attempts are made to induce teachers . . . to become purveyors of irreligious and immoral teachings."[6] According to the Holy Father, the remedy for this situation was for Catholic clergy and laymen in Mexico to organize in defense of the Church's sacred rights and to give "utmost attention to the question of education and the formation of the young."[7]

Learning of the encyclical, President Rodríguez charged the Pope with inciting agitation and warned that his government would act energetically at the least sign of disorder. In October 1932, at the request of the Chamber of Deputies, the president ordered the expulsion of Apostolic Delegate Leopoldo Ruiz y Flores, who had circulated Pius XI's encyclical throughout Mexico.[8]

While denouncing the Pope's declarations, Rodríguez agreed that it was imperative to give "utmost attention to the . . . education and

---

[4]NYT, December 14, 1931, p. 10; Mecham, Church and State in Latin America, p. 500; Alberto María Carreño, Páginas de historia mexicana (Pages of Mexican History) (México, D.F.: Ediciones Victoria, 1936), pp. 89, 91; CH 36 (September 1932): 723.

[5]William Weber Johnson, Heroic Mexico: The Narrative History of a Twentieth Century Revolution (Garden City, N.Y.: Doubleday & Co., 1968), p. 409; Hubert Herring, Latin America from the Beginning to the Present, 3d ed. (New York: Alfred A. Knopf, 1972), p. 358.

[6]Pius XI, The Church of Mexico: On the Persecutions of the Church by the Mexican Government (Washington, D.C.: National Catholic Welfare Conference, 1932), pp. 8, 12.

[7]Ibid., p. 8.

[8]Emilio Portes Gil, Autobiografía de la Revolución Mexicana: Un tratado de interpretación histórica (México, D.F.: Instituto Mexicano de Cultura, 1964), p. 674; CH 37 (November 1932): 206; Leopoldo Ruiz y Flores, Recuerdo de recuerdos: Autobiografía del excmo. y rvmo. Sr. Dr. don Leopoldo Ruiz y Flores (México, D.F.: Buena Prensa, 1942), pp. 102-103.

the formation of the young." Accordingly, in December, the president went a step beyond the Constitution of 1917, which required secular education only at the primary level; he decreed the secularization of secondary education. Responding to this presidential action, Archbishop Díaz warned parents within his jurisdiction not to send their children to lay secondary schools. He impressed upon Catholics their obligation to educate Mexican youth only in schools imparting "Christian education."[9]

By stressing the importance of Christian schooling, the Archbishop was restating an earlier papal pronouncement. In 1929, Pius XI had declared unsound any form of education not based upon the ideas of original sin and grace; and he had insisted that the Church has an inalienable right, which the State must respect: to "watch over the entire education of her children." His pronouncement admonished parents to provide their progeny with Christian education and informed Catholics that work promoting religious schools was meritorious.[10]

Was Mexico to have Christian or secular education? This question became a major issue in the 1930s when President Rodríguez and his successor, Lázaro Cárdenas, began implementing reforms designed to remove the country's educational system from clerical control. While governmental leaders endeavored to secularize education, the Catholic hierarchy, in accord with papal dictates, fought to preserve Christian education. Because neither the Catholic Church nor the Mexican government was willing to compromise on this point, the two institutions found themselves increasingly at odds for the greater part of the decade.

Aware that 1934 was an election year, Calles suggested in May 1933 that a written plan should be formulated to guide national development during the next presidential term. In June, a committee of trusted *callistas* drafted a document for submission to the national convention of the Partido Nacional Revolucionario (PNR) that was scheduled to meet later in the year. Convening early in December, the two thousand PNR delegates discussed, modified, and adopted the proposed Six Year Plan, which was designed "to raise the standards of living of workers, to establish a final minimal wage, to develop education vigorously, to complete Mexico's agrarian program and to help Mexico's relations with foreign countries."[11]

[9]James W. Wilkie, "Sexual Education and Socialist Education in Mexico—The Early 1930s," in *Revolution in Mexico: Years of Upheaval, 1910-1940*, ed. James W. Wilkie and Albert L. Michaels (New York: Alfred A. Knopf, 1969), p. 200; Verna Carleton Millan, *Mexico Reborn* (Boston: Houghton Mifflin Co., 1939), pp. 52-53.
[10]Pius XI, *Encyclical Letter of His Holiness Pius XI by Divine Providence Pope . . . on Christian Education of Youth* (Washington, D.C: National Catholic Welfare Conference, 1936), pp. 9, 32.
[11]*NYT*, December 4, 1933, p. 13; Michaels, "Mexican Politics," pp. 50-51; Herring, *Latin America*, p. 359.

At this time, Calles was becoming increasingly conservative. Thus, it is debatable whether he really believed in a plan that proposed such radical changes in many aspects of Mexican life. As a shrewd politician, he simply may have recognized the growing leftist element in Mexico and desired to woo this sector of the population.[12] Whatever Calles's motives, the Six Year Plan that resulted from his suggestion was allegedly the blueprint for Mexican development from 1934 to 1940.

In regard to education, the Six Year Plan provided guidelines for expenditures at the federal and state levels and promised the opening each year of 1,000 to 3,000 new rural schools. Recognized in the plan as a social institution, the primary school was to serve the people by imparting rational and scientific answers, rather than religious ones, to questions in the minds of students. To achieve this, the PNR pledged to sponsor the reform of Article III in order to insure governmental control of the educational system and instruction "based on the orientations and postulations of the socialist doctrine upheld by the Mexican Revolution."[13]

Having adopted the Six Year Plan, PNR delegates faced the task of selecting the man to implement it. Their unanimous choice was Lázaro Cárdenas, who had been a brigadier general at age twenty-five, governor of his home state of Michoacán, president of the PNR, and Minister of War and Navy.[14] Although there would be other candidates for the presidency, the PNR candidate was virtually assured of victory in the July 1934 election.

Desiring to reach the people, Cárdenas conducted a vigorous campaign involving travel to all of the Mexican states and speeches that emphasized his three main interests: agrarian reform, education based on socialism, and workers' cooperatives. He promised, "If the people make me president . . . I will not permit the clergy to intervene in popular education in any way. . . ."[15]

While Cárdenas campaigned, Narciso Bassols, an ardent revolutionary and Secretary of Education under President Rodríguez, proceeded with his own plans to create a school system more responsive to the needs of the masses. To accomplish this objective, Bassols considered a list of curriculum revisions suggested in 1933 by the Mexican Eugenics Society. Having studied a report by Mexican physicians describing national problems involving venereal diseases, un-

[12]Millan, *Mexico Reborn*, pp. 64-65.
[13]*The Mexican Government's Six Year Plan, 1934-1940: Complete Textual Translation of the Revised Plan* (México, D.F.: Trans Agency, n.d.), pp. 29-37, passim.
[14]*NYT*, December 7, 1933, p. 12.
[15]William C. Townsend, *Lázaro Cárdenas: Mexican Democrat* (Ann Arbor, Mich.: George Wahr Publishing Co., 1952), p. 80; Johnson, *Heroic Mexico*, p. 412; Howard F. Cline, *The United States and Mexico*, rev. ed. (New York: Atheneum, 1971), p. 218; Alberto Bremauntz, *La educación socialista en México: Antecedentes y fundamentos de la reforma de 1934* (México, D.F.: Imprenta "Rivadeneyra," 1943), p. 175.

professional abortions, and unwanted children, the Society had requested that public schools provide children with instruction in hygiene and physiology. In January 1934, Bassols responded to this advice by announcing a new sexual education program for grades one through six.[16]

Although the program was intended as a worthwhile project, the decision to entitle it sexual education proved unfortunate. Rumors regarding the content of "sex" classes circulated rapidly. Mothers were warned of the unclean acts that children would be forced to perform if they attended schools offering "sex" instruction. The Catholic Church added to this hysteria. In a confidential pastoral dated February 5, Archbishop Díaz warned of inherent dangers in sexual education. He informed Catholics that they would be unworthy of receiving the sacraments if they failed to remove their children from schools where danger of perversion existed. Reacting to rumors and clerical warnings, concerned Catholics formed parents' associations to coordinate their efforts and declared student strikes. Thousands of aroused parents gathered in Mexico City to demonstrate against the program through which they believed the now highly unpopular Secretary of Education wished to corrupt their children. When public pressure forced Bassols to resign in May 1934, he blamed the Catholic clergy for agitation within the country.[17]

Like Bassols, Calles also blamed the Catholic clergy for much of the turmoil in Mexico. Speaking in Guadalajara in July, he renewed his offensive against the Catholic Church by telling his countrymen that the Mexican Revolution was entering a psychological period in which it must destroy existing prejudices and form a new national soul. Warning that schools in many states were under the direction of reactionary, ecclesiastical elements, he insisted that Mexicans must eliminate clerical influence from education.[18] His speech had significant repercussions in succeeding months.

Adhering to the Six Year Plan and advice given by Calles in his Guadalajara speech, participants at a PNR caucus in September drafted a long-discussed revision of Article 3 of the national Constitution. The proposal declared that education should be socialistic, exclude all religious doctrines, combat fanaticism, and provide Mexican youth with a rational "concept of the universe." Religious corporations were

---

[16]Millan, *Mexico Reborn*, pp. 54-55; Lyle C. Brown, "Mexican Church-State Relations, 1933-1940," *A Journal of Church and State* 6 (Spring 1964): 203.

[17]Millan, *Mexico Reborn*, pp. 55-56; Brown, "Mexican Church-State Relations," p. 203; *La Palabra Nacionalista*, 28 January 1934; Michaels, "Mexican Politics and Nationalism," pp. 113-14; Carreño, *Páginas de historia mexicana*, p. 135, CH 40 (July 1934): 473; *NYT*, May 10, 1934, p. 13.

[18]*La Palabra Nacionalista*, July 21, 1934; Josefina Z. Vázquez Knauth, "La educación socialista de los años treinta," *Historia Mexicana* 18 (April-June 1969): 411-12; Michaels, "Mexican Politics and Nationalism," p. 150; Brown, "Mexican Church-State Relations," pp. 204-205.

not to interfere with or offer financial aid to public educational institutions, and private schools could operate only with official authorization. When this measure was submitted to the national congress for approval, debates in the Chamber of Deputies revealed confusion among revolutionaries over the meaning of "socialist education." Despite the ambiguity of the phrase and the variety of interpretations presented, the Chamber approved the proposed amendment on October 10. Nine days later the Senate did likewise.[19] The amendment to Article 3 was then presented to the states for ratification.

Discord resulted from the proposed amendment. The exiled Apostolic Delegate, Archbishop Leopoldo Ruiz y Flores, stated on October 24 his conviction that religious rights and the right of parents to determine their children's education were superior to any constitution. Warning that no Catholic could be a socialist or even a member of the PNR, Ruiz y Flores asked all loyal Catholics to organize peacefully and assert their rights. His flock responded. Conservative newspapers published editorials opposing the proposed amendment. Concerned Catholics circulated leaflets warning of the evils of socialist education. Mass meetings and public demonstrations, usually dispersed by policemen and firemen, were held to protest possible ratification. Catholic parents warned that they would not send their children to schools imparting socialistic education.[20]

For every Mexican who attempted actively to prevent passage of the amendment, many others either supported the government or remained neutral in the matter. In Mexico City on October 28, more than 150,000 Mexican laborers and government employees demonstrated in support of Rodríguez and Cárdenas. Reviewing the procession of demonstrators, the President and the President-elect saw placards reading "We demand socialistic education" and "Socialistic education means freedom from Catholic oppression."[21] As time passed, it became increasingly evident to everyone—except the Catholic clergy and their more zealous followers—that a sizeable number of the Mexican people were not going to abide by clerical dictates.

Whether those Mexicans who backed the government did so of their own free will is a moot point. For reasons of idealism, self interest, or a combination of the two, many Mexican citizens shared the desire of those in power to see reforms achieved. Members of this group naturally aligned themselves with the government during the

---

[19]Carreño, *Páginas de historia mexicana*, pp. 165, 167, 169; Vázquez Knauth, "La educación socialista," pp. 412-13; Bremauntz, *La educación socialista*, pp. 305, 307, 309.
[20]Brown, "Mexican Church-State Relations," pp. 206-207; Carreño, *Páginas de historia mexicana*, p. 149; NYT, October 20, 1934, p. 6; see also the issues of *La Palabra Nacionalista* published in October and November 1934.
[21]NYT, October 29, 1934, p. 9; *La Palabra Nacionalista*, October 29, 1934.

altercation over religion and education. Others took this stand because it was the only realistic choice open to them. Federal employees who failed to participate in the October 28 demonstration subsequently lost their jobs. Some educators were also dismissed because they would not support governmental policies. During the controversy surrounding the amendment of Article 3, certain states began to rid their schools of personnel who opposed socialistic education or held strong religious convictions. As a requirement for keeping their positions, teachers were at times forced to sign pledges in which they denied having any religious beliefs.[22] This type of pressure, combined with other, more subtle forms of persuasion, undoubtedly caused some Mexicans to think twice before taking sides in the church-state dispute.

While the Mexican people expressed their views on the religious issue, the gulf between the episcopate and the government widened. When a group of congressmen visited Calles in October, he informed them of his belief that the clergy was in the process of organizing a rebellion. Calles's accusation appeared in the press and was answered by Archbishop Díaz, who denied that the Church authorized the use of armed force. Unimpressed by Díaz's denial, Calles instructed Rodríguez that action should be taken to expel churchmen guilty of sedition. Desiring to act with moderation and within legal channels, President Rodríguez asked Attorney General Emilio Portes Gil to determine which of the Catholic prelates, if any, were responsible for the upheaval in Mexico. Early in November, following a brief investigation, Portes Gil informed Rodríguez that two prelates—Apostolic Delegate Ruiz y Flores and José de Jesús Manríquez y Zárate, the Bishop of Huejutla—had blatantly provoked unrest in Mexico. After Portes Gil compiled a formal document containing charges against these two clerics, a judge in the Federal District issued warrants for their arrest. Both of the clergymen, however, were already in exile in the United States and were outside the jurisdiction of the Mexican courts.[23]

By November 1934, two-thirds of the Mexican states had ratified the amendment to Article 3; however, events during that year had revealed to PNR leaders that they must move slowly and carefully in implementing this controversial reform. Hoping to calm the tense

[22]NYT, November 5, 1934, p. 2; Townsend, *Lázaro Cárdenas*, p. 79.
[23]Carreño, *Páginas de historia mexicana*, pp. 177, 179, 181; John W. F. Dulles, *Yesterday in Mexico: A Chronicle of the Revolution, 1919-1936* (Austin: University of Texas Press, 1961), p. 564; Emilio Portes Gil, *Quince años de política mexicana*, 3d ed. (México, D.F.: Ediciones Botas, 1954), p. 502; NYT, October 31, 1934, p. 1; NYT, November 16, 1934, p. 15; Brown, "Mexican Church-State Relations," p. 208. See Emilio Portes Gil, *The Conflict between the Civil Power and the Clergy: Historical and Legal Essay by Emilio Portes Gil, Attorney General of the Republic* (México, D.F: Press of the Ministry of Foreign Affairs, 1935), p. 115-35.

situation in Mexico, the PNR announced that it would not act in haste.[24]

This declaration did not calm Catholics upset by the allegations in Portes Gil's report and fearful of eventual implementation of socialist education. Having unsuccessfully tried legal means of opposition to revolutionary schemes, the Church's more fervent followers concluded that armed insurrection was the only remaining method for protecting their rights. On November 20, a group of Catholic laymen in Cerro Gordo, Vera Cruz, proclaimed the formation of a Popular Liberating Army to overthrow the Calles-dominated government. This second Cristero uprising, which gradually spread to nine other states, suffered from three basic weaknesses: insufficient public backing, lack of qualified leadership, and refusal of the Catholic hierarchy to support the movement publicly. Despite these handicaps, the Cristero guerrillas, while they never posed a serious threat, managed to sustain their rebellion until 1937.[25]

Inaugurated on December 1, Cárdenas became president of a country torn by religious strife. Plutarco Elías Calles, through his Guadalajara speech and his insistence that Rodríguez act against the episcopate, was at least partially responsible for the difficulties that the new executive faced. While president from 1924 to 1928, Calles had revealed his compulsion to subject the Catholic Church to governmental control. Thus, it was not out of character for him to criticize the hierarchy, to warn against clerical influence, or to insist that repressive action be taken against the Church. Perhaps, then, Calles's actions in 1934 require no further analysis. However, one must ask why the political boss chose to renew his assault upon the Roman Catholic Church precisely in the six-month period immediately preceding Cárdenas's inauguration.

Calles delivered his speech in Guadalajara just two months after Narciso Bassols, a staunch *callista*, had been forced to resign as Secretary of Education. Calles may have felt the need to repay members of the clergy for the trouble he believed they had caused his partisan.[26] This presumed personal desire for revenge may suffice to explain the timing of Calles's outburst of open aggression against the Church. Nevertheless, there may have been a less obvious but more significant explanation for his actions.

Since 1928, Calles had been active behind the scenes in the three presidential administrations succeeding his own. From 1928 to 1934 his own political views had become increasingly conservative, especially in regard to labor and agrarian reform. In 1934 Calles found himself faced with a President-elect who not only was radical in

[24] NYT, November 16, 1934, p. 15.
[25] Brown, "Mexican Church-State Relations," p. 208; Michaels, "Mexican Politics and Nationalism," pp. 148–49.
[26] Carreño, *Páginas de historia mexicana*, p. 137.

political beliefs but also enjoyed a strong following among the Mexican citizenry. Under these circumstances, Calles may have seized the religious issue as a tool to achieve his own ends. Jealous of his political power and desirous of hampering Cárdenas's reform program, Calles may have chosen deliberately to aggravate the church-state conflict in hope of forcing the new president to turn to him for guidance.[27] If this were indeed Calles's goal, he was partly successful. His acts did worsen the religious crisis in Mexico; however, Cárdenas proved himself capable of handling problems without the assistance of the *Jefe Máximo*.

The new president's original cabinet was composed of an interesting assortment of Mexicans, many of whom had been involved in various phases of the church-state dispute. Narciso Bassols was appointed Secretary of Finance and Emilio Portes Gil became Secretary of Foreign Relations. Tomás Garrido Canabal, a violent anticlerical from Tabasco, was Cárdenas's selection for Secretary of Agriculture.[28]

As virtual dictator of Tabasco since the 1920s, Garrido had almost eliminated the Catholic Church from that state. Coming to the national capital in November 1934, he brought a contingent of his followers, known as Red Shirts, who marched in a parade honoring Calles. The *Jefe Máximo* congratulated the young men and their sponsor for the fine work they had done in Tabasco, and he cited it as an example for other states to follow. Garrido interpreted this statement as an inducement for the Red Shirts to extend their activities to Mexico City. Consequently, after he formally assumed his cabinet post, Garrido watched with approval as his small brigade organized "Red Saturdays" and "Red Sundays" during which they spread antireligious and anti-Catholic propaganda.[29] These activities created tension in and around the capital.

Mexico City was only one of many areas experiencing stress caused by the church-state conflict. In Jalisco, Nuevo León, and elsewhere, alarmed Catholic parents kept their children from attending schools that allegedly offered socialist education. Indignant Catholics in Durango reportedly kidnapped any teachers willing to impart socialist instruction. Through fear, ignorance, and misunderstanding, violent action spread; and some teachers were beaten, abducted, mutilated, or murdered.[30]

[27]Johnson, *Heroic Mexico*, pp. 403-403; Michaels, "Mexican Politics and Nationalism," pp. 11, 150.
[28]Silvano Barba González, *Lázaro Cárdenas*, vol. 4 of *La lucha por la tierra*, 4 vols. (México, D.F.: Editorial del Magisterio, 1964), p. 163.
[29]Alan M. Kirshner, "A Setback to Tomás Garrido Canabal's Desire to Eliminate the Church in Mexico," *A Journal of Church and State* 13 (Autumn 1971): 480-81; Townsend, *Lázaro Cárdenas*, pp. 103-104.
[30]NYT, December 3, 1934, p. 11; NYT, December 4, 1934, p. 14; Vázquez Knauth, "La educación socialista," p. 420; Bremauntz, *La educación socialista*, pp. 328-30. See also David L. Raby, "Los maestros y los conflictos sociales en México," *Historia Mexicana* 18 (October-December 1968): 190-226.

Reacting to conditions in Mexico, Apostolic Delegate Ruiz y Flores issued a statement on December 12 concerning both armed rebellion and socialist education. Asserting that the clergy neither promoted nor prohibited armed insurrection, he explained that they could not stop Catholics from defending their rights, which included the right of parents to decide the kind of education that their children would receive. The papal representative then reminded everyone concerned that no Catholic could learn or teach socialist education.[31] These words may have served as encouragement for those Catholics acting outside of legal means in opposition to governmental policies.

While the clergy continued to oppose revolutionary designs, revolutionaries opposed clerical activities. By the end of 1934, thirteen Mexican states had forcibly closed most church buildings within their borders. A few states had completely abolished religious services. Whereas there had been more than four thousand active Catholic priests in Mexico in 1926, the combined state laws restricting clerical numbers allowed only 322 for the entire country by 1935.[32]

While various state governments moved to curb clerical influence, the Red Shirts continued their campaign against the Catholic religion. On December 30, members of the group gathered in front of the Church of San Juan Bautista in Coyoacán. Shouting anticlerical slogans, they planted their flag near the church building. Worshippers grew angry and tempers soared. A clash resulted. After killing five Catholics, the Red Shirts were forced to retreat to a nearby municipal building. Unaware of what had just happened, Ernesto Malda arrived tardily upon the scene. The sight of his red shirt infuriated the crowd, and he was lynched. When police arrived, they placed sixty-four Red Shirts in custody and arrested three other men for the murder of Malda. Learning of the incident, Cárdenas indicated his distress and pledged punishment of the guilty. Despite the President's statement and mounting sentiment against Garrido's followers, the Secretary of Agriculture gave his personal support to the forty Red Shirts formally charged with inciting the Coyoacán riot.[33]

In early January 1935, angry university students sacked the headquarters of the Red Shirts, who fired into the crowd and wounded five

---

[31]Leopoldo Ruiz y Flores to the episcopate, clergy and Catholics of Mexico, December 12, 1934, Reel no. 41, Archivo de la Liga Nacional Defensora de la Libertad Religiosa, Latin American Collection, University of Texas at Austin (hereafter cited as Archivo de la L.N.D.L.R.); Brown, "Mexican Church-State Relations," p. 209; Charles S. MacFarland, *Chaos in Mexico: The Conflict of Church and State* (New York: Harper & Bros., 1935), p. 133.

[32]Charles Cumberland, *Mexico: The Struggle for Modernity* (New York: Oxford University Press, 1968), p. 283; James W. Wilkie, "Statistical Indicators of the Impact of National Revolution on the Catholic Church in Mexico, 1910-1967," *A Journal of Church and State* 12 (Winter 1970): 97-98.

[33]*NYT*, December 31, 1934, p. 1; Kirshner, "A Setback," pp. 482-85; Comité "Asesinados de Coyoacán," *Los sangrientos sucesos de Coyoacán* (México, D.F.: n.d.), pp. 2-15, passim.

students. Confronted with this explosive situation, Cárdenas realized the need to restrain the over-zealous youth group in order to prevent additional trouble. Consequently, he announced that in the future the official party would control all propaganda activities and demonstrations. This presidential announcement, coupled with public indignation, effectively curbed the Red Shirts' activities.[34]

Within a month of the Coyoacán incident, President Cárdenas clarified his own position regarding the Roman Catholic Church. He informed newspapermen: "The conflict between church and civil power has had but one meaning for the government—the absolute submission of the clergy to the laws as a means to put a stop to their collective or personal interference in political, legal, economic, and social fields."[35] The chief executive contended that his administration desired not persecution of religion but execution of the law.

On January 26, Díaz refuted Cárdenas's statement and charged that "Persecution does exist." Subsequently, a presidential decree published in February 1935 appeared to Catholics to be proof that persecution did exist in Mexico. It prohibited circulation in the Mexican mail of any materials or correspondence containing religious propaganda.[36] Although short-lived, this prohibition worsened the already tense church-state situation.

The seriousness of this situation did not escape the American ambassador to Mexico. Josephus Daniels realized that PNR leaders condemned the clergy for active involvement in politics. To counteract clerical influence, the government felt the imperative need to indoctrinate Mexican youth with principles of the Revolution; hence, emphasis had been given to socialist education. On the other hand, the Catholic hierarchy believed that the government not only persecuted the Church but also sought to impose atheist education on the country. Determined to block governmental efforts, the hierarchy had appealed to Mexican Catholics for support. The real tragedy of the situation, the diplomat realized, was that members of both factions were sincerely committed to their conflicting beliefs.[37]

Acting upon his own beliefs, the Mexican head of state signed the enabling act for the amendment to Article 3 of the Constitution in March 1935. For the remainder of his term, Cárdenas worked whenever possible to make socialist education a reality. He encouraged modification of the school curriculum to instill in students a "spirit of cooperation." Textbooks were printed which stressed understanding of the workers' condition, the vices of bourgeois society, and the need for a more equitable social system. Hoping that the

[34]Kirshner, "A Setback," pp. 489-90.
[35]NYT, January 26, 1935, p. 14; *La Palabra Nacionalista*, January 26, 1935.
[36]NYT, January 27, 1935, p. 24; *La Palabra Nacionalista*, February 13, 1935.
[37]Josephus Daniels, *Shirt-Sleeve Diplomat* (Chapel Hill: University of North Carolina Press, 1947), p. 189.

public school would replace the Church as the center of the Mexican community, Cárdenas increased educational allotments, opened new school buildings, hired additional teachers, made textbooks subject to state inspection, and sponsored cultural missions to train rural schoolmasters in the methodology of the "new" education.[38]

Political occurrences in June 1935 temporarily distracted Cárdenas's attention from educational reforms. During that month he found himself challenged by Calles. Deploring the radicalism of the existing administration, Calles criticized Cárdenas for allegedly attempting to divide Congress into factions of *callistas* and *cardenistas*. Noting that similar circumstances had resulted in the resignation of President Ortiz Rubio, Calles hinted that the same thing might happen to Cárdenas. Unlike Ortiz Rubio, Cárdenas proved himself capable of meeting Calles's challenge. At the President's request, his cabinet, which included several *callistas*, resigned. Majority blocs in both the Chamber of Deputies and the Senate indicated their allegiance to Cárdenas rather than Calles. Portes Gil, newly elected head of the PNR, declared that he would "second the policies of the President." Having received this strong support, Cárdenas countered the powerplay by Calles, who then departed for the United States.[39]

While successful in this initial confrontation, the President realized that Calles would not relinquish easily the power he had exercised for so many years. Aware of the need to strengthen his own position as much as possible, Cárdenas worked to win the loyalty of all sectors of Mexican society, including the Catholic hierarchy and the faithful. Turning Calles's anticlericalism against him, the President made overtures to the Church. While insisting upon his determination to enforce religious laws in Mexico, he proclaimed amnesty for Mexicans exiled for political or religious reasons, encouraged state governments to modify restrictions on the Catholic Church, and replaced Secretary of Agriculture Garrido Canabal with General Saturnino Cedillo of San Luis Potosí. While Garrido Canabal had been one of Mexico's most vociferous anticlericals, Cedillo was a protector of Catholics and a champion of religious rights.[40]

Despite these actions, Cárdenas encountered difficulty in improving church-state relations. Through a joint pastoral in September

---

[38] J. H. Plenn, *Mexico Marches* (Indianapolis, Ind.: Bobbs-Merrill Co., 1939), p. 168; Michaels, "Mexican Politics and Nationalism," pp. 118-19, 124, 132-33; Vázquez Knauth, "La educación socialista," p. 418; Cline, *The United States and Mexico*, p. 224-25; Townsend, *Lázaro Cárdenas*, pp. 81-82; Nathaniel and Sylvia Weyl, *The Reconquest of Mexico: The Years of Lázaro Cárdenas* (New York: Oxford University Press, 1939), p. 324.

[39] Johnson, *Heroic Mexico*, p. 415; NYT, June 13, 1935, p. 1; NYT, June 15, 1935, p. 1; NYT, June 16, 1935, p. 3.

[40] Michaels, "Mexican Politics and Nationalism," pp. 68, 149, 176; Cline, *The United States and Mexico*, p. 220; CH 42 (September 1935): 638; Townsend, *Lázaro Cárdenas*, pp. 105-106, 117.

1935, the Mexican episcopate recommended that faithful laymen form associations to work for the repeal of persecutory legislation. The following month, Catholic clergy themselves petitioned for modification of constitutional articles restricting the Church's rights. In response, the President charged the Church with responsibility for most of the "bloody internal warfare" that had transpired in Mexico and vowed enforcement of laws affecting religious worship and education.[41]

While Cárdenas upheld the government's educational policies, extremist elements persisted in terrorizing school teachers. Distressed by a number of attacks on rural teachers, the Secretary of Education requested that the War Department allow teachers to arm in self defense. In early December, thousands of militant teachers demonstrated in Mexico City. Assuring the demonstrators that they were the mainstay of the Revolution, Cárdenas agreed to give them arms.[42]

Adding to the President's worries, Calles returned to Mexico from the United States on December 13. Calles insisted that he had intended to stay out of Mexican politics after his exit from the country in June, but he explained that the "storm of insults and calumnies" unleashed against him during his absence had caused him to change his mind.[43] Calles's return and his subsequent remarks indicated that he still considered himself an active participant in Mexican politics.

The beginning of 1936 found Cárdenas faced with continuing opposition from Calles, the Catholic hierarchy, and a large segment of the Catholic laity. Under these circumstances, Cárdenas made overtures to the Church in a speech delivered at Ciudad Guerrero. Distinguishing between religious beliefs and fanaticism, he asserted that his government did not desire to combat religion. Socialist education, he explained, challenged not religion but fanaticism and prejudice. Cárdenas labeled as liars those who claimed that religious persecution existed in Mexico; he stressed that his government sought only "fulfillment of the laws."[44]

A month later in Guadalajara, the Mexican chief of state explained some of his reasons for modifying his attitude concerning the Catholic Church. He declared that his government's main concern was to promote economic and social reform. Contending that antireligious campaigns hampered progress in this direction, Cárdenas claimed that

---

[41]Mexican episcopate to Mexican Catholics, September 8, 1935, and Petition, Mexican episcopate to the President of the Republic, September 29, 1935, Reel no. 37, Archivo de la L.N.D.L.R.; Plenn, *Mexico Marches*, pp. 205-207; Michaels, "Mexican Politics and Nationalism," p. 158; NYT, November 6, 1935, p. 10.

[42]NYT, November 22, 1935, p. 15; NYT, December 6, 1935, p. 16; Michaels, "Mexican Politics and Nationalism," p. 131.

[43]NYT, December 14, 1935, p. 6.

[44]Brown, "Mexican Church-State Relations," pp. 213-14; Michaels, Mexican Politics and Nationalism," p. 160; NYT, February 18, 1936, p. 5.

he would avoid the mistake of earlier presidents who had treated "the religious question as a problem preeminent to other issues."[45]

Events in Mexico during March testified to the sincerity of the President. Under his influence, eight states reopened Catholic churches. At the end of the month, Secretary of Gobernación Silvano Barba González informed the press that the federal government would neither provoke the Church nor allow it to be persecuted. He promised that the religious rights of Catholics would be respected as long as they obeyed existing laws.[46]

Although attempting to alleviate the church-state crisis so that his government could concentrate on other matters, Cárdenas acted and spoke forcefully when necessary. In late March, Catholics who were protesting socialist education rioted in Ciudad González and killed eighteen members of a cultural mission. The President immediately conducted a personal investigation. Speaking to the townspeople, Cárdenas claimed that the local priest had incited the bloody incident by spreading propaganda against socialist education. After making several remarks in defense of the government's educational reforms, he ordered the cleric to leave Ciudad González within twenty-four hours.[47]

Shortly after this riot, Cárdenas visited the state of Jalisco. There he was approached by a group of rural teachers who complained that their lives were endangered by hostile peasants. In his reply, Cárdenas revealed his awareness that blame for agitation in Mexico did not rest wholly upon the shoulders of the clergy. He advised the educators that anticlerical movements provoked resistance and were a "waste of the efforts of public servants." Declaring that antireligious propaganda must be removed from the classroom, the President insisted that "All ... attention must be concentrated upon the great cause of social reform."[48]

By April 1936, Cárdenas had outlined his position toward the Roman Catholic Church. He would not allow members of the clergy to intervene in matters outside their sphere nor would he permit Catholics to block governmental programs. However, the President was aware that prolonged church-state conflict accomplished little of value and consumed much of the government's energy. Thus, he was willing to adopt a more conciliatory approach.

It was in April 1936 that the final encounter developed between Cárdenas and Calles. Since his return from the United States, the *Jefe Máximo* had frequently criticized radical aspects of the Cárdenas ad-

---

[45]NYT, March 6, 1936, p. 10; Brown, "Mexican Church-State Relations," p. 214.
[46]Michales, "Mexican Politics and Nationalism," p. 161; NYT, March 19, 1936, p. 6; NYT, March 31, 1936, p. 14; Brown, "Mexican Church-State Relations," p. 215.
[47]Michaels, "Mexican Politics and Nationalism," pp. 161-62. See Lázaro Cárdenas, *Escuela socialista y religión* (México, D.F.: Talleres Gráficos de la Nación, 1936).
[48]Plenn, *Mexico Marches*, p. 207; Townsend, *Lázaro Cárdenas*, p. 135.

ministration. These remarks had caused labor and agrarian groups to call for Calles's expulsion from Mexico. As feeling against Calles began to grow, Cárdenas decided to act. On April 10 he deported his former mentor along with a few noted *callistas*. Justifying this action, the President accused Calles of having conspired to undermine achievement of the Six Year Plan.[49]

With Calles gone, Cárdenas could devote more of his energies to implementing the principles embodied within the Six Year Plan. During the remaining years of his term, basic areas of disagreement continued to exist between the Mexican government and the Catholic Church. While the President required obedience to Mexican laws and acceptance of educational innovations, Catholic prelates still requested constitutional reform and emphasized the sanctity of Christian education. Nevertheless, church-state relations did improve.

Without modifying existing legislation, the federal government relaxed enforcement of the more stringent religious restrictions and influenced state governments to do the same. Leadership in the Mexican Catholic Church also underwent a change and the hierarchy began to act in a more moderate manner. When Pascual Díaz died in May 1936, Luis María Martínez y Rodríguez became Archbishop of Mexico. Martínez, former auxiliary bishop of Michoacán, knew and respected Cárdenas. In 1937 Ruiz y Flores resigned as Apostolic Delegate, and his duties also fell to Archibishop Martínez. For the first time in many years, Church authority in Mexico centered in one man, a prelate who defended Catholic interests but who was a realist. Since 1925 the Church had vainly resisted subordination to political authority. Believing that nothing could be gained by prolonging this struggle that divided the people of Mexico, Martínez accepted as a major aim the attainment of "concord, harmony, and unity" in his country.[50] Under the leadership of Martínez and Cárdenas, the Roman Catholic Church and the Mexican State began a slow, painful, but steady move toward a type of "peaceful coexistence."

---

[49]NYT, April 11, 1936, p. 1; *NYT*, April 19, 1936, sec. 4, p. 6; Johnson, *Heroic Mexico*, pp. 416-17.
[50]NYT, February 26, 1937, p. 15; Brown, "Mexican Church-State Relations," p. 219; Plenn, *Mexico Marches*, p. 208.

10. Mexican Catholics and Socialist Education of the 1930s

SISTER MARIA ANN KELLY, C.S.J.

After outlining the Mexican political scene at the beginning of the 1930s, Dr. Kelly describes the nature of Mexican Catholicism at that time and discusses the Catholic philosophy of education, particularly as set forth by the Vatican and by the Mexican hierarchy. The principal focus of this study is the government's program of socialist education together with responses by the Catholic prelates, priests, and laity.

In an address to the Third Congress of Mexican and North American Historians held in Oaxtepec, Morelos, in 1969, Jean Meyer underscored the fact that until the role of religion in the life of the masses has been clearly defined, it is impossible to understand adequately the history of a people. He indicated that the relationship between religion and social tensions is in need of study. This ought to be examined in the light of two questions which Meyer posed: "What is the activity of religious bodies confronted with social tensions?" and "Is religion a factor of conflicts?"[1]

It is within such a framework that this present study rests. If one is to interpret properly the activities undertaken by the Mexican people when their government implemented a program of socialist education in 1934, it is essential to understand the philosophy of the Catholic Church with regard to education and socialism as well as the manner in which the Mexican bishops applied and interpreted this philosophy at a given moment in history. Consideration must also be given to responses and attitudes assumed by various sectors of the Mexican population.

---

[1]Jean Meyer, "Historia de la vida social," *Investigaciones contemporáneas sobre historia de México: Memorias de la tercera reunión de historiadores mexicanos y norteamericanos* (México, D.F.: Universidad Nacional Autónoma de México, 1971), pp. 395-96.

The Mexican Scene In 1930

At the Convention of the Partido Nacional Revolucionario (PNR) held in Querétaro in December 1933, convention delegates called for the reform of Article 3 of the Constitution to insure control by the state over primary and secondary education, which they hoped to see rooted in the orientations and postulates of the socialist doctrine sustained by the Mexican Revolution.[2] Such a resolution was the culmination of radical movements that had been seeking establishment of the rationalist as well as of the socialist school during the late 1920s and early 1930s. Professor Josefina Vázquez, a distinguished authority on the history of Mexican education, credits strong antireligious movements with achieving this proposal for the reform of Article 3 in the Querétaro Convention.[3]

After vigorous debates in the Congress and certain adjustments in the original proposal, Article 3 of the Constitution was amended to read as follows:

> The education that the state gives will be socialist, and besides excluding all religious doctrine, it will combat fanaticism and prejudices. For this reason, the school will organize its teaching and activities in such a way as to permit the creation of a rational and exact concept of the Universe and of social life.[4]

The article also prescribed that only the State could give primary, secondary, and normal instruction. If private schools submitted to government regulations and programs, they would be authorized by the Ministry of Education and remain under its close scrutiny. Members of religious communities or ministers of any creed were prohibited from any type of participation in school affairs.

Former President Plutarco Elías Calles and President-elect Lázaro Cárdenas wanted to take over the minds of the youth, to rid them of their prejudices, and to prevent the clergy from interfering in any way in the educational process. Their hope was that the school would no longer be used by the clergy to retard the progress of the country or to convert the young people into enemies of both the working class and the Revolution.[6]

Mexico had been embroiled in a bitter religious war from 1926 until 1929, when a *modus vivendi* was arranged between the Mexican government and the Catholic Church. Nevertheless, difficulties

---

[2]Carlos Alvear Acevedo, *Lázaro Cárdenas: El hombre y el mito* (México, D.F.: Editorial Jus, 1972), p. 100.
[3]Josefina Vázquez de Knauth, *Nacionalismo y educación en México* (México, D.F.: El Colegio de México, 1970), pp. 152-53.
[4]Quoted in José Bravo Ugarte, *La Educación en México (. . .-1965)*, (México, D.F.: Editorial Jus, 1966), p. 160.
[5]Ibid.
[6]*Excelsior*, July 21, 1934; Partido Nacional Revolucionario, *La educación socialista* (México, D.F.: n.p., 1935), p. 22.

between the two entities did not abate; and, once more, severe restrictions were placed upon the Church. Its properties were seized, and state and federal legislative bodies enacted drastic laws that severely limited the numbers of priests permitted to function. Hostile actions toward bishops resulted in exile for many, while private schools continued to suffer from a host of resrictions, regulations, and confiscations.[7]

During the 1930s, Mexicans were bombarded with Marxist propaganda. Recognized Marxists assumed high positions in the administration of President Lázaro Cárdenas, and many teachers joined the Communist Party. These teachers voiced anti-God slogans, taught that God does not exist, and used textbooks that condemned the clergy and lauded Marx. Opponents of socialist education circulated reports concerning the immorality of government teachers and charged that graphic sex lessons were being given in the schools.[8]

Mexican Catholicism

Statistics reveal that in 1930 approximately 97.8 percent of the Mexican people identified themselves as Roman Catholics.[9] Let us consider the nature of this Catholicism and of the individuals who professed it.

After study, observation, and consultation with many Mexicans, this writer believes that Mexican Catholicism should be interpreted in the following manner: Because Mexican Catholicism has never been monolithic, it cannot be understood without distinguishing among the various sectors that comprise the Church. The Pope, the bishops, and the clergy set forth Church doctrine. A relatively small number of laymen, distinguished by their faith as well as their knowledge of doctrine, formed an elite leadership group. Comprising a third sector were the majority of Mexican Catholics, who had a very inadequate knowledge of religion. For many members of this latter group, religion was an inheritance of various religious-social customs that consisted of ceremonies and fiestas celebrated at periodic intervals. Deprived of solid instruction in the Catholic religion, the Mexican masses slipped into exaggerated, superstitious, and fanatical practices. Yet, despite the lack of doctrinal knowledge that led to certain exaggerations, most

---

[7]Joseph H. L. Schlarman, *Mexico: Tierra de volcanes*, trans. C. de María y Campos (México, D.F.: Editorial Porrua, 1969), p. 636; J. Lloyd Mecham, *Church and State in Latin America: A History of Politico-Ecclesiastical Relations*, rev. ed. (Chapel Hill: University of North Carolina Press, 1966), pp. 404-405.

[8]Alvear Acevedo, *Lázaro Cárdenas*, pp. 301-306; Schlarman, *Mexico*, pp. 54-60; "Moscow in Mexico," Bulletin no. 43, September 1936, Reel no. 39 in Archivo de la Liga Nacional Defensora de la Libertad Religiosa, Instituto Nacional de Antropología e Historia, México, D.F. (hereafter cited as Archivo de la L.N.D.L.R.).

[9]James W. Wilkie, "Statistical Indicators of the Impact of the National Revolution on the Catholic Church in Mexico, 1910-1967," *A Journal of Church and State* 12 (Winter 1970): 91.

Mexicans had an intense faith which was not dependent upon a profound understanding of Catholic religion. This unshakeable faith in God and in Our Lady of Guadalupe dominated their life.

The Catholic Philosophy of Education

On January 17, 1932, Mons. Pascual Díaz, the Archbishop of Mexico, reminded parents of the seriousness of their obligation to give their children a proper education. Díaz asserted that a Christian education ought to form the child in such a manner that throughout his life he would bear a striking resemblance to Christ Himself. The Bishop explained that man's immediate purpose in life is to serve God and thus attain his final goal, which is the salvation of his own soul and the glorification of God.[10]

On November 21, 1935, the Mexican bishops reaffirmed the goals of Christian education and emphasized the educational doctrine of the Catholic Church as Pope Pius XI had developed it in his encyclical of December 31, 1929.[11] The encyclical teaches that education is social in nature because a child is born into three societies: the family, the Church, and the state; and each has its own particular function and purpose. The family exists for the purpose of creating and educating children; but because it lacks all the means to accomplish this, it must seek the aid of the state and the Church. Civil society exists to provide for the temporal good of its members, while the mission of the Church is to bring all men to eternal salvation. Because education is concerned with the whole man, both as an individual and as a member of society and in his natural life as well as in his supernatural life, the Church explains that all three societies have educational rights appropriate to their own particular ends.[12]

The Church insists that her rights in education are of the supernatural order, that they come from God Himself and are above any rights in the natural order. The Church has the express command of Christ to teach and to baptize all nations, and it has the assurance of Christ that in this work it will be free of error because Christ will be with the Church until the end of time. As spiritual mother, the Church asserts her right to bring souls to supernatural life and to nourish and educate them in the divine life of grace.[13]

Because the Church is independent of any earthly power in her

---

[10]Pascual Díaz, "Instrucción pastoral: A los padres de familia del Arzobispado de México sobre la educación cristiana de sus hijos," January 17, 1932, in *Pastorales, edictos y otros documentos*, ed. Alberto María Carreño (México, D.F.: Ediciones Victoria, 1938), p. 163.

[11]"Carta pastoral colectiva que el episcopado mexicano dirige a los muy Iltres. Cabildos, al Vble. Clero Secular y Regular y a todos los fieles, sobre la doctrina educativa de la Iglesia," November 21, 1935, in *Christus*, December 1935, p. 27.

[12]Ibid., p. 27; Pius XI, *Divini Illius Magistri*, December 31, 1929 (Washington, D.C.: National Catholic Welfare Conference, 1936), p. 76.

[13]*Divini Illius Magistri*, p. 7.

origin and in her mission as educator, the Mexican bishops cited the Church's right to maintain schools to carry out her mission. For this same reason, the Church reserves the right to judge what is profitable or detrimental to a Christian education.[14]

The Church did not claim that the state may not issue regulations for the schools, but it did insist that these should be within the legitimate dispositions of civil authority. Pius XI stated clearly that the Church "is in every way ready to cooperate with this authority and to make provision for a mutual understanding should difficulties arise."[15]

The family, too, has rights in education that are undeniable; thus, Pius XI stated: "God directly communicates to the family, in the natural order, fecundity, which is the principle of life, and hence also the principle of education to life, together with authority, the principle of order."[16] In the light of this teaching, the Church refuses to give credence to the argument of those who contend that man is born into civil society directly and, therefore, the state has the right to control education. The Church insists that children are born into the family from whence they enter into civil society.[17] However, the state has rights in education because of its God-given authority to promote the temporal welfare of society. Nevertheless, it has no right to monopolize education and to absorb either the individual or the family or to become a substitute for them. When the family and the Church need assistance in providing an adequate education for their children, the state, which is supported by the contributions of all citizens, is in turn obligated to support the needs of its citizens. Coupled with this supportive role of the state in education, the Church recognizes the right of the state to ensure that all receive physical, moral, and intellectual training as well as a formation in civics and politics, because these have direct bearing upon the good of the entire nation.[18]

The Mexican prelates repeatedly denounced the philosophy of socialism and pointed out its errors. Apostolic Delegate Leopoldo Ruiz y Flores and Archbishop Pascual Díaz explained that in condemning socialism they did not condone the evils of society. The Apostolic Delegate indicated on October 24, 1934, that liberalism, which the Church had condemned, was the cause of the grave evils that socialism now sought to remedy with even greater evils.[19] Insisting that the resolution of Mexico's social question lay in pacifying and

---

[14]"Carta pastoral colectiva . . . sobre la doctrina educativa de la Iglesia," p. 28.
[15]*Divini Illius Magistri*, p. 9.
[16]Ibid, p. 12.
[17]Leo XIII, Rerum Novarum, quoted in *Divini Illius Magistri*, p. 13.
[18]*Divini Illius Magistri*, pp. 16-17.
[19]Leopoldo Ruiz y Flores, "Mensaje de protesta del Excmo. y. Rvmo. Sr. Delegado Apsotólico a los católicos mexicanos," October 24, 1934, Reel no. 36, Archivo de la L.N.D.L.R.

uniting the antagonistic classes of society, Archbishop Díaz denounced the idea of class struggle. Socialism was in error because it insisted that the good of the state ought to take precedence over the rights of individuals. Socialism considered all religion as its enemy because the interests of God and of morality were opposed to the idolatry of a God-state.[20]

One of the most outspoken opponents which the Mexican government faced was the bishop of Huejutla, José de Jesús Manríquez y Zárate. In a letter to his people he stated that the government's Six Year Plan was directly headed toward the erection of a Communist nation.[21] In another treatise he cited the inherent errors of the philosophy of socialism. He condemned it for seeking to remedy social evils by destroying social institutions and creating a worker's paradise. Society became an end in itself instead of being the means by which man could further his eternal destiny. That socialism was rooted in atheism became evident in its rejection of matrimony, thus making it nothing more than a civil contract. Although socialism wished to appropriate the youth to itself, the Bishop argued that the state was not capable of making adequate provision for their sustenance and education from infancy. And, lastly, he condemned socialism because it denied the individual the right of private ownership.[22]

Although the Church insists on the right of private ownership, it maintains that the individual has an obligation to use his property for the common good of all and not to reserve it for his own selfish ends. Archbishop Ruiz emphasized that the Church opposes neither a just redistribution of riches nor expropriation when it is for the common good. What the Church does ask is that the lawmaker exercise both justice and equity and offer proper indemnization to the owners. He warned against using such measures for either political exploitation or antireligious propaganda.[23]

Sexual education in the schools was a separate issue in Mexico prior to the official adoption of the socialist school, but it came to be closely associated with the new school. The Apostolic Delegate denounced any program of sex education in the school because it trampled upon the sacred rights of parents.[24] On November 21, 1935,

[20]Pascual Díaz, "Instrucción que dirige a sus sacerdotes sobre el problema de la enseñanza socialista, April 30, 1934, in *Pastorales, edictos y otros documentos*, pp. 209-15.
[21]José de Jesús Manríquez y Zárate, "Orientaciones para mis diocesanos," July 2, 1935, Reel no. 54, Archivo de la L.N.D.L.R.
[22]José de Jesús Manríquez y Zárate, *El socialismo* (México, D.F: Ediciones PAGF, 1939), pp. 16-18.
[23]Leopoldo Ruiz y Flores, "Al episcopado, clero y católicos de México," December 12, 1934, Reel no. 41, Archivo de la L.N.D.L.R.
[24]Ruiz y Flores, "Mensaje de protesta del Excmo. y Rvmo Sr. Delgado Apostólico, October 24, 1934, Reel no. 36, Archivo de la L.N.D.L.R.

the Mexican bishops explained why the Church did not approve of a sexual education program in the schools. To use purely natural measures as a way of preventing young people from falling into the pitfalls of concupiscence is erroneous. A premature exposure to the mysteries of sex, especially when it is devoid of all relation with the supernatural, would place the child in grave danger.[25] Pius XI rejected the argument that accustoming children to sex and its mysteries at an early age would discourage them from lapsing into premature sex. He explained that its proponents failed to recognize that such lapses generally occurred because of the weakness of human nature rather than because of ignorance.[26]

The bishops' concern for the education of children was reflected in their reminder to parents that it would be reprehensible for them to entrust their children to evil or ill-prepared instructors. The teacher is the direct representative of the parent while the school is an extension of the home.[27] In his encyclical on education, Pope Pius XI stressed the right which every child has to expect that the instruction he receives is in full accord with the Church's teaching. This does not conflict with the liberty of teaching which the Church acknowledges. Liberty of teaching is not an absolute right, and the Church sees herself responsible for preventing instruction from lapsing into error.[28] In the 19th century, Pope Leo XIII explained that liberty is a property of rational creatures only and he defined it as the "faculty of choosing the means fitted for the end proposed."[29] In developing this, Leo stated that if man's intellect and will were perfect, he would always choose that which was truly good and certain to bring him closer to his final objective. However, man is an imperfect being and needs the guidance of law to aid him in selecting the good. Thus, according to papal teaching, liberty and freedom are characterized not by an absence of law but by law which engenders true freedom.[30]

In the pastoral of November 21, 1935, the bishops discussed the Church's understanding of a Christian education. Students must find in the school not only scientific knowledge but the moral training that harmonizes with their religion. Although religion should occupy the prime position in the school, the entire program and the entire atmosphere of the school must possess a totally Christian quality. Teaching personnel and students alike must be penetrated with the spirit of Christ. If such conditions do not prevail, then the school will bear little fruit.[31]

[25] "Carta pastoral colectiva ... sobre la doctrina educativa de la Iglesia," p. 33.
[26] *Divini Illius Magistri*, p. 25.
[27] "Carta pastoral colectiva sobre los deberes de los padres de familia en materia de enseñanza," December 12, 1936, Reel no. 55, Archivo de la L.N.D.L.R.
[28] *Divini Illius Magistri*, pp. 22-23.
[29] Leo XIII, *Libertas Praestantissimum*, June 20, 1888, in *The Great Encyclical Letters of Pope Leo XIII* (New York: Benziger Brothers, 1903), p. 137.
[30] Ibid., pp. 135-40.
[31] "Carta pastoral colectiva ... sobre la doctrina educativa de la Iglesia," p. 33.

A National Protest

Resistance to socialist education assumed diverse manifestations throughout Mexico. The ecclesiastical authorities, who took on an advisory and didactic position, issued norms and directives to the laity so that they might know what position to take relative to the socialist school. The laity, too, responded. Civic organizations and parents' groups attempted to arouse the public conscience by publicizing the evils of the socialist school and by scheduling meetings, rallies or strikes. Others expressed their disapproval of the new program by resorting to sporadic acts of violence directed against the representatives of socialist ideas. Another segment of the people strove to organize a Cristero liberation movement comparable to that of the late 1920s. The final years of the 1930s saw the rise of thousands of Mexican Catholics in a massive, nationalistic movement dedicated to reestablishing a government rooted in Christian social principles.

Before examining the various ways in which popular opposition was manifested, it must be stated that resistance to socialist education did not develop with the same degree of intensity or uniformity throughout the country. All regions of Mexico do not evidence the same depth of religious fervor. The central parts of the country are generally held to be more "Catholic" than the states on the periphery. The most vehement opposition to the school appears to have been in those areas that were also the regions of the most significant Cristero activity from 1926 to 1929. Further, some state governors were staunch advocates of the socialist school while others were opposed to the federal government's program.[32] Similarly, individual bishops determined the manner of applying and interpreting the norms of the Holy See and the National Episcopate according to the peculiar circumstances of their individual dioceses.

Ecclesiastical Norms

On December 12, 1934, the Apostolic Delegate indicated that the bishops' task was to protest with prudence against unjust laws, to teach and direct the people in doctrinal matters, to search for an accommodation with the civil government, and to demonstrate with positive deeds the good will of the Church. He reminded the laity that as citizens they had the grave obligation to defend themselves and the Church by utilizing all the licit means available to them.[33]

All Catholics were reminded that they had an obligation to resist the establishment and spread of socialist education. They could

---

[32]Guillermo Ruiz Vázquez, private tape-recorded interview held in Guadalajara, September 20, 1972, and in Mexico City, October 18, 1972; Silvino Robles Gutiérrez, tape-recorded interview held in León, Guanajuato, May 2 and 4, 1972. Cárdenas praised Tabasco and Sonora as bastions of socialism; see *La Prensa* (San Antonio, Texas), September 21, 1934.

[33]Ruiz y Flores, "Al episcopado, clero y católicos de Mexico."

neither open or sustain schools where socialist education was taught nor could they attend such schools or permit their children to do so. It was strictly forbidden for a Catholic to learn, to teach, or to cooperate in the imparting of this socialist education to others. Parents or those in charge of children were reminded that if they sent their children to a socialist school they would sin gravely and be subject to excommunication. This same norm also applied to young people who were sufficiently mature to select the school they desired to attend. Professors and directors of schools were directed that they could take no part in the socialist school. The teaching of socialism involved instructors in the propagation of heresy because socialism contained much heresy. If directors permitted socialism to be taught, they were told that they, too, would be under suspicion of heresy. There were certain conditions under which a professor might teach in a socialist school. If he were to give instruction in a subject that contained none of the heresies of socialism and if he were not required to sign a declaration admitting to socialism, then, for a serious reason, this employment was permissible. Yet, even then, he had to ascertain that his action would not give scandal to others. In general, the same norms were given for school directors and teachers; and the penalties for both entailed serious sin and excommunication.[34]

On December 20, 1936, Cardinal Pacelli, as representative of Pius XI, advised the Mexican bishops to continue their vigilance in regard to the socialist school even though he had received information that in many areas the laws were not being enforced or that they could be avoided. Parents were reminded that only the bishop in their own diocese could determine whether or not there was a sufficiently serious reason for permitting their children to attend an official school. In granting such permission, the bishop had to insure that proper measures would be taken to counteract evil effects of the school.[35]

Although the word excommunication appeared frequently in the norms issued by Mexican bishops, as late as November 21, 1935, no parents had been punished by excommunication. The penalty of excommunication did not apply unless a person were warned that he was in error and that he must rectify his actions within six months or be excommunicated.[36]

The Mexican bishops consistently insisted upon the necessity of prayer and the efficacy of daily mass and the rosary as means of pre-

[34]Ibid.; Díaz, "Instrucción que dirige a sus sacerdotes sobre el problema de la enseñanza socialista," p. 222; Leopoldo Ruiz y Flores, "Normas del Comité Ejecutivo Episcopal a los sacerdotes y a los católicos," January 4, 1935, in *Orientaciones y normas dadas por la Santa Sede y por el Excmo. y Rvmo. Sr. Delegado Apostólico* (San Antonio, Tex.: Imprenta Mundial, 1935), pp. 20-21.

[35]Eugenio Pacelli, "Instrucciones sobre la conducta que el episcopado y los fieles han de observar acerca de la enseñanza socialista impuesta por el gobierno mexicana," December 20, 1936, Reel no. 39, Archivo de la L.N.D.L.R.; Comité Ejecutivo Episcopal, "Instrucción pastoral," May 12, 1937, Reel no. 55, Archivo de la L.N.D.L.R.

[36] "Carta pastoral colectiva sobre la educación de la Iglesia," p. 34.

serving themselves and their children from dangers threatening all Mexicans. The bishops inaugurated a "Spiritual Campaign for the Mexican Children" involving the recitation of special prayers for the safety of young people faced with so many evil influences. They fostered catechetical programs and centers of religious instruction, and they encouraged publication of literature to instruct the faithful.[37]

The Bishops themselves recognized that not all Catholics had heeded their oft-repeated exhortations about the socialist school. In December 1936, they expressed concern that many parents were not fulfilling their obligations to instruct the youth properly. Some parents, in the opinion of the bishops, were permitting their children to be taught error, possibly because of ignorance or indifference toward parental obligations. Others might be ignoring their responsibilities for reasons of expediency. But, for whatever reasons, the bishops indicated that parents were not evidencing that spirit of union which was so necessary if the errors of socialism were to be neutralized.[38]

A National Response

The laity also responded to the socialist school. Well-organized parents associations such as Unión Nacional de los Padres de Familia (UNPF), Asociación Nacional Pro-libertad de la Enseñanza (ANPLE), and Frente Unico Nacional de los Padres de Familia (FUNPF) attempted to alert parents to the dangers of the socialist school and the need for presenting a united front to indicate their disapproval. By means of leaflets, flyers, bulletins, magazines, meetings, rallies, and strikes these organizations effected a creditable if not a wholly satisfying response. Newspapers of the time indicated that many parents' groups in various parts of the Republic refused to accept socialist education and did not send their children to the schools.[39]

Professor Joaquín Camacho, in Guadalajara, believes that UNPF greatly aided the Church in its work of informing parents of the dangers of the socialist school. He stated that the association possessed capable lawyers who negotiated with the authorities so that private schools might continue to function.[40]

One layman who lives in Puebla has different thoughts on the effectiveness of UNPF. Dr. José Aurioles Diaz, one of the founders of

[37]Ruiz y Flores, *Orientaciones y normas dadas por la Santa Sede y por el Excmo. y Rvmo. Sr. Delegado Apostólico,* p. 5.
[38]"Carta pastoral colectiva sobre los deberes de los padres de familia en materia de enseñanza."
[39]See *La Prensa,* August 8, 11, 19 and 26, 1934; September 21 and October 27, 1934. Also, see *La Palabra,* August 23 and September 5 and 11, 1934; *El Universal,* October 17, 1934, and July 5, 1935; *Excelsior,* September 12 and October 27, 1934; *Noticias de la Provincia de México,* October 1934 and July 1935.
[40]Joaquín Camacho, tape-recorded interview held in Guadalajara, Jalisco, September 25, 1972.

ANPLE and of FUNPF, indicated that he and others were dissatisfied with UNPF because of its policy of accommodation with the government. The members of ANPLE insisted that one should not beg for one's rights but instead should demand them.[41]

Parents' groups throughout the country stimulated the establishment of home schools. Some parents who refused to send their children to socialist schools opened up their homes so that classes might continue. Although many private schools were closed by the government, the students continued to study in clandestine schools. To enable their students to receive certificates giving them official recognition of their studies, the Christian Brothers often arranged for students in home schools to appear on the rosters of one of the incorporated schools.[42] A Marist Brother, who is now living in Querétaro, reported that students were taken to San Luis Potosí because Governor Saturnino Cedillo allowed the Christian Brothers to conduct classes without interference.[43] Dr. Aurioles of Puebla revealed that home schools in his city often had the outright support of government leaders, who at times actually aided them.[44]

In reading the newspapers and magazines of the 1930s, one finds evidence that some parents did respond to the efforts of parents' organizations and did heed the counsels of the Church. One authoritative statement in this regard is that of Juan B. Salazar, who was the head of the Department of Secondary Education in the Ministry of Education. He reported that in March 1935 the majority of the schools of Puebla were empty because most of the parents, either through personal conviction or fear of reprisals, did not send their children. He added that because of the intense religious feeling in Puebla, perhaps the situation there was more drastic than elsewhere.[45]

In other areas, also, there were significant decreases in school attendance. Juan Sánchez Azcona, a prominent Mexican, wrote that the lack of attendance in primary and secondary public schools, both in the capital and in many of the states, was alarming. He pointed out that the majority of parents rejected socialist teaching and the mixed school that enrolled both male and female students.[46]

Despite the fact that parents did (in some places and for a period of time) refuse to send their youngsters to socialist schools, there are evidences that the cooperation was considerably less than it could have been. An article in *La Defensa del Hogar*, the official magazine

---

[41] José Aurioles Díaz, tape-recorded interviews held in Puebla, Pue., May 16, August 29, and October 7, 1972.
[42] Luis Lozano, tape-recorded interview held in León, Guanajuato, May 3, 1972.
[43] Santiago Gutiérrez, tape-recorded interview held in Querétaro, October 13, 1972.
[44] Aurioles Díaz, interview.
[45] *La Prensa*, March 3, 1935.
[46] *El Universal*, February 25, 1935.

of FUNPF in Puebla, attributes the apathy of the people either to a fear of fighting in defense of their sacred right to educate their sons or to a fear of losing material goods. The article indicates that some were unwilling to exert themselves or to make sacrifices and endure privations. In the final analysis, this article lays the principal fault to a lack of union and organization among the majority of Mexicans.[47]

In discussing this apathy, Dr. Aurioles Díaz has stated that it was a national defect of his people because, unfortunately, they had become accustomed to having things done for them either by the Church or by the government. Above all, he believes that the people lacked an adequate understanding of the problem, were ignorant of their rights, and were satisfied with confining their activities to petitioning the government and seeking no more than tolerance from it.[48]

The opposition to socialist education which the university students manifested is well known. In interviews with individuals who took part in student movements against the government's attempt to impose a particular philosophy on the schools, there is general agreement that it was for religious reasons as well as for the right of liberty of teaching. One professor who took part in the student strike in the University of Guadalajara indicated that the majority of students opposed the government because of religion. Yet, he and others who belonged to a radical socialist group had joined the Catholic students because they were opposed to the imposition of any philosophy.[49] Benito Coquet, president of the Unión Nacional de Estudiantes Católicos stated in August, 1934: "What the university wishes is to think freely, investigate freely, criticize freely, and not under the command of an official mandate."[50] Another gentleman who had participated in the Guadalajara movement said that liberty of teaching, not religion, had been emphasized but that the religious leaders had been behind the student strike.[51]

The Liga Nacional Defensora de la Libertad Religiosa, a vigorous civic organization, had come into existence in the mid-twenties. It provided the leadership and the organization for the Cristeros during the religious conflict of 1926-1929. Many of its members felt that they had been betrayed by the Mexican bishops whom they believed had "sold out" to the enemy, the Mexican government. Lic. Miguel Palomar y Vizcarra, one of the Liga's principal leaders, specifically blamed the educational problems of the 1930s on the two bishops, Pascual Díaz and Leopoldo Ruiz y Flores, who had agreed to an ar-

---

[47]*La defensa del hogar*, March 8, 1936, p. 2; also see ibid., January 17, 1937; April 10, 1938; and February 19, 1939.
[48]Aurioles Díaz, interview; also noted by Camacho, interview.
[49]Alfonso García Ruiz, tape-recorded interview held in Mexico City, August 8, 1972.
[50]*Excelsior*, August 1934.
[51]Ali Chumacero, tape-recorded interview held in Mexico City, November 2, 1972.

rangement which left education under the control of the government and the Mexican children in the hands of the enemy.[52]

One of the principal goals of the Liga was to achieve liberty of teaching. On July 2, 1935, the Liga denounced the new persecution of Cárdenas in the schools and indicated its own determination to organize and consolidate Mexicans so that they might develop sufficient power to take for themselves those basic liberties to which they had a right.[53]

The Liga published a magazine entitled *Reconquista* which carried news of various efforts to rally the people, reminding them of their rights and obligations while exhorting them to join the Liga in the fight for liberty. They believed that vigorous civic action was necessary if this liberty were to be achieved.[54]

According to a memorandum issued by the Popular Liberation Army, the Liga had no direct involvement in the second Cristero movement which arose in Mexico in the 1930s.[55] That it had not discarded the possibility, however, seems to be indicated by a questionnaire sent from the Republic of El Salvador to the Directive Committee of the Liga in 1937. It is a detailed questionnaire seeking to ascertain the probabilities of success for an armed movement.[56]

There were various attempts to create a new liberation army, however, but the response to these efforts was minimal. The Directive Committee of the Popular Liberation Army in Mexico City indicated that there were about 6,000 men in arms by mid-1936.[57]

A more spontaneous type of violence occurred sporadically in Mexico's rural areas and was directed principally toward the federal rural teachers who symbolized for the campesinos the evils of socialist education. Federal teachers, in some areas at least, were rejected before they arrived in a village because of what they symbolized. So that such teachers would be recognized readily as purveyors of evil, the campesinos often marked them by cutting off their ears.[58] Others were harassed and run out of town while the less fortunate were killed.

It is not easy to determine whether such violence was perpetrated because of religious beliefs or if other considerations dictated these

[52]Alicia Olivera de Bonfil, *Miguel Palomar y Vizcarra y su interpretación del conflicto religioso de 1926*, Archivo Sonoro no. 2 (México, D.F.: Instituto Nacional de Antropología e Historia, 1970), 39-40.
[53]R. Castañares, "Orientaciones oficiales que da la Liga Defensora de la Libertad," Reel no. 54, Archivo de la L.N.D.L.R.
[54]"Importante documento," *Reconquista*, 3a. Epoca, December 1935.
[55]Comité Especial del "Ejercito Popular Libertador," "Memorandum," Mexico, D.F., Reel no. 41, Archivo de V.I.T.A. Mexico (Archive of the Liga delegation in Rome, Italy).
[56]Carlos Alberto Siri, "Cuestionario al Comité Directivo de la Liga," followed by response of Liga on April 17, 1937, Reel no. 39, Archivo de la L.N.D.L.R.
[57]Comité Especial del "Ejercito Popular Libertador," "Memorandum."
[58]José María Vargas, tape-recorded interview held in Guadalajara, Jalisco, September 23, 1972.

actions. However, one historian, who compiled a list of some 223 incidents of violence from 1931 to 1940, notes that most of them occurred in areas especially noted for religious fanaticism, in the regions of the greatest Cristero activity, and in that part of the country where Sinarquismo had flourished.[59]

Why campesinos resorted to this type of activity was explained in an interesting manner by one of the members of Mexico's National Congress. Diputado Guillermo Ruiz Vázquez said that because there has been no history of political activity, pacific defense has never brought results. Either the people must surrender or resort to violence. In rural areas where the campesino is less enlightened and less able to reflect on the form in which he manifests his rejection, he resorts to violence.[60]

One of the most significant demonstrations of the influence of Mexican Catholicism in the lives of the people is evident in the rise of the *Sinarquista* movement. Born in León, Guanajuato, on May 23, 1937, it grew to tremendous proportions and numbered some 500,000 in 1940.[61] José Trueba Olivares, one of the founders of the organization, explained during an interview that *Sinarquismo* had a positive program rooted in Christian social principles. Socialism and Communism entailed a suppression and a denial of man's liberty while *Sinarquismo* respected the dignity of the individual and supported his right to liberty, justice, and private property.[62] As Professor Michaels has shown in his treatment of this subject, *Sinarquismo*, which attracted the campesinos and the middle class, was an overwhelming rejection of Cardenas's government and a call for a Christian nation.[63]

Let us conclude with this brief observation. During the 1930s, the social tension created by the adoption of the social school elicited a firm response from the Mexican hierarchy as well as from numerous lay organizations which supported the Catholic philosophy of education. A significant portion of the popular elements responded in one or another fashion. In view of the evidence presented, one must conclude that religion was an overriding influence in this conflict between Mexicans and their government.

---

[59]David L. Raby, "Rural Teachers and Social and Political Conflict in Mexico, 1921-40" (Ph.D. diss., University of Warwick, 1970), pp. 179-80.
[60]Ruiz Vázquez, interview.
[61]Albert L. Michaels, "Fascism and Sinarquismo: Popular Nationalisms Against the Mexican Revolution," *A Journal of Church and State* 8 (Spring 1966): 239.
[62]José Trueba Olivares, tape-recorded interview held in León, Guanajuato, May 4, 1972.
[63]Michaels, "Fascism and Sinarquismo," p. 241.

SOCIAL SCIENCE

Population, poverty, and power are dealt with in the following three essays. Each of these topics is of importance to the social scientist who is concerned with social groups, economic deprivation, and power relationships in Mexico.

11. Evangelical Expansion in Mexico: A Study of the Number, Distribution, and Growth of the Protestant Population, 1857-1970*

JULIAN C. BRIDGES

This study traces the historical development of Protestantism in Mexico, provides data concerning the number and geographical distribution of Protestants in 1970, analyzes factors affecting regional and rural-urban distribution of Protestants, and describes the growth of Mexico's Evangelical population before 1950 and from 1950 to 1970. Ten basic conclusions are presented at the end of the study.

This study is an analysis of the absolute and relative importance of Mexico's Protestants, their geographic distribution, and their numerical increase from 1857 to 1970. Ten years ago almost none of the general works on Latin America mentioned the existence of the Protestant movement in Iberoamerica. Today, however, Evangelicals (as Protestants in Latin America prefer to be called) have become the object of comment in major works; and, recently, specialized publications have begun to appear.[1]

*This study is based primarily on the author's *Expansión evangélica en México* (El Paso, Tex.: Editorial Mundo Hispano, 1973).

[1] Some of the more significant of these are MARC, *Brazil Protestant Handbook* (São Paulo: Missionary Information Bureau, 1973); John H. Sinclair, *Protestantism in Latin America: A Bibliographical Guide*, 2d ed. (Pasadena, Calif.: William Carey Library, 1973); Roger Greenway, *An Urban Strategy for Latin America* (Grand Rapids, Mich.: Baker Book House, 1973); William R. Read, Victor M. Monterroso, and Harmon A. Johnson, *Latin American Church Growth* (Grand Rapids, Mich.: Eerdmans, 1969); Emílio Willems, *Followers of the New Faith: Culture Change and the Rise of Protestantism in Brazil and Chile* (Nashville, Tenn.: Vanderbilt University Press, 1967); Donald McGavran, John Huegel, and Jack Taylor, *Church Growth in Mexico* (Grand Rapids, Mich.: Eerdmans, 1963); and Prudencio Damboriena, *El protestantismo en América Latina*, 2 vols. (Friburgo, Suiza: Oficina Internacional de Investigaciones Sociales de FERES, 1962-1963).

Concerning the size of the Evangelical movement in Latin America, the Institute of Church Growth, a Protestant organization which is quite realistic about its estimates, states:

> If the current rate of growth does not decrease, Evangelical Churches in Latin America will have more than doubled in communicant membership in the ten year period between 1960-1970. There is every reason to expect this to happen again in the decade between 1970 and 1980. If the Church continues to grow at the present rate, there will be over thirteen million communicant members by 1980. This will give the Evangelical community more than twenty-seven million members, or 8 per cent of the population.[2]

Such growth will undoubtedly motivate more research on Protestants in Latin America. Authorities generally concede that the Evangelical minority wields much more influence than its actual members represent.[3] Research by social scientists indicates also that adherence to Evangelical religion in Latin America is linked to significant social and cultural change. Emílio Willems, for example, discovered that conversion to Protestant faith often brings about increasing prosperity and enhanced social status. His research indicates that Max Weber's economic ethic seems to apply to Latin American Protestantism.[4]

The Historical Development of Protestantism in Mexico[5]

Antecedents. — Protestantism as a movement actually dates from the granting of freedom of worship in the Mexican Constitution of 1857. Prior to that time the movement was technically illegal. Even before Mexico won independence in 1821, however, there were traces of Protestant ideas and influence in the country. For example, the father of Mexican Independence, Don Miguel Hidalgo y Costilla, was once charged with "Lutheranism," although it has never been determined whether this accusation was justified in the ideological sense.[6]

After the War for Independence, copies of the Bible were sent into

---

[2]William R. Read, Victor M. Monterroso, and Harmon A. Johnson, "Growth in Latin America," *Church Growth Bulletin*, September, 1969, p. 6.
[3]See, for example, the Roman Catholic authority on Protestants in Mexico, Pedro Rivera R., *Protestantismo mexicano*, 3d ed. (México, D.F.: Editorial Jus, 1961); and *Instituciones protestantes en México* (México, D.F.: Editorial Jus, 1962).
[4]Willems, *Followers of the New Faith*, pp. 173-210.
[5]For a more extensive treatment of the history of Mexican Protestantism, see Gonzalo Báez-Camargo and Kenneth G. Grubb, *Religion in the Republic of Mexico* (New York: World Dominion Press, 1935); Marvin J. Penton, "Mexico's Reformation: A History of Mexican Protestantism from Its Inception to the Present" (Ph.D. diss., State University of Iowa, 1965); and Julian C. Bridges, "A Study of the Number, Distribution, and Growth of the Protestant Population in Mexico" (M.A. thesis, University of Florida, 1969), pp. 7-33.
[6]Báez-Camargo and Grubb, *Religion in the Republic of Mexico*, p. 87.

Mexico by the British and Foreign Bible Society and were privately circulated as early as 1824. The great Mexican reformer, Dr. José María Luis Mora, became an active member of this Society and participated in prayer meetings of the organization, together with some priests and other liberals.[7]

Origins of the Evangelical movement. — Prior to 1857, only Roman Catholicism had been legal in Mexico; but Benito Juárez, Melchor Ocampo, and Miguel Lerdo de Tejada were able to prevent establishment of the Roman Catholic Church as the country's official religious body in the new Constitution of 1857.[8] Two years later, a specific statement of separation of church and state was added to the document.

The first form of any organized Protestantism took place in 1859, when five Mexican Catholic priests began to hold meetings in Mexico City. They formed a group that was called the "Constitutionalist Fathers," because they were in sympathy with the new national document.[9] On January 30, 1864, the first Mexican Protestant congregation was formally organized in Monterrey as the First Baptist Church. By 1870 there were seven Baptist churches in northern Mexico.[10]

Meanwhile, in Mexico City, the work of the Constitutionalist Fathers (later the Episcopal Church) had grown to about 6,000 members by 1870.[11] Government leaders (including Benito Juárez, Matías Romero, Guillermo Prieto, and Ignacio Ramírez), along with their families, attended some services of this group. President Juárez went so far as to suggest the creation of a "Mexican Church" (non-Roman Catholic) devoted to the principles of his reform movement. He is quoted as having stated on one occasion, "The future happiness and prosperity of my nation depend on the development of Protestantism."[12] Justo Sierra, the noted Mexican educator, declared that Juárez once commented to him: "I should like Protestantism to Mexicanize itself by winning the Indians. They need a religion that compels them to read and not spend their savings on candles for the saints."[13] The death of Juárez in 1872 slowed the expansion of Protestantism in the capital, although seventy-two congregations of the Episcopal Church

---

[7]Pedro Gringoire [pseud.], "El 'Protestantismo' del Dr. Mora," *Historia Mexicana* 3 (January-March 1954): 328-66, passim.

[8]J. Lloyd Mecham, *Church and State in Latin America: A History of Politico-Ecclesiastical Relations*, rev. ed. (Chapel Hill: University of North Carolina Press, 1966), p. 364.

[9]Fay S. Greenland, "Religious Reform in Mexico: The Role of the Mexican Episcopal Church" (M.A. thesis, University of Florida, 1958), p. 11.

[10]American Baptist Home Mission Society, "A Century Is Not Enough" (n.p. and n.d.), pp. 1-2.

[11]Greenland, "Religious Reform in Mexico," p. 30.

[12]Quoted in Baez-Camargo and Grubb, *Religion in the Republic of Mexico*, p. 89.

[13]Justo Sierra, *Evolución política del pueblo mexicano*, 2d ed. (México, D.F.: La Casa de España, 1940), p. 423.

had been planted there and in southern and southwestern Mexico by that time.[14]

During the era of Porfirio Díaz (1876-1910), a more conciliatory policy toward the Catholic Church was established and sustained. While Díaz did not close the door to the entrance of Protestants, for the most part he left enforcement of the Constitution to local authorities. Generally, this meant that the more remote areas of Mexico offered less opportunity for Protestant penetration.[15] By 1910, however, most of the major Protestant bodies had established themselves in Mexico's larger cities.

The period of instability. — From 1910 to 1917, the period of most intense revolutionary struggle, there was little progress for Protestants or any other religious group. Then, from 1917 until 1940, several turbulent events caused Protestant development to be quite unstable.

The first of these events was the adoption of the Constitution of 1917, a document which limited the influence of all religious groups. At first, articles on religion were not frequently enforced; but in 1926, President Elías Calles announced that all foreign clergy were to be deported. Although the law was to be applied to Protestants as well as Catholics, there is evidence to indicate that favoritism was shown to the former group, particularly in the cities. Calles is quoted as saying publicly, "Actually the Protestant ministers are working in Mexico without harming anyone for they have always adjusted themselves to the Law."[16] Calles' strict enforcement of the Constitution, however, resulted in the Cristero Rebellion (1926-1929). In certain areas, particularly in the very conservative states of central and southwestern Mexico, some violent attacks were made on Protestants and many Protestant missionaries felt compelled to leave the country.

In 1934 the government announced that education in Mexico would be "socialist," although it was not quite clear what this term implied. Nevertheless, some states went so far as to require public school teachers to sign a statement saying that they were atheists. Consequently, some Protestant groups closed their mission schools. Gonzalo Báez-Camargo and Kenneth Grubb state that in 1935 there were only about 2,000 pupils in primary schools that at one time had been associated with an evangelical group, and they report only about 100 students in secondary and normal schools of this type. These numbers compare with 8,704 and 2,135 students, respectively, in 1921.[17] By the latter part of the 1930s, however, tension had eased considerably.

[14]Greenland, "Religious Reform in Mexico," pp. 37-38.
[15]See Mecham, *Church and State in Latin America*, pp. 458-59; and William Butler, *Mexico in Transition* (New York: Hunt and Eaton, 1892), p. 301.
[16]Mecham, *Church and State in Latin America*, p. 393.
[17]Báez-Camargo and Grubb, *Religion in the Republic of Mexico*, p. 111.

The period of extensive development. — There has been a decided change in the religious atmosphere of Mexico since 1940. In that year Manuel Avila Camacho succeeded Lázaro Cárdenas in the national presidency; and in his first press interview the new president made his now famous declaration, "I am a believer." This public confession of Avila Camacho's Catholicism was the beginning of greatly improved relations between church and state in Mexico.

One consequence of this relaxation of restrictions against religious organizations has been the great influx of foreign clergy, both Catholic and Protestant, into the country. From 1940 on, this flow has been steady; but it increased significantly after the Second World War and the closing of mainland China to Christian missionary organizations. The *Directorio evangélico de México, 1970* lists thirty-nine distinct Protestant denominational headquarters located in Mexico City. In addition, forty-eight other Evangelical organizations are included, and undoubtedly there are many more.[18] Some Protestant missionaries, particularly those of smaller denominations and independent groups, live within the United States but commute frequently to their assignments in northern Mexico. Thus, a great deal of evangelistic and social service work is being conducted by persons who often are not included in statistics on foreign personnel.

This writer's survey of major Protestant denominations in Mexico reveals that there has been rapid expansion on the part of most of them since World War II. In particular, Presbyterians, Methodists, Seventh-Day Adventists, and Southern Baptists have expanded their institutional work since 1950. The latter group, for example, has opened a hospital in Guadalajara, constructed hostels for university students in several cities, and initiated cultural centers for students in Mexico City and Monterrey. Numerous bookstores have been established throughout the nation, and extensive radio and television ministries, with accompanying correspondence courses, are now being conducted. Camps, retreats, children's homes, at least one home for the aged, and numerous seminaries and other theological training schools are flourishing across the country. In the national capital, various denominations have located seminaries in a new Protestant theological community that is situated near the campus of the National Autonomous University of Mexico.

These developments are representative of the extension of the Protestant movement as a whole. In particular, Pentecostal groups have experienced great numerical and geographical expansion since 1950.[19] The numerical aspect of this expansion will be more fully dis-

---

[18]Mexico Missionary Services, *Directorio evangélico de México* (Cuernavaca, Mor.: Tipográfica Indígena, 1970), pp. 99-101, 121-25.

[19]See McGavran, Huegel, and Taylor, *Church Growth in Mexico*, pp. 33-35, 113-24. Specific data on the various Pentecostal groups and other evangelical denominations

cussed below under a section entitled "Growth of the Evangelical Population."

The Number and Distribution of Evangelicals in 1970

Because statistical information from the various Evangelical denominations is incomplete and often lacks uniformity in defining which persons are full members, the most reliable data on the Protestant population as a whole are obtained from official enumerations in the published volumes of the national censuses. Not all of the data from the general census of population conducted in 1970 have been published at the time of this writing. Nevertheless, enough information is available, when combined with an analysis of data from earlier censuses, to make important observations and to draw some significant conclusions.

The number of Evangelicals. — The most significant single fact concerning the Protestant population in Mexico is its size. According to the census of 1970, there were 876,879 Evangelicals among a total population of 48,225,238.[20] Although Evangelicals comprised only 1.8 percent of the total population, their absolute number is now of a magnitude that cannot be ignored.

At the time of this writing, all official data from the 1970 censuses of other republics in Latin America have not been published. In 1960, however, Mexico ranked third, behind Brazil and Chile, with respect to the total number of Protestants in Latin America. The size of the Evangelical population in Mexico was more than the combined Protestant populations of Colombia, El Salvador, Bolivia, Dominican Republic, Uruguay, Panama, Nicaragua, Paraguay, Honduras, Venezuela, Costa Rica, and Ecuador.[21] Thus, it was larger than that of more than half of the countries of Latin American taken together; and it is probable that by 1970 the Evangelical population of Mexico occupied second position in all of Latin America.[22]

Geographical distribution. — Second in importance only to the absolute number of Evangelicals in Mexico is their geographical location within the country. Figure 1 and Table 1 have been prepared to show the distribution of Mexico's Protestants among the nation's thirty-two major civil divisions.

The Federal District was the civil division with by far the largest number of Evangelicals in 1970. It contained almost 112,000, or 12.8

were obtained; but because they are both incomplete and unreliable, they were not presented in this study.

[20]México, Dirección General de Estadística, *IX censo general de población, 1970: Resumen general abreviado* (México, D.F.: Secretaría de Industria y Comercio, 1972), p. 55, Table 8.

[21]Compiled and computed from H. Wakelin Coxill and Kenneth Grubb, eds., *World Christian Handbook, 1962* (London: World Dominion Press, 1962), pp. 109-42.

[22]See Read, Monterroso, and Johnson, *Latin American Church Growth*, p. 49.

Table 1

Absolute and Relative Importance of Evangelicals in Mexico, by Region and Major Civil Division, 1970

Region and civil division	Total population	Evangelicals Number	Percent of total	Percent of all Evangelicals in Mexico
Mexico	48,225,238	876,879	1.8	100.0
North				
Baja California	870,421	20,406	2.3	2.3
Sonora	1,098,720	16,188	1.5	1.8
Chihuahua	1,612,525	41,811	2.6	4.8
Coahuila	1,114,956	25,255	2.3	2.9
Nuevo León	1,694,689	47,714	2.8	5.4
Tamaulipas	1,456,858	41,911	2.9	4.8
North Central				
Baja California T.	128,019	1,106	.9	.1
Sinaloa	1,266,528	14,148	1.1	1.6
Durango	939,208	10,805	1.2	1.2
Zacatecas	951,462	6,197	.7	.7
San Luis Potosí	1,281,996	23,431	1.8	2.7
Central				
Nayarit	544,031	5,516	1.0	.6
Aguascalientes	338,142	1,358	.4	.2
Jalisco	3,296,586	19,082	.6	2.2
Guanajuato	2,270,370	6,797	.3	.8
Querétaro	485,523	1,447	.3	.2
Hidalgo	1,193,845	18,544	1.6	2.1
Colima	241,153	1,021	.4	.1
Michoacán	2,324,226	14,982	.6	1.7
México	3,833,185	54,193	1.4	6.2
Federal District	6,874,165	111,957	1.6	12.8
Morelos	616,119	22,685	3.7	2.6
Tlaxcala	420,638	8,160	1.9	.9
Puebla	2,508,226	43,030	1.7	4.9
Veracruz	3,815,422	88,031	2.3	10.0
South				
Guerrero	1,597,360	19,471	1.2	2.2
Oaxaca	2,015,424	30,177	1.5	3.4
Southeast				
Chiapas	1,569,053	75,378	4.8	8.6
Tabasco	768,327	63,732	8.3	7.3
Campeche	251,556	13,914	5.5	1.6
Yucatán	758,355	21,610	2.9	2.5
Quintana Roo T.	88,150	6,822	7.7	.8

Source: Compiled and computed from data in México, *IX censo general, 1970: Resumen general*, pp. 55-56, Table 8.

percent of all Protestants in Mexico. The states of Veracruz and Chiapas each had over 75,000 Evangelicals and occupied second and third places, respectively. Together these three civil divisions contained almost one-third of all the country's Protestants. If the Evangelicals in the states of Tabasco, México, and Nuevo León are added to the group, it can be noted that approximately one-half of all Evangelicals live in only six of the country's thirty-two civil divisions.

Another way of stating this information is that the Federal District had more Evangelicals than fourteen other civil divisions combined. At the same time, it can be noted that the total population of these civil divisions is 65 percent higher than that of the Federal District. Thus, it is obvious that the distribution of Protestants among Mexico's major civil divisions is far from even. This fact indicates that the proportion of the total population which is Evangelical in each entity is also of significance.

Data in Table 1 show that Tabasco has the highest proportion of Protestants in its total population, with Quintana Roo, Campeche, and Chiapas next in order. States in which Evangelicals are of least relative importance are Querétaro, Guanajuato, Aguascalientes, and Colima, in ascending order. The proportion of Protestants in Tabasco is almost twenty-eight times higher than is that in Querétaro.

It is also significant to observe the degree to which an entity is Protestant in comparison with its share of the national population. This information is obtained by dividing the percentage of the civil division which is Protestant by the corresponding figure for the nation: 1.8 percent. Such a computation reveals that Tabasco has almost five times its due proportion. In comparison, Querétaro and Guanajuato have only a sixth part of the number of Protestants which would correspond to them if the Evangelical population were distributed in the same manner as is the total population of Mexico. This type of contrast becomes even more evident when it is noted that Jalisco (the fourth most populous state in the nation, having thirty-seven times more residents than the territory of Quintana Roo) had less than three times the number of Evangelicals than did the territory. In other words, Quintana Roo had about twelve times more Evangelicals per 100 inhabitants than did Jalisco in 1970.

Factors Affecting the Distribution

What are some of the major reasons for the very disproportionate distribution of Evangelicals in Mexico? The answer to this question can best be discussed relative to four main geographical areas of the country: the southeast, the central region (including the north central, southwestern, and southern states), the Federal District and Morelos, and the northern border states.

The southeast. — By observing Table 1, it can be noted that the

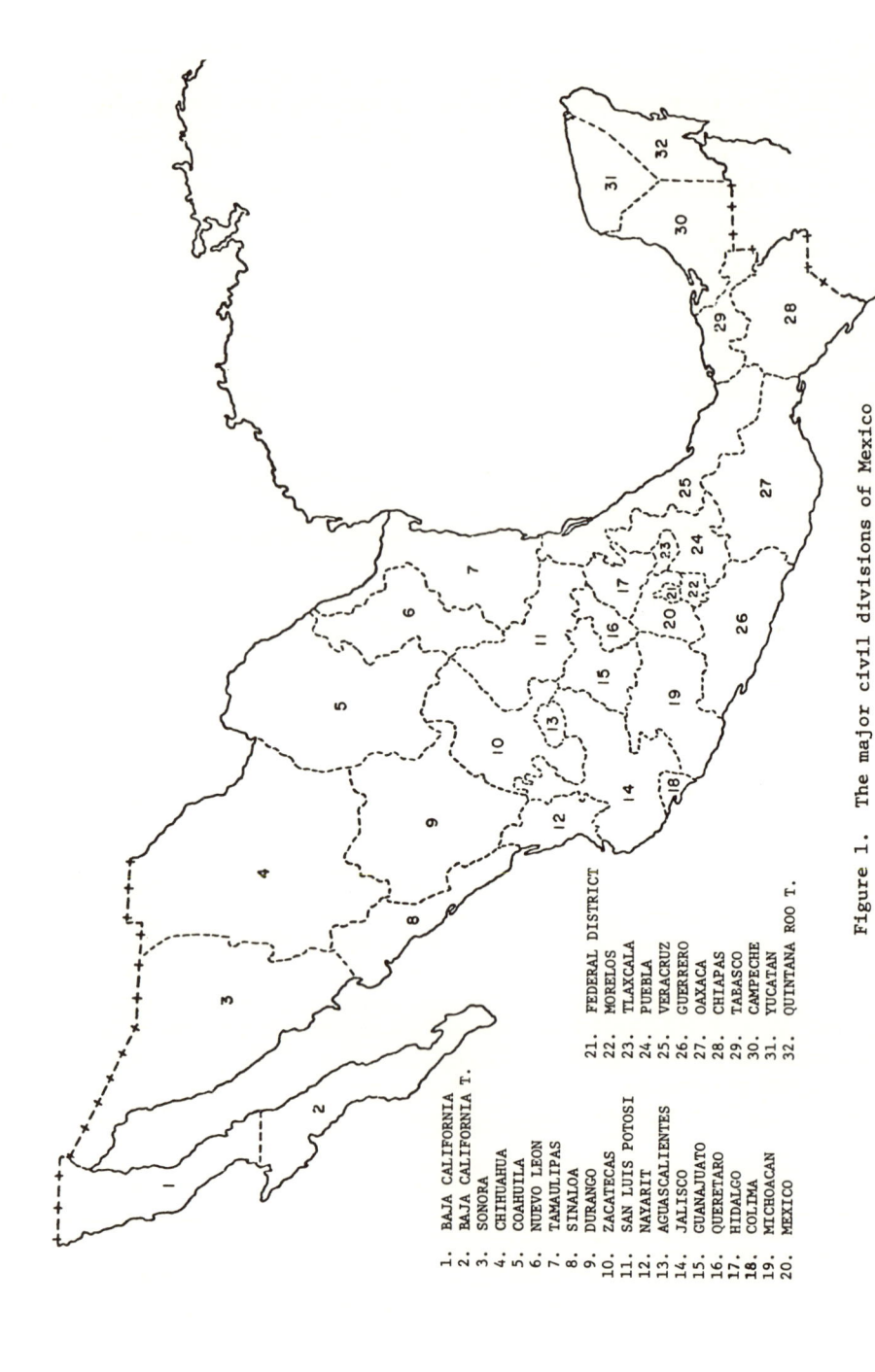

1. BAJA CALIFORNIA
2. BAJA CALIFORNIA T.
3. SONORA
4. CHIHUAHUA
5. COAHUILA
6. NUEVO LEON
7. TAMAULIPAS
8. SINALOA
9. DURANGO
10. ZACATECAS
11. SAN LUIS POTOSI
12. NAYARIT
13. AGUASCALIENTES
14. JALISCO
15. GUANAJUATO
16. QUERETARO
17. HIDALGO
18. COLIMA
19. MICHOACAN
20. MEXICO
21. FEDERAL DISTRICT
22. MORELOS
23. TLAXCALA
24. PUEBLA
25. VERACRUZ
26. GUERRERO
27. OAXACA
28. CHIAPAS
29. TABASCO
30. CAMPECHE
31. YUCATAN
32. QUINTANA ROO T.

Figure 1. The major civil divisions of Mexico

civil divisions with the highest proportions of Protestants in their populations are, with one exception, all located in southeastern Mexico. In all of these entities—Tabasco, Quintana Roo, Campeche, Chiapas, and Yucatán—at least 2.9 percent of the total population is Evangelical. This is significant because (1) the national average of 1.8 percent is considerably lower, and (2) only in the case of the exception, Morelos, does any other civil division in all of Mexico have a percentage higher than those of the civil divisions of the southeast. The case of Morelos will be discussed below.

Several characteristics that distinguish the southeastern section of Mexico from the remainder of the country help to explain the relative importance of Protestants in this region. First, most of the area formed part of the ancient Maya empire, and many of the inhabitants speak Maya dialects even today.[23] This fact has made it difficult for Catholicism to be readily accepted, particularly in rural areas of the southeast where priests have penetrated infrequently and with little knowledge of the Maya language.

Second, southeastern Mexico has historically been quite independent from the remainder of the republic. Concerning this area, one historian states:

> Nowhere in all America was resistancce to Spanish conquest more obstinate or more nearly successful.... Occasionally the Spaniards would meet them in open battle and their superior weapons would give them the victory; but the Mayas would never accept defeat.... Parts of the interior ... remained independent until the end of the following [seventeenth] century. And even though they were finally crushed by superior force, the Mayas preserved their spiritual independence....[24]

Until very recently a third characteristic of the southeast has been its geographical isolation. Most travel in Mexico has historically moved north and south or between the center and the west. Not until the 1960s have highway facilities permitted automobiles to reach the southeastern peninsula throughout the year. Thus, problems of transportation have also made it more difficult throughout Mexican history for this portion of the country to be thoroughly catholicized. In 1960, for example, while the national average for the number of inhabitants per priest was 5,057 to one, in the southeast there were about 9,000 persons for every priest.[25] As a result, pre-Cortesian rites and customs from the Maya religion are still widely practiced in part

---

[23]See Julian C. Bridges, "The Population of Mexico: Its Composition and Changes" (Ph.D. diss., University of Florida, 1973), pp. 106-107.

[24]Henry Bamford Parkes, *A History of Mexico*, 3d ed. rev. (Boston: Houghton Mifflin Co., 1960), pp. 70-71, 176.

[25]Rutilio Ramos, Isidoro Alonso, and Domingo Garre, *La Iglesia en México* (Friburgo, Suiza: Oficina Internacional de Investigaciones Sociales de FERES, 1963), pp. 63 and 67.

of the Mexican peninsula.[26] It is also interesting to note that the percentage of the population in the southeastern civil divisions that indicates either no religious creed or a creed other than Catholic, Protestant, or Jewish was approximately twice as high as that of the national average.[27]

While sections of the southeast remained relatively uncatholicized (compared with the rest of Mexico), Protestants penetrated the area as early as 1896 and their work spread quite rapidly.[28] Evangelical missionaries often learned the indigenous dialects and thus were able to minister to and evangelize Indian groups living in some of the most remote rural districts. During the religious persecutions of the 1930s, when the number of priests was reduced almost to nil in the southeast and all priests were excluded from Tabasco, Protestantism flourished in the rural areas of that state.[29]

The central area. — In sharp contrast to the progress of Protestantism in southeastern Mexico, its growth in central and southwestern states has been slow. As of 1970, Evangelicals amounted to not more than 1.0 percent of the population in Guanajuato, Querétaro, Aguascalientes, Colima, Jalisco, Michoacán, Nayarit, and the neighboring north central state of Zacatecas. (See Table 1.) Catholicism has always been strong in this region. It is precisely in this part of Mexico where the ratio of the number of inhabitants to each priest in 1960 was by far the lowest in the nation, only 3,892 to one.[30]

The Federal District and Morelos. — One reason for the concentration of Evangelicals in the nation's capital is the fact that the first organized Protestant work began there in 1859. Most Evangelical denominations established their national headquarters in the Federal District relatively early. Generally there has been greater religious freedom in Mexico City than elsewhere in the country, because federal government protection always has been accessible to members of the Protestant faith. The state of Morelos, which borders the Federal District on the south, has become a resort center for retired North Americans, many of whom are Protestants. This has resulted in an unusually high concentration of Evangelicals in that civil division and has contributed an additional spirit of religious liberalism to the state which was the birthplace and residence of Emiliano Zapata, one of the most famous generals of the Mexican Revolution.

[26]See, for example, Robert Redfield, *A Village That Chose Progress: Chan Kom Revisited* (Chicago: University of Chicago Press, 1950).
[27]See Bridges, "The Population of Mexico," pp. 123-24.
[28]Ezequiel Lango, "La Siembra," *Libro histórico de las bodas de oro del Sínodo General de la Iglesia Presbiteriana en México: 1901-1951* (México, D.F.: Comisión de Literatura, 1956), p. 18.
[29]McGavran, Huegel, and Taylor, *Church Growth in Mexico*, pp. 89-90.
[30]Ramos, Alonso, and Garre, *La Iglesia en México*, p. 63.

The northern border states. — Mexican civil divisions located contiguously to the United States have a relatively high proportion of Evangelicals. In the states of Tamaulipas, Nuevo León, Coahuila, Chihuahua, and Baja California, at least 2.3 percent of the population is Protestant. All of these civil divisions border on either Texas or California, where there are large Protestant majorities which have sponsored missionary ministries in northern Mexico since the inception of Protestant work in the 1850s. Sonora, the other border state, is located across from Arizona, where American Protestants are much fewer in number and where the sparse settlement of the population in general lends itself to less frequent communication with Mexico than do the dense concentrations of persons on the borders of Texas and California.

The Rural-Urban Distribution of Protestants

R. Livi, an Italian scholar, was the first to formulate the sociological principle that rural populations are recruited primarily from the immediate vicinity and are thus homogeneous in composition, while urban populations are recruited from comparatively distant places and are therefore relatively heterogeneous.[31] There is a corollary of this principle: social characteristics that are common or native to an area will be found in higher proportions in rural than in urban populations. Pitirim A. Sorokin and Carl C. Zimmerman claim that persons affiliated with the established or native religion of a region will be found in greater proportions in rural districts, while adherents to non-native religious bodies or groups will be found in higher proportions in urban areas.[32] If this hypothesis is correct, and is applied to Mexico, one would expect to find Protestants—a non-native religous group—concentrated in higher proportions in the cities rather than in the countryside.

The Mexican census defines the concepts "rural" and "urban" according to a quantitative criterion. A rural population is one whose members live in localities of less than 2,500 inhabitants, while an urban population is constituted by persons who reside in localities of 2,500 inhabitants or more.[33]

When Sorokin and Zimmerman's hypothesis is tested for Mexico as a whole, the data do not substantiate it.[34] However, it must be remembered that the proposition applies only where a religion, in this

---

[31]Pitirim A. Sorokin and Carl C. Zimmerman, *Principles of Rural-Urban Sociology* (New York: Henry Holt and Co., 1929), pp. 108-109, 142.

[32]Ibid., p. 420.

[33]México, Dirección General de Estadística, *VIII censo general de población, 1960: Resumen general* (México, D.F.: Secretaría de Industria y Comercio, 1962), p. xiv.

[34]Julian C. Bridges, "How Religiously Homogeneous Is the Rural Population of Mexico?" *Rural Sociology* 37 (June 1972): 245-47.

case Roman Catholicism, has been native or common to a rural population. As stated earlier, it is very doubtful that Catholicism was ever firmly planted in the rural sections of the civil divisions in southeastern Mexico, where a large part of the entire nation's rural population resides. Thus, the hypothesis cannot be applied to this section of the country.

In the southeast. — When an analysis is made of all of Mexico's county-like *municipios*, it is found that 41 were at least 10.0 percent Protestant in 1970. Of these, 28 were located in the 5 civil divisions of the southeast. Only 4 (all located in Tabasco) of the 28 *municipios* had populations of 5,000 inhabitants or more. Even in these 4 *municipios*, more than 70 percent of the population lived in rural localities, which means it is probable that a large part of the Evangelicals living there also resided in rural areas.[35] These data tend to confirm the historical evidence that Roman Catholicism never has been the primary native religion in sections of the rural area of southeastern Mexico.

In the southwest and center. — It is possible to test Sorokin and Zimmerman's proposition in a region of Mexico where Roman Catholicism clearly has been the native religion even in the most remote rural areas. If one travels to the states of the southwest and to those civil divisions in the center which border on the southwest, he immediately becomes aware that Catholicism historically was the faith of the entire population. Whereas today in the southeast one can travel through towns and villages and never see a Catholic church, in the southwestern states there are churches and chapels even in the smaller villages and in the open countryside. Protestant work was established earlier in the southwest than in the southeast, but it has prospered little in the cities and towns of the southwest and center.

Table 2 indicates absolute and relative importance of Protestants in the states of this area in 1960, according to the size of their *municipios*. It can be observed that the highest proportions of Evangelicals are found in the categories of *municipios* which have the most inhabitants living in urban localities. One exception is the category for *municipios* which have from 25,000 to 49,999 inhabitants, but this difference is not significant. Existence of a higher proportion of Protestants in the urban areas is shown even more clearly in the analysis of data for the state of Jalisco, which probably has the strongest Catholic influence in the entire region.[36] Therefore, Sorokin and Zimmerman's proposition is operative when the religious creed of a population is native to the area under study, and their hypothesis is

---

[35]Compiled and computed from 1970 data supplied to the author by the Dirección General de Estadística of the Mexican government.

[36]See Bridges, "How Religiously Homogeneous Is the Rural Population of Mexico?" p. 251.

Table 2

Absolute and Relative Importance of Evangelicals in Selected States of Mexico by Size of Municipios, 1960

Size of municipios	Number of municipios*	Total	Urban Number	Urban Percent	Evangelicals Number	Evangelicals Percent
Total	387	8,001,245	3,722,696	46.5	43,867	.5
250,000 and over	2	1,001,027	950,422	94.9	8,245	.8
100,000 to 249,999	4	538,773	392,040	72.8	3,669	.7
50,000 to 99,999	22	1,367,274	675,656	49.4	8,253	.6
25,000 to 49,999	51	1,687,775	697,656	41.3	7,288	.4
10,000 to 24,999	155	2,383,799	785,440	32.9	11,543	.5
5,000 to 9,999	122	898,989	209,089	23.3	4,684	.5
2,500 to 4,999	30	115,827	12,968	11.2	185	.2
0 to 2,499	1	1,945	0	.0	0	.0

*The 100 percent rural municipio, Susupuato, Michoacán, which had 5,836 inhabitants and 680 Evangelicals, is omitted as a rare exception, in order not to distort the data presented above.

Source: Compiled and computed from data in México, Dirección General de Estadística, VIII censo general de población, 1960: Aguascalientes, Colima, Guanajuato, Jalisco, Michoacán, Nayarit, Querétaro, and Zacatecas (México, D.F.: Secretaría de Industria y Comercio, 1962-1964), Tables 5 and 15 in respective volumes.

established in the region of Mexico where Roman Catholicism is clearly the common religion of the people.

Growth of the Evangelical Population

One objective in the study of a population is to determine how it changes over periods of time. In the case of the Protestant population of Mexico, extraordinary growth has been a major characteristic.

Growth before 1950. — Table 3 indicates the absolute and relative importance of Protestants in Mexico from 1900 to 1940. The census of

1910 revealed a net gain of 17,043 Prootestants (32.9 percent) over the census of 1900, while in the 11 years preceding the 1921 enumeration only 5,112 Evangelicals were added (a mere increase of 7.4 percent). However, these latter data demonstrate something of the durability and vitality of the Protestant movement, because Mexico's total population actually decreased 825,589 during the revolutionary years between 1910 and 1921.

The surge of growth in the Protestant population from 1921 to 1930 is worthy of comment. While the national population increased only 14 percent, Protestants increased 76 percent. In large part, this is probably due to two factors: First, a sizeable number of Protestants, mostly Mennonites, migrated to Mexico during this decade. (Whetten estimates that there were about one thousand families.) Second, the national government's opposition to the Catholic Church, particularly from 1926 to 1930, may have encouraged Evangelical growth.[37]

Protestant growth continued from 1930 to 1940, but at a somewhat reduced pace. Whereas the increase in the previous decade had been 76 percent, from 1930 to 1940 it was only 36 percent. Decline in rate of growth was probably due in part to the partial recovery of strength made by the Roman Catholic Church during the latter part of this period. However, the rate of increase for Protestants was still approximately twice that of the national population during the same ten years.

In the decade from 1940 to 1950, the highest percentage growth in the history of Protestantism in Mexico was realized. The number of Evangelicals grew 152,157, an increase of 86 percent, while the nation's total population had a growth of 31 percent. This means that the Protestant population increased almost three times as rapidly as the total population during the decade. The reader will remember that it was in the 1940s, after World War II, that many American Protestant denominations sent more missionaries and mission funds to Mexico.

Growth from 1950 to 1970. — Some very interesting changes in the growth pattern of Protestants took place in the two decades prior to the 1970 census. Table 4 shows changes in both the absolute and relative bases during this period. It will be noted from these data that there was an increase of almost 550,000 Evangelicals during the twenty-year span. This means that a figure equal to 62 percent of the 879,241 Evangelicals in 1970 was added after 1950.

Absolute growth occurred in all civil divisions from 1950 to 1970; however, only five divisions accounted for more than one-half of the Protestant increase: the Federal District, Veracruz, Chiapas, Tabasco, and the state of México. Twenty-eight of the thirty-two federal entities had higher proportions of Protestants in their populations in 1970

---

[37]Nathan L. Whetten, *Rural Mexico* (Chicago: University of Chicago Press, 1948), pp. 160-61.

Table 3
Absolute and Relative Importance of Evangelicals in Mexico, 1900-1940

Census year	Total population	Evangelicals Number	Percent of total
1900	13,607,259	51,796	0.38
1910	15,160,369	68,839	0.45
1921	14,734,780	73,951	0.52
1930	16,552,722	130,322	0.79
1940	19,653,552	177,954	0.90

Source: Compiled and computed from data in México, Dirección General de Estadística, Anuario estadístico, 1938 (México, D.F.: Secretaría de la Economía Nacional, 1939), pp. 56-57. Table 21; México, Dirección General de Estadística, Compendio estadístico, 1958 (México, D.F.: Secretaría de Industria y Comercio, 1959), p. 61, Table 26; and México, VIII censo general, 1960: Resumen general, p. 282, Table 18.

than in 1950. The four exceptions are the Federal District and three relatively strong Roman Catholic states: Durango, Michoacán, and Zacatecas. Due to difficult economic conditions, there were large migrations from these latter civil divisions during the 1960s.[38]

While increasing considerably in absolute numbers from 1950 to 1970, the Federal District's Protestant population failed to keep pace with the large total population growth in that political entity during the same period. This may have been due to a small proportion of Protestants found among those migrating to the capital from relatively strong Catholic areas nearby. Growing secularization among the Federal District's residents is probably also a factor, and it is possible that in recent years some of the older Protestant denominations have reduced their efforts to evangelize the urban masses. In 1940, the civil divisions with the highest proportions of Protestants were the northern border states (except Sonora) and the Federal District;[39] but by 1970 the most heavily Protestant areas were the remote and once highly isolated entities of southeastern Mexico.

Between 1950 and 1970, in the nation as a whole, the Protestant population increased by 166 percent. This should be compared to an 88 percent increase in the country's total population during the same period. In other words, since 1950 the Evangelicals have increased almost twice as fast as the rapidly growing total population of Mexico.

Protestant population growth should always be compared to changes in the total population. This can be accomplished with ap-

[38] See Bridges, "The Population of Mexico," pp. 279-83.
[39] Bridges, "A Study of the . . . Protestant Population in Mexico," pp. 83-84.

Table 4

Growth of Protestant Population of Mexico, by Region and Major Civil Division, 1950-1970

Region and civil division	Number of Protestants			Percent of total population Protestant		
	1950	1960	1970	1950	1960	1970
Mexico	330,111	578,515	876,879	1.3	1.7	1.8
North						
Baja California	4,351	12,450	20,406	1.9	2.4	2.3
Sonora	6,693	12,616	16,188	1.3	1.6	1.5
Chihuahua	16,572	26,481	41,811	1.6	2.2	2.6
Coahuila	15,580	22,514	25,255	2.2	2.5	2.3
Nuevo León	16,679	25,747	47,714	2.2	2.4	2.8
Tamaulipas	20,222	34,336	41,911	2.8	3.4	2.9
North Central						
Baja California T.	131	487	1,106	.2	.6	.9
Sinaloa	4,574	7,673	14,148	.7	.9	1.1
Durango	7,657	10,942	10,805	1.2	1.4	1.2
Zacatecas	4,447	6,914	6,197	.7	.8	.7
San Luis Potosí	11,029	18,078	23,431	1.3	1.7	1.8
Central						
Nayarit	1,372	2,621	5,516	.5	.7	1.0
Aguascalientes	536	898	1,358	.3	.4	.4
Jalisco	4,475	10,498	19,082	.3	.4	.6
Guanajuato	2,261	6,489	6,797	.2	.4	.3
Querétaro	529	688	1,447	.2	.2	.3
Hidalgo	9,012	17,661	18,544	1.1	1.8	1.6
Colima	376	423	1,021	.3	.3	.4
Michoacán	9,820	16,116	14,982	.7	.9	.8
México	12,935	23,849	54,193	.9	1.3	1.4
Federal District	54,884	77,152	111,957	1.8	1.6	1.6
Morelos	6,323	10,291	22,685	2.3	2.7	3.7
Tlaxcala	4,704	6,514	8,160	1.6	1.9	1.9
Puebla	20,584	34,422	43,030	1.3	1.7	1.7
Veracruz	30,936	51,569	88,031	1.5	1.9	2.3
South						
Guerrero	7,662	14,431	19,471	1.2	1.2	1.2
Oaxaca	9,468	18,433	30,177	.7	1.1	1.5
Southeast						
Chiapas	19,292	50,877	75,378	.3	.3	.4
Tabasco	19,607	33,228	63,732	5.1	6.7	8.3
Campeche	2,645	6,546	13,914	2.2	3.9	5.5
Yucatán	8,012	14,903	21,610	1.6	2.4	2.9
Quintana Roo T.	658	2,668	6,822	2.4	5.3	7.7

Source: Compiled and computed from data in México, *Compendio estadístico*, 1958, pp. 61-64, Table 25; México, *VIII censo general, 1960: Resumen general*, pp. 282-89, Table 18: and México, *IX censo general, 1970: Resumen general*, pp. 55-56, Table 8.

proximate results by comparing Protestant percentages of the total populations in each of the civil divisions for 1950, 1960, and 1970 (see Table 4).[40] All but one (the Federal District) had higher proportions of Protestants in 1960 than in 1950. In 1970, however, nine civil divisions had lower proportions of Protestants than in 1960; and four others (the Federal District, Guerrero, Puebla, and Tlaxcala) merely maintained the same percentage, that is, kept pace with the rapid rate of increase in the total population. Whereas the Evangelical population of Mexico grew 2.1 times as rapidly as the total population from 1950 to 1960, the increase was only 1.4 times as great in the decade before 1970. Only field research will uncover factors that can explain this decline in the rate of Protestant growth, although more extensive analysis of 1970 census data, when they are published, can indicate in which municipios the decline was the greatest.

Conclusions

This study analyzes the number and distribution, the relative importance, and growth of the Protestant population of Mexico. It also considers factors that account for the distribution and increase of Protestants in that country.

Basic conclusions are as follows:

(1) Since their official entry into Mexico in 1857, Protestants have expanded their work from a ministry to a small number of believers in only a few states to many churches, schools, hospitals, student hostels, and other institutions located in all of Mexico's thirty-two major civil divisions.

(2) Of the almost 900,000 Evangelicals in Mexico in 1970, approximately one-half were concentrated in only six of the country's thirty-two major civil divisions: the Federal District, Veracruz, Chiapas, Tabasco, México, and Nuevo León.

(3) The four civil divisions that had the highest proportions of Protestants in their total populations in 1970 are located in southeastern Mexico. These entities are Tabasco, Quintana Roo, Campeche, and Chiapas.

(4) Civil divisions where the absolute and relative importance of Protestants is least are those states located in the southwestern and central parts of Mexico.

(5) Cultural, historical, and geographical factors have influenced variations in the absolute and relative importance of Protestants in Mexico's population. Where such factors have caused the Roman Catholic Church's influence to be weak, as in the southeastern entities, Protestants are found in greatest numbers and highest propor-

---

[40]For a more detailed and precise analysis, using index numbers, see Bridges, *Expansión evangélica en México*, pp. 54-57.

tions. Conversely, where the Catholic Church has been strong, as in the southwestern and central states, Protestants are relatively few.

(6) With respect to the rural-urban distribution of Protestants, some distinct differences are observed. In the major political entities of the southeast, where Roman Catholicism never fully penetrated rural areas, Protestants often make up higher proportions of rural than of urban populations. However, in the states of the southwest and central area, where traditionally even the most remote rural areas have been catholicized, greater concentrations of Protestants are located in urban than in rural districts.

(7) Growth of the Protestant population prior to 1940 was both steady and significant. The period of greatest growth was from 1921 to 1930, when the number of Protestants increased five times as fast as that of the total population of Mexico. The smallest absolute and relative changes occurred during the years of the Mexican Revolution.

(8) Mexico's Protestant population almost tripled between 1950 and 1970. Moreover, its rate of growth was about twice that of the total population of the country during the same time.

(9) Prior to 1940, the northern border states and the Federal District were entities showing the largest numbers and highest proportions of Protestants. Since 1940, however, the most rapid increase of Evangelicals has been in the eastern and southeastern civil divisions.

(10) From 1960 to 1970, the Protestant population increased only 1.4 times as rapidly as the rate of growth in Mexico's total population. This is probably the lowest relative growth in any decade of Mexican Protestant history, with the possible exception of the period of the Mexican Revolution (1910-1917). Thus, it becomes evident that even the dynamic Evangelical movement in Mexico has recently encountered difficulty in keeping pace with the very high rate of growth in the country's burgeoning total population.

12. La Religión como Transfondo en la Vida Familiar del Mexicano Pobre: Respuesta a Oscar Lewis

MANUEL MENDOZA

Few books by social scientists have been as widely read and hotly discussed as the works of Oscar Lewis, a cultural anthropologist who tape-recorded numerous life histories of Cubans, Puerto Ricans, and Mexicans. Lewis's *A Death in the Sánchez Family* has prompted this essay by Professor Mendoza. Although a teacher of modern languages and literature, not a social scientist, Professor Mendoza writes with the personal experience of a man who was born and reared among Mexico's urban poor.

> Yo sé que hay autores que han dicho que el mexicano sabe cómo enfrentar la muerte y no le importa la muerte ni la vida, y que hay muchos chistes y bromas y canciones sobre la muerte, pero yo quisiera ver a estos escritores famosos, verlos en nuestro lugar y haber padecido con nosotros paso a paso los sufrimientos tan enormes que tenemos en nuestra clase, y ver si es posible que acepten ellos con una sonrisa en los labios el que uno de nosotros muera, sabiendo que tiene remedio. Eso es una gran mentira.[1]

Esto es lo que Consuelo Sánchez, la principal protagonista del drama que Oscar Lewis titula *Una muerte en la familia Sánchez*, reclama en contra de quienes escriben tranquilamente de la vida real sin percatarse siquiera de cómo vive y muere el pobre en México o en cualquier parte. Consuelo continúa:

> ¿Cómo dar a entender el dolor que absorbe hasta la última gota de alegría que pudo haber quedado en mi corazón? De ninguna manera me resigno a que los míos, tan aplastados ya, mueran así. Todos vamos a morir, sí, ¿pero por qué en esas circunstancias tan inhumanas y miserables? . . . Porque la muerte, desde mi punto de vista, no es nada

[1] Oscar Lewis, *Una muerte en la familia Sánchez* (México, D.F.: Mortiz, 1970), p. 79. Los textos son reproducción de grabaciones directas y versiones taquigráficas. Referencias a esta obra se darán con cita del número de página después de la letra M.

gracioso ni nada a lo que estemos acostumbrados porque se le haga fiesta a la muerte o porque comamos calaveras de azúcar o juguemos con esqueletos. (M., p. 79).

Tal es su denuncia contra los escritores que convierten una tragedia real en fantasiosa diversión de diletantes del folclor y yo no pude dejar aquí de acordarme del folclorísimo "laberinto" de un poeta.

La segunda "Gran mentira" sobre México, que esa real y verdadera mujer que Lewis llamó Consuelo Sánchez nos echa en cara, es la ficción de un bello y próspero país inventado por los dueños del poder económico y político. Ella se pregunta:

> Por qué empecinarnos en la farsa tan absurda, la mentira gigantesca que esconde la verdad en "mi república" ¿mexicana? Me llena de horror el drama de nosotros mismos ante la escena: "Los mexicanos progresan... la hermosa, prosperante base política y económica"... Ya mi viejita está muerta. Ahí en su nido, lleno de piojos, ratas, mugre, basura y desperdicios; escondido entre los girones del vestido de etiqueta de la bella dama, la Ciudad de México. (M., p. 80).

Yo creo que cualquiera de nosotros puede encontrar en sí mismo, en el pensamiento como en la acción, un cierto remordimiento por este abandono del pobre del que Consuelo nos hace justamente responsables. Pero ahora viene la tercera acusación que es la más delicada y la que debo tratar de entender y compartir con amor y sinceridad. Sus palabras son éstas:

> En la generación anterior es probable que hayan tenido otra filosofía, de no darle importancia a la muerte, pero creo yo que sea debido al aplastamiento que sufrió por parte de la Iglesia, que les condenaban por completo la mente, haciéndoles pensar que no eran nada, que no valían nada; que aquí en la vida no iban a ganar nada y que su premio estaba en la eternidad. Yo creo que llegaba el grado en que esas mentes las aplastaban por completo, las sumergían y no tenían esperanza ni tampoco ilusión de nada. O sea, que vivían ya muertas; las hacían creer en la muerte, viviéndola. (M., pp. 79-80).

Estas son palabras textuales, según se apunta en la edición de la obra. Resumen claramente y con gran intensidad una sensación aniquilante de impotencia ante la miseria de los seres queridos. Esta sensación es más punzante y vívida que la angustia existencial del individuo o la pasión ideológica por una clase social.

Antes de colocar estos puntos extremos de sensibilidad humana, quiero apuntar algunos rasgos de religiosidad que parecen destacarse en *Una muerte en la familia Sánchez*.

En general, los individuos y el medio social de esta obra que, según Lewis, son "better representatives of the way of life which I have called the culture of poverty than were Jesús Sánchez and his children," muestran una religiosidad más dramática y comprensiva que la de otros estudios. En *Los hijos de Sánchez*,[2] que fue el libro de Lewis más popular y discutido en México, la familia tiene un fondo problemático más bien de carácter moral y jurídico que religioso. En sus otras obras mexicanas,[3] tampoco he visto algún sentido de religiosidad que sobresalga.

En la obra que comentamos, Lewis destaca la conciencia religiosa de Guadalupe Vélez dentro de un contexto sociológico de extrema pobreza y nos da este resumen: "Guadalupe died as she had lived, without medical care, in unrelieved pain, in hunger, worrying about how to pay the rent or raise money for the bus fare for a trip to the hospital, working up to the last day of her life . . . leaving nothing of value but a few old religious objects. . . ."[4]

Con esto entendemos cómo, dentro de su privación extrema de bienes materiales, la tía Lupe tenía algo muy valioso para ella como eran sus "viejos objetos religiosos." Respecto a su vida de sufrimiento y probreza, debo confesar que me impresionó de tal modo que no supe qué entresacar de ella para presentar aquí.

De interés y significación social-religiosa igualmente registra Lewis en esta obra observaciones como las siguientes: "As one moves up the economic and social ladder, the more formal Catholic beliefs begin to predominate. . . . In 'Panaderos' [la vecindad de Guadalupe], 91% of the heads of families believed in the coming of the dead whereas in the 'Casa Grande' [la vecindad de 'los hijos de Sánchez' y sobrinos de Guadalupe] only 34% believed in this." (D. p. xxxi) En la vecindad de "Panaderos," que tenía 14 cuartos de adobe, había 14 altares y un total de 147 imágenes de santos (p. 118) y los únicos trajes de vestir eran los de dos niños que se los compraron para la Confirmación (D., p. 119). Ahí, "Guadalupe ranked . . . lowest in clothing. . . . She ranked first, however, in number and value of religious objects . . . 23 religious pictures and other objects with a total value of $35.12 (dlls.)." (D., p. 115) Estos haberes religiosos de la economía de la miseria se presentan en el recuento de un apéndice final que desentona con el tema del libro como podría desconcertar una cuenta a quien no puede pagarla.

La segunda característica de la religión que se puede apreciar en esta obra es que consiste en ideas y costumbres no sólo de carácter popular, sino también de significación formalmente católica. Sin em-

---

[2]Oscar Lewis, *Los hijos de Sánchez* (México, D.F.: Fondo de Cultura Económica, 1964).

[3]*Life in a Mexican Village: Tepoztlán Restudied* (Urbana: University of Illinois Press, 1951); *Tepoztlán, Village in Mexico* (New York: Holt, Rinehart & Winston, 1960); *Five Families: Mexican Case Studies in the Culture of Poverty* (New York: Basic Books, 1959); and *Pedro Martínez, A Mexican Peasant and His Family* (London: Secker and Warburg, 1964).

[4]Oscar Lewis, *A Death in the Sanchez Family* (New York: Random House, 1969), p. x. Las citas en inglés, de la Introducción y el Apéndice de esta edición, son originales de Oscar Lewis. Referencias a esta obra se darán con cita del número de página después de la letra D.

bargo, a la hora de calificar este modo de religiosidad, Lewis acude al concepto de "folk Catholicism." Por ejemplo, hablando de la familia de Guadalupe, dice: "Her parents were religious and had been properly married in church. . . . As far as we know, they followed no tradition other than Mexican folk Catholicism. . . . The parents required all the children to rise at three in the morning to haul water for the garden before attending Mass at four." (D., pp. xi-xii)

Como crítica incidental quisiera advertir aquí la contradicción o incongruencia del concepto "folk Catholicism" con las afirmaciones de que los papás se casaron debidamente por la Iglesia y llevaban a sus hijos a misa todos los días. En verdad, respecto a lo primero, en México no se dice casarse "en" la iglesia con referencia al lugar ("in church") sino se dice casarse "por" la Iglesia para significar casarse "por las leyes de la Iglesia," ya que al matrimonio católico se le considera, principalmente en el campo mexicano, como algo sagrado (un sacramento) que hay que respetar y cuyo respeto lo garantizan precisamente las leyes eclesiásticas por las que uno se casa. Respecto a lo segundo, yo diría que la misa no es algo folklórico sino la manifestación litúrgica más alta de la religión católica. Y es precisamente en esta pura y rigurosamente católica religiosidad de la familia donde me inclino yo a ver el origen de la fe inquebrantable y del ánimo que nunca decayó en esa víctima de la miseria que fue Guadalupe Vélez.

Aquí entra el objetivo final de mi estudio que consistirá en ver cómo en las instancias últimas de la vida es donde la religión se nos manifiesta con más vigor. Para ello espero que un breve examen de los límites que alcanzó la probreza de Guadalupe nos permita descubrir un poco el verdadero papel de la religión en la vida del pobre.

Nuestro análisis incluirá dos puntos: 1o.- Desarrollar un poco lo indicado antes sobre la idea de "colocar los extremos de sensibilidad humana dentro de un marco de pobreza familiar y no sólo individual." 2o.- Cambiar nuestra perspectiva de la probreza del ángulo socio-económico al ángulo religioso.

Respecto al primer punto diremos que la experiencia de la pobreza en el propio ser individual es tan necesaria para entenderla realmente como que sus efectos de hambre, frío o enfermedades se sufren realmente en carne propia. Sin embargo, estas experiencias físicas son de suyo acicates que mueven a salir de pobre rompiendo muchas veces límites "a como dé lugar," en el decir mexicano. En la pobreza individual no hay drama moral, hay un imperativo físico que no puede aplazarse indefinidamente.

Pero la experiencia de la pobreza en la familia es otro cantar. La familia la entendemos aquí en dos sentidos: a) el sentido original de un grupo humano en cuyo seno vive alguien su niñez y su juventud; b) el sentido derivado de la familia que sostiene uno como adulto.

La familia en que vivimos la niñez y adolescencia nos suele dejar ciertos modos de sentir y pensar que constituyen la base de nuestra sensibilidad y criterio en la edad madura. Si esa familia es pobre y vive al estilo del Bajío o del centro de México, ya sea en un medio rural o urbano, no se da en ella el sentimiento individual de un "yo" malherido por la pobreza. Lo que se forma es un tremendo sentido del "nosotros" familiar como cuerpo orgánico en el que cada miembro siente y comparte sus carencias y sus haberes. Ahí nadie trabaja para sí mismo; se trabaja, así en impersonal, para todo lo que se necesite en "la casa."

Yo nací en una ciudad del centro de México donde no había sino gente rica o pobre. No había "middle class" en su sentido económico. De origen pobre, me identifiqué con él espiritualmente. A la separación del tiempo y la actitud vital de ahora, la pobreza sigue siendo para mí algo moralmente muy valioso que, sin embargo, no tiene valor cultural, no constituye un modo de cultura ni aun de "sub-cultura." La llamada por Oscar Lewis "culture of poverty" o "sub-culture of poverty" yo propongo traducirla en castellano por "economía de la pobreza" a aun "economía de la miseria," según sea su nivel económico.

Si soy pobre, la pobreza es una condición o estructura incidental que me impuso o me impone la sociedad. Pero ni ésta ni su economía pueden imponerme un modo familiar o un estilo personal de vida. Aun cuando me encuentre o me dejen en la mayor miseria, conservo todavía la inalienable libertad de elegir y realizar culturalmente mi vida personal y familiar. Cultura es libertad interior. Y esta libertad interior es lo que se conserva en el hogar. No es en la sociedad sino en la familia donde se armonizan los intereses de mi libertad personal y por ello, en caso de conflicto, podría yo dejar un trabajo, por ejemplo, pero no abandonar a mi familia.

Antes de volver con "los Sánchez" y ver el valor moral que la pobreza pudiera tener en sus condiciones de vida, quisiera aquí apuntar de paso otra razón para cambiar "culture" por "economía" en los términos de Lewis.

Lo que quiero es advertir que dentro del concepto latino-hispánico de "cultura" no pueden admitirse contradicciones de incultura, barbarie o miseria que destruyan valores de la vida humana. Y es que dicho concepto no deriva de un orden social y externo sino sólo en cuanto de ese orden externo y social se tomen los elementos que puedan asimilarse y cultivarse interiormente—la cultura es siempre cultivo—sea en el seno de la tierra (agri-cultura) o del alma (animi-cultura). De los cultivos de la naturaleza y del alma humana es de donde se abstraen, por así decir, los "valores" que caracterizan a una cultura en su sentido estricto y la distinguen de los meros "hechos sociales" en bruto.

El valor moral de la pobreza se relaciona con la segunda condición que apuntamos antes como necesaria para entender el papel de la religión en la vida del pobre. Esta condición requiere un cambiar de golpe nuestro ángulo de visión.

En vez de contemplar la pobreza o la muerte en su marco social, como lo hace Lewis, las buscaremos en el fondo moral y religioso del propio existir. Nuestra visión gira así en torno totalmente, de adentro hacia adentro. Aquí ya no vemos las realidades últimas a través de una imagen prestada y extraña o al menos externa, en los demás, sino que las palpamos en nosotros mismos, en la propia y muy personal indigencia y en el sentido temporal de nuestro ser. Estas instancias extremas, que se nos presentan como urgencias de que la vida no se nos acabe sin hacer algo en ella, se delimitan en la fuerza de su drama según el tiempo y circunstancias en que a cada quien le corresponda vivirlas. De ahí es de donde nace su dimensión moral.

Desde un punto de vista religioso, esta contradicción existencial con que vivimos la muerte o encontramos un valor positivo en las carencias, es uno de los inagotables sentidos dinámicos del vivir que la fé cristiana puede descubrirnos a todos, y que de hecho le está descubriendo al pobre en su pobreza. Indudablemente que fue uno de esos sentidos el que sostuvo a Guadalupe Vélez en firme hasta el momento de su muerte.

La dimensión cristiana de la pobreza la dan la Fé y la Esperanza en un Dios Providente, que no sólo nos promete una recompensa espiritual para la otra vida, sino que ya nos está dando y fácilmente puede darnos una mayor ayuda moral y material en ésta.

Doña Lupe parece haber sido un tanto cuanto fatalista y no solamente cristiana en su aceptación de la pobreza como un carácter a modo de ser que se hereda al nacer y en él se vive hasta la muerte. ¿O era, quizá, un encariñarse con su pobre casa y sus pobres cosas lo que la hizo responder a su sobrino, cuando la invitó a irse a vivir con él: "No, hijo, yo de aquí no salgo hasta que me saquen en hombros con los pies pa'delante"? (M., p. 66).

Fuera como fuere, fatalista o cristiana, los valores familiares de un catolicismo "formal" (y no solamente "folclórico," como quiere Lewis) alcanzaron a pervivir, de la infancia a la vejez, en la vida miserable de Guadalupe Vélez. "Folclórica" puede decirse la manera en que la casaron sus padres por la fuerza y "por la Iglesia," con el hombre que la raptó a los 13 años. Ese más forzoso que forzado matrimonio le sirvió de norma absoluta de conducta, pues ya después no quiso casarse.

Por otro lado, el matrimonio eclesiástico de sus padres, tan formal en el estilo campesino del Bajío, y la práctica litúrgicamente formal, y campesina también, de madrugar al trabajo y a misa, sin duda dejaron algún rastro indeleble en el alma niña de Guadalupe. De otro modo no podría entenderse esa honda religiosidad suya (¿"folclórica"? ¿"barroca"? ¿"tradicional"? ¡Qué importa!), que luego se manifestó en altares y velas, crucifijos e imágenes (se sentía especialmente orgullosa de los que habían sido de su familia por muchos años) ante los que Doña Lupe sin duda lloraba y oraba intensamente.

Sin duda, también, ella fue la que sentó ejemplo y estableció el modelo de vivienda en su vecindad de la calle de Panaderos, donde ocupaba un cuarto "que tenía el número 1" en más de un sentido. Muy fácilmente posible me parece que esa promoción devocional de Guadalupe haya sido en gran parte responsable de que los 14 cuartos de la vecindad se llenaran de 14 altares y 147 imágenes de santos, como mencionamos antes. Mas, ¿podría este "hecho religioso" explicarse sociológicamente como un segundo ejemplo de que en esa pequeña vecindad se daba, junto con el "compadrazgo," "an interesting *reversal* of the usual trend toward secularization" de la gente que emigra del campo a la ciudad? (D., p. xxx).

Sin una verdadera *reversión* en nuestro enfoque de adentro-por-fuera-hacia-dentro, en que vayamos hacia los visiblemente pobres "objetos religiosos" y volvamos a la invisible, pero abundante y efectiva fe y culto interior, es difícil que podamos entender "el fondo religioso en la vida familiar del mexicano pobre."

Como una pequeña muestra de esa fé, flor tierna y delicada que aparece en medio de la suciedad y miseria del tugurio de Guadalupe, quiero sólo mencionar un rasgo, para mi gusto, sumamente conmovedor. Lo recuerda su sobrina Consuelo cuando le lleva flores a su féretro: "... entré a dejar las flores al pie de la caja. Ya tenía varios ramos. Recordé su carita chiquita cuando mi tía arreglaba las flores para el Señor, que durante toda la vida de mi linda, nunca dejó de ofrecérselas en su día. Y le decía: 'Aquí están tus flores, papá. Están lindas, ¿verdá? Le traje sus flores a mi papá.' "

Terminemos. Pero antes, ¿cómo podríamos responder a las tres acusaciones que ha lanzado el personaje central en esta obra de Lewis?

La primera se dirigió contra los intelectuales insensibles a esa miseria humana que todos somos y no queremos aceptar. Yo creo que Lewis respondió bien no sólo como investigador social sino principalmente como amigo de la gente pobre que trató en sus estudios. Por ello me parece que sus obras no son laudables tanto por algún valor, científico o literario en particular cuanto por lo universal humano que nos ha descubierto en la pobreza.

La segunda denuncia va contra los poderosos que no tienen conciencia de su poder económico o político. Pocos de ellos llegan a imaginar ni mucho menos que sus grandes empresas o decisiones puedan tener alcances funestos para infinidad de miserables a quienes ni siquiera conocen. Me gustaría enviarles una simple copia de las páginas biográficas de la tía Guadalupe, y ver luego sus respuestas, (pero, ¿a quienes?)

La tercera acusación, contra la Iglesia, nos afecta a muchos más. A unos porque al creer nos hacemos también Iglesia. A otros porque, si las varias iglesias del cristianismo actual, como también de otras religiones, ya no matan sino que avivan el sentido de lucha en la conciencia del pobre, es claro que tenemos que hacer algo más que culpar a las agrupaciones eclesiásticas.

Finalmente, yo creo que no serán la revolución social, ni los poderes económico o político quienes resuelvan el problema en su origen, sino necesitamos dejar que la contradicción cristiana nos descubra en el alma el dinamismo moral de la pobreza.

13. The "Politics" of Iván Illich and Small Group Political Behavior at CIDOC—Cuernavaca, 1972

WILLIAM R. GARNER

This study is based on the author's experiences at the Centro Intercultural de Documentación (CIDOC) in February and March 1972. After Professor Garner's article was written, Iván Illich phased out CIDOC and donated its library to the Colegio de México, claiming that the purpose of CIDOC is now being carried out by other institutions.

The Setting and Clientele

The Centro Intercultural de Documentación (CIDOC) is operated out of a large white villa on a hill overlooking Cuernavaca, fifty miles south of Mexico City. Its extensive well-landscaped campus is the perfect location for what has become known as the world's foremost Latin American think-tank. It was the present writer's fortune to be able to go directly to Cuernavaca and CIDOC from a six-month sabbatical in Quito, Ecuador, where a book manuscript was prepared for publication. On the basis of this work, a seminar on psychological variables in Latin American politics was given during February and March 1972.

CIDOC began as the Center for Intercultural Formation. It was established in 1961 by Dr. Iván Illich, who was then a priest with the Roman Catholic Diocese of New York. The purpose of Illich's endeavor was the preparation of Catholic missionaries for work in Latin American nation-states. Intensive programs in the Spanish language and Latin American Studies were offered. The entire process was to be carried out in the light of one overriding imperative— "deyankeefication" of persons seeking to be of spiritual and earthly assistance to Latin American populations. Associated with the Center was a library (CIDOC) which also published a bulletin, *CIDOC Informa*, for distribution in Latin America. Gradually, the bulletin and the library became more important than the other activities pursued at the Center. Thus, in 1966, the name was changed to CIDOC and the ever-popular language school was associated with it. In 1967, the Catholic hierarchy forbade priests and other religious to attend the Center; subsequently, the hierarchy also suspended the functions of priesthood for Illich. Concerning this action, Illich stated, "The Club of Rome placed its Papal ban on both me and the Center."[1] Thus, the Center, while remaining extremely normative and in the broadest sense "spiritual," was formally secularized. Bruce Rusk, an Anglican priest from Toronto, wrote about the campus during the same period of time as my stay: "One of the few traces of its religious origins is an outside altar which during my first visit [as well as his subsequent visits and this writer's first] served as a stand for selling fresh fruit and as a student mailbox."[2]

At the time of the present writer's experience at CIDOC, with the beautiful old home and unused swimming pool as a constant reminder of pre-Revolutionary opulence in the now-fading age-old resort city of Cuernavaca, there were approximately 150 to 200 young people and academics/dilletantes "in residence." The term "residence" signifies that these individuals had paid the yearly rates for entrance to and use of the grounds, the library, and the bookstore; also, they had the right to avail themselves of any one or a combination of three segments comprising the Center's thrust: (1) the intensive Spanish language school, (2) the ICLAS seminars, and (3) the CICLO series representing special presentations given each day at 11 A.M. This writer was asked to give a CICLO on the first Monday of his stay in Cuernavaca. Tuesdays at that hour are reserved for the special Illich CICLO, with compulsory attendance on the part of all persons taking advantage of any of the CIDOC programs.

Intensive Spanish classes—one month in duration—are attended by both young and old from all over the world, but primarily by persons from the United States. Language students represent the most varied, and hence "least controllable," group from the standpoint of the official ideological orientation of CIDOC (that collage of values expounded verbally and in print by Illich and supported both by permanent institutional and informal "Illich" groups in Cuernavaca or elsewhere). The language program also carries much of the financial burden for the more ideologically-oriented parts of the Center's operation.

[1]Interview with Iván Illich, Centro Intercultural de Documentación, Cuernavaca, Mor., March 8, 1972. The author is uncertain as to whether Illich referred to the Papacy or the worldwide organization of intellectuals who met first in Rome (1968) to discuss the ramifications of many of the same problems with which Illich has dealt. In the context of the highly theological conversation of March 8, however, the metaphor appears aimed at sanctions imposed by the Roman Catholic hierarchy.
[2]Bruce Rusk, "CIDOC Revisited," (Windsor, Ont., Canada, 1972), mimeographed by CIDOC with CIDOC citation 72.03, p. 1.

The ICLAS series draws persons whose interests are somewhat avant garde, and the seminars bear provocative titles such as "The Bhagavad Gita and the Parables of Christ," "Blaming the Manstitutions: Female Phenomenology Undermines Male Empiricism," "Alternatives to Jails and Mental Hospitals," and the seminar which this writer offered: "Toward an Interpretation of Latin American Political Processes: A Value Orientation."[3] Generally, Illich's more devout followers are found in these seminars, but this is certainly not always the case. A more heterogeneous clientele becomes obvious when one looks at the physical positioning at the Tuesday-Illich CICLO, where the most ardent audience is found literally at his feet. Others position themselves in significant geometric circles that radiate out from the wooden platform upon which Illich makes his statements and fields questions.

As stated earlier, it was the writer's privilege to be a part of this intellectual environment every day for one month. In the process he came upon a leadership and, by default, followership pattern which constantly reminded him of the hypotheses and discussion presented in a study by Sidney Verba that was published some years earlier.[4] The leadership models in Verba's work were found to be congruent with the personality and influence of Iván Illich, the constant variable and bulwark of the Center's operations, and with other persons employed at the Center. Using Verba's study as a foundation both for testing his hypotheses and for presenting impressions received through personal encounters and interchange within the CIDOC milieu, this essay constitutes an attempt to explore and describe the power relationships which revolved around the controversial priest who draws so many to Cuernavaca and to the Center for Intercultural Documentation.

This study of CIDOC is representative of similar applications of small-group political theory and is to be viewed as nothing more than a case study. Academics in other relatively small and somewhat controlled situations might use similar case studies as a basis for increasingly rigorous generalizations concerning the generation or loss of political power by leadership personalities in both informal settings, such as that described here, and those of a more formal nature.

Most certainly, the single case study is perceived in this instance as being the safest vehicle for the expansion of relevant theory. Throughout the 1961 study, Verba stressed the relativity of leadership-followership patterns:

> Abstract models have a certain elegance and appeal, but unless such models can be related at some point to reality they will have a seriously

---

[3]CIDOC Catalogue No. 14, pp. 12-28, passim.
[4]Sidney Verba, *Small Groups and Political Behavior: A Study of Leadership* (Princeton, N.J.: Princeton University Press, 1961).

limited value to social analysis. One of the major tasks of small group experimental research is that of connecting small group models more closely with actual social situations. . . . The constant process of testing small group findings in the real world should increase our knowledge of the real world at the same time that it sharpens our use of the experimental method.[5]

Likewise, with respect to any perceived bias in the approach, it should be proper at this point to stipulate, as has Verba, that there is no assumption of a "natural superiority for democratic over autocratic [leadership] methods."[6] Verba continues in this vein by cautioning the would-be-researcher: "There is no 'best' leadership structure. What structure is best must depend upon the group setting, task and membership—in short, upon the total situation."[7]

CIDOC and the No-conflict Assumption

As indicated earlier, Illich's least important problems are likely to come out of the ICLAS seminars and from those who lead them. Many seminar leaders make their permanent home in Cuernavaca and offer courses throughout the year. Others, keeping in touch with Illich and the Center through publications and personal correspondence, come regularly—either as seminar leaders or as students—from literally every part of the world. It should be reiterated, however, that generalizations concerning ideological consensus are not verifiable.

Early in 1972, Illich was plainly on his guard with respect to the more obviously "unenlightened," that is, Catholics, Protestants, and others of more "conservative" bent. Yet, it should be stressed that the professionals in business, education, and organized religion did not constitute a monolithic group. Many came out of curiosity, some out of boredom, many simply for a learning/vacation experience in the pleasant climatic and physical environment of Cuernavaca and the Center; others came to pursue the torturous but functional language programs. Thus, there were factions and personalities to "juggle" if the assumed *Weltanschauung* of CIDOC were to be maintained and utilized for ends known most clearly to the leader and his coterie but perceived through a glass only darkly by the majority of residents. That these ends are perceived only darkly in no way implies dangerous or "sinister" motives but refers simply to the constant, open-ended barrage of stated problems with little or no attempt to develop specific ameliorative social programs. As The Reverend Bruce Rusk described the situation in the Spring of 1972: "Illich pointed out that it is the main task of the philosopher to state the obvious in as or-

[5]Ibid., pp. 246-48.
[6]Ibid., p. 242.
[7]Ibid., p. 243.

dinary terms as possible. This has been the role of CIDOC. It is left to others to concretize and implement the ideas developed there."[8]

Placed in the perspective of the theoretical model, the above description of a not-so-consensual group of persons does not mesh with Verba's statement of the so-called "no-conflict" assumption: "that there is a single group goal or a single method of attaining a group goal that is in the interests of all concerned—both leaders and followers . . . suggested by the group's expert leadership using the proper technique of presentation—[leading] to a recognition by the followers that it [the single group goal or method of attaining it] is in their best interests."[9] Further, Verba suggests that the assumption is valid *only* "in a large number of experimental groups artificially insulated from external pressures" but is *not* valid in the "myriad complex [of] social situations in which the goal of some members of the system may not be the same as that of the others, and the best solution for some participants will not be the best for others."[10]

Illich vis-à-vis Verba's Requisite Leadership Functions

Leadership structures in Verba's model perform a dual function in order that the group being organized and effectively controlled may continue to be viable and achieve its goals. The two types delineated are termed *instrumental* and *affective*. The instrumental component of leadership deals with tasks external to but including the internal work of the group; that is, it concerns tasks which are directly connected with the goal-orientation of the organization. On the other hand, the affective function is concerned with internal systems maintenance and the psychic-intellectual satisfaction of the needs of individual group members.[11] It is clear that the performance of *both* functions relating to system/group maintenance may represent an onerous task, as Verba observes:

> The difficulties of the leadership position derive not merely from the fact that the leader must be active in both the instrumental and affective group tasks, but from the fact that these two tasks are closely related. The way in which the group functions in one area will influence functioning in the other. If group members have a strong affective relationship with the leader, they will be more likely to accept his instrumental directives.[12]

This, of necessity, relates to the problems of organizational equilibrium and an ordered pattern of human behavior on the part of the group as a whole or factions found within it.

---

[8]Rusk, "CIDOC Revisited," p. 5.
[9]Verba, *Small Groups and Political Behavior*, p. 222.
[10]Ibid., p. 223.
[11]Ibid., p. 142.
[12]Ibid., pp. 145-46.

In consideration of the equilibrium problem, Verba and others suggest that not one but *two* leaders are, in practice, required to bring about the optimal relationship between instrumental and affective leadership functions. This is very much the case in the CIDOC structure. Illich's primary purpose is that of providing the goal-set for the Center as well as that charismatic force which is so necessary for success in affectivity. His flamboyance of speech, mannerisms, and "body language" all contribute to the establishment of rapport with those who hear him in his weekly CICLO or as he rushes to sit in on one of the seminars of the ICLAS series. In the Tuesday CICLO, Illich sits cross-legged on an old wooden table, gesticulating energetically while at the same time performing verbal acrobatics of a gargantuan magnitude. The semantics, the look in his eyes, the scalding derision aimed at those sitting around him who ask "wrong" questions or make "wrong" remarks all contribute to the functional performance of his affective role.

The affectivity of Illich's leadership is heightened by the *mysterium* surrounding the official Registrar for the campus, who signs all correspondence from CIDOC to inquirers with the name Esperanza Godot. This name is sooner or later seen as a very trenchant *nom de plume* by those who come to CIDOC "looking for her." Certainly, the euphemistic appellation was given away by a slip which Illich probably made unwittingly in *Celebration of Awareness* (1970). In the concluding section of this work (widely acclaimed and capped with a personal interview of Illich by Hugh Downs, then of NBC's "Today" broadcast), the author writes that "development-mad Brazil and ... humanist Cuba" are futilely "waiting for Godot [without] a radical change in their institutions."[13] Thus, the intriguing name of the Registrar is clarified somewhat.

Actually, the functions of "Esperanza Godot" were performed by or under the direct supervision of Valentina Borremans (whom this writer knew to exist but never met on the Center's campus). Miss Yolanda Guadarrama, who was either Valentina Borremans' and/or Illich's "Girl Friday," served as appointments and seminar coordinator as well as general "shield." She was the only *visible* evidence of the actual existence of Borremans or—for the "troubled" or naive— Esperanza Godot. Rusk has described Valentina Borremans, who has been with the Center since its founding in 1961, in the following context:

> While Illich as the charismatic visionary [has] gained prominence through talks and publications, the driving force behind CIDOC has been Valentina Borremans.... On my first visit [to the Center] I heard Valentina referred to as the enigmatic power-behind-the-throne, but I

[13]Iván D. Illich, *Celebration of Awareness: A Call for Institutional Revolution* (Garden City, N.Y.: Doubleday & Co., 1970), p. 185.

never saw her. On my second visit I spent an hour with this charming, intelligent, obviously strong-willed woman who has a very clear conception of the role of CIDOC, but who prefers the obscurity of the administrator to the limelight of the teacher.[14]

One must go through the office of Miss Guadarrama, also a quiet, extremely sensitive, aloof but strong-willed individual, in order to have any person-to-person relationship with Illich. Therefore, under the tutelage and with the aid of Valentina Borremans, she is viewed as performing the instrumental leadership function referred to by Verba. If the affective-emotional-ideological function is in the main performed by Illich, instrumental systems-maintenance is reserved for the trinity of Borremans-Guadarrama-"Godot" (to isolate Esperanza Godot empirically amid the camouflage of the written, formal information disseminated by CIDOC).

At each non-Illich CICLO (every day except Tuesdays at 11 A.M.) it was Miss Guadarrama who was constantly in the background, feverishly taking notes on a steno pad, keeping a record of the behavior of those in the audience as they related positively or negatively to the speaker of the day. Others of Illich's inner circle would be sitting near the front, some with tape recorders or cassettes, making sure that the presentations of persons like myself were on record for replay and discussion. It was Miss Guadarrama to whom all persons took procedural problems concerning the ICLAS series. If one wished a room or tree change for his/her seminar, it had to be effected by Guadarrama. If one wanted to see Iván Illich privately, it was in her power to decide if and when. This writer tried for three weeks to obtain an appointment with Illich, but not until the last day of responsibilities with the seminar was a meeting scheduled. It was most probably Guadarrama, sufficiently impressed by the author's persistence, who consulted with either her mentor (Illich) or her instrumental supervisor (Valentina Borremans) and arranged the interview. That appointment, over a modest lunch served on Illich's private terrace outside his sumptuous, private quarters, was a memorable occasion that will be described later. Mention of the appointment at this point, however, is meant to indicate the locus and power of instrumental leadership inside the CIDOC structure.

Illich's ability to make an audience for himself outside the CIDOC compound (e.g., on U.S. television, in various U.S. and foreign periodicals and publishing houses such as Doubleday, Harper and Row, and others) is due to what appears to be a smoothly running cooperative effort involving himself and the two women wielding instrumental power. Theoretically speaking, according to Verba:

The ability of the leader to relate the group to the external environment

[14]Rusk, "CIDOC Revisited," p. 2.

and manipulate that environment for the benefit of the group increases his acceptance and interpersonal influence. Communications from the external environment to the group and from the group to the external environment will tend to go through the group leader, who becomes in this way an opinion leader or "gate keeper."[15]

As has already been indicated, personalities like Illich are faced with a dilemma stemming from incompatible expectations placed upon them. "If the leader conforms to [novel] demands of the external environment, he risks rejection by the group. If, on the other hand, he rejects adjustments to [such novel pressures], he may cease to be an effective leader...."[16] Thus, the requisite stability inside the organization may be jeopardized by that lack of optimal equilibrium between the two facets of functional leadership. Verba states, "Insofar as the group can achieve some satisfactory balance between the instrumental and the affective aspects of its interaction and a stable leadership structure is developed, the group will be effective and contribute to the satisfactions of its members."[17] It would appear—certainly from this account and Rusk's—that the necessary "balance" was struck between the instrumental or "task leader" and the "socio-emotional" affective leader forms.[18] The role differentiation and explicit (or implicit) role assignments performed by Borremans-Guadarrama-"Godot" and those functions executed by Dr. Illich are representative of the requisite Verba coalition.

Conformist-Charismatic Qualities of the Leader

The small group theoretical analysis used here suggests that the leader is by nature a conformist in that

> the relationship between conformity and rank is mutual—the higher one's rank the closer one conforms to the norms [of the group]; the closer one conforms to the group norms, the higher one's rank. The group's demand for conformity to its norms and the special need of the leader for acceptance by the group combine to place stronger demands for conformity upon the leader than upon any other group member.[19]

Thus, deviant behavior on the part of the group must be assessed within the framework of cost and risk factors involving such behavior. Conversely, with respect to deviation or substantive change initiated by a personality like Illich, any novel ideological "products" or structural innovations must be "sold" in the marketplace of the CIDOC universe. If the supply of new material or procedure is not in optimal

---

[15]Verba, *Small Groups and Political Behavior*, pp. 152-53.
[16]Ibid., p. 155.
[17]Ibid., p. 159.
[18]Ibid., pp. 162-66.
[19]Ibid., p. 186.

relationship with the demand for or acceptance of such, then the "presence" or Weberian charismatic function must be brought into play.

When following closely the limitations of Max Weber's definition of charismatic leadership form (e.g., perception by the group of supernatural, superhuman, God-like or God-given qualities in the spirit-mind, body, and general behavior of a leader), we are not merely making statements relating to the rapport of the leader with the strivings and desires of the followers.[20] The interrelationship must be seen, in addition, as a more functional technique for insinuating innovation. Paul Halmos, as quoted by Verba, builds upon the norm that "charisma derives from [perceptions by the group] of the internal sufferings of the leader" and observes further that "the charismatic leader is no other than the one whose private misery is the ideal type of the misery prevalent in his culture."[21] If "his culture" is changed to read "his power universe," then the CIDOC organization and its audience provide an excellent example of an ongoing process of innovative thought patterns and intellectual evolution through dialogue with the clientele of the Center made possible by those clearly charismatic qualities of Illich's personality. Verba clarifies the argument in elaborating the leader's "acceptance capital":

> We have suggested ... that there is a wide variety of ways in which leaders conform to the expectations of the group members. Through this conformity leaders build up a fund of acceptance by the group which allows them some leeway for deviation. Thus the degree to which the charismatic leader identified himself with the masses gives him leeway to act in ways quite different from the average group member. If the leader can develop sufficient high, generalized status by conforming to the expectations of his followers, he will be able to deviate in some respects from the group without facing rejection.[22]

This writer could give numerous examples regarding Illich's high acceptance capital as evidenced in the introduction of new subjects for discussion and new procedural requirements for either the most significant or the most elementary changes in functions within the Center's structure. It is observed, therefore, that the charismatic element is exemplified with respect to deviation from priorly-accepted norms of the group.

A separate but equally important issue is seen in group member deviation and the manner in which it is dealt with by the leadership.

---

[20] Note *From Max Weber: Essays in Sociology*, trans. and ed. H. H. Gerth and C. Wright Mills (New York: Oxford University Press, 1946), pp. 245-62; see also Reinhard Bendix, *Max Weber: An Intellectual Portrait* (New York: Doubleday & Co., 1962), pp. 300-305.

[21] Paul Halmos, *Towards a Measure of Man: The Frontiers of Normal Adjustment* (London: Routledge and Kegan Paul, 1957), p. 134, quoted in Verba, *Small Groups and Political Behavior*, p. 187.

[22] Verba, *Small Groups and Political Behavior*, p. 201.

Leaders like Illich are at times under strong pressures to conform to novel norms emanating from factions *within* the group. What does he do to evade violation of those norms when they represent—both qualitatively and quantitatively—demands for change which cannot be easily neutralized by his charismatic function? For example, what did he do in February-March 1972, when confronted by a schism? This development involved a group of malcontents who voiced opposition to others who, feeling somewhat the same pangs, formed an "opposition," though probably not a significant one from the standpoint of danger to group stability on the campus. In addition, there was a more important sub-group representing a continuing and permanent "loyal opposition" to Illich's ideological position as well as to his personal behavior or "style." Whether the opposition came from temporary residents of the Center or those perennially *within* CIDOC's circle, the response was essentially the same. Illich and the instrumental team of Borremans-Guadarrama-"Godot" reacted in patterns that evolved continuously from an ever-shifting but well coordinated charismatic-instrumental potential.

In the case of deviation by the international editor of *Guideposts* magazine from Pawling, New York, the reported response was a stand-off in private conversation with Illich. With an attractive middle-aged female professor (doctorate in Religious Education) teaching at an American Baptist seminary in New York State, the style of reaction was a "cool treatment" which persuaded the woman to make her stay in Cuernavaca shorter than she had first anticipated.[23] With other persons (who were usually in the language school and/or the ICLAS seminars), typical behavior of Illich was failure "to see hands" or to recognize questioners at his CICLO. In some instances, when questions went too much against the grain, Illich would scathingly denounce the individuals with counterquestions aimed at ridicule and instant embarrassment.

During this writer's luncheon interview with Illich, the latter implicitly conceded an error in logic and proceeded to a series of martyr-like histrionics which was aimed, probably, at what might have appeared to Dr. Illich as an opening in his adversary's softer side. When the behavior did not bring sufficient contrition, the luncheon was abruptly terminated by Illich, who then accompanied this writer to the first floor reception area. After Illich had been thanked both for the meal and month's experience on the CIDOC campus, he quickly disappeared into his quarters upstairs. As long as he was in the reception area, he continued to weep. With feelings of unrest and ambivalence about the preceding scene, this writer walked out of the

---

[23]The individual in question was known at the Center as being responsible for distributing a journal issue with an article critical of Illich's philosophy and of his attack on contemporary education. The article in question was Theodore A. McConnell's "Ivan Illich's Assault on Education," *Religious Education* 67 (January-February 1972): 42-48.

Center compound for the last time to wait for a taxi. At that point, a young Canadian woman (a permanent Cuernavaca-CIDOC resident who termed herself a Christian Buddhist and was always attired in a *sari*) asked if she could offer transportation from the Center. This writer explained the problem of having already called a taxi and refused politely. She then said that she was aware of the fact that Illich had had "a bad time of it" over our lunch; also, she stated that Illich was in one of the larger, more popular seminars on "deschooling" and had been heard to say that "Garner had asked him to discontinue the Tuesday CICLO." This charge was false, and the young woman was told so. Illich's behavior after the noon interview was disquieting. He had apparently conceded victory. This writer has not and does not question Illich's intelligence. He is a brilliant man. And this personal experience and other examples of reactive behavior described above point to quite functional manipulative action with which the writer has little quarrel, as a political scientist.

Conclusions

The task of evaluating Iván Illich's behavior as *líder máximo* of the Centro Intercultural de Documentación is somewhat difficult because of the writer's negative experiences. It would seem appropriate, therefore, to make the following clarifications: This participant-observer did not feel "at home" in the Center due to an increasing uneasiness over the substance of ideas presented there and the manner in which they were presented. On the other hand, observation of general behavior on the part both of affective and instrumental leadership was quite positively appreciated from the standpoint of theory *qua* theory. Hopefully, this essay contributes one more case study in a Latin American environment—a case study which may add to the knowledge gleaned from numerous studies done in more advanced nation-states. The hypotheses set forth by Sidney Verba and others concerning small-group-political behavior have been put to the test and found helpful in explaining the leadership forms found at CIDOC.

Thus, additional applications of Verba's leadership model have been provided. The dual-leadership coalition type seems to have been substantiated. Problems perceived with regard to equilibrium maintenance in the small-group system, or attempts at equilibrium change together with the methods utilized by leadership to maintain an internally-defined stasis (or something approaching it), are given a more precisely delineated theoretical focus. The interchange potential of Illich with respect to groups outside the Center is made clearer. In Mexico, he was either ignored or most probably tolerated as harmless by the government and the Partido Revolucionario Institucional (PRI) because of his close ties with the liberal Bishop of Cuernavaca as well as with the world-renowned psychoanalyst, Eric Fromm, who has made nearby Mexico City his permanent home. With respect to the intellectual arena in the Western world at large, Illich is highly respected by important innovative groups. Hopefully, for any readers of this paper who have been in correspondence with CIDOC and have received letters from Miss Esperanza Godot, the mystery of her name as well as her identity have been clarified somewhat in the discussion of instrumental leadership.

To conclude with one final statement concerning the substantive orientation of the ideological environment, the foundation of the Center remains normative and, therefore, in the broadest sense, spiritual. On the other hand, there appears to be an extremely interesting psychological base for the informal theocracy prevailing in such a milieu of spirituality. Nonetheless, the religious concerns are clearly demonstrated in Illich's numerous publications dealing with such subjects as the "seamy side of charity," celibacy for the priesthood, the "powerless Church," schools as "sacred cows," and "the vanishing clergy."[24] These writings give Illich's position on a variety of religious institutions and spiritual attitudes. His many articles in the U.S. periodical *America*—along with his books: *Celebration of Awareness* (1970),[25] *The Church, Change and Development* (1970)[26] and *Deschooling Society*[27]—represent a totally religious philosophical attitude within the framework of an avante garde Roman Catholic point of view. In spite of the fact that he has been "banned" by some, as he accused this writer of attempting to do to him, his position is thoroughly stimulating. When one speaks of the totality of the Latin American religious, socioeconomic, and political milieu, the questions which Illich raises cannot be avoided. Over and above the frustrations experienced because of the constant open-ended dialogue/monologue, this writer found Illich's personality extremely interesting from an academic viewpoint and his statements thoughtful and thought-provoking. Both this observer and CIDOC's leader are normatively oriented, and the fact that our norms failed to mesh is not the issue here.

Written by a political scientist, this essay has attempted to clarify some of the ramifications of a psychology of messianism and of the particular form it took at CIDOC, which is an extremely important center for interchange and introspection about contemporary social problems in Latin America.

---

[24]These separately published articles are printed in Illich's *Celebration of Awareness*.
[25]Ibid.
[26]*The Church, Change and Development*, ed. Fred Eychaner (Chicago: Urban Training Center Press for Herder and Herder, 1970).
[27]*Deschooling Society* (New York: Harper & Row, 1971; Harrow Books, 1972).

LITERATURE

While lacking the documentation of historical investigation and the manipulation of data that is characteristic of much research in the social sciences, poets, dramatists, and novelists make important contributions to the knowledge of history and society. As cases in point, authors of the following essays have examined religious themes and subjects treated by Mexican men of letters from the early days of the colonial era to the present.

14. The Virgin of Guadalupe in Mexican Culture

HARVEY L. JOHNSON

In the early years of the colonial era, an Indian woodcutter named Juan Diego reported to Bishop Zumárraga the apparition of the Virgin Mary in the form of an Indian maiden. Professor Johnson explains that this event has been the very center of Roman Catholic culture in Mexico, as may be illustrated by millions of Mexicans who have made pilgrimages from all parts of the country to venerate or to worship the Virgin's image housed in the Basílica of Guadalupe in the Federal District.*

If you have been to Mexico City, you probably visited the shrine of the Virgin of Guadalupe. If you did not go there, you most assuredly saw her image in churches, chapels, niches, stores, almanacs, books, Christmas cards, neon lights; viewed her likeness on liquor and medicine bottles, saddles, plastic shopping bags, melon seeds, silver bracelets, coins, paper weights; and heard her name cited in ballads sung in the streets or given to schools, small seminaries, religious orders, congregations, hotels, villages, rivers, lakes, mountains, islands, etc. She appears in all sorts of materials: canvas, glass, wood, plaster, stone, clay, beads, tissue paper, and cooked delicacies (cakes, cookies, candies). Countless lips murmur her name every day. A medallion of Guadalupe is every Mexican child's birthright. At least 50 percent of the females and numerous males of the Republic have Guadalupe as one of their names. A chapel dedicated to her is found at every bullring where Mexican toreros fight; moreover, they frequently have her image woven into their capes. Her likeness is tatooed on more male arms and bodies than any other figure in Mexico. A copy of her picture or a clay figurine, luminous with the sun's rays and painted with the colors of her original image, is cherished in almost every dwelling. The taxicab driver, lunging and veering with a dangerous lust for pedestrian and private car alike, speeds down

*Chapters from a forthcoming book of the same title.

streets honking and bluffing his way, while the bus operator whips his overloaded vehicle along, causing it to careen like a drunken roller skater, the passengers holding their breath as they gaze instinctively toward the Virgin's serene portrait attached above the windshield and illuminated in both taxi and bus by a tiny electric light. For she is the First Lady of Mexico, the Nation's Captain, the Republic's Most Holy Mother, the North Star of Mexico, The Dark Virgin, the Indians' special Protectress, the Queen of Mexico, and, finally, the Empress of America. Hence it is not surprising that historian, theologian, mystic, sociologist, anthropologist, psychologist, artist, poet, novelist, dramatist, author of movie scripts, and musician be interested in her. To tell the story of the Indian Virgin is to recount in a sense the cultural history of Mexico. For almost four and one-half centuries, her shrine has been the center of worship of Mexico. In short, she is the warp and woof of many Mexicans' daily existence. Nowhere else but in Mexico is worship of the Virgin so much a part of individual lives and national feelings.

Veneration of the Virgin of Guadalupe

The North American historian Hubert H. Bancroft pithily wrote of her: "In 1531 an event occurred which greatly contributed to the suppression of idolatry, which was the miraculous appearance of the Virgin of Guadalupe...."[1] From that time on, Our Lady of Guadalupe began to exercise the profound influence she has had on the destiny of Mexico. In her role of defender of the oppressed, she early inspired a strong feeling of Mexicanism. One of the more beautiful stories of Catholicism in flower, her worship most certainly offers something that has captured the emotions and spirit of the people. On December 12, masses and various festivities are held in her honor throughout the Republic. For many years the Lottery of Our Lady of Guadalupe served to finance her cult in her sanctuary. In the smallest communities, towns, and cities, the populace "goes all out," as it were, praying, shouting, feasting, drinking, quarreling, fighting, even killing in celebration of her special day. As explained by one of Mexico's best known essayists,

> During the days before and after the twelfth of December, time comes to a full stop, and instead of pushing us toward a deceptive tomorrow that is always beyond our reach, offers us a complete and perfect today of dancing and revelry, of communion with the most ancient and secret Mexico. Time is no longer succession, and becomes what it originally was and is: the present in which past and future are reconciled.[2]

---

[1]*History of Mexico: 1521-1600*, vol. 2 of 6 vols. in *The Works of Hubert Howe Bancroft*, 39 vols. (San Francisco: A. L. Bancroft and Co., 1882-1890), 10: 403.
[2]Octavio Paz, *The Labyrinth of Solitude: Life and Thought in Mexico*, trans. Lysander Kemp (New York: Grove Press, 1961), pp. 47-48.

The Catholic Church very wisely put her hermitage and later churches at Tepeyac, a barren hill approximately one hundred and thirty feet high, because it was the site of the Aztec shrine dedicated to Tonantzin, Mother of the Aztec Gods and Goddess of the Earth, whose fiesta was celebrated in September or October. This shrine had enjoyed a wide cult before its destruction ten years prior to her appearance.[3] By appearing to a native to whom she gave her message in Nahuatl, the apparitions of the Virgin of Guadalupe strengthened the contention that the Indians, even though people without faith, were not born to be slaves—as many Spaniards, particularly conquistadors, maintained in order to justify their exploitation. Arguments of the Indians' defenders rested on the premises that the natives were human beings and, therefore, equal before God and that the Spaniards, their brothers, were responsible for the Indians' welfare.[4] It became increasingly more difficult to deny the pleas for human liberty after the Virgin's appearance to Juan Diego, a symbol of the Indians.

Worship of the Dark Madonna resulted in reconciliation of two opposing worlds—in the fusion of two religions, two traditions, and two cultures. She offers an excellent example of accommodation of

---

[3]Destruction of shrines and idols after the conquest did not prevent the Indians from reverting to their idolatrous habits. Coincidences in detail existed between their religion and Catholicism; these similarities undoubtedly expedited their conversion to the new faith. The Aztecs had practiced rudimentary forms of baptism, confession, and communion before their subjugation by the Spaniards; and their rich polytheism readily lent itself to the worship of the saints, a custom learned from the missionaries. It came as something of a disappointment to the friars to discover that pagan practices did not cease in spite of catechetical instruction and baptism: "However, they encountered what proved the greatest difficulty and needed more time to root it out. This was the assembling of the Indians at night and their calling upon and feasting the demon with numerous and diverse ceremonies which they had formerly observed. Such was especially the case at the time when they planted and harvested corn and also at the end of the twenty days that made up their months. On the last of these twenty days a general feast was held in the entire land. These feasts were dedicated to one of the chief demons, to whom they did honor with several human sacrifices and with many other ceremonies." See Toribio Motolinía, *History of the Indians of New Spain*, trans. and annotated with a bio-bibliographical study of the author by Francis Borgia Steck (Washington, D.C.: Academy of American Franciscan History, 1951), p. 106. Vestiges of pagan cults still persist in Mexican Catholicism, especially among Indians in small towns and villages, and are manifested in the following ways: continuance of certain pagan feasts as Christian festivals; retention of their superstitions, talismans, and charms; offerings to the images of copal and wild animals; adoption of pagan shrines or deities under Christian names; worship of saints and madonnas, with the incorporation of native dances and music. See Charles S. Braden, *Religious Aspects of the Conquest of Mexico* (Durham, N.C.: Duke University Press, 1930; reprint ed., New York: AMS Press, 1966), pp. 280-308; Anita Brenner, *Idols Behind Altars* (New York: Payson and Clarke, 1929), pp. 141-48.

[4]Lewis Hanke, *The Spanish Struggle for Justice in the Conquest of America* (Philadelphia: University of Pennsylvania Press, 1949); and idem, *Aristotle and the American Indians: A Study in Race Prejudice in the Modern World* (London: Hollis and Carter, 1959).

Christian practices to deep-rooted Indian beliefs and customs. In a sense, the Catholic Virgin and the Aztec Goddess joined hands at Tepeyac to satisfy the spiritual needs of two conflicting societies from which the Mexican people were to emerge. The Dark Virgin's apparitions added a national element to the creed imported from Spain, thereby making it more readily acceptable as an instrument of catechism to the Aztecs, who had evolved a sophisticated, complex concept of god (each god had multiple forms and attributes) and cosmology before the Conquest. Her veneration contributed a fervor to the Mexican faith that was sorely lacking in the petrified, defensive Church of Europe, just as her worship in replacement of Tonantzin offered a respite to the ritual violence of the priest-driven drama which spilled sacrificial blood over the steps of the pyramids.

Mexico is a matriarchy in its religion because "it is the Virgin representing what Plato termed the female éros (the emotional, passionate, metaphysical principle in the nature of things) and not the Christ representing the male lógos (the rational, doctrinal principle, formalized explicitly for Orthodox Catholicism by St. Thomas Aquinas) who has for the most part caught the imagination and the devotion of the Mexicans."[5]

The Church did not dare to interfere with the spontaneous feeling of devotion generated in the Indians' spirit. The Brown-skinned Virgin is in La Villa in her own right; she is the object of a devotion divorced from her relation to her son. On journeying through the Republic, one becomes conscious of the absence of images of the Christ in the countryside and finds few of them in the churches. On the other hand, the image of the Virgin of Guadalupe appears everywhere, further confirmation of the unorthodoxy that has been observed about the sanctuary in La Villa. The lone Indian, standing before the Virgin's tiny shrine in a remote village or on a parched, barren hillock pitched up against a clear blue sky, with face lifted, eyes half closed, arms outstretched in the sign of the cross, offers irrefutable testimony of veneration of her. Obviously, Mexican Catholicism centers around the cult of Our Lady of Guadalupe. Worship of her entails a personal relationship generating love, devotion, and loyalty. In no sense is this relationship dependent on the Catholic Church. Thus, Octavio Paz has written:

> We know that the Conquest coincided with the apogee of the cult of two masculine divinities: Quetzalcoatl, the self-sacrificing god, and Huitzilopochtli, the young warrior-god. The defeat of these gods—which is what the Conquest meant to the Indian world, because it was the end of a cosmic cycle and the inauguration of a new divine kingdom—caused the faithful to return to the ancient feminine deities. This

---

[5]F. S. C. Northrop, *The Meeting of East and West: An Inquiry Concerning World Understanding* (New York: Macmillan, 1946), p. 28.

phenomenon of a return to the maternal womb, so well known to the psychologist, is without doubt one of the determining causes of the swift popularity of the cult of the Virgin. The Indian goddesses were goddesses of fecundity, linked to the cosmic rhythms, the vegetative processes and agrarian rites. The Catholic Virgin is also the Mother (some Indian pilgrims still call her Guadalupe-Tonantzin), but her principal attribute is not to watch over the fertility of the earth but to provide refuge for the unfortunate. The situation has changed: the worshipers do not try to make sure of their harvests but to find a mother's lap. The Virgin is the consolation of the poor, the shield of the weak, the help of the oppressed. In sum, she is the Mother of orphans. All men are born disinherited and their true condition is orphanhood, but this is particularly true among the Indians and the poor in Mexico.[6]

When Father Miguel Hidalgo y Costilla launched the war for Mexican Independence from Spain (1810) in his church in Dolores, Guanajuato, with the cry "Long live the Virgin of Guadalupe and down with the bad government"—words echoed annually every September 15 by the president of the Republic—he acted in keeping with the popular will. From the time he seized an oil painting of her image in the sanctuary in Atotonilco and made it his banner, she has been the emblem of independence. On being proclaimed generalísimo by the rebel leaders, he wore around his neck a large gold medal bearing her image. During the ten years of strife, the insurgents carried banners stamped with the portrait of the Virgin of Guadalupe, whom Hidalgo affectionately called captain general. As for the royalists, they had flags emblazoned with the likeness of the Virgin of Remedies, who was named captain general by the viceroy. She had been brought to Mexico by the conquistadors who, incidentally, called her The Conqueress. A banner captured by either side was shot as a traitor. Father José María Morelos y Pavón, successor to Hidalgo and a more fervent follower of the Mother of Tepeyac, commanded in a proclamation of March 11, 1813, that all towns should have on the twelfth of every month a special mass in her honor and display her picture on the doors and balconies of the houses. All males over ten years of age were to wear on their hats a cockade of blue and white, the national colors, and a badge with which they declared themselves soldiers and defenders of the Virgin's cult and their country; any who might fail to comply with the aforesaid orders, after being reprimanded three times, would be declared traitors. Picked troops formed Morelos's crack Guadalupe Regiment. The Guadalupes, a secret society, supported the independence movement in Mexico City. Even the royalists had an armed schooner, the *Guadalupe*, named for the Virgin.

Agustín Iturbide, who established a monarchy with himself as emperor in 1821, named one of his sons Felipe Andrés María de Guadalupe. Iturbide's inauguration of the Imperial Order of

---

[6]Paz, *The Labyrinth of Solitude*, pp. 84-85.

Guadalupe in La Villa on August 13, 1822, with its knights in mantles and plumage, was likened by Fray Servando Teresa de Mier to the barbarous dance of "The Little Old Men," performed at festivals by preposterously dressed Indians. The ceremony was carried out in front of the Virgin's image with much pomp. The knights took the oath of allegiance at the conclusion of the pontifical mass. Establishment of the Order contributed to the eventual collapse of the empire. Upon Iturbide's abdication, he laid his general's baton at her feet. The Order was reinstituted during Antonio López de Santa Anna's presidency and Maximilian's ill-fated reign. The first act of the Congress (1822) of the newly founded Republic was to proclaim December 12 a national holiday. In 1824, this legislative body agreed to place her image as Queen and Patroness in the Chamber of Deputies.

Manuel Félix Fernández, the first president of Mexico (1824-1829), changed his name to Guadalupe Victoria in honor of the Virgin and the victories he had won under her protection. In 1828, General Vicente Guerrero deposited on her altar the banners taken from the Spanish invader, Isidro Barradas. Devotion to the Dark Virgin became so fervent that it was customary during the nineteenth century for presidents and victorious generals to go to her sanctuary to give thanks and invoke her guidance. After signing the peace treaty between Mexico and the United States on February 2, 1847, in La Villa de Guadalupe, the signatories entered the sanctuary to give thanks for the successful conclusion of their work. Benito Juárez declared December 12 a national holiday in 1859, an uninterrupted custom since then. In 1862 was fought the celebrated battle of the 5 de Mayo on the Hill of Guadalupe near to Puebla. Maximilian and Carlota attended a most solemn *Te Deum* in the Basilica on June 11, 1864, the day before making their formal entrance into Mexico City. By visiting the sanctuary before beginning to govern, they were emulating the practice followed by the viceroys from the end of the sixteenth century. In 1867, General Porfirio Díaz stored his guns and other materiel of war in the Sanctuary of Guadalupe. During the first half of the nineteenth century, the Virgin of Tepeyac even penetrated the Masonic Order, particularly the York rite. Many days of indulgences were granted for displaying her effigy in windows and balconies and for special prayers, genuflections, and masses in her honor.

One of the causes of disagreement between the *Carrancistas* and *Zapatistas* in the late stages of the Revolution was the attempt of the former to wrest from the latter the image of the Virgin of Guadalupe, which was carried into battle beside the national flag. Zapata's soldiers also wore her likeness on their straw hats. During the cataclysmic years of the Revolution (1910-1917) when peasants rose up against the landed oligarchy and the proletariat rebelled against industrial capitalism and Big Power imperialism, the survival of Mexico as a nation was due in great part to her unifying force. Venustiano Carranza's constitutionalist document disavowing General Victoriano Huerta's regime was signed March 26, 1913, at the hacienda of Guadalupe in Coahuila and was called the Plan of Guadalupe because of the site of its approval by the signatories. Over a decade later, President Plutarco Elías Calles carried out an antireligious campaign that produced the Cristero Rebellion (1926-1929). During these troubled years, churches, convents, and monasteries were closed; religious services were suspended; the number of priests was limited; foreign ecclesiastics were deported; and the government increased its control over the peasants and began dividing vast landholdings. Under these conditions, some believers have credited the Virgin's influence with saving the nation from splitting asunder.[7]

La Villa de Guadalupe is situated about four miles north of the Zócalo, Mexico City's main square. Because of national fervor produced by the War of Independence, the name was changed to La Villa de Hidalgo. A century later, at the end of the Revolution of 1910, its name became La Villa de Madero, but the people continue to speak of it as la Villa de Guadalupe or simply as La Villa. Quite naturally, the first railroad line built in Mexico would lead to it. The town has grown up around the collection of buildings that constitute the sanctuary; these temples exemplify Mexican colonial art, a particular form of baroque that justifiably might be labeled "Guadalupan."

Hundreds and hundreds of books, articles, and sermons by Mexican scholars, theologians, and popular writers have related the story of Guadalupe's appearances to Juan Diego and his uncle. Apparently, the first reference to the Virgin of Guadalupe in English comes from Miles Philips, a member of Sir John Hawkins' slave-hunting expedition to Africa. As a captive of the Spaniards, he visited Tepeyac in 1568—thirty-seven years after the apparitions. In his report, Philips

---

[7]Brantz Mayer, *Mexico: Aztec, Spanish and Republican: A Historical, Geographical, Political, Statistical and Social Account of that Country from the Period of the Invasion by the Spaniards to the Present Time; with a View of the Ancient Aztec Empire and Civilization; A Historical Sketch of the Late War; and Notices of New Mexico and California* (Hartford, Conn.: S. Drake and Co., 1851), pp. 63-69; Mariano Cuevas, *Album histórico guadalupano del IV centenario* (México, D.F.: Escuela Tipográfica Salesiana, 1930), pp. 227-70; John Anthony Caruso, *The Liberators of Mexico* (Gloucester, Mass.: Peter Smith, 1967); José María Roa Bárcena, *Recuerdos de la invasión norteamericana (1846-1848)*, 3 vols. (México, D.F.: Editorial Porrúa, 1947), 3: 301; Lucas Alamán, *Historia de Méjico*, 5 vols. (México, D.F.: Editorial Jus, 1942), 1:350, 448-49; 2:202, 226, 510-14; 5:422-23, 593-600, 630-31, 809; Antonio García Cubas, *El libro de mis recuerdos* (México, D.F.: Editorial Patria, 1945), pp. 453-54; William Weber Johnson, *Heroic Mexico: The Violent Emergence of a Modern Nation* (Garden City, N.Y.: Doubleday and Co., 1968), pp. 150-51; 385-402; Frances Parkinson Keyes, *The Grace of Guadalupe* (New York: Julian Messner, 1941), pp. 116-20; José Vasconcelos, *Bolivarismo y monroísmo: Temas iberoamericanos*, Biblioteca América, No. 5 (Santiago de Chile: Ediciones Ercilla, 1934), p. 128.

says the shrine had no Spanish houses around it, mistakes a silver and gilt statue (probably one donated to the hermitage in 1566) for the sacred image, and comments on the people's marked devotion, the healing water of the well, and the miracles performed there. His recollections of imprisonments, misfortunes, and escapes conjure up many scenes of colonial Mexican life:

> The next morning we departed from thence on our journey towards Mexico, and so travelled till wee came within two leagues of it, where there was built by the Spaniards a very faire church, called our Ladyes church, in which there is an image of our Lady of silver & gilt, being as high, & as large as a tall woman, in which church, and before this image, there are as many lamps of silver as there be dayes in the yeare, which upon high dayes are all lighted. Whensoever any Spaniards passe by this church, although they be on horse backe, they will alight, and come into the church, and kneele before the image, and pray to our Lady to defend them from all evil; so that whether he be horseman or footman he will not passe by, but first goe into the church, and pray as aforesayd, which if they doe not, they thinke and beleeve that they shall never prosper: which image they call in the Spanish tongue, Nuestra sennora de Guadalupe. At this place there are certain cold baths, which arise, springing up as though the water did seeth: the water whereof is somewhat brackish in taste, but very good for any that have any sore or wound, to wash themselves therewith, for as they say, it healeth many: and every yeere once upon our Lady day the people use to repair thither to offer, and to pray in that church before the image, and they say that our Lady of Guadalupe doeth worke a number of miracles. About this church there is not any towne of Spaniards that is inhabited, but certaine Indians doe dwell there in houses of their own countrey building.[8]

Among North Americans who have written about Our Lady of Guadalupe are Willa Cather, Frances Parkinson Keyes, Helen Behrens, Edith Hoyt, Donald Demarest, Coley Taylor, and John Steinbeck. Her influence has made itself felt also in Mexican-American writings. For example, the setting of *Bless Me, Ultima*, Rudolfo A. Anaya's novel that won the Second Annual Quinto Sol literary award in 1971, reflects Chicano culture in a New Mexican town named Guadalupe for its Patroness. The mother in the story has a statue of the Virgin and directs her supplications to the Dark Virgin, also loved by the youngest son who is wont to pray before her altar.

---

[8]Miles Philips, "A Discourse Written by ... One of the Company Put on Shoare Northward of Panuco, in the West Indies by Mr. John Hawkins 1568, conteining Many Special Things of That Countrey ... An. 1582," in Richard Hakluyt, *The Principal Navigations, Voyages, Traffiques & Discoveries of the English Nation*, 12 vols. (Glasgow: James McLehose and Sons, Publishers to the University; New York: Macmillan, 1904), 9:419-20.

The Virgin in Song and Poetry

In song and poetry, the Queen of Mexico belongs uniquely to the people, to popular verse and folk music—in no sense pretentious but permeated with sensitive tenderness. Patently, she has stirred a few poets with a fervor that transcends the temporary and enters into the timeless world. Since her apparitions to Juan Diego, she has been acclaimed in ballads, jingles, and songs. Guadalupan poetry was born in the sixteenth century and continues to the present. Recitation of the poem was often accompanied by dancers, splendidly outfitted in feathers and plumes, who advanced in a circular movement, swaying the body to music played in a slow measure on primitive drums by a couple of old men. These traditional story-dances are still performed in the open air as part of the ceremonial festivals in December. The earliest Nahuatl songs or poems about the Virgin are rich in metaphors, inspired in flowers and their aroma, and in precious stones or brilliant objects employed in a figurative sense. Meaningless interjections aid to create a metrical effect. One of the ancient Aztec songs, attributed by some critics to Bishop Zumárraga and therefore contemporary with the Virgin's appearances, welcomes her as God's perfect creation and acknowledges that her spirit lives in the sacred portrait exposed to view at the bishopric. At the same time, the song expresses hope that the poet's flowers, i.e., his verses, will be acceptable to her along with the other plants that bloom in her honor. Through symbolism peculiar to Aztec literary language, this song conveys what the Dark Madonna's image already means to the Indians. The accompaniment to this chant was on the *teponaztli*, a hollowed-out log drum with three grooves cut in it, which the player struck with sticks that had rubber balls attached at the ends. Father Mariano Cuevas titles this song "El pregón de ataval" ("The Proclamation of the Drum"), which is included among the *Cantares mexicanos (Mexican Songs)*, a collection that goes back to the end of the sixteenth century. He opines that it announced the appearance of the image and served to call the faithful to take part in the procession on December 26, 1531. Other scholars believe that it is an adaptation of an old song originally composed to honor the corn-goddess. These few verses convey some idea of the beauty of its poetic imagery:

> I am the plant of the loveliest buds,
> The creation of the one, the perfect God,
> I am the most perfect of his creations.
> Thy soul comes to life in the painting.
> We sing to your venerated picture
> As we follow behind it.[9]

[9]Daniel G. Brinton, *Ancient Nahuatl Poetry* (Philadelphia: D. G. Brinton, 1887), pp. 109, 144; Cuevas, *Album histórico guadalupano*, pp. 21-30; Donald Demarest and Coley Taylor, eds., *The Dark Virgin: The Book of Our Lady of Guadalupe, A Documentary Anthology* (Freeport, Me.: Coley Taylor, 1956), pp. 201-202.

The *corridos* (ballads), sung to the accompaniment of a guitar or harp and printed with crude woodcuts, were distributed as broadsheets handed out by medicine men, street singers, and beggars, or were published in small-town newspapers. Born during the war for independence from Spain, they were the outpourings in verse and music of a mestizo population, of which the large majority longed to establish its own identity and nationality. Out of poverty, out of suffering came these outpourings. Written for the populace, these narrative songs carried messages of sadness and cheer, of historical events, of political movements, of legendary bandits and heroes or reportorial news of crimes, disasters, praise of towns and the nation. They enjoyed their widest popularity from 1880 to 1930—particularly during the years of the Revolution. More recently, they can be heard on phonograph records or radio programs. Most of the *corridos* are anonymous short compositions. A variety of strophic and metric forms occurs in a goodly number, but the most typical have stanzas of four octosyllabic verses. They emphasize equally the trivial and the sublime in singing about the Virgin of Guadalupe. Simple trust, absolute faith, and staunch devotion characterize the sentiments felt for Our Lady, who came from heaven to watch over the Mexicans. Some ballads take the form of morning songs to greet her and request her blessing; others, like hymns, beg her never to abandon Mexico or the Indians. Airs of the soil, colloquial phrases, and everyday speech fuse in them. The flavor of the *corridos* varies from region to region.[10]

Mexican singers, who cross the border with ballads about the Mother of Tepeyac in their repertoires, invoke her care at the fiestas celebrated in Los Angeles, Chicago, and Detroit. A Mexican priest recalls that in the Convent of the Holy Sepulchre in Jerusalem he heard an old Turkish servant singing in Spanish a ballad about the Dark Virgin, probably taught to him by a friar from San Fernando in Mexico, who resided in the past in Israel:

> Brunettes have pleased me
> Since I have known
> That a brunette
> Is Mexico's own.
> Come hasten, and so
> Let us all go

---

[10]Brenner, *Idols Behind Altars*, pp. 175-84; *Visita y oraciones a María Santísima y colección de cantos religiosos populares* (San Juan de los Lagos, Jal.: Imprenta Carlos Gallardo, n.d.), pp. 28-32; Vicente F. Mendoza, *El corrido mexicano: Antología, introducción y notas*, Letras Mexicanas, No. 15 (México, D.F..: Fondo de Cultura Económica, 1954), pp. vii-xliv; Merle E. Simmons, *The Mexican "Corrido" as a Source for Interpretive Study of Modern Mexico (1870-1950)* (Bloomington: Indiana University Press, 1957), pp. 380-415, 568-70; Mario Colín, *El corrido popular en el estado de México* (México, D.F.: Biblioteca Enciclopédica del Estado de México, 1972), pp. 463-90.

> To the newly built convent
> At San Fernando.[11]

Whether singing in the streets, parks, *pulquerías* (bars that vend a fermented drink made from the juice of the maguey or cactus plant) or country fairs at home or abroad, the balladeer was accustomed to doff his hat in respect upon pronouncing the Virgin of Tepeyac's name.

A typical *corrido* about the Virgin of Guadalupe is the one illustrated by José Guadalupe Posada, artist-caricaturist-engraver. Many of the ballads—most of them anonymous—merely repeat the story of Our Lady of Tepeyac's apparitions and the miracle of her image. An example of such simple songs is the following:

> Oh, chosen Juan Diego
> She appeared to your eyes
> When you crossed the hill
> Of the queen of the skies.
>
> On your fine ayate,
> She of the Indies
> Left us her image
> The Guadalupe Virgin.[12]

Another ballad, composed in 1931, "IV centenario guadalupano" ("Guadalupe's Fourth Centenary"), relates the story of her appearances; veneration accorded to her by the Viceroy Núñez de Haro, Emperor Iturbide, Fathers Hidalgo and Morelos, and General Villa; and homage rendered to her by dignitaries who came from all parts of the world for the celebration.[13] Daniel Castañeda's "Gran corrido a la Virgen de Guadalupe" ("Grand *Corrido* to the Virgin of Guadalupe"), truly popular in speech and feeling, alludes to the brown-skinned Lupes, small and charming; says that all citizens spit on their hands to put on festivals worthy of their Patroness; refers to her motherly affection for Juan Diego and how he happily carried the proofs to the bishop, announcing that the Mexicans now have their mother and North Star. "De las apariciones de la Virgen de Guadalupe" ("About the Virgin of Guadalupe's Apparitions"), by Silvino C. N. Martínez, was handed out as a broadsheet with a poor woodcut of the Dark Madonna's picture in the Plaza de Coyoacán, a suburb of Mexico City, in April, 1954. The two following strophes furnish some idea of its narrative style and colloquial speech:

> The Bishop answered promptly;
> "You have to show me a sign
> That it was the Virgin sent you

---

[11] Keyes, *The Grace of Guadalupe*, pp. 104, 179.
[12] Brenner, *Idols Behind Altars*, p. 153.
[13] Mendoza, *El corrido mexicano*, pp. 388-92.

> And that you haven't been drinking wine."
> ....
> And to this day we hymn her
> Guardian of our soil;
> In every Mexican breast she reigns,
> Queen of all our toil.[14]

Balladeers have also exalted The Virgin in her role as defender and protectress of the nation in its war for independence from Spain, resistance to Emperor Maximilian, uprising against Porfirio Díaz, fear of an attack by the Axis, and resentment against the United States for its intervention: "Don't let the foreigner come in and ruin our lives." Too, the singer appeals to her as an intercessor with God because of fear of an erupting volcano, a flood, or other natural phenomena. One soldier prays to her that no harm come to him in battle; another begs her to spare his life long enough to see his little son before dying; a third commends his mother to Guadalupe. A worker departing for the United States advises his wife to pray to her to bring about their reunion. A smoker asks her for marihuana. Bandits and miners appeal to her in song for protection. Laments that combine religious and revolutionary feelings over the slaying of a leader are directed to her. Still another *corrido* speaks of the indignation aroused in the country over the attempt to destroy her image with a dynamite bomb. Commending President Portes Gil for assuming a more reconciliatory stance toward the Church, one balladeer prays that Our Lady take him under her protection. In general, however, there is total silence with regard to the Church and clergy, an indication of the lack of confidence in or fervor for the institution and its priests. Several ballads proclaim with joy the triumphs of revolutionary leaders.[15] Felipe Carrillo Puerto, governor of Yucatán and a mestizo, mostly of Maya blood, infuriated a reactionary group by reforming state laws, building roads and school houses, and effecting changes beneficial to the Indians, children, and oppressed. In these typical strophes, the balladeer laments the death of the martyred governor:

> Mother mine, Guadalupana,
> You who wept for poor Juan Diego
> When you saw him with bare feet,
> Half naked, hungry and weak.
>
> Where were all your angels gone,
> Where are they now, that below
> They did not see treason done?
> And Carrillo Puerto is dead.

---

[14]Demarest and Taylor, *The Dark Virgin*, pp. 208-12.
[15]Brenner, *Idols Behind Altars*, pp. 176-226.

Felipe believed the traitor;
Felipe was caught in a trap;
He had gone only two paces
When he was shot in the back.

Shot in the back by a coward
Stabbed in the neck with a knife,
Staining with his blood the paving,
Felipe gave up his life.

Mother mine of Guadalupe,
The blood of that execution;
Colors for us to remember,
Red and black of the revolution.[16]

Conclusion

In the four and one-half centuried evolution of the Dark Virgin's influence on Mexico, one sees not merely collision but clashing conflict; not merely a succession of happenings but colossal events; not merely humanity but divinity; not merely devotion but a great passion that surges through a nation's heart. In spite of details, often unseemly, often ridiculous, often absurd, one finds in the mass of structure the dignity, the grandeur of divine design. One hears cadences that form a music fitting for a celestial choir. This mighty drama, not brooded by one poetic brain but rather a production of composite authorship, comes to life every time one sees the pageantry; the breathing, moving figures; the reverence and adoration reflected in the enrapt faces in the Basilica—attachment to the Dark Virgin for her maternal mercy. In sum, she is a novel, vibrant, spiritual force born into a New World, the incarnation of the beauty of meekness, the grace of forgiveness, the redemptive power of love. She embodies the Christian history of Mexico, assisting in the conversion of the autochthonous race during the colonial era and making a forceful impact on almost every facet of the Republic's existence. The Mexicans' consistent devotion to Guadalupism is truly a great national power. She is the molder of Mexican culture, having contributed to all of the arts, the intimacies of feelings and a popular spirit not perceptible in other countries. She has given to creative artists a prodigious impulse. Against the lurid background of Mexican national history, veneration of the Virgin appears constantly with qualities unique in ritual, religious practice, and belief.

The spirit of Our Lady of Heaven dwells in the blue of the Mexican sky, in the peaks of the Mexican mountains, in the depths of the Mexican soul, in the hearts of the Mexican people, in all aspects of

---

[16]Simmons, The Mexican "Corrido," pp. 393-94; Brenner, Idols Behind Altars, pp. 222-24.

Mexican life. She hovers over Mexico like the gentle breeze that passes over the green fields. She is a dreamy fantasy over the concrete world. She is invisible like the night, impalpable like the wind. She pervades and permeates everything. She is everywhere in Mexico. She fuses harmoniously the seen and the unseen, the religious and secular, Aztec myth and Catholic belief, past and present. Everything spiritual revolves around her. She reconciles two vastly different races. She transmits a vision far removed from this technologically oriented world. She is the light that illuminates. She offers fundamental proof of Mexican unity. Millions pray to her and invoke her aid in time of despair. What matters this revolving planet with its petty cares if an understanding mother whose benevolence is as unfading as the light of moon and stars waits ready to comfort, nourish, and strengthen them in their faith! Upon her, Mexicans rest their hopes. She heals their hurts. She has no rival in Mexico. She is a definite, permanent, vital, active, creative force in the life of our neighboring Republic. Finally, Guadalupe's Mexico is the real nation. Countless are the nuggets of pure gold in the Guadalupan story. One cannot help but wax poetic in finishing this work about Mexico's Dark Virgin, for she, as Carlos Pellicer so beautifully puts it, is the Universe:

> Ella es el Universo: las estrellas
> anidan en su manto y todas cantan.[17]

> (She is the Universe: the stars
> nest in her mantle and all sing.)

Two strophes of one of the songs that Aztec pilgrims sing to the accompaniment of their primitive instruments on arriving at the Basilica provide a fitting conclusion to this study:

Tonantzin Icuic	Song to Our Mother
Amo yuhquin quichihuili	No other nation on earth
ac cequin nepapan tlaca	Has been so blessed by God
Ipampa tech tlazotili	For that the Indians of Mexico
Huan iyoloztin yech maca.	Carry thee in their hearts.
Coatlalupej, Coatlalupej,	Guadalupe, Guadalupe,
Motzopelica tocatzin	The name that brings us joy,
Totenco cemicac mani	May it be ever on our lips
Ica mama huizticatzin.	With great devotion.[18]

---

[17]Carlos Pellicer, "Ansia de las rosas," *Material poético (1918-1961)* (México, D.F.: Universidad Nacional Autónoma de México, 1962), p. 573.
[18]Helen Behrens, *The Virgin and the Serpent God* (México, D.F.: Editorial Progreso, 1963), p. 206.

15. Calderón de la Barca in Nahuatl

NORRIS MacKINNON

Transplanting Catholicism to the New World was an important objective of the Spanish conquest, and religious drama was one of the devices used to indoctrinate the Indians. This essay discusses the adaption of Calderón de la Barca's *El gran teatro del mundo*, one of his many *autos sacramentales*, to Nahuatl by Padre Bartolomé de Alva Ixtlilxóchitl, a seventeenth-century descendant of the kings of Texcoco.

For some three hundred years Spain ruled Mexico as her colony of *Nueva España*. During that extended period, the Spaniards employed widely varying methods, including drama, to transplant their culture to the New World. The purpose of this study is to extend the analysis and the publicity that has already been given to a specific case in which a famous Spanish work took root in the Mexican environment.

Religion was one of the primary elements of European culture brought to Mexico. In the very act of conquest, the Spaniards provided friars to convert the Indians. It is well documented that these evangelists went far beyond teaching the catechism; they studied the native languages and wrote works for the edification of their charges. As part of these activities, it is no surprise that we find a traditional Spanish didactic dramatic form, the *auto*. This term is variously applied to short religious plays and represents the continued development of a religious theater dating back into the Middle Ages. Some *autos* were merely simple dramatizations of Biblical stories in Spanish or an indigenous language. Such dramatizations were probably a common form of religious instruction in Mexico. The *auto sacramental*, however, focused on the Eucharist. *Autos* of this type appearing in Spain toward the middle of the seventeenth century were complex allegorical works, couched in the elaborate forms of baroque poetic expression and staged with all the amazing richness and technology that engineers of the period could muster. Pedro Calderón de la Barca, one of the several great dramatists of Spain's Golden Age, was, and is, recognized as the master of the *auto sacramental*. He and other poets were commissioned annually to compose *autos* for major urban centers of Spain where performance of such works was a traditional part of the celebration of the feast of Corpus Christi. In his long and active life, Calderón wrote some seventy of these one-act plays.

El gran teatro del mundo, one of Calderón's earlier *autos*, is probably best known to modern readers. The *auto sacramental* is at best an esoteric genre when removed from its natural habitat, but *El gran teatro del mundo* comes closer to bridging gaps of culture and time than most works of its type. The universality of its theme, the beauty of its poetry, and the simplicity and precision of its construction have combined to establish this drama as a major work and to commend it to the attention of scholars and public.

El gran teatro del mundo was first staged in 1649 but was not published until 1655. Some scholars have speculated that this *auto* was written only a few years prior to its first performance. Angel Valbuena Prat, however, after repeated examination of internal and other evidence, has concluded that the play is much older, dating perhaps as far back as 1633.[1]

Our knowledge of a Nahuatl adaptation of *El gran teatro del mundo* is due primarily to the work of William A. Hunter, who has published an edition and study of the *auto*.[2] Hunter's work contains an extensive discussion of the manuscript, its author, the state of the theater in New Spain, the genre of the *auto sacramental*, the Nahuatl language, and the comparative similarity of Spanish and Mexican versions. The edition of the Nahuatl text is combined with an interlinear translation into modern Spanish; further, the full text of the 1655 Spanish *editio princeps* is included as an appendix.

The version of the *auto* in the Aztec language exists only in a single manuscript copy in the Bancroft Library of the University of California, Berkeley. It is bound with manuscripts of two other Spanish plays adapted to Nahuatl, all the work of a Mexican priest descended from the kings of Texcoco: Bartolomé de Alva Ixtlilxóchitl, who is known to have published at least two other religious works in Nahuatl. The manuscripts of the plays probably passed through private collections after Mexican ecclesiastical libraries were dispersed during the Reforma period, and thence into the California library, where they lay unnoticed for many years. A year, 1641, is found on only one of these manuscripts, but examination of the paper and handwriting indicates that all are from about that time. This poses the mystery of Bartolomé de Alva's access to the original

---

[1] Pedro Calderón de la Barca, *Autos sacramentales*, vol. 3 of *Obras completas*, ed. Angel Valbuena Prat, 3 vols. (Madrid: Aguilar, 1959), pp. 201-202.
[2] William A. Hunter, "The Calderonian Auto Sacremental, *El Gran Teatro Del Mundo*: An Edition and Translation of a Nahuatl Version," in *The Native Theatre in Middle America*, ed. Margaret A. L. Harrison and Robert Wauchope, Middle American Research Institute, no. 27 (New Orleans: Tulane University, 1961), pp. 105-201. Subsequent references to this source are by page number only.

Spanish work. The Mexican priest apparently translated Calderón's *auto* not only before it was printed in Spain, but even before it was publicly performed. Alva served as parish priest in the village of Tzumpahuacán from about 1641 until his death nearly thirty years later. How the *auto* reached him there we can only guess, but it is clear that literary works spread through the Spanish domain considerably faster than is suggested by official records. This probable date of Alva's adaptation supports the idea that *El gran teatro del mundo* was written much earlier than it was performed. Alva's version carries no title in Nahuatl, nor is there a reference to Calderón. Although there is no record that the adapted *auto* was ever performed, its value and that of companion pieces lies not only in their own merit, but also in the fact that they are important documents of Nahuatl literature. Hunter states that "the absence of evidence to the contrary seems to justify the view that the Nahuatl manuscripts in the Bancroft Library are unique. For there are no other examples of Nahuatl versions of familiar European literary works known to be extant. There is no proof, in fact, that any others were ever produced" (p. 121).

To compare the Mexican adaptation of *El gran teatro del mundo* to its Spanish source, let us begin by summarizing the latter. Calderón's *auto* is usually called a "play-within-a-play," though "play-about-a-play" might be a more accurate description. Its single act is divided into five distinct moments, or scenes, in which God, assisted by the World, plans the drama of human life, distributes the roles, observes the performance, recalls the actors, and finally evaluates and rewards them. God is represented by the allegorical figure called *el Autor*, a theatrical term which in the Golden Age referred to the overall authority and prime mover of a play, somewhat like our modern producer. Wishing to celebrate his power, *el Autor* calls the personification of *el Mundo* out of the created world and commands him to begin preparations for a play of human life in *el teatro del mundo*. El Mundo, acting as a sort of stage manager, then delivers a long speech in which he outlines the production. The drama of human life is to be composed of three *jornadas*, or acts, as was typical of Spanish plays of the period. The first of these is to be governed by *la ley natural* and will portray human history from the Garden of Eden to the time of the Flood. The second act, *la ley escrita*, will take mankind from the time of Moses through the remainder of the Old Testament period. The final act, under the heading of *la ley de gracia*, will cover the Christian Era. El Mundo will provide all the properties required so that no man will lack what he needs to play his assigned role. The stage will have two doors: an entrance bearing a cradle as a label, and an exit bearing a sepulcher.

In the second scene the actors, still undifferentiated, are called out. *El Autor* explains that each will be given a role to play in the drama, and that each will think he is living a life. Then the actors receive their parts, which are allegorical human types. *El Rey, el Rico, la Hermosura,* and *la Discreción* accept happily. *El Pobre* bitterly laments his lot, and *el Labrador* grumbles sarcastically. One other character, *el Niño*, is to die before birth. Note that *Discreción* in this play represents what we might call spiritual insight. When asked what the title of the play will be, *el Autor* replies that it is to be called "Obrar bien, que Dios es Dios." He announces that there will be no rehearsal but that all, high and low alike, will have the prompting of his Law. Also, each should be prepared to exit at any time, even unexpectedly. *El Mundo* then gives each actor the clothing and equipment needed for his role.

The third scene is the performance itself. The prompter enters and is specifically identified as *la Ley de Gracia*. *El Mundo* takes a seat, commenting that he will be *el vulgo*, the critical audience. In their various encounters on stage, the characters show their foibles; and each in turn, when troubled by uncertainty, hears the same words from the prompter: "Obrar bien, que Dios es Dios." One by one their roles are ended by the voice of death. In the fourth scene, *el Mundo* demands of the characters the properties given them before their play began. He explains that the items were only lent and could not be removed from his theater. Possession, like life, is only an illusion. Divested of their earthly roles, the characters are now equal, uncomfortably so in some cases. In the final scene *el Autor* appears at a table set with the Eucharistic chalice and Host, which are to serve as eternal sustenance and glory for those who acted their roles well in the theater of the world. *El Pobre* and *la Discreción* are invited to the table immediately; but *el Rey, la Hermosura,* and *el Labrador* must wait until they are cleansed in Purgatory. *El Rey*, however, is soon in glory after *la Discreción* pleads his case because he had supported religion. *El Rico* is cast directly into eternal torment because of his total selfishness.

In comparing the texts of the Spanish and Nahuatl *autos*, Hunter notes that the most obvious difference is that Alva shortened the work considerably. Also, he wrote in prose, substituting simpler, more Mexican imagery for the long and elaborate classical and Biblical allusions of the Calderonian work. The most striking variation in the plot is the complete omission of the role of the *Labrador*, which is one of the longest and most developed parts in the original. Alva deleted this character quite skillfully, however, so that few weak spots are discernible in the resulting abbreviated dialogue. Calderón's prompter, *la Ley de Gracia*, is changed in Nahuatl to what Hunter translates as *el Orden*. He finds other variations to be of only minor importance.

While it is true that Alva followed the Calderonian plot quite closely, careful examination shows that some of his changes significantly alter the import of the whole *auto*. For example, the changing of *la Ley de Gracia* to *el Orden* brings with it the harshness of legalism, an element not found in the original. Indeed, Hunter seems to emphasize this aspect of Alva's allegorical figure when he states in a note that the meaning of the Nahuatl word is close to our modern term "law-and-order" (p. 153). Although the Spanish expression "obrar bien, que Dios es Dios" places importance on good behavior, the fact that it is heard from the mouth of *la Ley de Gracia* gives it a gentler tone. The Law of Grace, after all, is the rule of love as expressed in the life and death of Christ. The admonition in Nahuatl, of significantly different wording, is translated as "Haz bien, que te mira Dios." This is almost threatening in tone and sounds much like "Big Brother is watching you." In his handling of this character, Alva also loses some of the structural precision typical of Calderón's work. In the latter it is *la Ley de Gracia*, and only she, who prompts the actors always by chanting the same words, "Obrar bien, que Dios es Dios." Alva varies the wording somewhat—"Haz bien," "Bien debéis vivir," "Vive bien," etc.—and does not limit these lines to his character *el Orden*. In fact, the third time an actor is so advised, *el Mundo* remarks, "A cada uno le avisa" (p. 165). This is a direct translation of Calderón's line, but in Alva's *auto* it refers to the first time *el Orden* himself has delivered the warning.

Perhaps the most important factor which distinguishes Alva's adaptation from its Spanish source is the absence of the theatrical context. The Nahuatl *auto* is not a play-within-a-play at all, but simply an allegorical play about human existence. Judging by Hunter's Spanish translation, there is an almost complete lack of the theatrical terms so common in the original. The word *teatro* does not appear at all, nor does *comedia*, though *drama* is supplied once in parentheses (p. 155). Only the terms *representar*, "to act or perform," and *papel*, "role," are used. *Representar*, of course, is a word commonly used with no dramatic connotations. It seems doubtful that the occasional use of the word *papel* reflects a Nahuatl word that implies a dramatic role. In this context Hunter uses a variety of words such as *tarea* and *parte*, and on one occasion, after *obligación*, he puts *papel* in brackets (p. 159). The figure called *el Autor* by Calderón has a Nahuatl title rendered simply Señor by Hunter. This expresses accurately enough the character of *el Autor* but fails to suggest the theatrical function of the original role. Throughout Calderón's *El gran teatro del mundo*, the characters frequently express themselves in a way that repeatedly underlines the fact that they are dealing with a theatrical work. The long speech by *el Mundo* early in the *auto* makes it clear that he envisions the staging of a standard three-act drama in his theater. The corresponding speech in Nahuatl is a much shorter and quite beautiful description of the Creation. In the Spanish play, *la Ley de Gracia* is specifically and frequently referred to as a prompter. In the Nahuatl drama, *el Orden* is said only to advise. Finally, as each character dies, Calderón has them speak merely of ending their roles, though they do exit through the sepulcher door. Alva is not so subtle. His king, the first to go, says, "Voy a morir"; and *el Mundo* observes, "Pereció, pero a la vez se dió cuenta de sus pecados" (p. 168). Calderón's characters are never said to sin, but rather to play their roles badly.

We can speculate that the reason for Alva's having abandoned the theatrical context in his adapted plot was that his audience was probably unfamiliar with terms relating to the highly popular commercial theater of Spain. As a result of this change, the Nahuatl *auto* lacks the important concept of the illusory nature of human life. Perhaps this is why Alva did not head his version with a translation of Calderón's title, *El gran teatro del mundo*.

Belief in the unreality of so-called "real life" is central to the whole meaning of the original *auto* and is the very basis of the theater metaphor which structures it. Calderón, to insure that his audience will understand, states the idea directly in the dialogue. For example, as *el Autor* is about to distribute the roles, he comments:

> Todos quisieran hacer
> el de mandar y regir,
> sin mirar, sin advertir
> que en acto tan singular
> aquello es representar,
> aunque piense que es vivir.[3]

Likewise, *el Mundo*, after recovering his properties from the characters following their performance, tells them: "Al teatro pasad de las verdades,/que este el teatro es de las ficciones."[4] Calderón's interest in the theme of the illusion of life finds its most famous expression in his play, *La vida es sueño* (1635), close to the probable time of composition of *El gran teatro del mundo*. Many ideas found in the two plays are similar and in some cases are expressed in nearly the same words. Curiously, the only direct reference in the Nahuatl *auto* to life as an illusion is a suggestion that life is a dream, a specific metaphor not found in the original work. In spite of this one remark, Alva in general portrays human life as simply the business of Man, as decreed by God, his creator.

The Nahuatl *auto* also differs greatly in tone from its Spanish source. Calderón gave this work the gravity and ornate poetry for which he is famous. Alva's version seems to be much more of a folk play, even when read in Hunter's Spanish translation. This, of course,

---
[3] Calderón, *Autos sacramentales*, p. 207.
[4] Ibid., p. 220.

would be in keeping with the historical origins of the Spanish *auto* genre. It is clear that the Mexican priest was intent on relating his work to the experience of his parishioners. Early in his *auto*, in a speech corresponding to an elaborate statement by Calderón's *Autor*, Alva's *Señor* calls on *el Mundo* saying, "Estás embellecido de flores de cacao y flores muy finas y de otras varias (flores). Tú también, O Cielo, resplandeces en las estrellas. Por medio de ti vuelan el pájaro verde, la paloma, el pato, y el pinzón" (p. 154). In several places characters speak in a folksy manner entirely alien to the Calderonian style. This is seen even when Alva follows his source closely, as when his *Rico* reacts to the death of *la Hermosura*: "Pues ella era una flor; apenas floreció cuando tuvo que marchitarse. Es un agüero, un ejemplo, para que mañana no nos pase a nosotros la misma cosa. Gocemos, llenemos las tripas, mientras que vivamos un rato" (p. 169). The first lines of *el Orden* also seem to have a special localized interest. At the corresponding moment of the original *auto*, *la Ley de Gracia* merely introduces herself and her function and chants, "Ama al otro como a ti,/y obra bien que Dios es Dios."[5] Alva's *Orden*, however, sings a song:

> Quiere a tus vecinos
> así como a ti,
> así como a ti,
> para disponerte
> con el agua de la vida,
> con el agua de la vida.
> Hay riqueza (felicidad) en el Cielo.
> Allá está Dios.
> Te dará contento
> cuando mueras,
> cuando perezcas (p. 162).

This has the simplistic ring of what we might call a Sunday School song, and we may surmise that it was well known to Alva's congregation.

These folk elements and other bits of evidence invite us to conclude that this Nahuatl *auto* was actually performed in Alva's village of Tzumpahuacán, though such a performance cannot be documented. We can imagine the church steps and courtyard being used as a theater, just as was done in medieval Europe, and Alva's stage directions support this hypothesis. In Calderón's work *el Autor* watches his play from his throne in a *globo celeste*, which closes at the end of the performance. At this point in the Nahuatl version *el Señor* withdraws and the stage directions read, "Aquí se cierra la iglesia" (p. 171). In a number of places characters seem to speak directly to the audience. After *la Hermosura* has passed through the sepulcher door and ap-

---

[5]Ibid., p. 211.

pears before *el Mundo*, he describes what has happened to her: "Aquí notad, vosotras todas las gentes. Era sólo una flor, y se marchitó en mi mano. Los gusanos se comieron la belleza; nada dejaron" (p. 173). Early in the play, before the other actors have entered, *el Mundo* names the characters and speaks to them in such a familiar way that they seem to be standing in front of him, perhaps in the first rows of the audience. Then, as all is in readiness, *el Señor* gives the order to begin: "que comience (el drama). Aquí, Chalchiuhatenco Quetzalatzalan, he aquí lo que has de hacer, pinzón. Has las debidas tareas por tu parte" (p. 155). Hunter has no explanation for these Nahuatl words, which are apparently an Aztec proper name, except to suggest that they could refer to a particular stagehand. This may well be so, or perhaps we have here the name of one of the Indian actors. In either case, the line suggests the intimacy of a folk play written for a specific audience with which the author was familiar.

The important characteristics of this *auto* by Bartolomé de Alva are several. It is historically significant because it helps date an important work by Calderón and because it testifies to the mobility and richness of the cultural milieu within the Spanish empire. The play is no routine translation but an adaptation done with skill and understanding. The Christian doctrines of love and grace are not so strongly stated as in the Spanish source, but Alva clearly asserts the importance of loving one's neighbor. In *El gran teatro del mundo*, Calderón combines the familiar themes of life as a fiction and death as a leveler with the idea of Man's responsibility to God, his creator. When Alva omits the theatrical references, he loses Calderón's basic metaphor of the world as a theater, and with it the emphasis on the illusoriness of life. The rest of the meaning of the original *auto* remains essentially intact. With its intrinsic merit and its folk play charm, Alva's *auto* is an interesting product of the colonial culture of Mexico and an attractive example of Nahuatl literature.

16. General and the Lady: Two Examples of Religious Persecution in the Mexican Novel

VIVIAN M. GRUBER

In this essay, Professor Gruber examines a nineteenth-century novel by Vicente Riva Palacio, *Monja y casada, virgen y mártir*, and a twentieth-century novel by Rosario Castellanos, *Balún-Canán*. The former work concerns social and psychological responses to the colonial Inquisition, and the latter work deals with religious repression during the decade of the 1930s. Comparison of passages in these novels offers interesting parallels in methods and attitudes that predominate when religious beliefs are suppressed by church or by state.

Religious persecution has appeared in many guises in all ages and in all inhabited areas of the world. As religion in man is universal, so is its repression and abuse. These conflicts have been recorded in every manner: from the most objective, carefully investigated treatise to violently prejudiced and inflammatory pulp novels. Religious persecution has been one of the frequently used motifs in artistic literature, and the Hispanic novel has been no exception. The Inquisition in Spain and in some Spanish colonies spawned myriad plots and counterplots, not often contemporary to that institution. In nineteenth century Mexico, the Inquisition became a symbol of repressive authority; and Vicente Riva Palacio made that obvious in his romantic historical novel, *Monja y casada, virgen y mártir*.[1] In Mexico, however, there was another moment of religious repression that was at times equally as violent as the era of the Inquisition in New Spain. This was the era that engendered the first novel, the epoch of the Constitution of 1857 and its revisions and implementation. The Constitution of 1857 incorporated earlier decrees secularizing church

---

[1]Vicente Riva Palacio, *Monja y casada, virgen y mártir*, edición de lujo, 2 vols. (México, D.F.: Editorial Nacional, 1953).

properties. To these provisions, other liberalizing laws were added by President Benito Juárez, only to be abrogated by General Felix Zulóaga, re-instituted by Juárez, abrogated by Maximilian, restored by Juárez, amended under Díaz, etc., until finally, after a tempestuous struggle, a new Constitution of 1917 was adopted in the aftermath of the Revolution of 1910.[2] The second repression of religion, especially as President Lázaro Cárdenas carried out a strong anti-clerical policy in the 1930s, provides the setting for another Mexican novel. Mexico's outstanding contemporary feminine novelist is Rosario Castellanos and, although her techniques and motifs are vastly different from those of Riva Palacio, her novel *Balún-Canán*[3] effectively interprets for us the persecution of the clergy and the faithful of the Catholic Church during the 1930s. Nearly a century separates the times of writing; far more separates the points of view.

Vicente Riva Palacio (1832-1896) had a many-faceted career. He was a liberal lawyer, a general under Juárez, and a defender of the Constitution of 1857; but he was also a supporter of the Plan of Tuxtepec that led to the *pan o palo* dictatorship of Porfirio Díaz. Riva Palacio finally chose the pen and the political arena for his personal *combate*. He was poet, journalist, cabinet minister, governor, magistrate, and even minister plenopotentiary in Spain and Portugal; but it is in the romantic historical novel that he excelled, although some critics dispute the quantity of his writing. One of them, Carlos González-Peña,[4] has called his work *la novela folletinesca* (pulp novel), although he also refers to Riva Palacio as the creator of the historical novel in Mexico and its chief exponent during his short literary career.[5] Riva Palacio's interest in the historical novel comes naturally, one would conjecture, from his labor as an historian. He was general editor of the monumental *México a través do los siglos*[6] and author of its second volume, *El virreinato*, which he wrote while in prison as a result of his opposition to President Manuel González. Riva Palacio's *folletinesca* tendency perhaps comes from his experience as journalist and publisher. The novel from which we take our first example of religious repressions is one of these pulp novels.

General Riva Palacio relied on his skills as reporter and historian to write what he subtitled *Historia de los tiempos de la Inquisición*, first published in 1868 during the short period of relative tranquility

---

[2]Alfonso Teja Zabre, *Guide to the History of Mexico: A Modern Interpretation* (México, D.F.: Press of the Ministry of Foreign Affairs, 1935), pp. 42-53.

[3]Rosario Castellanos, *Balún-Canán* (México, D.F: Fondo de Cultural Económica, 1957; reprint ed., Colección Popular 92, 1970).

[4]Carlos González Peña, *Historia de la literatura mexicana desde sus orígenes hasta nuestros días*, 5th ed. (México, D.F.: Editorial Porrúa, 1954), p. 335.

[5]Ibid., pp. 336-37.

[6]Vicente Riva Palacio, ed., *México a través de los siglos: Historia general y completa del desenvolvimiento social, político, religioso, militar, artístico, científico y literario de México desde la antiguedad más remota hasta la época actual*, 5 vols. (Barcelona: Espasa, 1888-97).

under Juárez and the restored republic. It was written with five other novels[7] during the three-year period and seems to have been his second novel. This one and the four which followed it are historical in their perspective and portray the colonial period. Perhaps these works were inspired by his research for *El virreinato*. Historical data and detailed descriptions of Mexico City, its customs, buildings, streets, and general atmosphere all attest to his minute and exact historical knowledge. There are frequent references (none flattering) to the Inquisition, to the *Gran Inquisidor de México*, and to the *Santo Oficio* with its dreaded banner bearing the *cruz verde*. The author describes a general attitude of fear and a feeling of utter despair on the part of those who were detained by the Inquisition or the *Santo Oficio*. This is summed up in the proverbial statement that "era más fácil sacar un ánima del Purgatorio que un acusado de las garras del Santo Oficio."[8] Underlying fear is a recurring theme throughout the long, two-volume novel.

Two major episodes involve the Inquisition. Both are instigated by Luisa, a mulata slave of base motives. The first episode is told in retrospect by Teodoro, slave of Doña Beatriz. He is a giant of a man with great physical and moral strength. Teodoro relates the story of his life to explain why he has refused a reward for having rescued the oidor, don Fernando de Quesada. Teodoro's former owner had been accused of blasphemy and witchcraft by Luisa, who is greedy and ambitious beyond imagination. With the help of an equally avaricious and convetous neighbor, Luisa is able, through various deceits, to assure the arrest and conviction of her owner by the Inquisition while she escapes to a better life. Teodoro discovers a way to visit his master secretly; but to do so, he must travel at night through many locked doors and winding tunnels, much as Virgil led Dante down through the various levels of the inferno through scenes of agony and horror:

> Descendimos por una escalera á unos espacios subterráneos; Santiago abría y cerraba luego grandes puertas de madera, abiertas de planchas y barras de hierro, inmensas rejas, cadenas que impedían el paso, y con gran admiración mía, encontramos carceleros encerrados en los corredores, que no podían salir para tenerlos más seguros cerca de los presos.... los calabozos ... eran unas especies de cuevas, ... los reos estaban atados á gruesas cadenas ... llevaban grillos y esposas y no tenían cama, ni una mala silla.... Se les veía casi desnudos, pálidos, con los cabellos y la barba largos y enmarañados. Aquellos calabozos exhalaban insorportable hedor....[9]

These scenes are much worse, in one sense, than those of Dante's *Inferno* because their characters are the living dead, tortured, waiting for

---
[7]González Peña, *Historia de la literatura mexicana*, pp. 336-37.
[8]Riva Palacio, *Monja y casada*, 2:680.
[9]Ibid., 1:135-36.

the public *auto de fe* or the private execution by garroting or whatever unbelievably cruel fate might await them in the name of religion.[10]

The other episode is far more graphic and impressive, and it forms an integral part of the novel. The episode is complex, with implications extending beyond the Inquisition itself. Several subordinate themes are interwoven in the overriding emphasis on complete condemnation of the Inquisition and its functions. First, the context is set in the political rivalry of 1623 between the viceroy, don Diego Fernández de Córdoba, along with his followers, and the archbishop of Mexico, don Juan Pérez de Varais, *alcalde mayor* of Metepec. Luisa has concealed her identity as mulata and former slave. The cruel irony is that her machinations plus the vengeance of her longstanding enemies place her in the same cell of the secret Inquisition jails as doña Blanca de Mejía, the object of her jealous revenge. One of the themes is the strong contrast between the interrogation hall of the *Tribuna de la Fe* and the world of horrors beyond the dreaded "*puertecilla que tenía encima escrita la prohibición de entrada para los que no fuesen del secreto.*"[11] The hall is "*magníficamente adornada, rodeado de columnas ... con ricas colgaduras de damasco encarnado ... un gran dosel de terciopelo carmesí con franjas y borlas de oro; ...*"[12] There are also rich furnishings, the coat of arms of Spain, and an ornate crucifix with the motto of the Inquisition: *Excurge Dios, judica causam tuam*. The crucifix is flanked by two angels: "*uno con una oliva en la mano derecha ... el otro ángel con una espada en la mano derecha....*"[13] They proclaim the two choices of the accused: *Sed ut convertabur, et vivat* or *Ad faciendam vindictam, in nationibus increpationis, in polulis*. Beyond the dreaded, forbidden door is a horror chamber with a light that is "*rojiza e incierta.*"[14] The walls are blackened, and the author explains: "*No es posible describir con exactitud aquel antro de la crueldad humana.*"[15] The cells are perpetually dark. Following the torture sessions, the accused is cast on a "*húmedo lecho de paja*" and for covering is given a "*sucio y roto lienzo.*"[16] All this is in strong contrast to the red and gold velvets and rich ornamentation of the interrogation room.

Yet another motif is the contrast between the pathetic condition of the accused (his pallor, craven fear, and plea for pity) and the utter indifference on the part of the inquisitors. Doña Blanca Mejia makes an impassioned plea that is heightened in effectiveness by her beauty and exaltation, but to no avail. She is condemned to torture and

---

[10] Ibid., vol. 1, bk. 1, chaps. 13-15.
[11] Ibid., 2:617-18.
[12] Ibid., p. 609.
[13] Ibid., p. 610.
[14] Ibid., p. 619.
[15] Ibid.
[16] Ibid., p. 683.

dragged away through that awful door by hooded jailers as the inquisitors "como si nada estuviera pasando allí, seguían tratando de otros negocios."[17]

Another theme is the contrast between the gentle, well-bred Blanca and her rough-handed jailers. After having been forced by her covetous brother into a cloistered convent, she is accused not only of breaking the cloister, but also of consorting with the devil and of witchcraft, marriage, and lechery. Every sensibility of the noble, pure, and gentle young woman is offended as the jailers prepare her for torture, stripping her and strapping her to the rack. There are constant allusions to the effects of the torture on her beauty[18] and of the indifferent brutality of the executioners. Further, we see that *poderoso caballero es don Dinero* when her brother is released by the Grand Inquisitor after he has promised to found and endow "una o dos capellanías ... dando el patronato a la Santa Inquisición,"[19] even though he is, in truth, the one guilty of every conceivable sin while his innocent sister is tortured and condemned to death. Riva Palacio uses the cumulative effect of these and related incidents to heighten the horror and disgust in the reader's reaction to the Inquisition. The author also enhances his melodramatic story with rich documentation as he chronicles the history of the Inquisition from creation to growth in Spain and establishment in New Spain under don Pedro Moya de Contreras.[20] For one who might not believe and who might wish to defend the Inquisition, he asserts: "Documentos irrefutables tenemos para confundirle."[21]

The author has exploited highly inflammatory questions concerning the church, the Spanish government, the Inquisition, and the *Santo Oficio* in order to produce a romantic, historical novel placed within the context of a moment in Mexican history when the official position of the government was anti-clerical, reflecting the convictions of President Juárez and his supporters. With enactment of the Reform Laws, the atmosphere was appropriate for condemning the Catholic Church. What better place to open fire than the colonial church, which symbolized for the nascent Mexican nationalism an evil foreign domination?

The lady of our title, Rosario Castellanos, set her novel in the aftermath of the Revolution of 1910 and the Constitution of 1917 as implemented in the administration of Lázaro Cárdenas in the 1930s. She pinpoints the time: "Pero Felipe había recortado de un periódico el retrato de Lázaro Cárdenas. El presidente parecía borroso, entre una

---

[17] Ibid., p. 618.
[18] Ibid., pp. 619-29.
[19] Ibid., p. 728.
[20] Ibid., p. 669.
[21] Ibid., p. 670.

multitud de campesinos."[22] Mexico still faced many of the same problems as those described by Riva Palacio: social classes in conflict, witchcraft, religious persecution, abuse and ignorance, poverty, and racial conflict. By law, slavery has been abolished but the Indian is little more than a slave of the landowner whose lands are about to be confiscated and divided. The Catholic Church has lost its wealth and power, and it has been changed into a clandestine, forbidden organization whose clergy, in spite of all this, remains the absolute arbiter of the destinies of the faithful. All this we see dimly through the eyes of a young girl who narrates most of the novel. In the child we see the influence of her Indian *nana* as the latter narrates Indian myths and legends. For example, the fear of taking communion is inspired in the girl and her younger brother by one of the tales of the Indian demon Catashaná, "el diablo de las seite cuerdas . . . el padre de la mentira,"[23] who converted "la hostia . . . en una bola de plomo"[24] to punish a child in the story. This threat hangs over the two children as they are prepared for their first communion, and fear that the host would become a leaden ball as they try to swallow it provokes the climax of the novel. These legends become more real to the narrator and her brother than the Christian faith.

Her mother is caught up in the superstition and witchcraft of the *curanderas* and *brujos* to the extent that she is persuaded that Mario, her only male child, will die. His death will destroy the only remaining bond between her and her husband. Suddenly, in this atmosphere, the underground church enters. The feeling of fear at being discovered by the government is somewhat similar to fear of the Inquisition—a feeling that others had felt centuries earlier during the colonial era. By night the mother and her two children are taken to the home of a friend who has arranged for a priest to come. The parlor has been converted into a chapel.[25] Amalia, the friend, promises Zoraida, the mother of the children, that she will be the first to see the priest in spite of the crowd ("Mujeres humildes, tapadas . . . descalzas. Niños . . . sudorosos . . . Señoras. Erguidas, aisladas . . .")[26] because, says Amalia, "De algo me ha de servir correr los riesgos que corro. Imagínate si ahora vinieron los gendarmes a catear la casa . . . a la cárcel íbamos a parar todos. . . ."[27] Finally, after they have waited for three hours, the priest arrives, exhausted and hungry. He is a very strong man ("alto, fornido")[28] and at the moment is completely

---

[22]Castellanos, *Balún-Canán*, p. 159.
[23]Ibid., p. 259.
[24]Ibid., p. 260.
[25]Ibid., p. 246.
[26]Ibid.
[27]Ibid., p. 247.
[28]Ibid.

frustrated by the lack of religion in his flock. Of the Indian, he says: "Me trae las criaturas para que yo las bautice, no porque quieren hacerlas cristianas, pues nadie jamás piensa en Cristo, sino por aquello del agua bendita que sirve para ahuyentar a los nahuales y los malos espíritus...."[29]

Now his faithful among the white upper class seek his aid for the same purposes: "No he conocido dureza de corazón igual a la de la gente de este pueblo."[30] For them he must risk life and freedom. In his frustration, he reveals the situation a bit more clearly than the child-narrator: "¿Valdría la pena aguantar hambre?... ¿Soportar el cansancio, el frío? ¿Consumirse luchando contra el terror de esta persecución inicua y sin sentido?..."[31] The result of this senseless persecution we see when the child-narrator is told at the death of her brother that the priest "Alcanzó a llegar. Pero los gendarmes lo detuvieron a salir de la casa. Ahora está preso."[32] Mario died before his first communion, which he feared so much that he became mortally ill; and he met death without the solace of the priest, who had been imprisoned by the *gendarmes*. Because the narrator of this novel is a child who recounts experiences in the first person, and because this is a *nueva novela*, experiences of the detained priest cannot enter into the novel as did some of the experiences to which Riva Palacio so vividly alludes: fear, interrogation, injustice, and inhuman tortures.

Rosario Castellanos (wife, mother, writer, teacher, critic, and diplomat) writes this novel and others of her "Chiapas cycle" to present the Indian to her reading public.[33] Thus, the episode reflecting religious persecution is only a part of the rich tapestry of the background of Comitán and Chiapas, which is the scene of the novel and home of the Tzotzil tribe that is portrayed. Her purpose is to present the Indian, not as a stereotyped, one-dimensional figure but as a fully developed, four-dimensional human being, albeit at times shadowy and ill-defined by the child-narrator. Her central motif does not emphasize religious persecution; rather, it is a somber leitmotiv in *Balún-Canán* ("place where the nine stars meet") like the black threads that run through the beautiful weaving of the Indians.

General Riva Palacio had as his central motif the historical portrayal of an institution that he abhorred; or perhaps he sought to destroy the influence and memories of three institutions which he found distasteful and foreign to the atmosphere of the Juárez regime: the peninsular Spanish influence in government, the ecclesiastical

---

[29]Ibid., p. 249.
[30]Ibid.
[31]Ibid.
[32]Ibid., p. 281.
[33]Walter M. Langford, *The Mexican Novel Comes of Age* (Notre Dame, Ind.: University of Notre Dame Press, 1971), pp. 184-85.

hierarchy, and the Inquisition manipulated by both. Riva Palacio effectively portrays the full range of political intrigues in the rivalry between the archbishop and the viceroy, but Rosario Castellanos merely reveals these intrigues as they affect the daily life of the child whose father is away in Tuxtla trying to see the Governor and whose mother suffers an almost pathological fear that "los brujos se comerán"[34] her only male child. There is no direct awareness of the intrigue at the state capital in Tuxtla or in the national capital as Lázaro Cádenas struggled to impose agrarian reform on the large landholders who were fighting to maintain the status quo.

Rosario Castellanos' work is more somber, perhaps more effective, than the colorful, sensational novel of Riva Palacio. Yet, however much the two novels differ, they offer evidence that the abuse of religion—witchcraft, ignorance, superstition, persecution, injustice—is tragically a part of humanity and its imperfections; nevertheless, man eternally seeks guidance and solace from his religion and its leaders—or from a substitute for them—regardless of personal danger involved. Religion and repression are two universals in man.

---

[34]Castellanos, *Balún-Canán*, p. 249.

17. "Así en la Tierra como en el Cielo": Religión, Mito, Superstición y Magia en las "Novelas de la Tierra" de Agustín Yáñez

ROBERTO BRAVO-VILLARROEL

Agustín Yáñez has figured prominently in the political and literary life of twentieth-century Mexico and of his native state, Jalisco, in particular. Here, Professor Bravo-Villarroel analyzes Yáñez's treatment of religon (*Al filo del agua*), myth (*La tierra pródiga*), and magic and superstition (*Las tierras flacas*).

Si, como asevera Octavio Paz, "el novelista no demuestra ni cuenta: recrea un mundo",[1] Agustín Yáñez es sin duda el novelista que más ampliamente recrea el mundo de Jalisco, su estado natal. Yáñez, en efecto, ha utilizado como materia para su mejor narrativa no sólo los pueblos jaliscienses, sino además la ciudad de su nacimiento, Guadalajara, capital del estado. *Flor de juegos antiguos* (1942), *Al filo del agua* (1947), *La tierra pródiga* (1960) y *Las tierras flacas* (1962), integran la tetralogía novelística en que este escritor retrata la topografía geográfica y espiritual de Jalisco.

No es ésta ocasión para analizar extensamente las novelas que acabamos de mencionar. A la vez, *Flor de juegos antiguos* quedará al margen de este comentario, ya que en realidad este libro es más bien una evocación lírica, de tono autobiográfico, que pretende asir las esencias de la niñez tapatía durante las dos primeras décadas de nuestro siglo. Es cierto que pretende además reinventar a Guadalajara por medio de una crónica infantil hecha de recuerdos asociados a momentos lúdicos y corros de niños, pero creemos que su verdadero propósito es presentar el reencuentro de la propia infancia y el despertar del erotismo adolescente.

[1] *El arco y la lira* (México, D. F.: Fondo de Cultura Económica, 1950), p. 222.

Nos ocuparemos, por tanto, de las llamadas "novelas de la tierra," a saber, de los relatos en que Yáñez toma tres regiones jaliscienses que, según él, ejemplifican tres modos de vida dentro del contexto semiurbano y rural de su estado natal. Analizaremos la religión en *Al filo del agua*, el mito en *La tierra pródiga*, y la magia y la superstición en *Las tierras flacas*.

Yáñez, desde sus años iniciales de escritor, programó un plan ambicioso de relatos que cubrieran los diferentes aspectos de la vida de Jalisco. Esquematizó su obra narrativa llamándola "El plan que peleamos", y en la segunda sección de este planteamiento, llamada "El país y la gente", incluye las tres obras recién aludidas. Con estos relatos traza una línea narrativa que une el oriente y el occidente de su provincia para darnos un vasto mural literario que tiene como centro a Guadalajara, vientre de Jalisco.

Al filo del agua

En 1947 aparece *Al filo del agua* y pasa desapercibida por cierto tiempo. Meses más tarde, casi al unísono, es saludada como la obra iniciadora de una etapa en la novelística mexicana. Constituye, en efecto, una piedra miliar y un punto de arranque para la narrativa que le sucederá. Por primera vez en la literatura imaginativa de México, perspectivas y técnicas del realismo y regionalismo ceden su lugar a la presentación de la realidad interior afectada de manera diferente por las coordenadas de tiempo y espacio. El tiempo deja de ser simple secuencia de eventos cronológicamente presentados, para adquirir la relatividad y el diacronismo que la conciencia psicológica suministra. El espacio, antigua matriz de toda realidad novelada, es ahora preferentemente modo de sentir o de ser que interpreta la vida de manera no locativa. El amor, que generalmente era fuerza redentora o fuente de gozo, es ahora estímulo pesimista y fugaz, causa de tormento y frustración. Los protagonistas heroicos y verticales son sustituidos por anti-héroes, seres sinuosos, solitarios y a veces villanos. El mundo se torna mítico mediante la yuxtaposición de lo físico y lo fantástico. Y, finalmente, el lector es llamado a participar en la creación literaria al delegarle interpretaciones, complementos y conclusiones.

Con *Al filo del agua* la novela mexicana se libera de su lastre documental, de su tono de denuncia y de su función, a veces hábilmente disfrazada, de alegato y propaganda. Por primera vez los medios expresivos—palabra, sintaxis, imagen, semántica—sirven no de integumento para el asunto, sino de objeto primario del relato. Bajo estas premisas Yáñez compone su novela. Es bien sabido que *Al filo del agua* tiene un marco seudohistórico, es decir, relata una serie de sucesos acaecidos entre el mes de marzo de 1909 y los últimos días de 1910 en un poblado del estado de Jalisco, muy posiblemente Yahualica, tierra de los antepasados del escritor. Sin embargo, este marco sirve sólo de canevá para mostrar cómo el pueblo, durante esos veintidós meses, vive el agobio de la rutina, el erotismo soterrado, el calendario litúrgico, el crimen y la expectación de algo desconocido e inminente. El pueblo está al filo del agua, es decir, ante el borde de la guerra civil conocida como la Revolución Mexicana.

El libro, estructurado mediante un "Acto preparatorio" y dieciséis capítulos, nos presenta un tema central: la lucha entre el deseo y el miedo. En este pueblo "de perpetua cuaresma", la libertad y los anhelos en vano intentan galopar. La reclusión, el temor a la vida, la omnipresencia de la muerte, la represión del amor y, sobre todo, la falsa religiosidad, perfilan la psicología inhibida de casi todo el pueblo. El "Acto preparatorio", de fuerte barroquismo, con intensas apoyaturas en alusiones bíblicas y frases litúrgicas,—que con cierta profusión aparecerán también en el cuerpo de la novela—nos sumerge de inmediato en la tónica del libro y condiciona la caracterización de los personajes. A partir del primer capítulo, Yáñez nos hará sentir la lucha entre la asfixia impuesta por la tradición y la religiosidad mal entendida, y la exigencia de liberación reclamada por legítimos deseos.

Los eventos de que está hecho el relato son de dos clases: unos pertenecen a la esfera de la conciencia, tanto psicológica como moral; otros supuestamente podrían ser calificados de seculares o arreligiosos. Si examinamos los eventos de conciencia, vemos que el pecado, tanto como acción vitanda cuanto como fuente de gozo prohibido, empapa la novela entera. Es decir, la religión adquiere un carácter eminentemente ético. Sacerdotes y feligreses—en realidad no hay otra categoría de personajes—son protagonistas de una lucha en el orbe moral. Todos ellos aparecen pensados y realizados *sub specie aeternitatis*, bajo una perspectiva transcendente, como posibles trofeos en la pugna entre el vicio y la virtud, el infierno y la gloria. Esta condición los hace a todos ser personajes agónicos, esto es, luchadores trágicos. Las pasiones que los sacuden no son estímulos que conduzcan a una conducta de resonancia puramente terrenal; ahí se juega nada menos que la salvación o condenación de un alma. Su conflicto interior no se resolverá en esta vida sino en la futura. Se enfrentan a un dilema medular que trasciende tiempo y espacio.

La otra clase de eventos es de carácter externo. Muchos de ellos aparecen condicionados a las campanas de la iglesia parroquial y al cielo litúrgico: los ejercicios espirituales durante la cuaresma, catarsis espiritual en la que el autocastigo y el recuerdo de las postrimerías extenúan a los penitentes; la celebración de la Semana Santa, con su doliente liturgia eucarística y redentora; la Pascua de Resurrección, que débilmente refuerza la fe en Cristo redivivo; las "juntas" de la Asociación de Hijas de María, para quienes el celibato es un voto cuasi-religioso, rígidamente impuesto y exigido por el escrupuloso padre Islas; el día de la Santa Cruz, de perfumes vegetales, en el que retoñan en colores y plegarias todas las cruces del pueblo; los funerales, que hacen recordar a los feligreses el "día de la ira" y el polvo, común y final destino del hombre; el día de la Ascensión, fiesta de naturaleza jubilosa y promisoria, pero en el que se insinúan la tragedia nacional de la Revolución y la de algunos personajes. Todos estos acontecimientos y situaciones impregnan la vida colectiva e individual de "este lugar del Arzobispado, cuyo nombre no importa recordar", como escribe el novelista. Paralelos a estos acontecimientos hay otros aparentemente seculares, pero que son en realidad antítesis de aquéllos: circulación de periódicos anticlericales y novelas eróticas, infiltración de ideas masónicas y liberales. Llegan también corrientes ideológicas antiporfiristas y nuevos módulos morales importados por los "norteños", antiguos emigrados a los Estados Unidos que retornan al pueblo. Los sacerdotes tratan de consolidar la situación tradicional que han impuesto, a base de controlar las vías de acceso de esas ideas disolventes, pero subrepticiamente todos esos factores se cuelan y producirán un colapso moral en varios de los personajes principales.

Entre éstos se encuentran los representantes oficiales de la religión católica, es decir, tres sacerdotes: el párroco don Dionisio María Martínez, el padre Islas y el padre Reyes. Resulta oportuno señalar aquí que Yáñez, en contraste con la mayoria de los novelistas que tratan el tema de la Revolución Mexicana, que adoptan una actitud definidamente anticlerical, perfila al párroco de manera digna aunque interiormente trágica. Don Dionisio es virtuoso, ascético, guía auténtico de la vida moral del pueblo, compasivo hasta con los criminales, incorruptible frente a la presión porfirista, conservador de un justo medio entre el fanatismo y el liberalismo de sus principales vicarios, celoso protector de sus sobrinas y del huérfano Gabriel, incólume defensor de la ortodoxia católica, de vida interior intensa y sana. Estas notas individuantes, a la vez, no lo hacen un prototipo a la manera de la novelística tradicional. Don Dionisio es un personaje muy humano, con desmayos interiores, expectante y temeroso, asediado por sobresaltos que afloran en sus pesadillas nocturnas y en sus delirios febricitantes. Su gran tragedia reside en el reconocimiento de que es muy difícil cambiar la naturaleza humana, proclive a la pasión y al pecado. Paulatinamente se va dando cuenta de la derrota de sus esfuerzos sacerdotales. Advierte claramente que varios cambios están en gestación en el pueblo: las ideas advenedizas impondrán nuevas actitudes; el sexo se desembocará; su sobrina María y Gabriel buscarán aires más libres; la Revolución empezará a rodar. Al final de la novela el párroco aparece celebrando misa. Frente a su feligresía, que llena el templo parroquial, el presbítero recuerda sus años de sacerdote joven al escuchar el hemistiquio que completa el primer versículo del salmo del Introito: *Ad Deum qui laetificat iuventutem meam.* Evoca con tristeza sus treinta y cuatro años de sacerdocio, que hoy le saben a cáliz amargo pues no sabe si "podrá vencer el vértigo que lo derrumba, la caída que esperan con sádico silencio."[2] Y la novela termina con el deseo reprimido del anciano sacerdote por repetir el versículo, síntesis de su idealismo de presbítero recién ungido.

El padre José María Islas tipifica el catolicismo neurótico y cerrado. Ha hecho de la castidad la virtud nuclear de su vida, pero ha caído en la anormalidad al ver ocasión de lujuria en estados, situaciones o actos moralmente lícitos. Tiene un concepto sombrío de la existencia, nunca ríe, su vida es impenetrable. A pesar de que su actividad principal es la dirección de la Asociación de las Hijas de María, es en el fondo un clérigo misógino. El noviazgo y el matrimonio de los feligreses lo llevan a estados ridículos de cólera. Jamás habla a solas con una mujer; nunca confiesa a una si no hay luz del día. La virginidad es para él el estado perfecto; no celebra misa en la capilla de la Sagrada Familia; tiene disimulada fobia a San José y a San Antonio, patrono de los novios. Su rigidez en cuestión de sexo hace mella en varios feligreses: algunos sufren terriblemente cuando ven juntarse, al impulso del viento, ropas masculinas y femeninas puestas a secar. Otros dudan sobre si no han pecado de pensamiento al introducir la llave a la cerradura o al enhebrar una aguja. Algunas mujeres evitan ir a los ranchos para no tener ocasión de ver a los animales refocilarse y ayuntarse. Toros y gallos han sido desterrados de varios establos y corrales.

El padre Islas crea así una atmósfera letal que ataca los orígenes mismos de la vida: "Los niños van adquiriendo uso de razón en este clima de penumbra, inhibitorio. Sus pasos y risas tropiezan en mitad de silencios. Hallan que todo en la vida es un misterio. Escuchan frecuentemente la idea de que mejor hubiera sido que no vinieran al mundo. Flota en la atmósfera una difusa certidumbre de que han venido por caminos de tristeza. Presienten que bajo el rostro de sus padres y tras la apariencia de las cosas, un esfuerzo leve pondrá en descubierto algo terrible, cuyo nombre tratan de ocultarles los mayores".[3]

El presbítero Abundio Reyes es la contrapartida del vicario anterior. Inquieto, bromista, dinámico, con don de gentes, llega al poblado con muchas prevenciones, pero el párroco le recibe con comprensión y franqueza. Después de un tiempo de cauteloso ajuste, su temperamento extravertido lo fuerza a un apostolado religioso de ritmo alegre y simpático. Dinamiza la vida espiritual y se aproxima a las "ovejas negras" del lugar. Hubiera querido fomentar actividades y festejos profanos como instrumentos de atracción religiosa, pero el carácter del pueblo y las experiencias desagradables en su anterior

---

[2]Agustín Yáñez, *Al filo del agua*, Colección de escritores mexicanos, 72 (México, D.F.: Editorial Porrúa, 1971), p. 387.
[3]Ibid., p. 232.

parroquia le cohiben. Se le tilda de tolerante, liberal y modernista por sus ideas y métodos renovadores.

Consiguientemente, el pueblo presentado en *Al filo del agua* no está del todo regulado por prácticas e ideas de signo negativo. Cierto es que el padre Islas es un elemento inhibitorio de legítimas aspiraciones, pero éste es también objeto de escarnio de parte de muchos feligreses, especialmente cuando, después de un ataque de histeria, queda paralítico, acaba confinado en un manicomio de Guadalajara, y le despiden del pueblo escasos vecinos. Cierto es también que el párroco se inclina hacia la severidad moral, pero su bonhomía vence la rigidez de sus principios. El padre Reyes guarda un justo medio en su religiosidad abierta pero ortodoxa. Creer que Yáñez quiso sentar la tesis de que el pueblo se encuentra en condiciones de atraso únicamente a causa de la religión y sus ministros, equivale a analizar la novela con prejuicio monístico y sin inquirir la verdadera intención del novelista. Yo creo que Yáñez siempre ha escrito para mostrar, no para demostrar. A la vez, su actitud como escritor es de conmiseración o simpatía, nunca de hostilidad o repugnancia. Es siempre indulgente con la humanidad, especialmente con la que desgasta su vida en las zonas oscuras de la provincia porque en ésta generalmente ve, a pesar de sus defectos y su vida insular, autenticidad y cierta felicidad genuina. Él mismo lo ha reconocido en páginas autobiográficas: "Fuimos así educados en un sentido rural de la existencia, tan amplio, tan sano, tan fuerte y libre como la naturaleza, lejos de toda pequeñez, refractarios a todo ámbito confinado, a toda mezquindad".[4]

La tierra pródiga

De 1953 a 1959 Yáñez desempeñó el puesto de gobernador en su estado natal. Este escritor constituye uno de los casos, cada vez menos frecuentes en el mundo hispánico, del intelectual llamado a participar en la vida política de su país. Desde hacía tiempo él había concebido el trabajo intelectual "como servicio público y como deber civilizador", y ahora se le presentaba una oportunidad para poner en práctica en su provincia ideales y convicciones e intentar remediar males que había expuesto como hombre de letras. Su sexenio político tuvo un carácter definidamente humanista, que se manifestó en la intensificación de la vida cultural de Jalisco y en el espíritu de concordia, ecuanimidad y limpieza de su gobierno. Su lema quedó grabado en la rotonda de Minerva, fuente monumental de Guadalajara: "Justicia, sabiduría y fortaleza custodian a esta leal ciudad".

Durante su gubernatura, la política presidencial de Adolfo Ruiz Cortines estableció el programa llamado "la marcha hacia el mar".

---

[4]*Alfonso Gutiérrez Hermosillo y otros amigos* (México, D.F.: Editorial Occidente, 1945), p. 59.

Jalisco está integrado en su zona occidental por más de 18,000 kilómetros cuadrados situados en el litoral del Océano Pacífico, y Yáñez entusiasmadamente trabajó en la incorporación de esa región a la vida económica y social del estado y del país. Como producto de sus viajes a la zona costera nace *La tierra pródiga*.

Esta novela se ocupa de un mundo muy distante del presentado en *Al filo del agua*. La región ahora retratada es de mundo virgen, violenta, primitiva y trepidante como el mar que la limita. Los personajes son seres duros y poderosos, afectados por la vieja dicotomía de civilización contra barbarie, razón contra instinto. Este tema, de larga progenie en la letras hispanoamericanas, tiene en Yáñez un tratamiento peculiar al asignarle a la naturaleza una función cuádruple: es circunstancia, no protagonista; suministra abundante substancia lírica al novelista; es instrumento de actualización de la historia y, finalmente, forma con la mujer un "símbolo biforme". Desde *Facundo* hasta *Doña Bárbara* ninguna novela hispanoamericana había sido concebida con tan generosa amplitud de intenciones en el tratamiento de la naturaleza.

En *La tierra pródiga* creo que se debe ver una novela que funciona básicamente sobre el supuesto de dos mitos. Conviene aclarar que por mito aquí se entiende la recreación literaria de una saga heroica y el intento de encarnación de un símbolo. Concretamente, este relato, a través de una serie de eventos ocurridos en la zona marítima de Jalisco, reconstruye la conquista española en América y, además, ejemplifica el binomio clásico naturaleza-mujer. El propio novelista, en su artículo "Cómo escribí *La tierra pródiga*",[5] señala esta dualidad mítica que acabamos de introducir.

El paralelismo que el autor traza entre los conquistadores hispánicos y los caciques de esta "tierra caliente" es justo y vigoroso. Ambos tipos humanos se enfrentaron a tierras retadoras, innominadas y paradisíacas, que parecían como si acabaran de surgir del tercer día de la creación. El júbilo del descubrimiento y de dar nombre a las cosas, como Adán, aunado al sobrecogimiento que les producen las bellezas naturales que les llenan las retinas, hacen que la vida de estos hombres no sea otra cosa que una tarea de lucha, posesión, defensa y goce. Todos estos hombres están hechos de una misma levadura: gente de acción, aventureros, tenaces, ambiciosos, padres de pueblos, rutas y genealogías. La evocación de los conquistadores asoma a menudo en el relato, implícita o explícitamente: "Aquellos hombres eran gigantes, nadie me lo quita de la cabeza; y gigantes se necesitan", dice Sotero Castillo, uno de los caciques, refiriéndose a los españoles. A esto replica Ricardo Guerra Victoria, apodado "El Amarillo", pro-

---

[5]Agustín Yáñez, "Cómo escribí *La tierra pródiga*," *La cultura en México* (Suplemento cultural de *Siempre!*), February 21, 1962, p.v.

tagonista de la novela: "Yo y tú somos gigantes. Para mí no hay imposibles".

Esta novela contiene páginas que más parecen referirse a la epopeya conquistadora que a los métodos de dominio de los jaliscienses de estas tierras bravías:

> No puede decirse que su fortuna salió de la nada, porque nada tuvieran cuando llegaron y emprendieron el avance sobre la costa. Traían arrojo y tesón, malicia y mañas, con que amasar sangre, sudor y lágrimas, cogidos como factores de riqueza, frente a tierras mostrencas o abandonadas, entre gente dispersa, abúlica, corroídos de miserias morales y físicas.
>
> Los señores entraron como ventarrón y algunas veces como la humedad, como reptiles que se arrastraban, caminaban, se distendían lentamente. Raudos o premiosos, ha sido dura su lucha, como es dura la realidad que arrostran: gente, naturaleza, problemas. Muchos años de fatigas.
>
> No era no más tomar posesión con los ojos y el deseo de aquellas extensiones. Había que asentar el pie y la mano dominantes. Entregarse a la tierra, vivir con ella para vivir de ella, explotándola.[6]

Nadie, que yo sepa, ha explorado el simbolismo del nombre del protagonista, Ricardo Guerra Victoria. Aparejada a la significación del nombre de pila—"el fuerte"—, vienen los apellidos, de obvia significación. Yáñez debió pensar, al bautizar a este personaje, en una gradación intencionada en su simbología: el hombre fuerte—que lucha— obtiene el triunfo. Pero a la vez, irónicamente, como aconteció con casi todos los conquistadores peninsulares, Guerra Victoria acaba despojado de lo que obtuvo a base de tenacidad, audacia e intrepidez. Termina vencido por las estructuras burocráticas impuestas por el programa de industrialización de la costa. "El Amarillo" razona rudamente:

> El pleito es con un fantasma que todos mientan y nadie conoce bien a bien; se la sacan con él, con él se limpian: ora le dicen "la institución", luego, que "la marcha" o "el plan", o "el consejo"; que su chucha madre. Impulsos no me han faltado de agujerar alguno para saber, para descubrir de qué se trata. Lo he reflexionado: aunque a todos esos, y a sus achichincles, ingenierillos, técnicos, me los echara al pico, de nada serviría: "la institución" seguiría en pie, caminando en mi contra con más ganas. Es como una máquina, que se echa encima sin contemplaciones.[7]

Tiene extensa estirpe en la mitología universal la asociación de tierra y mujer, en su bipolaridad de fertilidad y esterilidad. Los ritos de la vegetación y la agricultura de los misterios eleusinos, dedicados

---

[6]Agustín Yáñez, *La tierra pródiga*, Colección popular, 19 (México, D.F.: Fondo de Cultura Económica, 1971), p. 112.
[7]Ibid., p. 305.

a Deméter, Perséfone y Triptolemo, son solo una de las múltiples variantes de ese núcleo mítico. En *La tierra pródiga* hay también otra trilogía: Elena, Gertrudis y Guerra Victoria. La primera, esposa de éste, es estéril y se suicida sin dejar descendencia; la segunda le proporciona el orgullo de la paternidad. Ambas, a la vez, representan una bipolaridad erótica que, en el fondo, es sólo una forma de posesión en los personajes masculinos de este relato. Por medio de estos símbolos "se conjugan la idea de conquista de la mujer, la idea de propiedad y el afán de dominación que impulsa a estos hombres".[8]

"Si domino a una, dominaré a la otra," se promete "el Amarillo", lo que equivale a confesar que mujer y tierra son no sólo recíproco estímulo para la posesión, sino también un mismo elemento. Por ambas presas—hembras y costas—luchan Guerra Victoria y Sotero Castillo. Esta mentalidad, producto del "machismo", hace que aquél se complazca tanto en la sumisión de Elena, esposa noble pero estéril, como también en el disfrute de Gertrudis, manceba hosca pero fecunda. Elena era "la razón, el deber, la difícil facilidad, el bienestar. Gertrudis: apetito, capricho, peligro, desquite, imaginación, difícil gozo, tentación dolorosa."[9] Al final, Gertrudis, como la tierra que ella simboliza, acaba venciendo a su dominador, el cual confiesa a aquélla que "ninguna mujer, a pesar de que era eso lo que andaba buscando en ellas, en todas, sin excepción, ninguna me había hecho sentir lo que tú: el mismo gusto de dominar y ser dominado por la tierra caliente . . ."[10] En último análisis, creo que Guerra Victoria ve en la mujer, más que una entidad femenina, un mito y un instrumento: el viejo mito cíclico de la muerte y resurrección de la naturaleza, y el instrumento de la perpetuación de la especie. Bien dice "el Amarillo": "Por un hijo seré capaz de hacer otra vez la tierra caliente, caso de que desapareciera o se acabara".[11]

Veo finalmente en *La tierra pródiga* una última intencionalidad simbólica: el enfrentamiento entre las fuerzas telúricas y las fuerzas técnicas, ambas necesarias en el desarrollo humano. Gea, diosa de la tierra, y Prometeo, el titán creador de la civilización, aparecen recreados implícitamente en esta novela. Guerra Victoria de nueva cuenta resume mi interpretación cuando dice al ingeniero planificador de la costa jalisciense: "Es que, perdóneme la presunción, creo que nos completamos: usted, arriba, yo abajo; usted la inteligencia, yo, la naturaleza en bruto".[12]

---

[8]Citado en Emmanuel Carballo, *Diecinueve protagonistas de la literatura mexicana del siglo XX* (México, D.F.: Empresas Editoriales, 1965), p. 306.
[9]Yáñez, *La tierra pródiga*, p. 66.
[10]Ibid., p. 304.
[11]Ibid.
[12]Ibid., p. 161.

Las tierras flacas

El último intento novelístico de Yáñez por interpretar la realidad de Jalisco—formas de vida, lengua, personajes—está representado por *Las tierras flacas*. El ambiente de este relato hace retornar al lector a la atmósfera de *Al filo del agua*. Son de nuevo las zonas tristes, erosionadas, a las que el novelista regresa para insertar sus personajes, aunque con una diferencia: en *Las tierras flacas* Yáñez se ocupa de la vida rural: en *Al filo del agua*, de la vida municipal. El contraste de la novela que ahora analizamos con *La tierra pródiga* es obvio, como lo revela el título mismo. A la vez, ambas novelas se enlazan por el tema: el cacicazgo que sojuzga a las dos regiones, y el poder redentor de la máquina, la cual impone la dependencia del hombre frente a la técnica. La tierra juega un papel central, aunque opuesto: en *La tierra pródiga* es reto para la conquista; en *Las tierras flacas*, objeto de abandono. En aquella novela sirve de estímulo para el esfuerzo; en ésta, de fuente de fracaso. El cacicazgo es de diferente origen, naturaleza y métodos de acción. En *La tierra pródiga* está fundado sobre el derecho primitivo que da la posesión de *res nullius* (tierra de nadie); en *Las tierras flacas* lo está sobre el apoderamiento progresivo a base de dolo y usurpación. En aquella novela el cacicazgo está basado en el poder individual; en ésta, en el familiar. Los métodos de acción en el primero son energía y astucia; en el segundo, fuerza adquirida a base de endogamia y patriarcalismo.

Esas "tierras flacas" que forman el "Llano de los Tepetates" o, como alguien las llamó, quizá con ironía o piedad, "Plan de la Tierra Santa", están ubicadas, literariamente, en el noreste de Jalisco. Están constituidas por ranchos que tienen toponimias bíblicas y que dan nombre a los cinco capítulos o "estancias", como las llama el novelista: Betania, Jerusalén, Belén, Babel, Damasco y Galilea. Ahí manda Epifanio Trujillo, déspota polígamo, que impone un patriarcado basado en la sangre y la fuerza. Dos campesinos, Rómulo y Merced, padres de la difunta Teófila, se enfrentan al dilema de entregar a Trujillo, como pago de sus deudas, una máquina de coser que pertenecía a su hija, o un misérrimo trozo de tierra, última posesión que les queda en la vida. Alrededor de esta anécdota banal gira un mundo violento en que aparecen, entre otras figuras, los hijos bastardos del déspota rural; la máquina de coser, que se convierte en objeto mítico; el libertador Jacob Gallo que renueva la vida de la comunidad y, especialmente, Matiana, que es la que regula, con sus hechicerías, el mundo elemental en que viven los personajes.

La magia y la superstición predominan sobre la religión en este relato. La primera está encarnada en Matiana, zahorina rural, de rica psicología, uno de los mejores personajes creados por Yáñez. Esta mujer es una viuda solitaria—muy débilmente aparece en sus recuerdos la imagen de su esposo que, siendo joven, fue arrastrado por la "leva" de la Revolución—, pero que sublima su maternidad frustrada al convertirse en "madre" de los lugareños. Hace el bien a base de consejos, adivinaciones, conjuros, remedios corporales, valiéndose de una riquísima farmacopea. Su magia es blanca, benévola, sin sombra de satanismo, la cual hace que a Matiana se le respete, no que se le tema. Su figura personifica el sincretismo religioso, hecho de catolicismo y superstición, que prevalece en muchas comunidades rurales y semiurbanas de México. La "taumaturgia" de Matiana a menudo se realiza a base de exorcismos, hechizos, ensalmos y otras prácticas esotéricas. En un mundo sin calendario ni campanas, ella impone las fechas propicias para la recolección de hierbas terapéuticas, cumplimiento de mandas y promesas y celebración de fiestas cristianas. Ella es sacerdotisa de sus propios ritos y acaba siendo también su víctima al ser cegada por sus enemigos. Esto no le arredra y prosigue en su misión de velar por el pueblo. "Pobre carne vieja que no ha podido curtirse para dejar de temblar en presencia del miedo y del dolor", dice de sí mismma.[13] Esta celestina campesina, sibila de la "Tierra Santa", tiene como frecuente ministro a la muerte pues vaticina a su modo el deceso, algunas veces trágico, de algunos miembros de las comunidades agrarias. A la vez, es profundamennte religiosa y no se arroga poderes sobrenaturales, aunque modestamente se atribuye ser instrumento de Dios:

> De mí quieren sacar secretos que sólo Dios conoce, porque los justos juicios de Dios no más Dios, y porque sin su voluntad no se mueve la hoja del árbol, menos una hoja seca como yo. A mí acuden cuando se les cierra el mundo. Desde una aguja o una res perdida, hasta que resucite muertos y les lea el futuro. Yo no me determino sola y Dios no siempre se vale de mí, no diario me ilumina, por más que viendo las necesidades yo se lo pida con ganas de remediarlas. Estudien su catecismo, les digo. No le entendemos, responden. Métanselo de memoria, y en momentos de aflicción el apuro hará que lo entiendan y apliquen; así podrán solos leer el futuro, como seguido lo hago, sin molestar a Dios, no más con la práctica de contemplar bien las caras y los actos. El refrán lo canta claramente: Al que se ayuda, Dios lo ayuda; y también: a Dios rogando ...[14]

La farmacopea de Matiana se basa principalmente en la herbolaria y la ungüentaria del campo, las cuales constituyen un inventario vastísimo y exótico. Ella guarda en su choza, en cuya puerta hay una cruz que saluda al visitante, todo un extraordinario muestrario de materiales que le sirven para sus alquimias:

> Olor, por de pronto, a viejo; gradualmente: a húmedo; a cerrado; a estancado; a mucho tiempo guardado en cajas de maderas fragantes, en-

---

[13]Agustín Yáñez, *Las tierras flacas*, Biblioteca Básica Salvat, 47 (Estella: Salvat Editores, 1971), p. 224.
[14]Ibid., pp. 95-96.

tre yerbas no por secas menos penetrantes; mezclado a raras esencias desconocidas o vagamente reconocidas: copal, cera consumida, resina de ocote, mezquite o palo santo; agua florida y esos que llaman perfumes; yerbas, flores, maderas, aceites y grasas medicinales; aceite de comer y aceite de lámparas encendidas; unto de ardilla, de puercoespín, de jabalí, de coyote, de leopardo, de mil animales fabulosos; infundia de gallina, de pato salvaje, de golondrina, de cotorra, de tecolote, de gavilán, de zopilote, de aguililla; el misterioso, vasto reino de bálsamos y ungüentos, arómaticos unos, otros apestosos, y de polvos, en coro de nombres mágicos: Bálsamo de Fierabrante, de Judea, de María, de Guayacán, de Aloe, de Almizcle, de Lágrimas de Incienso y Mirra, de Almendras Vírgenes; Bálsamo Magistral; Ungüento de la Misericordia; Oleodeángeles; Unción de Arcángeles, Tronos y Dominaciones; Santaunción del Serafín; Pomada del Querubin; Leche de la Doncella; Linimento de la Peregrina; Agua de Oro Cocido; Agua de Contraespanto, de Contracólera, de Contralatido, de Contrarrotura; Bizma de Redaños de Toro; Emplasto del Profeta; Polvos de la Buenaventura; Polvos de la Madre del Amor Hermoso; Polvos de la Dichosamuerte, hechos con cenizas de palma, algodones, trapos y otras materias consagradas o benditas; Polvos de Ánimas, hechos con huesos de muertos insepultos; Polvos del Juicio Final, hechos con huesos, pelos, plumas, pezuñas y uñas de animales rapiegos.[15]

La magia de Matiana es una magia sin ceremonial que, como sucede siempre en estas prácticas esotéricas, pretende controlar el mundo exterior para satisfacer fines prácticos de los habitantes del "Llano". Como he ya señalado, esta mujer no se atribuye propiamente poderes de control interior. Si la mayoría de los miembros de la comunidad así lo creen, es porque la magia siempre presupone un auditorio mentalmente receptivo y sobre todo dispuesto a ser siempre engañado. En realidad, la magia de Matiana opera no por ser eficaz, sino porque los rancheros la aceptan como condición básica para justificar y complacer su propia credulidad.

La superstición, otra manifestación del mundo de la fábula, aparece también en la novela, representada en el poder mítico que, en las últimas páginas del relato, es atribuido a la máquina de coser que había pertenecido a Teófila, ahora difunta, quien empieza a ser reconocida como "santa". Esa "reliquia", prolongación mecánica de la supuesta virtud de la doncella, comienza a ser venerada y a obrar "milagros". Podría parecer del todo inverosímil esta sacralización de la máquina de coser si no supiéramos que en toda sociedad hay elementos, quizá más primitivos y menos mecánicos, que son objetos de veneración y culto. Este fenómeno siempre se da en mentes proclives a la irracionalidad y que desconocen o rechazan las leyes de la causalidad. Ni las sociedades más técnicamente desarrolladas están del todo inmunes, por lo menos en algunos de sus estratos, a ciertas

[15]Ibid., pp. 97-98.

supersticiones, religiosas o laicas. En consecuencia, no nos debe parecer extraño el que Yáñez inserte en su relato un fenómeno de esa naturaleza. Recuérdese además que en las capas sociales populares mexicanas todavía están activos muchos residuos de creencias y prácticas procedentes de las antiguas religiones mesoamericanas, Sirviéndonos de un verso de López Velarde podemos decir que en México todavía sollozan las viejas mitologías.

Como consideración sumaria debo indicar que Agustín Yáñez ha creado a los personajes de estas tres novelas desde un ángulo doble: modela seres de carne y hueso, verosímiles, bien plantados en la tierra, pero, al mismo tiempo, los concibe desde una perspectiva ultraterrena al hacerlos súbditos de la religión, del mito, de la magia y la superstición. Los coloca así en la tierra como en el cielo de lo trascendente. En la trilogía novelística que parcialmente he analizado, su autor recrea en *Al filo del agua* el México de ideología colonial y tradicionalismo católico; en *La tierra pródiga* moderniza la épica violenta de la conquista española en nuestro continente y ejemplifica, a lo mexicano, el mito de la recurrencia de vida y muerte; y en *Las tierras flacas* nos regresa a la historia prehispánica, con sus señores tribales y su mundo de pronósticos y arúspices. En verdad estas novelas nos muestran tres momentos y modos de ser de un país, es decir, tres culturas distintas en un solo pueblo verdadero: México.

18. El Tema Religioso en *Al Filo del Agua* de Agustín Yáñez

LINO GARCÍA

Like the preceding essay by Professor Bravo-Villarroel, this essay deals with the work of Augustín Yáñez; but the focus of Professor García's essay is restricted to one book: *Al filo del agua*. In particular, Professor García analyzes the quality of Mexican religious life as portrayed in a novel that has as its setting a village in Jalisco during the months immediately before and after the outbreak of the Mexican Revolution.

El año 1947 significa un paso adelante de gran trascendencia en la novela mexicana y marca la cumbre en el arte creativo de Agustín Yáñez. En ese año se publicó *Al filo del agua*, su obra sobresaliente y, al mismo tiempo, una de las creaciones más logradas de la novelística hispanoamericana.[1] El autor explora la subconciencia colectiva de un pueblo mexicano en la etapa anterior al inicio de la Revolución. Como muchos pueblos mexicanos de aquel entonces y de hoy, vivía pendiente de las campanas de la iglesia, con todos sus sentimientos opresivamente suprimidos por esta institución. Bajo esta opresión religiosa, se desbordan las pasiones humanas de los habitantes. El amor, la ambición, el deseo sexual y lo humano en general pide un cauce por donde manifestarse.[2]

Desde el momento en que el lector se engolfa en las primeras páginas de *Al filo del agua*, se revela ese pueblo lóbrego, hermético, conventual, regido por ese ambiente religioso. Es "un pueblo de mujeres enlutadas", "pueblo triste y oscuro", en el cual aparecen esos personajes sacados de la realidad mexicana, cuya existencia se determina bajo la influencia de la iglesia. Los conflictos de estos seres humanos y las acciones que se desarrollan dentro de la novela revelan

[1]Emilio González López, *Historia crítica de la literatura hispanoamericana* (New York: Holt, Rinehart and Winston, 1968), p. 679.
[2]Ibid.

ciertas ideas que se convierten en temas que reflejan el ambiente mexicano. El pueblo que describe Yáñez en su novela es un pueblo anticuado antes de la Revolución de 1910.

En este pueblo, como en muchos otros pueblos mexicanos, la Revolución era una esperanza; era la esperanza que el mexicano esperaba para que lo salvara de su tristeza y de la supresión de sus deseos. En esta obra novelística existe la frustración y monotonía que son ocasionadas por la iglesia y por la rigida tradición impuesta por la cultura del país. Esta frustración provoca el deseo de revolución, y esta rebeldía pronto estalla en forma de la Revolución de 1910.

Este pueblo es de gente bastante religiosa, convertida por supersticiones que ahoga—e impide—a todos los habitantes que vivan más alegres. Es un pueblo conventual, de vida triste, hipócrito, hermético, en el cual el jefe político, el sacerdote y las familias más importantes sostienen al pueblo dentro de convenciones. Es un pueblo lleno de perjuicios, de sospechas que llegan de afuera trayendo nuevas ideas que pueden degenerar a la juventud. Es un pueblo sin fiestas. No se oye ninguna clase de música alegre, ni se ve gente bailando. La única clase de música alegre que se oye es la de las campanas de la iglesia, y éstas son más importantes que cualquier otra música porque se considera casi un pecado oír algo alegre. Cuando las campanas doblan, la gente se postra en las calles o en la plaza. Cuando doblan éstas a las doce y a las tres, los hombres se quitan los sombreros. Al oír la Campana Mayor, los ancianos madrugadores van a la iglesia arrodillados en oscuros lechos.

El sol es la única alegría del pueblo. Cuando oscurese, suben los miedos y deseos de la gente de este pueblo.Todos los deseos sexuales se consideran algo malo que se debe de esconder en lo oscuro. Nunca se oye alguna conversación de amor en la plaza o en el parque de noche y menos de día. Nunca se ve una pareja agarrados de las manos. De noche solo los habitantes pasan el tiempo esperando el amanecer para empezar otro día igual que el pasado. La alegría que presenta el sol es una alegría que casi no se nota porque la disimula la gente de este pueblo tan solemne. Es un pueblo de perpetua cuaresma: "Primavera y verano atemperados por una lluvia de ceniza. Oleo del Dies Irae inexhausto para las orejas. Agua del Asperges para las frentes. Puas del Miserere para las espaldas. Canon del Memento, Homo, para los ojos. Sal del Requiem Aeternam para la Memoria. Los cuatro jinetes de las Postrimerías, gendarmes municipales, rondan sin descanso las calles, las casas y las conciencias. De Profundis para lenguas y gargantas".[3]

Es una vergüenza casarse en este pueblo de deseos oprimidos. La pareja que se case siente mucha vergüenza al salir de su casa los primeros días después del casamiento. La mujer no quiere salir con su

---

[3]Agustín Yáñez, *Al filo del agua* (México, D.F.: Editorial Porrúa, 1963), p. 9.

marido, y el hombre no quiere ni platicar con sus amigos. Pero esto no es raro, sino que es lo más normal en el pueblo. La atmósfera de este pueblo es una de tristeza, de desconsuelo, de vidas amargas llenas de pena, y de desilución. No hay alegría en este pueblo; no hay música, ni risas, ni chismes, ni canciones, ni gritos, ni llantos. La iglesia es suprema, es lo más importante en las vidas de los habitantes.

La unidad de *Al filo del agua* que hace llamarla novela es la atmósfera. Antes del primer capítulo, en el "Acto Preparatorio" Yáñez describe la atmósfera en la que actúan los personajes. En estilo poético describe la atmósfera como un pueblo de "mujeres enlutadas", un pueblo seco, sin árboles, ni huertos, un pueblo sin alameda, un pueblo de ánimas donde las calles son puentes de necesidad para ir a la iglesia. La atmósfera se caracteriza por una monotonía. Hay gran frustración cuya causa principal es la iglesia, que ejerse una fuerte influencia sobre los habitantes del pueblo, especialmente sobre las muchachas, ocasionándoles complejos y sentimientos de frustración e inhibición.

Es un esfuerzo destacado del autor de indagar en el subconciente de sus criaturas, ahondar allí, captar sus frustraciones, deseos y aspiraciones, para presentar al lector un trozo de la condición humana mexicana. El crítico norteamericano John S. Brushwood ha dicho:

> It would be reasonable to say that the town's hermeticism is ecclesiastical, for its rhythm and its apparent reason for being are controlled by the Church. However, the Church itself is as circumscribed as any inhabitant of the town. The members of the clergy do not move in a common direction, have only glimpses of the quality of being. Neither ritualism, nor organizationalism, nor even ordinary human understanding can break the spell of restraint, fears, death, cast by the circumstances which past attitudes and actions have created.[4]

Dentro de este pueblo lóbrego está siempre la presencia del poder de la iglesia, que contrarresta los deseos interiores de los feligreses. Dentro de este cuadro surge la influencia de la religión. Cada acción dentro del hilo narrativo, cada conflicto, sea interior o exterior (de los personajes) que se encamina hacia lo positivo, provoca una reacción por parte de la iglesia. Así, pues, el tema religioso se destaca en un pueblo de Jalisco, un pueblo fanatizado, ignorante, supersticioso, y amodorrado por cuatro siglos de dominación católica. Carece, sin embargo, de sectarismo católico y clerofobia. El autor se echa fuera del tema, y lo contempla con serenidad estética. Yáñez convierte ritos religiosos, atmósfera de incienso y beatería, personajes ascéticos torturados por las tentaciones y vidas humildes torturados por el de-

---

[4] John S. Brushwood, *Mexico in Its Novels* (Austin: University of Texas Press, 1966), pp. 9-10.

seo de la carne en un tema de arte y en forma de novela que retrata fielmente el paisaje mexicano de aquel entonces.

Tienen en práctica los sacerdotes la antigua guerra de la iglesia católica hacia lo sexual. Desde tiempo pasado se había exaltado la castidad como virtud máxima. Así, pues, todo contacto con la mujer debe evitarse. Fue una reacción, desde siglos pasados, contra el libertinaje y la orgía sexual en que había caído la sociedad pagana en Roma. Entonces, el pueblo mismo se convierte en una evocación angustiosa de la vida de un pueblo que reniega de la vida en busca obstinada de una monstruosa santidad. Con el tema religioso Yáñez ha logrado ser mexicano así como universal.

El tema religioso se mueve no solamente dentro de las acciones de los personajes, sino que es parte intrínseca también de la realidad objetiva que rodea al pueblo. El deseo de existir, de vivir, de cambio, de nueva vida revelado en estos seres infunden en el pueblo un choque inmediato con las restricciones, lo negativo y lo tradicional que proviene de la iglesia. Es este conflicto primario entre lo deseado y lo prohibido que produce, inevitablemente, un cambio. Los acontecimientos dependen en ese impulso vital creado por las tradiciones ecclesiásticas que niegan la vida normal en pugna constante con los deseos suprimidos de los habitantes. Asímismo, los personajes contribuyen a percibir y sentir la anticipación que forma el eje de la novela. Esta anticipación dará resultado en un cambio en el existir del pueblo.

Al filo del agua presenta al hombre mexicano en su frustración, la frustración que se apodera del hombre cuando algo le falta o cuando no es dueño de su propia libertad, la "libertad humana" de la que tanto hablan la mayoría de los países mundiales. La narración está fragmentada porque son muchos los personajes que presentan sus vidas desde sus propios puntos de vista. Yáñez no se contenta con presentarnos el exterior y el interior de sus personajes, sino que profundiza verdaderamente en los caracteres de éstos y nos presenta un análises, casi se puede decir clínico, del personaje, mediante el uso del hilo de conciencia. El monólogo interior ofrece una imagen psicológica de la vida de los personajes. Cada uno de los personajes más importantes dice lo que hace, y por qué lo hace y también lo que siente al hacerlo. Esto queda claro mediante la presentación de los diferentes niveles de los procesos mentales.

Don Timoteo Limón, uno de los primeros personajes con que nos encontramos en la novela, revela sus deseos escondidos en las primeras páginas de esta obra. El desea la muerte de su tullida esposa porque la pobre ha sufrido mucho, pero luego se pone a pensar que "él ya lleva muchos años de martirio y si ella se muere, él podría casarse con alguna muchacha lozana todavía".[5] Veremos este choque

---

[5]Yáñez, *Al filo del agua*, p. 20.

constante entre los deseos ocultos de los habitantes en conflicto con la realidad objetiva de gran influencia religiosa. Después de este personaje, el autor nos presenta a Merceditas Toledo, Hija de María recién recibida. Esta chica, por medio de monólogo interior, nos revela su psicología. El recibir una carta de un pretendiente le causa tormento—pues es ella Hija de María—por lo consiguiente, no puede ni debe pensar en nada amoroso. De nuevo aqui la influencia religiosa del pueblo que, por muchos años, ha podido suprimir los deseos normales de sus feligreses, pues Merceditas, Celadora de las Hijas de María, atormentada por sus pensamientos impíos y por los deseos que la impulsan hacia lo normal, se siente arrastrada por la fuerte tradición religiosa. Al recibir la carta de Julián, su primer impulso sería de romperla y hacerla pedazos—pues ella es Hija de María. Distintas sensaciones le allegan a su pensamiento; le llama "la maldita carta, algunas de cuyas palabras tenía pegadas en el cerebro: "amor", "tristeza", "deseo", "poder hablar", "comprendernos", "toda la vida".[6] Pero, en desesperación, como para convencerse de su fortaleza, al fin exclama, y vence otra vez la tradición religiosa contra los deseos normales de esta joven.

Poco a poco se nos presentan los varios personajes dentro de la novela, y el autor revela una tensión dentro de cada personaje que está al filo de algo, es decir, para explotar. Es el ambiente religioso que busca una salida para sus sentimientos y pasiones. El crítico Joseph Sommers ha dicho: "*Al filo del agua* is a novel of imminence. Set on 'the edge of the storm', during the year and a half leading to and including the first outbreak of 1910, it has the Revolution as a presiding presence".[7]

Dentro de este ambiente religioso aparece el cura del pueblo, don Dionicio Martínez. Como representante de la iglesia, se siente obligado y responsable por la conducta de sus feligreses. El, más que nadie del pueblo, representa la rígida influencia religiosa en las vidas de los habitantes. Su lucha es mantener el pueblo libre de toda influencia extranjera que puede dañar la vida conventual de ese pueblo de mujeres enlutadas. Su presencia representa la iglesia dominante en las vidas de los personajes. Bajo la dominación de él se desarrollan los ejercicios de encierro a los cuales acuden los varones del pueblo. Allí, juntos con los demás, se encuentran haciendo ejercicios espirituales los hombres de este pueblo. Gran madrugador, al levantarse por la mañana ya tiene en sus primeros pensamientos las primeras oraciones del día: "Ave María Purísima del Refugio, sin pecado original concebida. En el nombre del Padre, y del Hijo, y del Espíritu Santo." Después de esto, "Peccavi, Domine, Miserere Mei".[8] Después le viene

---
[6]Ibid., p. 27.
[7]Joseph Sommers, *After the Storm* (Albuquerque: University of New Mexico Press, 1968), p. 37.
[8]Yáñez, *Al filo del agua*, p. 40.

todo el pensamiento de su responsabilidad, el desenfreno de las costumbres, la descristianización del universo, la amenaza en contra de su pobre rebaño que se le ha encomendado. Su vida representa total abstinencia en los asuntos sociales. Jamás recibe a solas a las mujeres. Hombre de conciencia estricta, humilde, retraído, y rígido en sus creencias. El conduce a sus feligreses por los ejercicios espirituales de encierro. Predica contra la lujuria, sobre las penas del infierno, usa el hedor de azufre y brea que llena la capilla esa noche, para crear el ambiente de estos ejercicios espirituales. Pero, será difícil detener el paso del tiempo, pues ya llegan voces ajenas del extranjero a cambiar el ambiente del pueblo.

Uno de estos personajes que trae este deseo de cambio es Micaela. Acaba de llegar de Guadalajara y de la Ciudad de México donde ha conocido un ambiente mejor, todo contrario al que existe en su pueblo. Se convierte en coqueta del pueblo que pronto incita a ciertos individuos. Uno de ellos es el hijo de don Timoteo Limón, Damián, que acaba de regresar del norte. Con ellos llegan al pueblo otros puntos de vista, otra manera de pensar. Así, pues, se revela Micaela como uno de los personajes más humanos y más rebeldes. Ella y Damián son los primeros en rebelarse contra las tradiciones religiosas que habían regido el pueblo por muchos años. Son los instrumentos que utiliza Yáñez para presentar la reacción contra la influencia de la iglesia que tanto había dominado el pensamiento y las vidas de los feligreses. Para vengarse de ella, Damián concluye no solamente matándola sino que causa la muerte de su propio padre, don Timoteo Limón.

En cierto modo la muerte de Micaela por Damián es el resultado directo de su provocación, así como el resultado indirecto del hermeticismo y supresión que sufre el pueblo. En estos dos personajes se capta una intensa frustración y angustia interior causada, en parte, por la supresión de los deseos normales. Otras causas del estallido que ocurre en el pueblo son el aislamiento del pueblo de las corrientes culturales, la represión sexual, la falta de libertad de pensar y el predominio de la iglesia sobre las actividades de los personajes. Son estas criaturas almas en penas, atormentadas, en conflicto consigo mismas, motivadas por el deseo sexual y otras pasiones humanas.[9] Revelan también sus estados psicológicos: el estado morboso en que se encuentran los habitantes del pueblo, y por extensión la situación de la Republica, que se encontraba en 1910 al filo del cambio socioeconómico más importante de su historia.[10]

Son dos los otros sacerdotes que componen parte de este ambiente religioso dentro de este pueblo. El Padre José María Islas,

---

[9] Luis Leal, *Breve historia de la literatura hispanoamericana* (New York: Alfred A. Knopf, 1971), p. 281.
[10] Ibid., p. 282.

fanático a lo extremo. Es él, más que nadie, quien impone lo negativo a todo aspecto sexual de la vida humana. Con el nace toda vigilancia que, aun entre familias, se hace contra este deseo normal, hasta que se torna en algo asqueroso, aun en los matrimonios. Por culpa de él se establece las estricta separación de los sexos, en las calles, en la iglesia, aun los recién casados tienen vergüenza de salir fuera de sus casas por temor de miradas frías dirigidas por miembros de sus familias. Lleva consigo el padre Islas una obsesión con todo lo sexual en la vida. Es él quien sirve de director espiritual de las Hijas de María, y utiliza su importancia suprimiendo en ellas todo deseo de normalidad. Su estado psicológico contiene una nota negativa, pues él comparte con don Dionicio Martínez parte de la culpa por el ambiente rígido que existe en el pueblo.

Dentro de este ambiente religioso aparecen varios y distintos personajes, todos los cuales prestan autenticidad al desarrollo de los conflictos dentro de los cuales aparecen los temas. María, la sobrina de don Dionicio, ha podido vivir en un mundo subjetivo bajo la protección de su tío. La supresión que él mantiene sobre las acciones de ella le produce una constante frustración, que le dirige hacia la rebelión, y al fin de la novela la encontramos en camino con unos revolucionarios que pasan por el pueblo. Al fin, ella también encuentra su libertad, aunque es todo lo contrario de los deseos de su tío cura. El campañero Gabriel, criado bajo la influencia del cura don Dionicio, también sufre ese dolor de frustración al no saber quién fue su madre y al no poder comunicar el amor pueril que él siente por María. La falta de cauce para sus sentimientos hace que se envuelva en sus campanas. Allí pasa mucho de su tiempo, y el pueblo se rige pendiente de su tocar. Sin embargo, toda su expresión artística, así como su deseo de comunicar sus sentimientos, le producen una frustración muy similar a la de los demás personajes dentro de la novela.

Toda la novela enfatiza lo negativo, hasta el punto de romperse y seguir la libertad. El tono anticlerical percibe la supresión como el mayor mal infligido en los habitantes. Rechaza un dogmatismo fanático que en toda manifestación subraya lo negativo sobre vida y progreso.[11] Al final de la novela, cuando todo está al filo del agua, es decir, cuando la Revolución está para estallar, rompen sus cadenas los personajes, y al mismo tiempo, se llena el pueblo de un nuevo espíritu de libertad. De todos los personajes, el que sufre mayor tormento es el mismo padre Dionicio Martínez, quien aun ya viéndose lo inevitable de la historia, no hace más que celebrar misa, pues es todo lo que sabe hacer, aun mientras sus parroquianos le van buscando señas de su destrucción. Es inútil detener el correr de la historia, y el pueblo, como muchos más de la República Mexicana, espera el cambio que traerá la Revolución.

[11]Sommers, *After the Storm*, p. 62.

Con gran maestría y arte Yáñez ha hecho un cuadro de este ambiente tan mexicano. Por medio de las prácticas religiosas medievales de un pueblucho aislado ha surgido de la pluma de este novelista mexicano una obra de arte que pinta el paisaje del país. Hace un estudio de las ceremonias religiosas y de la repercusión que en la conciencia y en la conducta de los habitantes tiene la prédica sacerdotal y el exceso de fanatismo y superstición. Dentro de este ambiente de ritos religiosos; de atmósfera de incienso y beatería; de personajes ascéticos, torturados por las tentaciones y el constante terror del infierno—se presentan los personajes de la novela. Las acciones de ellos, sus conflictos y la interrelación unos con otros producen los varios argumentos que sirven de vehículos para llevar acabo el pensamiento central que se propone presentar el novelista. Este pensamiento central se nos convierte en el tema religioso. Presentando este tema dentro de la novela, Yáñez presta una visión vívida a este pueblo mexicano, como muchos otros que abundan en la Republica mexicana. Así como la Revolución trajo cambio a la nación, del mismo modo una nueva época llega a este pueblo de mujeres enlutadas.

19. Octavio Paz: Mexico, the United States, and the World

JOHN HADDOX

Octavio Paz, Mexico's best-known poet, social critic, and interpreter of Mexican life and thought, views his country, the United States, and the world from a humanist perspective that enjoys popularity among many Latin American intellectuals who no longer look to the Catholic Church for spiritual direction. It is his hope that modern man will discover a new holiness that is nonreligious but aesthetic and moral in nature.

Born in 1914, Octavio Paz, essayist-poet-diplomat, has been at once a man of Mexico and a man of the world, very Mexican and very much an international figure. The latter title is due not just to the fact that he has been active all over the world: in Spain during the Civil War in the 1930s, in California for two years as a Guggenheim Fellow in the early 1940s, in New York with Mexico's United Nations staff, and with the Mexican diplomatic service in France, Japan, Switzerland, and India (where he was Ambassador until the autumn of 1968); even more, it is due to the fact that his concerns have clearly extended beyond Mexico to those of the human situation.[1]

The origins of Paz's most widely read book of essays, *The Labyrinth of Solitude* (1950), can be traced, at least partially, to experiences during the years of his fellowship in California and his vigorous reaction against assumptions of racial superiority that he discovered in many North Americans. This work, which includes brilliant, incisive explications of differences between the cultures and values prevalent in Mexico and in the United States, is concerned basically with the problem of resolving the imperfection of human

---

[1]Paz's activities in the diplomatic field are part of a Latin American tradition that includes such literary figures as Pablo Neruda of Chile and Miguel Angel Asturias of Guatemala. The blending of literary and philosophical endeavors is in no way unique in Latin America: witness such writers as José Pereira de Graça Aranha of Brazil, José Enrique Rodó of Uruguay, and José Vasconcelos of Mexico.

solitude into a condition of wholeness or health characteristic of communion. In this book his "dazzling talent for blending elements of prose and poetry together on the same page"[2] is strikingly evident.

The objective of this essay is to examine Paz's reflections on what has happened in Mexico since he wrote *The Labyrinth*. These reflections have appeared primarily in *The Other Mexico: Critique of the Pyramid* and *Alternating Current*.[3] *The Other Mexico* was inspired by events of the autumn of 1968 when large numbers of students were imprisoned, wounded, and killed by Mexican authorities. About that time Paz (along with other Mexican poets) was asked to compose a poem to submit to the cultural committee of the Olympic games, which were to take place in Mexico City and which the authorities feared would be disrupted by dissident students. Paz angrily resigned his position as Mexican Ambassador to India and wrote a bitter poem in which he speaks of "a whole nation come to shame."[4]

Among the questions concerning Mexico and the Uniited States that will be examined here are the following: Can we speak? Can we listen? Can we, speaking and listening, communicate and possibly achieve (or at least approximate) an international, human community based on a philosophy of communion?[5] In attempting to answer these questions, we will look briefly at Paz's views of the Mexican character[6] and that of the North American, at the relations between us as they have been and are and could and can be, and at the philosophy of history that is the basis for his views.

The Problem of Mexico

Early in *The Other Mexico*, Paz proclaims that in Mexico there has been "a horror—it would not be too much to call it a sacred horror—of anything like intellectual criticism and dissidence";[7] yet without these a pluralistic democracy appropriate for a multiple culture like that of Mexico is impossible. He comments with irony that every dictatorship leads to two forms of expression: the

[2]Martin S. Stabb, *In Quest of Identity* (Chapel Hill: University of North Carolina Press, 1967), p. 197.

[3]"Recently published" in English that is; actually the essays included date from two periods: 1959 to 1961 and 1965 to March 1967. They were published first as a book in Mexico in 1967.

[4]This is dicussed in Muriel Rukeyer's introduction to Paz's *Configurations*, trans. G. Aroul et al. (New York: New Directions, 1971).

[5]In *The Labyrinth of Solitude: Life and Thought in Mexico*, the same issue is raised in a different way when Paz writes that "we must join together in inventing our common future. World history has become everyone's task, and our own labyrinth is the labyrinth of all mankind." (New York: Grove Press, 1961), p. 173.

[6]In an interview of Paz by Rita Guibert, published in *Seven Voices*, trans. Frances Partridge (New York: Alfred Knopf, 1973), Paz remarks that most of what he says about Mexico applies to the whole of Latin America.

[7]*The Other Mexico: Critique of the Pyramid*, trans. Lysander Kemp (New York: Grove Press, 1972), p. 30.

monologue and the mausoleum—"Moscow and Mexico City are full of gagged people and monuments to the Revolution."[8]

A second major need, Paz insists, is for an open and honest search for Mexican identity, which need results partly from the nation's mixed heritages—Indian and Spanish—and partly from the propensity of Mexicans to imitate others (an effect of a colonial mentality that has lingered in Mexico long after the expulsion of Spain). Further, Paz notes that Mexico is not one nation, but two, and that the two Mexicos, a developed and an undeveloped, differ not merely economically but also psychically, historically, and culturally. In addition, he complains that the developed Mexico forces its model on the other Mexico "without noticing that the model fails to correspond to our true historic, psychic, and cultural reality and is instead a mere copy (and a degraded copy) of the North American archetype."[9] Thus, he argues that development should correspond to the real situation in Mexico in order that it be a natural unfolding, a free and harmonious growth.

Paz views as incompatible the three major goals of twentieth century Mexico: creation of a new state, social reform, and economic progress. (At least this is true of the last two.) To explain why they are incompatible, and to show why the conflict was decided in favor of economic development at the expense of social justice, he turns to the history of Mexico.

Paz notes that the Mexican is "Castilian streaked with Aztec"[10] and that Spanish power merely replaced Aztec power and continued it, leaving a "thread of domination" from Aztec rulers, through Spanish viceroys, to Mexican presidents, a system that is centralist and authoritarian.[11] In *Alternating Current*, Paz explains that the Institutional Revolutionary Party (the PRI, "that monumental logical and linguistic invention of Mexican politics")[12] is the natural product of a centralist and authoritarian point of view.

---

[8]Ibid., p. 11. He further notes that "the experiences of Russia and Mexico are conclusive: without democracy, economic development has no meaning." Ibid., p. 10.

[9]Ibid., p. 73.

[10]On this point Stephen Clissold, in his *Latin America, New World, Third World* (New York: Praeger, 1972), writes: "Some, like the poet and thinker, Octavio Paz (b. 1914), hold that the Mexican mind is still scarred by the Aztecs' deeply rooted obsession with violence and death and by the traumatic experience of the Spanish Conquest" [p. 308]; and in *The Other Mexico*, Paz objects to the Mexican penchant for extolling the Aztecs as the highest culture of the pre-Hispanic world in that area (witness the Museum of Anthropology in Mexico City). He urges, rather, for Mexicans to seek an archetype, an Indian heritage model, in the Zapotecs, Olmecs, Mayans, Tarascans, or Otomi.

[11]In the interview by Rita Guibert published in *Seven Voices*, p. 247, Paz criticizes *caudillismo* and notes that "The caudillo is an extraordinary being and I want for Latin America the opposite: to be an extraordinary people governed by ordinary leaders!"

[12]Octavio Paz, *Alternating Current*, trans. Helen R. Lane (New York: Viking, 1973), p. 18.

He urges that the Mexican's concern be for an economic development that is proper to a plural Mexico and compatible with social justice. Even more he feels that Mexico is moving toward a condition of crisis in which the two possible alternatives would be "democratic social reform or reactionary violence." If the ways to find independent and original means of growth are not discovered or developed, he fears the results would be, first, violent anarchy, and then a pyramid of power topped by a dictatorship of Mexican capitalists, the military, and U.S. business interests—with the masses at the bottom, helpless!

The Problem of Relations Between the United States and Mexico

The Mexican philosopher, Samuel Ramos, in his *Profile of Man and Culture in Mexico*, has discussed at length the unfortunate (and undeserved) but real "inferiority complex" of the average Mexican in relation to the North American. Ramos has observed a resulting tendency for these Mexicans to imitate the "colossus of the north," which is the source of the failure to solve their own problems. Paz thus asks hopefully: "Will we now, at last, be capable of thinking for ourselves?"[13]

As was noted earlier, Paz feels that developed Mexico often copies the most degraded aspects of cultural and social life in the United States. He proclaims, however, that one characteristic of many North Americans ("Blacks and Chicanos, women and the young, artists and intellectuals") that should be emulated is a great capacity for criticism, socio-political criticism and self-criticism, that has been largely absent in Mexico and in Latin America generally. In fact, he comments that most persons in that part of the world have not learned to think with real freedom and that this is a moral, more than an intellectual, problem because "the world of a spirit is measured by its capacity for enduring the truth."[14] Thus, paradoxically it seems that one of the most important things Mexicans can learn from North Americans is to think for themselves (i.e., not to learn from or at least not to copy them).

In an interview with Rita Guibert, Paz expressed a great truth: "the opposition between Latin America and the United States is not reducible to economic and political differences, such as development and underdevelopment, imperialism and colonialism, capitalist democracy and feudal caudillismo, etc. If these differences were to disappear, other more profound ones would persist: two contradictory views of time, work, the body, leisure, death, good and all things in this and the next world."[15] In *The Other Mexico* he identifies civiliza-

---

[13] Paz, *The Other Mexico*, p. x.
[14] Ibid., p. xi.
[15] Guibert, *Seven Voices*, p. 256.

tions as "styles of living and dying."[16] These factors make it particularly unfortunate, Paz believes, that Mexico has only known two recent models of development: United States-capitalist or Soviet Union-Marxist. He remarks that these are equally disastrous, but the previously mentioned lack of intellectual-moral freedom makes it difficult (though not impossible) to discover alternatives that are unique and proper to Mexico.[17]

Problems of the Modern World

Paz notes that it is the young people (and some not so young Blacks, Chicanos, women, artists, and intellectuals) of "the most advanced and progressive society in the world, the United States" who are questioning the validity of the very principles that underlie their society: "progress and prosperity."[18] He argues that many persons are seeing that the true face of the philosophy of progress is "a featureless blank" and that we are now becoming aware that the kingdom of progress promises a future that is "impalpable, unreachable, perpetual." Progress has peopled history with the marvels and monsters of technology but it has depopulated the life of man. It has given us "more things but not more being."[19]

Speaking of "underdeveloped lands" in *Alternating Current*, Paz complains that the very term is a result of our fixation on the idea of social and economic progress. Aside from the fact that he opposes both cultural uniformity and any attempts to reduce all men to a single model (industrial society), he also doubts whether the tie between economic prosperity and cultural excellence is one of cause and effect. Moreover, he insists, "the rush to 'develop' reminds me of nothing so much as a frantic race to arrive at the gates of Hell ahead of everyone else."[20]

Paz urges that a part of man that has been humiliated and buried by the morality of progress, the part that reveals itself in art and love, must become dominant. Thus the definition of man as a "worker" should be replaced with that of "a being who desires." A concern for the "implacable phantasm of the future" must be replaced by a concern for "the spontaneous reality of the now." He argues that the other alternative is "to perish in a suicidal explosion or to sink, deeper and deeper, into the current process in which the production of goods is in danger of becoming less than the production of refuse."[21]

---

[16]Paz, *The Other Mexico*, p. 38.

[17]In the introduction to *The Other Mexico*, Paz notes that, while Mexico needs to find her own way, communication with the United States is important and true dialog between these nations will be possible if each can freely dialog with itself.

[18]Ibid., p. 8.

[19]Ibid., p. 7. Later (on p. 68) he exclaims: "Whoever builds a house for future happiness builds a prison for the present."

[20]Paz, *Alternating Current*, p. 19.

[21]Paz, *The Other Mexico*, pp. 8-9.

Philosophy of History

In *Alternating Current*, Paz argues, in opposition to two dominant theories, that history is not rectilinear-progressive and it is not a circular process. In explaining his view of history he points out that until recently the developed nations (mainly European and the United States) have been the *agents* of history, while the Third World Nations (much of Latin America, Asia, and Africa) have been the *objects* of history. Now this has changed (or is changing); now no race or nation or economic class has a monopoly on the future. Rather, "history," he proclaims, "is a daily invention, a permanent creation: a hypothesis, a game, a wager against the unpredictable. Not a science, but a form of wisdom; not a technique, but an art."[22] With history as "art, wisdom, invention," we are *all* its agents. We can *choose* our history, thus moving against what Paz terms (in the interview with Rita Guibert) "our disastrous progress toward uniformity among men." After explaining to Guibert that preserving cultural diversities in a society (or among societies) does *not* necessarily mean preserving economic hierarchies and that what must be opposed is a static cultural homogeneity, he announces: "What sets worlds in motion is the interplay of differences, their attractions and repulsions. The ideal of a single civilization for everyone, implicit in the cult of progress and technique, impoverishes and mutilates us. Every view of the world that becomes extinct, every culture that disappears, diminishes a possibility of life."[23] Carlos Fuentes has pointed out the similarity of Paz's notion to Nietzche's concern about "the physiogomy of cultures, the particular form and the unique mission of each of them."

Paz urges a plural world and argues that the task of our times is to conceive, discover, develop "viable models of development, models less inhuman, costly, senseless than those we have now."[24] For an example of what is beginning to happen, he notes that a radically new art is dawning, an art unrelated to rectilinear time:

> There is no one center, and time has lost its former coherence: East and West, Yesterday and Tomorrow exist as a confused jumble in each one of us. Different times and different spaces are combined in a here and now that is everywhere at once. A synchronic vision is replacing the former diachronic vision of art.... The works of the new time that is aborning will not be based on the idea of linear succession, but on the idea of combination: the conjunction, the diffusion, the reunion of language, spaces, and times. Fiesta and contemplation. *An art of Configuration.*[25]

[22]Paz, *Alternating Current*, pp. 192-93.
[23]Guibert, *Seven Voices*, pp. 267-68. In his *Claude Levi-Strauss, An Introduction*, trans. J. S. Bernstein and Maxine Bernstein (Ithaca: Cornell University Press, 1970), pp. 95-97, Paz is caustic in his criticism of the North American "melting-pot" ideal.
[24]Paz, *The Other Mexico*, p. 68.
[25]Paz, *Alternating Current*, p. 21.

Paz argues that a model for such an art (and for a world in which such an art would flourish) is non-Western. The basic unit in Western life and thought is the individual, often indivisible, entity: in metaphysics (being), in psychology (the self), in social sciences (political bodies, class, nation). He insists, moreover, that this model is erroneous and continually denied and destroyed by reality: "dialectics, poetry, eroticism, mysticism, and in the realm of history, war and internal conflicts are the violent, spontaneous forms whereby Otherness reminds the One of its existence." Now the basic unity is insubstantial, multiple, ever-changing. The archetype of this reality is found, Paz notes, in India where plurality, flux, and relation are emphasized and "just as elements are combinations, the individual is a society."[26]

Finally, in the interview with Rita Guibert, he insists that modern man needs to discover a new (nonreligious) holiness that would be the point of convergence of art and poetry, of freedom and love; and in *Alternating Current* he suggests that persons in the United States lack a philosophy of such holiness but many are seeking one, while, with a sorely needed freedom and spirit of self-criticism, the Third World could well move toward one. In fact, after noting that many persons deny poetic or artistic achievement among Latin Americans because of an unconscious extension of the notion of "underdevelopment" to the area of artistic creation, and after admitting that it has been a continent of "obtuse, grasping oligarchies, bloody dictatorships, oppressed peoples, and governments that are puppets of Washington," Paz reminds us that "since the days of Rubén Darío, this somber world has produced a series of good poets"[27] (and, this writer would add, artists).

Because, as William F. Cooper puts it, for Paz the aesthetic-moral experience "is one which shatters barriers that separate one human being from another and any given individual from himself," and because this experience "delivers the individual from the fragmentation and emptiness of life by engendering wholeness in one's attitude toward himself and love in his relationships to others,"[28] the lands of Latin America, lands of poets and artists, might well be the birthplace of a new whole-holy philosophy.

This is the dream of Octavio Paz. May it come true!

---

[26]Ibid, p. 123.
[27]Ibid., p. 34.
[28]William F. Cooper, "The Moral Quality of Aesthetic Experience as Developed by Octavio Paz," in *Filosofia*, vol. 3 of *Anais do VIII Congresso Interamericano de Filosofia e V da Sociedade Interamericano de Filosofia*, 3 vols. (São Paulo: Instituto Brasileiro de Filosofia, 1974), p. 279. In his *Claude Levi-Strauss*, Paz writes: "It is a phenomenon common to all the arts: man communicates with himself, discovers himself and invents himself, by means of the work of art" (p. 68) and "Human nature, while not an essence or an idea, is a concerto, a harmony, a proportion." (p. 133).

PART III

SPANISH SOUTH AMERICA AND THE CARIBBEAN

Spanish South America and Caribbean islands were colonized in much the same manner as was Mexico, but there were differences in the ways natural and human resources of these areas were exploited, in relationships between crown and colony, and in the way the Roman Catholic Church took root. In recent years, one of the distinguishing features of South American Catholicism has been the militancy and reform-mindedness of some of its clergy, as may be illustrated by the *tercermundistas* in Argentina and the Golconda movement in Colombia. Contributions to Part III feature the work of historians who have examined topics in both the colonial and national periods, essays dealing with twentieth-century political thought and practice relating to religious affairs, and studies of the religious aspects of selected prose and poetry.

HISTORY

Judgments vary greatly concerning methods and objectives of Catholic clergy who participated in the Spanish conquest and who struggled for centuries to consolidate and protect the accomplishments of their missionary effort. Given the vast geographic area involved, the problems of confronting differing indigenous cultures, and the dangers posed by diverse environmental conditions, this missionary and pastoral effort represents an important chapter in the history of Roman Catholicism. Although contemporary advocates of religious liberty and cultural pluralism find much to criticize in the church history of Spanish South America and the Caribbean, traditional Catholic intolerance and authoritarianism were not altogether different from characteristics of some non-Catholic institutions of pre-twentieth-century times.

20. Colonial Education and Indoctrination of the Andean Indians

BROTHER ROBERT D. WOOD, S. M.

The religious and vocational education of the Indians living in the northern Andean regions was well planned by the missionaries of the early colonial period. On the basis of policies developed in Queen Isabella's court, Indians were relocated into centers referred to as *resguardos* and *doctrinas*, wherein they received religious instruction and training in useful crafts. Professor Wood's article describes this program and its implementation.

Religion in Latin America and the role and status of the Indians during the colonial period are themes that have suffered from longstanding, unchallenged statements. Frequently, these statements have been exaggerations, one-sided appreciations, or worse, half truths. Much of what has been written is more passionate than profound, more emotional than factual. For example, the Peruvian writer, Javier Prado, states that the Spaniards "did not kill the Indian, but barbarized him";[1] and Pío Jaramillo of Ecuador claims that Christianity as an element of culture did very little or nothing for the Indian.[2] Others have stated that "neither the King, nor the Viceroy, nor the *Audiencia* was interested in native education,"[3] and that there was a "systematic exclusion of the Indian from all intellectual enterprise."[4]

It is part of the historian's task to challenge oversimplified judgments and, through diligent investigation, to search into the recesses of the past with a brighter light from the torch of truth. This writer's year of intensive archival and bibliographical research in South

[1] Javier Prado, *Estado social del Perú durante la dominación española* (Lima: Imprenta de El Diario Judicial, 1894), p. 182.
[2] Pío Jaramillo Alvarado, *El indio ecuatoriano* (Quito: Casa de la Cultura Ecuatoriana, 1954), pp. 417-18.
[3] César Angeles Caballero, *Historia de la educación peruana* (Ica: n.p., 1964), p. 28.
[4] Gabriel Giraldo Jaramillo, *Estudios históricos* (Bogotá: Editorial Santafé, 1954), p. 320, quoted in Luis A. Bohórquez Casallas, *La evolución educativa en Colombia* (Bogotá: Litografía Villegas, 1956), p. 43.

America produced results that are both surprising and revealing: surprising in that it becomes clear that much was done in legal and practical ways to educate the Indians (in both academic and nonacademic ways), although relatively little has been said about it; and revealing, in that there is positive documentary evidence of efforts as well as achievements. The sixteenth century was a period that produced the foundation, organization, and consolidation of Andean Indian education. In this essay, special attention is given to the religious indoctrination of Indians.

Referring to the native inhabitants of the Indies in her last will and testament, Queen Isabella stated: "Our principal intention ... was to win over the people there to Our Holy Catholic Faith ... and to send devoted and God-fearing people to instruct the inhabitants ... to indoctrinate them, and to teach them good customs...."[5] The Spanish Crown had two basic aims: evangelization of the peoples of the New World, and incorporation of these peoples into the cultural mainstream of Spain, into a new civilization which, henceforth, was to be their way of life. These aims come through clearly in this quotation and in the early instructions given to the conquerors and colonists, as well as in the prolific royal decrees of the colonial period. They are well summed up in the *Statutes Concerning New Discoveries and Settlements*, dated July 13, 1563:

> Teach them good manners; have them dress and wear shoes and let them have many other good things heretofore prohibited to them. Take away their burdens and servitude; give them the use of bread, wine, oil and other foodstuffs, cloth, silk, linen, horses, cattle, tools, arms and all the rest that Spain has had; and teach them the arts and trades by which they may live honestly, and that all of these things may be enjoyed by those who come to the knowledge of our holy Catholic faith and to Our obedience.[6]

From this it can be seen that transculturation of the Indians was to be brought about in a threefold manner: 1) education in daily living, emphasizing social and civil customs; 2) education in religion; and 3) education in some of the simpler secular branches of knowledge, especially crafts and trades.

Education of the Indians began as an almost immediate consequence of Spanish settlement in the Andean area. Indians were forced to fit into Spanish organization, government, and daily life. Simply by being told what to do and how to do it, they were already learning new ways and being educated in the broad sense of the term. The *Laws of the Indies* stated that after pacification, the *adelantado*

---

[5]Quoted in Carlos Pereyra, *Breve historia de América*, 2 vols. (Santiago: Editorial Letras, 1938), 1:208-209.

[6]Luis Torres de Mendoza, ed., *Colección de documentos inéditos del Archivo de Indias*, 10 vols. (Madrid: Imprenta de Frias y Compañía, 1867-1873), 8:533.

should divide the Indians among colonizers who, in turn, should provide a teacher to instruct them in Christian doctrine and civic life.[7] Thus, in the beginning, education and indoctrination of the Indians were made the responsibility of the *encomenderos*, partly because of the scarcity of religious personnel, and partly because most of the Indians were on the *encomiendas* that had been distributed to the conquerors and first settlers. King Ferdinand indicated that an *encomendero* with more than fifty Indians was obliged to teach one of them to read and write, as well as the basics of Christian doctrine. Bishop Tomás Ortiz of Santa Marta decreed in 1531 that from each *encomienda* one or two Indians, preferably sons of chiefs or other important persons, should be sent to the city to learn so that they, in turn, could teach their parents and other people of their villages.[8] Archbishop Jerónimo Loayza of Lima suggested the same thing for Peru in 1542, [9] and this practice was enforced by Vaca de Castro in the Cuzco area.[10]

Spain was not content merely to demand and encourage the education of Indians. In addition to promoting earnest endeavors and legislation for indigenous education, the Crown sent people who were culturally best prepared to educate them. Indian education received its real impetus and force from increased numbers of religious missionaries, who were the main agents of transculturation for Spain.[11] This explains in part why education had such a highly religious character. On December 8, 1535, Charles V gave orders to the *encomenderos* of Peru to take the sons of *caciques* and principal Indians to the religious convents.[12] Further decrees of December 17, 1551, and October 8, 1560, indicated that where this was not possible, the *encomenderos* had to keep and to pay a religious to teach the Indians.[13] In 1550, Franciscans, Augustinians, and Dominicans were ordered to teach the Indians religion, Spanish, and "everything else that is necessary to their way of life."[14] In the same year, Valdivia obligated the *caciques* in Chile to let the religious educate their children.[15] Two years earlier, Pedro de la Gasca had sent Juan Núñez del Prado to

---

[7]Bohorquez, *La evoluciión educativa en Colombia*, pp. 46-47.

[8]Juan Friede, ed., *Documentos inéditos para la historia de Colombia*, 3 vols. (Madrid: Artes Gráficos ARO, 1954-1956), 3:206.

[9]Emilio Lissón Chaves, ed., *La Iglesia de España en el Perú*, 6 vols. (Seville: Editorial Católica Española, 1943-1956), 2:142.

[10]Pedro Borges, O.F.M., *Métodos misionales en la cristianización de América, siglo XVI* (Madrid: Raycar, S.A., 1960), p. 401.

[11]Pedro García y Sanz, ed., *Apuntes para la historia eclesiástica del Perú*, 2 vols. (Lima: Tipografía de "La Sociedad", 1872-1876), 2:141ff. García cites several colonial documents on the preparation and good work of the missionary religious.

[12]Borges, *Métodos misionales*, p. 408.

[13]Juan Manuel Pacheco, S.J., *Los Jesuitas en Colombia*, 2 vols. (Bogotá: Editorial "San Juan Eudes", 1959), 1:37.

[14]National Archives of Colombia, Section "Conventos", 19:00363.

[15]Borges, *Métodos misionales*, p. 402.

Tucumán with "religious of letters and conscience" to teach the Indians there.[16]

In 1550, the king was informed that conversion and education of the Indians had been slow because there were not enough monasteries of religious. The Crown responded with a decree of December 6, 1565, which ordered the erection of monasteries wherever they were necessary in order to make instruction and education in Spanish ways available to the Indians.[17] When religious orders were unable to support or build monasteries, the Crown would offer its assistance. At the same time, the Crown would order the *encomenderos* to help pay for new monasteries that the Indians helped to build.[18] There arose in America, therefore, a situation similar to that of Europe in the Middle Ages: monasteries and convents became centers of instruction and civilization, and various kinds of educational institutions sprang up in connection with them. From these convents the religious spread out to the rural areas.

Because they felt the Indians would be more accessible and approachable in communities, the Spaniards decided from the outset of colonization to bring together the Indians into villages or *reducciones*, some of which were parts of *encomiendas*. In this they were supported by the Crown, and from 1538 on there were laws regarding the "reducing" of the Indians.[19] These rural villages were known in Nueva Granada as *resguardos*, and throughout the rest of the Andean region they were called *doctrinas*. The aspect of "reduction" is important because the diffusion of education was in direct proportion to it. In Peru, Ecuador, Colombia, and parts of Bolivia where Indian villages were formed on a rather solid basis, education was more widespread and more permanent in its effects. In Argentina, Chile, and Venezuela, much less was achieved.

As villages, the *doctrinas* were part of the political pattern and civil government which Spain adopted in order to colonize and organize the newly-discovered territories as efficaciously as possible. This explains the interest of the Viceroys, *Audiencias*, and other civil authorities in the *doctrinas*. In addition, as ecclesiastical units they came under the Royal Patronage, or rights of the king in ecclesiastical affairs; also, they were part of the highly centralized organization of

---

[16]Roberto Levillier, ed., *Gobernantes del Perú: Cartas y papeles*, 14 vols. (Madrid: Sucesores de Rivadeneyra, S.A., 1921-1926), 1:188.

[17]National Archives of Colombia, Section "Conventos," 19:00362; Alonso de Zamora, O.P., *Historia de la Provincia de San Antonio del Nuevo Reino de Granada* (Caracas: Parra León Hermanos, Editorial Sur América, 1930), p. 243.

[18]Consejo de la Hispanidad, *Recopilación de leyes de los reynos de las Indias* (Madrid: Ediciones Cultura Hispánica, Gráficas Ultra, S.A., 1943), 1:18, 95. The laws are in bk. 1, tit. 3, law 3 and in bk. 1, tit. 13, laws 1 and 2; National Archives of Ecuador, Cédulas Reales, tomo 1, folio 130, no. 9.

[19]Rafael Gómez Hoyos, *La Iglesia de América en las Leyes de Indias* (Madrid: Gráficas Orbe, S.L., 1961), pp. 146-47.

the Church and were dependent on the bishoprics in which they were located. During most of the sixteenth century, the *doctrinas* were in the hands of the religious orders and were likewise under the jurisdiction of the monasteries that provided personnel for them. The *Laws of the Indies* decreed that the monasteries of a given province should be of one order only and should be six leagues apart. The same laws also stipulated that where religious were the *doctrineros*, there should be no secular clergy, and vice versa. Thus, the number of *doctrinas* was indirectly regulated.[20]

Once the initial stage of colonization had passed, the Crown made efforts to enlarge upon the simple, broad, basic education demanded from the *encomenderos* and the missionary religious. An attempt was made to establish more permanent centers of learning, in addition to the monasteries. Instructions which Viceroy Francisco Toledo received before his departure for Peru stated: "In order to establish the Indians and to implant in them the Christian doctrine with more foundation and root, a very solid means is that of schools where the children can learn. . . ."[21]

Schools established in the New World were of various types. There were the private and boarding schools, mainly for Spaniards, and the *colegios* or academies that existed for those who aspired to the priesthood or some civil career. For the Indians, there were free schools in or near the convents, because the town councils required a school if a convent were to be established.[22] There were schools for education in various arts and trades, and special institutions for the education of the sons of Indian chiefs and nobles. In the cities there were free private schools for both Spaniards and Indians, as well as schools created by the *cabildos* and cathedral chapters.[23] Most of the Indians, however, received their education in the *doctrina* schools.

As early as 1503, Governor Obando of Hispaniola had been given orders to organize Indian villages and to build churches in them, "and together with the said churches, see to the building of a house in which all of the boys . . . may be brought together twice a day so that the said chaplain may teach them to read and write and bless themselves. . . ."[24] With regard to their work with the Indians, instructions given to the first Augustinians were applicable to other religious orders as well:

---

[20]These laws are found in the same sources cited above in note 18.
[21]Lissón, *La Iglesia de España en el Perú*, 2:452.
[22]Vicente D. Sierra, *El sentido misional de la conquista de América* (Madrid: Consejo de la Hispanidad, 1944), p. 555.
[23]Danilo Nieto Lozano, *La educación en el nuevo reino de Granada* (Bogotá: Editorial Santafé, 1955), pp. 23-24, 64-65, and 74.
[24]José Tudela, ed., *El legado de España a América*, 2 vols. (Madrid: Ediciones Pegaso, 1954), 2:460.

> Create schools where they may learn to read, write and count. Have them learn the public trades and occupations in such a way that they can become useful. Teach them honorable crafts: to be painters, carpenters, tailors and blacksmiths; to make the best of their talents in order to become important personages in their respective villages.[25]

In the Andean rural villages, a parish priest, or *doctrinero*, was placed in charge. "Under his care was the school of reading, writing and counting, obligatory in all of the churches, and at its side, for the more talented, one of vocal and instrumental music, the most powerful support of cult and devotion."[26]

The *doctrina* schools were primitive institutions, with little ventilation or light. Pupils brought their own "benches" of woven straw or small boards, or more often than not simply sat on the ground. The small schoolhouse had two rooms, one of which was a classroom and the other served as a lavatory or a storeroom and punishment room. Where possible, students used goose quills, loose sheets of paper, the juice of the indigo plant for writing, and sand for drying.[27]

Primary education given in Spain at this time dated from rules set down by Henry II in 1319. Under these rules, children learned to read, write, and count; but instruction was essentially religious in character.[28] The same kind of education was imparted in America. Teachers wrote the alphabet in small and capital letters on papers that were fastened to a board with a handle. These were called *cartillas*. The first *cartilla* for reading was made in 1533 by Dr. Bernabé de Busto and was called *Manual for Learning to Read and Write Perfectly*. Similar *cartillas* were published in 1534, 1552, 1565, 1588, and 1589.[29] There were also a number of pious books from which children often spent long hours copying. Copy work was checked once each morning and each afternoon, particularly to correct spelling mistakes. The daily schedule varied from place to place and from school to school. In general, however, the morning was devoted to reading, writing, arithmetic, and music; and the afternoon was reserved for learning prayers and the catechism, and singing.[30] Children were expected to attend Mass in the early morning hours and to say the rosary together in the afternoon.

For Spanish authorities, both lay and religious, education in religion was the prime concern of the process of transculturation. Royal

---

[25]Antonio de la Calancha, *Crónica moralizada de la Orden de San Agustín en el Perú* (La Paz: Artística, 1939), pp. 356-57.
[26]Tudela, *El legado de España a América*, 1:197.
[27]Levillier, *Gobernantes del Perú*, 9:62, 78.
[28]Bohorquez, *La evolución educativa en Colombia*, pp. 33-34.
[29]Manuel Antonio Ponce, *Reseña histórica de la enseñanza de la lectura en Chile (Siglos XVI-XIX)* (Santiago: Imprenta, Litografía i Encuadernación Barcelona, 1905)), pp. 3-6.
[30]Lissón, *La Iglesia de España en el Perú*, 3:137, 151, 168, 519-25.

decrees insisted on the point, but it was left mainly to the ecclesiastical authorities to work out the details. This was done in Peru in 1567 and 1583, in Nueva Granada in 1556 and 1576, and in the Kingdom of Quito in 1570, 1594, and 1596. The same general rules prevailed everywhere and provided for uniformity in the method of teaching doctrine to the Indians. Men, women, and children were to be taught the Our Father, Hail Mary, Credo, and Commandments in Spanish and in the native languages, along with the observance of good Christian customs. Doctrine was to be learned by memory, but with understanding according to the ability of the learner. The custom of teaching doctrine through singing was popular and widespread; thus, one visitor reported: "In the Indies in general, almost everything is taught by singing. In that way, they understand it better, and also since they are fond of song, they study and learn it with more pleasure and without boredom."[31]

Boys and girls were obliged to attend doctrine classes every day until they were ten years old. Adults were to be taught catechism three times a week — Sunday, Wednesday and Friday — and were to be separated by sex into groups of twelve to fifteen to be instructed by the priest or lay cathechist.[32] Viceroy Toledo added the requirements that older boys should receive doctrine three times a week before going to work in the morning and that girls over ten should accompany their parents to doctrine classes.[33] The *Laws of the Indies* also provided for the founding of schools for Indian girls who were otherwise exposed to immoral traffic or given to the Indian chiefs by their parents. In these schools, girls were taught doctrine and the Spanish language.[34]

Often the *doctrinero* needed assistance. Sometimes the sacristan was given the job of teaching. Bilingual Indians, called *ladinos*, were taught doctrine and were sent back to their villages to teach other Indians.[35] Some became professionals. In Quito in 1568, San Andrés had eight Indians on the faculty teaching reading, writing, singing, and making instruments.[36] In 1586, the Governor of Santa Cruz de la Sierra wrote that doctrine was being taught by youths assigned for the

---

[31] Bernardo Recio, S.J., *Compendiosa relación de la cristiandad de Quito* (Madrid: Consejo Superior de Investigaciones Científicas, 1947), p. 467.

[32] Lissón, *La Iglesia de España en el Perú*, 3:185, 200; Alonso de la Peña Montenegro, *Itinerario para párrocos* (Amberes: Henrico y Cornelio Verdussen, 1698), p. 88-89.

[33] Francisco de Toledo, *Ordenanzas* (Madrid: Imprenta de Juan Pueyo, 1929), p. 361.

[34] Rafael Gómez Hoyos, "El Indio en la Conquista," in *Historia de Colombia* (Bogotá: Editorial ABC, 1950), 5:209.

[35] Levillier, *Gobernantes del Perú*, 4:128-29; José Toribio Medina, *Colección de documentos inéditos para la historia de Chile* (Santiago: Fondo Histórico y Bibliográfico José Toribio Medina, 1963), 6:40-41, mentions the *ladinos* being used in Tucumán also.

[36] José María Vargas, O.P., *La cultura de Quito colonial* (Quito: Editorial "Santo Domingo", 1941), p. 152.

purpose and that they were having success.[37] Royal decrees stated that where there were no *doctrineros* the bishops should appoint a competent and qualified person to take care of teaching the Indians. Viceroy Toledo did this in Peru and paid them from the royal treasury.[38]

Of special importance and interest were the schools dedicated to educating the sons of the Indian chiefs and nobles. In the organization of its overseas empire, the Spanish Crown preserved many indigenous social institutions, such as class distinctions to which the Indians had been long accustomed and which Spaniards, from their own heritage, could very much appreciate. There was a natural and understandable reluctance on the part of the *caciques* to have their sons mix with boys of the lower classes and be taught on an equal level with them, especially when they saw the Spaniards themselves making distinctions. The Crown wanted to preserve the authority of the Indian chiefs in order to influence the masses and to protect national dignity and character. The *Laws of the Indies* provided "that the Academies founded for the raising of the sons of *caciques* be favored, and that others be established in the main cities," especially in Mexico and Peru.[39] In time, these academies existed in the Andean region in Bogotá, Quito, Lima, Cuzco, Charcas, Santiago, and Chillán. Most of them were in the care of the Jesuits, though the Franciscans also "maintained a school exclusively for the sons of the *caciques* and other principal wealthy men" in each *doctrina*.[40]

By the time Viceroy Toledo arrived in Peru (1570), there were schools for the Indians throughout the country. The Dominicans alone had sixty of them, and in 1581 Viceroy Enríquez confirmed the presence of schools throughout the viceroyalty.[41] They also existed in La Paz, in the Franciscan *doctrinas* in Charcas and Santiago del Estero, in the Jesuit missions in Tucumán, and in all of the Indian villages of the central region of Chile.[42] The Franciscans, Dominicans, and Augustinians had schools throughout Nueva Granada; and President

---

[37]Marcos Jiménez de la Espada, ed., *Relaciones geográficas de Indias* (Madrid: Tipografía de Manuel G. Hernández, 1897), 2:162.

[38]National Archives of Ecuador, Section "Cédulas Reales," t. 1, fol. 77; Fernando de Armas Medina, *Cristianización del Perú, 1532-1600* (Seville: Escuela de Estudios Hispano-Americanos, 1953), p. 393.

[39]Consejo de la Hispanidad, *Recopilación de leyes*, 1:212.

[40]Tudela, *El legado de España a América*,1:458-59; Antonine Tibesar, O.F.M., *Franciscan Beginnings in Colonial Peru* (Washington, D.C.: Academy of American Franciscan History, 1953), p. 83.

[41]Levillier, *Gobernantes del Perú*, 9:62; Armas, *Cristianización del Perú*, p. 391.

[42]Guillermo Monje, "Breve historia del desarrollo educacional en la ciudad de La Paz," in *La Paz en su IV Centenario*, 3 vols. (Buenos Aires: Imprenta López, 1948), 3:163; Bruno Avila, O.S.B., *La Iglesia en la Argentina* (Buenos Aires: Editorial "San Benito," 1949), p. 44; Domingo Amunátegui Solar, *Chile bajo la dominación española* (Santiago: Sociedad Imprenta y Litografía Universo,1925), p. 57.

Andrés Venero de Leiva in 1564 organized primary schools in all of the villages for both Indians and Spaniards.[43] In addition to the famous Colegio San Andrés, there were other schools in Quito for Indian children; and the *cabildo* informed the king in 1577 that there were many schools for Indians in villages throughout the kingdom. The Augustinians, for instance, had schools in all twenty-three of their *doctrinas*.[44]

The number of Indians in the *doctrinas* varied widely. In 1568, Bishop de la Peña in Quito agreed with the civil authorities that each *doctrinero* could take care of 800 to 1,000 parishioners. In 1588, Archbishop Toribio de Mogrovejo of Lima informed the king that a Provincial Council had decided that each *doctrinero* should have no more than 300 Indians in his *doctrina*; and the king approved this limitation. Bishop Trejo y Sanabria of Tucumán raised the number to 500 in 1607.[45] At the end of the sixteenth century, there were over 800 *doctrinas* in the Andean region.[46] If we suppose a minimum of 500 people in each *doctrina*, then by 1600 around half a million Indians were being educated.

[43] José Manuel Groot, *Historia eclesiástica y civil de Nueva Granada* (Bogotá: Editorial ABC, 1953), pp. 272-74; J. M. Fernández and Rafael Granados, S.J., *Obra civilizadora de la Iglesia en Colombia* (Bogotá: Editorial Nueva, 1936), pp. 196, 313.

[44] Oscar Efrén Reyes, *Breve historia general del Ecuador*, 4 vols. (Quito: Editorial "Fray Jodoco Ricke," 1955), 1:308; Vargas, *La cultura de Quito colonial*, p. 22; Julio Tobar Donoso, *La Iglesia, modeladora de la nacionalidad* (Quito: La Prensa Católica, 1953), p. 221.

[45] José María Vargas, *Historia de la Provincia de Santa Catalina Virgen y Mártir de Quito de la Orden de Predicadores* (Quito: Tipografía y Encuadernación Salesianas, 1942), p. 40; Lissón, *La Iglesia de España en el Perú*, 3:484-87; Miguel Angel Vergara, *Estudios sobre historia eclesiástica de Jujuy* (Tucumán: Universidad Nacional de Tucumán, 1942), p. 62.

[46] Any attempt to estimate the number and location of the *doctrinas* must encounter a series of obstacles. Sources of information are limited or specialized, and they seldom coincide with one another. In trying, for instance, to form an idea of the growth of *doctrinas* in the Archdiocese of Lima, one discovers that mid-sixteenth century statistics include *doctrinas* as far north as Panama and south into Chile; at the end of the century they extend to the northern frontier of present-day Peru and sometimes include the bishopric of Quito but omit the whole southern section of Peru beginning with the bishopric of Cuzco. Superiors of the religious orders also sent lists of their *doctrinas* to the king; but these lists are generally divided according to the canonical provinces of the Order, which often overlapped several dioceses. Reports from civil authorities were frequently limited to the boundaries of a particular *audiencia* or province. The effort to combine this statistical information is rather frustrating. If our study is to have any historical value, however, we must in some measure have an idea of the number of *doctrinas* because Indian education was so intimately related to them. Relying on eighteen different sources, we can arrive at the following approximation for the end of the sixteenth century:

Peru-Charcas: religious *doctrinas*, 165; secular, 300; total 465
Tucumán-Chile: religious, 28; secular, 40; total 68
Nueva Granada: religious, 65; secular, 50; total 115
Kingdom of Quito: religious, 83; secular, 97; total 180
                    Andean grand total: 828

What about those Indians not in the *doctrinas*? For most of them, it was the broad, general education in daily living that was insisted upon most. With time, all kinds of customs were introduced, and the Indians accepted and adopted an astonishing number of them. Sometimes these customs were learned in the service of the Spaniards in the cities, sometimes in special districts set aside for the residence of urban Indians.

Religious education was often given to servants in the home. There was even a provision that school children deserving punishment could be pardoned once a week if they taught doctrine to an Indian or Negro and brought a signed statement to that effect from their father. Hospitals were likewise centers of religious instruction.[47] The major means of solving the problem of Indian religious instruction in the cities, however, was the foundation of parishes exclusively for Indians. In 1571, there were seven such parishes in Cuzco; others existed in Lima, Bogotá, and Quito.[48] An extremely interesting and important feature in the Indian parishes was the establishment of the confraternities (*cofradías*), which were a religious version of the medieval craft guilds. These organizations played an important role in the religious education of the Indians along both doctrinal and practical lines.

Nonacademic education included agricultural tasks such as cultivating the fields, planting fruit trees and vines, and raising large and small herd animals from Europe; also included was training in various crafts and trades. This training was important to the Indians because it provided many of them with a means of livelihood and a useful place in society. Indians became the colonial carpenters, tailors, shoemakers, plasterers, hat makers, weavers, blacksmiths, waxchandlers, and tanners, to mention a few occupations. Already in the sixteenth century a judge of the *Audiencia* in Lima could write, "All the benefit of this kingdom in cultivation or in factories, mills, coca fields and other crafts and trades depends upon these Indians."[49]

In the fields of the fine arts, Indians likewise learned rapidly the use of Spanish instruments of music and the diatonic and chromatic

---

[47]José Antonio del Busto, "Un curioso reglamento para los Maestros de Escuela," *Boletín del Instituto Riva Agüero*, no. 2 (Lima, 1953-1955), p. 145. The teaching of doctrine to domestic servants was provided for in the *Laws of the Indies*, Libro VI, Título XIII, Ley 22; Roberto Levillier, ed., *Audiencia de Lima* (Madrid; Imprenta de Juan Pueyo, 1922), 1:28.

[48]Jesús M. Covarrubias Pozo, "Tercer libro del Cabildo de Elección de Alcaldes y Regidores Indios, Ingas y Yanaconas del Distrito de San Jerónimo y San Blas, jurisdicción del Cuzco," *Revista del Museo e Instituto Arqueológico*, no. 20 (Cuzco, 1963), p. 120; Pacheco, *Los Jesuitas en Colombia*, p. 42; José María Vargas, O.P., *Historia de la Iglesia en el Ecuador durante el patronato español* (Quito: Editorial "Santo Domingo," 1962), p. 63.

[49]Levillier, *Gobernantes del Perú*, 7:287; Jiménez de la Espada, *Relaciones geográficas de Indias*, 3:248, 251.

scales which were unknown to them previously. In architecture, the Spaniards relied heavily, if not entirely, on Indian labor for colonial construction; and the Indians had to learn how to make buildings of European design and architecture, including even the more complicated forms, such as baroque. Missionaries also taught the Indians the techniques of painting and the use of the brush and colors, mainly in their own convents. Cuzco and Quito became famous centers of indigenous art and produced schools of true excellence. Viceroy Toledo was so impressed with the Indian painters that he thought of sending some of them to Spain.[50]

These are some of the facets of Spanish education of the Indians, remnants of which still exist in the Andean region in religious practices, language, adapted forms of dress and other customs, musical instruments, works of art and architecture, and various trades. Not only did the Indians learn but they also transmitted their knowledge to succeeding generations. In this sense, Spanish education of the Indians was eminently successful. If there was a flaw, it was that the Indian was educated to *be*, and never to *belong*, to "fit into" the Spanish system, but not to share in it. This was the great tragedy in an otherwise splendid enterprise.

---

[50]Levillier, *Gobernantes del Perú*, 3:542-43.

21. The Jesuit Settlement Frontier in Southern Brazil

C. GARY LOBB

Professor Lobb's description of the early seventeenth-century Jesuit *reducciones* in South Brazil adds to our knowledge concerning one of the most extraordinary Spanish missionary efforts in Latin America. Expansion of Jesuit missionary activity eastward from Asunción, organization of the *reducciones*, and economic and administrative interrelationships are explored in this essay.

The Jesuits played a significant role in advancing the cause of Spanish and Portuguese political expansion in the New World. In 1626, their mission-building expanded eastward from Asunción (Paraguay) and crossed the Uruguay River into what is now Brazil, thus culminating over fifty years of Jesuit activity restricted to the Plata-Paraguay region. Initially, in 1588, an unsuccessful attempt was made to establish a mission among the Guaraní at Asunción. Eleven years later, however, the Jesuit Provincial dispatched missionaries to Guairá, Paraná, and Guaycurus. To avoid the transient, ineffective results of the first attempt to Christianize the Indians of these regions, missionaries gathered the Indians into permanent settlements or *reducciones*, taught them the Holy Faith, cared for them spiritually and materially, and imposed upon them the work ethic of the Benedictine Code. Indians were instructed how to cultivate the land and then were "kept busy working in the fields so as to avoid laziness."[1]

Success of mission settlements was directly related to fertility of the land and farming traditions of the Indians who worked it. Only among agricultural Indians were the *reducciones* successful. Thus, the mission to the Guaycurus, a non-agricultural Chaco tribe, failed and was abandoned around 1613. The first successful *reducciones* established in the Guairá region were San Ignacio Guazú and Loreto, which were founded in 1610. Situated on the Paranapanema River in

---

[1]Gregorio D. Funes, *Ensayo de la historia civil del Paraguay, Buenos Aires y Tucumán*, 2 vols. (Buenos Aires: Talleres Gráficos de L. J. Russo, 1910-1911), 1:291.

the upper Paraná basin, these *reducciones* were not far from the Spanish towns of Ciudad Real (Guairá) and Villarica. By 1617 the two *reducciones* had populations of 800 and 700 families, respectively.[2] As agricultural settlements, the *reducciones* on the Paranapanema were successful. Land around Loreto was especially fertile. In addition to high yields of the native staple, bitter manioc (*Manihot esculenta*), these settlements produced wheat from which ordinary bread could be made; by 1626, there were even some cows to provide milk from which cheese could be made.

Shortly after the founding of the Guairá missions, the Jesuits established *reducciones* among the Guaraní, southeast of Asunción. Roque González de Santa Cruz, a Spanish Jesuit who was well acquainted with the language and culture of the Guaraní, spearheaded expansion of mission settlements to the southeast. Granted permission by the authorities in Asunción and encouraged by Governor Hernandarias de Saavedra, González founded the first *reducción* at Itapuá, on the banks of the Paraná River, in 1615. That same year, he established Santa Anna Itatý slightly to the north. In 1620, he founded Concepción in the mesopotamian region within the Uruguay drainage. It was the first mission of that region.[3]

While most of the impetus for expansion into the Uruguay basin came from the Jesuit *colegio* in Asunción, church leaders and government officials in Buenos Aires displayed considerable interest as well. Governor Hernandarias toured the newly established *reducciones* of the Paraná in 1616 and noted the role these settlements could play in the security and development of the Spanish colonies. In a letter to the king, Hernandarias pointed out that the new missions would protect navigation and provide the Indian peoples of the region with a means of exporting their products to Buenos Aires.[4]

Hernandarias's successor, Governor Francisco de Céspedes, entrusted Padre González with the task of bringing inhabitants of the upper Uruguay region into the Catholic Church and under Spanish rule. Government support of missionary activities east of the Uruguay River was an attempt to revitalize the old ambition of Governor Hernandarias: the development of a Spanish-controlled corridor from Asunción to the coast of Santa Catarina and the founding of a city on the *Mar del Brazil*.

Padre González and the Spanish Jesuits were given exclusive rights to manage the spiritual and material affairs of the *otra banda*,[5]

---

[2]"Décima carta de Pedro de Oñat," in *Documentos para la historia argentina*, 45 vols. (Buenos Aires: Facultad de Filosofía y Letras, Instituto de Investigaciones Históricas, 1913-1974), 20:146.

[3]"Duodécima carta de Padre Nicolás Mastrillo Durán," in ibid., p. 20:304-305.

[4]*Revista de la Biblioteca Nacional* (Buenos Aires), 2 (January-March 1938): 10-11.

[5]The east side of the Uruguay River or what is today the Republic of Uruguay and the Brazilian State of Rio Grande do Sul.

and the padres remained the unchallenged landlords of the Indian domain until their expulsion from the Western Hemisphere in 1768. Governor Céspedes stated:

> I give them [the Society of Jesus], in the name of His Majesty, ample authority and unlimited and unrestricted power to organize and establish all the reducciones they can. I give them authority to select chiefs and judges as they see fit and to give them laws and authority in my name and in the name of His Majesty. And because it may be that our Lord will open the door that the Society may enter other provinces beyond Uruguay which do not pertain to another district or governor, I give them the same power and authority to take possession of these lands in the name of His Majesty and to group [reducir] the inhabitants so that they can learn the Holy Faith.[6]

With this carte blanche, Roque González crossed the Uruguay River; and in May 1626, he established San Nicolás, the first mission on the east bank.[7]

The following year, two more reducciones were founded among the agricultural Guaraní along the Uruguay River. To the south lived the warlike and non-agricultural Charruas, described by one observer as "inhumane and barbaric Indians, who have neither houses, agriculture, nor a permanent residence, and who live only by hunting and fishing."[8] González was responsible for much of the organizational work of the mission settlements in the Paraná-Uruguay region. While the same general plan was used that had also been employed in other parts of the Americas, the Uruguay reducciones provided González with an opportunity to organize the relatively sedentary Guaraní of this region without pressure from Spanish landlords vying for Indian labor and tribute. González clearly realized that a stable economic foundation was essential for every reducción, and the Society had sufficient resources to develop adequately the newly founded settlements. The Jesuits possessed huge tracts of property, and profits from the rental of lands and from textile factories provided the Society with capital to buy additional land and to develop the reducciones.

As the Indians were assembled in the reducciones, they were provided with agricultural implements and given a piece of land on which to grow maize and manioc. At first, they were supplied with iron hoes and axes that were brought from Asunción; later, these tools were manufactured in the reducciones. This early organization of Indian lands and resources evolved into a complex system of private and communal properties. There was also a rather strict division of

---
[6]Rio de Janeiro, Biblioteca Nacional, Secção de Manuscritos, "Colecção de Angelis," MSS I-29, 7, 25-26.
[7]"Duodécima carta de Padre Nicolás Mastrillo Durán," p. 365.
[8]Ibid.

labor among individual Indian families and among the *reducciones*.

Some of the mission settlements produced both cattle and wheat; thus, the surrounding missions were able to obtain meat and bread, relieving the monotony of a diet made up largely of manioc and maize. Except in *reducciones* where cattle were available and where *yerba mate* was grown and sold, the new Jesuit system did not provide the abundance that had been anticipated. The Jesuits did not understand the basic requirements of the Guaraní system of agriculture. Grouping of the Indians in the mission settlements concentrated the agricultural population and, in many cases, resulted in a complete breakdown of the Indian system of slash and burn (*roza*) agriculture. San Nicolás, the first *reducción* established on the east side of the Uruguay River, is a good example. Shortly after its founding in 1626, there were 280 families living in this *reducción*; a year later, the settlement had grown to 500 families.[9] But the mission suffered terribly from famine during that year. According to one account, "The large number of people immediately reduced were afflicted by the Lord with a famine that was so severe that Padre Roque admitted he had never seen one so awful."[10]

At first, the Jesuits were mystified by the itinerant nature of Guaraní agriculture. Writing from the newly established *reducción* of Nuestra Señora de los Reyes del Yapeyú in 1627, González commented on exaggerated population estimates for the Uruguay region. Because there were many agricultural clearings, the first Jesuit missionaries in the area had supposed that agricultural settlement was dense. Not understanding the energetics of tropical long-fallow cropping and low rural densities, González was perplexed by the Guaraní practice of shifting fields. He speculated that indiscriminate cutting of forests prior to Jesuit missionary activity had resulted in lowering the population:

> The Indian population may have been greater before, but because they have destroyed the forest [*mattos*] and used them up, there are only *capoeira* [second growth] now, and the Indians are forced to plant between hills and cliffs. As a result of this, they are widely spread over the countryside, the largest groupings being not over one hundred Indians.[11]

Following the Río Ibicuí, González led his group of missionaries into the interior of what is now the state of Rio Grande do Sul. Travelling up tributaries of the Ibicuí, he looked for proper sites for

---

[9]Ibid.
[10]Ibid.
[11]"Descripción de la Provincia del Uruguay y Tapé desde Buenos Aires hasta las Tierras del Guairá y del Brasil, hecha personalmente y a vista de ojos por el V. P. Roque González de Santa Cruz, año de 1627," vol. 56, Colección Mata Linares, Acadêmia de la Historia, Madrid, quoted in Carlos Teschauer, *História do Rio Grande do Sul dos dous primeiros séculos*, 3 vols. (Pôrto Alegre: Globo, 1918-1921), 1:45-46.

reducciones, sites where there were "sufficient people, the land of good quality and the location a healthy one."[12] González described the region in terms of its possibilities for future *reducciones*, and his report must have contributed to the zeal of the Jesuit officials to settle and Christianize the region east of the Uruguay. In almost every case, mission settlements were located in forested areas along the major streams where *roza* agriculture could be practiced by Indian residents.

Jesuit desire to settle the interior regions increased with the knowledge that Portuguese merchants were active in the riverine areas and were apparently carrying on a brisk commerce with the Indians of the Jacuí valley. To curb the influence of the Portuguese in this region, the Jesuits attempted to establish a *reducción* in the area known as the Tierra de los Tapes, located well to the east of the Uruguay River. Because of Tapé Indian hostilities and the general remoteness of the settlement, however, the mission was abandoned after only a few months.

The padres were determined to establish a chain of missions from the Uruguay to the Atlantic. Foundations were laid among responsive Indians for three more *reducciones*: San Nicolás, Asunción del Ijuí, and Caaro. But when González and two of his companions were killed in an Indian uprising in 1628, the newly established missions were sacked and burned. This brought expansion to a temporary halt.

Forced to abandon the mission settlements of Guairá because of *paulista* raids in 1629, the Spanish Jesuit missionaries were transferred to work in the Uruguay region. There followed a rapid expansion of the Jesuit state into the region of Tapé. The course of the Río Ijuí served as a major route of penetration eastward as *reducciones* were established in the Tapé region. From the headwaters of the Ijuí and its tributaries, missionaries crossed the drainage divide and founded settlements in the valleys of the Río Jacuí, Río Pardo, and Río Ibicuí.

In 1632, the first permanent mission of the Tapé region, San Miguel, was established on the upper Toropý. That same year, San Tomé and San José were founded in the Ibicuí valley. The three missions experienced such a rapid growth that their agricultural capabilities could not keep pace with the expanding population. San Miguel remained rather prosperous, while San Tomé and San José suffered disease and famine from the beginning.[13]

By 1633, missionaries were establishing settlements in the more

---

[12]Nicolás del Techo, *Historia de la Provincia del Paraguay de la Compañía de Jesús por el Padre Nicolás del Techo*, 5 vols. (Madrid: Librería y Casa Editorial A. de Uribe y Cía., 1897), 4:189.

[13]Antonio Ruiz de Montoya, *Conquista espiritual hecha por los religiosos de la Compañía de Jesús en las provincias del Paraguay, Paraná, Uruguay y Tapé* (Madrid: Imprenta del Reino, 1639), pp. 81-82. (On microfilm, University of California Library, Berkeley.)

Jesuit Expansion 1628-1634

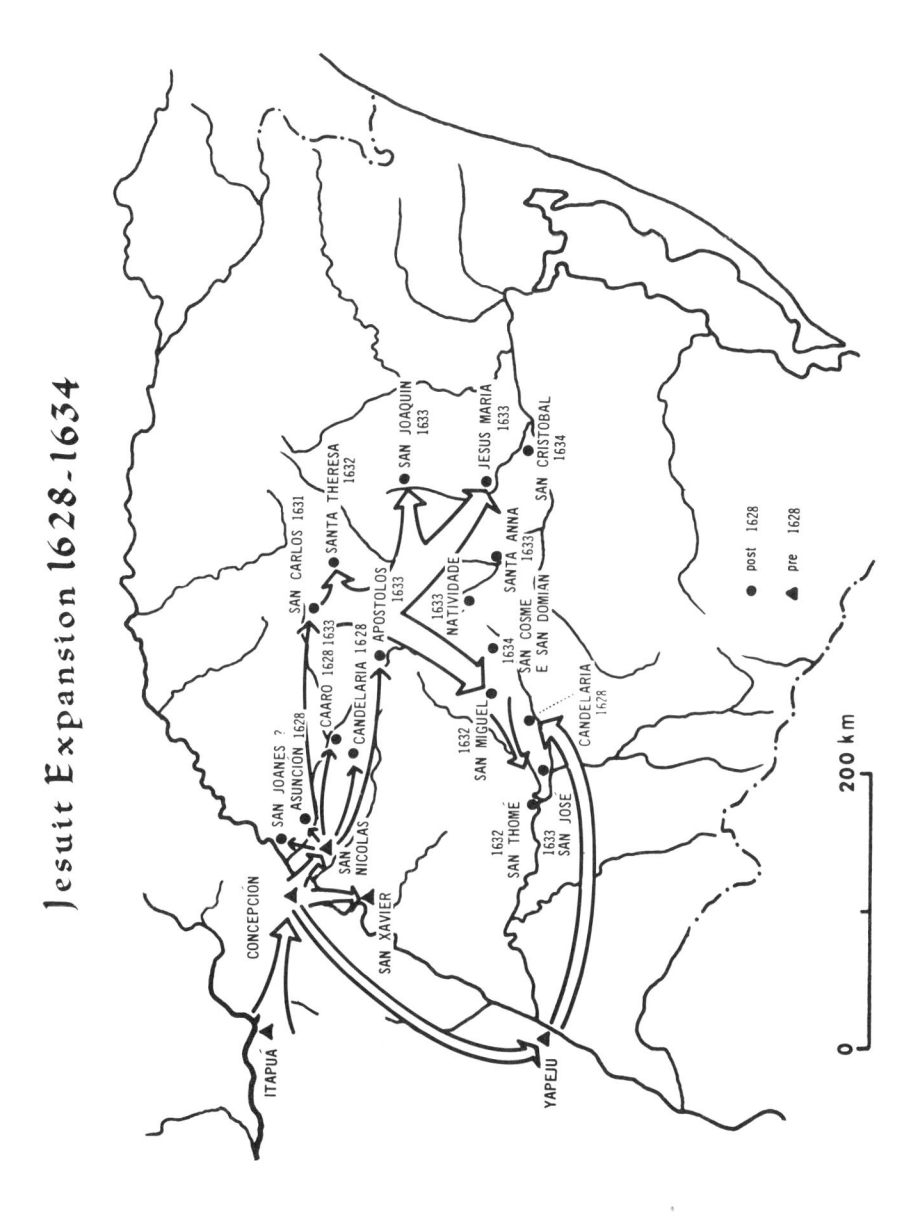

fertile valleys of the Jacuí and its tributaries. Missions on the Jacuí were well-located. Santa Ana, located on the Jacuí near the confluence of the Vacacaí Mirim, was on a "good and fertile plain," and the population grew to about 7,000 residents.[14] Santa Teresa, also founded in 1633, was probably in the best location of all the Tapé reducciones for the development of the Jesuit-Guaraní system of agriculture. Located near the headwaters of the Jacuí in the Serra dos Tapes, Santa Teresa was surrounded by extensive forest lands and the rich volcanic soils of the upland region. Because of its elevation, European grains did much better in Santa Teresa; and, in addition to maize and vegetables, the grain of this region was used to supply other reducciones during times of famine. Santa Teresa was apparently the only reducción with significant surpluses. Because this settlement was somewhat isolated, the Jesuits located the San Joaquín reducción on the upper reaches of the Río Pardo. Another settlement in the same area, Jesús-María, became the largest of the Tapé reducciones. Within three years, its population exceeded 10,000; and the community was reported to have the appearances of a "true city."[15]

The Jesuit state's expansion to the east came to an end in 1634, when the last two reducciones were founded. San Cosme y San Damián, established on a very poor site, was soon abandoned. San Cristobal, last of the missions to be built, was established on the Río Pardo near its confluence with the Jacuí. San Cristobal's population was reported to be about 2,300 in 1636, and the community was said to possess "the most elegant of all the churches in the region."[16]

The same conflicts over agriculture that were present at the founding of the original settlements by Roque González persisted with the establishment of the Tapé missions, though to a lesser degree. The Jesuits' ability to deal with Indian farming had improved as Guaraní practices were assimilated and as the mission reducciones tended to be smaller with more land available for long-fallow roza activities. In a letter of 1626-1627, Father Durán described the Jesuit practice in the Tapé region:

> The first thing done when any reducción is established is to lay out the land for the plantings. The Indians are not accustomed to planting in cleared fields (campo descuvierto) [sic] because they believe that land in such a state is exhausted (más gastada) and as a result their plantings will not do well. But in the forests (montes), they believe the land has been protected by the trees which are very dense, conserving the moisture and producing high yields (buenos frutos).
>
> As a result of this practice, large amounts of land are needed around the reducciones, depending upon the number of families, and each

---

[14]Del Techo, Historia de la Provincia de Paraguay, 4:276.
[15]Ruiz de Montoya, Conquista espiritual, p. 87.
[16]Del Techo, Historia de la Provincia de Paraguay, 4:314.

family is assigned a separate piece of land for their plantings. Much land is needed, for after five or six years the land is abandoned, useless and worn out, and they clear another piece. As a result, it is important and necessary that where a pueblo is founded there be considerable forest land nearby.[17]

Even with these adaptations by the Jesuits, only a few of the agricultural settlements were even moderately successful in producing manioc, maize, and the introduced vegetables and grains. Sedentary agriculture in gardens adjoining the mission churches was carried on without the use of animal fertilizers and was not at all successful. As mentioned previously, only at Santa Teresa were there any significant agricultural surpluses. Nevertheless, populations of the missions increased rapidly as more and more Indians were "reduced"; in 1634, there were reported to be 95,000 baptized Indians living in the missions of the Uruguay.[18]

Precisely where and at what time livestock were first introduced into the cattle regions of southern Brazil is not certain. Jesuit documents indicate that large-scale, deliberate introductions into the mission *reducciones* of the present state of Rio Grande do Sul did not take place before 1634. Apparently cattle were not utilized when the mission settlements were first established in this region. In response to generally deteriorating conditions, however, the Jesuits decided early in 1634 that cattle should be introduced into the mission settlements in large numbers. At this time, the nearest true *estancias* were in the *campos* of Entre Ríos and Corrientes. This mesopotamian area was populated with cattle as early as 1588, when over 1,500 head were brought to San Juan de Vera de las Siete Corrientes from Asunción.[19] The padres first obtained stock for their *reducciones* of the Uruguay from the *vacarías de Corrientes*.

Accompanied by Cristobal de Mendoza, Father Superior Pedro de Romero traveled to Corrientes to buy cattle. Mendoza was a *criollo* priest from Santa Cruz de la Sierra, the western-most *reducción* of the Jesuit state and an important seventeenth-century cattle center. Ranching had been an important activity in this region for over seventy-five years. As a result, Mendoza was well prepared to initiate the industry in southern Brazil. He had surveyed the possibilities of the land and was convinced that cattle would do well on the grassy interfluves between the major rivers of the mission region; also, he believed that cattle would help solve the production problems of the Jesuit missions. Mendoza was confident that these animals would be highly beneficial to the Indians. Besides providing meat, cattle would

[17]"Duodécima carta de Padre Nicolás Mastrillo Durán," p. 368.

[18]"Carta annual de Diego de Boroa, 13 de agosto de 1637," in *Documentos para la historia argentina*, 20:547.

[19]Emilio A. Coni, *Historia de las vaquerías del Río de la Plata* (Buenos Aires: Editorial Devenir, 1956), p. 15.

produce fertilizer, would serve as draft animals for plow agriculture, would provide transportation, and would supply leather and tallow to stimulate local industries. Therefore, with San Miguel serving as a central distribution place, the Jesuits initially introduced ninety-nine head of cattle into each of the *reducciones* of the Uruguay.[20] It became immediately apparent that mission settlements with broad open grasslands were better equipped to develop a viable ranching industry than those near streams and rivers.

Although the cattle venture was a failure in *reducciones* such as Apóstoles, San José, and Santa Teresa, the animals did exceptionally well in many of the settlements. By 1635, there were some 400 cows in Jesús-María, near the Río Pardo and within the Jacuí Valley. Candelaria, located on the grassy interfluve between the Ijuí and the Piritaní had 200 head. Such results encouraged the padres to introduce cattle into the foothills of the Serra Geral, the lowlands of the Jacuí (*depressão central*), and, finally, into the *campanha*.[21] Because cattle did so well on the natural pastures of the *campanha*, the padres introduced many more. In the years from 1634 to 1636, over 5,000 additional head were introduced, the bulk of these being cows.[22]

Jesuit settlement activity in the *otra banda* was dealt a serious blow by the *paulista* raids of the 1630s, and this region was abandoned in 1638. A successful pattern of settlement activity had been worked out, however; and when the eastern *reducciones* were reestablished in 1687, a combination of ranching and agriculture provided the basis for successful management of the *siete pueblos* of the upper Uruguay.

New settlements made in 1687 were not located in close proximity to the feral herds of the *campanha*; instead, they were selected for their agricultural capabilities. As was the case in the earlier *reducciones*, sites were selected near streams and on the margins of the *galería* forests. In such locations, Indians could utilize the *mato* for slash and burn agriculture; and areas of less dense vegetation, near the missions, could be cleared for the community gardens and plantings.

Organization of the new *reducciones* was similar to that of their antecedents, although greatly expanded and perfected throughout sixty years of experimenting and planning. It was bureaucratic and extremely paternalistic, but undoubtedly efficient. The Jesuits had been named sole protectors of the Indians in the provinces of Paraná,

[20]"Colecção de Angelis," MS I-29, 7, 31. This *anua* written by Padre Romero and dated April 3, 1636, has been transcribed in Roberto C. Simonsen, *História económica do Brasil, 1500-1820*, 2 vols. (Rio de Janeiro: Companhia Editora Nacional, 1937), 1:229.

[21]The *campanha* is the grasslands environment of southern Brazil, a northern extension of the Argentine *pampa*.

[22]Aurélio Porto, "Martirio do Veneravel Padre Cristovão de Mendoze S. J.," in *Anais do III Congresso Sul-Riograndense de História e Geografia*, 4 vols. (Pôrto Alegre: Globo, 1940) 2:794.

Uruguay, Yabebirí, and Itatines. They were responsible for the "protection and defense of these humble natives,"[23] and they took their commission very seriously.

In a tight chain of command, each *reducción* was assigned two Jesuit missionaries, a *cura* or chief parish priest and a vicar, both of whom were subject to the Mission Superior and provincial authorities. In each village, a council (*cabildo*) was organized. It was composed of Indians and presided over by an Indian *corregidor*, who was usually the military commander as well. While the *corregidor* was nominally elected, his election had to be confirmed by the Spanish government upon recommendation of the *cura*. There were eleven minor village officials—all of whom were subject to the local *cura*, who was consulted in all matters and who intervened everywhere.[24] These village officials were also farmers.

In the case of the first new *reducciones* (San Miguel, San Nicolás, and San Luis Gonzaga), each had a well-developed political organization at the time of its founding. Once a site had been selected for a new community, distribution of agricultural plots could be made immediately. Individual plots called *abambaes* (*aba*: Indian; *mbae*: possession) were never actually owned by Indian families but were worked under a stewardship arrangement. In conjunction with Indian officials, the local *cura* measured the amount of land necessary for a family. Punishment was forthcoming if all of the land was not worked.

Although the *abambaes* were the closest thing to private holdings that existed in the *reducciones*, they may have been worked communally. During times of planting and harvest, teams of workers were organized, headed by their *caciques*. One or two of the village officials (*cabildantes*) were assigned to each team to keep a record of all who did not work. In this way a good harvest was often achieved.

After the harvest, only a portion of the produce was kept by the farmer. Community storehouses called *percheles*, which were apparently used in pre-Spanish times, were available for storing maize and *habas*. A farmer was required to bring two large sacks of maize to the *percheles* after each harvest. The name of the owner was attached to each sack, which was stored for use during periods of deficiency. Food and seed were considered safer in the *percheles*, where the Indians could not use these items unwisely or trade them for alcohol or manufactured goods and then suffer from hunger. Even when Indians stored grain, many required assistance from the church at the end of the year.

[23]"Auto del Presidente de la Audiencia para nombrar protector de indios al Provincial del Paraguay," quoted in Pablo Hernández, *Organización social de las doctrinas guaraníes de la Compañía de Jesús*, 2 vols. (Barcelona: Gustavo Gil, 1913), 1:511-12.
[24]Guillermo Furlong Cardiff, *José Cardiel, S. J. y su carta-relación 1747* (Buenos Aires: Escrituras Coloniales Rioplatenses, 1953), pp. 137-38.

Although agriculture in the new *reducciones* was better organized and more productive than it had been in pre-*paulista* times, food was frequently in short supply. Insects, particularly ants, attacked the vegetables; parrots took a heavy toll of maize after it ripened.

First, the Jesuits introduced the iron hoe; then, with the availability of draft animals obtained as calves from the feral herds, the common European iron-tipped plow was manufactured locally and used. Near each of the pueblos, a large corral was built; oxen were kept there during the planting season. These animals were made available to the Indians to assist them in preparing their fields. This practice has been described as follows:

> When it is time to plow the fields, 600 to 800 oxen are rounded up and are distributed among the Indians. The secretary lists each Indian who receives oxen, and when they are returned their names are checked off. This is to make sure the animals are not lost or killed and eaten by the Indians.
> The Indians treat the animals very badly; they overwork them and do not allow them to eat or drink. As a result the total number of oxen in the mission corral is never made available all at once. After three months of work one group is retired and a fresh group is utilized.[25]

Large parcels of land held communally were known as *tupambae* (*tupa*: God; *mbae*: possession). Such holdings fell under two major classifications: 1) vast cattle lands of the *campanha*, owned in common by all the pueblos; and 2) individual mission properties, consisting of agricultural lands and the mission buildings and factories.[26] In some cases, the *tupambae* devoted to agriculture were subdivided into land utilized for royal tribute, land used to support the church and to sustain widows and orphans, and land used to support the entire pueblo in times of famine.

Among the lands devoted to royal tribute were the extensive *yerbales*, often located over 100 kilometers from the mission. Each of the pueblos possessed a large *yerbal* where a number of Indians were sent during the months of the dry season to harvest the wild *mate* (*Ilex paraguaiensis* St. Hil.). Attempts to cultivate the plant nearer the pueblos met with little success; the natural *yerbales* always produced a better crop. The leaves were dried, toasted, and pulverized, and then brought to the pueblos in large sacks. Because they felt that Indian laborers were being exploited by the padres, the *provinciales* attempted to limit activity in the *yerbales*. In 1647, the royal tribute had been reduced for the Indians of the *otra banda* because "they had valiantly defended their lands against the Portuguese of Brazil";[27] but they were

---

[25] José Cardiel, "Breve relación de las misiones del Paraguay," quoted in Hernández, *Organización social*, 2:531.

[26] Small *talleres* in which cotton textiles were made and wool spun and woven or the processing sheds for the harvested yerba mate.

[27] "Cédula Real de 1647," quoted in Hernández, *Organización social*, 2:514-15.

still required to pay one peso of eight *reales* for each Indian male between the ages of eighteen and fifty. *Mate* was one of the commodities that could be readily marketed to satisfy the demand for tribute. As a result, a brisk trade in *mate* developed in the early eighteenth century between the pueblos of Uruguay and the cities of Santa Fé and Buenos Aires. According to one account, "Each year a shipment of tribute was sent from the pueblos to Santa Fé and Buenos Aires by boat. In these cities there were *procuradores* who put the goods in warehouses. They always sent more than the tribute required to exchange the surplus for iron, swords, guns, powder, medicine, and rope."[28] In addition, *mate* from the missions was exported to Chile, Potosí, and Peru. Using barter, the pueblos exchanged cotton for wool and sugar cane for cattle.

Most of the pueblos maintained large plantings of cotton. After this fiber and a textile industry were introduced into the *reducciones*, cotton and cotton textiles from the mission area were used to pay the tribute debt. Usually, cotton was grown in the *tupambae* as a community project. San Miguel had extensive cotton plantings as early as 1691, as well as a substantial cloth and textile industry. As many as 6,000 *quintales* of cotton per year were harvested from the San Miguel plantations.[29] In addition to cotton, there were also community fields of maize, sugar cane, tobacco, and, to a lesser degree, rice; however, an attempt to cultivate vines and to produce wine failed.

All Indians in a pueblo were expected to contribute to the cultivation of the *tupambae*. Each tributary male was supposed to spend Mondays and Saturdays working in the common fields during the six months of the growing season. Food items harvested in the *tupambaes* were stored in the *percheles*; and from this source, food was made available for persons making trips to Buenos Aires and to the *yerbales*. The produce of the *tupambae* also supplied food and seeds for many of the mission Indians who used up their private supply each year.

Each of the mission settlements possessed a garden *tupambae*, which usually occupied the best section of land near the mission church. Located close to the communal corrals, these gardens could utilize manure for fertilizer. Mission gardens abounded with European vegetables and fruit trees. Thus, Anton Sepp, an Austrian Jesuit, was impressed with the variety of fruits and vegetables that he encountered in Yapejú on his way from Buenos Aires to San Miguel in 1691:

> There is a large garden next to the mission full of vegetables and fruit trees. There were cabbage, chickory, parsnip, spinach, couve, Munich style turnips, parsley, anise, . . . melons, cucumbers and Indian

[28]Furlong Cardiff, *José Cardiel*, p. 150.
[29]Padre Antonio Sepp, *Viagem as missões jesuiticas e trabalhos apostólicos* (São Paulo: Livraria Martins Editora, 1943), p. 199.

plants. Every mission is also well supplied with sugar cane, oranges, lemons, apples, pears, nuts, peaches, pomegranates, quince and other fruit known in Germany.[30]

Mission gardens were worked by Indians who were selected for their diligence and good work and were closely supervised by the padres. They were constantly struggling with ants. These insects and the periodic droughts of the upper Uruguay region were the most serious agricultural problems that the Jesuit farmers encountered.

None of the new *reducciones* was more than ten leagues (a Spanish league equals six kilometers) from its neighbor; most were much closer together. A signal light displayed from the tower of one *reducción* could be seen from the tower of another. Such visual communication was designed to provide warning in the event of a surprise attack such as those inflicted by *paulistas* on earlier settlements. Roads connecting the *siete pueblos* were relatively good. Bridges were constructed; and way-stations, where travelers could stay, were built five leagues apart. Indians were kept busy building and repairing these roads and bridges during the five or six months when they were not working in the fields.

Many of the *reducciones* grew to be impressive communities. In 1691, Padre Sepp reported that "each *pueblo* has an ample and beautiful common, about 400 feet square, located next to the church. The houses form streets just as they do in European cities, but these houses are of very different construction with straw or thatch roofs and a few have tile roofs.... Every *pueblo* has a large and beautiful church."[31] By 1697, San Miguel had become one of the largest *reducciones* of the Jesuit state. The population exceeded 6,000. As a result, it was divided; a new site was selected for about half the inhabitants. Sepp was one of a contingent of padres from San Miguel and nearby San Lorenzo who selected the site for the new settlement, which was called San Juan Bautista.[32] Lands at the new site were distributed by

[30] Ibid., pp. 115-16.
[31] Ibid., pp. 119, 122.
[32] Ibid., p. 189. Although writing after the *siete pueblos* had been established, Cardiel outlined the criteria he considered essential for a mission settlement. "A nearly flat plain should be selected with the following attributes: 1) It must be at least one-fourth league wide so the streets can extend long enough; 2) it should be somewhat high, so that drainage will be good and the inhabitants will enjoy good air circulation; 3) it must not be near a swamp where there are mosquitoes, toads and poisonous snakes; 4) a supply of good water should be nearby to drink and to use to wash and bathe; 5) it should be near forests to obtain firewood and lumber; 6) it must be open to the south to receive cool breezes during the summertime."

During the era of the early settlements (before the *paulista* raids), the padres did not pay much attention to these factors; as a result, almost all the *reducciones* had to be moved two or three times or else they had to be abandoned altogether. In 1747, Cardiel wrote: "Construction is more permanent now. There are no straw houses; all are of adobe brick. Settlements are armed this time, too, and provided with a well-trained militia supplied with horses and equipment." Furlong Cardiff, *Cardiel*, pp. 153, 154, 157.

Mission Estancias and Yerbales After 1735

Map taken from BRUNO GARSCH middle 18th century

the *caciques* (chiefs) to their respective subjects, and crops were planted in both the *tupambae* and *abambae* before the women and children were allowed to join the men. It was customary for nearby settlements to contribute labor, seeds, and horses to a new *reducción*.

In addition to the oxen used as draft animals in the mission fields, other domestic animals were kept in the *reducciones*. Each pueblo, shortly after its founding, received a large flock of sheep to supply the inhabitants with wool. Unlike oxen, which were badly cared for, sheep were well taken care of because their wool was so highly valued. Some of the pueblos, particularly those in the central portion of the Uruguay valley, were better suited for sheep than those of the upper Uruguay. A relatively cool winter in the pueblos of Yapejú, San Borja, Santo Tomé, and La Cruz produced a sufficiently thick fleece to make the central area the center of wool production for the entire Jesuit state. Sepp reported that in 1691 there were over 40,000 sheep in the corrals of the *reducción* of Santo Tomé, and that each head of sheep was considered to be worth three times more than a steer because of its wool. All the *reducciones* of southern Brazil had domestic chickens, milk cows, sheep, goats, and, of course, horses and mules.[33]

Before 1700, few domestic cattle were kept to supply the pueblos with meat, hides or tallow. In order to meet the demand for these items, feral cattle were hunted and killed in the vast *campanha* grasslands. Meat was super-abundant and was eaten by almost everyone at every meal, yet very little of it came from domestic supplies. Sepp reported, "There are so many steers, cows, and calves in the *campos* that in many places you can see nothing else except cattle, fat and beautiful cattle. Animals are sold from pueblo to pueblo or to the Spanish, but not to individuals, because within the pueblos meat is distributed by the padres twice a day to the Indians, free of charge."[34]

When Padre Sepp arrived at Yapejú in 1691 to begin his first assignment among the mission Indians, he was shocked at the amount of beef available. There was so much that "only the very best quality beef was offered to the padres, most of it being veal."[35] People of that area were so accustomed to eating veal that they would not eat older beef (*carne de boi*). On a short horse-back excursion into the interior, Sepp observed the "uninterrupted fields covered with nothing but cattle."[36] While the padres watched, the Indians killed six cows and four calves. They skinned them and cut them into pieces—all in the space of about one hour. During the barbecue that followed, the meat was served almost raw; and the Austrian priest lamented that it was not

[33]Sepp, *Viagem as missões jesuiticas e travalhos apostólicos*, p. 133.
[34]Ibid., p. 130.
[35]Ibid., p. 103.
[36]Ibid., p. 105.

"well-cooked and prepared with a sauce of rosemary and marjoram."[37]

The *campo* around Yapejú was particularly productive, especially the lands on the eastern side of the Uruguay. Indians of that *reducción* had been given permission to hunt cattle on the east bank since the 1660s, and they knew where the large concentrations were to be found. Sepp reported:

> There are innumerable herds of cattle and they feed in the areas of *capim verde* [a certain quality pasture composed of a number of species]. They do not have barns or stables but leave the cattle in the *campo* day and night, winter and summer. Neither do they cut the grass to make hay [*feno*] because it is able to serve all year for pasture. And there is no need to have cattle guards, for there are no rustlers.[38]

In two months during 1691, Sepp relates that 50,000 head of cattle were rounded up around Yapejú; and he reports that a few months earlier, 90,000 head had been taken. Such round-ups were for the purpose of obtaining hides, which were shipped down the river to Buenos Aires and eventually exported to Europe. In what is perhaps an exaggerated report, Sepp states that three Jesuit ships transported some 300,000 hides to Europe in 1691.[39] Profits accruing to the Jesuits must have been enormous. Hides obtained without spending one penny could be sold in Buenos Aires for the same price that an entire animal brought. In Europe, these hides were worth considerably more.

Availability of a seemingly unlimited number of cattle took pressure off the agricultural base of the mission settlements. Although some of the pueblos did not have easy access to the *campanha* cattle, animals captured there were sold or otherwise distributed among all of them. While the *campanha* was considered the common property of the pueblos, those that supplied men for the round-ups had the best claim. Pueblos that contributed little or nothing usually had to pay for the cattle. Such security, however, was not long-lasting. The wealth of the *campanha* was eventually tapped by non-Jesuit groups, and it proved to be insufficient for all who sought to use its resources. The cattle lands and the *reducciones* were eventually turned over to the Portuguese with the Treaty of Madrid in 1750, and the Jesuits withdrew from Rio Grande do Sul.

---

[37] Ibid., p. 106.
[38] Ibid., p. 128.
[39] Ibid., p. 131.

22. The Inquisition and the Enlightenment Library of Antonio Nariño

JERROLD S. BUTTREY

Antonio Nariño was the creole son of a viceregal officer who served in Bogotá during the late eighteenth century. At the age of twenty-nine, Nariño was arrested by agents of the Inquisition. He was charged with possessing unauthorized publications and holding unacceptable views. This article examines details of that event and analyzes available information concerning Nariño's library.

An inventory of Antonio Nariño's library was made in August 1794 at the time of his arrest in Bogotá for allegedly seditious activities. It has long been published and referred to in scholarly papers but has not been treated in an orderly and critical manner, perhaps because the inventory does not lend itself easily to such treatment.[1] Nonetheless, much of the writing about Nariño tends to stress the connections between his books and his important acts in the pre-revolutionary and early independence periods of New Granada.[2] Were

[1] Eduardo Posada and Pedro M. Ibáñez, eds., *El Precursor: Documentos sobre la vida pública y privada del General Antonio Nariño* (Bogotá: Imprenta Nacional, 1903), pp. 146-50, 164-79, and 183-91. Bernard Moses wittily calls it an "enlightening document." See Moses, *Spain's Declining Power in South America* (Berkeley: University of California Press, 1919), p. 283.

[2] The most important biographies of Nariño, in order of appearance, are the following: José María Vergara y Vergara, *Vida y escritos del General Antonio Nariño*, 2d ed. (Bogotá: Imprenta Nacional, 1946); Soledad Acosta de Samper, *Biografía del General Nariño* (Pasto: Imprenta Departamental, 1910); Raimundo Rivas, *El andante caballero don Antonio Nariño: Juventud (1765-1803)* (Bogotá: Editorial ABC, 1938); Jorge Ricardo Vejarano, *Nariño, su vida, sus infortunios, su talla histórica* (Bogotá: Editorial Centro, 1945); Alberto Miramón, *Nariño* (Bogotá: Editorial Kelley, 1960); Thomas Blossom, *Nariño, Hero of Colombian Independence* (Tucson: University of Arizona Press, 1967). Most useful are the volumes by Rivas and Blossom, but the latter's treatment of Nariño's library is very misleading. In an attempt to present a list of "damnable works," Blossom chose titles of one orthodox book after another in an exercise of uncanny inaccuracy.

the collection extant, the library probably would have been amply described. The Inquisition ordered Nariño's books to be publicly burned in Bogotá's main square. Although there is no evidence that the burning was effected, the library never reappeared.

Nariño, the creole son of a Spanish viceregal official, was an imposing figure at the age of twenty-nine in late eighteenth-century Bogotá. Socially prominent, intellectually stimulating, entrepreneurially aggressive, he was treasurer of the tithes of the archdiocese and an ex-*alcalde ordinario* of Bogotá. At the same time, he was enjoying—if not profiting from—an extensive export business based on sugar and cinchona. Nariño was easily the most important of the several young men implicated in the putative republican plot against the viceroyalty which occasioned his arrest.[3] His true role in the plot has remained a matter of debate. Nariño's milieu in 1794 is well described in contemporary documents. He had established a *tertulia* in his home, in the room which housed the impressive library. Although he stated that the primary purpose of the *tertulia* was to read the most important periodicals of the day, obviously the library itself, which Nariño had been expanding through the convenience of his export business, furnished basic sources that complemented the readings of the group.[4]

In December 1793, a book had come to Nariño which was to have a profound and immediate impact on his life. For him, the most important part of this book on the history of the French Constituent Assembly by Galart de Montjoie was the Declaration of the Rights of Man, adopted by the National Assembly in 1789.[5] The French monarchy had endorsed the natural rights of liberty, property, and freedom from oppression and had further acknowledged the sovereignty of the people.

Nariño soon translated the Declaration of the Rights of Man into

---

[3]There is serious doubt in this writer's mind whether the plot existed in the minds of the "revolutionaries" or in the imaginations of the viceregal officials. The question will never be settled, for the authorities generated enough documents over the next several years of litigation—after which all of the surviving conspirators were set free for lack of proof—to convince republican historians that the abortive uprising should be celebrated in text and tradition.

[4]Rivas, *El andante caballero*, pp. 50-51; and Posada and Ibáñez, *El Precursor*, p. 607.

[5]The volume used by Nariño for the translation has never been precisely identified. It was most likely a part of Felix-Louis Christophe Montjoie's *Histoire de la Révolution de France et de l'Assemblée nationale* (Paris: Gattey, 1792). The book belonged to Viceroy Ezpeleta, but how it came into Nariño's possession is not known. In his defense before the Audiencia, Nariño said that the book "vino de las manos menos sospechosas que se puede imaginar." Posada and Ibáñez, *El Precursor*, p. 95. While reviewing the case, the Council of the Indies claimed that Captain Ramírez de Arellano of the Viceroy's guard delivered the book. Ibid., p. 605. But in a request to the Crown for Nariño's release, in 1800, his wife insisted that Nariño had received the book from Ezpeleta himself. José Manual Pérez Sarmiento, ed., *Proceso de Nariño* (Cádiz: Imprenta de M. Alvarez, 1914), p. 183.

Spanish and began working in secret to publish the document on his own press. Soon after printing one hundred copies, Nariño was warned by a friend of the necessity of destroying them. Some say the burning was effected in December, others, as late as February 1794. At any rate, distribution of the impression was extremely limited: only two copies are known to have passed out of Nariño's hands, and neither civil nor ecclesiastical authorities could produce a copy to be used later in the case against him. Nonetheless, Nariño's surreptitious translation and publication of the Declaration of the Rights of Man of the French Constituent Assembly were the primary grounds for his sentence of eight years in prison in Ceuta, perpetual exile from the Americas, and forfeiture of all personal property.[6]

R. R. Palmer has noted that for publishing the Rights of Man, "Nariño was transported to Spanish Africa."[7] Had Nariño actually reached Africa, had he been kept destitute and in exile from the Americas, he would present us with few historical problems. The library also would be more easily dealt with, for in it are found a number of seditious works ample for any self-respecting revolutionary of the era. But Nariño was to inconvenience historians by jumping ship as it entered Cádiz harbor, to strut across the stage of Colombian history again and again, often in seemingly contradictory roles.

Delineation of the intellect of the "Precursor" of Colombian independence is not the purpose of this paper. The original goal of working with the inventory was simply to put the books in an order that lends itself better to scholarly consideration.[8] Works that could be identified were categorized by subject, language, publication date, and relationship to the Enlightenment and to the Inquisition. By comparing these characteristics, data were obtained which throw new light on the library. These data are held to be valid only for Nariño's library, but they may serve as a departure point for further speculation on Nariño's ideology. Hopefully, the information will also offer suggestions for additional research in the relationship between the Enlightenment and the Inquisition in Spain and Spanish America. The data seem to indicate that the Inquisition had, at most, minimal influence in protecting those areas from the rapidly spreading ideas of the eighteenth century Enlightenment.

The inventory of the confiscated library listed exactly 700 title entries, including 28 works smuggled out of Nariño's house on the eve of

[6]While Nariño's sentence was severe, it was not extraordinary. As early as 1752, King Ferdinand VI had indicated perpetual exile and confiscation of goods for the crime of publishing without royal consent. Marcelin Defourneaux, *L'Inquisition espagnole et les livres francais au XVIIe siecle* (Paris: Presses Universitaires de France, 1963), p. 37.

[7]*The Age of the Democratic Revolution*, 2 vols. (Princeton, N.J.: Princeton University Press, 1965), 2:512.

[8]Jerrold S. Buttrey, "A Revisionist Approach to an Enlightenment Library," (Master's thesis, University of Texas, 1967), pp. 80-133.

his arrest and later recovered by viceregal authorities.[9] The total number of volumes in the inventory is 1,891. The following analysis is based on the works which were identifiable, not on the library as a whole. Because of the size of the library, and because positive identification was possible for more than 60 percent of the titles, there is adequate data for at least a tentative re-evaluation of the collection.

Nariño's books were printed in six languages: Spanish, French, Latin, Italian, English, and Greek (in diminishing order of occurrence). Spanish is predominant, with a total of 271 works out of 425 works for which language could be identified. One hundred and eight—or 25 percent—are French. This considerable amount compares with the even more surprising 28 percent of French works in the library of Archbishop-Viceroy Caballero y Góngora.[10] There are 21 works in Latin, and there would be many more if the classics identified (45 in number) were included. The many translations of the classics preclude language classification. Fourteen of the works are Italian, ten are English, and one is Greek.

There is no precise information regarding when Nariño acquired the books in his library. Publication dates are grouped in rather arbitrary categories so that hypotheses might be based on periods most frequently represented. Books written prior to the introduction of printing to Spain (ca. 1500) comprise 11 percent of the 402 titles for which publication dates could be ascertained. Three percent are from the sixteenth century, and the seventeenth century provides almost 10 percent. Three-quarters (304) of the books were published in the eighteenth century, and one-third of these (109) were printed between 1780 and 1794.[11]

Of the 614 titles for which subject identification was made, 5 percent (31) were philosophical works. Interestingly, all of these works for which dates are identified were first published in the eighteenth century. Works by D'Holbach, Voltaire, Montesquieu, and Condillac indicate that the French philosophers were present, as has been generally held. Almost 40 percent (12) of the philosophical works were in the tongue of the philosophers, but the French were not all *aficionados* of the modern ideas. In fact, opposing the four

[9]The hidden books were soon discovered in the room of a priest who was a friend of Nariño but who recanted before being expelled from the viceroyalty. Many of the works bore the signature of Vargas, who had by this time been forced to flee Nueva Granada. These works—which included Montesquieu, Voltaire, William Robertson, and Raynal—have traditionally been considered a part of Nariño's library. They are so treated in this paper.

[10]José Torre Revello, "La biblioteca de Virrey-Arzobispo del Nuevo Reino de Granada Antonio Caballero y Góngora," *Boletín del Instituto de Investigaciones Históricas* (Buenos Aires), July-September 1929, pp. 27-45.

[11]There is evidence that Nariño inherited some of his library from his father. The many works published from 1780 to 1794, after the elder Nariño's death, are the only subgroup that can be safely considered to have been collected by Nariño.

enlightened works mentioned above are five French books that were written for the very purpose of confounding the new philosophy.

By far the largest category of books in the library is that of religious works, which contains 220 (36 percent) of the 614 titles identified.[12] The Spanish Inquisition ordered condemnation or expurgation of ten of the religious works. Condemnation of religious works was aimed more at errant Catholics than at Protestants, of whom two are represented. Among the former is a work of Louis-Antoine Caraccioli, the writer considered by Richard Herr to have been the most popular representative in Spain of the conservative position.[13] Of the latter, Necker's *De l'importance des opinions religieuses* was recommended to Floridablanca by a Spanish diplomat as a work which might, with proper changes, be used in the struggle against Protestantism and atheism.[14] While fifteen (7 percent) of the religious works were written precisely for the purpose of refuting the Enlightenment, only one is considered to have been written by a protagonist of the new ideas—the work of Necker mentioned above.

It is possible that no type of literature more influenced eighteenth century Europe than the social sciences. The 91 titles in this category make up almost 15 percent of the 614 works identified for subject matter in the library. Fifty-one of the 59 books (86 percent) for which publication dates were identified were printed after 1700. Twelve (20 percent) were published by mid-century, 19 (32 percent) from 1750 to 1779 and 20 (34 percent) from 1780 to 1794. Periodicals comprise seven of the 20 entries in this latter group, including three of the most important Spanish journals of the day: *Memorial literario de la Corte de Madrid*, *El Mercurio de España*, and *El Espíritu de los mejores diarios*.[15]

Although there is a rather even distribution of works within

[12]Titles of religious works often lend themselves to identification more easily than those of other groups, i.e., *Semana Santa*; therefore, this percentage would probably prove to be a little high should positive identification of all the works in the collection be possible.

[13]*The Eighteenth Century Revolution in Spain* (Princeton: N.J.: Princeton University Press, 1958), p. 214. The practice of expurgation was the most widely implemented method of censorship by the Holy Office. Its use has often been exaggerated: for example, Herr lists Cervantes among several authors whose works were "prohibited or ordered expurgated" (p. 205). Yet just one sentence, from *Don Quixote*, was ordered removed from all the prolific genius's work. *Indice de los libros prohibidos por el Santo Oficio de la Inquisicion Española*... (Madrid: Imprenta de D. Antonio Pérez Dubrull, 1873), p. 164.

[14]Jean Sarrailh, *La España ilustrada de la segunda mitad del siglo XVIII*, trans. Antonio Alatorre (México, D.F.: Fondo de Cultura Económica, 1957), p. 301. This recommendation came in December 1789. By then the Crown had already enlisted the aid of the Holy Office in combatting French revolutionary ideas; it would have been impolitic, if not impossible, for the civil to have overruled the ecclesiastical authority on this point as it might have done a year or so before.

[15]The ample work of Luis Miguel Enciso Recio has focused attention on the periodical press of the era; for examples, see his *Nipho y el periodismo español del*

several subgroups of the social sciences, economics has easily the largest number with 30 percent of the titles. Throughout the eighteenth century in Spain, political economy was the most vital branch of the social sciences. Many of the major works in this field are present in the library, ranging from the neo-mercantilism (influenced by Colbert) of Uztáriz, Bernado de Ulloa, and Ramos to the rebuttal of the physiocrats by Nicolás de Arriquibar, who recommended that more attention be paid to Spain's industrial base than to her agriculture.[16]

The Spanish crown took an active interest in developing economic societies comparable to those in France and England. In 1765, a royal license was granted for the Sociedad Vascongada de los Amigos del País.[17] A history of the society, *Ensayo de la Sociedad Vascongada de los Amigos del País*, probably written by Peñaflorida, was published in 1768. By that time, societies were being founded throughout Spain, which could boast of 56 by 1789. Indicative of their influence in the Indies is the essay by Quito's precursor (and Nariño's co-conspirator), Eugenio Espejo, *Discurso dirigido a la Sociedad Patriótica de Quito*. Writing from exile in Bogotá, Espejo vainly encouraged the founding of such a society in his home city.[18] The primary purposes of the societies were two-fold: to build up libraries, thereby encouraging reading and discussion of the latest ideas from abroad, and to present papers and books so that Spain might herself contribute to this body of knowledge.

In the field of customs and folklore, there are several important commentaries on past and contemporary Spain. Two of these are replies to Masson's denigrating articles on Spain in the *Methodical Encyclopedia*, those of Juan Pablo Forner and Antonio Caballines. In education, opposing the more traditional positions of Madame de Genlis and the Marqués de Caraccioli, is the French translation of John Locke's *Some Thoughts Concerning Education*.[19]

Attempts by the Spanish establishment to control the influence of

siglo XVIII (Valladolid: Universidad de Valladolid, Secretariado de Publicaciones, 1956) and *Prensa económica del XVIII; El correo Mercantil de España y sus Indias* (Valladolid: Facultad de Filosofía y Letras de la Universidad de Valladolid, 1958).

[16]Herr, *The Eighteenth Century Revolution*, pp. 48-49.

[17]This was only three years after the founding of the Paris society. Sarrailh, *La España ilustrada*, p. 232.

[18]Although Espejo's attempt was frustrated, these societies enjoyed important success in other parts of Spanish America. See Robert Jones Schafer, *The Economic Societies in the Spanish World, 1763-1821* (Syracuse: University of Syracuse Press, 1958).

[19]Roland D. Hussey was the first to note that Rousseau was not in the Nariño collection as had been previously reported; but he further indicated, this time incorrectly, that neither was Locke to be found. See Hussey's "Traces of French Enlightenment in Colonial Hispanic America," in *Latin America and the Enlightenment*, ed. Arthur P. Whitaker, 2d ed. (Ithaca: Cornell University Press, 1961), p. 42. Locke's friend and translator, Pierre Coste, appeared as the author "monsieur Poste" in the inventory, making immediate identification most difficult. Posada and Ibáñez, *El Precursor*, p. 189.

Enlightenment ideas in the social sciences were as ineffective as the data in the category regarding religious work suggest. While there are two works that were written to discredit the Enlightenment, there are seven which take pro-Enlightenment positions, and 19 more may be said to be disseminators of Enlightenment ideas of one sort or another. The fact that only two of these works—Condillac's *Commerce and Government* and Montesquieu's *Spirit of the Laws*—were condemned by the Spanish Holy Office clearly indicates that if the Inquisition were sincerely attempting to curb these intellectual trends, its shots were wide of the mark.[20]

While he thought it something of a bother, the greatest Spanish source for the ideas of the "century of genius," Benito Feijóo, was not to be deterred by the Inquisition. Two great works, *Teatro Crítico* and *Cartas Eruditas*, made Feijóo the most important transmitter of foreign ideas at that time. His function might be compared to those of Bacon and Bayle in their countries; Feijóo tied together the social and natural sciences in the most reasonable and popular manner. Later in the century, Miguel Jerónimo Suárez was to continue to battle against overwhelming odds to popularize the sciences. Journalism was Suárez's forte; and through this medium he attempted to relate new materials in the social, natural, and applied sciences. His *Memorias instructivas y curiosas sacadas de las obras de varios autores extranjeros, señaladamenta las Reales Academias y Sociedades de Francia, Inglaterra, Alemania, Prusia y Suecia* was published weekly from 1778 to 1791. A major disseminator of Enlightenment ideas, particularly in the field of political economics, the periodical includes essays by Condillac on commerce, Necker on corn laws, and Turgot on distribution of wealth.[21]

The two naturalists of the eighteenth century, Buffon and Linneaus, are in the collection—an appropriate tribute to the important position biology enjoyed in Nueva Granada. The 39 volumes of Buffon's *Historia natural* indicate that Nariño was probably faced with a problem common to learned Americans. Buffon's hypothesis that American species were younger and therefore inferior to those of the European continent was popular among Old World intellectuals of the day. It clearly implied the inability of the American environment to fashion progress in the European mode. Nonetheless, the work of Buffon and his disciples was admired and collected by Americans of both

---

[20] An example of the Inquisition's inadequacy is found in the appearance of Montesquieu's *Letras familiares*, which deals with his earlier condemned work but was not itself anathematized. The above work was not even condemned in Rome. *Index Librorum Prohibitorum* (Rome, 1948), p. 329.
[21] Robert Sidney Smith, "The Wealth of Nations in Spain and Hispanic America, 1780-1830," *Journal of Political Economy*, 65 (April 1957): 104.

hemispheres, who could make selective use of enlightened sources.[22]

In the field of history there are 74 titles, 12 percent of the 614 works identified for subject matter. Of the histories identified by publication date, more than 75 percent (48) were published in the eighteenth century. There are only four seventeenth-century titles and none at all from the previous century.

Contemporary history about the New World is not found in great quantity in the collection, but its selection reflects awareness of the most important writing being done in Europe. There are two copies of Robertson's *History of America*, for which the Scottish author was offered a chair in the Real Academia de la Historia, only to have the invitation withdrawn when the work was found so offensive that the Council of Castile ordered it banned from Spain and the Indies.[23] Two works that were prohibited by the Inquisition, Raynal's *Histoire philosophique et politique* and de Pauw's *Recherches philosophiques sur les américains*, vied with Robertson for popularity and overshadowed him in their adherence to Buffon's hypothesis of the innate inferiority of the American species. De Pauw's work, the most enthusiastic espousal of these ideas, was to be refuted in the work of Giovanni Carli, who attempted to continue Antonio de Ulloa's notes on America. Ulloa's travels in America and those of his companion, Jorge Juan, are salient works among the 23 comprising the geography and travel collection. The comments of James Cook on his voyages, perhaps the most popular of this genre in the century, are present in four titles.

Although five of the historical titles were condemned by the Holy Office and two more by the Council of Castile, it is interesting to note that one of these works, the faithful Caraccioli's *Vida de Clemente XIV*, was written by an opponent of the Enlightenment. Nor are all of the other histories on the *Index* by enlightened authors: the condemnation of Gregorio Leti and William Robertson appear to be more the result of their Protestantism than their liberalism. Opposing the single apologist are three works closely connected with the Enlightenment, while no fewer than ten can be considered disseminators of these ideas. Here it becomes evident that the combatants are never to meet in head-on conflict; however, it should be granted that in the field of history the ecclesiastical authorities appear to have recognized the immediacy of the challenge more than in the other social sciences or even in philosophy.

One of the more interesting parts of Nariño's library is his collec-

---

[22]The definitive work on the "Buffonian problem" is the classic by Antonello Gerbi, *La disputa del nuovo mondo: Storia di una polemica, 1750-1900* (Milan: R. Ricciardi, 1955).

[23]Ricardo Donoso relates this interesting story at some length in his *Un letrado del siglo XVIII, el Doctor José Perfecto de Salas* (Buenos Aires: Universidad de Buenos Aires, Facultad de Filosofía y Letras, 1963), pp. 469-77.

tion of literature, some 68 titles representing 11 percent of those identified. Periods represented in greatest number are the classical, the seventeenth century, and the last half of the eighteenth century. There is a marked absence of *siglo de oro* works that one might expect to find in such a collection, and the first half of Nariño's own century also has a surprisingly small representation, particularly when considered in the light of the excellent selection of works published after mid-century.

There is a vitality to the literature of late eighteenth-century Spain that is not immediately obvious in retrospect. The new philosophy had made an impact on the literary community, and most of its members were convinced that Hispanic society was lagging behind those societies north of the Pyrenees. There was a general feeling of a need for social renewal. This was reflected in the tendency to stress the importance of literary content, somewhat to the detriment of form.

This literary urge for renewal and direction was in reality a search for identity. Some writers, such as the Duke of Almodovar in his *Década epistolar sobre el estado de letras en Francia*, would remind Spain that she must respond to the new trends of the continental tradition of which she was a part. Others, like Cadalso, fearing that Spain would revolve around France as a cultural satellite, demanded that Spain fully exploit and appreciate her own cultural heritage. Many of the proponents of this position were nonetheless well versed in contemporary French literature.

The interest of foreign authors at the time is found in the fourteen literary works by non-Spanish authors. Among the French works are Montesquieu's risqué *El Templo de Gnida*, Marmontel's banned *Belisario,* and Diderot's dramatic work, *El padre de familias.* There are two works by Englishmen, both from the seventeenth century: Milton's *El paraíso* and the popular verses of John Owen. Italian literature is also represented by Ponziano Conti and Muratori.

A quarter of the literature collection is composed of classical works, all of Latin origin, with the exception of Homer and Atheneus. Cicero contributes six and Virgil two of the nineteen titles. They are the only authors encountered more than once in this group. Included are the *Loves* of Ovid, the *Fables* of Aesop and Phaedrus, and a work of Plautus.

Spanish classics do not fare nearly so well. There are only two sixteenth-century works: Ercilla's *La Araucana* and the works of Fray Luis de Granada. *Don Quixote* opens the seventeenth century and sounds the death knell for the romance. That genre, which was forbidden to and so common in the Indies, is not found again in the library. The picaresque novel survives, however, in the works of Enríquez Gómez and Jerónimo de Alcalá. The only drama of these two centuries, which were so very productive for the Spanish stage, is that of Molière—a fact which in itself should bring suspicion on Nariño.

The presence or absence of given works have resulted in lengthy and heated debate over the intellectual formation of Nariño. In the last century, José Manuel Groot took Rousseau's predominant position in Nariño's time so much for granted that he listed Rousseau among the authors of the works spirited out of Nariño's house the night before his arrest. More recently, Raimundo Rivas named the work, among several he singled out of the collection, the *Social Contract*, naturally.[24] Closer imspection finds Rousseau absent, so Thomas Blossom concludes that the works of the philosopher were "probably destroyed."[25]

It must be emphasized that Nariño and his colleagues did have access to virtually all of the basic ideas of the Enlightenment—if not in the original, at least by second or even third hand. In this, the role of the periodical press of the Peninsula was particularly important; but it also disseminated orthodox ideas and theories, with direct and indirect support by the Crown.[26] In sum, there was virtually no genre of literature available on the Peninsula that could not be obtained in the New World—anathematized or not. It should be emphasized, however, that both Nariño and his library were products of a creole elite. The works which made up this atypically large collection were available, but only to a very small portion of the population.

What is most striking about the literature accessible to some Spanish Americans is its very catholicity. The range of subjects, languages, and ideologies tempts one to deny characterization of the Spanish regime as a truly despotic one that exercized a significant amount of thought control. There is little evidence that the civil and ecclesiastical authorities made serious effort to shield Spanish subjects from the main thrust of Enlightenment thought from the time Charles III came to the throne in 1759 until the French Revolution began in 1789. It was only at this later date that the throne would begin to work in concert with the Inquisition in order to stem the flow of revolutionary works entering Spain. Tension that existed between the Holy Office and the crown almost always precluded their working closely, except when the future of the monarch was in question—and that was precisely to be the case in the 1790s. The absence of French

---

[24]Rivas, *El andante caballero*, p. 50; Groot, *Historia eclesiástica y civil de Nueva Granada*, 2 vols. (Bogotá: Editorial ABC, 1953), 2:392.

[25]Blossom, *Nariño, Hero of Colombian Independence*, p. 13.

[26]Given the severity of punishment handed out for publishing anything, save marriage bans, without royal consent, it must be assumed that all imprints made public had at least the tacit approval of the civil authorities. In his defense before the viceroyalty in 1784, Nariño proved again and again that virtually each of the basic stipulations in the Declaration of the Rights of Man had been published explicitly in the Spanish periodical press freely circulating in Colombia at that time. Posada and Ibáñez, *El Precursor*, pp. 51-110.

revolutionary books from Nariño's collection is probably an indicator of the degree of success enjoyed by the dual monarchy of cross and crown during the most difficult period.

Overall success of these authorities in the period prior to 1789 is more difficult to judge. The considerable numbers of works that were truly subversive to the Old Regime but were controlled by neither the State nor the Church lead one to consider with some seriousness the following hyperbolic claim of Father Miguel de la Pinta Llorente:

> Apoyado en nuestras investigaciones sistemáticas puede el autor de este libro constatar el espíritu amplio y humano de la Inquisición española en sus funciones censorias, hasta el punto de poder concluirse que el Santo Oficio no prohibió libro verdaderamente importante, salvadas siempre y definidas, debe enterderse así, la ortodoxia y la pureza de la fe, que era su cometido especial.[27]

While it is difficult for this writer to consider the censoring duties of the Inquisition to have been of "ample and humane spirit," one might hold that—in the light of the evidence in Nariño's library—the Holy Office did in fact prohibit very few important books save those that attacked orthodoxy and the purity of the faith. It may be further posited that the Inquisition failed to anathematize a great number of potentially dangerous works because it failed to recognize the danger of works that were essentially secular, but were ultimately to undermine its position.

By the time Nariño was fashioning his library, the late eighteenth century, the battle between the old order and the new had essentially been decided. The French Revolution, and the later wars for Spanish-American independence, signalled the end to the institutionalized religious orthodoxies—the end to inquisitions—which had existed since the Middle Ages. Yet the Enlightenment was to create new problems in the nineteenth and twentieth centuries, as secular orthodoxies replaced traditional religions.

---

[27]*La Inquisición y los problemas de la cultura y de la intolerancia*, 2 vols. (Madrid: Ediciones Cultura Hispánica, 1953 and 1958), 1:277-78.

23. Spain and the Spiritual Reconquest of Santo Domingo, 1861-1865

JESS H. STONE

Based on archival research, this study describes and analyzes attempts to give the Catholic Church a monopoly over religious activity in Santo Domingo during the brief period when the country was reincorporated into the Spanish Empire. The author focuses on efforts of Archbishop Benvenido Monzón to cause the Spanish authorities to ban non-Catholic worship and on efforts by Protestants to regain a chapel that had been used as a military hospital.

On March 18, 1861, President Pedro Santana of the Dominican Republic proclaimed his country's reincorporation within the Spanish Empire. This act was precipitous for Spain, although imperial considerations dictated acceptance of the Dominicans as colonial subjects. For President Santana and his followers, the propitious pronouncement signaled the end of their seventeen years of hostilities with Haiti. Re-absorption by Spain, they believed, was the only means to preclude Haitian reconquest and to preserve Dominican culture.

During the years between Santo Domingo's experience as a Spanish possession and this third colonial epoch, various differences in culture, values, outlook, and life style had developed. These discrepancies had to be reduced to a minimum if reincorporation were to succeed. For their part, the *Santanistas* had attempted to prepare the way. One of the last alterations of the old Dominican order was President Santana's proclamation establishing Roman Catholicism as the state religion only two months before reincorporation.[1] This alteration

[1] A copy and translation of Santana's decree establishing Roman Catholicism's exclusivity within the Dominican Republic is found in British Consul Martin T. Hood to Lord Russell, No. 8, Santo Domingo, February 12, 1861, Foreign Office (Public Records Office, London), 23/43, pp. 67-74. Hood's copy of this decree is dated January 19, 1861. The Spanish documentation, Dirección de Ultramar, "Extracto—Tolerancia del culto protestante durante la república," dates the decree March 2, 1861. This date cannot be

of the law was not reflected in the Constitution and did little to affect spiritual practices. The *Santanistas* were too busy with other matters to attempt enforcement of Catholicism's spiritual monopoly. It is very likely that their thinking on the matter was not well developed. They were concerned more with appearances than with realities. Because of their geographical isolation, the few hundred Protestants, of some 250,000 Dominicans, probably never learned that their religious freedom had been outlawed by decree.[2]

This issue, as others, was left for the new Spanish authorities to resolve. Certainly President Santana envisioned no difficulties in the Spanish reformation of Dominican society when he stipulated that Spain honor all laws and treaties of the former republic. Neither did Spain.

Mindless of what complications might arise from laws inherited from the republic, officials of the new Spanish regime began with the assumption that Spanish values would have to be adopted by the Dominicans if the society were to be lifted from indolence and sloth to industry and prosperity. This assumption was bolstered by another: that the Dominicans were willing, perhaps eager, to adopt Spanish values. The social goals of the reforms they sought were expressed in the new penal code that was imposed.[3] This code was modeled in great part after the one then in existence in Spain. Its typical Spanish character was revealed by the first two chapters. Chapter 1 established the Spanish Catholic Church and obliged all parents to instruct their children in the religion under penalty of law. Article 129 of this chapter outlawed all other religious practices, thus giving the state religion a spiritual monopoly. Chapter 2 established the nonspiritual but church-influenced legal norms of public morality, among which were several prohibitions against nudity, even that of children. Such norms made sense to the more prosperous officials from a temperate climate, but they proved burdensome to the impoverished tropical subjects, especially those in the outlying areas of the new colony.

Before the new code was a year old, its unsuitability for Dominican society was apparent. While perhaps an accurate state-

checked against the original document because it has been separated from the *extracto* and presumably lost. The *extracto* is found in the Archivo Historico Nacional (Madrid) Ultramar/Santo Domingo 3530 [hereafter cited as AHN-U/SD].

[2]Nowhere in the Spanish documentation is there mention of the number of Protestants in Santo Domingo. Spanish Consul Mariano Alvarez asserted that the Dominican population was 250,000 in 1860. He was more concerned with racial composition than religious groupings. Spanish officials in Madrid may have been surprised that some Dominicans were Protestants when they first demanded the government's attention in 1861. The question posed by Protestantism for Spain, however, was one of principle not numbers. For Alvarez's population figures, see Mariano Alvarez, "Memoria, Santo Domingo ó la República Dominicana," Santo Domingo, April 20, 1860, AHN-U/SD 3526.

[3]*Bando de Policía y Gobernación* (Santo Domingo: Imprenta Nacional, January 1, 1863), AHN-U/SD 3526.

ment of the goals sought, it was wide of the mark as a guide for the reformation aspired to by the Spanish authorities. On October 26, 1863, about two months after the Dominican rebels began overcoming factionalism and were rallying to their provisional government dedicated to the reestablishment of the republic, Madrid finally realized that the code might be retrograde to Spanish aspirations and ordered the code revised. Santo Domingo's Government Council studied the matter and finally reported suggested modifications on August 9, 1864.[4] The modified version of the code did not, however, affect those portions that sought to establish the Spanish Catholic Church as the spiritual and moral force within society. Not only was the Church's monopoly unaffected, the modified code strangely ignored exceptions to the Church's exclusivity which by this time Madrid was being forced to admit.

Undoubtedly the reason that the modified code failed to better reflect religious pluralism was the influence and personality of Archbishop Benvenido Monzón. The first cathedral in the Americas had been without an archbishop until Spanish rule was reimposed. Strong church leadership was needed if the imperial experiment was to succeed. The clergy needed to be reinvigorated. Dominicans had to be brought back to a stricter observance and practice of Catholicism. In short, the Catholic Church had to undertake the spiritual reconquest of Santo Domingo. To lead this crusade, the Archbishop-designate of Toledo was selected and elevated to the Archbishopric of Santo Domingo. Monzón's religious devotion and discipline were his recommendations for this arduous job.

Archbishop Monzón sought to cooperate with secular authorities to whom he was beholden for financial support of the Church. He persuaded the state to authorize an additional six parishes, which brought the total to thirty-nine. Within a year after his arrival, Monzón had priests in all of the Dominican parishes, and Mass was being celebrated on a regular basis.[5] While Monzón was succeeding in mobilizing the Church, a more difficult obstacle in the path of spiritual harmony was developing. This was Protestantism, and its practice was later discovered to have legal sanction.

When the Spanish expeditionary force first landed on the island preparatory to the establishment of the new regime, General Manuel Buceta had to requisition private buildings for his troops until military facilities could be constructed at Samaná de Santa Bárbara on the Samaná peninsula. Lacking a hospital in which to lodge troops stricken by disease that was prevalent in the area, Buceta took over a

[4]Consejo de Gobierno de Santo Domingo to Sr. Ministro de la Guerra y de Ultramar José María Marchessi, Santo Domingo, August 9, 1964, AHN-U/SD 3526.
[5]Gobernador Capitán General Felipe Ribero to Sr. Ministro de la Guerra y de Ultramar Leopoldo O'Donnell, Santo Domingo, September 22, 1862, AHN-U/SD 3530.

Protestant chapel to use as a hospital until a more suitable facility could be erected. Upon dedication of the military hospital and transfer of the patients in September 1861, the Protestants wanted their chapel returned. Their struggle was not eased by former President, now Captain General, Santana. Fortunately for the Protestants' cause, they found a ready champion in British Consul Martin T. Hood.[6] Santana, an astute politician who took advantage of the hierarchy of command of which he was not a member, simply remitted to the Ministry of Colonial Affairs in Madrid all petitions requesting the chapel's return.[7] This stifled the native Protestants but not the dauntless British Consul, who persisted until his side prevailed.

The Colonial Affairs Ministry studied the chapel problem and sought to resolve it in a manner conducive to domestic tranquility. Two issues were involved: private property and religious freedom. On June 14, 1862, the ministry announced that the chapel had to be returned because it was private property. The announcement was silent about the problem of religious freedom.[8]

While the Colonial Affairs Ministry was studying the problem of the chapel, Dominican Protestants in Samaná and elsewhere continued to worship publicly—much to the consternation of Audiencia Regent Eduardo Alonso y Colmanares and Archbishop Monzón. The Archbishop saw the Protestants as dangerous to both Santo Domingo and Spain, despite the fact that they apparently had freely lent their chapel to General Buceta. Defining his spiritual opponents as a danger to the state, the Archbishop counseled Madrid on how the menace could be eliminated. Civil authorities, he proposed, could publish Article 129 of the new penal code that outlawed non-Catholic religious practices. Then this ban could be enforced, simply and without fear of conscience, against the Protestants. The Regent of the Audiencia was in silent agreement, but the Fiscal of the Audiencia urged caution. He saw the matter frought with consequences adversely affecting Spain's international relations and the colony's tranquility. But Archbishop Monzón would not budge from righteousness. He had succeeded in suppressing the Masonic threat to the Church and was now intent on suppressing heresy.[9] On October 20, 1862, Monzón

[6]Gobernador Capitán General Pedro Santana to Sr. Ministro de la Guerra y de Ultramar Leopoldo O'Donnell, Santo Domingo, January 28, 1862, AHN-U/SD 3530.
[7]Gobernador Capitán General Pedro Santana to Sr. Ministro de la Guerra y de Ultramar Leopoldo O'Donnell, Santo Domingo, March 28, 1862, AHN-U/SD 3530.
[8]Dirección de Ultramar, Estracto—Tolerancia del culto protestante durante la república, "Nota," June 14, 1862, AHN-U/SD 3530.
[9]The suppression of the Masonic Order in Santo Domingo occurred after Pedro Santana, the Order's Grand Master, retired from government. For Santana's long-smoldering resentment against those he considered responsible, see General Pedro Santana to Sr. Ministro de Ultramar, Cuartel General en Guárnica, October 1, 1863, Biblioteca Nacional (Madrid) Datos 20284-3.

again warned the secular authorities of Protestantism's revolutionary nature;[10] and the matter was referred to the Spanish Council of State.

On December 21, 1862, the Council of State issued a decision in a manner befitting its political nature. The council attempted to agree with all parties. The chapel was to be returned to its owners as the Colonial Affairs Ministry had commanded; moreover, owners of the chapel were to be paid four hundred pesos for needed repairs resulting from the military's use of the building. Practice of Protestant religions, however, was not to be tolerated.[11]

The question was not closed. Captain General Felipe Ribero, Santana's successor, forwarded to Madrid the British Consul's new protest against the Royal Order of December 21 which banned non-Catholic religious observances. Hood based his case on the treaty of March 5, 1850, between Great Britain and the Dominican Republic. The treaty provided for religious toleration.[12] This protest stunned the ministry in Madrid, but it had recovered sufficiently by the following August to inform Archbishop Monzón of Hood's contentions.[13] The case was referred to the Council of State for resolution. Final decision was delayed until a copy of the Anglo-Dominican Treaty could be located and studied. On August 12, a copy was finally found and sent to the Council, which resumed consideration of the case. By this time the United States' commercial agent, G. W. Jaeger, had joined Hood with protests of his own in support of religious toleration. In Madrid, the Council of State was forced to recognize the validity of Hood's contentions. Article 8 of the Anglo-Dominican Treaty did provide for freedom of conscience and allowed British subjects to observe their religion in their homes, their churches, or other religious sites. The Council had to yield to Hood's protestation of the closing of the English Church in Santo Domingo and to the American claim that religious freedom had been granted by Haitian President Jean Boyer well before the establishment of the Dominican Republic, which had long condoned the practice.[14]

These exceptions to the monopoly given the Spanish Catholic Church, of course, did not legally apply to Dominican Protestants. The question as to what impact these exceptions had on Santo Domingo's Protestants is moot. These Protestants were freed American slaves who had been settled in the country by the Haitians and whose

[10] Arzobispo Benvenido Monzón to Sr. Ministro de la Guerra y de Ultramar Leopoldo O'Donnell, Santo Domingo, October 20, 1862, AHN-U/SD 3530.

[11] Dirección de Ultramar, Extracto—Tolerancia del culto protestante durante la república, "Nota," December 12, 1862, AHN-U/SD 3530.

[12] Gobernador Capitán General Pedro Santana to Sr. Ministro de la Guerra y de Ultramar Leopoldo O'Donnell, Santo Domingo, March 7, 1862, AHN-U/SD 3530.

[13] Dirección de Ultramar, Extracto—Tolerancia del culto protestante durante la república, "Nota," July 6, 1863; "fechado agosto 1863," AHN-U/SD 3530.

[14] Dirección de Ultramar, Extracto—Tolerancia del culto protestante durante la república, "Nota," August 12, 1864, AHN-U/SD 3530.

numbers had been augmented by British West Indians; thus, they could have drawn out the contest by claiming to be British subjects or American nationals; but the case never reached this stage. By the time that Madrid finally decided that the Church did not have an ironclad monopoly within the colony, Dominican rebels controlled the greater part of Santo Domingo and Spain had already decided to withdraw from the island. Both the experiment in imperialism and the attempted spiritual reconquest of Santo Domingo had failed.

In conclusion, one can say that the assumptions upon which this imperial experiment in Santo Domingo was undertaken were erroneous. Spain's protective shield was not the only means to preserve Dominican culture. This culture, despite its Spanish origin, was not sufficiently similar to that of Spain to allow easy identification between the officials of the new regime and the new colonial subjects. The Dominicans, as Spanish subjects, were neither eager nor willing, beyond gratuitous lip service, to adopt Spanish values. Thus the penal code, regardless of the regime's ability to enforce it, was a source of irritation for all groups of Dominicans who, for whatever reasons, were not in harmony with the royal government in Santo Domingo.

The role originally projected by the Catholic Church was frustrated by the prelate selected for the job. Archbishop Monzón failed in his mission because of his zeal and devotion, the very traits which had prompted his rise within the Church. He failed to realize the cultural and attitudinal differences separating him and his Catholic beliefs from parishioners whose faith had weathered different storms. Monzón failed to realize that Dominican Catholics looked upon their Protestant neighbors as Dominicans, even if they might conceive Protestantism to be a revolutionary danger.

Monzón's attitudinal difference is underlined by his insistence, in the face of empirical evidence to the contrary, that Protestantism was a revolutionary danger. Confusing principle, as he envisioned it, with practical reality, the Archbishop sidetracked the spiritual reconquest of the Dominican masses while he gave himself to the suppression of a few isolated Protestants. In so doing, he sacrificed the chance to alter Dominican society for the better. Contrary to his contentions, Dominican Protestants played no significant part in the revolt against Spanish rule, other than momentarily distracting official attention from time to time. If anything, the Protestants only underscored Spain's inept management of the Dominicans. Those who initially supported the new regime could only look forward to their eventual estrangement because the regime's leaders failed to recognize reality.

SOCIAL SCIENCE

Fast-moving social, economic, and political changes in the twentieth century have produced new and different attitudes toward the Catholic Church in Spanish South America. As a result, Catholic institutions and religious personnel have been subjected to widespread criticism, both from within and without the Church. In particular, there have been charges of indifference toward the grinding poverty of large segments of the population, and there have been complaints that prelates and priests tend to support unjust social structures and repressive political regimes. Since the middle of this century, however, the official stance of the Catholic hierarchy has been modified in favor of greater sensitivity toward basic human needs. Particularly among seminarians and the lower clergy, there have been examples of those who have joined militant Catholic laymen, heretics (separated brethren), and infidels (atheist Marxists of various orientations) in efforts to bring about rapid reform or revolutionary change. Sometimes these efforts have been limited to peaceful protest demonstrations; at other times there have been acts of violence; and in a few instances clerics or ex-clerics have taken up arms to wage guerrilla warfare against the establishment.

24. Evidence of González Prada's Influence on the Attitudes Toward Religion of Mariátegui and Haya de la Torre

JUDITH WALKER

Manuel González Prada exercised a telling influence on the thought and attitudes of José Carlos Mariátegui and Víctor Raúl Haya de la Torre. In this essay, Professor Walker analyzes the impact of González Prada's attitude toward religion on the writings of these two political thinkers. Although religious themes were not central in their work, their attitudes toward religion seem to be similar. Both condemned prevailing religious practices and customs. In particular, they denounced the Roman Catholic Church as oppressive and life-denying. Professor Walker points out that Mariátegui and Haya de la Torre called for more honest social and moral commitments that would serve as the basis for social and political reform.

Religion is one of the major themes in the work of Manuel González Prada. Because José Carlos Mariátegui and Víctor Raúl Haya de la Torre were greatly influenced by Prada, one would expect their writings on religion to share evidence of his influence in this area. In order to identify and describe this influence, the published essays of all three writers have been analyzed.

González Prada's attitude toward religion is best summed up in this blunt statement: "De las religiones puede asegurarse lo mismo que de las enfermedades: ninguna es buena."[1] Of all religions, he held that Catholicism is the most militant and demanding. Even its hell, he claimed, is a posthumous inquisition.[2] Furthermore, he complained that Catholicism teaches resignation and seeks to establish itself as the highest authority on earth.[3]

[1] *Prosa menuda* (Buenos Aires: Edit. Imán, 1941), p. 51.
[2] *Nuevas páginas libres* (Santiago de Chile: Edit. Ercilla, 1937), p. 59.
[3] *Anarquía* (Santiago de Chile: Edit. Ercilla, 1936), p. 25.

Prada was convinced that those who have discovered the truth about religion must fight to destroy it. Regarding Catholicism, he concluded that there was no middle ground; either it must be totally accepted or completely rejected.[4] Because religions evolve slowly, Prada explained that reformers cannot expect them to be destroyed instantaneously.[5] It was his belief that fanaticism can be cured with truth but not with threats.[6]

Prada asserted that the link between church and state in Peru was dangerous.[7] He was certain that the power of the Catholic Church was greater than the constitutional protection it was guaranteed. Prada charged that, in fact, the clergy governed Peru;[8] and he complained about the expenditures of public funds for the benefit of the Catholic Church.[9]

Although religion received much attention in González Prada's works, Mariátegui touched on it only superficially and within specific areas. As a Marxist, he criticized his master's stand:

> González Prada se engañaba, por ejemplo, cuando nos predicaba anti-religiosidad. Hoy sabemos mucho más que en su tiempo sobre la religión como sobre otras cosas. Sabemos que una revolución es siempre religiosa. La palabra religión tiene un nuevo valor, un nuevo sentido. Sirve para algo más que para designar un rito o una iglesia. . . . González Prada predecía el tramonto de todas las creencias, sin advertir que él mismo era predicador de una creencia, confesor de una fe. La que más se admira en este ateo, un tanto pagano, es su ascetismo moral. Su ateísmo es religioso.[10]

Of course Mariátegui's emphasis on the semantic question is not appropriate because Prada rarely used the term "religion." When he did, it was usually synonymous with Christianity, and he made his stand against the Catholic Church quite clear.

Mariátegui's position here as well as his whole circumvention of the religious issue has been studied and attacked or defended by several scholars. Chang-Rodríguez, for example, has compared him with other Latin American leftists who have encountered difficulty in their attempts to overcome the Church's powerful influence in those countries.[11] Several authors have mentioned Mariátegui's mystic tendency, describing an early interest in the Church and in the Spanish mystics. One of these, Germán Arciniegas, wrote, "José Carlos es el

---

[4]*Propaganda y ataque* (Buenos Aires: Editorial Imán, 1939), p. 60.
[5]*Nuevas páginas libres*, p. 48.
[6]*El tonel de Diógenes* (México, D.F.: Editorial Tezontle, 1945), p. 129.
[7]*Horas de lucha* (Buenos Aires: Editorial Americalee, 1946), p. 215.
[8]*Prosa menuda*, p. 60.
[9]*Horas de lucha*, p. 162.
[10]*Siete ensayos de interpretación de la realidad peruana* (Santiago de Chile: Edit. Universitaria, 1955), p. 196.
[11]Eugenio Chang-Rodríguez, *La literatura política de González Prada, Mariátegui y Haya de la Torre* (México, D.F.: Ediciones de Andrea, 1957), p. 159.

hombre que lucha entre el anticlericalismo ineludible, fatal, y el místico impulso."[12]

Whatever his personal or subconscious motives for evading the religious issue, Mariátegui's expressed ideas are easily studied, for he wrote only one essay on the topic: "El factor religioso," which was published in *Siete ensayos*.[13] Unfortunately, this essay does not adequately clarify his position. Basically, it is a historical survey of the role of the Catholic Church in the conquest and colonization of Peru and of the early years of his country's national independence. Prada saw the conquest as a crusade that was both military and religious; therefore, he explained, colonization was political and ecclesiastical. In his opinion, the priests did not impose Roman Catholicism dogmatically; instead, they adapted the Church's teachings to the culture of the Indians. According to Mariátegui, the liberal attitudes of the Peruvian clergy prevented development of any strong anticlerical movements. Only with Vigil did an antireligious movement begin. He was followed by González Prada and his disciples, but they were bound to fail because they had no socio-economic program.[14] At the end of the essay, Mariátegui identifies his position by aligning himself with the socialists:

> El socialismo, conforme a las conclusiones del materialismo histórico— que conviene no confundir con el materialismo filosófico—considera a las formas eclesiásticas y doctrinas religiosas, peculiares e inherentes al régimen económico-social que las sostiene y produce. Y se preocupa, por tanto, de cambiar éste y no aquellas. La mera agitación anticlerical es estimada por el socialismo como un diversivo liberal burgués.[15]

In this essay on religion, Mariátegui employs several lengthy quotations to back up his statements. He does not criticize the religion of other persons, rarely editorializes, and seldom adds a personal interpretation to his brief chronicle of the history of the Catholic Church in Peru. His explanation for this approach is that conditions had changed to the point where personal statements about religion were unnecessary.

In another essay, however, he recalls with reverence his trip to Europe because it had led him to discover God at the same time that he discovered humanity.[16] One is to surmise, therefore, that his redefinition of religion was merely a method of avoiding differences that would surely arise in working with the issue—especially for Marxists and followers of González Prada.

[12]"González Prada, Mariátegui y Haya de la Torre," *Cuadernos Americanos* 16 (May-June 1957): iii, reprinted as Introducción, in Chang-Rodríguez, *La literatura política*, p. 12.
[13]*Siete ensayos*, pp. 120-43.
[14]Ibid., p. 122.
[15]Ibid., p. 142.
[16]Ibid., p. 261.

Other essays by Mariátegui provide fragmentary information about his religious attitudes. For example, in his article on José Santos Chocano he identifies Rome as the center of Catholicism and "ideologically, the historic citadel of reaction." Further, he states, "Los que peregrinan por sus colinas y sus basílicas en busca del evangelio cristiano, regresan desilusionados; pero los que se contentan con encontrar, en su lugar, el fascismo y la Iglesia—la autoridad y la jerarquía en el sentido romano—, arriban a su meta y hallan su verdad.... El [Chocano], que nunca ha sido cristiano, se confiesa finalmente católico,"[17] Thus, Mariátegui indicated that he is not against Christianity but rather against the reactionary Church. This is reminiscent of Prada's statement that one can be anti-Catholic without being a personal enemy of Jesus Christ.[18] Prada believed that the cult following Jesus had degenerated into Catholicism.[19] Mariátegui seconded that belief.[20] Also, both thinkers discussed the reactionary role of the Church in politics. Like Prada, Mariátegui assumed that religion is a dying issue and that science is the cause: "La decadencia de las religiones tiene su origen demasiado visible en su creciente alejamiento de la experiencia historica y científica."[21]

To González Prada, the religious question is not a personal problem to be left for history. Although recognizing that it is something many people resolve for themselves in their youth, he asserted that religion also must be resolved socially.[22] Prada objected to all religions that became well established in society.[23] Mariátegui indicated his agreement with this attitude when he wrote that religious dogma could provide direction for change "mientras el dogma no se transforma en un archivo o en un código de una ideología del pasado."[24]

Now that religion, in the traditional sense, is a dead issue, the problem, according to Mariátegui, is to create a new myth. He declared that bourgeois civilization lacks a faith, a hope—because science has destroyed religion and the political state is decaying. Only a myth can fill the need that mankind has for something infinite. Disagreeing with Prada's ideal, he insisted that science and reason cannot fill the depth of man's being.[25]

Asserting that modern life requires action rather than thought,

[17] Ibid., p. 204.
[18] *Propaganda y ataque*, p. 19.
[19] *Nuevas páginas libres*, p. 30.
[20] *El alma matinal y otras estaciones del hombre de hoy*, vol. 3 of *Ediciones populares de las obras completas de José Carlos Mariátegui* (Lima: Edit. Amauta, 1959), p. 71.
[21] *En defensa del marxismo*, vol. 5 of *Obras*, p. 57.
[22] *Propaganda y ataque*, p. 59.
[23] *Horas de lucha*, pp. 216-17.
[24] *En defensa del marxismo*, p. 104.
[25] *El alma matinal*, pp. 18-22.

Mariátegui contended that the only faith acceptable to contemporary man is an active, combative faith. He found a new Latin American generation that was full of his faith and hope,[26] and he described Prada as sharing that mentality.[27]

Neither essayist minimized the role of religion in social reform. For Prada there was no doubt that "de toda cuestión social o política surge siempre una cuestión religiosa."[28] Mariátegui believed that the artist must create new myths for his time and that a genius must translate the intuition of his era into a new religion.[29]

Both men viewed religion as the opposite of liberty. Prada defined "propaganda de libertad" as "propaganda irreligiosa."[30] He repeatedly opposed dogma with reason, contending that faith in dogma kills the soul.[31] Mariátegui played another semantic game when he spoke in favor of dogma: "Para pensar con libertad, la primera condición es abandonar la preocupación de la libertad absoluta."[32] Direction and purpose are necessary, he explained. Dogma could furnish that direction, provided the dogma was a doctrine of social change.[33] Freedom was not the problem for Mariátegui. Therefore, he did not find it objectionable to hold a passionate belief to the point of excluding portions of possible alternatives. It is in this sense that he thought Prada was religious. Prada's call for everyone to believe only in himself[34] demonstrates the opposition of the two writers in this area, in spite of their similar views of religion as loss of liberty.

One of the greatest differences of opinion lies in each man's view of the role of religion in Peruvian history. Prada wrote that colonial Lima was channeled between the walls of religious fanaticism and lust. The priest was king. The cruelty of the conquistadores continued in the Church and in other segments of the society.[35] Mariátegui disagreed, stating, "En cuanto a religiosidad, la colonización española no pecó de exceso."[36] He described the work of the priests as being not only ecclesiastical but also educational and cultural.[37]

The differences between Mariátegui and González Prada in the area of religion are the basic differences in their outlook as Marxist and as individualist. They agreed that organized religion was dying because of scientific discoveries. Prada thought that reason would fill

[26]Ibid., pp. 17, 28.
[27]Siete ensayos, p. 195.
[28]Horas de lucha, p. 216.
[29]El artista y la época, vol. 6 of Obras, p. 37.
[30]Ibid., p. 217.
[31]Propaganda y ataque, p. 52.
[32]En defensa del marxismo, p. 105.
[33]Ibid., p. 104.
[34]Nuevas páginas libres, p. 86.
[35]El tonel de Diógenes, pp. 21-25.
[36]Siete ensayos, p. 83.
[37]Ibid., p. 127.

the void left by the death of religion; Mariátegui thought that socialism would become the new myth. Both believed that religion played a large role in society and in the social changes they wanted to see made.

Like Mariátegui, Haya de la Torre wrote little about organized religion. Both used the term "religion" to mean a passionate belief. Like his Marxist teacher, Haya believed that a myth was necessary for modern man and especially for Peruvians. Alianza Popular Revolucionaria Americana (APRA) was to become the passion that was lacking.[38] Just as González Prada called anarchy the new religion[39] and Mariátegui considered socialism the new religion,[40] Haya claimed that APRA should be considered a religion of justice, a creed of liberty.[41]

Unlike Prada, Haya and his party claimed they never attacked the beliefs of the Catholic Church.[42] "Otros son los problemas que reclaman solución en el Perú," Haya explained.[43] The Apristas did, however, work for the separation of church and state, which was an important principle for Prada. Haya once stated, "La conciencia religiosa debe ser libre. Los Gobiernos no deben atacar ni proteger credo alguno."[44]

Haya de la Torre suffered attacks from the pulpit as had Prada. One priest reportedly identified Haya as Satan because of his curved nose and sharp eyes.[45]

Haya did attack the clergy's exploitation of the Indian in much the same way that Prada had done. He wrote, "El cura católico, aliado y partícipe de la explotación, coadyuva a este implacable retorcimiento de la vida de tres millones de hombres, ofreciendo las llamas del infierno a los insumisos y las venturas del cielo a los genuflexos."[46]

While Mariátegui's personal ambivalence on the religious issue is probably the key to why he could continue neither Prada's nor the socialists' work in this area, Haya de la Torre's personal beliefs seemed to enter rarely. He wanted a plan that was realistic according to the Peruvian scene. Being a traditionally Catholic country, Perú was not going to drop its religion; but Haya believed separation was a way of bringing new vitality for both government and the Catholic

[38]*Cartas de Haya de la Torre a los prisioneros apristas* (Lima: Edit. Nuevo Día, 1946), p. 12.
[39]*Anarquía*, p. 25.
[40]*Siete ensayos*, p. 143; *El alma matinal*, p. 22.
[41]*Política aprista*, 2d ed. (Lima: Edit. Imp. Amauta, 1967), p. 110.
[42]Ibid., pp. 185-86.
[43]Felipe Cossío del Pomar, *Biografía y gráficos de Haya de la Torre* (Lima: Edit. Américas Unidas, 1946), p. 19.
[44]Ibid., p. 19.
[45]Luis Alberto Sánchez, *Haya de la Torre y el Aora* (Santiago de Chile: Edit. del Pacífico, 1955), p. 278.
[46]*Por la emancipación de América Latina* (Buenos Aires: M. Gleizer, 1927), p. 43.

Church.[47] Perhaps the young reformer remembered Prada's remark that the clerical issue would be increasingly less important because science was replacing religion. Prada had also predicted that the Church would lose its power in the government to the military.[48]

One of González Prada's major themes, to which Mariátegui gave little attention, was an emphasis on the importance of morality. This, however, was one of Haya de la Torre's main themes. Prada defined morality as a personal commitment to truth and mutual agreement.[49] In this sense, morality came before religion in the development of societies.[50] In fact, Prada claimed that the morality of Catholicism was based on egotism and hypocrisy.[51] The morality that Prada advocated would be based on truth.[52] He wrote that with this new morality, love could be emancipated from the carnal instinct.[53]

Haya de la Torre combined the master's emphasis on a new morality with Mariátegui's call for a new myth. APRA was Haya's answer to the moral crisis, because it could be a moral source of intelligence and culture.[54]

One of the key positions of both Prada and Haya was that morality was the basis of society. Haya contended that strong, moral citizens were essential to a democracy. To him, moral education became as important as the material reorganization of the country.[55] This education would teach Peruvians how to love, which cannot be done without a moral outlook.[56] Also, he insisted that a moral man conquers temptation.[57] Haya believed that one of the faults of Peru was that the people wasted themselves with sensual pleasures.[58] Moral integrity became a central idea in Haya's writings and speeches to his Aprista followers.

Chang-Rodríguez has written that González Prada took an anticlerical stand because it was in vogue in Europe, but he explains that Mariátegui and Haya took from their predecessor only his ideal of and struggle for separation of church and state.[59] Certainly, European thinkers influenced Prada to a large extent, but the Catholic Church's large role in Peruvian society and government was a hindrance to

[47] Política aprista, pp. 185-86.
[48] Anarquía, pp. 37-38.
[49] Horas de lucha, p. 209
[50] El tonel de Diógenes, p. 150.
[51] Prosa menuda, pp. 51, 112.
[52] Ibid., pp. 64-65.
[53] Nuevas páginas libres, p. 107.
[54] Política aprista, pp. 94-95.
[55] Ibid., p. 201.
[56] Coloquios de Haya de la Torre, ed. Ignacio Campos (Lima: Univ. Popular González Prada, ca. 1964), p. 214.
[57] Ibid., p. 231.
[58] Ibid., pp. 229-31.
[59] Chang-Rodríguez, La literatura política, p. 341.

social changes that Prada thought necessary. Examples of this belief appear in the works of the two younger Peruvian essayists.

It is interesting to note that in writings where Mariátegui and Haya de la Torre have reflected Prada's influence directly, the tone and style of Prada's works are also reflected. This is further evidence of the master's impression on the younger men.

Each essayist formulated religious ideas based on his attitudes toward and goals for society. It was in this sense that Prada influenced the religious thought of Mariátegui and Haya de la Torre.

25. The Catholic Church and Political Development in Colombia

STEVEN J. BRZEZINSKI

Professor Brzezinski describes those factors that have caused the Catholic Church to become a moderate agent of change in Colombia. After dealing with the limitations of Catholic Action, he explains the impact of Father Camilo Torres and the Golconda movement, which are described as extremist challenges to Catholic Action as a developmental strategy.

For serious students of Latin American politics, one of the most striking and potentially significant developments of the last quarter-century has been the changed nature of Roman Catholic involvement in political and social development. Historically a bulwark of the existing social order and highly resistant to all forms of change, the Church has evolved into an organization explicitly committed to modern values and directly involved in the search for solutions to the problems of underdevelopment—particularly among the poor, underrepresented elements in the political system. This case study examines the new approach as it has been applied in Colombia.

Our principal objectives are to examine the attitudinal and programmatic commitment of Catholic religious elites to the modernization[1] of Colombian society and to describe the internal fragmentation of Church structures that reflects disagreement about implementation of this new commitment. Historical antecedents of this policy change, as well as its relation to shifting channels of political access at the national level, provide additional points of reference, though they remain subordinate to the principal focus of the case study: the policy commitment of religious elites to a modern Colombia and the result-

---

[1]"Modernization" is used here to refer to the impact of change experienced by a country undergoing rapid industrialization. It involves the processes of urbanization, secularization, democratization, education, and media participation. See Daniel Lerner, *The Passing of Traditional Society* (New York: The Free Press, 1958), p. 438.

ing fragmentation of Church structures over the specifics of this commitment.

Historical Antecedents

Earlier studies of the Colombian Catholic Church have classified it among the most politically traditional national churches in Latin America.[2] A basic question arises when this accepted view is compared with recent developments. What factors altered a long-established commitment to traditional values and helped propel the Catholic Church into its new role as an active, though quite moderate, change agent in Colombian society? The answer to this question is complex and has important antecedents in Colombian history.

Church espousal of a developmental strategy has been dependent on several interrelated factors: 1) a favorable social role and resulting political access were enjoyed by traditional religious agencies before the 1930s, when the full impact of modernization began to be felt in Colombia; 2) as a result of high political influence before the 1930s, Church structures became rigid and were unable to respond to the profound changes in the political environment wrought by modernization; and 3) by the 1940s, severe losses in social prestige and political influence resulted from this organizational rigidity. These losses were epitomized by the failure of ecclesiastical moral sanctions aimed at preventing the political system from collapsing into civil war during the period 1948-1953. Each of these factors needs to be examined in greater detail.

High political influence of the traditional Church. The Catholic Church has played an important institutional role in the politics and society of Colombia since the days of the Spanish conquest. During the colonial period, it performed administrative tasks for the Crown in addition to carrying out religious functions. Church and State never were mutually exclusive in Spanish political practice; thus, throughout the colonial period the Church shared power and status with lay political rulers. For example, the archbishop of Nueva Granada served also as viceroy on a number of occasions.[3] After Independence in 1819, the Church continued its association with the dominant political elites. Its hierarchy was recruited from members of the same large-landholding minority who formed the Conservative Party. As a consequence, the highest-ranking religious leaders

---

[2]For explicit statements of this thesis, see J. Lloyd Mecham, *Church and State in Latin America: A History of Politico-Ecclesiastical Relations*, rev. ed. (Chapel Hill, N.C.: North Carolina University Press, 1966); Benjamin Haddox, *Sociedad y religión en Colombia* (Bogotá: Editorial Tercer Mundo, 1965); and Ivan Vallier, "Religious Elites: Differentiations and Developments in Roman Catholicism," in *Elites in Latin America*, ed. Seymour Martin Lipset and Aldo Solari (New York: Oxford University Press, 1967).

[3]Cornelia Butler Flora, *Mobilizing the Masses: The Sacred and the Secular in Colombia* (Ithaca, N.Y.: Cornell University Press, 1970), pp. 67-68.

(bishops in the dioceses and abbots in the religious orders) tended to share the views and to identify with the interests of this group.

When the anticlerical Liberal Party held power between 1850 and 1884, the strong economic influence and, to a lesser extent, the political role of the Church were curtailed. Liberals were successful in depriving the Church of much of its wealth, but in the 1880s they accepted Church preeminence over education and social welfare as preconditions to the political stability they sought to achieve.

Political and social preeminence of the Church grew even stronger during the four decades after 1890, because of the virtual demise of the Liberal Party as a political force. Between 1890 and 1930 the Conservative Party, which supported the religious establishment's traditional role, dominated Colombia's government.

Throughout this forty-year period, the Church relied on favorable relations with the controlling political elites, providing in return a symbolic legitimacy for the government and exercising social control over the highly religious peasant majority of Colombia. The favorable position of the Church depended less on the internal coherence or effectiveness in its organizational structure than on the success of its *ad hoc*, informal bargaining with political elites.

Organizational rigidity of the traditional Church. As a result of dependence on external political connections to maximize political influence, organic weaknesses in traditional religious organizational patterns went uncorrected—particularly in such matters as authority delegation and chain of command. During the premodern period, these weaknesses did not seem vital to continued Church influence over social life, supported as it was by external political bargains. Indeed, they went unrecognized for the most part, until the cataclysmic effects of modernization made them apparent in the 1940s.

Only major social dislocation and, ultimately, a civil war forced the Church to face up to its organizational inadequacy. Recognition of these structural problems did not occur with the first disruptions caused by modernization in the 1930s. The initial response of the traditional religious elites to these changes was incredulity. Witnessing the accelerated population shifts and rapid emergence of new political and economic interests in the 1930s, the hierarchy clung to a belief that dislocations would be only temporary and looked toward eventual reestablishment of the traditional political environment.[4]

Through continued reliance on informal bargaining with political elites, the religious leadership attempted to minimize the negative effects of modernization on the Church's position. Social unrest accompanying modernization was denounced from the pulpit as "Communist-inspired"; and because religious leaders could see no rela-

---

[4]J. Ivan Cadavid, *Los fueros de la Iglesia ante el liberalismo y el conservatismo en Colombia* (Medellín: Editorial Bedout, 1955), pp. 93-114.

tionship between the inadequacies of the Church's mechanisms for sociopolitical reform functions and the country's deteriorating political situation, little or no structural reorganization was implemented.

During the first fifteen years of Colombia's modernization experience, roughly 1932 to 1947, the response of traditional religious elites was hesitation and misinterpretation. They watched the ever-growing social chaos and political instability with apprehension, but they held to a naive belief that the disequilibrium could be managed through existing means for conflict resolution. The traditional Church recognized that its position was under attack; it did not fully appreciate the extent, much less the nature, of the threat.

Civil war and the erosion of the traditional Church. Into the 1940s, religious leaders continued to minimize the potential danger of rapid social change to the stability of the traditional political system. Still hoping the bewildering array of new national problems could be resolved by existing means, they persisted in blaming the Communists for the burgeoning political discontent.

Resistance of religious elites to modifications in their own organizational structures, as well as in the existing political system, lasted until the outbreak of the *Violencia*, an amorphous, unchannelled civil war which broke out in 1948 and lasted until at least 1953.[5] During the *Violencia*, long-simmering antagonism against the Church erupted for the first time in the twentieth century. Priests were publicly shot, churches looted and burned, and Catholic universities ransacked. Church prestige suffered a precipitous decline.[6]

The hierarchy finally admitted what it had denied for twenty years: that the traditional political system was bankrupt and that new methods to effectively regulate political conflict had to be found. In addition to questions concerning the political system itself, the *Violencia* raised fundamental questions about the role of the Church in Colombian society, particularly concerning its efficacy as a social mediator. The religious leadership began to recognize the organizational weaknesses of the Church and initiated the task of slowly reorganizing its structures. Catholic elites, their customary channels of political access clogged and disrupted by civil war, now attempted to restore the Church's lost prestige through a new political strategy: Catholic Action.

Catholic Action originated in the European Church. When the local hierarchy gradually adopted it in Colombia, they accepted for

[5] Some Colombian scholars fix the end of the *Violencia* in 1953, when the dictatorship of General Rojas Pinilla came to power; others prefer to view it as lasting until the creation of the National Front in 1957.

[6] For a quantitative estimate of the extent of this decline, see Aaron Lipman and A. Eugene Havens, "The Colombian Violencia: An Ex Post Facto Experiment," *Social Forces* 44 (December 1965): 238-45.

the first time the concept of social change as a desirable national goal. But in doing so, the religious leadership attempted to regulate the tempo of progress by seeking to implement their own development strategy. Catholic Action sought to provide new orientation for Colombia's political system by imposing a peculiarly "Roman" cast on the country's modernization experience. Disagreements inherent in determining and later in implementing key factors in the Catholic Action development strategy, together with other approaches to change applied by dissident religious elements, comprise the main theme of this case study.

Catholic Action

The Colombian hierarchy introduced Catholic Action into Colombia in 1944, before the outbreak of the civil war; but it was not until after the shock of the *Violencia* that Church elites turned to it in earnest as a political strategy.[7] It would be misleading to view Catholic Action as a comprehensive developmental strategy initiated by the religious leadership at a given point to meet the crisis of modernization. Such a view of its function may have some validity for Catholic Action in the decade of the 1970s, but in no way corresponds to the early years of the movement. Catholic Action began as a loose collection of *ad hoc* programs for political and social development. Among them were programs for support of trade union movements in the cities and rural areas and for establishment of experimental radio schools among the peasants.

Different sets of religious elites, in most instances working independently of each other, developed these initial programs; ties between the various programs and the hierarchy were established only gradually. For example, the radio school program of *Acción Cultural Popular* (ACPO) did not originate with the hierarchy but was created and refined by a single parish priest, Father Salcedo, who acted on his own in the isolated mountain village of Sutatenza in 1947. Only after this program had enjoyed considerable early success in a number of communities did the religious leadership absorb it into the formal structure of Catholic Action.

This example illustrates the general pattern in the evolution of a Catholic strategy of development: various groups within the Colombian Church, acting largely on their own initiative, have implemented developmental schemes. Since 1944, the hierarchy has linked the most promising of these programs into the formal network of Catholic Action.

In the years since the *Violencia*, the Church has attempted to

[7]For the best short summary of Catholic Action in Colombia, see Gustavo Jiménez Cadena, S.J., *Sacerdote y cambio social*, Centro de Investigación y Acción Social (Bogotá: Editorial Tercer Mundo, 1967), pp. 101-19.

restore its former influential position in the social structure through implementation of its own approaches for handling change. These programs, funded by the Catholic Church and staffed by religious specialists, comprise Catholic Action. A number of programs have enjoyed considerable success. The urban trade union movement begun by the Jesuits in 1946, the *Unión de Trabajadores de Colombia* (UTC), has become the largest labor organization in Colombia, with over 500,000 affiliated members.[8] Recently, plans were completed to merge it with the other large labor federation, the *Confederación de Trabajadores de Colombia* (CTC), thereby increasing the influence of organized labor in the political system.

Acción Cultural Popular, the radio school program for the rural areas, expanded from one school with a handful of students in 1947 to 22,212 schools with 69,696 students in 1968.[9] Its newspaper, *El Campesino*, has achieved the largest circulation of any rural newspaper in Colombia, with over 50,000 copies sold each week. In spite of these important achievements, Catholic Action has not succeeded in restoring to the Church the status and influence that it enjoyed in the traditional political system. Neither has it been able to accelerate significantly the Colombian developmental process.

The objectives of the Catholic Church in entering the field of developmental policy were the effective restoration of Church prestige and political influence lost through civil war and unchannelled social change. These objectives have not been realized. The reasons are numerous. First, many of the programs of Catholic Action have never achieved the successes of those mentioned above. For example, the agricultural trade union movement of the *Federación Agraria Nacional* (FANAL) has never had much success in welding farm workers into an effective political force. Second, the success of the radio schools and the urban trade union movement is of limited impact. ACPO does not possess the resources to provide much more than basic literacy and technical skills to Colombian peasants, and the scope of its influence is restricted to the High Andean regions where the Church influence traditionally has been high. Although the UTC has indeed become the largest trade union movement in Colombia, actual influence of religious elites over union policy has declined from real direction at its outset in 1946 to the present symbolic roles of *asesores morales*, who exercise formal authority in policy formation.

The crucial deficiencies of Catholic Action as a comprehensive strategy of development are its insufficient economic base and lack of qualified technical personnel necessary to staff the various agencies

---

[8]This figure, which comes from the archives of the UTC, probably is inflated; it should be viewed only as an approximation of actual membership strength.
[9]*Acción Cultural Popular, Los campesinos trabajan por el desarollo* (Bogotá: Editorial Andes, 1970).

under its direction. Catholic Action decided to rely on internal strengths and resources of the Catholic system for its support, but did so at a time when these elements had already suffered serious erosion resulting from the disruptions of large-scale social dislocation, most particularly the *Violencia*.

Because traditional ties with political elites were weakened by rapid social upheaval and civil war, the Church has attempted to contribute to Colombian development through utilization of its own resources as the vehicle for a return to political prominence. This has not worked. Catholic economic, social, and political resources had diminished appreciably by the end of the *Violencia*. Given the insufficient human and economic capital that the Church could muster on its own behalf, the Catholic Action emphasis on self-reliance was doomed from the outset to exercise only a marginal impact on the national developmental process.

Handicapped by the modest capital resources available for investment in its programs, Catholic contributions to Colombian development have centered primarily on motivating development in rural areas where the Church is still influential. This "psychological cushion" identifies the goals of modern society with those of the Church, facilitating adoption of modern attitudes and technical innovations by the rural population; but it stops far short of providing the Church with major institutionalized responsibility in the national development network. The initial reason for espousing Catholic Action was the assumption by the hierarchy that the Church could play a dominant role in the national developmental process. The subsequent failure of Catholic Action to restore the Church to its traditional prominence in the political system can be traced to this overestimation of organizational capacity. Neither has the institution been able to assume a major role in the solution of the enduring problems of Colombian underdevelopment.

This dual failure eventually undermined the initial consensus maintained by Catholic Action among the Colombian clergy. Serious intra-organizational conflict developed over the proper role of the Church in the developmental process; increasingly militant counter-strategies of political involvement in competition with Catholic Action were offered by non-hierarchical elite groups. This internal fragmentation and the new strategies of the Catholic political activity generated by it will now be the subjects of our attention.

The Church and Development: The Extremist Challenge

As the official Church program of development, Catholic Action encountered no serious opposition within the religious elite system for almost twenty years. The first stirrings of protest, heard in 1964, were concentrated in the activity of a single influential priest, Father

Camilo Torres.[10] A mercurial personality with tremendous crowd appeal, Torres had studied sociology at the University of Louvain and returned to Colombia in 1959 as a lecturer in sociology at the National University in Bogotá. Beginning as a moderate reformer, his criticism of the Colombian government and the Church hierarchy began to assume militant proportions. First exposed to Marxist social categories while in Europe, Torres' reliance on them grew perceptibly greater after 1964. He castigated the bishops for their explicit support of a regime that he considered to be both coercive and repressive; also, he condemned the hierarchy for refusing to take a direct political role in precipitating the revolutionary overthrow of the government. Attacking Catholic Action at its first principles, Torres argued that the Church lacked resources necessary to achieve comprehensive developmental goals through independent efforts. His recommended course of action was to maximize Catholic resources through coalitions with groups seeking similar objectives, including the Communists. Most important, he did not exclude the use of tactical violence as a means for overthrowing a government whose legitimacy he did not accept.

Father Torres' platform touched off shock waves, both within the Church and throughout the larger Colombian society. The hierarchy refused to give it serious consideration, because it blatantly contradicted the highly institutionalized development strategy of Catholic Action. First, Torres advocated a return to direct clerical participation in the political process, a bargaining style previously rejected by Catholic Action in favor of a non-conflictual developmentalism. Second, Torres favored a strategy of coalition with Marxist groups that were wholly unacceptable to the official Church organization. Finally, he openly accepted violence as a legitimate political response, which his superiors immediately condemned as being antithetical to Catholic teaching.

The rift between Father Torres and the hierarchy widened after failure of the establishment to co-opt him by offering him a grant to do research abroad. The final blow came on May 22, 1965, when Torres publicly announced the formation of a new political coalition, the *Frente Unido,* a revolutionary popular movement that accepted support from any truly revolutionary group, including the Communists. The titular head of the Colombian Church, Cardinal Concha of Bogotá, condemned him for consciously separating himself from the doctrines and directives of the Church.

On June 24, 1965, Father Torres asked for laicization, which was granted. Covertly, he became a soldier in the Army of National Libera-

---

[10]Biographical information on Camilo Torres is taken from John Gerassi, ed., *Revolutionary Priest: The Complete Writings and Messages of Camilo Torres,* trans. June de Cipriano et al. (New York: Random House, 1971).

tion, a guerilla group operating in central Colombia. Publicly, Torres promoted the *Frente Unido* in lectures to all types of audiences, attracting a large urban following of leftist students and extremist trade-union members. Through these efforts and the extensive media coverage they received, Camilo Torres became one of the most famous and most recognizable individuals in Colombia. But his fame was relatively short lived, for he was killed in combat with government troops on February 15, 1966.

Since his death, Camilo Torres has acquired symbolic status in the eyes of many under-represented elements in the political system. Posters bearing his picture are still seen everywhere in Colombia. More important for our own examination of the eroding consensus behind Catholic Action within the Church, his personal example served as the model for a new radical movement within the Colombian clergy.

Called Golconda, this movement was initiated by forty-eight priests and one Colombian bishop, most of whom had been personal friends and sympathizers of Camilo Torres.[11] They adopted his platform intact and continued his criticism of Catholic Action's approach to the problems of Colombian underdevelopment, but Golconda's acceptance of an ethic of revolutionary violence hampered its growth as a major organizational alternative to Catholic Action. Golconda membership has been unable to branch out beyond the elite-cadre level. Nonetheless, the movement has exercised some influence over non-affiliated but sympathetic elements in the Colombian clergy.

The Camilo Torres-Golconda emphasis on conflict and direct clerical participation in the political process has been absorbed by groups and individual priests sympathetic to the basic approach, but who cannot accept its justification of violence as compatible with the Catholic ethic. These priests, many of them young Jesuits trained in the social sciences and not identified with the old Catholic Action wing of the order, have become increasingly involved in programs of *concienciación* and direct organization of peasants against large landholders in the countryside.

These extremist challenges to Catholic Action as the developmental strategy of the official Church have been largely ineffectual. Emphasis on clericalism and conflict have made them highly suspect to the major political parties, and their reception in the media has been almost wholly negative, for the same reasons. But for the purpose of studying the participation of Catholic religious elites in the developmental process, their failure is much less significant than the simple fact of their emergence. Existence of such a clearly defined counter approach attests to the systemic breakdown of intraorganizational consensus over Catholic Action as a viable strategy of development.

[11] Ibid., p. 53.

The cumulative consequences of modernization in the 1940s demanded that the Church formulate a new relationship with the political system. Its response was Catholic Action. This developmental strategy accepted moderate social change as a proper societal goal but eschewed direct political involvement. Catholic Action even avoided identification with governments by implementing its own development programs that were wholly dependent on Church sources for capital and personnel. As the official strategy of the Colombian hierarchy, Catholic Action enjoyed unchallenged hegemony within the Church for twenty years. Since 1964 it has come under serious attack from a competing Catholic ideology that stresses direct political participation of the Church in support of more accelerated social and political change. This extremist challenge to the majority status of Catholic Action within the Church organization has failed as a movement, but it has polarized the Catholic elite system into competing factions identified with distinct political strategies. Erosion of the consensus behind Catholic Action, and related fragmentation within the organizational apparatus of the Church, have combined to circumscribe further the already modest scope of Catholic Action as a program of development. As a consequence, there has been a reduction of political access to and influence of religious elites with the major policy-making elements in the Colombian political system.

Inability to maintain general support for Catholic Action as the proper response to modernization can be attributed to two mutually reinforcing defects in the Colombian Church's social doctrine and organizational structure: inadequacy of Catholic social ideology, and weakness of sanctions at the disposal of Church operating units to ensure compliance with their policy decisions. Catholic Action emerged from encyclicals and other Church documents which give expression to the social doctrine of the Church; however, this doctrine has been formulated in a highly general, abstract manner. It is not designed to serve as a blue-print for a concrete strategy of development, nor is it equipped to provide an ideological justification for the specifics of Catholic participation in development. When Catholic Action was challenged by elements within the Church seeking an alternative strategy, it relied on virtually the same Church documents to buttress its position as did its challengers. Each side emphasized an interpretation of the documents congruent with its own position. The potential for conflict in this process, along with the claim of Catholic Action to "official" status within the Church, seriously weakened the power of the bishops to maintain voluntary organizational consensus in support of their policies.

This breakdown in support for Catholic Action brings us to the second defect in the Catholic system, the weakness of hierarchical sanctions. In the absence of a voluntary acceptance of Catholic Action by all staff elites within the Church, the religious leadership has attempted to maintain consensus through use of coercive pressures that can be exerted by diocesan bishops. These pressures have not proved successful, because dissident priests are often members of religious orders that report directly to Rome or to their superiors within the order; therefore, they are relatively free from effective control by diocesan bishops. This weakness of hierarchical sanctions vis à vis behavior of dissident clergy has led to fragmentation of public interpretation of Catholic social ideology. Each contending view competes for majority support within the Church, but none possesses sufficient authority to effect such a consensus.

Previous discussion of this subject has tended to see the Colombian Church's development strategies as being essentially congruent and not in direct conflict, despite admitted differences in principles and tactics.[12] Findings of this case study place in doubt the assumption that all of the change-oriented factions within the Colombian Church share a core of commitment to modern values. Evidence presented here points to a need for substantial revision in this assumption. Within the Catholic elite system, substructures that support modernization do not possess cumulative, congruent bargaining strategies. On the contrary, their approaches are discordant and dysfunctional. For both theoretical and empirical purposes, these factions can be viewed more profitably as highly competitive and conflicting structures, each with its own specific ideological base competing for majority recognition within the Church.

Catholic Action does not "prepare" the clergy and the laity for the more militant revolutionary consciousness of Golconda; indeed, it actively opposes such a development and seeks to prevent emergence of such attitudes. This lack of cooperation holds not only for widely divergent political strategies like Catholic Action and Golconda, but also for the strategies of sub-organizations like FANAL, UTC, and ACPO.

Lack of a Catholic social ideology does not cause internal fragmentation of the Colombian Church, as previous research has argued.[13] The culprit is lack of any definitive interpretation of this ideology within the Catholic system, which is an entirely different matter. In other words, the Church's difficulties result not from failure to articulate Catholic social ideology but from inability to agree substantially on any one development approach. It is the proliferation of competing and incompatable values and activities that precipitates the crisis.

The problem, then, is not substantive but organizational. A single acceptable ideology and program could be evolved if an effective in-

---

[12]This is one of the assumptions in Vallier's "Religious Elites: Differentiation and Developments in Roman Catholicism," p. 217.
[13]Ibid., p. 217.

terest-aggregation and compromise structure existed, one capable of working out approaches acceptable to all modern elements within the Church. Obviously, this mechanism must be equitable enough to satisfy all interests if it is to re-establish organizational consensus around a coherent strategy of development. Given the high degree of fragmentation and ideological polarity within the Church, however, prospects for emergence of such a unifying structure appear dim; without it, the overall impact of Catholic participation in Colombia's development politics must remain marginal.

26. Catholic Radicalism and Political Change in Argentina

MICHAEL DODSON

After describing the origin and development of Argentina's Movement of Priests for the Third World, Professor Dodson explains the basic elements of *tercermundista* political theology and praxis. Then he traces *tercermundista* efforts from 1966 to 1970 as the activist priests sought to pressure the hierarchy to support their struggle against policies of President Ongania's military regime.

Religious traditions are flexible tools that can become sources of great innovation and change in times of social stress. Until recently, when they discussed the Catholic tradition in Latin America, most writers identified it with conservative politics and the status quo. Roman Catholicism in that political milieu evoked images of permanence, stability, and continuity rather than rapid change. Indeed, at least until the early 1960s, scholars could safely argue that by virtue of its traditional values, "Latin American Catholicism was synonymous with . . . conservative politics."[1] During the past fifteen years, however, Catholicism in Latin America has experienced internal convulsions of a scope and intensity that suggest profound change. In that time, a remarkable number of Latin American Churchmen have taken seriously the Second Vatican Council's call for religious and social change. The comparative suddenness and depth of this development have produced divisions and confusion; nevertheless, it is appropriate that we begin to reflect on this phenomenon and seek to locate whatever patterns may lie in the apparent chaos.

One fundamental question looms large: Can the Catholic Church maintain a coherent and viable role as a social actor while attempting

---

[1] Ivan Vallier, "Radical Priests and the Revolution," in *Changing Latin America: New Interpretations of Its Politics and Society*, ed. Douglas A. Chalmers, vol. 30 of *Proceedings of the Academy of Political Science*, no. 4 (1972): 15.

to come to grips with the religious reorientation that is so profoundly affecting its goals and activities, both religious and secular. This question becomes especially acute when the Church is being urged to immediate and drastic measures—pastorally, socially, and politically— by radicalized priests in its own midst. Focusing on the Argentine experience up to late 1973, this essay attempts to provide some tentative answers to the question. Particular attention is given to the way in which Catholic radicalism has forced the issue of rapid change. Through a brief examination of the rise of the Movement of Priests for the Third World (*Tercermundistas*) and its political theology and political action program, the writer outlines the nature of the challenge confronting the Argentine Church. Then, turning to responses of the hierarchy and the regime of General Juan Carlos Onganía, an attempt is made to assess the relation between rapid religious change and social and political change in this prominent Latin American country.

Rise of the Third World Priests

The Movimiento de Sacerdotes para el Tercer Mundo (Movement of Priests for the Third World) is basically an outgrowth of two converging influences. The first of these was the worker-priest experience, begun in France and imported to Argentina in the 1950s. Carried to Argentina, in part, by priests with direct experience in post-World War II France, Spain, and Italy, this approach to coping pastorally with the problems of the working class fell on fertile soil in post-Peronist Argentina.[2] A second influence was the somewhat more recent reorientation generated in world Catholicism by the Second Vatican Council, which, with its call for greater social awareness of the needs of the poor, reinforced lines of commitment and activity already under way in Argentina.[3] Initially, the Argentine hierarchy encouraged the worker-priest movement while political regimes of the 1950s ignored it. Gradually, however, and at an accelerating tempo, the worker-priest movement in Argentina began to transcend its early anonymity and to call attention to itself by virtue of activities among the country's urban working class. Because these priests served highly concentrated population clusters and were affiliated with working groups that were organized for the first time, their potential for influence was much greater than the size of their membership would have suggested. In 1959, they constituted less than 3 percent of Argentina's nearly 5,000 priests.[4] Therefore, when direct involvement re-

---

[2]"De Maritain a Perón," *Primera Plana*, January 18, 1972, pp. 12-13.

[3]Karl M. Schmitt, ed., *The Roman Catholic Church in Modern Latin America* (New York: Knopf, 1972), p. 25.

[4]Frederick C. Turner, *Catholicism and Political Development in Latin America* (Chapel Hill: University of North Carolina Press, 1970), p. 184. The figures are for the year 1959.

sulted in the dramatic conversion of many priests to the same sense of militancy as the workers, the tone of the worker-priest movement became seriously altered from what the hierarchy had envisioned; and enthusiasm for the project among most bishops swiftly cooled. When this attitude failed to halt the mounting wave of clerical activism, the hierarchy responded by threatening to defrock the most militant adherents. The Argentine government became involved at this point. It assisted the hierarchy by deporting several worker-priests. Rather than containing the growing militancy among priests, this series of actions seems, in retrospect, merely to have hardened the determination of socially involved priests. Thus, it foreshadowed the actual emergence of the Third World Priest Movement, which numbered more than 400 active members by 1972.

The religio-political movement of Priests for the Third World emerged as a consequence of both the worker-priests' experience and the great increase of interest in a socially relevant theology among Argentine Catholic priests, theologians, and university professors. Details of the Movement's formal birth and subsequent development are documented elsewhere.[5] Mention of the Movement's priestly composition is important, however, in understanding the nature and focus of its political commitment. Theologians and academicians among its membership have given it a highly sophisticated and articulate rationale for political involvement—a political theology whose scope, depth, and subtlety can be suggested here only in the barest outline. Worker-priests, seasoned through direct involvement with the working class poor (both urban and rural), have helped to provide its particular ideological flavor—especially its stress on action at the "bases of society," on participatory political structures for the poor, on a humanist socialism that "liberates the oppressed."

Political Theology and Political Praxis

The basic emphasis of *Tercermundista* theology requires a frontal assault on traditional dualist theology which "officially" separated the religious sphere from the profane. According to Tercermundismo, faith in God is directly and indissolubly linked to man "if what we are to believe is precisely that God does not exist either against or separated from man but rather dwelling within him." Humanity is perceived as God's temple; the relationship between God, Christ, and man is so fundamental that it is not possible to know God adequately through faith, independently of a knowledge of man. Rather, "in order to know God it is necessary to know man."[6] This proposition linking Christian

---

[5]Michael Dodson, "Religious Innovation and the Politics of Argentina: A Study of the Movement of Priests for the Third World" (Ph.D. diss., Indiana University, 1973), especially ch. 2.

[6]Rolando Concatti and Domingo Bresci, *Nuestra reflexión: Versión definitiva* (Buenos Aires: Publicaciones del Movimiento de Sacerdotes para el Tercer Mundo, 1970), pp. 133-34.

faith to a temporal knowledge of man implies, as *Tercermundistas* see it, an essential social dimension for pastoral action and is the basic building block in their political theology.

Their case is based on well-known Old Testament texts which treat of the close relationship one has with both God and neighbor. Proverbs 14:21, for instance, warns against despising one's neighbor and exploiting the humble. Deuteronomy 24:14 adds, "Thou shalt not oppress a hired servant that is poor and needy, whether he be of thy brethren or of the strangers that are in thy land." Amos 8:6 attacks those who "buy the poor for silver, and the needy for a pair of shoes." Finally, Isaiah asks: "What mean ye that ye beat my people to pieces and grind the faces of the poor?" (Isaiah 3:15) This prophet adds a somber warning: "Woe unto them that join house to house, that lay field to field, till there be no place, that they may be placed alone in the midst of the earth!" (Isaiah 5:8)[7] The conclusion *Tercermundistas* draw from these texts is that God is served only by doing justice to one's neighbor. To put the matter the other way around, men cannot simultaneously know God (meaning to love and serve Him) and knowingly do injustice to their fellow men.

We should note here that the *Tercermundista* case is a strong one, insofar as it goes, but that it does not, and probably cannot, go far enough; it leaves unanswered the crucial question of how to determine what constitutes justice and injustice in concrete instances. The Biblical texts cited give only very general guidelines for ascertaining concrete instances of oppression in the modern social milieu. Moreover, they are completely lacking in guidelines for the proposal of concrete alternatives in cases thought to fall within their condemnation. In short, while they may be an effective source of moral criticism, they do not constitute a substantial resource from which to draw political proposals. These shortcomings aside, however, we clearly are discussing an interpretation of the faith with a potentially important political dimension because this interpretation links the faith fundamentally to human relationships and to modes of conduct, both private and public.

To summarize, proper ethical conduct, not only religious but political, is grounded in the commandments to love both God and men; and it leads to the idea that "we have to meet men in order to find God." Faith involves a meeting of others; therefore, what men do to and for one another here on earth becomes critically important.[8]

From this conception of the Catholic faith, *Tercermundistas* have

---

[7] Gustavo Gutiérrez, *A Theology of Liberation: History, Politics and Salvation*, trans. and ed. Sister Caridad Inda and John Eagleson (Maryknoll, N.Y.: Orbis Books, 1973), pp. 289-94.

[8] Concatti and Bresci, *Nuestra reflexión*, p. 20; Lucio Gera and Guillermo Rodríguez Melgarejo, "Apuntes para una interpretación de la iglesia argentina," *Víspera*, February 1970, p. 74.

redeveloped the concept of a prophetic Church and a prophetic ministry. The Church as an institution and the priest as its representative are each called upon to "interpret the signs of the times," much in the manner of the Old Testament prophets. Clearly, this interpretive function is highly normative. On the one hand, it involves promotion of Christian values among men in a manner that emphasizes the totality of the human person, viewed as having salvation or liberation needs of both a physical and spiritual nature. *Tercermundistas* contend vigorously that, in promoting these values, the proper mission of the Church is not exclusively, but only specifically, religious. From this perspective, the Church has an ample role with respect to social affairs, for even granting "the legitimate autonomy of the temporal order cannot mean the disregard of the religious dimension of all human projects...."[9]

In its broadest sense, the Church role thus derived calls for critical examination of social and political structures and processes to determine their consistency with Christian soteriology (that is, with God's plan for the spiritual and temporal salvation of mankind). This entails "desacralizing" unjust structures. Where political domination or exploitation exists, the Church has a sacred duty, according to this theological perspective, to criticize and to call for reform—even revolution where conditions warrant it. But the position goes even further; it calls upon the individual priest himself to become engaged politically on behalf of the poor and the oppressed. This involves conscientizing the poor to their condition and even organizing them for political action to achieve the greater social and political justice portrayed in liberation theology, when no other political actors step forward to undertake the task. In *Tercermundista* theology, liberation replaces salvation because it depicts more compellingly the profoundly important political dimension of the overall emphasis of salvation.

Finally, all the political goals of the liberation effort can be resolved into two basic objectives. First, *Tercermundistas* are committed to the achievement of a democratic political framework within the context of which equality does not become overshadowed by liberty. Thus, although liberation consists of becoming free with respect to other men, this freedom must entail relationships that do not permit social and political domination. Their second objective is the establishment in Argentina of a humanist socialism that involves not just a redistribution of the wealth but, even more importantly, converts the ethic of "having more" into an ethic of "being more."[10] Let us now examine briefly how the Third World priests have at-

[9]Concatti and Bresci, *Nuestra reflexión*, p. 39.
[10]Ibid., p. 69. Each of these objectives is discussed in detail in Dodson, "Religious Innovation and the Politics of Argentina," ch. 3.

tempted to realize these principles in practice and then assess some of the consequences for the Argentine religious and political systems.

Tercermundistas in Politics and the Reactions of Hierarchy and Regime

We noted above that the early history of the worker-priest movement was characterized first by hierarchical support, then by increasing hierarchical opposition as it became clear that the movement was motivating priests to assist workers in the struggle for improvement of their social conditions. We noted, too, the collaboration of regime and hierarchy in the effort to quell the growing spirit of social reform among activist members of the clergy. Two other points are also important. First, the early thrust of the worker-priest movement and of *Tercermundismo*, as it evolved through the period from 1965 to 1968, was much less explicitly political than it was to become later. There was a dual emphasis in this early period: to bring the Church to the worker through the direct participation of priests in manual labor, and to interest the national Church (especially the hierarchy) in the plight of Argentina's working classes. In this stage, the focus was latently political; already, pamphlets, manifestos, and declarations of a political kind were beginning to appear in some quarters among the clergy. The basic emphasis, nevertheless, was religious; the priests sought to make the Church more relevant by urging it to change itself. Vatican II clearly provided the priests with a crucial source of legitimacy and encouragement. In the ensuing years, however, failure of the hierarchy to respond adequately to its pastoral responsibility stimulated evolution of the movement from a primarily religious program to a fundamentally political program.[11]

To be sure, the hierarchy did not enter this period totally unaffected by impulses radiating from Vatican II. Indeed, the prelates were already in a state of evolution. Some bishops were openly embracing the new currents of thought and social emphasis; but in June 1966, these members were unquestionably a minority. As a whole, the Church was moving slowly toward a moderately progressive position. The hierarchy would not have time, however, to make the transition smoothly. This was due partly to the "pull" of *Tercermundismo* and partly to the "push" of the military regime of Juan Carlos Onganía.

By virtue of political interests and associations, the Church was linked on numerous levels to the Onganía regime. Thus, in the light of the regime's overt, right-leaning Christian militancy, the Catholic hierarchy found it particularly difficult to respond to the urgings of

---

[11]For further discussion of this relationship between the hierarchy and the regime, see Michael Dodson, "The Catholic Church in Contemporary Argentina," *New Perspectives on Modern Argentina*, ed. Alberto Ciria et al. (Bloomington: Indiana University, Latin American Studies Program, 1972), pp. 57-67.

the *Tercermundistas*. Traditionally, the Church had been able to accommodate itself to the disagreeable aspects of successive regimes. In this case, the disagreeable aspects of a military dictatorship were at least partially offset by the obvious attempts of this deeply Catholic administration to make an ally of the Church. This was a political game with which the Church was quite familiar;[12] however, the profound uncertainty and the rapid pace of transition (which characterized the period due to the influence of changes in world Catholicism and the growth in size and militancy of the Catholic left) put the Church on quite unfamiliar terrain. The remainder of this study concerns the following matters: the way in which the Church has coped with political cross pressures; the way it has dealt with rapid change within its own institutional framework; and, ultimately, its shift with regard to social and political issues.

The immediate prelude to the formal organization of the Movement of Priests for the Third World involved a series of incidents throughout Argentina over a three-year period. During this period, conservative bishops and/or the Onganía regime repeatedly interfered in and attempted to stifle initiatives for reform. In December 1965, a strike by priests in Mendoza resulted in resignations by nearly thirty priests who abandoned their pastoral functions in protest against the "pre-conciliar mentality" of their bishop. This catalytic event was followed by another strike in San Isidro in February 1966 and, shortly thereafter, still another in Tucumán. In retrospect, the priest's strike of 1965 appears to have marked a point of departure from the decidedly religious focus of priestly agitation to a more political focus. Evidently, this event hardened the attitudes of many who either had been worker-priests or had sympathized with them. As a result, the crises that followed the San Isidro clash became increasingly political in nature, directed less at Church reform and more at pulling the Church, perhaps against its will, into a commitment to social and political change. This commitment was effected largely through activities of already committed clergy. To make the commitment effective, coordination on a national basis was implemented; by May 1968, the Movement of Priests for the Third World had been formally created at a national conference held in Córdoba. Here, organizational machinery was created, leadership selected, an organ of communication was established, and the foundations were laid for concerted political action by priests throughout Argentina.[13]

One cannot help but feel the irony in these developments, given the fact that during this same period the Argentine hierarchy was in

---

[12]Ibid., p. 60.

[13]Rolando Concatti and Domingo Bresci, *Sacerdotes para el Tercer Mundo: Crónica—documentos—reflexión* (Buenos Aires: Publicaciones del Movimiento Sacerdotes para el Tercer Mundo, 1970), p. 10; and Jorge Vernazza, "Naturaleza y objectivos de nuestro movimiento," *Cristianismo y Revolución*, April 1970, pp. 25-26.

the process of making a sincere effort to come to grips with the ideas of Vatican II. True enough, there were bishops (like the ones in San Isidro, Mendoza, and Tucumán) who were opposed to change in virtually any form; but there were probably even more bishops who were at least attempting to understand the new currents of reform. Of course, given the swiftness with which the Council's influence penetrated and spread throughout Latin America, it is not surprising that change in the hierarchy did not come rapidly enough for the most socially militant priests. At the same time, it is clear that the hierarchy was moving away from traditional stances of the 1950s and early 1960s. Indeed, bishops were already delivering themselves of pastoral declarations which hinted that in time the extent of the hierarchy's changing attitude would be profound. In June 1966, for example, the Episcopacy issued a document that condemned economic and cultural discrimination in Argentine society and proposed the "profound transformation" of Argentina's social structure, calling for a much greater degree of social, economic, and political equality in the country.[14] The real test for Church change, however, would be the extent to which such declarations would be followed up in practice; this was the test to which *Tercermundismo* determined to put the Argentine hierarchy.

Four factors seem to have played a significant role in determining how the Church was to meet this test over the next half dozen years. These include the rather dramatic political impact of the Third World Priests as they attempted to implement their program of "Christian praxis." This factor entails not only the political visibility and articulateness of the Movement, but also its self-conscious strategy of taking measures carefully calculated to lead the Church leftward but not to put the hierarchy in an impossibly comprising position. A second factor was the hierarchy's own decision, albeit after several early confrontations, to allow the *Tercermundistas* room to maneuver. Through all the turbulent events of these years, the hierarchy never openly condemned the Movement—even in the face of intense pressure from the regime to do so. This leads to the third factor, the nature of the military regime itself, which proved to be quite impolitic in handling the challenge posed by the Catholic left. Perhaps because of the general quiescence of other political groups at this time, perhaps because its own rigidly ideological Christian militancy differed so greatly from that of the Movement, perhaps because the regime was politically inexperienced and was therefore ill-equipped to cope with such uncertainties as a radical priest movement—for these and possibly other reasons, the Onganía regime proved consistently inflexible and over-reactive in its response to the Movement. As a conse-

---

[14] "The Argentine Church after the Council; Pastoral Statement of the Argentine Episcopate," *CIF Reports*, July 16, 1966, pp. 7/21-7/28.

quence, the government played into the Movement's hands by offending the very hierarchy it so wanted as an ally (and might indeed have gained as an ally had it made some moves to recognize the demands of the moderates). Instead, the regime aligned itself with the most reactionary wing of the Church, and the result was that the center was pushed leftward. In short, the regime indirectly served the ends of the radical left it so bitterly opposed. Finally, moderates within the Church hierarchy were deeply influenced by the commitments undertaken by a small but growing number of their own bishops on behalf of the general position represented by *Tercermundismo*. In 1966, not more than two Argentine bishops were associated with the advocates of social change; but shortly after the fall of Onganía, a dozen of Argentina's approximately fifty bishops were openly identified with the program of the *Tercermundistas*.

The remaining paragraphs illustrate by reference to concrete events how this series of factors was related in the initiatives and reactions of these three actors. The *Tercermundistas* chose Christmas of 1968 to stage their first nationally concerted effort of political protest and leadership. Beginning on December 20, priests in major cities throughout the country participated in a hunger strike, accompanied by as many as 3,500 lay persons in Reconquista and groups of from several dozen to about one hundred in various parts of Buenos Aires. The striking priests refused to celebrate Midnight Mass on Christmas Eve; held a series of press conferences in which they described and criticized social, economic, and political inequalities in Argentina; and distributed a Movement document denouncing the Onganía regime for its lack of interest in remedying these ills. In Buenos Aires, the presidential palace was picketed by twenty-one *Tercermundistas* who delivered a copy of the denunciatory letter to a Presidential assistant. Needless to say, these events received great publicity in the Argentine press.[15] The effect of the "Rebel Christmas," as it was called by *Primera Plana*, a leading Argentine weekly news journal, was largely symbolic. It did, however, appear to have two substantive consequences. First, these protest actions demonstrated to both Movement and Church that the *Tercermundistas* could launch a concerted, nationwide political effort; and they "proved" that the Movement was viable and could act politically on a national scale. Second, the "Rebel Christmas" probably encouraged many *Tercermundistas* at the diocesan level to engage more actively in local political protests and demonstrations. Much of the concrete organizational successes did indeed come at this level.

---

[15]See "Argentina: Priests for the Third World," *IDO-C International*, North American Edition, December 12, 1970, p. 79; Tercer Mundo (Buenos Aires: Asociación de empleados de la Dirección Impositiva, n.d.); and "Dios protesta a través de sus ministros," *Carta Latinoamericana*, February 1969.

In March and April 1969, significant political events involving *Tercermundistas* occurred in Rosario, Santa Fe, and Tucumán. In Rosario, thirty priests resigned in protest against Archbishop Guillermo Bolatti's pre-conciliar attitudes and policies, which were believed to inhibit their efforts to organize and to educate politically the working class poor in that city's *villas miserias*. While priestly sentiment around the country congealed rapidly in support of Rosarian *Tercermundistas*, the Argentine hierarchy did not unite in support of Archbishop Bolatti. Indeed, on approval of their own bishops,[16] many dioceses quickly opened their doors to the resigning priests. Thus, the Rosario protest did not develop into a national crisis, pitting clergy against hierarchy throughout the country. Furthermore, coming closely on the heels of the Rebel Christmas, this event helped publicize the Movement throughout the country.

The events in Santa Fe and Tucumán were more typical of similar, less noteworthy, but still significant acts of priestly political involvement that were taking place in many areas of Argentina. In each city, *Tercermundistas* had taken a leadership role in organizing unemployed and underemployed workers to conduct acts of protest against local industries, much in the fashion of unions. Where these activities were carried out, the response of local authorities was swift and severe: workers and priests alike were beaten and jailed.[17]

As these events were occurring, Argentine bishops were gathering in San Miguel for the Second Assembly of the Argentine Episcopate. Few in the assembly would have forecast at the outset how far-reaching would be the positions ultimately adopted—positions that reflected a remarkable degree of coincidence with the views already associated with *Tercermundismo*. Official sessions were devoted to what was indeed a controversial set of issues and ideas for an assembly of Argentine prelates. Moreover, some of the most innovative (and *Tercermundista*-like) positions put forward came from the very highest levels of the hierarchy. For example, Monseñor Eduardo Pironio (one of Argentina's most prestigious bishops and former Secretary General of the Conference of Latin American Bishops) offered his *Reflexión Teológica*. Vigorously decrying the ills brought on by *dependencia*, Bishop Pironio argued: "It is the Church's place to denounce prophetically these injustices, to awaken the consciences of the governing classes and enlist its members in the transformation— rapid and profound—of such structures." In a sense, the positions finally adopted by the Second Assembly at large were even more in-

---

[16]See "Curas: El motín de Rosario," *Primera Plana*, May 25, 1969, p. 8; and Armando Amirati et al., "Qué está sucediendo en la iglesia de Rosario?" *Cristianismo y Revolución*, August 1969, p. 16.

[17]"Los trece de Tucumán," *Primera Plana*, May 25, 1969, p. 10; and Oscar Caballero, "Villa Quinteros también es América," *Primer Plana*, May 13, 1969, pp. 32-42.

novative, because they suggested that change should be heavily encouraged to take place on the initiatives and actions of the popular sectors.[18]

The bishops also agreed with the essentially Marxist interpretation put forward by *Tercermundista* writers: that unjust social structures in Argentina have been the product of a lengthy historical development encompassing all dimensions of social life. "Therefore, liberation must be realized in all sectors where there is oppression: the juridical, political, cultural, economic and social." In addition, liberation is to be based on authentic indigenous values. This position led the bishops, as it did the *Tercermundistas*, into a call for participatory democracy as the best means to actualize indigenous values.[19]

The timing of the San Miguel conference puts its declaration at a key juncture in the unfolding political panorama of 1969. The sociopolitical nature of the document was interpreted in highest government circles as an expression of Church dissatisfaction with the regime. Indeed, it was interpreted as an attempt to disengage the Church from the regime. The rift thus created was widened in May when the regime found itself beset with widespread strikes, demonstrations, and riots. Not only were *Tercermundistas* directly involved in these events (and some bishops as well), but also government officials were convinced that the San Miguel declaration had helped to trigger this direct action by arousing a desire for rapid social and political change.

In large measure, the regime's attitude was justified. Not only had the hierarchy lent its public support to progressive and even radical positions with respect to highly charged political issues, but also the bishops had moved well away from the "visible compromise" with the regime that had been characteristic in 1966. At a time when the government was hard pressed by dissent from many quarters, this defection was keenly felt—so keenly, in fact, that a high government official publicly denounced the San Miguel document as immoral. Shortly thereafter, the Minister of Interior issued a public warning to the Church that it should support the government "totally and without desertions."[20] This could be interpreted as an effort to pressure clerical moderates (who had been counted on as allies because of their reluctance to enter the social arena) to put their own house in order, i.e., bring the militants into line. To some extent, the hierarchy did attempt to do this; and, by implication, the bishops attempted to retreat somewhat from the commitment opened up at San Miguel. But

---

[18]*Declaración del episcopado argentino* (San Miguel: Ediciones Paulinas, 1969), pp. 35-40.

[19]Ibid.

[20]Arnaldo Cristiani, "La iglesia 'Tercerista' en los sucesos de mayo y junio de 1969," *Cuadernos de Marcha*, July 1969, pp. 20-21.

the events of the next several years (extending over to the Lanusse presidency) suggested that the hierarchy had made a commitment that could not be retracted. Government pressure served only to harden the determination of more militant elements of the Church; at the same time, heavy-handed tactics toward those militants served to force the hierarchy to their defense.

Throughout May and into June 1969, Argentina experienced a continuous sequence of related events that involved rioting, massive demonstrations, work stoppages, and the killing of civilians by harassed police in major cities of the interior. Rosario, Corrientes, and Córdoba were scenes of the most violent and prolonged of these activities which continued to envelop *Tercermundistas*, hierarchy, and regime in a triangle of cross-pressures and conflicts.[21] In all of these turbulent political conflicts, *Tercermunidistas* were evident in the front ranks of political protest, along with students and labor groups. They were consistently effective in drawing attention to working class demands and demands of what may be called the lumpenproletariat; also, through their publicity efforts, they underscored the political rigidity and the brutality that all too often characterized the government's handling of these events. *Tercermundistas* were somewhat effective in "conscientizing" their target groups to the need for political organization and in providing leadership and concrete organizational initiatives. On the whole, however, the Movement was relatively ineffective in seeing any of these conflicts through to the realization of concrete political gains for the poor. Of publicity, there was plenty; of tangible gains for the lower class, there were precious few.

In the short run, perhaps of more consequence was the effect these actions had on the hierarchy. Rather than being alienated, more and more prelates seemed to be persuaded of the viability of the *Tercermundista* position and of the need for such a voice within Argentine Catholicism. Increasingly, new bishops spoke out in behalf of the Movement. With a dramatic gesture in November 1969, President Onganía attempted to regain for his regime the rapidly dwindling support of the Church. He announced an attempt to unify the country around an essentially religious act, the "public and solemn consecration of Argentina to the immaculate heart of Mary." The regime, it seems, felt obliged to enter the religious sphere for the sake of its political welfare. This initiative failed rather strikingly. Less than half of Argentina's bishops acknowledged the event. Others spoke out openly against it.[22]

[21]For a fuller discussion of these conflicts and the *Tercermundista* role, see Dodson, "Religious Innovation and the Politics of Argentina," ch. 6.
[22]"Argentina: Mientras el Presidente Onganía consagra el país a la Virgen, algunos obispos y sacerdotes denuncian la miseria del pueblo," *Informaciones católicas internacionales*, December 2, 1969, p. 17.

In June 1970, Ongania was ousted from the presidency by yet another military coup; General Levingston, who was to last only a few months in office, replaced him. Official response of the hierarchy to this change was decidedly cooler than it had been when Ongania came to power. With Ongania's fall and replacement by yet another general, the hierarchy was determined to approach the new military government with care. In their declaration of June 10, the bishops drew attention to the "disturbed" nature of the Argentine condition. Peace, they argued, would only be possible "through the installation of a just order which fully respects the dignity of all men and which satisfies their legitimate aspirations." In an apparent reference to the recently deposed regime, they asserted that "The oppression exercised by powerful groups can give the impression of maintaining peace and order, but in reality it is merely the germ of rebellion." Responsibility for creating better communication between governors and the governed was charged directly to the new regime. Concerning the role of Christians, the bishops declared: "they must defend the rights of the poor and marginal, and eliminate everything that menaces justice: marginalization, oppression of groups . . . irritating inequalities in the distribution of goods, disproportion between prices and salaries."[23]

One need not be a *Tercermundista* to interpret this declaration as a warning to the new regime that the weight of the Church had swung toward a much greater concern for the temporal needs of the lower classes, particularly when compared to the attitude Ongania had encountered in 1966. Thus, *Tercermundismo* emerged from the Ongania period not only intact and vigorous among clergy, but significantly present in the thought of the moderate majority within the Argentine hierarchy.

Conclusions

What may we conclude from this brief survey of religious innovation and its role in recent Argentine politics? First, let us assess the role of the Movement of Priests for the Third World. The pattern of political involvements that has typified this movement strongly suggests that the denunciatory role aimed at discrediting (desacralizing) unjust social structures and publicizing the political needs of marginal working class groups has been generally effective. This can be argued in the dual sense that *Tercermundista* activities received constant and widespread attention in the public arena (from press, hierarchy, and regime alike) and that other interest groups, both lay and religious, picked up the *Tercermundista* cry with respect to issues on which they had hitherto been utterly silent. The very creation of a political theology is an important dimension of the denunciatory

[23]"Declaración del episcopado argentino después del derrocamiento de General Juan Carlos Onganía," *NADOC*, July 1, 1970, pp. 1-2.

role. Beyond this, *Tercermundistas* have shown themselves adept at discovering and exploiting opportunities to promote their political theology among target groups, including their own hierarchy. In this connection, a major achievement of the Movement has been its success in getting the *Tercermundista* program on the agenda of the national Church.

With regard to the organizational and leadership role, however, there is not a great deal of evidence to show that the activist priests have made significant headway in organizing the "oppressed classes" in Argentina for concrete, self-sufficient political action. Direct organizational efforts have tended to be random, decentralized, and aimed at resolution of immediate, temporary goals. Community-centered political groups organized and led by *Tercermundistas* have sought primarily to redress immediate economic grievances. There has been no coherent, nationwide effort on the part of *Tercermundistas* to create a unified political apparatus serving the poor. Admittedly, coordinating a nationwide effort of this kind would be much more difficult than coordinating the denunciatory effort. Nevertheless, if the political organization of the masses is an integral part of liberation politics, as *Tercermundista* political theology implies, then the priests must be judged to have made little concrete progress on this important front.

There is no doubt that initially the rapid rise to prominence of the Third World Priests traumatized the Argentine Church. Given the strength of pre-conciliar views as late as 1965, the hierarchy in general showed a remarkable flexibility in coming to the positions it had adopted by 1970. Two points are noteworthy in this regard. The first concerns the persistent adaptability of religious traditions in the face of change. The behavior of the Argentine Catholic Church cannot be attributed to mere opportunism. Rather, it is a manifestation of the richness of Catholic tradition that it contains resources with which to confront a time of profound change. The second point concerns the purely political skill exemplified by the hierarchy during this period. Strident demands of right and left served to present the Church with an insoluble dilemma in 1966, but the hierarchy adroitly negotiated its way between the horns of this dilemma, following *Tercermundismo*, but never patently enough to force an open rupture with the regime. The hierarchy even managed to provide *Tercermundismo* a degree of protection without bringing upon itself the expressions of governmental wrath it endured, for example, during the first Perón era.

What, finally, must be said of the regime's role? By its own admission, the regime of General Onganía was affected by the Movement of Priests for the Third World. The author would argue that the regime overestimated the direct threat represented by the Movement and therefore overreacted to the radical priests. The reason for this seems to lie in the fact that *Tercermundismo* arrived on the Argentine political scene at a time when some traditional political actors were hesitant and quiescent; others, such as the Peronist groups, were barred from formal participation in the political process. Something of a political vacuum had been created after the June 1966 coup; and within this vacuum the activities of *Tercermundismo* took on more sinister aspects, from the regime's point of view, than might otherwise have been the case. When *Tercermundismo* appeared to join forces with labor during the *Cordobazo*,[24] and when it became obvious that the hierarchy was moving toward a *Tercermundista* position of open criticism with respect to the regime, such bizarre behavior as the abortive "consecration" was the unfortunate result. Church disaffection, stimulated by *Tercermundismo*, was thus a factor in the demise of the Onganía regime; and in this respect, at least, Catholic radicalism played a significant role in effecting immediate short run political change in Argentina.

[24]*Cordobazo* here refers to the wave of strikes and street demonstrations that involved workers, students, and clergy in violent clashes with police in the industrial city of Córdoba in May and June 1969. Many observers have regarded the *Cordobazo* as a major factor in weakening the credibility of the Onganía regime.

LITERATURE

Literary and philosophical responses to religious issues reflect the variety of perspectives that characterize Spanish-American culture in South America. In regard to religious questions, this variety is especially noticeable. Martin Heidegger, German poets of the twentieth century, and the surrealists have exerted secular influences that have affected attitudes toward the human condition. These influences have had a telling impact on the understanding of the religious concept of redemption. At the same time, perceptive description and analysis of what some critics have held to be the sterile influence of certain phases of the work of the Catholic Church have an important place in the novel, drama, and short story. In addition, non-Catholic theological developments have added new dimensions to the religious life of Spanish South America.

27. Time and Eternity in Víctor Massuh's Philosophy of Religion

NIELS C. NIELSEN, JR.

This essay clarifies basic themes in Víctor Massuh's *Sentido y fin de la historia en el pensamiento religioso actual*. Massuh's work responds to the thought of twentieth-century philosophers such as Buber, Bultmann, Niebuhr, and Berdyaev as they have worked with eschatological issues. Professor Nielsen summarizes Massuh's thought and analyzes his claims that the meaning of historical events is based on an eschatological perpective.

Professor Víctor Massuh holds a chair in philosophy and the history of religions at the University of Buenos Aires. In his *Sentido y fin de la historia, en el pensamiento religioso actual*, he takes on an important contemporary religious theme, namely, eschatology.[1] Massuh considers the varied use of eschatology in the writings of Karl Löwith, Nicolas Berdyaev, Hans Urs von Balthasar, Martin Buber, Rudolf Bultmann, Reinhold Niebuhr and Josef Pieper. A wide spectrum of points of view (Roman Catholic, Orthodox, Protestant, and Jewish) is included in the survey that he makes before formulating his own conclusions. Each of the philosophers and theologians to whom Massuh gives chapters, has attempted to show the contemporary relevance of the theme of eschatology. Massuh does not detail the development of New Testament research since publication of Schweitzer's *Quest of the Historical Jesus*, which brought the theme of eschatology into new prominence.[2] Rather, he presupposes Schweitzer's work and attempts to treat apocalyptic as well as eschatological claims phenomenologically from the point of view of the philosophy of religion, not just confessionally.

---

[1]Buenos Aires: Eudeba (Editorial Universitaria de Buenos Aires), 1963.
[2]For the original edition of this work, see *Von Reimarus zu Wrede: Eine Geschichte der Leben-Jesu-Forschung* (Tübingen: J.C.B. Mohr, 1906).

Massuh recognizes not only the mythical world view of the sects, but the utopian expectations of political revolutionaries. Not to be overlooked is the present possibility of worldwide destruction by atomic and hydrogen bombs, a fact which must come into the purview of the most secular thinker, not given to myth or symbol. This spectre of a planet-wide catastrophe brings its own possible eschatology, at least an end to the world. How, Massuh asks, does the theme bear on the meaning of history, as life on the planet has been in the past and may be in the future? First, he cites Löwith's claim that historical consciousness belongs more to the West than to the East, and to the Hebrew more than to the Greek tradition.[3] Jewish interpretation was predominantly religious, concerned with God's activity in history. Deity was understood to have been present in the beginning at creation and at the end in fulfillment, even as divine Providence is conceived as active in the period between.

The Greeks in their mythology as in their teleology, according to Löwith, were more oriented to natural processes. Their doctrine of fate did not leave an open future which could evoke hope. By contrast, Jewish eschatological expectation premised God as acting freely in history and was more dynamic. Christianity, continuing this orientation, radicalized the expectation of the coming of the kingdom of God. For such a view, human life is not simply a record of progress. Massuh rejects a secularized version of so-called linear history, citing Ranke's remark that every generation is equidistant from eternity. Judged morally, in the long view, one must consider growth in wickedness as well as goodness, for there is the unhappy sequence from Caesar to Napoleon to Hitler. Massuh cites the outlook of the Swiss New Testament scholar, Oscar Cullman: the Christian lives between the times, between the first and the second coming of Christ. In consequence, profane and sacred history exist side by side. As against the Augustinian view, however, it must be argued that there can be no established Christian society as was often presupposed in the Middle Ages. On the contrary, Christian hope is superhistorical in its bases. Despair is overcome in faith, and from this perspective Christianity has left its legacy of historical consciousness.

Massuh is particularly impressed by Nicolas Berdyaev, the exiled Russian philosopher who also spoke of profane and sacred history, but not in the same sense as Cullman. Berdyaev's view is more profoundly ontological and at the same time millenial. Amid the growth of both good and evil, history cannot be reduced to its simply immanent meanings or realities. Berdyaev's perspective is eschatological but not just apocalyptic or mythical. Rather he emphasizes creative act as against a view which focuses simply on the end of time. Berdyaev's ontology is explicit in the claim that time cannot be

---

[3]Karl Löwith, *Weltgeschichte und Heilsgeschehen* (Stuttgart: Kohlhammer, 1953).

separated from eternity. Nor is the latter just everlastingness. Instead, there is an interaction between the two. Massuh agrees with Berdyaev that the course of events itself has been profoundly changed by the kind of historical consciousness that Christianity has brought. Its eschatology does not just look for the end of the world but for transformation. As there is cooperation between the will of God and the will of man, diversity of thought and life become unified. The kingdom of God becomes real. Berdyaev finds every human hope to be a request for the end of history in this qualitative sense. He does not deny that eschatology has a future orientation. The kingdom of God brings personal, social, and cosmic transformation. This means drastic discontinuity. Not a doctrine of progress which sublimates the present to the future but the resurrection of the dead will be the end of history, he asserts. At the same time, eschatology is not just future, but signifies a transcendent presence, the eternal in time. Rather than remaining ambivalent between the negation of apocalyptic destruction and the more positive affirmation of a millenium, Berdyaev invokes the "mysticism" of John's Gospel. Time and eternity are together in a promise yet to be fulfilled.

Of all the authors considered by Massuh, the Roman Catholic, Hans Urs von Balthasar, places the least stress on future expectation. His emphasis is on the past and present more than on the present and the future. Specifically, von Balthasar describes Christ as the archetype and center of history. Reality and events in the world are not self-contained. This means that their pattern is not one of eternal return as Nietzsche supposed. Christ is the union of the singular and universal, concrete and abstract, historical and superhistorical, temporal and eternal. By contrast, the eschatology of the Jewish thinker, Martin Buber, is clearly not ontological. Eschatology belongs to prophecy, he argues, as utopia belongs to philosophy. Buber avoids the apocalyptic. His view is determined even in his eschatology by his dialogical understanding of the relation between I and Thou. Eschatology arises from a quest for justice and righteousness as it looks to God for fulfillment. Buber's interpretation is radically personal rather than social or communal. Moreover, the individual rather than man in general is primary in historical relations.

The Protestant New Testament scholar, Rudolf Bultmann, denies any simple universal history. Like Buber, Bultmann's orientation is not on something "outside" of history; this he does not allow. Rather, eschatology must express an actual decision directed toward the future. Massuh is critical of Bultmann's outlook. It is difficult to relate his view to the course of history by way of any generalization. Indeed, he allows no unity of history apart from eschatology, claiming that such interpretation is an overintellectualized one. Prophecy and apocalyptic, like eschatology, are seen in the context of the radical temporality prescribed by Heidegger's view of being. Massuh also considers Reinhold Niebuhr's *Nature and Destiny of Man*.[4] Niebuhr seems to him to be pessimistic about history, minimizing freedom, and emphasizing judgment. But Niebuhr is optimistic about what is beyond history.

Massuh's book on Nietzsche and the end of religion was written after his study on eschatology and history.[5] Yet the two are not unrelated. Both writings raise the question of the relation of time to eternity. Massuh's work on Nietzsche is primarily expository. He takes careful note of the point of view of Heidegger as well as that of Fink with respect to Nietzsche interpretation. However, Massuh's own claim is that Nietzsche has not destroyed religion nor is his attack on it unqualified. In short, Massuh's position is more positively religious in the end than Heidegger's. The priority which Massuh gives to internalization in his own view of eschatology as well as his evaluation of religion in general appears in the background of his Nietzsche interpretation. Even after Nietzsche's polemic, religion remains a vital part of the inner life of man, Massuh believes. Primarily, it is religion as external authority, dogma, and institution which Nietzsche opposes in asserting that God is dead. If religion is a kind of inwardness, it may be said to live on in Nietzsche's own "mysticism." Nietzsche critics point out that a distinction must be made between Nietzsche's early and later outlooks; Massuh agrees. But in no case is his artistocratic, individualistic view to be equated with that of Marx on the one hand or of positivism on the other.

The really crucial components of Nietzsche's own view of time and eternity are to be found in his doctrine of eternal recurrence. A variety of critics have argued that he regarded this as his greatest achievement.[6] Whatever it means, eternal recurrence expressed the inspiration which came to him high in the Alps. All experience and the universe itself seemed to him to cohere in a kind of mystical unity. As he recognized the eternal "Now" he was able to accept time and history, the world with all its suffering and agony even in joy. Does Nietzsche's view mean that there is no ultimate distinction between time and eternity? Here I wish to go beyond Massuh's analysis in reference to Buddhism. In some types of Mahayana Buddhism, Nirvana is not only this-worldly but present. Nietzsche similarly—although rejecting Schopenhauer's appropriation of Buddhism as too world-denying—asserts no real difference between time and eternity. Of course, in such a context, no eschatology is necessary. What is the meaning of history? For Nietzsche, it is eternal recurrence and not Nirvana. Transcendence, fixed moral goals and values, and all dualism between time and eternity are invalidated. Massuh, along

[4] New York: Scribners, 1943.
[5] *Nietzsche y el fin de la religión* (Buenos Aires: Editorial Sudamericana, 1969).
[6] Cf. Walter Kaufmann, *Nietzsche* (Princeton, N.J.: Princeton University Press, 1950).

with others, points out that a kind of return to innocence is implied. Without Nirvana, the world alone is real and it is as if evil had never been encountered or the Four Noble Truths proclaimed. Eschatology is premised on a time-eternity tension. For Nietzsche, as in the case of Buddhism, all is becoming—but the becoming of eternal recurrence. There is no eschatology except for eternal return; the latter is without karma. The justification of good and evil must be in the human self. If there is theodicy, it is superman. But this is to stretch terms, for there is no need for theodicy if there is no real evil.

A time-eternity distinction appears in Massuh's *El Diálogo de las culturas*, as he speaks of Jaspers' categorization in the distinction: world, man, and Encompassing.[7] Massuh protests against any simply sociological, psychological or cyclical view of the life of culture. Spengler's outlook, for example, is incomplete in its view of history. Massuh urges that man has freedom in his encounter with transcendence. Nietzsche's life vitalism is incomplete; recognition of abiding goods and evil leads to questions of eschatology. If time is regarded as self-complete, the very real danger arises that history will become meaningless. So-called technological progress operates on only a superficial level and gives no lasting asylum from questions of good or evil. In justifying his reference to eschatology, Massuh rejects a variety of alternative positions. When the past itself is regarded as fullness, he argues, there tends to be a lack of emphasis on human initiative and will. By contrast, when the future is regarded as only the work of human reason and will, utopianism follows. Modern revolutions have been characterized by impatience with the present and illusions about the future. Collective enthusiasm has envisaged a mystical moment of eternity even as the achievements of the past have been destroyed.

At the same time that it envisages the end of history, eschatology raises the question of the total meaning of history. Massuh criticizes Paul Althaus' claim that our theme is simply a part of theology. Its full importance cannot be understood simply confessionally, he argues. Most of all, one must recognize that eschatology cannot be part of a system. Viewed in its fullness, history may require an eschatology. Massuh argues that so-called secular affirmations (social, philosophical, and scientific) use this idea. To be sure, the kingdom of God is replaced by the kingdom of man. As against many traditional religious views, it is clear to Massuh that a place must be left for human freedom even as it is affirmed that time itself is not absolute. The notion is of little value or illumination if it means only destruction of liberty or the process of history.

Eschatology becomes of relevance as it is recognized that pro-

[7]*El diálogo de las culturas* (Tucumán: Instituto de Filosofía, Universidad Nacional de Tucumán, 1956).

phetic, mythical, and utopian visions have their basis in the dialectic between present and future, understood not simply from itself but from the point of view of eternity. Of course, eschatology is not limited to temporality and the present but concerns the superhistorical also. As John's Gospel makes clear, it has to do not just with the future but the eternal now. Phenomenologically, it may be said that eschatological expectation is provoked by the presence of eternity to and with man along with his experience of finitude. One cannot reduce the dialectic between eternity and time simply to intermediate temporal stages. Man's deepest longings cannot be satisfied by a belief in progress.

Massuh's own evaluation and reinterpretation is based on a distinction between different types of eschatology: prophetic, mythical, apocalyptic, and mystical. Initially, he accepts that eschatology introduces a perspective that is not simply philosophical. The end of history cannot be known in the present; however, a claim for eschatology need be no more indefinite than the theory of progress which has affirmed a dynamic of history and direction without knowledge of an end. Massuh's basic affirmation is the interrelation of time and eternity; the latter is qualitatively and not just quantitatively different from the former. In principle, he agrees with Berdyaev, although not accepting in detail the Russian's interpretation. Massuh's question can be called hermeneutical: what do religious eschatological symbols mean? He seeks to treat them phenomenologically and critically, not reducing their existential reality simply to concept. How then is his own theory developed? It is mystical eschatology, not the prophetic, much less the mythical or apocalyptic, which Massuh believes can bring contradictions into positive relations with each other. Lasting coherence and unity of opposites appears only in the perfection of eternity. To be sure, all existential contradiction is not immediately resolved; however, this is of secondary importance. (Massuh notes that mystical eschatology has its secular counterpart in hedonism as it seeks a timeless moment.)

In his appraisal, Massuh seeks to avoid the problems of literalism while still explicating relevantly the category of eschatology. It is the weakness of many past interpretations of this theme that they have wavered between destruction and millenialism. Massuh rejects the utopianism of a futurized apocalyptic for the eternal "Now" of mystical eschatology. It is the superhistorical character of the latter, he believes, which opens the way to positive relations with a variety of cultural forms—art and poetry, for example. His claim that eschatology gives dynamic and meaning to history is not disputed in this paper; the question remains, however, as to the differences between the mystical, prophetic, apocalyptic, and mythical views. It must be emphasized that Massuh does not ask simply how religious knowledge is possible, much less attempt to "unpack" terms in the mode of some types of modern analytic philosophy. What he is attempting to do is clear enough from the thinkers, the exposition of whose ideas make up more than half of his book on eschatology. Eschatological statements are perennial in theism; to be sure, they are generally kerygmatic. Massuh does not believe that they can be reduced away naturalistically or dissolved in demythologizing. They not only signify that history remains open to the future, its meaning not exhausted simply by concept; they point to a present tension in man and his world.

History, freedom, and eternity present problems of context and not just the use of terms. Can such themes be clarified in philosophy of religion? Massuh's premise, assuredly debatable, is that they are not simply kerygmatic. In appraising his position, it is important to note that the Biblical perspective resists dissolution into non-temporal categories. The Hebrew Biblical material affirms God's everlastingness, not his eternity. Even the Fourth Gospel is not simply Platonic. How much is the Biblical concern for history destroyed in a mystical eschatology? At this point one cannot avoid the question of the meaning of religious language: How much is it necessarily symbolic, mythical, and temporal? How much is it mystical? Contemporary Protestant interpretation has emphasized that the basic Biblical categories are not time-eternity, finite-infinite, but sin and grace. Practically, one may ask how much meaning a simply mystical eschatology would have for a person living in the midst of persecution, as for example, at the time of the writing of the Book of Revelation? Would it be effective in sustaining faith or would time simply dissolve into eternity? Massuh does not propose a secularization of the religious view. The strength of his position is that he treats his theme phenomenologically. Interpreted philosophically, it is not reduced away existentially. The condition and reality which evoked it remain.

28. Religion in Colombia as Seen in the Works of García Márquez

BERTIE ACKER

García Márquez has written a series of stories in which the religious life of Colombia is the central theme. Generally, he views this religious influence as unhealthy, as life-denying, and as having a stultifying effect on the vitality and culture of Colombians. Professor Acker has analyzed García Márquez's works in order to establish his views toward the Roman Catholic Church and the religious life of his country.

Roman Catholicism is strong in Colombia. Colombians on the whole are devout—a fact often proclaimed in newspaper headlines. The Catholic Church, firmly entrenched, presides over the social life of the people from baptism to burial. Laws—anti-divorce, anti-birth control, to mention only two of paramount social important—adhere to officially sanctioned Catholic policies.

An author like Gabriel García Márquez, an astute observer who recreates a Colombian mini-cosmos in his Macondo, could hardly fail to include an account of the role that religion plays in the life of the individual and the community. And "Gabo" does indeed, in each of his works, provide a helpful understanding of the Catholic Church in Colombia as well as expressing his own attitude toward the church in relation to social and political circumstances.

Taking García Márquez's works chronologically, let us observe the Church's role in each.

La hojarasca (1955) has as its theme the contrast between a strong and charitable individual, the Colonel, and a town permeated with hatred and resentment—the same town of Macondo whose founding families brought with them their old religious practices and beliefs and carried images of saints in their trunks on the long journey in search of a place to settle. The colonel defies everyone, including his own family, to see that his old friend the doctor is buried. Inhabitants of Macondo want the body to rot as punishment for the doctor's unconforming behavior. (He had become a hermit, had lived openly with Meme without benefit of clergy, and once had refused to care for the town's wounded on a night of tragic violence—probably the kindest thing he could do, as he apparently was not actually trained in medicine.) But the people neither forgot nor forgave, for he was too different. When the doctor's strange, withdrawn and tormented spirit finally leads him to suicide by hanging, the merciless town rejoices. The new priest, Padre Angel, refuses permission to bury the suicide and atheist in holy ground, and the civil officials must be bribed to give authorization for the funeral.

La hojarasca probably has the least literary merit of all that García Márquez has written. The style is choppy. The theme is too blunt. Yet the author's preoccupation with the conflict between moral codes and human understanding is made patently clear. The colonel's compassion and understanding present a dramatic contrast to the lack of charity of the self-righteous citizens. The Catholic Church is not directly charged with responsibility for these attitudes—after all, the colonel is a religious man—but it must at least have failed to inculcate principles of acceptance and forgiveness in its members.

In *El coronel no tiene quien le escriba* (1961) the church regulates life in Macondo. Church bells indicate the time to awaken, to attend mass, to say the rosary or they toll the hour of a funeral. Before the nightly showing of the movie, Padre Angel indicates the show's moral rating by ringing the church bells. Usually he tolls twelve times, meaning that it is bad for everyone; then he seats himself at the window to see who goes in despite his warning. Social customs of respect for the dead are carefully observed, yet, in truth, the attitude toward death is strangely pagan. A young man has died at the beginning of the novelette. The colonel notes that it must be horrible to be buried in October. Women shout after the corpse as if the dead boy could hear. The colonel and his wife speak of their own dead son as if he were alive, as if he were greeting his friend who has just joined him in death—and together they would surely talk of the sport of cock fighting.

Religion is seen in this work as a part of the rhythm and structure of life, but the central concerns of the people are the struggle against poverty, police violence, political censorship, and a general lack of concern for the poor and the old. Veterans of the civil war grow senile and die waiting for their promised pensions. The rich, in collusion with the government, steal from the poor. The Church is not a dynamic force in combatting these problems. It concerns itself only with such questions as whether it is sinful to borrow money on a wedding ring or to sing on the day of a funeral, while crimes of vast dimensions committed by those in high places go unreproved.

In a collection of short stories, *Los funerales de la Mamá Grande*

(1962), "La siesta del martes" recounts the visit of a poor woman, accompanied by her young daughter, to the village of Macondo. She asks the priest for the key to the cemetery so that she may place flowers on her son's grave. The son had been shot and killed when the widow Rebeca thought he was trying to break into her home. He was a good man, according to his mother. He had been taught never to steal anything that someone else needed. But when he had tried to earn a living as a boxer, he would often spend days in bed after a beating. He lost all his teeth. Every mouthful his mother ate then tasted of her son's suffering. The priest's words of consolation, "La voluntad de Dios es inescrutable,"[1] are spoken without much conviction because experience has made him skeptical. The priest shows compassion, first by giving up his afternoon siesta to assist the mother, and second, by trying to dissuade the women from going into the streets to face the threatening crowd that has gathered there. But the self-righteous intolerance of the village compounds the social wrongs that led the dead man into a life of petty crime. The reader is left with the uneasy feeling that the Church is an ineffectual institution in a land of poverty and pride.

Christian precepts do not seem to affect human nature. "La viuda de Montiel" introduces us to a believer, José Montiel, who publicly promised to give the temple a life-sized statue of Saint Joseph if he won the lottery. Two weeks later his ticket won and he kept his promise. No mention is made that such bartering with God is frowned upon. Montiel, however, is a thief on the grand scale; but, unlike the poor boxer in "Siesta," Montiel may steal with impunity. He began as an informer against his own townspeople when the new mayor arrived with orders to liquidate the political opposition. The poor whom he betrayed were shot in the public plaza; the rich were given twenty-four hours to leave town. Montiel then offered to buy their property and cattle at a price he himself fixed. He died one day of a heart attack—leaving his widow lonely, embittered by the consciousness of her tainted inheritance, abandoned by their former "friends" and by her own children. Montiel may have given lip service to religion, but it did not inhibit his criminal way of life.

Father Antonio Isabel del Santísimo Sacramento del Altar Castañeda y Montero is ninety-four years old at the time we meet him in "Un día después del sábado," a story that contains all the logic of a dream or that matches the confused reasoning of senility. Birds have started falling dead in Macondo. They destroy window screens trying to enter the houses to die. Everyone is talking about the weird phenomenon—except the priest who is slow to recognize what is happening. Father Antonio Isabel is a man of regular habits. He is small,

---

[1]Gabriel García Márquez, *Los funerales de la Mamá Grande* (Buenos Aires: Editorial Sudamericana, 1970), p. 18.

insignificant, with pronounced and solid bones, slow gestures, and a silken voice. He loves the Greek classics, is imaginative, intrepid in interpretation, and rather nonsensical in his sermons. He does nothing except to say mass. Twice a week he seats himself in the confessional, although for years no one has confessed. He simply believes his parishioners are losing their faith because of modern customs. The people think he is a good man, gentle and kind, but that he habitually wanders about in a mental fog. Years ago they had asked that another priest be sent to replace him, partly because of his age, but especially because of his saying he has seen the devil on three occasions. He enjoys wandering through metaphysical mazes, and he, himself, does not realize that his thoughts have become so subtle that in his moments of meditation he no longer is thinking about anything.

One Saturday it occurs to him, as a marvelous revelation, that dead birds are raining upon the town, and he, the minister of God, has completely forgotten the Apocalypse. As he sits at the station waiting for the train to go by, his mind wanders through old memories, making strange associations, until he stands up, lifts a surprised hand, and exclaims with terror, "El Judío Errante."

Meanwhile, a penniless young man on his way to the capital gets off the train to eat. The train starts before he finishes his meal, and he is left without baggage or money in a strange town. Next morning he goes to mass. Father Antonio Isabel sees the stranger enter with his hat on and seat himself in the last row. The priest's heart overflows with gratitude and he begins to preach the great sermon of his life. The temple is gradually crowded with people devoutly listening to the sermon; they readily accept the tale of the Wandering Jew as an explanation for the dying birds. Father Antonio Isabel dimly realizes what is happening; for the first time in his life he knows the sin of pride, as pressing as thirst. Abruptly he directs the acolyte to collect the alms, to tell the people the money is to exile the Wandering Jew, and then to give it to the boy on the back row so he can buy a new hat. (The hat may have entered the story as part of the nebulous thinking of the priest who worried because the youth did not remove his hat in church.)

Ironically, Macondo had been indignant about the story of seeing Satan, but easily accepted the story of the Wandering Jew. Plausible supersititons permeate thinking from the altar to the street.

The appealing, funny-tragic Father Antonio Isabel may stand as a symbol of the church itself—sincere, good-hearted and well-meaning, learned, but totally impractical. The priest is almost a slap-stick figure, as several farcical incidents illustrate. His fuzzy mind and ineffectual ministry could stand in García Márquez's opinion for the anachronistic church as a whole.

In "Rosas artificiales," Padre Angel refuses communion to women who come to church with make-up or with bare arms; thus, girls hear mass while wearing false sleeves that can be removed as soon as they leave the church. For Mina, going to church is not so much a spiritual exercise as a matter of appearances. Church attendance serves, too, as a pretext for leaving the house to meet her sweetheart. In this story, only Mina's blind grandmother seems to understand faith as a spiritual orientation, for she observes that it is a sin to take communion when one is angry.

A rapid-fire caricature of the Church is presented in "Los funerales de la Mamá Grande." This brief, exaggerated sketch also points out the strong ties between the Church and those who hold political power. Big Mama is the absolute sovereign of the feudal kingdom of Macondo. When she dies in grace with God, the Pope himself comes to her funeral services. It is suggested that Big Mama, corrupt and powerful, has arranged and dissolved canonships, benefices, and sinecures—and may have influenced even the election of the Pope and his cardinals.

The most important themes in *La mala hora* (1962) are political oppression and hypocrisy. The town of Macondo is the protagonist of this novel, and the two great concerns of the people are politics and the anonymous defamatory notes—the *pasquines*—that are pinned to the doors of houses during the night. These notes bring tragedy in their wake. The novel opens with César Montero killing the young musician Pastor after César finds a *pasquín* on his door.

One of the prominent characters is Padre Angel. He is a good man, sincere in his ministry. He visits the sick, the poor, and the bereaved; and he concerns himself with the spiritual health of his parishioners. It grieves him to think that Pastor died too suddenly to allow time for confession; but he is equally anxious to see César Montero, oppressed by the burden of guilt the murderer must have on his conscience. Padre Angel leads a life of celibacy and extreme poverty. He is not much concerned with worldly things; he feels it is of minor importance to build a fine temple but of great importance to guard the morals of the community. It is here that we see Padre Angel's weakness. Unwittingly, he is fostering an atmosphere of hypocrisy that will destroy the peace of the town. His insistence on social decorum and decency, if it does not repress human nature, at least causes people to hide the truth. Those with something to hide are vulnerable and fearful of exposure, and the libel notes have a demoralizing effect. Scandal drives some families out of the town and brings about murder and broken marriages.

On the other hand, the poor families in Macondo seem rather gleeful about the discomfiture of the recipients of the *pasquines*. Apparently the affairs of the poor are much more open; scandal can only touch those who falsify appearances. Judge Arcadio's pregnant mistress refuses Padre Angel's pleas to urge marriage. "Pero será un hijo ilegítimo," he insists. "No le hace," she answers. "Ahora Arcadio me trata bien. Si lo obligo a que se case, después se siente amarrado y la paga conmigo." She tries to explain her attitude to the uncomprehending priest. "Don Sabas me compró por 200 pesos, me sacó el jugo tres meses y después me echó a la calle sin un alfiler. Si Arcadio no me recoge, me hubiera muerto de hambre. . . . O hubiera tenido que meterme a puta." Father Angel protests that as they are living now, not only is she in an insecure position but the couple constitute a bad example for the town. Still the girl insists that it is better to do things openly. Hasn't he read the *pasquines?* The priest asserts that they are calumnies and that she must save herself from gossip. She replies, "No tengo que ponerme a salvo de nada porque hago todas mis cosas a la luz del día. La prueba es que nadie se gasta su tiempo poniéndome un pasquín, y en cambio todos los decentes de la plaza los tienen empapelados."[2]

Padre Angel believes the *pasquines* are lies; if they were true, he would have known about these things in the confessional. Doctor Giraldo suggests that it is a bad sign that he does not know. Somewhat shaken by this idea, the minister forces Trinidad, a young girl who helps him in the church, to give a detailed confession from which he learns of an incident she has long hidden under a general confession of sins, fearing his reaction to specifics. It is thus confirmed in his mind that he is not as well informed about the private lives of the faithful as he has believed. A veneer of respectability is hiding much immorality. As the doctor has charged, Padre Angel is trying to stop up human instinct with steel plating without changing the truth beneath the surface.

The widow Asís, head of the wealthiest family in Macondo and the person who supplies food for the priest, insists that Padre Angel preach a sermon on the *pasquines*. In an effort to avoid this painful task, the priest calls the mayor and begs him to take some action to stop the notes. The mayor is very reluctant. Any overt show of force, now that peace is just being reestablished, could be disastrous. Finally, he yields, reinstitutes the nightly curfew, and organizes armed civilian patrols—but still the *pasquines* continue. On Sunday, Father Angel stumbles through his sermon but ends it without ever referring in a direct way to the *pasquines*. Intervention of the civil authority in this matter has been a great mistake. One night the patrol catches Pepe Amador carrying clandestine leaflets—news censored by the government. The boy is taken to jail, questioned, and tortured in an effort to discover the source of the material. He is killed by one of the police officers—all of whom are former criminals. The mayor directs them to bury the body in the courtyard, tells the angry populace that Pepe has escaped, and tries to repress the violent reaction of the town. The men

[2]Gabriel García Márquez, *La mala hora* (México, D.F.: Ediciones Era, 1966), pp. 79-80.

of Macondo slip away in the night to join the revolutionaries in the interior; there is shooting on the streets; the jails are full. A total state of war has grown from the priest's actions.

The Church's concern with morality and outward appearances creates an atmosphere of hypocrisy that is extremely harmful. But the really great evil in Macondo is the thieving and oppressive government—an evil with which the Church is careful not to meddle.

García Márquez's masterpiece, *Cien años de soledad*, was published in 1967. Religion in this novel exists as a part of the lives of the characters but is almost conspicuous by its absence as a theme. The handful of families who founded Macondo lived in a primitive Garden of Eden cut off from the rest of humanity. There was no constituted authority to govern them, no church to rule on spiritual matters. The people became accustomed to arranging their affairs directly with God and lost the malice of mortal sin.

The *corregidor*, don Apolinar Moscote, who arrived later in Macondo, had to teach his politically innocent son-in-law, Aureliano Buendía, about political parties. He explained:

> Los liberales . . . eran masones; gente de mala índole, partidaria de ahorcar a los curas, de implantar el matrimonio civil y el divorcio, de reconocer iguales derechos a los hijos naturales que a los legítimos, y de despedazar al país en un sistema federal que despojara de poderes a la autoridad suprema. Los conservadores, en cambio, que habían recibido el poder directamente de Dios, propugnaban por la establilidad del orden público y la moral familiar; eran los defensores de la fe de Cristo, del principio de autoridad, y no estaban dispuestos a permitir que el país fuera descuartizado en entidades autónomas.[3]

Most of the characters consider this party-church alignment to be rigid. When Colonel Aureliano Buendía orders the restoration of the church tower that has been destroyed by the cannons of the Conservative army, Father Nicanor comments, "Esto es un disparate: los defensores de la fe de Cristo destruyen el templo y los masones lo mandan componer."[4] Colonel Gerineldo Márquez, on presenting Amaranta Buendía with a prayer book, provokes the response, "Qué raros son los hombres. Se pasan la vida peleando contra los curas y regalan libros de oraciones."[5]

The funniest and most unsympathetic character in *Cien años* is Fernanda del Carpio, the beauty queen who marries Aureliano II. Reared in an old traditional church town by impoverished but pretentious parents, she has been shielded from all contact with reality. When Fernanda marries, she takes to her new home a calendar on

---

[3]Gabriel García Márquez, *Cien años de soledad* (Buenos Aires: Editorial Sudamericana, 1970), p. 88.
[4]Ibid., p. 119.
[5]Ibid., p. 143.

which her spiritual advisor has marked with purple ink the days of sexual abstinence. Only forty-two days in the year are free for intercourse with her husband. Needless to say, things do not go well in the nuptial bed. This eventually leads to Fernanda's agreeing that Aureliano II may keep Petra Cotes as his mistress, so long as no public scandal is created.

La increíble y triste historia de la cándida Eréndira y de su abuela desalmada (1972) shows an evolution of García Márquez's style toward ever more subtle and symbolic modes of expression. There is more fantasy than ever; yet, perhaps this very fantasy makes his view of the world the easier to capture. In the story, "Un señor muy viejo con unas alas enormes," Pelayo finds an ugly angel stuck in the mud of his patio. The creature is bald, toothless, and looks like a drenched great-grandfather with wings like those of a big buzzard, dirty and half-deplumed. Pelayo and his wife, Elisenda, observe it so closely that very soon they begin to find it familiar and they speak to it. The being answers in an incomprehensible dialect. A neighbor declares it is an angel. Probably it has come for Pelayo's sick child. In her opinion, it should be killed, for angels today are fugitive survivors of a celestial conspiracy. But Pelayo does not have the heart to kill the angel; instead, he locks it in the chicken-yard. When the baby awakens without fever, Pelayo feels magnanimous and decides to put the angel on a raft with water and provisions for three days and abandon it to its fate on the high seas. They find all the neighbors playing, without the least devotion, with the angel and throwing it things to eat as if it were not a supernatural creature but a circus animal. Before 7 o'clock Father Gonzaga arrives. He can hardly believe a real angel would not understand Latin, the language of God, or know how to greet His ministers. Nothing in its wretched appearance is in accord with the eminent dignity of angels. In a brief sermon, Father Gonzaga warns the curious against the risks of gullibility. He reminds them that the devil has the bad habit of resorting to carnival tricks to confound the credulous. He argues that if wings are not the essential element in determining the difference between a hawk and an airplane, much less can they be used to recognize angels. He promises to write a letter to his bishop, however, so that the bishop may write another to his primate and the primate may write another to the Pope so that the final verdict will come from the highest tribunal. Within a few hours, so many people have gathered in the patio that a troop of soldiers with bayonets must be summoned to frighten away the tumultuous crowd that is on the point of wrecking the house. Then Elisenda has the good idea of fencing in the patio and collecting five centavos entrance fee to see the angel. The curious come from as far away as Martinique. Sick people come to seek healing. The angel's only supernatural virtue seems to be patience. Hens peck it in search of the stellar parasites that proliferate in its wings; the infirm pull out its feathers to touch their defects; and even the most pious throw rocks to make it get up so they can see its whole body. When they burn its side with a branding iron, the angel awakens startled and gives a couple of mighty wing-flaps that provoke a whirlwind of chicken droppings and lunar dust. The angel is a cataclysm in repose.

While awaiting final judgment on the nature of the captive, Father Gonzaga tries to verify if the creature has a navel, if its dialect has anything to do with Aramaic, if it can fit on the top of a pin, or if it is simply a Norwegian with wings. One day a wandering Caribbean fair brings to the town the sad spectacle of a woman who has been turned into a spider for disobeying her parents. Interest in this human tragedy makes the crowds forget the angel; Pelayo's patio is solitary once again.

Pelayo builds a mansion with the money he has earned; also, he resigns from his job as constable and Elisenda buys satin high-heeled slippers and many dresses of irridescent silk. When the baby learns to walk, they are careful not to let him near the chicken yard. Later, they forget their fears and the boy begins to play with the angel. Both catch chicken pox at the same time. The doctor who attends the child cannot resist the temptation of using the stethoscope on the angel; he finds so many leaks in its heart and so many noises in its kidneys that it seems impossible to him that it should be alive. By the time the child starts to school, the chicken yard has fallen into ruins and the angel drags itself here and there. If they drive it out of the bedroom with a broom, a moment later they find it in the kitchen. It seems to be in so many places at the same time that the exasperated Elisenda, beside herself, shouts that it is awful to live in that hell full of angels. By now the angel can hardly eat; it seems half-blind and all its feathers have fallen out. Pelayo lets it sleep in the shed when he realizes it has fever and spends the night deliriously raving in old Norwegian. They are alarmed—not even their wise neighbor can tell them what to do with a dead angel.

The angel survives the winter, however; and in the spring some large, hard feathers begin to appear, though it is careful not to let anyone notice them nor to hear the sailor songs it sings beneath the stars. One morning, while Elisenda is slicing onions for lunch, a sea breeze blows into the kitchen. She looks out the window and sees the angel clumsily trying to take flight. It manages to gain altitude, and Elisenda are confronted with a succession of questions concerning the creature: What is it? Is it dangerous? What is to be done with it? How imaginary dot on the horizon of the sea.

Reactions of the characters are interesting to note. Pelayo and Elisenda are confronted with a succession of questions concerning the creature: "What is it? Is it dangerous? What is to be done with it? How are they to cope with the crowds? But they are delighted with the money they are collecting. Then the angel is forgotten until they wonder if it may be dangerous to their child. Later, they have other questions: How can they keep it out of the way? How could they dispose of a dead angel? Finally, there is relief that it is gone. Only after its disappearance does the reader feel that the angel inspires some awe. Practical problems have dominated their relationship throughout the story. The miraculous in flesh and blood is no longer miraculous, and an angel is an angel only when it is unseen.

Each character has used the angel for his own purposes. Father Gonzaga sees it only in the light of his theological notions, or as something to warn the people against or to report to his superiors. Interestingly, he never urges more humane treatment for it. The doctor finds it entertaining to examine but, like the priest, never considers treatment for the ailing creature. Sick people are merciless to the being from whom they hope for a cure. The curious stare, then abandon what may have been a real angel and turn to the fairly obvious hoax of the spider-girl. We can be sure that García Márquez is not trying to propose the real existence of angels. His story raises the question of what would happen if a real angel walked the earth. Despite the miserable condition and ridiculous appearance of the very old man with enormous wings, a few aspects suggest something superhuman about it: the "stellar parasites," the "lunar dust," its nature of a "cataclysm in repose," and its wild songs beneath the stars. If it is an angel (though different from popular conception of course), it quickly becomes familiar and loses the respect of everyone. All and sundry callously use the angel for their own purposes. García Márquez shows it exploited by the Colombian fondness for sensation. Crowds will form in carnival spirit at the slightest novelty. The people, credulous and skeptical at the same time, are irresistibly drawn to spectacle. Unable to distinguish between the real and the fantastic, they are also surprisingly unconcerned about making this distinction. The Church must sanction and designate what is to be truly revered. But the priest's efforts to inform Church authorities remind us of Kafka's *The Castle*—the infinite distance that separates man from supreme authority is unbridgable. Father Gonzaga's letter is lost as if it had fallen into the void. Even if a final answer to the question were given, how could official recognition settle the matter? Can the Pope know more than Pelayo does about the old man? We are left, then, with a picture of Colombian society rather than a picture of a divine visitor to earth, and the Church is ridiculed as an antiquated and impractical institution.

The title story about Eréndira contains a section concerning a mission in the midst of the desert. The missionaries are respected by everyone from civil officials to outlaws who deal in contraband. The missionaries rescue Eréndira from her cruel grandmother for a time, and she is happy among these hard-working people. But the self-sacrificing monks who endure so many hardships to Christianize the Indians of the region are also painted as imposing alien standards upon the people and as stooping to unworthy means to do so. The missionaries comb the area, chasing pregnant concubines to get them married. It is hard to convince the women, who defend themselves from divine grace by the true argument that the men will feel they have a right to demand rougher work of a legitimate wife than of a mistress. Priests bribe the women with trinkets of jewelry; and once a woman's consent is obtained, the men are beaten out of their hammocks with rifle butts and carried away, tied up, to be married by force. Children are bribed with money to take religious instruction and to make their first communion. The moral codes and outward forms of religious observation for which the missionaries strive seem strangely inapplicable—they are dealing with concepts that the inhabitants cannot grasp. Bribery and force hardly become the servants of God; rather, such acts reveal a desperate conviction that conformity must be enforced.

The pagan joy that is aroused by the sea that smells of roses in "El mar del tiempo perdido" seems to inspire some spiritual renewal. One night the air changes and the odor becomes solid. Everyone in the village goes down to the beach to enjoy it. By dawn the fragrance is so pure that it hurts to breathe. Couples make love all afternoon. Attracted by the scent of roses, people flock to the town as tourists, entertainers, and exploiters. A priest arrives. He goes about prohibiting everything that has preceded him: games, music, sleeping on the beach. He believes that the odor is the odor of God. The Holy Scripture is explicit in regard to this odor.

After the scent of roses disappears, all the visitors abandon the area. The priest now feels it is urgent to begin construction of the temple. Something must sustain the illusion of those who remain. From so much pleading for alms, he grows more and more diaphanous; his bones begin to fill with noises, and one Sunday he rises two hands above the level of the floor. Then he leaves forever, saying that the odor will not return. The town has fallen into mortal sin. So far as the reader knows, the scent of roses does not return. It may have been only an illusion all the time. But the villager Tobías follows Mr. Herbert, the gringo con man, to the bottom of the sea and there finds another magic world whose delight he cannot communicate to those who have not experienced it. This is a poetic story that contrasts the beauty of life, a sort of pagan ecstasy, with rigid moral codes.

"El mar del tiempo perdido" may sum up García Márquez's attitude toward established religion. The Church is a decaying institution frantically trying to dam up human instincts by offering the sterile substitute of formal rites, ceremonies, and rules in exchange for the love of life and the sense of mystery and wonder that life can awaken in man.

29. The Limits of Exorcism and the Poetry of Humberto Díaz Casanueva

S. ALAN SCHWEITZER

Humberto Díaz Casanueva, a Chilean poet, has written extensively in a tradition that has not developed widely in Latin American poetry. This essay analyzes some of his themes that echo perspectives in the philosophy of Martin Heidegger. The intensely introspective nature of the poetry and the dimensions of its main problems give Casanueva's work a broad range of human appeal.

The work of Humberto Díaz Casanueva (b. 1906), a Chilean poet, embodies two concerns: the quest for human origins and the attempt to communicate the experience of that quest through recourse to an esoteric, often obscure, imagery that recreates the poet's concept of a primordial reality. The poet conceives and elaborates his vision of an elemental, phantasmal, largely nocturnal universe wherein the poet comes in intimate contact with the enigmatic, primeval forces referred to consistently as the *potencias oscuras*. Religious implications become obvious in the consistent theme that dominates his poetry: the pursuit of ultimate knowledge and the image of man as developed and projected in its relationship with the eternal source of being.

From Casanueva's earliest poems, salient features and patterns appear and reappear throughout his work with marked consistency: the longing to return to a pristine, nuclear reality that is transcendent to historical, rectilinear time; the contact of the poet with a condition before the Creation of the universe; the polarization of opposites; and the persistence of a mythical cosmogony imposed upon the natural cyclic regularity—a response both individual and collective to a primordial, originative impulse as if some force or unknown forces within the depths of the poet's psyche were calling out to him in the form of a directive. While exploring those inner, latent mysteries within himself, the poet will establish his own elaborate system of signs and correspondences that link mind and matter in a universal convergence.

Casanueva's poetry appeals, moreover, to that experience which relates to the collective unconscious, to the myth of the eternal return—an experience derivative in part from the psychology of Jung. Yet the unfolding imagery (which defines the archetypal quest in Casanueva's metaphysical debates) proceeds, in large measure, along the rigors of dialectic, of intellectual inquiry. Just as the poet conceives a poetry impregnated with a volatile yet powerful nature, so does he project upon this primordial universe a parallel order that engenders a continual flow of hypothetical abstractions, a dimension of reality that infiltrates the visionary, almost hallucinatory, universe derived from the dream experience.

A central theme in Díaz Casanueva is seen in the poetic "mission" to project the human ego upon an incommensurate and monstrous entity, a leviathan which appears as chaos and chance.[1] Upon identifying the human ego with the ultimate mysteries (i.e., death, the prenatal experience), the poet discovers that these mysteries respond by absorbing the poet's being in a series of events that continually undermine and erode the original quest, that is, the search for origins. These events are the very limitations imposed by reason.

Casanueva invokes from within himself the demonic forces, the *potencias*, to ascertain the origin and destiny of man. The poet discovers that the purpose, the *fons et origo*, of being consists in an appeal to a primordial need in the form of a call, a temptation, an *oscuro mandato*[2] or dark imperative. In assuming this need, this *despierta indigencia*,[3] he discovers that his being is his own cause; he is, moreover, the source of all being. The poet himself thus needs to exorcize the will to determine why he is a finite being, a being condemned to die.[4] He longs to transcend his mortality, to comprehend the riddle of being and time; he can only realize this quest through exorcism in obedience to the *potencias*. The processes of logical thought thus find their consummation in the recourse to will, in the appeal to exorcism; yet the poet forces, or rather is forced to impose upon himself, the need to will his limitations, that is, his death—an act that becomes at once penitential or sacrificial, and, hence, ritualistic. This confrontation with death, a process that parallels the poet's ingress in-

---

[1] Some of the paradigms and images in Díaz Casanueva's work are also present in the speculative, archetypal themes that characterize the work of such diverse poets as Octavio Paz, José Gorostiza, and Vicente Huidobro, to mention a few. However, Casanueva's extended experience in Germany and his exposure to the works of Trakl, Heym, and Rilke oriented the Chilean toward German expressionism, a peculiarity evident in his earliest poetry and a trait which was to distinguish his poetry from that of his Spanish American contemporaries.

[2] Díaz Casanueva, *Sol de lenguas* (Santiago de Chile: Nascimento, 1966), p. 27.

[3] Díaz Casanueva, *Vigilia por dentro* (Santiago de Chile: Nascimento, 1931), p. 11.

[4] The existentialist themes are derived mainly from Heidigger. Díaz Casanueva studied philosophy with the German master and came to incorporate many heideggerian concepts into his poetry.

to primordial reality, is an event that is continual, endless. *Logos* and *mythos* became synonymous, coaxial in a poetic structure in which speculation, dialectic, and abstract thought evolve in juxtaposition with those levels of experience derivative of the revelatory orders of the spontaneous, the instinctual, and the intuitive.

In *Vigilia por dentro*, a typical pattern emerges. It is a rhythmic cycle whose pattern becomes more clearly defined later on as the quality and character of ritual, of incantation. The poet responds to a mandate or call that originates from the depths of his consciousness in the form of a temptation to probe and to confront the basic enigmas and mysteries within his psyche. The *Vigilia* becomes a nocturnal odyssey. It is a journey into an arcane, phantasmal world wherein primal forces lay siege to that part of the poet's being which is determined to woo and unravel the secrets of the universe.

> Ser mío consumes por tu exceso cuando hacia ti voy con esta mi despierta indigencia.
> Ah! Si reposaras como esa luz ya rendida que en las manos de un fundidor se revela.
> ....
> Desesperado apago en mi la aureola de los santos, quiero descubrir mis propias leyes.
> ....
> Que obscuridad caliente jadeo en mi eclipse íntimo, pierdo el presagio ay hacia mi corazón sería capaz de negar su pequeña crisálida y esas pavorosas alas que le asoman emergiendo de la nada. (*Vigilia*, p. 11)

In order to determine and to reveal the hidden, magical world of a corresponding, intuitive order of experience (a reality the poet frequently confesses to be incommunicable: "blanda cera que inútilmente junto al fuego busca forma," *Vigilia*, p. 10), Casanueva develops the poem on an intermediate level of perception which includes and reciprocates a dual order of reality: that of *vigilia* (wakefulness) and of *sueño* (dream). It is a duality that relates at once to corresponding analogues of being and nothingness.

> Tal vez porque estos repetidos sueños tiran de la nada esa parte mía que todavía no tengo,
> La unidad de mi ser no consigo aun a costa de su propio destino
> Mi cabeza tuvo una salida que daba al gozoso barro, pero crueles sueños me decapitan.
> ....
> Este es el testimonio doliente del que no puede labrar sus formas puras.
> Porque se lo impone su ser hecho de peligros y cruel sobresalto. (*Vigilia*, p. 10)

The *Vigilia* is a meditation or, as the title of the poem implies, an inner wake. It is a poem whose immediate design suggests a precarious synthesis between the diurnal reality of wakefulness and the nocturnal world of dream, a synthesis in the realm of the fantastic, the marvelous, with its "dinastías de secretos" (*Vigilia*, p. 47). Such a synthesis becomes increasingly tenuous and eventually inoperative, because the poet feels compelled to return to the rational world, a concession which forfeits the rewards gained from the exploration of the inner fissures of the self.

> Siento el corazón pesado, ciencia de santos he de aprender.
> Casi recuerdo cuando era apenas un pequeño aire entre mi padre y mi madre.
> Mas ya no puedo, que di mis venas a una sombra la que alarge sus ramas.
> Y los pies en el vino han perdido el rastro que seguían. (*Vigilia*, p. 15)

Despite the lure to explore the inner self, Casanueva yet acknowledges that his descent into the shadow world induces an intense fear, an unmitigating sense of dread, as he suddenly discovers the looming spectre of his death.

> Torné a lo oscuro, a larva reprimada otra vez en mi frente y un terror hizo que gozara de mi corazón en claros cantos.
> Estoy seguro que he tentado las cenizas de mi propia muerte, aquéllas que dentro del sueño hacen mi más profundo desvelo. (*Vigilia*, p. 51)

For Casanueva, the probe into the mysteries of the self ultimately determines the poet's knowledge and apprehension of human finality. The poetic act becomes limited and imposed upon by the poet's realization that he can never get to the roots of being, that he is denied access to the ultimate principles which constitute and control human consciousness.

> Un infante hijo aún de su abismo, busca la greda viviente,
> busca la frente febril para sus sueños en horda obscura,
> las prisiones para su corazón todavía anegado de dioses
> pues solo posee ese secreto que es anterior al alma.
> Se tienta una vena la madre, ahí nadan dos ojos sueltos
> que tal vez no atinan a fijar sus estambres invisibles,
> y esos pies que le golpean pidiéndole un camino terrestre
> los encuentra, cuando duerme, hallando su propio rumbo.
>
> Cuando la madre dormita, el niño le sopla su nombre
> y le ruega calme su miedo de aproximarse al mundo,
> porque ya vive, el destino terminó los nudos a su alma
> y su memoria está olvidando su verdadero origen. (*Vigilia*, p. 27)

Whereas the *Vigilia por dentro* is contemplative and restrained as the poet explores his inner self in silent vigilance, *El blasfemo coronado*[5] emerges in explosive fury. This work, perhaps Casanueva's

---

[5]Díaz Casanueva, *El blasfemo coronado* (Santiago de Chile: Ediciones Intemperie, 1940).

finest achievement, is an unequivocal, exhaustive statement of a poetic order patterned on the grand design of antithesis, regeneration, and transcendence. In the effort to overcome limitations imposed in the earlier poem, the *Blasfemo* assumes the originative, if not demiurgic, function of probing and fathoming the germinal stages of being. The poet appeals to the unconscious, often drawing upon the personal past as well as upon the ancestral memory equated with archetypal symbols and myths. In direct repudiation of the paradisiacal dream and divine grace, the poet embarks upon his Faustian mission as he invokes the *Daimon*, that legendary, archetypal image, the source of knowledge and wisdom that facilitates the poet-blasphemer's access to and passage within the ultimate mysteries.

> Hay un lugar que no menciono, todos estamos allí de cierto modo.
> Cátedras austeras y apuradas tablas que caen encadenadas y anatemas al oído del que se precipita al mediodía, sostienen el ser. (*Blasfemo*, p. 10)

The shadow image at the beginning of the poem is symbolic of the mysterious and the occult, a presence which bears a strong resemblance to the biblical story of the creation, and the fall from divine grace. The poet accepts the solitary route of exile in his descent into the aboriginal abodes of chaos and chance. In his voluntary descent into hell, the poet recreates the sacrificial hero of legend. Indeed, much of the poem's recurring imagery equates the unfolding *mythos* with a primeval form of Satan, the prototype of the rebellious angel.

El blasfemo coronado, a poem with several levels of meaning, develops central and ancillary themes related to the riddle of birth, the nature of time, the enigma of death, the nature of God, and other perplexing mysteries that haunt and tempt the poet. In the flow of the poem, two distinct levels predominate: a level consisting of speculative, analytical hypotheses, and a mythical, archetypal level. On the first level, the poet prevails upon reason to resolve the overwhelming antimonies that plague the poem. The result is an evolving ontology. Díaz Casanueva responds to a mandate in order to undertake the mission of self-definition, of self-realization. In that response, the poet attempts to determine and to define the mysterious need or impulse to carry out the inner probe. The mythical level of interpretation assumes a religious character. Casanueva conceives a vast, anthropomorphic theogony as an aprioristic structure, with the poet-*persona* at its vital center, animating and completing the emerging symbols in all their fullness. Thus, *El blasfemo coronado* is the collective dramatization of man's journey through hell. The reader participates in the infernal odyssey into the primordial regions of the cosmos, and he shares in the poet's torment and incessant challenge to God for recognition.

The quest for ultimate knowledge ends in the poet's guilt and frustration as he becomes ever more aware of his role as creator and sustainer of the universal tragedy of life and art. The poet suffers perpetual banishment from Paradise; in his exile he reenacts the myth of the eternal return in a constant search for God. Casanueva learns that he is responsible for the existence of God and that he is "condemned" to question his instinctive nature to discover the God he had created. The poet's experience with the unknown is mysteriously identified with his longing to be absolved of a primordial guilt, a guilt for which God is ultimately liable. What the poet (Satanás) demands is knowledge of self-creating self. His mission is to grasp the significance of his being that has been willed, for it does not exist by chance.

> Arrojad de los cuerpos la esperanza suprema, las estrellas/debajo de las cosas quiero.
> Obscurece en nuestros sentidos y la altura los derriba uno/a uno, los dioses
> nos destruyen como apurados.
> ¡Ah hombre, ay origen sin saberlo! (Blasfemo, pp. 34-35)

As the poem progresses, Casanueva substantiates the impossibility of winning Paradise. Because he is his own cause, he perpetuates his voluntary will into increasing stages of his guilt. The poet suggests that the infernal quest is mysteriously contingent upon the divine will. Indeed, Casanueva emphasizes that the poet (Satanás), Man, and God are one and the same: a force, an élan or cosmic intelligence that is sustained and conditioned upon exorcism. God and Man are synonymous. Likewise, the descent into the human psyche parallels a mission to extend the poetic quest into the limits of the physical universe. It is an act that enables the poet to comprehend and embrace all matter, potential and actual. Thus the poet, the created poem, and man become a tri-partite extension analogous to the structural whole of consciousness that unfolds existentially from its obscure origin in the anguish of the poet's understanding or awareness. This structural whole is perceived within the perspective of *hoc tempus*, of the specious present. The twenty-five cantos of the *Blasfemo coronado* prefigure the continuous descent of the poet within a sequence of multiple concentric circles, each circle emerging from the previous one and correlating symbolically to the poet's increasing exile from divine grace into successive and more intensive stages of blasphemy.

In *La Estatua de sal*,[6] the image of human intelligence parallels the poet's concept of a spatiotemporal continuum, an ontogenesis extended inwardly within the inner psyche and outwardly toward the limits of the physical universe. Within the dimensions of this continuum (at once process and event) to which the poet in frequent

[6]Díaz Casanueva, *La estatua de sal* (Santiago de Chile: Nascimento, 1954).

passages refers as "la casa del ser," animate and inanimate beings are conceived and actualized to inhabit the universe.

> He aquí mi fin mas he aquí también mi comienzo, he de velar todos los momentos de mi vida y luego engendrarlos
> Sólo hay un tiempo que prevalece
> Una marea sollozante arrolladora
> ....
> ... que me hace ser lo que soy (*Estatua*, p. 16)
> ....
> He de aullar asomado a mi casa hasta merecer los arrullos que llenan el silencio de chispas ... (*Estatua*, p. 49)

Against this continuum Casanueva imagines a compensating universe, an offsetting order of non-being, a category of nothingness which precariously exists contiguous to but in opposition to the *Casa*.

> ¿Lo invisible es apenas un lado de lo visible? ¿El muerto es el lado entornado de mí mismo?
> ¿Y no hay un muro que separe sino apenas una lampara tornadiza que nos alumbra a turnos? (*Estatua*, p. 55)

If the poet's being determines and perpetuates his death, then the reverse condition is realized in that the poet's non-being, that is, his death, becomes responsible for his *de facto* existence in time.

> El que guía la danza de la muerte no es la muerte sino yo mismo,
> yo soy el hijo y el padre de mí madre
> y mirándolo fijamente hago la vida,
> ....
> Soy el flanco de un mundo sin memoria
> La flor del éxtasis remoto, (*Estatua*, p. 56)

The poet is thus destined, or rather condemned, partly by his own volition (exorcism) and partly by an enigmatic force or forces to choose the paradox of his external life or his external death.

> Brazos magullados salen de la fría tierra, ciñen mi casa y me tornan ceniciento (*Estatua*, p. 31)
> ....
> Otra voluntad más poderosa me concita en favor suyo,
> otro tiempo consume mi tiempo,
> y me siento como dentro de un alud. (*Estatua*, p. 32)
> ¿Paz tendré? ¿Alianza? ¿Designio? ¿Que tengo yo contra mí para condescender con el miedo que me muestra lo que soy?
> No sé si he nacido eternamente y si he de morir eternamente (*Estatua*, p. 74)

Although *La Estatua de sal* develops the poet's *weltanschauung* partly along the lines of dream experience, whose revelatory powers link the poet's identity to a primordial reality, that same experience is never totally disassociated from the diurnal, secular world of practical activity. In short, the quest for origin is circumscribed by the poet's limitations: his finality and the corresponding *awareness* of his limitations. To fathom and to realize a truly primordial experience beyond the strictures of times is not possible, because the poetic act (and poetry itself, the very analogue and structure of human intelligence) can only be realized in time. Thus, Casanueva is emphasizing a theme suggested in his earlier work: his innate sense and understanding that he cannot exceed the restricting dimensions of his mortality. As the contingency of birth determines the temporal-spatial continuum within which the poet's being is to evolve, there ensues the corresponding vision of the poet's conception of those very confines which constitute and define the quest:

> y el fin decide tanto como el origen y al consumirnos renovamos lo que nos vuelve a consumir.
> Hasta que el desierto seca el arroyo que ha permitido penetrarlo!
> El hombre es órbita deshecha, llanto en que el otro
> se agiganta,
> Tierra que relampaguea sobre la tierra
> Casa en que pernocta el tiempo perseguido. (*Estatua*, p. 58)

The poet's origin is thus always behind him as his death precedes him.

> Aquí esta el mundo aparente y dentro el mundo
>   sellado y ambos me son recíprocos y en ambos
>   escarbo buscando la fuente que me derrama (*Estatua*, p. 26)

The poet contains the world as the world encloses the poet, a condition which precludes any possibility of ascertaining the ultimate enigma of birth. Casanueva thus acknowledges he may never return to that conjectural moment or event that is continually injecting him into being and time.

> Cada día es una venda que vamos quitando a la llaga
>   del corazón dormido
> El agujero está casi descubierto y de súbito nos
>   desplomamos
> Desde este mundo ajeno perdido sin poseerlo (*Estatua*, p. 26)

Coeval to the orders of being and nothingness, Casanueva suggests yet a third category of experience, an undefined, mysterious presence which remains impassive, silent, oblivious to the poet's mission.

> Alguien se acerca; pero no llega jamás, sus pasos
>   cubiertos de oro traen la tierra:
> "Eh, Tú, ¿quién eres Tú donde termina mi canto?"

> El que está solo se consume como la candela situada
> entre respiraciones silbantes
> e imagina más que sabe
> y piensa más que obra. (*Estatua*, p. 27)

In several passages of the poem, Casanueva further characterizes this presence as ominous and menacing, omnipotent and vigilant, an order both transcendent to and pervasive within the dimensions of his being. Thus God is both prolific and formless because he is the universal source and sum of all possibility and actuality, *fons et origo* of the phenomenal and noumenal universe. Paradoxically conspicuous and yet absent, God figures mysteriously as the foundation of the poet's existence. At the moment of the poet's death, his soul, along with myriad other souls, now de-individualized, now formless, descend anomalously in their silent journey toward the realm of God where all are fused in original unity.

> (*Nadie de ellos sabe cual será el primero en entrar desmemoriado a la Casa común*).
> Los muertos van atravesado como si no les bastase precedernos.
> ....
> Los vivos aguardan su plenitud
> y cada uno grande y solitario como un faro cegado
> sobre el mar inmenso. (*Estatua*, p. 22)

The recourse to pure logic, to dialectic becomes useless, because it is powerless to determine and to comprehend the implication and elusiveness of the divine manifestation.

> Y lo que se manifiesta, ¿Cómo comunicarlo? Lo que
> entra en mí ¿Cómo hacerlo sagrada compañía?
> ....
> ¿Cómo explicarlo con mis obras? (*Estatua*, p. 27)

In later passages of the poem, Casanueva links his quest with the divine image in terms of increasing mythical, archetypal resolutions.

> Hay un dios nefasto que amasa el barro blanco
> Sus dedos dejan huecos por donde la noche pasa
>   el postrer suspiro pasa,
> Me grita al oído "*Es bella tu agonía mientras permaneces solo.*
> *Busca tu origen o tu fin mas no lo que se encuentre*
> *entre tu origen y tu fin,*
> *eres mi reminiscencia,*
> *Yo soy tu mismo inacabable.*"
> ....
> El gemido del hombre es su memoria, la serpiente que
>   sale de los pazos eternos es su tiempo.
> ¡Arriesgar el origen! ¡Arriesgar el fin! El hombre
>   es la travesía (*Estatua*, p. 85)

The serpent image plays a dual symbolic role. On the one hand, it symbolizes the temptation to taste the fruit of knowledge; therefore, the serpent relates to Satan, the *Daimon*, the archetype of evil. Thus, the serpent is symbolic of death. Man is tempted to sin and to perpetuate the Fall and his awareness of the Fall. In the context of Casanueva's works studied here, the serpent represents the metaphysical temptation (*mandato*) to realize the poet's mysterious affinity to God in the perpetuation of God's existence to and from Himself. The serpent image is also identified with sexual pleasure because it has been traditionally suggestive of phallic connotations. Man is thus tempted sexually to reproduce himself. As the poet assumes the role of tempter-tempted, God tempts Himself, through the poet, to perpetuate Himself at the expense of the poet's anguish.

> Pero hay un dios que brinca en torno nuestro. ¿No
> escucháis la dulce copla?
> ¡Oh caminantes en los distruidos átrios! ¿No escucháis
> el caramillo hecho de raíz crujiente al
> comenzar el día,
> sus pies como truenos,
> sus labios encima de mi casa,
> su frente que llena el rocío,
> el arco de bronce de la tierra,
> el hombre como flecha de su arco
> La luz que emprende el vuelo?
> ¡Es el centauro!

The poet's expulsion from Eden occasions the recognition, the knowledge, and the awareness that he is mysteriously condemned for an undetermined, enigmatic event whose effort induces in the poet's consciousness a sense of uncompromising dread, namely, to assume the realization that the Godhead conceived the poet (Man) in order to pursue the endless quest for origin; and, in the undertaking of that quest, the poet will resort to the act of exorcism and to the perpetuation of the divine image.

PART IV

BRAZIL

The Roman Catholic Church's relationships with the governments of Portugal and Brazil have been somewhat different from its relationships with Spain and Spanish-American governments. This has been true especially since the 1750s, when the Marquis of Pombal, prime minister under José I, initiated important reforms. As examples of some of the influences that have been brought to bear on the Catholic Church and Brazilian society during the past two centuries, this section features studies of regalism, Positivism, Protestantism, and traditionalism.

30. The Roots of Brazilian Regalism

TARCISIO BEAL

Professor Beal describes with thorough detail the rise of regalism in mid-eighteenth-century Portugal. This domination of the Catholic Church by the Portuguese state continued into the nineteenth century, setting the foundation for the cultural life and church-state relations in republican Brazil. Although the full extent of this domination initiated in the eighteenth century did not persist, it changed the structure within which church-state relations were established in Brazil, thereby affecting the way in which the Catholic Church has functioned as well as the way Brazilian governmental policies have been formulated.

Portugal was isolated from the intellectual mainstream of trans-Pyrenean Europe from the Council of Trent in mid-sixteenth century to 1750. In that year John V was succeeded by José I; and the office of chief minister was given to Sebastião José de Carvalho e Melo, who became Count of Oeiras in 1759 and Marquis of Pombal in 1770. Carvalho (best known to most readers as Pombal) controlled Portugal from 1750 to 1777, during which time he initiated a period of accelerated change that profoundly affected Portuguese society as a whole, including the Catholic Church. As a result of his efforts, regalism became the predominating perspective in Portugal and, by extension, in Brazil. Regalism, in this context, refers to the dominating control of the Church by the state, concomitant with the loss of power by the Holy See.

In eighteenth-century Portugal, two institutions stood in the way of progress, as progress was understood by the regalists. One was the University of Coimbra; the other was the Society of Jesus, which monopolized education in Portugal onward from 1555 and served as a bulwark of the papal prerogative. Although the Society was expelled from Portugal's colonies in 1759, it continued to be the most powerful corporation within Portugal. With the support of many influential friends, it fiercely resisted Pombal's policies; however, there was much in the history of the Jesuits in Portugal that could be used against them. In the eyes of Pombal and his aides, most of whom were identified with the Enlightenment, the mere presence of the Society in Portugal had prevented progress in every sector of national life.

Despite outstanding leadership in the discovery of the New World, Portugal soon fell behind most European countries. Attachment to scholasticism and distrust of modern writers and thinkers restricted access to contemporary philosophical and scientific discoveries to a few privileged individuals. Because the writings of Descartes were placed on the Roman Index of Prohibited Books in 1663, and because Francis Bacon's *De dignitate et augmento scientiarum* was similarly designated in 1668, publication of these works in Portugal was hindered by the Inquisition.

Customarily, the Jesuits have been held responsible for the literary and scientific backwardness of eighteenth-century Portugal. From mid-sixteenth century, their *colégios* dominated secondary education almost completely, and their influence in the Universities of Coimbra and Evora was without effective opposition. Because Coimbra had been the main intellectual center of Portugal since the beginning of the fourteenth century, its leadership had greatly influenced the destinies of Portugal and Brazil. The Society of Jesus was entrusted with the direction of the *Colégio das Artes* on September 10, 1555; and control of the *Colégio* meant, for all practical purposes, control of the whole university.[1]

Founded during a period of bitter political and religious wars, the Society of Jesus stood as the main defender of Catholic orthodoxy. According to one Jesuit writer, "It adopted an attitude fundamentally apologetical of the Church, trying to preserve the grandiose and secular edifice of Scholasticism, which had been erected in defense of the Gospels."[2] Hernani Cidade argues that the Jesuits, as intellectual leaders of Portugal, "were endeavoring to make it more Catholic than Latin, shielding it from the speculative inquiries that were agitating Europe, defending it against involvement in any activity that might lead to apostasy."[3]

The Society of Jesus was so successful within the Portuguese empire that by the middle of the eighteenth century it had supplanted the nobility in social and political prestige and in influence on the King. One Jesuit historian declares that the Jesuits at the court "were not only the directors of the conscience of all princes and princesses

---

[1] Junta de Providência Literária, *Compêndio histórico do estado da Universidade de Coimbra* (Lisbon, 1771), pt. 1, prel. 1, p. 8. The *Compêndio* has been attacked as a compilation of slanders against the Jesuits; but whenever it quotes from royal decrees included in the legislation of Portugal and points to well-known facts about Coimbra, this source becomes unassailable.

[2] Francisco Rodrigues, *A Formação intellectual do Jesuíta* (Oporto: Livraria Magalhães e Moniz, Ed., 1917), p. 532.

[3] Hernani Cidade, *Lições de Cultura e Literatura Portuguêsas*, 2 vols. (Coimbra: Coimbra Editora, 1948), 1:278.

of the royal family, but they were also the consultants of the King and his Ministers regarding the most important matters. No appointment to administrative positions in Church or State was made without their previous advice; the high clergy as well as the nobility and the people competed with each other for their protection and favor."[4] This preeminence and power, along with their conservatism, set the Jesuits as the inevitable target of the eighteenth-century reformers, although outside of Portugal they were more open to the modern sciences.

During the reign of John V, there were some important developments in higher education. The King founded the Royal Academy of Portuguese History in 1720 and established the Academy of Surgery. He built and generously endowed the library of the University of Coimbra, patronized the study of astronomy, and, above all, protected and encouraged the work of the Oratorians.[5]

The Congregation of St. Philip Neri, or the Oratorians, was introduced into Portugal after the Restoration of 1640. It became well known through the work of several famous scholars, men of the Enlightenment who were open to new ideas and who were enthusiastic advocates of the scientific method. Francisco José Freire (Cândido Lusitano); Teodoro de Almeida, one of the most fascinating representatives of the Enlightenment in Portugal; António Pereira de Figueiredo; and Luís António Vernei were among the best known members of the order. John V apparently protected the Oratorians in order to counterbalance the influence of the Jesuits and to import into the country the didactic methods, if not the theology, of the French Jansenists. The Oratorians were given the Monastery of Necessidades in Lisbon and a library of thirty thousand volumes, to which the Congregation added a large number of works by contemporary authors, including Benito Feijóo's famous *Teatro Crítico Universal*. They made known in Portugal the ideas of Bacon, Descartes, Gassendi, Locke, and Antonio Genovesi. In 1747, John V granted them perpetual rights over the new Port-royalist pedagogical method, which was to supplant the old method of the Jesuit grammarian Manuel Alvares.[6]

Beginning about 1740, the Jesuits faced competition strong enough to threaten their dominance of Portuguese education. Their power was resented by other regulars with respected achievements in education, such as the Franciscans and Dominicans, and especially by

---

[4]Jean Francois Georgel, *Mémoires pour servir à l'histoire des évènements de la fin du dix-huitième siècle depuis 1760 jusqu'en 1806-1810*, 6 vols. (Paris, 1817), 1: (16) - (17). See also Francisco Rodrigues, *História da Companhia de Jesus na Assistência de Portugal*, 7 vols. (Oporto: Apostolado da Imprensa, 1931-1950), vol. 1, t. 4, pp. 447-53.

[5]José Silvestre Ribeiro, *História dos Estabelecimentos scientíficos, literários e artísticos de Portugal*, 18 vols. (Lisbon, 1871-93), 1: 169, 174, 179ff.

[6]Teófilo Braga, *História da Universidade de Coimbra*, 3 vols. (Coimbra: Imprensa da Universidade, 1915), 3:19.

the emerging Oratorians. Well entrenched in key positions, however, the Jesuits chose to hold their ground and fight rather than to reform or modernize. In 1746, Father José Veloso, Dean of the College of the Society of Jesus and of the *Colégio das Artes* of the University of Coimbra, issued a strongly worded decree against modern philosophy. He commanded:

> In examinations or courses, public or private lectures, no new opinions of limited acceptance and usefulness shall be taught or upheld, such as the opinions of René Descartes, Gassendi, Newton, and others; the same applies specifically to any science that might uphold the ideas of Epicurus or deny the reality of the character of the eucharist or oppose the Aristotelian system, which is to be followed in these schools, as it is repeatedly recommended in the Statutes of the *Colégio das Artes*.[7]

The ink of Veloso's decree had hardly dried when the *Verdadeiro Método de Estudar*, a revolutionary work written by the Oratorian Luís António Vernei, exploded like a bombshell in the intellectual circles of Portugal. It directly attacked the pedagogical methods of the Jesuits at the University of Coimbra.[8] Fearing the Inquisition, Vernei chose to remain anonymous; thus, an Italian Capuchin friar was presented as the author of the letters which make up Vernei's work.

Vernei argued that scholastic philosophy in the eighteenth century was founded upon the prejudices of Aristotelianism, namely, the theory of substantial and accidental forms, and consequently was not only superfluous but also harmful to explanations of the dogmas of Christianity.[9] He recommended adoption of modern authors such as Grotius, Fleury, van Espen, and Heinecke—all of them either condemned or considered dangerous by the Roman Index. Vernei emphasized need for experimentation and for adoption of new scientific methods, for critical thinking and abandonment of argument by authority, and for study of both classical and modern languages as well as history, geography, natural law, and the law of the nations—all of which were neglected at the University of Coimbra.

A heated and lengthy controversy followed publication of *Verdadeiro Método de Estudar*. By 1757, more than forty-two works defending or, more often, attacking Vernei had been published. The majority of the author's opponents were Jesuits. All this added fuel to the rivalry between Oratorians and Jesuits. Vernei's attacks deeply hurt the feelings of the Jesuits, whose educational system had been

---

[7]Archives of the University of Coimbra, Provisions, 5:145-46. This decree was published in the *Annuario da Universidade de Coimbra* (1880-81), p. 240.

[8]*Verdadeiro Método de Estudar, para ser útil à Republica, e à Igreja: Proporcionado ao estilo, e necessidade de Portugal. Exposto em varias cartas, escritas pelo R.P. . . . Brabadinho da Congregacam de Italia, ao R.P. . . . Doutor da Universidade de Coimbra* (Naples, 1746), edition of Livraria Sá da Costa Editora, 6 vols. (Lisbon, 1952).

[9]Ibid., 6:233.

the pride and glory of Portugal. They reacted by accusing Vernei of sponsoring dangerous ideas, especially the heresy of Jansenism.[10]

What had started as a purely academic dispute over grammatical methods was soon turned into an all-out battle over the Jesuit system of education. Henceforth, the Society of Jesus was made responsible for Portugal's literary and scientific backwardness. In his campaign against the Jesuits, the Marquis of Pombal took full advantage of the controversy initiated by publication of Vernei's *Verdadeiro Método de Estudar*.

Pombal earned international fame primarily as a result of his success in destroying the Society of Jesus, which was abolished by papal decree in 1773. In Luso-Brazilian history, however, he is best known as the statesman who tried to rebuild the Portuguese empire and who, through a number of decrees and the reform of the University of Coimbra, determined church-state relations in Portugal and Brazil for the rest of the eighteenth and all of the nineteenth centuries. Regalism, as implemented in imperial Brazil, was first and last of the Pombaline brand. In the following pages of this study an attempt is made to show why.

While serving as Portuguese ambassador at the Court of St. James and as envoy extraordinary in Vienna, Carvalho not only was exposed to new ideas of the time but he also learned about the political advantages of taking control of the national church. In Vienna he was in contact with the Jansenists, well-known adversaries of papal supremacy.[11] When he became chief minister of José I in 1750, Carvalho adopted policies aimed at deuniversalizing the Church to make it fit into the mold of the national state. He recognized the Pope's spiritual jurisdiction, but sought the support and justification of Portuguese jurists for restricting Rome's field of action. Pombal did not go as far as Buchanan or Hobbes, Bodin or Grotius, who advocated supremacy of the state in religious matters; but he accepted and practiced the regalistic ideas of his countrymen António de Gouveia, Gabriel Pereira de Castro, and Pascoal de Melo Freire, who extended jurisdiction of the Portuguese government over all that did not concern the Church's purely spiritual ministry.[12]

As long as the Jesuits were in Portugal, they opposed Pombal's abridgment of the Church's prerogatives and its subordination to the

[10] Vernei's attitude toward the papacy and toward the authority and jurisdiction of the Roman Church, which he tried to distinguish from the Universal Church, reveals some leaning toward Jansenism and Gallicanism.

[11] Miguel Sotto Mayor, *O Marquês de Pombal* (Oporto: Livraria Editora, 1905), p. 18. See also Antônio Ferrão, *O Marquês de Pombal e a Expulsão dos Jesuítas* (Coimbra: Imprensa da Universidade, 1932), p. 11.

[12] On Antônio de Gouveia, see Diogo Barbosa Machado, *Bibliotheca Lusitana*, 4 vols. (Lisbon, 1741-59), 1:291-96; on Gabriel Pereira de Castro and Pascoal de Melo Freire, see Inocêncio Francisco da Silva, *Diccionario bibliographico portuguez*, 21 vols. (Lisbon, 1858-1914), 4:107-110; 6:350-51.

state. Overconfident of their power and influence, however, the Jesuits failed to heed signs of trouble and even challenged the Marquis's economic policies and his plans to secularize the Indian reductions in northern Brazil.[13] Pombal first secured the Portuguese hierarchy's support in the form of published, pastoral letters condemning the Jesuits. Then he closed all of the Jesuits' schools; prohibited use of their textbooks, replacing them with books produced by the Oratorians; and, finally, on September 3, 1759, published the royal decree expelling all members of the Society of Jesus from the kingdoms and dominions of Portugal.[14]

With the Jesuits gone, Carvalho embarked upon a program designed to subdue the Catholic Church. A decree of May 6, 1765, which was confirmed by orders of April 20 and August 23, 1770, reestablished the requirement of the royal placet on all papal documents;[15] and a new catechism prepared by Bishop Colbert, a Jansenist, was imposed on the schools of the kingdom. Oratorian António Pereira de Figueiredo lent his talent to the dissemination of Pombal's regalistic and reforming policies. In 1766 he published his *Tentativa theológica*, which had been preceded by his *Demostração theológica* in 1761. These two works aimed at proving the legitimacy of "an ancient custom of the Portuguese Church" that granted a bishop nominated by the Crown the right to take over the administration of his diocese before receiving papal confirmation. This regalistic thesis advocated for the bishops rights that had usually been reserved to the Pope.[16]

Other religious communities hoped that elimination of the Society of Jesus would satisfy Pombal, but they were mistaken. In January 1764, a royal letter was sent to all religious Superiors ordering them to cease accepting new candidates and to furnish the Crown with a list of their members and houses along with an estimate of the value of their property.[17] In a dispatch denying the General of the Carmelties the right of appeal to Rome, because the action was viewed as incom-

---

[13]João Lúcio de Azevedo, *Os Jesuítas no Grão-Pará, suas Missões e a Colonização* (Lisbon: Nova Seara, 1901), pp. 338-42, and see also pp. 336-37; Marcos Carneiro de Mendonça, *A Amazônia na Era Pombalina, Correspondência inédita*, 3 vols. (Rio de Janeiro: Instituto Histórico e Geográfico Brasileiro, 1961-63), 1:22, 69-70, 415-18; 2:784-88.

[14]*Collecção dos Negócios de Roma no Reindado de El-Rey Dom José I, Ministro Marquez de Pombal e Pontificados de Benedito XIV e Clemente XIII, 1765-60*, 2 vols. (Lisbon, 1874), 1:1146-16; António Delgado da Silva, *Collecção da Legislação Portugueza, Legislação de 1750-62*, 2 vols. (Lisbon, 1830), 1:743:44.

[15]Fortunato de Almeida, *História da Igreja em Portugal*, 4 vols. (Coimbra: Imprensa Acadêmica, 1917), 4:227ff.

[16]*Collecção dos Negócios de Roma*, 2:248-50.

[17]"Capitania do Rio de Janeiro," letter from Father Manuel Ângelo, Superior of the Carmelites, to Francisco Xavier de Mendonça Furtado, August 20, 1764, in *Revista do Instituto Histórico e Geográfico Brasileiro*, 65 (1902): 118-19.

patible with the consitution of the Kingdom and the rights of the Crown, José I enumerated the following established policies:

> *First:* not to allow any appeals of vassals of this Crown to the Roman Curia, under the penalty of losing their citizenship and property.
> *Second:* not to tolerate that the said vassals indict other vassals to Rome, under the same penalties.
> *Third:* not to permit, under the same penalties, that the regular orders of this Kingdom and its domains receive direct or indirect visitations from their General or his delegates who are not born vassals of this Crown.[18]

Diplomatic correspondence between the Courts of Lisbon and of Paris during the 1760s reveals the existence of a concerted effort to control the Church. On March 23, 1769, Vicente de Sousa Coutinho, Portuguese Ambassador to France, wrote to Pombal:

> Mr. de Choiseul reiterated to me that in Portugal and Spain the ecclesiastics should be made to take an oath of obedience to the Four Propositions which provide the basis for the liberties of the French clergy; that this doctrine should be taught in the universities and become law of Church and State; that as long as it is not put into practice, there will be a perpetual conflict between the two hierarchies, and all will remain precarious, depending on the will of this minister or of that prince; that in France, now that it had been established, there was no fear of the imprudences of a pope, since the latter had his hands tied while his feet were being kissed.[19]

Pombal needed a rapprochement with Rome to legitimize his regalistic reforms in the eyes of the national Church. Late in 1769, ten years after the severance of relations between Rome and Lisbon, the Holy See agreed to send an apostolic nuncio to Portugal. This action spelled further trouble for the Society of Jesus, whose expulsion from the Portuguese empire had led to the rupture between the two Courts. The papal envoy Inocêncio (later Cardinal Conti) became a tool in the hands of Pombal, never lifted a finger to protest the regalistic policies, and even lent his collaboration to the Pombaline reforms.[20]

Pombal's next target was the Inquisition, a symbol of conservatism and ultramontanism. Not daring to attempt outright abolition of the institution, he deprived the Holy Office of its remaining function, that of censoring books and similar materials, by establishing a state board of censorship in 1768. The *Mesa Censória,* as the board was called, was granted jurisdiction over every form of printed material and was staffed by high-ranking governmental and religious officials—all of whom were eager propagandists of regalism

---

[18]Archivio Segreto Vaticano, Nunziatura Portogallo, 119A, copy of José I's message to the Marquis of Pombal.

[19]Arquivo Nacional da Tôrre do Tombo, Ministério da Justiça, pkg. 15, Dispatch of February 15, 1768.

[20]Archivio Segreto Vaticano, Nunz. Port., 119A, fols. 48-49. See also 119, fols. 212-13.

and of the new sciences.[21] Furthermore, the *Mesa* not only permitted but also advertised the writings of authors labeled by Rome as subversive. Included among these authors (most of whom had been blacklisted by the Roman Index) were Justinus Febronius, Louis Ellies Dupin, Peter de Marca, Bernard van Espen, Paul Joseph Ritter von Riegger, Johan Gottlieb Heinecke, Grotius, Samuel Puffendorf, Jean Barbeyrac, and Christian Friedrich Wolff.[22]

A large majority of the Portuguese bishops went along quietly with recommendations and prohibitions of the *Mesa Censória*. An exception was Miguel da Anunciação, Bishop of Coimbra, who issued a pastoral letter condemning Febronius and Dupin. The *Mesa* reacted angrily by deposing the prelate and sentencing him to prison, where he remained until the last days of Pombal's administration.[23]

Only one item in Pombal's program awaited implementation: reform of the University of Coimbra. To this reform he gave great importance. Reforms in secondary education and creation of the Royal College of the Nobility preceded establishment of the Junta of Literary Providence on December 23, 1770; the expressed purpose of the Junta was to prepare new statutes for the University. Headed by Cardinal João Cosme da Cunha, the Junta's distinguished members included Father Manuel do Cenáculo, Provincial of the Third Order of St. Francis of Assisi and President of the *Mesa Censória*; António Pereira de Figueiredo; José de Seabra da Silva, Court Judge and Crown Attorney; and two Brazilian brothers: Francisco de Lemos de Faria Pereira Coutinho, President of the University of Coimbra, and João Pereira Ramos, Judge of the Royal Court of Appeals.

The initial result of the work of the Junta was the *Historical Compendium on the State of the University of Coimbra*, published in 1771. As expected, it was an anti-Jesuit attack and was based largely on the *Chronological and Analytical Deduction* (1768), which was designed to convince Portuguese intellectuals and leaders that Jesuitism was the source of every national problem. Despite an anti-Jesuit slant, the *Historical Compendium* is important because it reveals the authors' new and revolutionary approach, their enthusiasm for the sciences, and their determination to implement a thorough reform.[24]

The greatest accomplishment of the Junta of Literary Providence was the formulation of new statutes for the University of Coimbra.

---

[21] Collecção dos Negócios de Roma, 2:88; Arquivo Nacional da Tôrre do Tombo, Mesa Censória, pkg. 591.

[22] Arquivo Nacional da Torre do Tombo, Mesa Censória, pkg. 591.

[23] Colleccão das leys promulgadas e sentencas proferidas nos casos da infame Pastoral do Bispo de Coimbra D. Miguel da Annunciacão. Das seitas dos Jacobeos . . . (Lisbon, 1769); Antônio Pereira da Silva, A Questão do Sigilismo em Portugal no Século XVIII (Braga: Editorial Franciscana, 1964), passim.

[24] Compendio Histórico do estado da Universidade de Coimbra, pp. ii-iii, 117, 176-204, 205-226.

Before publishing these statutes, the Marquis ordered suspension of all classes at the university on September 25, 1771, and retrieval of all copies of the old statutes. A royal letter of confirmation and publication of the new statutes, with an accompanying decree designating Pombal as Visitor and Founder of the new university, was issued on August 28, 1772. Shortly thereafter, on September 11, Dom Francisco de Lemos was made Reformer of Coimbra. Pombal traveled to Coimbra on September 22 and was lodged in the episcopal palace. On the following morning, accompanied by an impressive retinue, he entered the university grounds and reviewed the troops and assembled faculty. Finally, on September 29, in a most solemn ceremony in the Main Hall of the university, Pombal, in the name of His Majesty, proclaimed and delivered the new statutes to the President and the whole faculty. A "Te Deum" in the university chapel concluded the solemnities.[25]

After delivery of the new statutes, classes were resumed and members of the faculty took the traditional oath of fealty to the Church. Because, among other objectives, the Pombaline reform aimed at diminishing the Roman influence in Portugal, administration of the oath came as a surprise. The surprise vanished, however, with the royal declaration of October 10, 1772, in which His Majesty explained that in taking their oath the professors had in mind to observe "the Conciliar Constitutions, the Constitutions so far received by the universal Church, and the Constitution already accepted and received, and those that would be accepted and received by the Portuguese Church; always safeguarding, however, those untouchable limits established by the supreme Legislator to separate the spiritual power of the Church from the temporal jurisdiction of the Sovereigns."[26]

A series of royal resolutions, designed to expand the physical plant and to emphasize the study of the sciences, was also issued. The Marquis of Pombal made certain that not only Portugal but all of Europe would be fully informed of the reform and of Coimbra's new statutes. In November, editors of the royal printing press were ordered to deliver copies of the statutes to all bishops of continental and overseas Portugal, members of the Council of Literary Providence, members of the Council of State, all court judges, the Chief Justice of the Court of Appeals, the Crown attorneys, and the Rector of the College of the Nobility. Remaining copies were to be sold to the public.[27]

The new statutes were published in three volumes in both Portuguese and Latin. The first volume covers theology; the second, civil and canonical jurisprudence; and the third, natural sciences and

[25] Mario Brandão and M. Lopes de Almeida, *A Universidade de Coimbra: Esboço da sua História* (Coimbra: Imprensa da Universidade, 1937), pp. ii, 88f.; Silvestre Ribeiro, *História*, 1:370-71.
[26] Biblioteca Nacional de Lisboa, *Collecção Geral das Ordens*, fol. 85.
[27] Silvestre Ribeiro, *História*, 1:374, 376, 380.

philosophy. Volume 2 sets forth the ideas and doctrines of Pombaline regalism in clear, precise terms. The reformers of Coimbra considered the pope to be first among the bishops rather than lord of the Church. Thus, university professors were to teach students "that the Supreme Pontiff is the Visible Head of the Church; that Church government means that the Supreme Shepherd and Primate should rule it together with the Bishops; not as Lord and Monarch with free power and control over the Canons, even those established by Universal Councils of the Church; but as a good President, Administrator, and prudent Dispenser of all that might result in good example for the faithful."[28] Professors were also to distinguish "between the Power and the essential, proper, and inalienable Authority of the Church which it exercised from the time of the Apostles; and the other power, and accidental and adventicious Authority which was granted to the Church by the Christian emperors."[29] Furthermore, they should lead the students "to acknowledge the just Authority that always belonged to the Kings as Sovereigns of this Monarchy regarding mixed matters, the external Policy of the Church, the external administration of the Spiritual Rights, in view of the two unique and precise principles of avoiding and preventing any evil to the State, and of seeing that Canonical laws are obeyed and observed."[30]

Coimbra's new statutes recognized the Church's temporal power as a privilege granted by the State. The Crown was given the right to protect the national Church against Roman centralization; and Crown "regalia, rights, prerogatives, articles, and liberties of the Portuguese Church" were emphasized.[31] Sovereigns were called Protectors of the Church and Upholders of the Canons, and they were granted rights to administer the temporal property and control the discipline and treasury of the Church. Papal bulls and other Roman documents were to be analyzed and interpreted according to historical circumstances, intention, content, and acceptance by the faithful. Natural law was to serve not only as the foundation of Church law but was also to take precedence over positive law, not excepting divine law.[32]

Other religious orders, which after the expulsion of the Jesuits were charged with a heavier load in education, were compelled to reform their studies according to the model of Coimbra. Most of them went as far as to copy parts of the statutes as well as some of the accusations of the *Historical Compendium* against the Society of Jesus. The new plan of studies of the Franciscans of the Province of

[28]*Estatutos da Universidade de Coimbra* (Lisbon, 1772), bk. 2, tit. 4, chap. 4, par. 10. Pius VI's bull *Auctorem Fidei* of 1794 declared the title "President" as heretical when used in reference to the Pope.
[29]Ibid., bk. 2, tit. 4, chap. 1, par. 20.
[30]Ibid., chap. 2, par. 12.
[31]Ibid., par. 14.
[32]Ibid., tit. 8, chap. 8, par. 30.

Portugal, published in 1776, ordered adoption of textbooks and other books used at Coimbra. Each professor of moral theology was to have a copy of the *Chronological and Analytical Deduction*, while another copy was to be kept in each library of the Province.[33]

In addition, the following works were also used at Coimbra after 1772: (1) *Elementa Scientiarum metaphysicarum* and *Elementa Logico-Criticae*, by Antonio Genovesi, for the Chair of Philosophy; (2) *Elementa Iuris Naturae et Gentium*, by Johan Gottlieb Heinecke, for the Chair of Moral Theology; (3) *Ius ecclesiasticum universum*, by Bernard van Espen, along with his commentary on Gratian's decree, for the Chair of Canon Law. Extensive use was also made of Claude Fleury's *Histoire Ecclésiastique*, which had been specifically recommended by the *Mesa Censória*; Pereira de Figueiredo's *Tentativa theológica* and *Demostração theológica*; Pereira de Castro's *De Manu Regia tractatus*; and Melo Freire's *History of Portuguese Civil and Criminal Law*.[34] The library of the University also had copies of the works of Febronius, Dupin, Gmeiner, Riegger, Marca, Grotius, Wolff, Puffendorf, and others. Students at Coimbra had access to all the important authors identified with regalism and Gallicanism, and the list of works proscribed by the Roman Index simply was ignored.

The Holy See had full access to information about changes carried out in Portugal, because the papal secretary of state received copies of the new statutes; but he either attached no special significance to the statutes or failed to read them.[35] When regalistic ideas began to be fully applied in Brazil during the nineteenth century, bitter complaints on the part of the Holy See were indeed belated.

The Marquis of Pombal continued to be treated not only with respect but also as a benefactor by the Holy See.[36] First to denounce these reforms as Jansenist and Gallican was Cardinal Bartolomeo Pacca, Apostolic Nuncio in Lisbon from 1794 to 1802. He wrote that Pombal had turned the University of Coimbra into a "true chair of pestilence."[37]

[33]*Plano Geral pelo qual se hão-de observar literalmente na Província de Portugal dos Menores Observantes de S. Francisco às disposições que se acham determinadas nos Estatutos da Universidade de Coimbra* . . . (Lisbon, 1776), pp. vi-vii, 21, 46.

[34]The adoption of Heinecke's work at Coimbra was surprising, because he was a Lutheran. The textbook, however, underwent a few changes designed to clear it from "the poison of a few Lutheran principles." See Manuel Lopes de Almeida, *Documentos da Reforma Pombalina*, 2 vols. (Coimbra: Imprensa da Universidade, 1937), 1:167. See also Arquivo Nacional da Torre do Tombo, Mesa Censória, pkg. 714.

[35]Archivo Segreto Vaticano, Dispatches from Nunzio Conti to the Cardinal-Secretary of State, n.d. (probably September 1771), October 12, 1772, Nunz. Port. 119A, fols. 129-39; and 183, fols 232f. See also Archives of the Portuguese Embassy in Rome, bk. 2, fol. 256, Dispatch of August 11, 1774, from Ambassador Francisco de Almada de Mendonça to the Marquis of Pombal.

[36]Archivio Segreto Vaticano, pkg. 183, fols. 232f.; Archives of the Portuguese Embassy in Rome, bk. 2, fol. 319.

[37]*Mémoires Historiques du Cardinal Pacca* (Paris, 1844), pp. 269-70.

Despite a partial decadence of Coimbra and a few reactionary decrees issued during the reign of Maria I, the basic ideas of the Pombaline reforms remained unchallenged. The statutes of 1772 were retained; and Dom Francisco de Lemos, who was retained as Rector of the University until 1779 and then was reappointed and served from 1799 to 1821, did his best to preserve alive Pombal's work and program. Cardinal Pacca bitterly complained that nothing really changed at Coimbra after the removal of the Marquis of Pombal from the government in 1777, especially because Dom Francisco de Lemos carried on the ideas of his mentor and best friend.[38]

In fact, the works of regalistic authors continued as textbooks at Coimbra; and a few more were added, such as the *Institutiones iuris ecclesiastici*, by Franz Xaver Gmeiner, and the *Institutions théologiques*, by the famous Lugdunensis.[39] In a letter to Pope Leo XII, dated October 2, 1825, Carlota Joaquina, wife of John VI, made these observations about Coimbra:

> There is in this Kingdom one University, that of Coimbra. The textbooks used in the various schools are full of errors and therefore rightfully placed in the Indexes of books prohibited by the Apostolic See. The University, Holy Father, educates civil and ecclesiastic magistrates who demonstrate enough talent to serve the country; so that from the bishops, their chapters, and pastors to ministers, secretaries of State, whether secular, regular or monastic, all have directly or indirectly drunk the poison of this University. Consequently, rarely is there found in Portugal a well-educated person who possesses sound doctrine, not to mention free-masonry, which has flooded this country.... The reform of the University of Coimbra is a necessity, and without it we shall all become heretics.[40]

By 1825, the doctrines of regalism were being put to practice in earnest in Brazil, already in its third year of independence. Although the Jesuits had educated Brazilians for more than two centuries and had created among the clergy a mentality of orthodoxy and of obedience to Rome, Pombaline reforms resounded deeply in the hearts of the Brazilian elite and eventually became triumphant.

Since late sixteenth century, it had become a tradition among well-to-do Brazilian families to send a son to study at Coimbra, the only public university within the Portuguese empire. Coimbra was the

---

[38]Ibid., pp. 274, 283.
[39]Gmeiner's *Institutiones* was published and adopted at Coimbra in 1815, without the cuts made in an edition published at Venice in 1783. The Coimbra edition includes attacks on clerical celibacy. Antoine Malvin de Montazet, Bishop of Autun and Archbishop of Lyon (Lugdunum), was one of the four French bishops who refused to submit to the bull *Unigenitus* in 1765. He expressly taught that decrees of general councils regarding ecclesiastical discipline needed previous approval of the state to bind the faithful to obedience. His Institutiones theologicae was condemned by the Roman Index in 1792.
[40]Archivio Segreto Vaticano, Nunz. Port., Year 1829, pkg. 250.

door to the most coveted careers in the colonies, to importance and prestige in society, and to the magic title of doctor while holding only a bachelor of arts or bachelor of science degree. Coimbra exercised an immeasurable influence upon Brazilian thought, mainly because it educated the intellectual elite of Portuguese America. After the reforms enacted by the Marquis of Pombal, this influence became even more pervasive. The Crown made the university the ideological instrument of its regalistic policies; the mentality of Coimbra invaded the cloisters, monasteries, convents, and schools controlled by religious orders; and, finally, the same students who attended classes at Coimbra became leaders of independent Brazil and were given a unique opportunity to test their ideas concerning church-state relations.

The teaching of English and, especially, of French, made easier the propagation of the ideas of the Enlightenment, Gallicanism, and regalism in Brazil. In general, ecclesiastics had an easier access to forbidden or dangerous books, because not only the Inquisition but also the *Mesa Censória* recognized the argument that they must inform themselves to be able to advise the faithful.[41] No wonder then that clergymen were in the front lines of every Brazilian revolt, from the Mineiro conspiracy to the rebellion of 1842.

An examination of registration records of the University of Coimbra until 1825 reveals the names of many Brazilians who studied there and later became persons of importance in the social, political, and religious life of imperial Brazil. Among them were Bishop José Joaquim da Cunha de Azeredo Coutinho, Canon José de Sousa e Azevedo Pizarro, and Fathers Francisco Correia Vidigal and Antonio Maria de Moura. Also included were ministers and secretaries of state, such as the Marquises of Queluz (João Severiano Maciel), of Barbacena (Felisberto Caldeira Brant Pontes), of Sapucaí (Cândido José de Araújo Viana), of Caravelas (Manuel Alves Branco), and of Olinda (Pedro de Araújo Lima, who was regent of the empire in 1837). Likewise, there were three Andrada brothers and many others who became members of the imperial nobility, Supreme Court justices, presidents of provinces, senators, and members of the Chamber of Deputies. In general, one might say that Coimbra shaped the mentality of the elite of imperial Brazil, at least in the area of church-state relations.

Graduates of Coimbra were present everywhere in the imperial government. For example, the office of minister of justice, which was charged with guiding and regulating relations between church and state, was monopolized by graduates of Coimbra. During the first empire, the only minister of justice who was not an alumnus of Coimbra

---

[41] Arquivo Nacional da Tôrre do Tombo, Mesa Censória, pkg. 714: permissions granted to the Franciscans of the Province of Arrábida and the monks of St. Bernard.

was Father Diogo Antonio Feijó, but even he had been heavily influenced by the regalism of that University.[42]

From 1746 to 1827, seventy-four Brazilian ecclesiastics studied at Coimbra; sixteen belonged to religious orders and the others were identified as diocesan or secular clergy.[43] One of these ecclesiastics was Azeredo Coutinho, Bishop of Pernambuco and founder of the Seminary of Olinda. As the only institution that offered a combination of secondary and higher education in northeastern Brazil, the Seminary of Olinda attracted candidates for the priesthood and lay students from the whole area. Its program of studies was patterned upon what the statutes of 1772 had established for the University of Coimbra. Azeredo Coutinho wished it to be this way; and Olinda was the first school in Brazil to replace fully the program of the Jesuit colégios with a different orientation. Here emphasis was given to the study of physical and natural sciences, ecclesiastical history, and modern languages. There was a veritable enthusiasm for new and liberal ideas. Thus, it is not surprising that in 1817 the great majority of the seminary's students and professors adhered to the republican revolution of Pernambuco.[44]

Elections for the first Constituent Assembly of the Brazilian empire in 1823 represented an enormous triumph for liberals and regalists educated at Coimbra. Out of ninety delegates, forty-eight were lawyers and alumni of Coimbra, while twenty-one (three never took their seats) were ecclesiastics.[45] When the Assembly prepared a constitution that failed to satisfy the absolutist tendencies of Emperor Pedro I, he chose a committee of ten jurists to draft a new document. Nine of them were graduates of Coimbra, and provisions of the Consitution promulgated in 1824 established the traditional regalism of the Crown and reflected the ideology of Coimbra.[46]

Perhaps enough has been said about the roots and sources of Brazilian regalism. Not only did imperial Brazil train leaders in the traditions of the Portuguese system of union of church and state, but also it inherited the whole system—lock, stock, and barrel. A young, recently emancipated country, Brazil had only the Portuguese model

---

[42]Brasília, Supplement to vol. 4 of Revista da Faculdade de Letras da Universidade de Coimbra (1949), pp. 187-441.
[43]Ibid.
[44]Francisco Muniz Tavares, História da Revolução de Pernambuco em 1817 (Recife, 1884), pp. 235f. No less than forty-one clergymen, thirty-five secular priests, five Carmelites, and one Franciscan were indicted as participants in the Revolution of 1817; a number of them rose up again in the 1824 Confederation of the Equator. See also Henry Koster, Travels in Brazil (London, 1816), p. 33.
[45]Anais da Assembléia Constituinte, 1823, 1:iv-vi.
[46]José Carlos Rodrigues, A Constituição Política do Império do Brasil seguida do Acto Addicional (Rio de Janeiro, 1853), pp. 80, 91. See also Brasília, pp. 314-56.

to follow; and nativist feelings were always suspicious of any move made by Rome or by papal representatives.

Rome's intolerance of various doctrines of the Enlightenment exasperated many regalists, whose religious liberalism stood in sharp contrast with the tridentine conservatism of the ultramontanists. Furthermore, regalists resented what they considered to be unjust charges of heresy that were often raised against them. Brazilian regalists never entertained the slightest thought that their ways of thinking and acting could be harmful to the Church or in disharmony with Christian teachings. Following the example of the reformers of Coimbra, they constantly spoke of returning the Church to its primitive purity. One can understand the way that Portuguese and Brazilian regalists thought, if one recognizes their belief in the old Augustinian ideal; that is, they wished church and state to work closely together to bring about the Kingdom of God on earth. Men such as Manuel do Cenáculo, Dom Francisco de Lemos, and Diogo António Feijó gave ample proof of their dedication to the Church and to Christian ideals. Regalism in Portugal and in Brazil, although an enemy of Roman centralization, was not necessarily an enemy of the Catholic Church.

31. Brazilian Positivism and the Military Republic

DON WHITMORE

Positivism as understood by Auguste Comte exercised an important influence on nineteenth-century Brazil's political development. Professor Whitmore explores the beginning of this influence and shows how Positivism evolved and adapted to changing circumstances. Also, he describes the influence that Positivist perspectives have had in the education of military officers and how these perspectives have affected their political role in national affairs in recent years.

A century ago, Brazilians entertained various alternatives for governing their country. After 1860, they tried to use some aspects of Comtean Positivism but had mixed success. This essay summarizes elements of Brazilian Positivism, explains how it caught the fancy of some Brazilian leaders, and notes evidence of Positivist influence in contemporary Brazil.

Auguste Comte was the first to use the term "positive philosophy" and to develop Positivism as an organized system of thought. Analyzing the ills of Europe, he explained that his new plan for society called for a popular dictatorship. Positivism came to be known less in North America than in Hispanic America, where "the great teachers ... were Leroux and Comte, Guyau, Fouillée, Renan and Taine, rather than the Kantian, Hegelian, or pessimistic schools."[1] For example, several Brazilians who studied with Comte returned from France with his teachings. Alfredo de Taunay's professor at the Peter II College had learned from Comte. Nísia Floresta, who had an aristocratic school in Rio de Janeiro, worked with the French master. Luís Pereira Barreto and Francisco Antônio Brandão Júnior adopted the Comtean attitude while in Belgium, and they brought it back to Brazil. Raymon-

[1] William Rex Crawford, *A Century of Latin-American Thought* (Cambridge, Mass.: Harvard University Press, 1963), p. 8.

do de Rocha Lima was a fervent disciple of Comte who led students in Ceará. From the 1850s onward, other students presented Positivist theses at the national Military School, where Manuel Joaquim Pereira de Sá and Augusto Dias Corneira were chiefly responsible for delivering Comte's thought to the Brazilian military.[2]

The principal spokesman for the Brazilian military-engineer group that favored Positivism was Benjamim Constant Botelho de Magalhães. After spending time with Comte in his last months, Constant then studied at the Military School under Pereira de Sá and Dias Corneira. Later, Constant returned to the Military School as a mathematics teacher. When the government set up the new Military School at Praia Vermelha (1874), Constant moved there and continued his teaching. As a result of Constant's influence, Positivism became a cohesive factor among the young cadets.

Besides being a teacher, Constant played a leadership role in political affairs. In fact, his activities illustrate that Positivism did influence political and intellectual circles, although the number of Positivists was minimal. Some events in Constant's life reveal much about the pulse of the times.

Five years of war against Paraguay kindled concern among thinking Brazilians. They looked for new ways to tackle old problems. Some of these proto-Republicans in the 1860s came from the military cadre; Constant lived among them. He was Lieutenant Colonel when he signed the Republican Manifesto in 1870; Deodoro da Fonseca, Ruy Barbosa, and others put their names on the document, also. Constant believed he spoke for most army officers. Unhappy with affairs in the Empire, they backed technocratic Comtism for liberal control of the state. Constant tried to take a stand and to influence the military toward implementing objectives that were set forth in the Manifesto. Some members of the new middle class (families of the young military) gave moral support to Constant's stand; later they formed part of the Federal Republican Party. Thus, the citizen-soldier gained support from the Paraguay War, support that would persist into the days of the Republic. Young men went to the Military School not for training in warfare so much as to obtain pre-professional training in engineering, mathematics, and medicine—disciplines close to the Comtean science hierarchy. According to João Cruz Costa, Comte and his Brazilian followers urged these vocations as "definitive solutions for all problems."[3] Moreover, "By means of this group of Bachelors and Doctors of physical sciences and mathematics, but also men in uniform, Positivism would penetrate Brazil, acting as an ideology of a

---

[2]Umberto Peregrino, "Benjamin Constant, Líder Militar," in *Euclides da Cunha e Outros Estudos* (Rio de Janeiro: Gráfica Record Editôra, 1968), pp. 151ff.
[3]João Cruz Costa, quoted by Peregrino, "Benjamin Constant, Líder Militar," p. 151.

class which, having become rationalist by its university training, would seek to be affirmed as an original group."[4]

Politics makes strange bedfellows. Republican partisans used military discontent after the war, and the military bought time for the eventual rupture. Here we see a miniature of a grander break between the Emperor and the middle class.

Constant allied with Deodoro da Fonseca in interesting ways. For one, he pushed Deodoro into the Republican camp. Some historians blame Constant for starting the famous rumor of November 1889. This rumor moved the Republican uprising forward to the fifteenth of the month, a few days before the originally scheduled date. Earlier, Deodoro listened to military men who fed on Comte's philosophy. They suggested that "the establishment of a Republic would assure just respect of the military."[5] A second hope tickled the ear of Deodoro. Constant reportedly proposed that he become dictator. All the while, the younger military dared more and more to debate with politicians—first on party lines, then openly as military class versus civilians.

Raimundo Teixeira Mendes wrote that Benjamin Constant founded the Brazilian Republic; he gave him too much credit. The signers of the Manifesto in 1870 had varied backgrounds and ambitions, and so did the Republic's leaders in the years after 1889. Indeed, Ruy Barbosa befriended Comtist theories until about 1890; but after that time, he found much with which to disagree. Ruy Barbosa probably relied more on literary or juridical formalism, another philosophy of his day. Quintino Bocayuva also placed his signature under the Manifesto, but he became an ardent spokesman for democracy and combatted Constant at times.

It was Constant, Teixeira Mendes, and Miguel Lemos who managed to persuade the Republic's leaders to adopt the theme for the Brazilian Flag. "Order and Progress" is a set phrase from Comte. Despite opposition, the slogan was selected and has remained on the national banner. In his *Republic of the West*, Comte had described two flags. His religious flag showed a woman and child; the background was green, the color of hope. The religious formula read: "Love is our Principle, Order is our Basis; Progress our End." A second banner was political, also green. One side carried the political and scientific motto, "Order and Progress"; on the reverse side was the moral and ethical motto: "Live for Others." The common color of

---

[4]Tocary Assis Bastos, *O Positivismo e a Realidade Brasileira* (Belo Horizonte: RBEP, 1965), p. 43.
[5]Charles Willis Simmons, *Marshall Deodoro and the Fall of Dom Pedro II* (Durham, N.C.: Duke University Press, 1966), p. 102.

Comte's flags and Brazil's flag may be due to chance, but one can hardly deny the identity of emblem.[6]

Constant served as Minister of Education. Here, his greatest impact was to convert the Pedro II College into the National High School. This forward step broke with the past and gave the state greater control over student ideology, and it vexed the Catholic Church. Constant's program made Positivist mathematics the only major scientific study in the new education. After his changes, students became encyclopedic, not scientific. What Comte had seen as mainstream Positivism, namely, methodology of questioning and seeking, now entered Brazil's thought processes only in a thinned-out manner.

Although Teixeira Mendes did not smile on the military, he stood firm for the glory of Constant's name. As a Positivist advocate and "apostle of Humanity" of the Apostolate in Rio de Janeiro (established in 1881),[7] Teixeira Mendes outlived his hero and kept on writing and delivering Comtist lectures. He admired the military trend of Comtism less than the civilian trend. Of course, both types looked to science for orientation and applied sectarian bases in their doctrines; but Miguel Lemos and Mendes believed in the religious sector more and shied away from intellectualism. Such hair-splitting may seem academic elsewhere, but its effects in Brazil caused men to take sides. Overall, they viewed Positivism in three ways: speculative or metaphysical, religious, and political. The 1889 Republican outburst mirrored the political aspect; and the religious aspect showed up in 1876, when Constant and his followers formed the Positivist Society in Rio de Janeiro. The speculative aspect was the flimsiest of all.[8]

A few men, such as Tobias Barreto and Clóvis Bevilacqua, argued this metaphysical aspect of Positivism in different parts of the country: however, Sílvio Romero, in *A philosophia no Brazil* (1878), openly criticized Comte's ideas as unworthy and a danger to science. Citing errors in logic, Romero took a strong stand against unconvincing scientific interpretations of Comte. Romero's doubt blossomed more in a second book, *Doutrina contra doutrina*, in which he disapproved of religious Positivism, i.e., the Apostolate in Rio de Janeiro. (Some regional jealousy or pride was surely involved, in that day of federated Brazilian states.) Romero took to task the thinly-clad Catholicism of the religion, with its priesthood, sacraments, dogma, and calendar. Comte's division of sciences was faulty, too, contended Romero. In sum, he remarked, "Futile Jacobinism and sterile Positivism, such are

[6]Auguste Comte, *Republic of the West: Order and Progress*, trans. J. H. Bridges (Paris, 1848), p. 431.
[7]João Cruz Costa, *Positivismo na República* (São Paulo: Companhia Editôra Nacional, 1956), p. 13.
[8]Martín García Mérou, *El Brasil Intelectual* (Buenos Aires: Felix Lajouane, 1900, pp. 59-61.

the two great causes which derailed the Republic in Brazil."⁹ Evidently, Romero sought a controlled progress for his country; he did not trust it to dilettante apostles like Teixeira Mendes and Demétrio Ribeiro.

Along with other publications in Brazil during the latter part of the Empire, many magazines and journals had Positivist phrases in their titles. Again the names of Raimundo Teixeira Mendes and Miguel Lemos figured prominently. The two writers had opposed slavery, according to Gondin da Fonseca, even before Joaquim Nabuco's article in the *Abolitionist* of 1880.¹⁰ Along with Joaquim da Cunha, Lemos also helped edit the *Academic Review* of 1873, a Rio journal of politics, literature, and science, which became a mouthpiece for his philosophical persuasion.

The flame of the various Comtean sects grew or sputtered, according to the respective spokesmen's moment of power. Lemos held real power in the Republic of the select. One writer states that, although Lemos did not speak as an army officer, "if Lemos had participated in political militancy, he would have been an exceptional partisan leader."¹¹ Lemos acted as doctrinaire promoter for the support of Floriano Peixoto, who, in turn, wanted to nominate Júlio de Castilhos and Lauro Sodré for President rather than Prudente de Morais in 1894. But Castilhos was diverting energies to a regional war in Rio Grande do Sul, and Sodré had scant experience in politics. Thus, although Lemos's military Positivism did not die out completely, it flickered for a time. On the other hand, Teixeira Mendes banked the fire of his religious Comtism in Rio Grande do Sul. It broke into flames in 1930, via Castilhos, with Vargas's rise and the return of the middle class to power.¹²

During Constant's era, he controlled much of the thinking of the Military Club in Rio de Janeiro.¹³ Constant told the Club, for example, that he would find a solution to the crisis of mid-1889. The young members assumed that he meant to replace the monarchy with a republic. Constant was not the only luminary member, for Deodoro da Fonseca shared influence over the Club. After Constant riled him by defending freedom of the press, the old friends parted ways. This falling away, and the subsequent death of Constant, gave ample opening for Floriano to ascend in the government hierarchy. Even before Constant's death, Floriano became Vice President and dismissed Cons-

---

⁹Silvio Romero, *Doutrina contra Doutrina: O Evolucionismo e o Positivismo no Brasil* (Rio de Janeiro: Livraria Clássica de Alves & Co., 1895), p. 291.
¹⁰Gondin da Fonseca, *Biografia do Jornalismo Carioca* (Rio de Janeiro: Livraria Quaresma, 1941), pp. 195, 204.
¹¹Bastos, *O Positivismo*, p. 153.
¹²Ibid., pp. 155-61.
¹³Robert Ames Hayes, "The Formation of the Brazilian Army and Its Political Behavior, 1807-1930" (Ph.D. diss., University of New Mexico, 1968), passim.

tant's moderate counsel. Many officers in the Military Club supported Floriano, because they rejected slow progress and insisted on immediate change.

While the government kept the Club closed for a time, political activists opposed those who urged an apolitical role for the military. The latter gained strength against both the Florianists and the Positivists. When Campo Sales reopened the Club, there were still enough Positivists to act in favor of military politicization. Later, when the clash resulted from the issue of the 1904 vaccination, apolitical Club members won out over militants and Florianists. Throughout all the upheaval and confusion, Lauro Sodré continued Constant's task of catechizing cadets informally at his home.[14] He saw himself as a steady keeper of the flame.

What happened to Positivism in Brazil? After the immediate Comtist phase, Republicans sublimated it in liberalism and their blueprint for society. At the same time, official religious groups practiced their rites. They gave dates on letters for both the Comtist calendar and the Christian year: "Rio, ninth of Homer, 104/sixteenth of February, 1892."[15] The former dated from the start of the French Revolution. Likewise, they closed letters and lectures with "Health and Fraternity," echoing the French phrase that Comte had formulated. Still feeling the flush of success over the national flag, the Apostolate sent more proposals to the Constituent Assembly in 1890. One may question whether their pressure to separate church and state in December 1889 greatly aided the cause of separation. More likely, the cleft sprang from a lay movement for neutrality, not from sectarian Positivism. Even if no more than a formality, separation of church from state distilled Positivists' dream of state evolution. Ruy Barbosa rightly claimed that Positivism did not build the new federative Republic, but it did lend sturdiness and moderation to balance the petty federalism and attempts at anarchy.[16]

In a more diluted manner, students at the Military School tried to fan the Positivist embers after 1889. Some officers pressed for "the establishment of a voluntary republican dictatorship to lead the nation on an orderly path to material progress and prosperity."[17] Nevertheless, this bid for Comte's republican dictatorship fell on deaf ears. Brazil held to the liberalism and regionalism of the day.

Sublimated Positivism continued to change and develop in Brazil.

[14]Hayes, "Formation of the Brazilian Army," pp. 52-133, passim.
[15]Raimundo Teixeira Mendes, *Benjamin Constant* (Rio de Janeiro: Imprensa Nacional, 1936), p. xii.
[16]Fernando de Azevedo, *Brazilian Culture*, trans. W. R. Crawford (New York: Macmillan, 1950), p. 414.
[17]Rollie E. Poppino, *Brazil: The Land and People* (New York: Oxford University Press, 1968), p. 217.

Its disciples bred their variants into the military and the society at large after 1900. For example, in Rio Grande do Sul, Júlio de Castilhos passed the mantle to General Manuel Vargas and to his heir, Getúlio Vargas. In 1925, the latter made known his Castilhist traits in an interview published in The Country.[18] As President-dictator, he fashioned laws on immigration and labor that contained Positivist bases. His Estado Novo belonged to the same Positivist tradition. Vargas's inheritance was so clear that Gilberto Freyre has written, "Vargas was a Brazilian, marked to the end of his life by Positivist training."[19] Hermes da Fonseca's reforms grew out of Positivist schooling, and the glow lived on in the later Military School of Realengo. Influences like these flared up from time to time amid other writers and statesmen, and into a kind of sociology.

Over a generation later, Humberto de Alencar Castelo Branco gave his inaugural speech in Rio de Janeiro. He spoke in 1964 from the vantage point of a life dedicated to the Brazilian Army. Born in Ceará as the son of a brigadier general, Castelo Branco attended the Military School at Pôrto Alegre. At the age of eighteen he changed to Rio's Military School of Realengo. His hobbies of music, Chinese vases, foreign languages, and especially books showed his broad abilities. Seen as an intellectual by other officers, Castelo Branco prepared himself by studying Brazil's political, economic, and social problems.[20]

Most observers agree that, once in the Presidential palace, Castelo Branco was a conscientious administrator but not a popular leader. Freyre says that he was "one of the greatest Brazilian intellectuals not just in the armed forces but in the entire nation."[21]

By March 1964, Castelo Branco became uneasy about the tendency in Goulart's policies and ideas. As a result, he sent out a memorandum of caution known as the "Castelo Branco Analysis." This paper urged his peers to commit themselves to military action in defense of the Constitution. At his inauguration the following month, he also made statements that must be noted. Some of his phrases are as follows: "the sentiments and ideals that have accompanied and inspired us since our youth; . . . a revolution to insure progress without reneging the past; . . . economic development through moral, educational, material, and political elevation; . . . [quoting Ruy Barbosa] "If

---

[18]Ivan Lins, História do Positivismo no Brasil (São Paulo: Companhia Editôra Nacional, 1964), pp. 197-201.
[19]Gilberto Freyre, Ordem e Progresso, 2 vols. (Rio de Janeiro: Livraria José Olympio, 1959), 1:xxxiv.
[20]Milan J. Kubic, "Brazil's Adroit New Leader," The Reporter, December 17, 1964, pp. 21-23.
[21]Time, April 17, 1964, p. 50.

we give the example to the people, they will follow us."[22] Some of these terms mirror earlier military solutions. Certainly, the flavor of Barbosa's line recalls the dreams of a dictator republic in the late nineteenth century.

All this leads to the following conclusion. Poppino is right in part when he says, "Confidence in the future was elevated to an article of faith by the briefly influential minority of Brazilians who adopted Auguste Comte's philosophy of positivism [sic], with its formula for a regimented social order and unlimited material progress. [But] positivism did not prevail."[23] Poppino has glossed over certain traits in modern "influential" Brazilians. If Castelo Branco was an intellectual in uniform, Brazil's military came full circle to Constant's century-old scheme for an enlightened dictator. Thus, Positivist embers have continued to smolder.

---

[22]See "The Inaugural Speech of President Humberto Castelo Branco," in *A Documentary History of Brazil*, ed. E. Bradford Burns (New York: Alfred A. Knopf, 1966), pp. 380-83.
[23]Poppino, *Brazil: The Land and People*, p. 201.

32. Sources of Brazilian Protestantism: Historical or Contemporary?

JOHN L. ROBINSON

In seeking an explanation for the rapid growth of Protestantism in Brazil, Professor Robinson examines peculiar conditions of Brazilian Catholicism, elements of Brazilian national character, religious policies of the Brazilian government, and the effect of non-Portuguese immigration. He concludes that historical factors have had a greater influence on Protestant growth in Brazil than have sociological phenomena.

Brazil's great geographic expanse, with the world's largest Roman Catholic population,[1] also harbors the largest and most rapidly growing body of Protestants in Latin America.[2] What explains this remarkable upsurge of Protestantism in Brazil? Joachim Wach long ago warned against explaining religious movements solely by "economic and social factors and conditions."[3] Yet Emílio Willems, in his groundbreaking work on the rise of Protestantism in Brazil and Chile, contends that Protestantism "emerged as a by-product of changes affecting the social structures and values of nineteenth-century Brazil and Chile."[4]

This essay suggests that Brazilian Protestant growth, unexampled elsewhere in Latin America, may be explained more adequately by historical factors than by contemporary sociological phenomena. Even Willems notes that "the structure of Brazilian society has shown a degree of permeability to Protestantism" not found in Chile.[5] This

[1] Charles Wagley, *An Introduction to Brazil* (New York: Columbia University Press, 1963), p. 233.
[2] Benjamin Moraes, "Brazil," *Christianity Today*, July 19, 1963, p. 19.
[3] Joachim Wach, *Sociology of Religion* (Chicago: University of Chicago, 1944), p. 203.
[4] Emílio Willems, *Followers of the New Faith: Culture Change and the Rise of Protestantism in Brazil and Chile* (Nashville, Tenn.: Vanderbilt University Press, 1967), p. 13.
[5] Ibid., 253.

385

very "permeability" would seem to indicate that Brazil's past is surely as important, if not more so, than contemporary sociocultural changes. Thus, historical factors furnish pertinent information with which to approach the riddle of Protestant growth in Brazil.

An integral explanation of Protestant growth in Brazil can be written only after much more research is done. It seems essential, however, to point to key aspects of the Brazilian past which have created in that nation's people a receptiveness to Protestantism unique for Latin America. Without attempting to assign priorities, several conditions of the Luso-American experience demand attention as causal elements in the striking socio-religious transformation now occurring in Brazil.

Peculiar conditions of Brazilian Catholicism, partly inherited from Portuguese Catholicism, helped prepare the ground for Protestantism. The Portuguese Catholic Church showed a distinct flexibility.[6] More than merely tolerant, the Portuguese religion, perhaps mellowed by centuries of Moslem influence, fell also under the sway of regalist monarchs. During Brazil's colonization, secular authorities clearly dominated ecclesiastical affairs, effectively drawing the Catholic Church into its policy of centralization.[7] Consequently, the transculturation process worked with a church adjusted to secular domination.

In Brazil, the purity of Catholic doctrine and practice was eroded through syncretism. The Portuguese never insisted that the Negro or Indian surrender his cultural heritage,[8] so Brazilian Catholicism incorporated both African and autochthonous elements.[9] No doubt the spiritual malleability of the colonial Catholic Church facilitated the future acceptance of another foreign element, Protestantism.

The limited number of clerics for such an immense colony meant few parishioners enjoyed regular spiritual counsel, and they grew accustomed to its absence. As early as 1575 the citizenry of Rio de Janeiro resisted the establishment of a prelacy in their midst, fearing it might hinder their less-than-exemplary business arrangements.[10]

Out of this environment grew a familial and formal Catholicism guided by clerics more interested in secular than religious pursuits.

---

[6]William J. Entwistle, "Religion," in *Portugal and Brazil*, ed. H. V. Livermore (London: Oxford University Press, 1953), p. 82.

[7]Sérgio Buarque de Holanda, ed., *História geral da civilização brasileira*, 4 vols. (São Paulo: Difusão Européia do Livro, 1960), 1:51. The Jesuits successfully resisted this domination for some time.

[8]Donald Pierson, *Brancos e pretos na Bahia* (São Paulo: Companhia Editôra Nacional, 1945), pp. 153-54.

[9]Thales de Azevedo, *O catolicismo no Brasil* ([Rio de Janeiro]: Ministério da Educação e Cultura, 1955), p. 29.

[10]Buarque de Holanda, *História geral de civilização brasileira*, 1:62-63.

The result was a Church "more social than religious."[11] Should future events alter or fracture the social structure, religious too must suffer.

During the Empire, Catholicism hardly fared better. New problems appeared while old ones remained and even intensified. Observers of that time saw no improvement in the quality of the priesthood,[12] and the number of priests still lagged far behind the growth in population.[13] The hierarchy of the Catholic Church reflected this meager substructure as it struggled with but six bishoprics.[14] To add to these problems, Pedro II inherited the regalism of his ancestors.[15]

The emergence of the Republic and the dawn of the early twentieth century presented a new set of circumstances to a Catholicism now shorn of state supports. Although the hierarchy expanded substantially, adjusting to the burgeoning population with more than 150 dioceses, the Church did not move to solve some of its long-standing problems.[16] Numbers of new priests were recruited, but many were foreigners[17]—a fact hardly appealing to active Brazilian nationalism. Today, the shortage of priests still exists as perhaps the most serious in the Catholic world.

A greater awareness of social problems came in the twentieth century, but many observers contend the Catholic Church has failed to recognize the degree and extent of the problems. Student groups have shown a sensitivity to these problems and have attempted to cope with them, but the Catholic hierarchy has often reacted against the radicalization of student movements.[18] Catholic Action, a lay movement growing out of Catholic regeneration endeavors of the 1920s and 1930s, achieved success; but this very success made it unresponsive to the more radical demands of later generations.[19] The Catholic left, therefore, created the Popular Action Party in 1963 in order to

[11]Roger Bastide, "Religion and the Church in Brazil," in *Brazil: Portrait of Half a Continent*, ed. T. Lynn Smith and Alexander Marchant (New York: Dryden Press, 1951), pp. 336-37, 339.
[12]Louis Agassiz, *A Journey in Brazil* (Boston: Ticknor and Fields, 1868), p. 497.
[13]T. Lynn Smith, *Brazil: People and Institutions* (Baton Rouge: Louisiana State University Press, 1963), p. 518.
[14]De Azevedo, *O catolicismo no Brasil*, p. 20.
[15]João Dornas Filho, *O padroado e a igreja brasileira* (São Paulo: Companhia Editôra Nacional, n.d.), p. 268.
[16]Thales de Azevedo, *Social Change in Brazil* (Gainesville: University of Florida Press, 1963), p. 59.
[17]Clodimir Vianna Moog, *Bandeirantes and Pioneers*, trans. L. L. Barrett (New York: Braziller, 1964), p. 209.
[18]Leonard D. Therry, "Dominant Power Components in the Brazilian University Student Movement Prior to April, 1964," *Journal of Inter-American Studies* 7 (January 1965): 39-40.
[19]Thomas C. Sanders, "Catholicism and Development: The Catholic Left in Brazil," in *Churches and States; The Religious Institution and Modernization*, ed. Kalman H. Silvert (New York: American Universities Field Staff, 1967), p. 85.

respond to the more pressing social and political needs; but the military takeover in 1964 frustrated its aims.[20] Only in very recent times has the Catholic Church become more responsive to the radical demands of some of her children. Historically, then, Brazilian Catholicism has cultivated and watered the land for a different seed.

Protestantism has prospered in the culture developed by Brazilians. Many visitors to the giant republic have commented on the uniqueness of this people. Similarly, few Brazilian writers can resist the inclination to describe the native character. Gilberto Freyre's well-established reputation testifies to the sustaining interest in this topic. So if one admits, along with most students of Brazil, the existence of a national character,[21] this character bears scrutiny in terms of its receptivity to Protestantism.

Brazilian character consists primarily of three basic infusions: Portuguese, African, and Indian.[22] Many scholars have discussed the contributions of each of these elements and the acculturation process that produced the Brazilian type; their well-known conclusions need no retelling here.[23] In due course, other European strains, particularly Italian, flavored the mixture with additional attributes. Today's Brazilian character emerged from these diverse influences. The most frequently attributed traits include innate warmth and hospitality, resignation in the face of periodic natural calamities, a flexibility of spirit producing toleration, enchantment with charismatic personalities, individualism, and a distinct turn to emotionalism and mysticism.[24]

All these features of the Brazilian personality have heightened the response to Protestantism. A hospitable frame of mind finds it inexpedient, if not blatantly discourteous, to reject summarily a stranger who comes bearing a new religious message. The missionary can expect a courteous hearing at least. Brazilian expectation, perhaps shaken by frequent natural catastrophes, brightens at the prospects held out by a

[20]Ibid., pp. 95-97.
[21]José Honório Rodrigues, The Brasilians, trans. R. E. Dimmick (Austin: University of Texas Press, 1967), p. 9, warns that an essential character for a nation cannot be dogmatically drawn, but that certain general traits can be well delineated.
[22]Affonso Arinos de Mello Franco, Conceito de civilização brasileira (São Paulo: Companhia Editôra Nacional, 1936) gives an excellent discussion of the acculturation processes.
[23]Gilberto Freyre, The Masters and the Slaves, trans. Samuel Putnam (New York: Alfred A. Knopf, 1956) is the seminal work.
[24]As a sampling of the extensive bibliography on this subject, see such works as Fernando de Azevedo, A cultura brasileira, 4th ed. (São Paulo: Edições Melhoramentos, 1964); Francisco Oliveira Vianna, Pequenos estudos de psicologia social, 3d ed. (São Paulo: Companhia Editôra Nacional, 1942); José Honório Rodrigues, The Brasilians; Rui Faco, Cangaceiros e fanáticos (Rio de Janeiro: Editôra Civilização Brasileira, 1963).

new faith.[25] Traditional openness to new ideas reinforces this receptiveness to new concepts of religion.

Personalism also plays a crucial role, for dynamic religious leaders have always found followers in Brazil.[26] When such men preach a Protestant gospel, the effect is no less potent. The charismatic Protestant leader, unfettered by traditional ecclesiastical structures, may soon command a great band of followers.

Individualism, too, finds fulfillment in Protestantism. Catholicism places chief emphasis upon things "outside the individual."[27] Portuguese Catholicism of the colonial era stressed ritual[28] and was perhaps even more ritualistic and less individualistic than its Spanish counterpart. Brazilian Catholicism mirrors its heritage. This leaves the door ajar for Protestantism, which tends more toward emphasis on the individual.[29] Thus, the various facets of the Brazilian national character or, if one prefers, those traits that appear so frequently in Brazil, have been receptive to Protestantism.

Receptiveness of the Brazilian government reflects that of the people. The Portuguese monarchy, as noted earlier, held regalist theories of church-state relations. This condemned the colonial Catholic Church to a partnership that provided for a monopoly of religion by the Church but carefully restricted its freedom of action.[30] The Pombaline era brought new hindrances to the preferred religion. With the legislation of 1751, the state began restricting activities of the religious orders and in 1759 expelled the Jesuits from its realm.[31] Using a variety of techniques, the crown controlled ecclesiastical affairs by means of the royal patronage.[32] Though it certainly did not tolerate Protestantism,[33] the Portuguese government too often played the good Jewish mother to the Roman Church.

[25]Willems, *Followers of the New Faith*, p. 14, suggests that the Protestant standard "rewards ethical discipline by providing what the traditional society denies."

[26]Sue Anderson Gross provides a good summary of this situation in "Religious Sectarianism in the Sertão of Northeast Brazil, 1815-1966," *Journal of Inter-American Studies* 10 (July 1968): 369-83.

[27]Pierson, *Brancos e pretos na Bahia*, p. 257.

[28]Caio Prado, Junior, *The Colonial Background of Modern Brazil*, trans. Suzette Macedo (Berkeley: University of California Press, 1967), p. 413.

[29]Wach, *Sociology of Religion*, p. 29.

[30]Buarque de Holanda, *História geral da civilização brasileira*, 1:70.

[31]Serafim Leite, ed., *História da Companhia de Jesus no Brazil*, 10 vols. (Rio de Janeiro: Instituto Nacional do Livro, 1949), 7:338-43.

[32]Prado, *Colonial Background of Modern Brazil*, p. 388.

[33]Protestantism was actually introduced during the colonial era, but against the will of the state. In 1555 John Calvin sent preachers to Villegagnon's colony at Rio. See J. A. MacKay, *The Other Spanish Christ* (New York: Macmillan, 1933), pp. 231-32; and José Carlos Rodrigues, *Religiões acatólicas no Brasil, 1500-1900*, 2d ed. (Rio de Janeiro: Escriptorio de "Journal do Commercio," 1904), p. 16. Later the Dutch introduced their brand of Protestantism in Nassau's colony. See José Honório Rodrigues and Joaquim Ribeiro, *Civilização holandesa no Brasil* (São Paulo: Companhia Editôra Nacional, 1940). None of these efforts was permanently successful.

Throughout the era of the Empire, although the government supported Roman Catholicism as the nation's official religion, it initiated a polity of toleration of Protestantism. In 1810, the regent signed a treaty granting toleration to resident Englishmen. This agreement allowed construction of Anglican churches, provided they were not outwardly identifiable as such. Proselytizing, however, was forbidden.[34] The newly created Empire broadened this breach in the Catholic monopoly with the Constitution of 1824, which extended to other Protestants those rights formerly held exclusively by the Anglicans. Protestants, however, were excluded from legislative service.[35] In 1824, also, Dom Pedro I encouraged non-Portuguese immigration to Brazil and granted Lutheran settlers the right to build houses of worship.[36]

Dom Pedro II did little to hinder these practices. Nondogmatic in religious belief,[37] the emperor resisted Catholic efforts to establish suzerainty in the spiritual world. As a staunch regalist and firm believer in freedom of inquiry, Dom Pedro II helped strengthen the climate of religious freedom; and in this more permissive atmosphere, Protestant churches began missionary endeavors.[38] While the state did not oppose missionary efforts, persecution did sometimes arise.[39] Toleration remained the general rule for the Empire, however, as Protestantism laid a foundation for remarkable growth during the republican epoch.

The Constitution of 1890, incorporating an earlier decree of the Republic, disestablished the Roman Catholic Church.[40] Subsequent laws have maintained this separation, and republican Brazil has displayed an official disinterestedness in religion. While the Roman Church, of course, still maintains considerable political influence, the basic stance of the government is nonsectarian.

Latin American Protestantism has achieved in Brazil what may be

---

[34]José Carlos Rodrigues, *Religiões acatólicas no Brasil*, p. 105.
[35]Ibid., pp. 108, 129.
[36]MacKay, *The Other Spanish Christ*, pp. 233-34.
[37]Basilio de Magalhães, *Estudos de história do Brasil* (São Paulo: [Companhia Editôra Nacional], 1940), pp. 153-54. Chapter 2 of this work presents a discussion of church-state relations during the reign of Pedro II. Also see T. de Azevedo, *O catolicismo no Brasil*, pp. 19-20.
[38]F. de Azevedo, *A cultura brasileira*, pp. 264-65, provides a convenient list of dates for the establishment of various Protestant churches. Several denominations have published national histories which trace their development at length, e.g., Antonio de Mesquita, *História dos batistas do Brasil*, 2 vols. (Rio de Janeiro: Casa Publicadora Batista, 1940).
[39]Julio Andrade Ferreira, *História da igreja presbiteriana do Brazil*, 2 vols. (São Paulo: Casa Editôra Presbiteriana, 1959); David Gueiros Vieira, "Some Protestant Missionary Letters Relating to the Religious Question in Brazil: 1872-1875," *The Americas* 24 (April 1968): 345n.
[40]Smith, *Brazil*, p. 510.

its highest level of development.⁴¹ In their diverse functions, Protestant churches operate without hindrance. Traditionally, the state has done little to dampen the Protestant fire in Brazil.⁴² In fact, national immigration policy since the time of independence has been highly conducive to the growth of Protestantism. Staggering under the complexities of industrialization and the trauma of national unification, nineteenth-century Europe sent massive numbers of people to American shores. Much like the United States, Brazil shared bountifully in this population shift; it was not until 1934 that legislation inhibited this flow of immigrants.⁴³

Immigration by non-Portuguese in the nineteenth century began as colony-planting ventures. When Dom Pedro I encouraged the establishment of agricultural colonies in 1824, the Germans responded.⁴⁴ It appears that prior to the 1870s, most non-Portuguese immigrants were German-speaking settlers who were attracted to the agricultural colonies of southern Brazil. Although most were Lutherans,⁴⁵ they contributed little to Brazilian religious life, keeping largely to themselves and making few if any attempts to extend their faith to non-Germans. Only in recent times have they even held services in Portuguese.⁴⁶

The peak years of immigration for Brazil were between 1887 and 1934. During this period there were more than four million arrivals,⁴⁷ with the Italians easily topping the list. At least nominally Roman Catholic, Italians could easily have slipped into the mainstream of Brazilian religion, and many of them did so; but the Brazilian Catholic Church was completely unprepared to claim them. Lack of clergy meant that many Catholic immigrants never received a priestly welcome. Culturally dislocated and religiously disoriented, they were open to the Protestant message. This probably accounts for the great success of Pentecostal Protestantism among Brazil's Italians. Established in 1910, the Pentecostal movement gained strength and stability as immigrants settled into their adopted homeland. Currently boasting a membership of several hundred thousand, including many non-Italians, this movement clearly demonstrates the Protestant religious possibilities inherent even among immigrants.⁴⁸

⁴¹J. Lloyd Mecham, *Church and State in Latin America*, rev. ed. (Chapel Hill: University of North Carolina Press, 1965), p. 281.
⁴²Smith, *Brazil*, p. 526.
⁴³Rollie E. Poppino, *Brazil: The Land and People* (New York: Oxford University, 1968), p. 199. Chapter 5 provides a good survey of immigration.
⁴⁴José Carlos Rodrigues, *Religiões acatólicas no Brasil*, pp. 101-102.
⁴⁵G. P. Howard, *We Americans: North and South* (New York: Friendship Press, 1951), p. 51.
⁴⁶William R. Read, *New Patterns of Church Growth in Brazil* (Grand Rapids, Mich.: W. B. Eerdmans, 1965), p. 196.
⁴⁷Smith, *Brazil*, p. 118.
⁴⁸Much of the information for the Congregação Cristã may be found in Read, *New Pat-*

There can be no doubt that immigration has radically affected the Brazilian social climate. An isolated, ingrown culture relishes and carefully nurtures its religious forms and concepts. Immigration, at least after independence, prevented this in Brazil. Continuous arrivals of foreign peoples created a cosmopolitan population, one able and even anxious to open its socio-cultural structures to modification. In such an environment, Protestantism secured a ready hearing and encountered few obstacles to real conversion. Only recently have Brazilianists begun to examine the broad spectrum of social transformations occurring in Brazil as a result of immigration.[49] These studies fill a long neglected gap.[50]

Clearly, Protestantism fits well into the constantly changing mosaic of contemporary Brazilian society. The various Protestant churches play important roles in changing and perhaps being changed by Brazilian social and cultural patterns. As the great nation drives toward new configurations, Protestantism's place in the scheme grows larger. Unless this trend is reversed, even more remarkable and accelerated Protestant growth may lie ahead.

Not all types of Protestantism share equally in this unique growth rate. The greater portion lies with that "biblicistic-ecstatic revival movement" generally identified as Pentecostal. According to one authority, "The most outstanding characteristic of the Movement is the doctrine of Spirit baptism as an experience different from conversion, manifested by speaking with tongues. The Movement ... above all has emphasized the charismatic gifts such as glossalalia and supernatural healing."[51] Pentecostal churches, moreover, usually demonstrate a high degree of congregational autonomy, doctrinal elasticity, and charismatic emphasis. The broad spectrum of Protestantism[52] includes several different denominations that are Pentecostal in nature.[53]

It would appear, then, that Brazil has embraced Protestantism warmly in recent times, partly because of the type of Protestantism

terns of Church Growth in Brazil, pp. 24-41. See also Congregação Cristã no Brasil, Relatório e balanço (São Paulo: Congregação Cristã, yearly) for information on this group.

[49] See especially Willems, Followers of the New Faith; Read, New Patterns of Church Growth in Brazil; T. de Azevedo, Social Change in Brazil.

[50] T. de Azevedo, O catolicismo no Brazil, p. 3.

[51] Nils Bloch-Hoell, The Pentecostal Movement ([Oslo]: Scandanavian University Books, 1964), p. 2.

[52] A detailed statistical survey of Latin American Protestant mission activity is C. W. Taylor and W. T. Coggins, eds., Protestant Missions in Latin America: A Statistical Survey (Washington, D.C.: Evangelical Foreign Missions Association, 1961). See also Read, New Patterns of Church Growth in Brazil.

[53] Read, New Patterns of Church Growth in Brazil, pp. 122-43; Emilo Conde, História das Assembléias de Deus do Brasil (Rio de Janeiro: n.p., 1960); Cândido Procópio Ferreira Camargo, Kardecismo e umbanda: Uma interpretação sociológica (São Paulo: Livraria Pioneira Editôra, 1961).

that has been offered. The remarkable growth of Protestantism during the past thirty years seems closely linked to the attributes of Pentecostalism that speak to some of the elemental needs of the rapidly changing Brazilian society.

It is evidently for this reason that several writers have ascribed Protestant growth primarily to industrialization, internal migration, urbanization, and other factors of socio-cultural change in contemporary Brazil. Yet other Latin American nations experiencing similar changes have not had a similar Protestant growth. For this reason, historical factors would seem to have a decisive importance.

Perhaps in these historical factors we have a viable explanation for Protestantism's unparalleled growth in Brazil. Entering a Roman Catholic land where the Church had been established for generations, Protestantism might have been expected to experience in Brazil the same travails that it has had in most of Latin America. But historical factors intervened. Developments in the society of that country, associated with national character, prepared Brazilians for acceptance of Protestant doctrines. In Protestantism, many Brazilians find a faith warmly compatible with their needs, hopes, and aspirations.

33. The Catholic Right in Contemporary Brazil: The Case of the Society for the Defense of Tradition, Family, and Property (TFP)

THOMAS NIEHAUS and BRADY TYSON

The coauthors provide a brief history of Brazil's TFP and an outline of its campaigns against the Goulart government (1961-1964), the agrarian reform program of the Catholic Action group in Belo Horizonte, a proposed divorce law, "Red priests," and "modernist heresy" resulting from Vatican II. They also describe how the TFP has become an international movement with member societies in other Latin American countries and in the United States.

The Catholic Right has been largely ignored by American scholars during the past few decades.[1] Unlike the Catholic Left with its belief in popular mobilization, the Catholic Right avoids a high profile,

[1]There is an extensive literature on the Catholic Left and the role of the Church in social change. See Thomas Bruneau, "Power and Influence: Analysis of the Church in Latin America and the Case of Brazil," *Latin American Research Review* 8 (Summer 1973): 25-51; idem, *Political Transformation of the Brazilian Catholic Church* (New York: Cambridge University Press, 1974); Emanuel de Kadt, *Catholic Radicals in Brazil* (London: Oxford University Press, 1970); Ivan Vallier, *Catholicism, Social Control, and Modernization in Latin America* (Englewood Cliffs, N.J.: Prentice-Hall, 1970); Manoel Cardozo, "The Brazilian Church and the New Left," *Journal of Inter-American Studies* 6 (July 1964): 313-21; Luigi Einaudi et al., *Latin American Institutional Development: The Changing Catholic Church* (Santa Monica, Calif.: Rand Corp., 1969); Thomas G. Sanders, "Catholicism and Development: The Catholic Left in Brazil," in *Churches and States: The Religious Institution and Modernization*, ed. Kalman Silvert (New York: American Universities Field Staff Studies, 1967); Gary MacEoin, "The Church," in *Revolution Next Door: Latin America in the 1970s* (New York: Holt, Reinhart and Winston, 1971), pp. 107-31; Frederick C. Turner, *Catholicism and Political Development in Latin America* (Chapel Hill: University of North Carolina Press, 1971). Typical of statements about the Catholic Right is the following: "The rebels [the Left] constitute only a relatively tiny group within the Church. We still do not know what the representatives of the moderate or conservative groups think and write (and they are in the majority)." Gerhard Drekonja, "Religion and Social Change in Latin America," *Latin American Research Review* 6 (Spring 1971): 65.

believing that public debate or even discussion of significant issues by the populace can only debase the subject, and that the true elite has no need of popular approbation. North American scholars found Catholic Rightists to be "riding the wave of the past," reminiscent of Franco and Salazar, who were considered to be merely temporary and unhappy obstacles to the march of liberalism, representative rule, and education. The Catholic Left was seen as the door to the future, even if that future was at best only dimly perceived. But the anticolonial and antitotalitarian vision of inevitable historical progress that found its high point in the Universal Declaration of Human Rights in 1948 appears to be losing its momentum and self-confidence, while there is an increase in the number of authoritarian and openly antidemocratic regimes in Latin America and other parts of the Third World.

The purpose of this study is to begin to fill the many gaps in the scholarship on the Catholic Right in Latin America by presenting a case study of one organization: the Brazilian Society for the Defense of Tradition, Family, and Property (Sociedade Brasileira de Defesa da Tradição, Família e Propriedade). It is popularly known as "the TFP." The authors describe the TFP's organization, characteristics, influence, and ideology; also, they suggest its relationships and origins in the contemporary Brazilian social, political, and religious context. Included in this study are a history of the TFP, an account of its five major campaigns in Brazil, a brief description of its life-style, and a tentative assessment of its impact on recent Brazilian political and intellectual life. An attempt is made to begin to correct the interpretation that the "new church" of the post-Vatican II and post-Medellín conferences is the inevitable wave of the future, that it will have a tremendous effect on the culture and institutions of Latin America, and that it has changed or is changing the mentality of all or most Latin American Catholics. Although quick to acknowledge that there is a movement that can be called the "new church," the authors believe it is equally important to acknowledge the existence of the "old church," to understand its thought, and to attempt to measure its influence. Like the "new church," the "old church" is itself complex and fragmented. The TFP has been selected not because it is the largest or even perhaps the most important (politically or intellectually) of the Catholic Right groups in Brazil, but because it has so consciously tried to influence the nation and the government.

The History of the TFP

In 1960, the TFP was founded in São Paulo by Plínio Correa de Oliveira, a professor of modern history at the Catholic Pontifical University of São Paulo. He had been involved in conservative politics in Brazil since 1928. Educated by Jesuits, Correa de Oliveira became a journalist and edited the São Paulo archdiocesan newspaper, *Legionário*, from 1935 to 1947. That publication's name comes from its close ties with the Legion of Mary, an international Catholic organization. In 1951, Correa de Oliveira became a member of the editorial staff of the newly founded monthly *O Catolicismo*, where he joined efforts with its founder, Msgr. Antonio de Castro Mayer, Bishop of Campos. Castro Mayer was an early leader of the TFP, together with another cleric, Geraldo de Proença Sigaud, Archbishop of Diamantina in the province of Minas Gerais. These three men are the most important leaders of the TFP.[2]

It was no coincidence that the TFP was founded in 1960, because it was at that time that Correa de Oliveira and other Brazilian conservatives felt that the Left had gotten too powerful. Starting with a membership of 40 in 1960, the organization had grown to about 2,000 by the mid 1970s. Membership estimates vary, but there are many thousands of nonmembers who are in sympathy with the organization's aims and who contribute financially.[3] Its benefactors are said to be among the most influential persons in the country, including a number of top-level government officials such as Cabinet members.

The TFP consistently backs up the policies of the conservative government, and has done so since 1964. The organization has made a number of statements to this effect, one of which includes the following three points: 1) "the great majority of [Brazil's] citizens ... enjoy the most complete and private liberty.... A precipate [sic] return to complete constitutional normalcy would bring liberty to those who do not deserve it." 2) "The Government of Brazil has firmly denied that incidents of torture take place within the country, and up to this moment no one has been able to present conclusive proof and evidence that they exist." 3) Communists and Marxists within Brazil are free to spread their ideas, and are not jailed as long as they do not engage in violence.[4]

The last assertion has been directly contradicted by Archbishop Sigaud, a TFP leader, who asks and answers the following question in

[2]Brief biographies of Plínio Correa de Oliveira can be found in "The Founder of the TFP," *Crusade for a Christian Civilization* (New York), October-December 1971, p. 2; Other biographies are in Uli Schmetzer, "The Brotherhood," *Washington Post*, January 6, 1974, p. B3; Marcio Moreira Alva, "L'extrème droite catholique et la politique brésilienne" (Paper delivered at the Centre d'Etude des Relations Internationales, Paris, October 27-28, 1972), p. 7; and Plínio Correa de Oliveira, *Revolution and Counter-Revolution* (Fullerton, Calif.: Educator Publications, 1972), pp. 3-4.

[3]A figure of 1,500 members is cited by Correa de Oliveira in *Fôlha de São Paulo*, June 22, 1969; by Sigaud in *O Globo*, October 12, 1970; and by an article in *Veja*, May 20, 1970. These are listed in Moreira Alves, "L'extrème-droite catholique," p. 7, n. 7. A figure of 2,000 is mentioned in Uli Schmetzer, *Washington Post*, January 6, 1974, p. B3. A figure of 3,000 is given in Turner, *Catholicism and Political Development in Latin America*, p. 99, n. 7, where Turner mentions a letter he received from the vice-president of the TFP, Prof. Fernando Furquim de Almeida, on September 21, 1967. The letter apparently is Turner's source for the figure 3,000.

[4]"The Campaign Against Brazil," *Crusade for a Christian Civilization*, October-December 1971, p. 5.

his *Anti-Communist Catechism:* "Do the Communists have the right to spread their doctrines orally or in the press, on the radio, television, or other means of propaganda? No. According to the Catholic doctrine, an error does not have the right to be spread. It is the government's duty to prohibit such propaganda."[5] This statement seems to reflect more closely the real feelings of many TFP members, as will be shown in the discussion of the organization's five major campaigns in the 1960s. These campaigns were waged against the Goulart government from 1961 to 1964; against the Catholic Action group in Belo Horizonte over agrarian reform; against Brazil's proposed divorce law in 1966; against the "Red priests," like Hélder Câmara and Joseph Comblin, in 1968; and against the "modernist heresy" of the postconciliar Church in 1969.

The Campaign Against Agrarian Reform

The TFP's campaign against Goulart centered on the issue of the "socialistic agrarian reform" of that government. Perhaps the TFP's most important move during this campaign was to join with other rightist and religious groups to form the "Family march with God for liberty" on March 19, 1964. It was in protest of the march of "Communists" a few days earlier. The "Family march" was a massive cooperative venture of the TFP, the Movement for Women's Mobilization (a group of middle-class women who espoused anticommunism), the Women's Civic Union, the Women's Campaign for Democracy (CAMDE), the Family Rosary Crusade, the Marian Congregations of the Legion of Mary, and the Catholic Women's League. These groups converged for a march through the streets of São Paulo to demonstrate massive opposition to the Goulart Regime. Estimates range from 500,000 to 1,000,000 marchers. An analyst on the scene reported that "the army, it is generally agreed, would have been hesitant to move had there not been strong indications that public opinion was favorable, and it is quite possible that spectacular demonstrations, such as the March 19 'March of the Family with God for Liberty' in São Paulo, were decisive in convincing the strictly military sector of the 'Revolutionary Movement' that the time was ripe."[6] The TFP played a part in this important march; and the membership was no doubt elated when the Goulart regime fell a few days later on March 31, 1964. They take

---

[5]Geraldo de Proença Sigaud, *Catecismo anti-comunista*, 3d ed. (São Paulo: Editôra Vera Cruz, 1963), p. 34, question 76.
[6]James W. Rowe, "Revolution or Counterrevolution in Brazil?" pt. 1: "The Diverse Background," *American Universities Field Staff Reports Service*, East Coast South America Series, vol. 15, no. 4 (Brazil), June 1964, p. 12. Detailed accounts of the "Family march" can be found in *Crusade for Christian Civilization*, January-March 1972, pp. 3-4 (the TFP's version); and Charles Antoine, *Church and Power in Brazil*, trans. Peter Nelson (Maryknoll, N.Y.: Orbis Books, 1973), pp. 21-23.

much credit for it in their literature, but tend to exaggerate their influence.[7]

A most interesting sidelight to this affair is the role of Father Patrick Peyton, an American priest who heads the international Family Rosary Crusade. The TFP gives much importance to the rosary and devotion to Our Lady of Fátima, its central religious theme. At the time of the "March of the Family," Miguel Arraes, mayor of Recife, was running for the office of Governor of the State of Pernambuco. There was a strong campaign against him; he was too leftist for many, and was called an "atheistic Communist." When Arraes visited the city of També during his campaign, someone dropped a framed picture of the Sacred Heart of Jesus at his feet, breaking it to pieces. From then on he was called an "anti-Christ." Just before election day, Father Peyton came to Recife to hold a rally for the Family Rosary. His arrival hardly seemed a coincidence, and it is unlikely that the TFP office in Recife was completely unconnected to the affair.[8]

The Campaign Against Catholic Action in Belo Horizonte

The TFP's second major campaign was directed against the Catholic Action group in Belo Horizonte in 1964. This group had become too leftist for the TFP because of its support of agrarian reform, an issue that was also related to the TFP's opposition to Goulart. The three top leaders of the TFP (Correa de Oliveira, Castro Mayer, and Sigaud) had collaborated in 1960 on a book that became a guiding policy statement on agrarian reform for the TFP: *Reforma agrária: questão de consciencia*.[9] They used 19th-century papal documents to show that agrarian reform is wrong, that private property is a right based on the nature of man, and that confiscation of land against the

[7]TFP, *A Vigorous Effort of Modern Brazil against Communism: The Brazilian Society for the Defense of Tradition, Family, and Property* (n.p., n.d.), pamphlet published in Brazil in the late 1960s.

[8]Joseph A. Page, *The Revolution That Never Was: Northeast Brazil 1955-1964* (New York: Grossman Publishers, 1972), pp. 115-16.

[9]Geraldo de Proença Sigaud, Antônio de Castro Mayer, Plínio Correa de Oliveira, and Luís Mendonça de Freitas, *Reforma agrária: questão de consciência*, 3d ed. (São Paulo: Editôra Vera Cruz, 1962). For commentaries on this book, see David E. Mutchler, *Roman Catholicism in Brazil: A Study of Church Behavior under Stress*, Studies in Comparative International Development, vol. 1, no. 8 (St. Louis: Social Science Institute, Washington University, 1965), p. 104. See also Antoine, *Church and Power in Brazil*, p. 51. A Brazilian Leftist, Márcio Moreira Alves, made the following comment on *Reforma agrária*: "a book written to the effect that all social ills in the countryside would end if peasants controlled their sexual impulses better and if landowners organized proper religious services on their estates." Moreira Alves, *A Grain of Mustard Seed: The Awakening of the Brazilian Revolution* (Garden City, N.Y.: Doubleday, 1973), p. 159. The main ideas of *Reforma agrária* are summarized in Proença Sigaud, "Reforma agrária," Verbum (Rio de Janeiro), 10 (1953): 1-6. The authors of *Reforma agrária* wrote a sequel entitled *Declaração do Morro Alto: Programa de política agrária conforme os princípios de "Reforma agrária; questão de consciência"* (São Paulo: Editôra Vera Cruz, 1964).

owner's will causes the ruin of the structure of the family, which in turn is based on property.[10] Widely advertised in the Brazilian press, the book was distributed to many influential persons. Almost all Brazilian bishops were opposed to the book's ideas, and this was noted in the public statements of bishops in the São Paulo area, the southern provinces, the Northeast, and Minas Gerais, where Belo Horizonte is located. All supported land reform.

Isolated in its position, the TFP sent "a courteous, but firm interpellation addressed to the members of the Catholic Action of Belo Horizonte, asking them to define in what [sic] consisted such a position.... It was also by initiative of TFP that a demonstration of university students took place in Belo Horizonte, which in great measure, cooperated to bar the gathering of Latin American Communist congress of the CUTAL in that city under the patronage of Goulart's leftist brother-in-law, Leonel Brisola. Both of these initiatives played a decisive role in the ideological preparation of the March 31st movement which overthrew Goulart."[11] Thus, the first two campaigns of the TFP were closely linked; both centered on land reform.

The TFP communique to Belo Horizonte's Catholic Action group consisted of a petition signed by 209,000 persons. Another petition against land reform was signed by 27,000 farmers and presented to the National Congress. Other petitions were sent by conservative TFP students to the JUC (University Catholic Youth) and to a key Christian Democratic representative in the Congress.[12] These actions helped to strengthen the anti-Goulart forces and contributed to the fall of the government. Petitions have become a regular tool in the TFP's arsenal of ideological weapons.

Satisfied with the new military government in 1964, the TFP remained silent, for the most part, between 1964 and 1966.[13] The silence was broken with an open letter addressed to Cardinal Agnelo Rossi of São Paulo and published in the newspaper *O Estado de São Paulo* on June 2, 1965. The purpose of the letter was to make Rossi proclaim his allegiance to the conservative government, but it also outlined campaigns to be conducted by the TFP in the years ahead. Although the letter was issued "under a false signature," one authority has asserted that "the TFP movement can be detected."[14] The letter spoke against Rossi's "progressivism" and his pro-Câmara stance, against the Catholic University of São Paulo, against Catholic Action, against the Dominicans, against current teachings on sexual morality,

[10]Proença Sigaud et al., *Reforma agrária*, pp. 33-36.
[11]TFP, *A Vigorous Effort of Modern Brazil Against Communism.*
[12]Antoine, *Church and Power in Brazil*, p. 51, n. 21.
[13]Ibid., p. 75.
[14]Ibid., pp. 67-68.

and against "progressive" priests, who were branded as "traitors twice over, to their country and to their church."[15]

The Campaign Against the Divorce Bill

In its 1966 campaign against a divorce bill proposed in the Brazilian Congress, the TFP again used petitions to make its voice heard. Statistics publicized by the TFP show that the petition was signed by 570,000 people in the first twenty days, and by a million people within fifty days. Over 450 young TFP militants went to fifty towns where they canvassed on street corners. The divorce bill was defeated in Congress, and the TFP claimed credit for the victory. The TFP could hardly have chosen a more popular appeal, because devout Catholics of all political leanings were against divorce. Such popularity created an embarrassing situation for the bishops, many of whom were against the TFP and saw it as a meddler in Church affairs. Thus the Central Commission of the Brazilian Episcopate, most of whose members had disagreed with the TFP's stand on agrarian reform, issued a statement claiming that the members of the TFP "have the habit of taking up positions which directly touch upon the doctrine and discipline of the Church, but they certainly do not represent the thought of the Central Commission of the Brazilian Episcopate."[16]

Twelve years later, on June 24, 1977, the Brazilian Congress passed a divorce law. But times had changed, for the TFP did not play a major role in the debate. The TFP is not mentioned in the main newspapers and magazines that covered the 1977 divorce debates. Public opinion had changed, and the TFP's policies and tactics were outdated.

The Campaign Against "Communist Christians"

The TFP's fourth major campaign began in 1968 and was directed against the "Communist Christians" and "Christian progressivism" in Brazil. The two persons who headed its list of subversives were Dom Hélder Câmara, Archbishop of Olinda and Recife, and Father Joseph Comblin, a Belgian professor at Câmara's Recife Theological Institute. The TFP reports that in 1968 the Brazilian police made public a "highly subversive document" belonging to Comblin—a document which proved that the "Catholic progressives" sought the overthrow of Brazilian institutions. The TFP National Council then published "A reverent and filial message to His Holiness Pope Paul

---

[15]*O Estado de São Paulo*, June 2, 1965, quoted in Antoine, *Church and Power in Brazil*, p. 68. The reference of the Dominicans concerns their alleged cooperation with the urban guerrilla leader Carlos Marighella.

[16]Antoine, *Church and Power in Brazil*, pp. 76-77. The campaign against divorce is also mentioned in *The Educator* (later *The National Educator*), July-August 1971, p. 5; and see *Veja*, September 18, 1968, p. 56.

VI" requesting that strong measures be taken against the growing Catholic Left in Brazil. In fifty-eight days, claims the TFP, the statement was signed by 1,600,000 persons, including twelve bishops. Also the TFP states that similar campaigns were conducted in Argentina, Chile, and Uruguay; and a claim is made that the TFP in those countries increased the total number of signatures to over 2,000,000.[17] The TFP goes into some detail in presenting information about this campaign. When its members were in the streets with the petitions, according to the TFP, there were "829 different instances [street fights, etc., designed] to prevent the taking of more signatures. In 396 separate cases the violence was attributed to leftist clergymen and religious."[18]

The Church's official attitude toward these petitions and the TFP is illustrated by the fact that during this period the Pope's representative, Monsignor Benelli, refused to receive Archbishop Sigaud in Medellín, Colombia, when Sigaud tried to present to him the TFP petitions and all of the signatures.

One is not surprised that the TFP has opposed Hélder Câmara, the charismatic leader of the Catholic Left in Brazil. Both Archbishop Sigaud and Bishop Castro Mayer have verbally attacked Archbishop Câmara. Castro Mayer wrote a letter to his fellow bishops on October 5, 1967, saying that a statement issued by Câmara and other Northeast bishops in July of that year had grave consequences "for a country that desires to repel communism in a decisive way." He noted that the Northeast bishops' manifesto denouncing the unjust structures of government and society "does not avoid favoring in a certain way the creation of the materialistic and egalitarian mentality advocated by Marxist socialism." Through a series of speeches, Archbishop Sigaud alerted the public against "Communist infiltration" and named Câmara as one of those responsible for it.[19]

On October 1, 1968 (when Câmara was launching his movement called Action, Justice, and Peace), many pamphlets were distributed urging people to "Come, see the devil and protest!" Câmara's biographer speculates that the TFP may have been one of the organizations responsible for this distribution.[20] One of the reasons for this speculation may be the TFP's practice of characterizing its opponents as the personification of the devil. Archbishop Sigaud's *Anti-Communist Catechism* asserts, "The person who invented this regime [Communism] was Satan, and he knows that the best way of leading

---

[17]José Lúcio Araújo de Correa, "The Phenomenon Known as the TFP," *Crusade*, October-December 1971, p. 3.
[18]"TFP—God's Young Heroes War for Brazil," *The Educator*, July-August 1971, p. 5.
[19]José de Broucker, *Dom Hélder Câmara: The Violence of a Peacemaker*, trans. Herma Briffault (Maryknoll, N.Y.: Orbis Books, 1970), pp. 44-45. A detailed account of the TFP crusade against Câmara is found in Antoine, *Church and Power in Brazil*, pp. 84-89.
[20]Broucker, *Dom Hélder Câmara*, p. 64.

men to eternal perdition is to make them rebel against the order constituted by God." Sigaud then refers to the traditional Faustian idea that Satan deceives men by promising them happiness on Earth if they will renounce God.[21]

Câmara did not make many rebuttals to the attacks made on him by the TFP, because he did not want to give it the feeling that it was important enough to merit a reply. But the incident in October 1968, involving pamphlets that identified him as Satan, moved Câmara to speak back: "At present there is a movement in our country called 'Tradition, Family, Property,' which is spreading everywhere. They are collecting signatures. . . . I thought we should aid the humble people to distinguish between true and false tradition, true and false family, true and false property. To help the masses comprehend that some people who talk about the family say stupid things, all about the horrors of communism, which they say advocates free love, and all this without doing anything to create conditions that would permit a great many working-class couples to have any kind of family life." During his encounter with the TFP in October 1968, Câmara met Archbishop Sigaud at a meeting of bishops and thanked him for all the propaganda because in the long run it had been beneficial to the Catholic Left. Câmara told Sigaud that the masses in the Northeast now realize that private property is not an absolute dogma.[22]

Brazilian leftists have suggested that the TFP was in some way responsible for the murder of Câmara's associate, Father Henrique Pereira Neto, a young priest in charge of the student movement in Recife. His death occurred on May 26, 1969, but the case remains unsolved.[23] In spite of these accusations, it is almost certain that he was killed by the CCC (Comando Caça-Communistas or "Communist-Hunting Commandos").

The Campaign Against Post-Vatican II "Modernism"

The fifth campaign waged by the TFP was begun in 1969 "to denounce the modernist heresy which is everywhere triumphantly on the increase" as a result of Vatican II. As evidence of this trend, the TFP cited the "prophetic groups" fostering progressivism, such as

---

[21]Sigaud, Catecismo anti-comunista, pp. 26-27, questions 58-59.

[22]Broucker, Dom Hélder Câmara, p. 132. Other members of the Catholic Right have also vilified Câmara, especially Gilberto Freyre and Gustavo Corção. In 1967 Corção suggested that the Pope should not give Câmara a Cardinal's hat, but rather "a straw sombrero with two holes cut in it for his ass's ears." See ibid., pp. 44-46. For more on the denunciations of Câmara, see José Brasileiro (pseud.), "Brasil: Campaña contra Dom Hélder," Mensaje (Santiago de Chile), 19 (November 1970): 534-36; and Brady Tyson, "Hélder Câmara: Symbolic Man," New Catholic World, July 1971, pp. 178-82, and August 1971, pp. 235-42.

[23]Moreira Alves, A Grain of Mustard Seed, p. 159. For other accounts of the murder of Father Henrique, see Antoine, Church and Power in Brazil, pp. 242-44; and Thomas E. Quigley, "Cold Blood in Brazil," Commonweal, July 25, 1969, pp. 452-53.

IDOC (International Center for Documentation on the Conciliar Church) and IDC (International Catholic Information). To fight this heresy the TFP issued a special number of *O Catolicismo*, which young TFP militants sold on the streets of Brazil.

There seems to be a direct link between the rise of the fifth campaign and an incident that gave the TFP added coals for the fires of its militancy. On June 10, 1969, the headquarters of the TFP in São Paulo was bombed. Three days later a special issue of *O Catolicismo* denounced the modernist heresy because the TFP thought that the "progressives" and the "Communist Christians" were to blame for this action. The most significant result of the bombing was that the building became a holy place for the TFP. It was quickly rebuilt, and a shrine to Our Lady of the Immaculate Conception was placed in front of the building.[24] Moreira Alves reports, "Every afternoon [since 1969] they stand at attention in front of the TFP's São Paulo palace, reciting a Rosary that ends with raised fist and acclamations of 'Christ! Christ! Christ!' "[25] Thus the bombing gave the TFP new energy for its battle against the Left, and it created the usual martyr complex that results from acts of violence committed by those on either the Left or the Right. Young men of the TFP still hold nightly vigils before the statue, changing at hourly intervals. They continuously recite the prayer, "Our Lady of the Immaculate Heart, save Brazil from communism."[26]

Internal Dissension Within the TFP

In 1970 the TFP experienced a major shake-up in its leadership. Archbishop Sigaud left the organization. It happened in the following way: Early in 1970, when Rome approved Novus Ordo (New Ordinary) for the Catholic Mass, Sigaud took the document to the director of his diocesan seminary, giving him a week in which to express a reaction. At the end of the week, the director said he could not accept the Novus Ordo. He resigned his position, and took ten seminary students with him. They went to Bishop Castro Mayer, asking to be accepted in his diocese. Castro accepted them. Although it was a decision in accord with Castro Mayer's conscience, it was a political mistake. Sigaud, his longtime colleague in the TFP, was deeply offended.

A few months later, Sigaud was interviewed by a reporter for *Veja* magazine. In the interview, Sigaud explained that his decision to leave the TFP was based on two issues: land reform and the TFP's rejection of the Novus Ordo.[27] Apparently the land reform issue was the

---

[24]Antoine, *Church and Power in Brazil*, pp. 228-30; José Lúcio Araujo de Correa, "TFP Phenomenon," *Crusade for Christian Civilization*, October-December 1971, p. 3; "TFP—God's Young Heroes War for Brazil," *The Educator*. July-August 1971, p. 5.
[25]Moreira Alves, *A Grain of Mustard Seed*, p. 159.
[26]Uli Schmetzer, "The Brotherhood," *Washington Post*, January 6, 1974, p. B3.
[27]See *Veja*, October 14, 1970, pp. 3-5.

more serious cause of his break with the TFP, and the Novus Ordo issue was the actual occasion for the decision—in a sense, the last straw.

The Brazilian government had recently passed a land reform law (Estatuto da Terra), signed by President Humberto de Alencar Castelo Branco. Sigaud accepted the law because it did not include confiscation of large land holdings; rather it emphasized making the land more productive. So Sigaud went against some of the ideas that he, Castro Mayer, and Correa de Oliveira had advanced in *Reforma agrária: questão de consciência*. After Sigaud's break with the TFP, Correa de Oliveira branded as "Communists" both Sigaud and Castelo Branco because they favored land reform.

Sigaud's disassociation with the TFP made him more acceptable to the other bishops in the National Conference of Bishops (CCNB), and he was gradually welcomed into the mainstream. Late in 1974, he attended the 14th Assembly of the CCNB and was well received.[28] In October 1976, he was elected a regular representative to the CCNB. Castro Mayer remained isolated, and did not participate in the CCNB.

In 1977 Sigaud reverted to some of his former ways. For example, he created a scandal by applying the Communist brand to two fellow bishops: Dom Tomás Balduíno, Bishop of Goiás; and Dom Pedro Casaldaliga, Bishop of São Félix. The resulting controversy became the subject of front-page stories in Brazilian newspapers over a period of five months.

The TFP Life-Style and Organization

Perhaps the most fascinating aspect of the TFP is its medieval lifestyle. Use of heraldry is central in its ceremonies and public demonstrations. Marches feature display of large red standards with the motto "Tradition, Family, and Property" inscribed beneath a rampant lion. TFP members have a song about their standard, the first stanza of which declares:

> The Revolution faces a stumbling block:
> It is our standard
> Intransigent as a rock,
> So tremendously anti-egalitarian
> With gold lion rampant on a field of red,
> O our lion is anti-egalitarian in every respect![29]

TFP militants use megaphones when marching or distributing pamphlets in the streets. Each wears a red sash over a conservative suit. Their headquarters in São Paulo resembles a medieval castle in its splendor and use of elegant furniture. The founder, Correa de

[28] Ibid., December 4, 1974, pp. 85-86.
[29] *Crusade*, October-December 1972, p. 7.

Oliveira, "the Master," has a throne in the "Hall of Knights," a gilded council chamber located in the headquarters building. He explains, "I want these young men to live with a tradition around them. It is more real than going to a museum, don't you think?" he asked one of his visitors.[30]

Regular use of the term "Crusade" for TFP publications is another medieval aspect. The role of the medieval knight's lady is played by Our Lady of Fátima, who is the center of the group's religious devotion. Her revelations in 1917 to three Portuguese children centered around the need for the world to pray the rosary and convert to better ways lest the world endure a more terrible war. Anti-Communist tendencies are easily seen in the devotion to Our Lady of Fátima, for the menace to the world was interpreted by most Catholics to mean Communism. The 1917 date of the apparitions coincided with the Bolshevik Revolution in Russia.

The writers cannot resist describing a medieval pageant that was held at the headquarters of the TFP in the summer of 1973. It took place in a field outside São Paulo and was called "creative anachronism" by the TFP news service:

> TFP members wearing medieval costumes—with helmets, spears, and so on—participated in a bow and arrow championship. When a burning arrow hit the target (a large picture of the head of a hippie), it ignited a rocket which shot up in the air and exploded in myriad colors. At the end, Prof. Plinio [Correa de Oliveira] himself gave out prizes to the winners, which consisted of medieval standards with heraldic designs. At the same time several musicians seated within a colorful medieval tent played medieval music on flutes and pipes.[31]

Also part of the TFP life-style are the works of Christian charity performed in the community. Their literature lists the following four types of good works: 1) at Christmas they spend "millions of dollars" on the poor, and in putting Christ back into Christmas; 2) a TFP medical team in Rio de Janeiro provides free medical care to the poor living in the *favelas*; 3) they distribute millions of rosaries each year in hospitals and schools; and 4) they have an annual contest for "Model Worker of the Year."[32]

Emphasis is on youth in the TFP, male youth. They make up 75 percent of the members and are between the ages of 16 and 30. Many are single and live in houses or dormitories owned by the TFP. Entry into one of the houses comes after a period of probation in which the organization looks over the prospective member and decides whether he is suitable to join. They are especially interested in his religious

---

[30] Schmetzer, "The Brotherhood," p. B3; see also Michael Sieiawski, "The Militant TFP," *San Francisco Chronicle*, December 17, 1970, p. 20.
[31] *Crusade for Christian Civilization*, September 1973, p. 4b.
[32] *Educator*, July-August 1971, p. 5.

and political opinions. Once a member, he passes through two stages or ranks that are given the names of medieval battles ("Poitiers" and "Navas de Tolosa") and two that are appellations of the Virgin ("Consolatrix Aflictorum" and "Mater Martirum"). In the TFP houses, the young men pray three times daily, go to bed at 10 p.m., read only recommended books, and (according to one sarcastic Brazilian Leftist) "button their pajamas up to the neck."[33] Correa de Oliveira uses the following motto for the TFP youth: "Youth is not made for pleasure, but for heroism."[34]

Use of violence by the TFP youth needs to be discussed. In the late 1960s, training in karate, self-defense, parachhute jumping, and ideological warfare were added to the TFP program.[35] Correa de Oliveira denies that TFP groups use firearms, saying "we do not attack, we defend ourselves. The various times that we were attacked during street campaigns our young men defended themselves victoriously."[36] He adds that "some of them [TFP youth] have the right to carry arms but they do not exercise it. In our 'mother-houses' we have a system of security manned by relays of members."[37]

Another version of this story is given by an ex-TFP member: "They also possess arms that are less ideological, like revolvers and Winchesters with which to guard themselves and their houses throughout the country 'against the eventual attacks of the sons and followers of Lucifer.' " [38] When this is added to a report that the Brazilian secret police recruit members from the TFP group,[39] and to reports that the police are quick to protect the TFP when it battles with hecklers in the streets,[40] one gets a different picture than that painted by Correa de Oliveira.

It has also been said that in 1969 "many TFP members joined the Communist-Hunting Commandos (CCC), a vigilante group that shoots students, breaks up street demonstrations, wrecks theaters, and is very likely responsible for the torture and murder on May 26, 1969, of

---

[33]Moreira Alves, "L'extrême-droite catholique," p. 8.
[34]*Educator*, July-August 1971, p. 5; *Crusade for Christian Civilization*, October-December 1971, p. 4. The motto was originally used by Paul Claudel, a French Catholic writer.
[35]Moreira Alves, "L'extrême-droite catholique," p. 8.
[36]Schmetzer, "The Brotherhood," p. B3.
[37]*Veja*, May 20, 1970; interview with Correa de Oliveira, quoted in Antoine, *Church and Power in Brazil*, p. 230, n. 21.
[38]*Opinião*, February 19-26, 1973, p. 18. This is based on a series of five articles on the TFP published in *Jornal da Tarde* in late 1972 or early 1973.
[39]Moreira Alves, *A Grain of Mustard Seed*, p. 159.
[40]Moreira Alves, "L'extrême-droite catholique," p. 8, n. 18. Reference is to a letter to the editor of *O Estado de São Paulo*, October 9, 1971, in which a person living near a TFP house describes how TFP militants beat a young man in the middle of the street and how the police took him into custody but apparently did not take action against his attackers.

Father Henrique Pereira Neto, a young priest in charge of Catholic student movements in Recife."[41]

TFP Becomes an International Movement

The TFP has now become an international movement. In addition to member societies in Argentina, Uruguay, Chile, Colombia, Venezuela, Peru, and Ecuador, it also includes a United States TFP that held its first meeting in New York City on October 5-7, 1973, complete with medieval heraldry. The meeting was called a SEFAC: Specialized Education and Formation in Anti-Communism.[42] In March 1974, the United States TFP published the first issue of its newsletter, To See, To Judge, In Order to Act. This issue is devoted to the theme of Joseph Cardinal Mindszenty, symbol of anti-Communism in Hungary; 1974 marked the 25th anniversary of his imprisonment by the Communists. The issue contains three articles, two on Mindszenty and one written by Correa de Oliveira.[43]

In an attempt to make the TFP movement less Brazilian, Lucerne, Switzerland, has been designated as the international headquarters. Within Brazil there is one "section" of the TFP for each of the 11 States, and 52 cities have "subsections." There are 18 TFP houses in São Paulo, 10 in Belo Horizonte, and 8 in Guanabara (the Rio de Janeiro area). On the local level, separate chapters have been organized for intellectuals, professionals, workers, farmers, and university students.[44]

The wealth of the TFP is seen in the organization's properties and many expensive activities. Attention has been called to the palacial São Paulo headquarters with its luxurious furnishings. Also to be noted is the fact that "the TFP regularly promotes congresses, seminars, courses and lectures, and it maintains chapels, libraries, classes, and meeting rooms all over the provinces. Some of these buildings also have restaurant, crafts, and gymnasium facilities attached."[45]

The TFP places great emphasis on use of broadcast media, as well as the printed word, to communicate its message to the Brazilian people. Castro Mayer's O Catolicismo, a monthly magazine, is the official TFP organ. Editôra Vera Cruz in São Paulo, which has released many

---

[41]Moreira Alves, A Grain of Mustard Seed, p. 159.
[42]Crusade for Christian Civilization, December 1973, pp. 6-7. This issue contains a complete description of the meeting, including devotions to Our Lady of Fátima and a Way of the Cross devotion composed by Correa de Oliveira. Typical of other TFP groups, all the participants were men.
[43]Published by the American Society for the Defense of Tradition, Family and Property (41-09 Glenwood Street, Little Neck, New York 11363), this first issue was sent to subscribers of Crusade for a Christian Civilization along with the June 1974 issue of the latter publication.
[44]Educator, July-August 1971, p. 5; also, see TFP, A Vigorous Effort of Modern Brazil Against Communism, and the cover story on the TFP in Veja, May 20, 1970, p. 36.
[45]Educator, July-August 1971, p. 5.

books in addition to a large number of leaflets and pamphlets, is the TFP publishing house. The "TFP Press Release" is an information bulletin put out in many languages, including English. A weekly TFP radio broadcast is carried by 75 Brazilian stations, and news releases are distributed through the Boa Imprensa Agency (ABIM) to some 1,400 newspapers and magazines. Correa de Oliveira has a regular column in *O Catolicismo*, which is reprinted in the conservative *O Estado de São Paulo* and in *The National Educator* (Fullerton, Calif.), a conservative monthly tabloid.[46] Much TFP information in English also appears in the *Crusade for a Christian Civilization*, which is published in New York City by American Catholics for the Restoration of Christian Civilization, a group that is closely related to the TFP organization in the United States.

Conclusions

Three general conclusions can be drawn from this study: 1) The TFP is an activist organization that draws a majority of its young militants from Catholic males who, if they had been students at Notre Dame University in our time, might well have become members of some of the charismatic communities in that area. It captures and directs a particular type of adolescent, Catholic fanaticism/devotion that hungers for submission, ritual, authority, and a militant crusade rooted in a secret society.

2) On an intellectual level, TFP represents, along with several other groups in Brazil and other countries today, an attempt to assert traditional Catholic triumphalist-corporatist answers to the maladies of the 1970s. The ideology rejects pluralism, liberalism, rationalism, scientism, and democracy. It is humanist in its own sense of the word, but the organization is profoundly dedicated to a theocentric-organic-hierarchical version of society in which a Catholic intellectual elite plays a significant, if not dominant, role in setting the values and cultural norms for the whole society.

3) Due to the weakness of liberal institutions and the trauma of rapid social change ferociously resisted by an entrenched privileged class, the TFP has managed on several occasions to capture the headlines and attention of Brazil's governing elites and the masses; and it has been able to exert pressure far in excess of its few numbers during the past two decades. Its strength results from tight discipline and training, and from financial backing by some wealthy Brazilians who are interested in its goals. Using this power, the TFP has sought to discredit, or at least to neutralize, progressive elements in the Brazilian Catholic Church and liberal institutions and beliefs in general.

[46]José Lúcio Araujo de Correa, "TFP Phenomenon," *Crusade for a Christian Civilization*, October-December 1971, p. 3.

Overall, however, the TFP has not had a major effect on the religious and political history of Brazil. TFP influence in the 1970s is much less than it was in the 1960s. Always a fringe group, the TFP has functioned as such: not accepted by the Catholic Church, and not allied to any political party. Nevertheless, it is an interesting example of how religion and politics have been combined in modern Brazil.

EDITORS AND CONTRIBUTORS

Editors

BROWN, LYLE C. B.A., M.A., University of Oklahoma; Ph.D., University of Texas at Austin. *Professor of Political Science, Baylor University.* Currently Director of Graduate Studies in his department and Codirector of Baylor's Master of International Management degree program, he served as Vice-President (1972-73) and President (1973-74) of the Southwestern Council of Latin American Studies.

COOPER, WILLIAM F. B.A., M.A., Baylor University; B.D., Southern Baptist Theological Seminary; Ph.D., Indiana University. *Professor of Philosophy, Baylor University.* He served as Treasurer of the Southwestern Council of Latin American Studies (1967-75).

Contributors

ACKER, BERTIE. B.A., Texas Woman's University; M.A., Southern Methodist University; Ph.D., University of Texas at Austin. *Associate Professor of Spanish, University of Texas at Arlington.* She is Coordinator of Spanish Section, Assistant Chairman of the Department of Foreign Languages and Linguistics, and Undergraduate Adviser for that department.

BEAL, TARCISIO. S.T.L., Franciscan Theological School (Petrópolis, Rio de Janeiro, Brazil); M.A., Ph.D., Catholic University of America. *Associate Professor of History, Incarnate Word College.*

BRAVO-VILLARROEL, ROBERTO. Lic. en Letras, Universidad de Nuevo León (Monterrey, N.L., México); M.L.S., University of Texas at Austin. *Associate Professor of Spanish, Texas Tech University.*

BRIDGES, JULIAN C. A.B., University of Florida; B.D., Th.D., Southwestern Baptist Theological Seminary; M.A., Ph.D., University of Florida. *Professor of Sociology, Hardin-Simmons University.* He is Head, Department of Sociology and Social Work, at his university.

BRZEZINSKI, STEVEN J. B.A., College of St. Thomas (St. Paul, Minn.); M.A., Ph.D., University of Illinois-Urbana. *Assistant Professor of Political Science, University of Wyoming-Laramie.* He is Director, Government Research Bureau, at his university.

BUTTREY, JERROLD S. B.A., St. Edward's University; M.A., University of Texas at Austin. *Instructor in History and Spanish, Saint Stephen's Episcopal School* (Austin, Tex.).

COCHRANE, JAMES D. B.A., Morningside College; M.A., Ph.D., University of Iowa. *Professor of Political Science, Tulane University.*

CORTES, ROBERTO. B.A., Tennessee Temple College; M.A., Baylor University. *Instructor, Instituto Irlandés* (Monterrey, N.L., México).

DODSON, MICHAEL. B.A., University of South Dakota; M.A., University of New Mexico; Ph.D., Indiana University. *Assistant Professor of Political Science, Texas Christian University.*

GARCIA, LINO. B.A., St. Mary's University (San Antonio); M.A., North Texas State University; Ph.D., Tulane University. *Assistant Professor of Spanish, Pan American University.*

GARNER, WILLIAM R. B.A., Baylor University; M.A., Southern Methodist University; Ph.D., Tulane University. *Associate Professor of Political Science, Southern Illinois University at Carbondale.* He is Chairman, Latin American Studies Advisory Committee, at his university.

GREENLEAF, RICHARD E. B.A., M.A., Ph.D., University of New Mexico. *Professor of History, Tulane University.* He is Director, Center for Latin American Studies, at his university.

GRUBER, VIVIAN M. B.A., M.A., Ph.D., Florida State University. *Professor of Spanish, Stephen F. Austin State University.* She is Graduate Program Adviser for her department.

HADDOX, JOHN H. B.A., M.A., Ph.D., University of Notre Dame. *Professor of Philosophy, University of Texas at El Paso.*

JOHNSON, HARVEY L. B.A., Howard Payne University; M.A., University of Texas at Austin; Ph.D., University of Pennsylvania. *Professor Emeritus of Spanish and Portuguese, University of Houston.* He served as Vice-President (1968-69) and President (1969-70) of the Southwestern Council of Latin American Studies.

JOSEPH, HARRIET DENISE. B.A., Southern Methodist University; M.A., Ph.D., North Texas State University. *Instructor in History, Texas Southmost College.* She is Director, Oral History Program, at her college.

KELLY, MARIA ANN. B.A., M.A., College of St. Rose; Ph.D., Georgetown University. *Assistant Professor of History, College of St. Rose.*

KIRSHNER, ALAN M. B.A., Hofstra University; M.A., City University of New York; Ph.D., New York University. *Professor of History, Ohlone College.* He is Chairperson, Department of History, at his college.

LOBB, C. GARY. B.A., University of Utah; M.A., Ph.D., University of California at Berkeley. *Associate Professor of Geography, California State University at Northridge.*
MacKINNON, NORRIS. B.A., Davidson College; M.A., University of North Carolina at Chapel Hill; Ph.D., University of Kentucky. *Assistant Professor of Spanish, Eastern Kentucky University.*
MENDOZA, MANUEL. B.A., Universidad de San Luis Potosí (San Luis Potosí, S.L.P., México); Ph.L., University of Montreal; M.A., Texas Christian University. *Assistant Professor of Spanish, Stephen F. Austin State University.*
MILLETT, RICHARD L. A.B., Harvard University; M.A., Ph.D., University of New Mexico. *Professor of Political Science, Southern Illinois University at Edwardsville.* He is Chairman, Latin American Studies Committee, at his university.
NIEHAUS, THOMAS. B.A., Xavier University, Cincinnati; M.A., University of Cincinnati; M.L.S., Ph.D., University of Texas at Austin. *Director, Latin American Library, Tulane University.*
NIELSEN, NIELS C., JR. B.A., Pepperdine University; B.D., Ph.D., Yale University. *Newton Rayzor Professor of Philosophy and Religious Thought, Rice University.*
REDMOND, WALTER B. B.A., M.A., Aquinas Institute of Philosophy; M.A., Aquinas Institute of Theology; M.A., University of Texas at Austin; Ph.D., Universidad Nacional Mayor de San Marcos (Perú). *Research Professor, Universidad Autónoma del Estado de Puebla* (Puebla, México).
ROBINSON, JOHN L. B.A., Abilene Christian University; M.A., Pepperdine University; Ph.D., Texas Christian University. *Professor of History and Political Science, Abilene Christian University.*
SCHWEITZER, S. ALAN. B.A., Centre College of Kentucky; M.L.S., University of Pittsburgh; M.A., Ph.D., Rutgers University. *Instructor in Spanish, Lorain Community College.*
STONE, JESS H. B.A., M.A., Colorado State University; M.A., University of Oregon; Ph.D., University of New Mexico. Formerly *Assistant Professor of History, College of William and Mary.*
THEISEN, GERALD. A.B., M.A., Marquette University; Ph.D., University of New Mexico. *Assistant Professor of Education, Eastern New Mexico University.* He is Director, Bilingual/Multicultural Program, at his university.
TORRE, TEODORO DE LA. S.T.D., Gregorian University (Rome); Dr. in Philosophy and Letters, University of Havana. Formerly *Professor and Chairman of the Department of Philosophy and Theology, Dominican College* (Houston, Tex.).
TYSON, BRADY. B.A., Rice University; B.D., Perkins School of Theology, Southern Methodist University; Ph.D., American University. *Professor of Latin American Studies, American University.*

WALKER, JUDITH. B.S., University of Kansas; Ph.D., University of Florida. *Assistant Professor of Education, University of Houston.*
WHITMORE, DON. B.A., North Texas State University; M.A.T., Ph.D., University of New Mexico. *Assistant Professor of Spanish, Texas Woman's University.* He is Coordinator of Graduate Bilingual Education Program and Faculty Consultant to Federal Bilingual Training Resource Center of the Federation of North Texas Area Universities.
WOOD, ROBERT D. B.S.Ed., University of Dayton; M.A., Ph.D., Catholic University of America. *Associate Professor of History, Saint Mary's University* (San Antonio). He served as Vice-President (1977-78) and as President (1978-79) of the Southwestern Council of Latin American Studies.

INDEX

Abascal, Salvador: 117
Acevedo, Aurelio R.: 99
Acción Católica de la Juventud Mexicana (ACJM): 92, 95
Acción Cultural Popular (ACPO): 308, 309
ACJM. See Acción Católica de la Juventud Mexicana
Adie, Robert F.: 6, 10, 11, 15, 16
Aguirre, Jesús M.: 98
Alegría, Isabelino: 115
Alexander, Robert J.: 5
Al filo del agua: religion in, 221-225, 233-240
Almazán, Juan Andreu: 99
Alonso y Colmanares, Eduardo: 292
Alva Ixtlilxóchitl, Bartolomé de: 205, 206, 210
Alvarez, Mariano: 290
Andean Indians:: indoctrination of, 251-261
ANPLE. See Associación Nacional Pro-libertad de Enseñanza.
Anticlericalism: 110-120, 128, 131, 133
Aquinas, Saint Thomas: 25, 43, 193
Archdiocese of Santa Fe: archive of, 85-88
Argentina: 58, 254; Catholic Church in, 3, 53; Catholic radicalism in, 316-330; Lutherans in, 53; Priests of the Third World in, 2; support of Catholic Church in, 19-20
Aristotle: 25
Army of National Liberation: 311-312
Assman, Hugo: 42, 47, 48, 49
Associación Nacional Pro-libertad de Ensenañza (ANPLE): 144, 145
Atheism: 112-113, 140
Augustinians: 255, 258, 259
Aurioles Díaz, José: 144, 145, 146
Avila Camacho, Manuel: 154

Báez-Camargo, Gonzalo: 153
Balduino, Tomás: 404
Balún-Canán: as example of religious persecution in fiction, 216-218
Bancroft, Hubert H.: 191
Baptists: 60; in Mexico, 152, 154
Barbosa, Ruy: 378, 379, 382, 383
Barreto, Tobias: 380
Bassols, Narciso: 123, 124, 127

Beltrán y Mendoza, Luis: 103
Benedictine Code: 262
Bevilacqua, Clóvis: 380
Bloc of Young Revolutionaries (Red Shirts): 112, 116, 128, 129, 130
Bocayuva, Quintino: 379
Bolatti, Guillermo: 325
Bolivia: 21, 254
Borremans, Valentina: 182, 183
Boyer, Jean: 293
Brazil: 19, 56, 262, 361-405; Catholic Church in, 17, 386-388; Catholic Right in, 394-409; Constitution of (1890), 390; Lutherans in, 53; Positivism in, 377-384; regalism in, 362-376; support of Catholic Church in, 19-20
Brazil Para Cristo Church: 59
Bricker, Victoria R.: 73
Brazil para Cristo Church: 59
Bricker, Victoria R.: 73
Bruneau, Thomas C.: 2, 17
Buceta, Manuel: 291, 292
Busto, Bernabé de: 256
Busto, Luis G.: 92

Cabildos: 255
Caciques: 253
Calderón de la Barca, Pedro: 204-211
Calles, Plutarco Elias: 98-99, 106, 107, 116, 120, 122, 123, 124, 126, 127, 128, 131, 134, 136, 153
Camacho, Joaquín: 144
Câmara, Hélder: 26, 37, 397, 400, 401, 402
Cano, Valencia: 23
Capistrán Garza, René: 96
Capitalism: 36
Cardenal, Ernesto: 51
Cárdenas, Lázaro: 99, 106, 116, 117, 118, 122, 123, 125, 127, 128, 130, 131, 132, 134, 136, 137, 147, 148, 154, 213, 218, 219
Carlota Joaquina (queen of Portugal): 373
Carrillo Puerto, Felipe: 201
Cartillas: 256
Carvalho e Melo, Sebastião José. See Pombal, Marquis de.

Casaldaliga, Pedro: 404
Case, Bradley W.: 74
Castro Mayer, Antonio de: 396, 398, 401, 403, 404, 407
Castellanos, Rosario: 213, 216, 218, 219
Castelo Branco, Humberto de Alencar: 383, 384, 404
Castilhos, Júlio de: 381, 383

Cather, Willa: 85
Catholic Action: 32, 33, 307-313
Catholic Church: and community development, 20-22; and liberation, 24-27; and Revolution, 22-24; as an agent of modernization, 2-18; diversity in, 27; support of: 19-20
Catholic elites: 8-12
Cedillo, Saturnino: 96, 100, 116, 131, 145
CELAM. See Conference of Latin American Bishops.
Ceniceros y Villarreal, Rafael: 92
Centro Intercultural de Documentación (CIDOC): 177-188
Céspedes, Francisco de: 263, 264
Chang-Rodríguez, Eugenio: 297, 302
Chardin, Teilhard de: 49
Charles III (king of Spain): 287
Charruas: 264
Chile: 56, 58, 254; Christian Democratic party in, 34
CIDOC. See Centro Intercultural de Documentación.
Cifuentes, Serapio: 94
Class struggle: 25
Cofradías: 260
Coimbra, University of: 363-375
Colégio das Artes: of the University of Coimbra, 363, 365
Colombia: 21-23, 34, 254; Catholic Church in, 22-24; Golconda movement in, 2, 23, 24, 34; political development in, 304-315; political influence of Catholic Church in, 305-308; religion in, 339-350; violence in, 307
Comando Caça-Communistas (CCC): 402, 406
Comblin, Joseph: 397, 400
Communism: 20, 53, 148
Communists: 311, 396
Comte, Auguste: 377, 378, 379, 380, 384
Concha, José Vicente: 22, 311
Conference of Latin American Bishops (CELAM): 40; in Lima, 39; in Medellín, 26-27, 38; in Rio de Janeiro, 26
Congregation of St. Philip Neri (Oratorians): 364, 365, 367
Constant Botelho de Magalhães, Benjamin: 378, 379, 380
Conversos: 80
Cooper, William F.: 247
Coquet, Benito: 146
Cordobazo: 330, n. 24
Correa de Oliveira, Plínio: 395, 396, 398, 404, 405, 406, 407
Costa Rica: 117
Costas, Orlando: 59, 61
Council of Literary Providence: 370
Cristeros: 90-105, 127, 153
Cruz Costa, João: 378

CTC. See Trade unions: Confederación de Trabajadores de Colombia.
Cuba: Catholic Church in, 14; support of Catholic Church in, 19-20
Cuevas, Mariano: 198
Culture of poverty: 173

Daniels, Josephus: 130
David, W. W. H.: 83
Declaration of the Rights of Man: translation and publication by Nariño: 280
Degollado Guízar, Jesús: 100, 104
Developmentalism: 41
Díaz, Porfirio: 153, 195
Díaz Casanueva, Humberto: poetry of, 351-360
Díaz y Barreto, Pascual: 93, 114, 115, 116, 121, 122, 124, 126, 130, 134, 139, 146
Doctrinas: 254, 255, 259, 260
Doctrineros: 255, 256, 257
Dominicans: 258
Durán, Nicolás Mastrillo: 268
Durango: diocesan seminary in, 86, 87, 88
Dussel, Enrique: 31, 42, 49

Ecuador: 21, 254
Ecumenical movement: 57
Edelmann, Alexander T.: 14
Education: Catholic philosophy of, 138-141; socialist, 124-126, 128, 129, 130, 132, 136, 137, 142-146, 153; sexual, 124, 140-141
Effio, Domingo: 21-22
Encomiendas: 254
The Enlightenment: 364, 374
Episcopal Church: in Mexico, 152
Escobar, José Gonzalo: 98, 99
Escobar, Samuel: 61
Estado Novo: 383
Exorcism: and poetry of Humberto Díaz Casanueva, 351-360

Faith and Joy (Fe y Alegría) movement: 21
FANAL. See Trade unions: Federación Agraria Nacional.
Fátima, Our lady of: 405
Fernández, Manuel Félix: 195
Fernández Aguado, Macario: 107
Fernández Manero, Víctor: 117, 118
Fernández San Vicente, Agustín: 88
Ferdinand (king of Spain): 253
First Baptist Church, Monterrey: 152

First Encounter of Christians and Socialists: 26
Fitzgibbon, Russell H.: 5
Fonseca, Deodoro da: 378, 379
Franciscans: 88, 258
Fraternidad Teológica Latinoamericana: 65
Frei Montalva, Eduardo: 3, 33
Frente Unico Nacional de los Padres de Familia (FUNPF): 144, 145, 146
Frente Unido (Colombia): 311, 312
Freyre, Gilberto: 383, 388
FUNPF. See Frente Unico Nacional de los Padres de Familia.

Galilea, Segundo: 31, 38
Gallegos, José Manuel: 84, 86-87
Gallicanism: 374
García Márquez, Gabriel: works of, 339-350
Garrido Canabal, Tomás: 106-118, 128, 131
Gasca, Pedro de la: 253
Gasparri, Pietro: 91
Gibson, Charles: 74
Godot, Esperanza (pseud.): 182, 183, 188
Golconda movement: 2, 23, 24, 34, 312, 314
González de Santa Cruz, Roque: 262, 264, 265, 266, 268
González-Peña, Carlos: 213
González Prada, Manuel: views on religion, 296-303
González Punaro, Manuel: 110
González y Valencia, José Maria: 91
Gorostieta y Velarde, Enrique: 96-97, 100
Goulart, João: 18, 383, 397
El gran teatro del mundo: Nahuatl version of, 205-211
Greene, Graham: 107, 117
Gregg, Josiah: 85
Grubb, Kenneth: 153
Guadalupe, Virgin of: 190-203
Guadarrama, Yolanda: 182, 183
Guaraní: 262, 264, 265
Guaycurus: 262
Guerrero, Vicente: 195
Guibert, Rita: 244, 246, 247
Gutiérrez, Gustavo: 24, 45, 47, 50, 51

Haiti: 56
Halmos, Paul: 185
Haring, Clarence: 79
Haya de la Torre, Víctor Raúl: attitude toward religion, 301-303
Heidegger, Martin: 50

Henry II (king of Spain): 256
Heretics: 71, 75, 76, 81, 143
Hidalgo y Costilla, Miguel: 151, 194
Hollenweger, Walter: 59
Holy Office of the Inquisition: See Inquisition.
Honduras: 56
Hood, Martin T.: 292
Huampaní Conference: 63
Hübner Gallo, Jorge Iván: 3
Huerta, Adolfo de la: 110
Huitzilopochtli: 193
Hunter, William A.: 205

Illich, Iván: 177-188
Imperial Order of Guadalupe: 194-195
Inquisition: 368; and the library of Antonio Nariño, 278-288; and the Indians, 71-75; influence of, 79-82; and Jews, 75-76; procedures of, 78-79; and Protestants, 75-76; scholarly analysis of, 76-78
Institute of Church Growth: 151
ISAL. See Latin America Board on Church and Society.
Isabella (queen of Castile), 252
Iturbide, Agustín: 194

Jacobinism: 380
Jaeger, G. W.: 293
Jansenists: 364, 366, 367, 372
Jaramillo, Pío: 251
Jesuits: 21, 258, 262-277, 362, 363, 364, 365, 366, 368, 395
John V (king of Portugal): 362, 364
John VI (king of Portugal): 373
José I (king of Portugal): 362, 366, 368
Juárez, Benito: 152, 195
Judaizantes: 75, 76

Kadt, Emanuel de: 7
Kamen, Henry: 80, 82
Kant, Immanuel: 50
Kennedy, John J.: 4

Ladinos: 257
Lalive d'Epinay, Christian: 59
Lamy, Jean Baptiste: 84, 88
Las Casas, Bartolomé de: 31
Las tierras flacas: magic and superstition in, 229-232
La tierra pródiga: myth in, 225-228
Latin American Board on Church and Society (ISAL): 63, 64, 65

Latin American Conference on Evangelism (Bogotá, 1969): 64
Latin American Plenary Council (1889): 32
Laws of the Indies: 252, 253, 255, 257, 258
Leagues of Resistance: in Tabasco, 111; in Yucatán, 111
Legion of Mary: 396
Lemos, Miguel: 379, 380, 381
Leo XIII (pope): 6, 32, 141
Leonard, Irving: 73
Lerdo de Tejada, Miguel: 152
Lewis, Oscar: 169-173
Liberalism: 139
Liberation movement: rise of, 31-40
Liberation theology. See theology of liberation.
Liga Nacional Defensora de la Libertad Religiosa: 146, 147
Livi, R.: 161
Loayza, Jerónimo: 253
López Ortega, Antonio: 93-94
López Trujillo, Alfonso: 39
Lutherans: 53, 391

Machebeuf, Joseph P.: 84, 88
Malda, Ernesto: 129
Manríquez y Zárate, José de Jesús: 126, 140
Manzo, Francisco R.: 99
Mariátegui, José Carlos: attitude toward religion, 297-303
Maritain, Jacques: 10, 32
Martínez, Antonio José: 87, 88
Martínez, y Rodríguez, Luis María: 134
Marx, Karl: 31, 42, 48, 49, 50
Marxism: 11, 25, 32
Marxists: 298, 301, 396
Massuh, Víctor: eschatology, 332-338; philosophy of religion, 332-338
Materialism: 53
Maxmilian (emperor of Mexico): 195
Medellín: 26, 27, 38
Melo, Manuel de: 59
Méndez del Río, Jenaro: 91
Mendoza, Cristobal de: 269
Mesa Censória: 368, 369
Methodists: 55, 60; in Mexico, 154
Mexican Communist Party: 137
Mexico: 19, 258; Constitution of 1857, 151, 152, 212-213; Constitution of 1917, 124-126, 130, 132, 136, 153, 213; geographical distribution of evangelicals in, 155-163; growth of evangelical population in, 163-167; historical development of Protestantism in,

151-154; Inquisition in, 70-89; number of evangelicals in, 155-163; poverty in, 169-173; Protestants in, 52
Michaels, Albert L.: 148
Míguez-Bonino, José: 65
Miranda, José Porfirio: 45, 46, 48, 49, 50
Missionaries: 57, 62
Modernization: in Colombia, 304-315; obstacles to, 13-18; techniques of, 13
Monja y casada, virgen y mártir: as example of religious persecution in fiction, 212-216
Monzón, Benvenido: 291-294
Morais, Prudente de: 381
Morelos y Pavón, José María: 194
Morner, Magnus: 73
Múgica, Francisco J.: 109

Nabuco, Joaquim: 381
Nariño, Antonio: library of, 278-288
National Conference of Bishops (CCNB): 404
National Defence League of Religious Liberty: 90, 91, 95, 102
National Liberation Army: in Colombia, 22
Navarro Origel, Luis: 94
Needler, Martin C.: 6
New Mexico: Catholic Church in, 83-89
Nichols, Glenn A.: 14
Nueva Granada: 254, 257, 258, 278
Núñez del Prado, Juan: 253

Obando, Nicolás de: 255
Obregón, Alvaro: 97, 106, 107, 110
Ocampo, Melchor: 152
Ochoa, Dionisio Eduardo: 95
Olaya, Noel: 240
Olinda: Seminary of, 375
Onganía, Juan Carlos: 317, 321, 323, 327, 329
Oratorians. See Congregation of St. Philip Neri.
Orthodox Catholic Apostolic Mexican Church: 90
Ortiz, Juan Felipe: 87
Ortiz, Tomás: 253
Ortiz Rubio, Pascual: 53, 98, 115, 120, 121, 131
Otero, Miguel A.: 84

Pacelli, Eugenio: 143
Palomar y Vizcarra, Miguel: 92, 146
Panama: 21
Papal encyclicals: 6, 32, 91, 121, 138-141

Paraguay: 58
Partido Nacional Revolucionario (PNR): 113, 122, 123, 125, 136
Paul VI (pope): 39, 400-401
Paulista raids: 266, 270
Paz, Octavio: 193, 220; reflections on modern Mexico, 241-247
Pedro I (emperor of Brazil): 375, 390, 391
Pedro II (emperor of Brazil): 390
Peixoto, Floriano: 381, 382
Pentecostals: 56, 58, 59, 391, 392, 393
Pereira de Figueiredo, António: 367, 372
Pereira de Sá, Manuel Joaquim: 378
Pereira Neto, Henrique: 402
Pérez H., Arnulfo: 112, 113
Perón, Juan Domingo: 3
Peru: 21, 253, 254, 255, 258; Catholic Church in, 16, 17; Priestly Movement ONIS in, 35
Phipps, Helen: 79
Pike, Frederick B.: 16, 17
Pironio, Eduardo: 325
Pius XI (pope): 91-92, 115, 121, 122, 138, 139, 143
Plan of Hermosillo: 98-99
PNR. See Partido Nacional Revolucionario.
Political parties: Catholic Electoral League (Brazil), 14; Christian Democratic (Brazil), 33; Christian Democratic (Chile), 33, 34, 39; Conservative (Colombia), 306; Electoral Alliance for the Family (Brazil), 14; Federal Republican (Brazil), 378; Liberal (Colombia), 306; Mexican Communist, 137; National Revolutionary (Mexico), 113, 122, 123, 125, 136; Popular Action (Brazil), 387; Society for the Defense of Tradition, Family, and Property (Brazil), 394-409
Pombal, Marquis de: 362-374
Poppino, Rollie E.: 384
Popular Liberating Army: 127, 147
Portes Gil, Emilio: 97, 100, 102, 104, 115, 126, 128, 131, 201
Portugal: 362, 363
Positivism: in Brazil, 377-384
Prado, Javier: 251
Presbyterians: 55, 60; in Mexico, 154
Priests for the People: 24
Priests for the Third World: 2, 24, 34, 317-330
Priestly Movement ONIS: 24, 35
Protestant churches: 20; immigrant, 60; mainline, 60
Protestantism: and Brazilian immigration, 391; growth of, 55; identification with the middle class, 61; socioeconomic crisis and, 58-60
Protestants: 37, 52-66; and the Inquisition, 75-76; cultural alienation among, 54; in Brazil, 385-393; in Mexico, 150-168; in Santo Dom-

ingo, 290-294; political influence of, 56; second generation, 60; social status of, 56; their attitudes toward Roman Catholicism, 53; their medical programs, 54; their social welfare programs, 54
Provisional Commission for Latin American Evangelical Unity (UNELAM): 64

Quetzalcoatl: 193
Quito, Kingdom of: 257

Red Shirts. See Bloc of Young Revolutionaries.
Reducciones. 254, 262.
Regalism: 362, 386, 389
Resguardos: 254
Revolutionary Vanguard: 112
Ribero, Felipe: 293
Rio de Janeiro: Military Club in, 381, 382
Riva Palacio, Vicente: 212, 213, 218
Rocha Lima, Raymondo de: 377-378
Rodríguez, Abelardo: 121, 122, 125, 126, 127
Romero, Pedro de: 269
Romero, Sílvio: 380
Rossi, Agnelo: 399
Royal Patronage: 254
Ruiz y Flores, Leopoldo: 93, 100, 101, 102, 121, 125, 126, 134, 139, 146
Ruiz Vázquez, Guillermo: 148
Rusk, Bruce: 182

Sáenz, Aarón: 115 n
Salazar, Juan B.: 145
El Salvador: 21
San Andrés, Colegio de: 257, 259
Sánchez Azcona, Juan: 145
Sánchez, Rafael G.: 95
Sanders, Thomas G.: 8, 10
Santa Anna, Antonio López de: 195
Santana, Pedro: 289, 290, 292
Santo Domingo: 289-294
Santos Chocano, José: 299
São Paulo: Catholic Pontifical University of, 395, 399
Sartre, Jean Paul: 50
Segundo, Juan Luis: 35, 49
Seminaries: Protestant, 61-62
Sepp, Anton: 273, 274
Seventh Day Adventists: 56, 61, 154
Sierra, Justo: 152

Sigaud, Geraldo de Proença: 396, 401, 403, 404
Silva Henríquez, Rául: 17
Sinarquistas: 117, 148
Six Year Plan: 122, 123, 124, 134, 140
Social action programs: Protestant, 61, 62
Socialism: 11, 36, 140, 148, 301
Society for the Defense of Tradition, Family, and Property (TFP): 394-409
Society of Jesus. See Jesuits.
Sodré, Lauro: 381, 382
Sorokin, Pitirím A.: 161
Sousa Coutinho, Vicente de: 368
Southern Baptists: in Mexico, 154
Spiritualism: 53
Statutes Concerning New Discoveries and Settlements: 252

Tabasco: 106-118, 128
Tamarón y Romeral, Pedro: 86
Tercermundistas. See Movement of Priests for the Third World.
TFP. See Society for the Defense of Tradition, Family, and Property.
Theology of liberation: 24-26, 29-51, 65; historical experience in, 41; intellectual influences on, 41; Marxist thought in, 36; salvation in, 36
Theology: political, 318-321
Toledo, Francisco de: 255, 257, 258, 261
Tonantzin: 192
Topete, Fausto: 98 n
Topete, Ricardo: 98 n
Torres, Camilo: 22, 24, 34, 38, 310-312
Tovar, Mariano: 113
Trade unions: 5; in Colombia, 309, 314
Treaties: Anglo-Dominican (1851), 293; of Guadalupe-Hidalgo (1848), 83; of Madrid (1750), 277
Trueba Olivares, José: 148

Unión Nacional de Estudiantes Católicos: 146
Unión Nacional de los Padres de Familia (UNPF):144
UNPF. See Unión Nacional de los Padres de Familia.
Uruguay: support of Catholic Church in, 19-20
UTC. See trade unions: Unión de Trabajadores de Colombia.

Vaca de Castro, Cristobal: 253
Valbuena Prat, Angel: 205
Valdivia, Pedro: 253
Valverde y Téllez, Emeterio: 91
Vargas, Antonio C.: 95

Vargas, Getulio: 381, 383
Vargas, Manuel: 383
Vasconcelos, José: 97, 98, 99
Vásquez, Josefina: 136
Vatican I: 32, 34
Vatican II: 9, 10, 34, 38, 57, 316, 317, 321, 402
Vekemans, Roger: 39
Velaz, José María: 20
Veloso, José: 365
Venero de Leiva, Andrés: 259
Venezuela: 21, 254
Verba, Sidney: 179, 180, 181, 182, 184, 185, 187
Vernei, Luís António: 365, 366
Victoria, Guadalupe: 88, 195
Villa de Guadalupe: 193, 196
Villahermosa, Tab.: 109, 110
Violence: 37
Virgin of Guadalupe: 120; subject of song and poetry, 198-203
Volunteers of Tabasco: 111

Wagner, C. Peter: 65
Weber, Max: 185
Wilkie, James W.: 103 n, 104
Willems, Emílio: 59, 151, 385
Worker-priests: 317

Yáñez, Agustín: analyses of works by, 220-240

Zubiría, José Antonio Laureano de: 86, 87
Zimmerman, Carl C.: 161